Praise for *A Long Long War* by Ken Wharton

"In this excellent and wide-ranging selection of first-hand accounts from the British Army in Northern Ireland, Ken Wharton has assembled testimonies from men of all ranks that are invariably informative, sometimes humorous and often deeply moving. A fitting tribute to the British soldier in a campaign that lasted nearly three decades."
Adrian Gilbert, author of *POW: Allied Prisoners in Europe 1939–1945*
(The *Sunday Times* Best Military Books 2006)

"A compelling story, told in the refreshingly simple prose of a soldier-scribe. This is the tale of that other war on terror – one fought over several, bloody decades, and largely in the shadows. Lest we forget."
Damien Lewis, bestselling author of *Operation Certain Death* and *Bloody Heroes*.

"Here at last is the authentic voice of the veterans of a gruelling and thankless campaign. Powerful, revealing and moving."
Patrick Bishop, bestselling author of *3 Para* and *Bomber Boys*.

A LONG LONG WAR

Voices from the British Army in
Northern Ireland 1969–98

Written and compiled by

Ken M. Wharton

Helion & Company Limited

Helion & Company Limited
26 Willow Road
Solihull
West Midlands
B91 1UE
England
Tel. 0121 705 3393
Fax 0121 711 4075
Email: info@helion.co.uk
Website: www.helion.co.uk

Published by Helion & Company 2008

Designed and typeset by Helion & Company Limited, Solihull, West Midlands
Cover designed by Bookcraft Limited, Stroud, Gloucestershire
Printed by Cromwell Press Ltd, Trowbridge, Wiltshire

Text © Ken M. Wharton
Maps of Belfast and Londonderry originally appeared in *The British Army in Northern Ireland*
by Michael Dewar (1985) and are © Weidenfeld & Nicolson, a division of The Orion
Publishing Group (London).
Photographs – where known, images are credited to copyright holders. If no credit shown, we have
been unable to trace the copyright holder – the publishers would be pleased to hear from such.
Front cover image: 'Alert in Belfast' 1986 © Paul Crispin.
Rear cover image: 'Thoughts of Home', Belfast 1986 © Paul Crispin.

ISBN 978 1 906033 18 7

British Library Cataloguing-in-Publication Data.
A catalogue record for this book is available from the British Library.

For details of other military history titles published by Helion & Company Limited contact
the above address, or visit our website: http://www.helion.co.uk.

We always welcome receiving book proposals from prospective authors. We would particularly
like to hear from Northern Ireland veterans who are interested in producing book-length
accounts of their experiences in the Province. Our contact details are above.

'Then it's Tommy this, an' Tommy that, an' Tommy how's yer soul?
But it's "Thin red line of 'eroes" when the drums begin to roll,
The drums begin to roll, my boys, the drums begin to roll.
O it's "Thin red line of 'eroes" when the drums begin to roll.
For it's Tommy this, an' Tommy that, an' 'Chuck him out, the brute!' But it's
'Saviour of 'is country,' when the guns begin to shoot; An' it's Tommy this, an'
Tommy that, an' anything you please; But Tommy ain't a bloomin' fool – you
bet that Tommy sees!'
(Rudyard Kipling)

'So I'll wait for the wild rose that's waitin' for me where the Mountains of
Mourne sweep down to the sea'
(William Percy French, 1854–1920)

FACT: Since the end of the Second World War in 1945, there has only been one year in which British soldiers have not been killed on active service. That year was 1968, the year before Northern Ireland went insane.

I phoned home and said: 'Mum, I've been shot.' She replied: 'Don't be so stupid. Don't tell lies and don't make jokes like that!'
(Lance Corporal Mark Overson, D.E.R.R. who was shot and wounded on April 3rd, 1993, near Crossmaglen)

Contents

List of photos

List of maps

Maps of Belfast and Londonderry originally appeared in *The British Army in Northern Ireland* by Michael Dewar (1985) and are © Weidenfeld & Nicolson, a division of The Orion Publishing Group (London)

Foreword

When I was asked to write the foreword, I felt unsure, as the book is mainly about soldiers telling their stories, and I am merely a sister of a soldier. My brother, Bombardier Terence Griffin, RA, was tragically killed through the Northern Ireland Troubles in the M62 coach bomb blast 4 February 1974. Upon reflection, I realised that most of us who are civilians did not know just how dangerous the situation in Northern Ireland was for those out there, trying their utmost best to keep peace. The reason I say this, is that my own brother, whilst coming home on leave had his stories to tell, but they were indeed much sanitised stories. I realise that this was probably to protect us, his family, from ever realising just how bloody and dangerous this war was. Upon reading many of the soldiers' stories in this book, you get a sense of just how much the British Army and the Irish community had to go through. The terrible stories of bombings, killings and heartache that endured for over 30 years; stories which have never been written before. They need to be written, so that people will be able to get a perspective of what war and the evils of terrorism does to each and every person. This book is not for the faint-hearted; Ken Wharton has written this book depicting the true horrors of war. I sincerely hope and pray that this particular war never raises its ugly head ever again. I dedicate this book to my brother; to all those soldiers, their families and friends, the community of Northern Ireland and all those who have lost and suffered because of the Northern Ireland troubles.

Mo Norton, 2007

Preface

Jason Hughes, formerly King's Regiment

I think it would be a good place to start by introducing myself and telling a little about myself and why I contacted the author – Ken Wharton – to include my stories in amongst this landmark work.

I have been a soldier for eighteen years and recently left as part of the normalisation process under the guise of Op Banner. However this was not where it began for me; this was with the now consigned-to-history 1st Battalion the King's Regt, where I served from during years 1987–1992. The years 1990–1992 were the tour dates in NI and were the beginning of a love affair with the country, but not all its people. There was a large number of us so called 'limeys', 'channel swimmers', 'money mercenaries' or just plain old 'Brits' – it's a good thing squaddies have a thick skin or they would be easily offended.

I wanted to recount some of the things I have seen and experienced but to also look at the often darkly humorous side of a soldier who chose to live in amongst the problem. I hope it will give the readers who are not in the military and had little or no idea of what it was like to be part of the process of change. I must count my own parents in this, as more often than not the lack of reporting back in the mainland meant they relied only on what I passed to them – which was often very little as I didn't see the point. Let's be honest, you can only mention there was another shooting yesterday so often before the answer becomes the same, 'oh, right.' It's not their fault that the media is doing much the same now with the world's other problems; if it goes unreported then it doesn't exist

I must comment that the process of integration was a long hard process of acceptance not always easy and often met with 'why?' and 'what do you know?' I can say I still don't fully understand the problem nor do I confess to offer any political points of view. All that I do know is the country is a much better place and the only way must be forward, however that happens. It will take a generation to even begin to heal the deep wounds left by this conflict.

Acknowledgements

THE VOICES

(Listed in order of material contributed, from first to last)
John Flexman
John O'Brien
Mark Overson
Martin 'Starsy' Starsmore
Philip Beale
Ray Gascoyne
Mrs Lita Overson
Charlie McGrogan
Doreen Gilchrist
Mike Day
Keith Hudson
Nigel Crosby
Dave Von Slap
Terry Friend
Bernie Homer
Richard Hall
Geoff Smith
Jim Parker*
Paddy Larkin
David Hardy
Andy Bennett
Bernard Loughran
Bill Jackson
Jim Mackenzie
Major Ross
Pat Moir
Andy Warren
Darren Ware
Dennis Gilpin
Pete Townend
Mike Gomersal
Paul Muspratt
Andrew MacDonald
Marcus Lapsa
Ernie Taylor
Stevie UDR
Alex Veteran
Paul Empey
James Kirkby

Pete Guild
Tim Castle
John Moore
Philip Gilbert
William Taylor
Rachel Hardy
Richard Dornall
Barry Crane
Allan Bolton
Hadyn Davies
Stephen Griffiths
Michael Thomasson
Steve 'Taffy' Horvath
Scott Buchanan
Geoff Moss
R.P. Mason
Dave Smith
David Hallam
Mick Low
Kevin Stevens
Allan Poole
Nigel Denford
Kenneth Donovan
Ken Draycott
Allan Harrdy
Roy Davies
Arfon Williams
Ken Haslam
Andy Anonymous
John Silkstone
Philly Morris
Jason Benn
Jason Hughes
Rocky Evershed
Richard Nettleton
Mike Hewlett
Lawrence Jagger
David Creese
Steve Atkinson
Paddy Leneghan
George Prosser
Carol Richards
Mike Morgan
Tom Clarke
Brian Bounsell
Gordon McClurg
Keith 'Tiny' Rose

Paul 'Scouse' Hughes
Derek Parsley
Stuart Martin
Ronnie Gamble
Chas Hawley
Mo Norton
Russ Slater
Barry Hughes
Alistair Keenan
Eddie Bright
Hugh Heap
Martyn Horton
Mike Edwards
Nick Bagle
Perry Lusher
Richard Peacocke
Mike Evans
Ossie Osbourne
Neil Evans
Lawrence Bowman
Phil Winstanley
Ian Jones
David Smith
'Buzzy'
The twenty unamed Squaddies who told me their stories not seeking recognition

(*All accounts by Jim Parker are copyright to him and may not be reproduced without his express permission)

I would also like to say a profound thanks to the following people, without whom this book would have never been written and for their tireless help, patience and understanding.

As an ex-squaddie myself, I am, unashamedly biased in my respect and affection for the Army in which I served; I have to record my thanks to the legion of both serving and former soldiers and their families for the incredible help they gave me.

Mike Day, for his tireless advice, his expertise in all things photographic and internet web sites and for his endless encouragement and sourcing of material for me. For his help in trips to Edinburgh and Aberdeen to talk to veterans and to his gorgeous wife, Josie, the deepest possible thanks. Without him, I could have never achieved all that I did.

Mike Heavens (who is so old, his first C.O. was Boadicea and, instead of an SLR, he carried a spear) for his tireless work and writing.

Profound thanks to Andrew Macdonald for countless hours of interviews, use of photographs and his hospitality.

A really big thank you to my Aussie Green Jacket mate, Dave Hallam for the hours he must have spent composing e-mails and bombarding every known Army website (including some that I hadn't even heard of) TV and Radio stations and just for being a great mate; good on ya' cobber!

An enormous thanks to Arfon Williams and the South Wales Borderers Museum in Brecon for some superb catering, guarded car parking, the run of an excellent museum on its closing day, great facilities and for bringing in some great former soldiers to help me.

I gratefully acknowledge Elley Mytton of Andre Deutsch, part of the Carlton Publishing Group for their kind permission to reprint parts of Nicky Curtis's *Faith and Duty* (1998, ISBN: 0 233 00006 2). Sections were used from the following pages of the 2003 paperback: 42-43; 43-44; 66-67.

I gratefully acknowledge Ronnie Gamble's *The History of E Company 5 UDR: The Last Coleraine Militia?* (Regimental Association of the UDR, Coleraine Branch, Coleraine, 2007).

I am also indebted to Darren Ware for allowing me to use long extracts from his proposed book on the death of his Guards regiment brother; his writing is powerful and poignant. His wife isn't bad either!

Jim 'people who talk to me get flat ears' Parker for endless telephone conversations and countless photographs and detailed accounts of his Army life.

My profound thanks to Steve Horvath for his story and the undoubted pain he had to re-live in telling me that story. He is still alive and lives in East Anglia with his wife Sarah, son, and daughter; he may never be cured of his PTSD but nowadays he has a motto. As he wrote:

> It has been both painful and helpful to have been asked to contribute to the Forgotten Voices. My sincerest thanks for being given this opportunity to tell my part of the story. To my beloved wife Sarah who has stuck by me, even though I have put her and my children through hell. I now live by 2 rules: Rule 1: I will wake up tomorrow. Rule 2: There are no other rules and if unsure, refer to Rule 1.

Lesley (at RGBW Regimental Office) John Flexman (again) because of the effort he put in as I questioned him constantly in an effort to ensure that I didn't make any mistakes. John O'Brien (again) for his endless patience and for quenching my endless thirst for information and a wonderful cup of tea at his house in Yorkshire.

Pat Moir for the loan of books and press material relating to the troubles.

Ray Gascoyne for his superb Green Howards web site www.ex-greenhowards.com.

Those amazing guys at the Coldstream Guards web site www.coldstreamers.co.uk. Thanks to Mannie and Reg Varney and Mac Boro.

I am very grateful to the Bombardier (Andy Warren) and his marvellous site www.militaryimages.net.

Sandy at Royal Highland Fusiliers museum.

Special thanks to Mark Overson; I spent a wonderful afternoon with him and his lovely partner Alison, in a Berkshire pub where the cost of a pint and a pastie would buy a 2 bedroomed house in Yorkshire. Thanks also to his Mum and Dad for their kind hospitality and for the words of an anxious Mother.

To Pete and Felicity Townend, now ensconced in Australia; killed off by a former comrade's book, I am happy to report that he is alive and well.

My profound thanks to Doreen Gilchrist, now living in Australia, for her moving description of the night that Gunner Robert Curtis became the first British soldier to be killed during the troubles. Her accounts were wonderfully moving. Thank you also for caring about the squaddies who patrolled your street.

I must acknowledge the kindness and the hospitality of the Hardy family – David who was very badly injured at Ballygawley, his lovely wife, Leigh and his Mum, Rachel who gave me a very moving account of a Mother's fears for her soldier son; thank you for your time.

Major Ross and Wilma and Judy of the Gordon Highlanders Museum

There has to be mention of Andy Bennett of the Northern Ireland Veterans Association not only for his incredible contribution to this book but for the amazing and constructive way that they support ex-squaddies and act as their legal voices. The tireless Keith Hudson NIVETS' press officer for all his help. To Dave Von Slap and Dave Langston of NIVA; long may this organisation continue to care about NI soldiers and their lives.

Geoff Smith for saving me a whole week of interviewing and telephoning. See www.lightinfantryreunited.co.uk. I am absolutely indebted to Geoff for his generous offer – gratefully accepted – to use his site for specialist accounts. Absolutely is a bloody hard word to argue with.

Tony Martin of the IJLB for his co-operation.

Another mention of Jim Mackenzie for the use and application of *Rose and Thistle* the journal of the Scots Guards.

Helen MacDonald, Helen Cheshire, Trevor Dawson, Jerry Wood, L.J. Franklin, Ian Wright, my friend Graham 'Pie eater' Watson and Phil, my neighbour, for their endless encouragement and giving me the belief in my own capabilities as a writer. To all 7 of my children for giving me the heart to put my words and thoughts in print.

I also commend the music of Terry Friend who has composed and sings some beautiful and haunting stuff about the troubles; see: http://www.anothercountrysong.com

We ALL owe, however, the biggest thanks to the young men and women who served their country in Northern Ireland, especially those who fell and those who still carry the scars of that 28 year period where an entire country went mad.

Publishers' Acknowledgements

The publishers would like to acknowledge the assistance they received from the following individuals:

David Barzilay, for generously placing at our disposal his books of negatives and prints taken during his time as a journalist in Northern Ireland, and for his unfailing and enthusiastic support for this project.

Guy Adams, for working so hard to make this book a success.

Paul Crispin, for responding at short notice to our inquiries and requests for photographs and information. His images are a testament to the soldiers on the streets of Northern Ireland.

Major Keith Scott and Mr David Zwirek of the Ministry of Defence, for their help in guiding the manuscript through to publication.

Dr Martin Melaugh, CAIN Director at the University of Ulster, for his assistance on a number of key parts of the book, without which this work would be the poorer.

Darren Croucher, for helping out with some photographs at very short notice.

Thank you to you all.

Glossary of Terms

2IC	Second in command
Angle Iron	Soldier of Royal Anglians
ASU	IRA Active Service Unit
ATO	Army Technical Officer (bomb-disposal)
Bandit Country	South Armagh and especially the area around Crossmaglen
Barrett.50	High velocity sniper's rifle (US-made)
Brick	4 men under a Corporal (4 bricks under a Sergeant)
B-Special	Part-time Police auxiliaries
Btn/ Bn	Battalion (generally 480 – 600 men in an infantry unit)
Bullet Catcher	Either the lead man or the tail-end Charlie in a foot patrol
Bullshit	The expression for the rigorous spit 'n polishing routine
Casevac	Casualty evacuation
Cas-Rep	Casualty Report
CGM	Conspicuous Gallantry Medal
CO	Commanding Officer (Lieutenant-Colonel)
GOC	general Officer Commanding
Contact	Shot fired by enemy
COP	Close Observation Platoon
CP	Check Point
CPC	Civilianised Patrol Car
Crap Hat	To a Para, this meant any other Regiment
CSM	Company Sergeant-Major
CSU	Civilian Search Unit
DERR	Duke of Edinburgh's Royal Regiment (see also DoE)
Det 14/The Det	Undercover British Army unit (also 14th Detachment)
Dicking	Being observed by gunman's helpers prior to a shot being set up. Also: being dicked
ECM	Electronic counter measure (to block radio signals intended to detonate bombs by remote control)

F.P	Foot Patrol. Also firing point; the reader needs to check the context of the incidents.
Full Screw	Full Corporal
GC	George Cross
GOC	General Officer Commanding
GPMG	("Jimpy") General Purpose Machine-Gun (1960s successor to LMG or Bren)
Green Bottles	Term used by soldiers to describe the RUC
GS	Garda Síochána (Irish Republic Police Service)
GSM	General Service Medal (awarded to British soldiers who have served a tour of active service)
HED	High explosive device
Hen patrol	Women looking out for soldiers and then alerting others by usually banging dustbin lids noisily.
IA	Immediate action
IC	In command
ICP	Incident Command Post
IED	Improvised Explosive Device
INIBA	Improved Northern Ireland Body Armour
INLA	Irish National Liberation Army
Int	Army Intelligence (thought to be a contradiction in terms)
IRA	Irish Republican Army (Óglaigh na hÉireann)
Irish Cocktail	Petrol Bomb
IRSP	Irish Republican Socialist Party (political wing of INLA)
IWS	Individual Weapons Sight (sniper scope)
Lance-Jack	Lance Corporal
Left-footer	Catholic (see also 'Taig')
Lift	To arrest
LMG	Light Machine Gun
LVF	Loyalist Volunteer Force
MC	Military Cross
MiD	Mentioned in Dispatches
MM	Military Medal
Mob	Usually a reference to the Army as a whole, used by soldiers
Multiple	12 man grouping (3 x 4 man teams) 2 multiples = a platoon

MQs	Married Quarters
ND	Negligent Discharge (premature or unnecessary firing of a weapon)
NIFSL	Northern Ireland Forensic Science Laboratory
NITAT	Northern Ireland Training Advisory Team
NORAID	American fund raising organisation which financed the IRA
NTH	Newtownhamilton
OC	Officer Commanding
Officials	Volunteer in the Official wing of the IRA (see also 'Stickies')
OP	Observation Post
Operation Motorman	Army operation in 1972 to forcibly end the "no go" areas of the province
Ops	Operations
ORBAT	Order of Battle
Overwatch	One unit giving support or protection to another (esp at VCPs)
Own Goal	Where a terrorist bomb might explode prematurely killing the bomber
PIG	Armoured personnel carrier (Patrol Infantry Group) produced by Humber
PIRA	Provisional IRA
Player	Army slang for known or suspected terrorist.
PPW	Personal Protection Weapon
Prod	Protestant
Provie/ Provo	Member of the Provisional IRA as the Nationalists would call them
Proxy	Bomb carried to point of detonation by a person under duress.
PTI	Physical Training Instructor (also known as the 'SS')
PVCP	Permanent vehicle checkpoint
QCB	Queen's Commendation for Bravery
QRF	Quick Reaction Force
RCIED	Remote controlled Improvised Explosive Device
RIRA	"Real" IRA (behind the Omagh atrocity)
RMC	Royal Marine Commando
RMO	Regimental Medical Officer
RN	Republican News (*An Phoblacht*) Republican newspaper
RPG	Rocket-propelled grenade
RT	Radio Transmitter

RUC	Royal Ulster Constabulary
RVH	Royal Victoria Hospital, Belfast
Rupert	An unofficial British Army term for Officer
SA80	Current British Army standard assault rifle
Sangar	Heavily fortified protective guard post
Sarry	Saracen Armoured Vehicle
SD	Suspect device
SDLP	Social and Democratic Labour Party (Páirtí Sóisialta Daonlathach an Lucht Oibre)
SF	Security Forces
Sf	Sustained fire (automatic weapons firing on fixed lines)
Shankhill Butchers	A Protestant murder gang who targeted only Catholics
Shebeen	Illegal drinking dens run on sectarian lines and offering all hours drinking
Sinn Fein	"We Alone/ Us Alone" (so-called political wing of the IRA)
Slot	To kill
SLR	Self Loading Rifle. 7.62mm standard British Army rifle
SMG	Sub Machine Gun
SOPS	Standard operating procedures
SOTAT	Security Operations Training Unit; N.I. street training in Germany
Squaddie	British soldier
Stag	Period of guard duty (i.e. a 2 hour stag)
Stickies	The derisive nickname for an Official IRA volunteer
Storno	Radio transmitter
SUSAT	Sight Unit, Small Arms Trilux
Taig	Protestant term to describe a Catholic (see also Left-footer)
The 'Murph'	The Ballymurphy estate in West Belfast
The Badge	Regimental Sergeant Major
The Bog	Northern Ireland or Ireland as a whole
Tom	Another word for squaddie
Tout	IRA term for an informer or spy
UCBT	Under car booby trap (see also UVBT)
UDA	Ulster Defence Association (Protestant paramilitary force)
UFF	Ulster Freedom Fighters (see also UVF)
US	Useless !
UVBT	Under Vehicle Booby Trap

UVF	Ulster Volunteer Force
VBIED	Vehicle-borne improvised explosive device
VCP	Vehicle Checkpoint
VISA	Vehicle Incendiary: South Armagh
Wad	Sandwich
WO	Warrant Officer (Sergeant Major)
Woodentop	Soldier in the Guards Brigade
Wriggly Tin	Corrugated iron
XMG	Crossmaglen

Regimental Abbreviations

17/21 L.	17th/21st Lancers
A. & S.H.	Argyll & Sutherland Highlanders
A.C.C.	Army Catering Corps*
A.P.T.C.	Army Physical Training Corps
B. & R.	Blues and Royals
B.W.	Black Watch
C.G.	Coldstream Guards
C.R.	Cheshire Regiment
D & D.	Devon & Dorsets
D.O.E.	Duke of Edinburgh's Regiment
D.W.R.	Duke of Wellington's Regiment
G.G.	Grenadier Guards
G.H.	Gordon Highlanders
G.Hr./XIX	Green Howards
GLOS	Gloucestershire Regiment
K.H.	King's Hussars
K.O.B.	King's Own Border Regiment
K.O.S.B.	King's Own Scottish Borderers
K.R.	King's Rifles
L.I.	Light Infantry
P.O.W.	Prince of Wales Own Regiment of Yorkshire
P.W.R.R.	Princess of Wales' Royal Regiment
PARA	Parachute Regiment
Q.D.G.	Queen's Dragoon Guards
Q.L.R.	Queen's Lancashire Regiment
Q.O.H.	Queen's Own Highlanders
Q.O.H.	Queen's Own Hussars
Q.R.	Queen's Regiment
Q.R.L.	Queen's Royal Lancers
R.A.	Royal Artillery
R.A.F.	Royal Airforce
R.A.M.C.	Royal Army Medical Corps
R.A.O.C.	Royal Army Ordinance Corps *
R.A.R.	Royal Anglian Regiment

R.A.V.C.	Royal Army Veterinary Corps
R.C.S.	Royal Corps of Signals
R.C.T.	Royal Corps of Transport*
R.D.G.	Royal Dragoon Guards
R.E.	Royal Engineers
R.E.M.E.	Royal Electrical & Mechanical Engineers
R.G.B.W.	Royal Gloucester Berkshire & Wiltshire Regiment
R.G.J.	Royal Green Jackets
R.H.F.	Royal Highland Fusiliers
R.H.R.	Royal Highland Rifles
R.I.R	Royal Irish Rangers
R.L.	Royal Lancers
R.L.C.	Royal Logistics Corps
R.M.	Royal Marines
R.M.P.	Royal Military Police
R.N.	Royal Navy
R.P.C.	Royal Pioneer Corps*
R.R.W.	Royal Regiment of Wales
R.S.D.G.	Royal Scots Dragoon Guards
R.T.R.	Royal Tank Regiment
R.W.F.	Royal Welsh Fusiliers
S.G	Scots Guards
Staffs	Staffordshire Regiment
T.A.V.R.	Territorial Army & Volunteer Reserve
U.D.R.	Ulster Defence Regiment (Northern Ireland's T.A.)
W. & S.F.	Worcestershire & Sherwood Foresters
W.G.	Welsh Guards
W.R.A.C.	Women's Royal Army Corps

* Merged into R.L.C. 1993

Army Chain of Command (Infantry)

Brick	4 men under a Lance-Corporal
Section	Generally 8 men led by a Sergeant
Platoon	Generally 30 men led by a Lieutenant
Company	120–160 men, led by a Captain or Major
Battalion	600 men led by a Lieutenant-Colonel
Brigade/ Regiment	1800 men led by a full Colonel or Brigadier

Maps

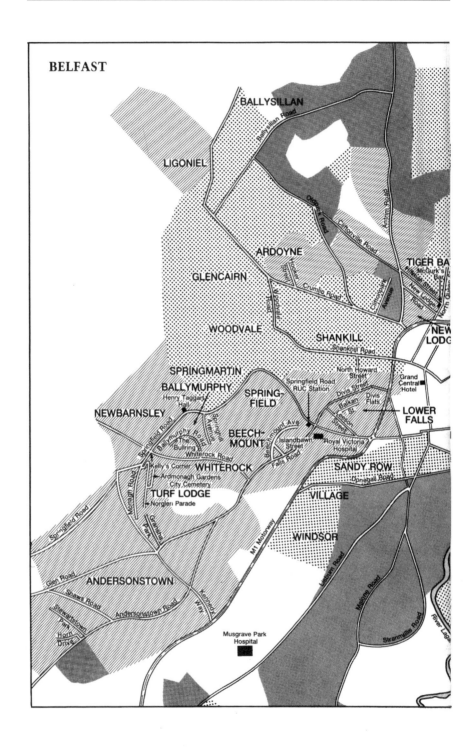

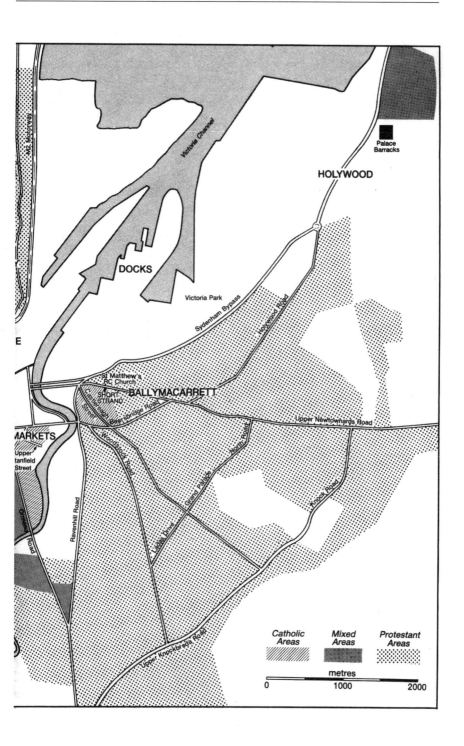

Palace
Barracks

HOLYWOOD

DOCKS

Victoria Park

Sydenham Bypass

Holywood Road

St Matthew's
RC Church

SHORT
STRAND

BALLYMACARRETT

Albertbridge Road

Upper Newtownards Road

MARKETS

Upper
Stanfield
Street

Woodstock Road

North Road

Grand Parade

Knock Road

Ravenhill Road

Eliza Drive

Ormeau Road

Upper Knockbreda Road

Catholic
Areas

Mixed
Areas

Protestant
Areas

metres

0   1000   2000

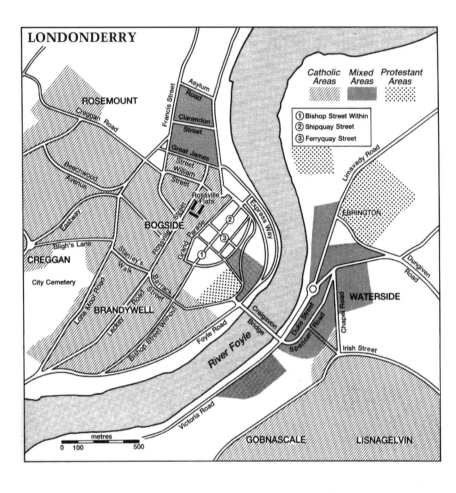

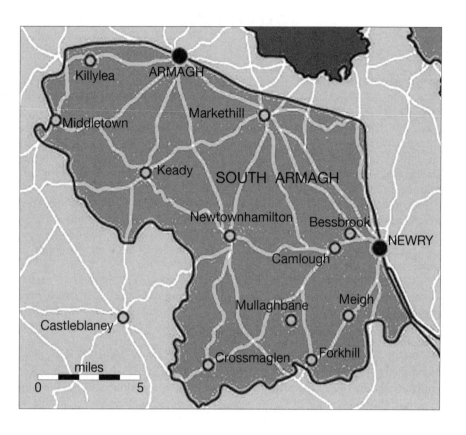

Introduction

On the 6th February, 1971 whilst patrolling in the New Lodge area of Belfast, Gunner Robert Curtis of the Royal Artillery was shot by an IRA gunman; he was just 20 years of age and left a young, pregnant, widow.

Nine days later, a fellow R.A. comrade, Lance Bombardier, John Laurie aged 22 who had been wounded in the same firefight as Gunner Curtis, died of his wounds. The killing spread to Londonderry. A mere 2 weeks later, a Military Policeman, Corporal William Joliffe who was just 18 years old, died of his wounds after being attacked with a petrol bomb.

By the end of that year of 1971, a further 45 British soldiers would have been killed, making it the worst year for Army fatalities since the end of the Korean War in 1953. That figure, sadly, would be surpassed several times more. The following year, 1972 it would hit a peak of 129, dropping to 66 in 1973 and then, thankfully, it would never again hit those awful heights.

In the year of Rob Curtis's death and the following year, the Army recorded 2,404 bomb incidents and a staggering 12,387 shooting incidents in a country of just 1.5 million people.

That there had been, officially, no deaths prior to the loss of Gunner Curtis was utterly incredible; but it was coming and once it did, tragically for the soldiers, the floodgates would open. Immediately prior to Robert's death, the Army had been on the streets of Northern Ireland, supplementing and in most cases, supplanting, the role of the hard-pressed RUC, for 18 months. In the days up and until his shooting, over 700 British soldiers – in the same period, over 800 RUC members – had been injured in riots and other forms of violence. Most Britons had been thankful that despite the injury rate, there had been, mercifully, no deaths. But, one Monday in early February, 1971, a gunman's bullet would change, forever, the face and complexion of Northern Irish – and, inextricably linked as it was – British politics.

26 years on from the death of Robert Curtis, almost to the very day, Lance-Bombardier Stephen Restorick was shot dead whilst manning a permanent vehicle checkpoint (PVCP) near Bessbrook Mill army base in Armagh. Although 16 months later, Corporal Gary Fenton, QCB, of the Royal Gloucestershire, Berkshire & Wiltshire Regiment was knocked down and killed whilst manning a vcp at Crossmaglen, Restorick was the last squaddie known, definitively, to have been killed by the IRA.

Gary Fenton was inspecting a truck which drove forward and killed him. Unbelievably, the driver received only a 6 months suspended sentence and loss of his driving licence for just one year!

This collection of voices will, I trust, fill in the tragic gap between the deaths of Robert Curtis and Stephen Restorick. That gap was marked by the passing of 9,503 days and nights and on every one of those days and nights, British troops sought to keep the peace in Northern Ireland.

One sad statistic, however, will never change, and that was that Gunner Rob Curtis would be accorded a legacy, a major one, in the history of what is somewhat euphemistically known as 'the Troubles'; he would be the first of over 1,000 British soldiers to be killed or die over the course of the next sad and tragic 27 years.

The author attended East Ardsley Secondary Modern School, a 'gasworks Lane' kind of Secondary Modern, leaving in 1964 as the school was closing and the village Primary school would relocate onto that hallowed ground vacated by the author and his contemporaries. Amongst the bright-eyed, collective innocence of the new term in September of that year, was a 9 year old boy called Tommy Stoker. Little did he know that he had already lived half of his life, because 9 years later, whilst in an observation post (OP) overlooking Berwick Road, Ardoyne in Belfast, with the Light Infantry, Tommy was accidentally shot in the back and badly wounded on the 29th July. After a courageous fight against death, he succumbed to his wounds 7 weeks later. At the time of the shooting, he had only been with the battalion for 2 days.

On that date, 19th September, 1972, Tommy became one of three Light Infantry squaddies killed in a matter of weeks, and the 154th British soldier to give his life for peace in that troubled province. On the roll of honour, his name is enshrined between those of Lance Corporal John Davies (Royal Regiment of Fusiliers), killed in Londonderry's Bogside and a Para, Frank Bell, who, like Tommy, was only 18 and who was killed on the notorious Ballymurphy Estate in west Belfast.

I visit Tommy's grave in St Michaels Parish Church at least once a year in order to place flowers for a fallen comrade and, on the grave he shares with his Mum, are the words 'Died 19th September, 1972, aged 18 years' Without the slightest embarrassment, I confess that I cry every time I visit his grave. On a nearby war memorial, commemorating the names of East Ardsley's fallen of two world wars, is the simple inscription – finally placed there, I understand as a result of his family's perseverance and persistence – which reads 'T.A. Stoker: Killed in Ireland 1972'

As one reads the engraved names of the young boys who perished on the Somme and 'Wipers' and a myriad number of other places on the fields of Flanders, the names in both wars are depressingly, the same. Indeed, it could be the morning register at my village school which Tommy also attended. In the event of another war, one supposes that the names of its fallen would be, tragically, the same ones.

This book is dedicated not only to the memory of every one of my fellow squaddies killed as a result of the madness which was inflicted, forcibly, upon Northern Ireland for such a large part of my life, but especially to Tommy Stoker. It is also dedicated to those who were injured and suffered debilitating and career-ending wounds.

Further, it will be a collection of accounts and photographs of those who served their country in that sad place where Britain lost more service personnel than it did in the Korean War. We must not lose sight of the fact that men fell, not only in areas of the province which would become, tragically familiar, but also in other places, not renowned for violent death. Men fell in places such as the Murph, Turf Lodge, Short Strand, Lower Falls Road and Springfield Road in Belfast, the Creggan and Bogside a little further north in Londonderry, also in Enniskillen and, of course, in that terrible bandit country of Crossmaglen and South Armagh, and there were other towns and cities, away from Northern Ireland.

Let us not forget the killings in Hyde Park, and on the same tragic day, in Regent's Park; in Deal, at Army and RAF barracks in Holland, Belgium and Germany and even on the streets of Derby, where Sergeant Michael Newman was assassinated outside the Army Careers Office. Let us not forget those squaddies and their families, cruelly murdered, on an Army bus on the M62 motorway in my native West Yorkshire. Let us also hold dear to our hearts 19 year old Private William Davies of the Royal Regiment of Wales who was shot dead at Lichfield railway station in Staffordshire whilst off duty and waiting for a train, in June, 1990. Of all the cowardly acts of murder committed against British troops, this atrocity cuts to the very core of our civilisation.

One remembers the nightly news during 1972, when 129 soldiers were killed in that insane year, with a soldier's death on average every three days or so – reports of a soldier shot in the head by a sniper in the Ardoyne or a soldier covering Army engineers being shot in the chest in the Falls Road or of another soldier being shot in the back in the Markets area whilst on foot patrol. Did we all become inured to the tragedy of Northern Ireland as it unfolded in our own living rooms on an almost daily basis?

As these words are written, it is well over 10 years since Stephen Restorick was gunned down manning that PVCP on a fateful day in Bessbrook and in those intervening years, we have had the Good Friday agreement, early release from prison of convicted terrorists, supposed decommissioning of arms and a new power-sharing Northern Ireland Executive; in short: reconciliation. There will, inevitably, be criticism of my insistence on writing this book from the perspective of the British soldier, the 'squaddie' and the 'Tom'. There will be no apologies for this stance and I ask you, the reader, to judge that stance.

Even today, quite a few years after my own unremarkable Army career ended, like many an ex-squaddie, ex-Tom or ex-Rupert, every time I hear on the nightly news of the loss of a British soldier, whether or not it is Iraq, Afghanistan, or in the past, in Sierra Leone, Bosnia, Serbia, Kosovo, or over in 'the Bog' and, course, in the South Atlantic, I die, just a little, inside.

During the writing of this book, I received an e-mail from an old squaddie who served with the Glorious Glosters on Imjin Hill in Korea in the 50s and he told me that he too, still grieves all these years later. I met and spoke with David Hardy who survived the appalling carnage which followed the IRA's attack on a Light Infantry coach bringing returning soldiers to Northern Ireland; by some miracle – despite the pain still suffered almost 20 years later – he lived; 8 of his comrades did not. It was an honour to have this ex-squaddie contribute to this book.

I apologise for any distress which might be caused through mis-spelling of soldiers' names, or the use of a wrong Christian name, or rank. But all the facts were checked on reputable sites prior to publishing. I am aware that distress can be caused. Indeed, a former Lieutenant Colonel of the Glosters implored me to make sure of my facts; I trust that I have indeed done so.

I think that it was a former Airborne soldier, Anthony Deane-Drummond, M.C. who once said, following the tragic but heroic failure at Arnhem in

September 1944: 'If you meet a man who fought at Arnhem, then buy him a drink.' I say the same about the lads who served in Northern Ireland.

I hope that, through these voices, you will begin to understand – those of you who were fortunate enough not to have been there – what life was like on the streets of Belfast and Londonderry and Crossmaglen and a dozen other places in Northern Ireland. You will read the words of the voices behind the statistics; maybe you will not see the faces behind the statistics, but be sure, every squaddie who served in Northern Ireland during those terrible years has a voice.

David Hallam, my good friend and former comrade wrote:

Our tour had been full of both the expected and unexpected; sadness and funny times, and some days were very long. No sleep and long nights both wet and cold. At some stage you say to yourself 'what am I doing here?' But you get on with it. You see the news on TV and it's about the bombing or shooting we had been involved in that day; and the report is nowhere near what had really happened. The BBC or ITV had cut it to bits just to make people's consciences clear.

People sit down to have their tea and the newsreader says that 'another soldier has been shot' but they don't show what a mess it has made of the man and the effect it has on his mates and the happiness of the other side when they sing 'one nil'. The people just get on eating their meal and then go to bed. We were young when we left for Ireland and came back older and changed men for life. We had seen things that you don't really see on TV or read in the newspapers.

We met people whom the everyday man and women will never get to meet. The anger towards us was a result of years of history that had been rolled up into a ball and it was now our turn to play and it was a game with one-sided rules.

All of us who served there became closer; we shared something in those four months which will last for the rest of time. Anyone who has ever been involved in something like this will understand what I am saying. When I look back and see what has gone on, in respect to the soldiers who have lost their lives; what was it all for; did we really achieve any thing; was it worth it, I wonder? Only time will tell.

To all those of you who are reading this introduction who may not have been aware of the violence and hatred, the prejudice, the open hostility or the resentment that the British soldier had to endure in Northern Ireland: read on. To those of you who were not aware of the tricks and devices the IRA employed to kill and maim British soldiers: read on. If you want to understand what it was like to fight almost on your own doorstep: read on.

Perhaps, if these voices strike a chord, you, the reader might just understand the stories behind the words which, for so many years of our lives, echoed around our living rooms with the evening news, particularly on News At Ten, when, between sombre chimes of Big Ben were sandwiched the words:: 'In Northern Ireland, another British soldier has been killed.'

Ken Wharton, Yorkshire, June, 2007

Chapter One

The Stage is Set

The last British soldier – officially – to be killed on active service in Northern Ireland – I pray, in later years that the fickle hand of history does not prove me wrong – was Lance-Bombardier Stephen Restorick of the Royal Artillery. Whilst manning a permanent vehicle checkpoint (PVCP) in Armagh, he was shot by an IRA sniper and lay dying, cradled in the arms of a woman he had never met before and whose car was stopped at the PVCP. He died later in hospital and the woman said 'He was there smiling and a while later, he was dead.' That tragic event took place on February 12, 1997, some 10 or more years ago now, as I start this book.

For those of you interested in such statistics, Stephen's death took the toll of British soldiers killed, to over 740 – although there is evidence which suggests that the figure is well over 1,000 – and their blood was spilled not only on Northern Ireland's streets, roads, fields and country lanes, but also in two of London's Royal Parks, on a motorway near Huddersfield, in a band practice session in Kent, in a Hampshire railway station, in pubs in the South East of England, in a street in Derby city centre, in Wembley, London and on the streets of Holland, Belgium and Germany.

Night after night, all readers over the age of 21 must have heard the news emanating from a BBC or ITV newsreader, spoken over images of riots and mobs and steel-helmeted, plastic-visored soldiers fending off petrol bombs – or 'miscellaneous incendiary devices' as Army-speak described them. Those black and white images becoming ever so much whiter as an 'Irish cocktail' exploded over the top of a PIG (Patrol Infantry Group, an armoured personnel carrier) or against one of the grim-faced soldier's riot shield. The sharp crack of a baton round – or a rubber bullet as the flak-jacketed news reporter called them as he crouched anxiously down behind the PIG or around a wall – and an entire cacophony of sounds which we came to recognise as 'normal' for Belfast and Londonderry.

Hands up any reader who has not heard of the Lower Falls or the Divis Street flats, or the Unity Street flats or the Turf Lodge in Belfast ? Hands up any readers who have never heard of the Bogside or the Creggan or of Crossmaglen? Who doesn't remember the bombings in Enniskillen on that most sacred of days to the British Commonwealth: Remembrance Sunday?

Who, among you had even heard of Warrenpoint until that terrible day in August, 1979, when 16 Paras and 2 Queen's Own soldiers were killed by an IRA landmine?

Now tell me, had the 'Troubles' never started, would you know where Anderstown or the Springfield Road or Ormeau Road or the Ballymurphy Estate or the Shankhill were? Would the name Omagh mean anything at all to you, had not the so-called Real IRA decided that a ceasefire and long term peace was not what they wanted?

How many of the Green Howards would have even heard of the Ardoyne or the Crumlin Road had fate not decreed that they be sent there to keep the peace?

But it was all so different, all those long years ago in the summer of 1969, when Harold Wilson's Labour government sent troops out to Northern Ireland on 'peace-keeping' duties. The squaddies, the 'Toms', even our officers – or 'Ruperts' as they were called – were all welcomed with open arms as the outrageously suppressed Catholics saw them as liberators; rather like Tom Courtenay's brilliant portrayal of a Walter Mitty-like character in *Billy Liar* where, at the head of a diverse and battered army he liberates the fictional country of Ambrosia. Unlike the fictional character in that movie, this was real. 'This is it, boys, we're going in to save the Catholics!' But, like lots of things in life, once the 'honeymoon' period was over, things were so much different; so very different. Like a doomed love affair, once the romance is gone, there's emptiness and then hatred; was it ever thus in Northern Ireland!

On what seemed like a nightly basis on our TV screens, we had watched those black and white images being broadcast from Northern Ireland depicting the plight of the Catholic community, clearly being repressed institutionally by the ruling Protestant politicians. The shouts and screams and cries of rage and hatred. If you are old enough, how can you forget the images of the RUC officers liberally using their truncheons and punching Civil Rights marchers as they protested against their second-class citizen status? The nightly cries of 'one man, one vote' echoed across our living rooms and was splashed across the front pages of every newspaper.

On the mainland, with our inherent and accepted equality in housing, education, employment and voting rights, we watched, somewhat bemusedly, as, in another part of the United Kingdom, the legitimately elected Government was actually bestowing the same rights as we enjoyed, on one part of the electorate and yet denying them to another – on the basis of religion!

Daily, our newspapers explained – a little too glibly in my opinion, almost as though it were acceptable – how often Protestants would enjoy two votes in certain situations and the Catholics would be denied even one. How the allocation of Council housing stock was on the basis of Protestants first and the Catholics not at all. How in education terms, the Protestant kids would receive the better education of the two communities. And, finally, how jobs were offered, purely on the basis of which church the applicant either prayed at, or nominally was involved with.

I was brought up a Jehovah's Witness and suffered as a result through lost friendships, through being considered some sort of social leper and through religious shunning. As a consequence, there was immediate solidarity with the Catholics – not thinking for a moment that one day that many might detest the community for the spawning and protection of the IRA – and myself, in common with millions, took their side.

So, from 1968 and through into that glorious summer of the following year, black and white scenes from the film *Mississippi Burning* were re-enacted on the streets of Belfast and Londonderry on a nightly basis. We soon discovered that the latter had two names! Londonderry if one was a Protestant or this new term which emerged, Loyalist and Derry if one was on the opposite side of the sectarian divide or, again, a new word which joined the lexicon of Northern Ireland, a Nationalist! One former soldier – of Irish descent, although proudly having worn the uniform of the British Army – wrote to the author expressing the long held views of his Father. 'He would rather drink acid than call it Londonderry.'

We were soon to learn that the newly emerging lexicon would grow and continue to grow. The next term to confront us would be 'B-Specials' (or 'B-spashools', as a big RUC sergeant would pronounce it one day as he explained to me why the Protestants were the 'good' guys) and these police auxiliaries would fill the vacuum created by the disbanding of the infamous Black and Tans. The Black and Tans, known as such because of their mix 'n match uniforms were a collection of former British soldiers, unemployed in the wake of 1918's peace dividend and early-released convicts of the worst type. Their barbarity, cruelty and systematic violence against Irish citizens in the run up to Irish independence is legendary, but it is not for debate here.

It is sufficient to say, that the B-Specials of 1968 and 1969 clearly drew on the activities of their mentors in the mixed uniform of nearly 50 years earlier. Wearing their black uniforms, these bully boys used the crudest of violence, wanton vandalism and blatant attacks on the Catholic communities throughout the province. It is no coincidence that the ranks of NICRA (Northern Ireland Civil Rights Association) swelled, commensurate to the increase of what was perceived as state violence against them by the RUC and B-Specials.

Their violence and repressive methods, which included mob attacks and deliberate arson attacks on the 'Taigs', as they called the other half of the sectarian divide was so blatant, that it was obvious that their longevity as an institutionalised force would be short lived.

In Londonderry – I use this term based on its description in my atlas and not in terms of my political leanings – 15,000 people held a sit-down protest and brought the city centre to a halt despite the liberal use of police batons. Another march was held with 5,000 people and, in protest against the brutality of the police, the next one attracted 20,000. New characters began to emerge and Bernadette Devlin, a firebrand of a girl with her dulcet Northern Irish accent popped up on the BBC and ITV news almost nightly. Later, Loyalists would try to kill the, then, Bernadette McAliskey and, as British troops ran into her house to save her, she would cynically remark 'What; have ye come to finish me off?'

Other names were starting to emerge, people such as Gerry Fitt, SDLP MP for West Belfast and John Hume. But, of the legendary IRA, there was as yet, no mention. It was, somewhat apocryphally believed that, after the Border wars of the late 1950s, the dormant IRA had sold all their weapons to the Free Wales Army (FWA)

In a period of almost constant tension, with parades and processions by both sides of the sectarian divide being seen as provocative, the Ulster government, led by William Craig, was quick to arbitrarily ban Catholic marches but openly sanction Protestant ones. In particular, the loud, triumphalistic bands of orange-sashed Protestants celebrating their historical victories over the Catholics, marching along and insulting them were especially volatile, provoking largescale backlashes with violence quick to start. The Orange Order leaders seemed to delight in routing their marches through Catholic areas and deliberately seeking flashpoints.

They did, of course, assert that these marches traditionally went through other sectarian areas and were backed by both Craig and the RUC. Somewhat ironically, when the RUC tried to keep the warring factions apart, however half-heartedly, their officers often came off worse as they were the meat in a sectarian sandwich!

One of the final straws for Harold Wilson's Labour government came, one feels, with the ambushing of a Civil Rights march at Duke Street in the city-with-two-names and later on a country bridge in the province, by the RUC.

This, the most violent incident to date, occurred at Burntollet Bridge where the marchers were attacked by about 200 unionists armed with iron bars, bottles and stones while police did little to protect them. The sight of the NICRA marchers being cut down as they marched for equality was simply too much for the Wilson Government, which had sat on its hands for far too long.

There is no doubt that the RUC were heavy-handed and violent and the whole scene was captured on film by an RTE camera crew from the Irish Republic – the rest, as they say, is history.

The question on the lips of the world was: how much longer can the British tolerate the nightly televising of Protestant or Loyalist mobs burning out entire Catholic streets forcing them to grab their meagre possessions and flee to what, in effect, were Catholic enclaves? The reverse was also true, as Catholics in retaliation, turned on their former friends and neighbours simply because they worshipped at a different denomination's Church.

In fact, although this was still a year down the line, a photograph of a soldier of the Green Howards carrying an injured woman over his shoulder after she was attacked by a Catholic mob, burned into the psyche of any decent-minded person who looked at it. That, and the sight of two more of the 'Yorkies' carrying an elderly man in his chair away from the burning ruins of his house did much to haunt both those of us with clear consciences and those, like the Wilson cabinet, who had stayed on the fence for far too long.

The whole world continued to watch and then wondered how long it would be before the trickle of dispossessed and burned-out families, their few bits of salvaged furniture and clothes piled on hand carts soon became a raging torrent and resembled the sad French and Belgian parades of refugees streaming away before the onslaught of the German Blitzkrieg in 1940!

The riots and the gradual collapse of social order as B Special–led mobs attacked entire streets of Catholics and the injuries sustained by both the RUC and civilians alike could not be allowed to go on. Thus was set the stage for the biggest tragedy in modern British history.

In the summer of 1969, British troops were deployed to the province and, for the first time since the General Strike of 1926 (other than the exigencies of 1939–45) armed soldiers would play a role on the streets of the United Kingdom.

Ever since the Easter Rising in Dublin 1916 – and even earlier with the emergence of the Irish Republican Brotherhood in the 19th century – the IRA had existed to varying degrees in terms of manpower and firearms. There had been border campaigns and even a wartime bombing campaign on the British mainland, but the motley crew of dissident Republicans had been largely quiet for well over a decade until the well-publicised problems in Northern Ireland from 1968 onwards.

In 1969, the expediently re-formed IRA had split into the Official wing and the far more militant, Provisional wing. The latter, the hot-heads and radicals had been disheartened as the IRA had been quiet and had not lived up to its traditional role of 'defending' the Catholic, or Nationalist communities. It was pointedly made clear to the dissenting Provisionals that the initials I.R.A. in many Catholics' eyes, in view of their acquiescence, or certainly, lack of resistance, to the attacks by the Protestants and, particularly, the B-Specials now stood for 'I Ran Away.'

For the first few years of the conflict, both wings vied for the role of being the bigger killer of security forces, but this mantle was quickly accorded to the highly militant Provisionals who clearly had few scruples when it came to killings. Their hollow apologies at bungled bombings and shootings and 'wrong targets' never did quite ring true, even nearly 40 years after they began the killing.

The IRA demand for a 'United Ireland' wasn't at first recognised by the British – both Government and Army – but in the end, after initially presenting themselves as defenders of the Catholic communities, they were actually able to hijack the 'one man-one vote' campaign for their own particular objectives. Did we, therefore, possibly just 'sleepwalk' our way into the bloodiest event to hit the British Isles since the Luftwaffe Blitz and Cromwell's tiff with Charles I over the concept of divine rule?

Whatever the cause – and here I have no intention of becoming bogged down in all the so-called historical perspectives – by the July of their third year in a 'peace-keeping' role, a peak deployment of 30,300 British and UDR soldiers were stationed in Northern Ireland. By the end of that third year, 243 British soldiers had been killed and 243 Army CVOs (Army Casualty Visiting Officers) had been forced to make that sad visit to 243 anxious families on the British mainland.

On it rumbled, depressing year after depressing year; a Catholic killed at random one day and a Protestant murdered a day or so after, in the same random manner, just because his address or location signified his religion. And, squeezed seemingly in between each killing, another squaddie met a violent end and another local officer was receiving instructions to drive to a house somewhere on the mainland to inform the lad's family and loved ones.

Tit-for-tat, a game we played during our childhoods suddenly assumed more sinister connotations in that sad and violent province.

After Wilson, Edward Heath (1970–74), Wilson again (1974–77), James Callaghan (1977–79), Margaret Thatcher (1979–90) and finally John Major (1990–97) continued to send out troops to the province – it was, after all, part of the United Kingdom. They were sent to fight and to die on what were, ostensibly, the streets of Great Britain. Five separate Prime-Ministers tried and failed and British soldiers paid the price for the sectarian hatred and for the failure of successive Governments. In the end, Tony Blair's Labour Government presided over peace and, to date, no squaddie has been killed on active service since he came to power. I firmly believe that this would have happened anyway, and that, whilst we should pay credit to Blair, I do not believe that he was solely responsible.

Why then, did all the killing, the shootings and bombings stop when it did?

The Army's perseverance, their inability to give in – after all, the last war they had lost was in the fields of Georgia back in 1783 – the stirling work of the much put-upon RUC, the sacrifice of the brave men of the Ulster Defence Regiment (UDR), The Royal Irish Regiment and, in the end, the sickened public all brought about an uneasy peace. It might be uneasy, but, please God it is holding and has held for over 10 years now.

Did the IRA and the Irish National Liberation Army (INLA) on the Catholic side of the community and the Ulster Volunteer Force (UVF) and Ulster Freedom Fighters (UFF) on the Protestant side realise, one morning that it couldn't go on?

I cannot answer that question; only they – the men in the hoods with their (generally) American-financed weapons – can. Did they wake up one misty morning, the air thick with the smoke and burned fuel of the riots of the night before, or were the roads of both communities stained with the fresh blood of a soldier, or gunman, a rioter, or perhaps, even some innocent passer by and know that enough was enough?

Will we ever know? Far greater minds than mine, far more eloquent writers than I have tried – and failed – to answer that one. Perhaps one day, an astute writer, a scholar of history in the next century will write a definitive account of that 28 year period of troubled history. Will they ask the question: how in God's name, did we British allow what was, in effect a civil war to happen and claim over 3,700 lives? Perhaps, he might reason, it was because a third of the Northern Ireland public felt that they were Irish, and not British?

As one soldier contributor wrote to me, a young man who had witnessed things in his military career that no-one should see in a waking moment, only in some awful nightmare from which we always awaken, 'Sort that lot out, Mr Historian!'

Perhaps that future historian might reason that successive British governments had to act in the same way as if an armed insurrection was taking place on the streets of Leeds, or Manchester or Nottingham or Hull?

Perhaps he might pose the question, why did it take the deaths and injuries to over 50,000 before it all suddenly stopped?

The author well remembers his first day in the Army; the wide-eyed innocence, the butterflies, the pride, the fear all mingled into one heart-thumping feeling. Every squaddie who fought, died or was wounded in that place which one former officer described as the, then, most dangerous place in the world, had, on their first day as a soldier, felt those same emotions.

Let me now turn over the pages of this book to the Squaddies and Toms and Ruperts who did the dirty work required by our Government and then let history and you, the reader, judge.

Chapter Two

1969

(Note: the figures relating to British Army deaths, by year, include UDR losses and Royal Irish Rangers)

A year of 10 bombs, 73 shootings, 1 RUC officer, 2 Terrorists and 10 civilians killed.

The first RUC officer to be killed during the present troubles was Constable Victor William Arbuckle, shot dead during rioting in Belfast. This fatality, on October 11 of that year was the first through political violence of an RUC officer for 8 years, and marked a turning point in the history of the trouble to come. PC Arbuckle was a Protestant but he was shot by the Loyalist UVF on the Shankhill Road in Belfast. That he was shot by Loyalist paramilitaries from his own community was to be one paradox in a long chain of paradoxical events which blighted this land.

A British soldier was killed whilst on home leave, but this will never be acknowledged as a death on active service, instead deemed simply a tragic accident. Thankfully, on the Armed Forces memorial at Alrewas the soldier – Hugh McCabe – is acknowledged.

On July 14 of this year, a 67 year old pensioner, Francis McCloskey of Dungiven died of injuries sustained in disputed circumstances. Some claim that he was hit in a baton charge by the RUC; whilst others maintain that he was hit by a stray brick and was already dying before the police charged. His death was the first of any type in the troubles.

BURNTOLLET COMMENT
Flight Sergeant Reginald Smith, RAF, Ballykelly

At the time of the ambush the Civil Rights Movement was about 40% Protestant (who had realised that the Catholics were badly treated, and wanted a better deal for them). They (the Civil Rights people) organised a march along the Irish M1, which passed through a cutting at Burntollet, with high banks either side.

Ian Paisley's second-in-command, a Major Smith (I think), organised truck loads of stones to be delivered to the banks of the cutting, from where his thugs stoned the march as it passed. Members of the RUC looked on, or even took part. The Head of the Electrical Department at Derry Tech (A Protestant) turned up for work the next morning with a large plaster on his head, where he had been hit by one of the stones.

A reporter for one of the local papers was on the march, which stayed at a school-house that night. During the night he got up to answer a call of nature and was confronted three times by men armed with shotguns, patrolling the school 'to protect their own people' – the IRA were back in business, having been effectively dormant for many years; they had lost the support of the reasonable Catholics (and now regained it).The Protestants were now no longer wanted, and the movement became almost entirely Catholic, with the IRA becoming better and better armed, largely from America.

This, of course, bred the loyalist terror gangs who, it must be said, were very quiet for the first few months, most atrocities being carried out by the IRA. The Loyalist terrorists learned from the IRA, and in due time were every bit as bad. The British soldier was, as usual, in the middle and hated by both sides.

In my opinion almost every death during the 'Troubles'; Protestant, Catholic or British, can be laid firmly at the door of Ian Paisley. Had he kept his mouth shut and controlled his thugs the 'Troubles' would not have happened as they did, with so much bloodshed. The IRA would not have had the opportunity to re-programme the Catholic people to support them and McGuinness and his friend Adams would have stayed in the gutter where they belong.

I do have quite strong feelings on this subject, and think that the only reason that Ian Paisley is still alive is that he was the best ally the IRA had. Every time he opened his mouth, another big tranche of moderate Catholics became IRA supporters. I can still remember him on TV nearly every night with his bigoted views and cries of 'No Surrender'.

The only reason the Troubles have gone away is that the moderate Irish Catholics have realised that the IRA, far from protecting them, have more or less united world opinion against them and they have therefore shown the IRA less support than before. Long may this continue.

This next account – and the first from a soldier – describes the initial welcome that the soldiers received from the Catholic community and confirms that the Army did, indeed, receive injuries when protecting Catholics from Loyalist attacks. Let us also not forget, that the Green Howards were also helping Protestant families up in the Ardoyne area of Belfast when they were being burned out, also, but this time by Republican gunmen.

BELFAST: 1969

Squaddie, Infantry Regiment

It was about 5 or 6 days into the tour that we were shipped into Belfast from the Lisburn garrison, in Bedford 3-tonners and Land Rovers, to familiarise ourselves with the planned patrol territory. We had 2 magazines (mags) with only 5 rounds, one locked into the SLR [Self Loading Rifle; standard NATO and British issue rifle] and one in an ammo pouch, and bayonets in scabbards at our sides and we had taken off our berets and donned instead steel helmets. We were told that we couldn't return fire in the event of being fired upon. There was a yellow card with all the rules of engagement on; honestly, it was such bollacks!

We arrived at Springfield Road police station (one of the most attacked and beleaguered stations in Belfast) and told that this would be our 'home' later on in

Springfield Road RUC Station (photo courtesy of Roy Davies)

the tour, although we had spells at a barracks in Omagh (site of that terrible atrocity by the 'Real IRA' some years later) the name of which, I cannot remember. And there we were briefed by a tall RUC officer (we called them 'green bottles' because of the bottle green of their uniforms) who was about 45, (we were kids of 19 and 20) and we thought how ancient he was at the time. It turned out that he had been fighting against the IRA for almost 20 years! He told us that there were only two kinds of people in his Belfast: Prods and Taigs! He briefed us on a big wall map and showed us the Shankhill Road (Prod) Falls Road (Taig) and Crumlin Road (Prod) and Divis Street (Taig), Turf Lodge (Taig) and, of course, the notorious Catholic housing area, the Ballymurphy estate. He didn't even pretend to be neutral but was clearly anti-Catholic and this may well have influenced some of us.

For several weeks afterwards, it was something of a honeymoon as we patrolled around the Falls Road, Divis Street and, around the Grosvenor Road, and got on famously with the Catholics. We rarely ventured into any Prod areas but we guessed that, whilst they alluded to be 'British', they saw us as 'Taig-lovers'. The Catholic men (largely unemployed) were in the main, sullen and sometimes we got a grudging 'Good morning' from them but the women and the kids were fantastic. 'What about ye, soldier boy?', 'Yerse Mammies will be proud o'youse lads 'God bless ye, Tommy' 'Be having a cuppa tea an' a wee biscuit, Tommy' were comments I can remember so well as the summer turned really hot by the end of August.

We weren't overly impressed with the RUC lot – somewhat unfairly, I think – and just thought that the whole bunch of them were u.s [useless in army-speak!]. The areas we patrolled were very working class, slum terracing, outside lavs and the like and it was a lot like the places most of the lads – me included – had been brought up.

Anyhow, we patrolled in shirt sleeves because of the heat and lack of danger. Some of us wore steel helmets (one lad actually fainted from wearing the heavy lid in that heat) but berets were the generally accepted headgear. 5 or 6 weeks in and although we had heard shots fired in other parts of Belfast, we had neither fired in anger nor been fired at. The *Daily Mirror* back in England ran a campaign to get us to remove our bayonets, which we did, but we sensed that the 'honeymoon' would soon be over.

All too soon, the cups of tea, biscuits and the odd plate of sandwiches stopped! Had they not, what with their attitudes changed, we would have suspected that they would have gobbed in them anyway!

Major Ian Kilmister meeting the locals
(photo courtesy of Regimental Museum of The Royal Welsh)

BELFAST: THE LULL BEFORE THE STORM: 1969

Bill Taylor, 1 Para.

I joined the Paras in 1969, starting my training in April and I passed out in, I think, September, after which we were sent on leave prior to joining the battalion (1 Para). I had been on leave a few days when I answered a knock at the door, to be confronted by a policeman asking for me by name, which I confirmed as me. He then informed me I was to return to Aldershot as I was going to Northern Ireland.

I duly returned. After the usual briefing and stuff, we found ourselves on a coach to Liverpool to get the ferry to Belfast, (passing my home on the way,) arriving the next morning. We joined our respective companies, which in my case was 'A' Coy, driving about in open-backed 4 tonners which were full of coils of barbed wire. After being shunted about for a few days, still sleeping on camp beds in derelict buildings with no running water etc, we ended up in an old mill in Northumberland Street (as you probably know this is a road that joins the Shankhill Road & Divis/Falls Road).

We obviously started patrolling both sides of the divide getting fed & watered by both Prods and RCs, in particular a woman (Roman Catholic) who lived off Divis Street. She started by leaving a tray of sandwiches and a flask of tea out for our patrols, 24 hours a day, and eventually passed a front door key with which we could let ourselves in to her house to make our own! And then, there was the gentleman who used to supply us with the occasional Ulster fry-up when we were in the O.P. [observation post] on the top of Divis flats, which was passed to us through the access hatch to the lift gear. Things hadn't deteriorated at that stage, and we were even able to leave our Dennison smocks and denims in the dry cleaners on the Falls Road. It would be much different later in the year when we returned for a 2 year tour and things changed for the worse.

FIRST ON THE FALLS: 1969

Major Ken Draycott, RRW

The battalion was stationed at Lydd when it all kicked off and due for a posting to West Germany, but in July, the Battalion [Bn] was told that we were going to Ballykinler to stand in for 3 LI. [Light Infantry] We had a brief NI training session but we didn't think too much of it and none of us really thought that it would blow up.

I think that we were expecting a 6 week 'holiday' and we didn't even take flak jackets – not that they were even heard of, mind – and we couldn't take the whole thing seriously. I was Sergeant at the time but I was called upon to do the duties of a Colour Sergeant for the duration of the tour. When we got to Ballykinler, we were dumped in a weekend (TA) camp and the first couple of weeks we relaxed on the ranges and got in some shooting practice. We were able to spend some quality off-duty time in and around Newcastle, Co Down, around Dundrum Bay and Clogher which was just across the water from the camp. It was notable for a pub which doubled as a bookie and stayed open for 12 hours a day and the

LCpl Bresslin (left), Lt John Quinton Adams (right), August 1969
(photo courtesy of Regimental Museum of The Royal Welsh)

number of drunken squaddies who nearly drowned as they capsized canoes on their way back to camp.

On the night of August 13, we were about to settle down for a meal and I made a quick phone call to the Mrs and she had seen on the News that troops were going in the next day. I can remember as though it were yesterday saying to her: 'It'll never happen; if they call the troops in, it will last 30 years'. [Major Draycott was almost prophetic; it lasted 39] I went back to my seat but before the first morsel had passed my lips the C.O. called the entire Battalion (Bn) to parade on the square in 30 minutes.

We were soon at Violet Street police station on the Falls Road and I set off to collect food and equipment from Palace Barracks, but every unit in Belfast had the same idea at the same moment! The first night was like Bonfire night with explosions, flames and gunfire lighting up everywhere. British troops went in with steel helmets, with camouflage scrim and fixed bayonets. As we had no flak jackets – the British Army had not used them since Korea – I was detailed to go to the QM's store and collect them. I had never seen one before, let alone used one and I foolishly tried to pick up ten at once; they weighed an absolute ton. They would shortly prove their value.

FIRST SOLDIER ON DIVIS STREET: 1969

Sergeant Roy Davies, Royal Regt of Wales

I can lay claim to being the first British soldier on Divis Street on the day that we went onto the streets of Northern Ireland on August 14, 1969. I was driving the Adjutant of the RRW and we were followed by a convoy of lorries.

In those dark days, when all law and order appeared to have broken down, our next point of call was to the RUC station on the Springfield Road. When we arrived outside the station we found not a trace of the RUC themselves. They had simply disappeared unable to cope with the constant anarchy on the streets; the notorious 'B' Specials, however, were still much in evidence. They were still prowling around wreaking havoc and we spotted an old lady being pushed in a wheelchair by what turned out to be her grandson. She was crying her eyes out and she was covered in blood and it was explained to me that she had been attacked and beaten up by thugs in the 'B' Specials; they were completely out of control.

I helped push her into the sanctuary of the RUC station and I just whispered to her: 'You're safe now' and we took care of her. On that first day, one of our lads was shot and wounded by a 12 bore shotgun but thankfully, he fully recovered. I now believe that he was the first British soldier to be shot and wounded during the troubles and I also firmly believe that he was shot by a 'B' Special thug. We managed to stop them in the end but they were almost uncontrollable.

One abiding and awful memory I have is of seeing literally hundreds of Catholics, women and children in the main, streaming towards us and past, to the safety of the Catholic church 50 or 60 yards behind the police station. I simply couldn't believe how many houses were on fire; there was smoke and flames everywhere. Our officers told us that we were the police now as all law and order had broken down and we were to act as policemen but never to forget that we were soldiers also.

That night, I was on sentry duty outside the front of the station when all of a sudden, a woman came running towards me in total distress from the houses opposite, pursued by an angry man armed with a carving knife. She got round the back of me, clinging on for protection and screamed 'He's going to kill me!' I was armed with an SMG and I quickly cocked it and pointed it at him and shouted 'If you come any closer, I'll shoot you!' He was incoherent with rage and his words were largely unintelligible and he looked at me and then just turned around and disappeared. I pushed this poor wretched woman inside the station for her own protection and then carried on doing my sentry duty.

'B' SPECIALS: 1969

'Taffy', Royal Regiment of Wales

My first memories, see, were the smoke and the flames and all the screaming going on; there were no RUC about; just mobs, running about throwing whatever they could lay their hands on. It was chaotic and I hadn't ever seen anything like that in my life before I went to Ireland. There were loads of people, some with bags and cases and prams, and some of the prams had clothes and bedding on them; I even seen a man with a baby's cot on his back coming out of all the smoke, his face blackened from all the soot, see.

Me and three of the lads were patrolling down some of the side streets near the RUC station on the Springfield Road. We heard shouts and whacking noises coming from another street, so we legged it over there and we seen two men in black uniforms hitting this woman with what looked liked a hockey stick, and the other fellow had a big stick and they was smacking this woman as she lay on the

Belfast City Centre, 1969
(photo courtesy of Regimental Museum of The Royal Welsh)

floor. They stopped when they saw us and then, funny it was, they smiled at us and started whacking the woman again, a girl really. I was angry but calm and I cocked my SLR, flicked off the safety and pointed it straight at the bigger of the two and just said: 'If you hit her again, my friend, I will f*****g shoot you right here and now.' They stopped and ran away down the street, stopping only at the end to give us the two-fingered salute and then they disappeared. I'm thinking, 'is this why I joined the Army?'

NEWTOWNARDS ROAD – BELFAST: 1969

Drummer Richard Nettleton, Grenadier Guards

During my first tour, I found myself stationed at the RUC barracks at Newtownards Road in Belfast, just down the road from the Harland and Wolff shipyard. Whilst there, we had the unenviable task of patrolling the night-time streets, and I, the pleasure of sitting in the back of a Land Rover operating the radio. Thankfully, nothing much occurred on these patrols but the tension was electric; then one grey, misty morning, there was an incident at the barracks where our Bn was stationed, reported the following day in the *Daily Mirror*.

It would appear that a soldier in the Royal Engineers attached to our Bn went missing whilst on guard, and was later found dead in the grounds. It was reported that he committed suicide but few believed that. I remember a suspicious looking 'B' Special standing on guard at the gates of the RUC barracks as we returned in the early hours saying: 'Well, it's finally started. Mark my words, lads, it'll only get worse from now on.'

How right he turned out to be.

' On 14 September, 1969, Craftsman Christopher Edgar of REME – there is some confusion here between this regiment and the RE – was reported to have died, but only NIVA record his death on their Roll of Honour. Neither *Lost Lives* nor even the Palace Barracks Memorial Garden record his death, which was apparently an RTA.

THE FIRST YEARS:

Major Ronald Gilpin, Royal Corps of Signals (TA)

I belonged to 40 Ulster Signal Regiment (Volunteers) and had been trained to maintain communications in mainland Europe in the event of an attack by the Red Army, but found myself needing to be constantly alert in my homeland of Northern Ireland. Living here, you were always cautious about who knew what you were and what you did, and security even after 1969 and as late as 1971 was still pretty lax. Although the IRA had said that they would kill men who were in, or associated with, the British Army, it was not uncommon for us to travel from our homes in uniform to TA meetings.

My uniform was often in the back of the car open to view, and we would still receive mail with our names and ranks on the outside and thus our security was open to prying eyes. On one occasion, files listing our personal details, telephone numbers etc were found in a supermarket trolley, presumably by a careless officer!

From 1970 onwards, members of the TA in Northern Ireland had to take precautions because the IRA would shoot anybody wearing British Army uniform and, as we wore the same uniform as the Ulster Defence Regiment (UDR), whose main role was to deal with the terrorist threat, we were targets too. We were allowed to grow our hair longer so that we didn't stand out – a group of three Scottish soldiers were identified as such because of their hair and they were murdered – it was a dead giveaway. We were forced to use soft-skinned military vehicles and were not issued with flak jackets.

BELFAST: 1969

Major Mick Sullivan, Prince of Wales' Own Regiment of Yorkshire

As a teenager, I joined the Army in the summer of 1966, and fully expected to be posted to some serious conflicts around the world. What I had not counted on was being asked to keep the peace in my own back yard – on British home soil in Northern Ireland.

Back in April 1969, as a young corporal, it was quite a surprise to find myself being deployed to the province, I must admit. Corporal Sullivan – as I was then – had been in Colchester with the 1st Battalion Prince of Wales' Own Regiment which recruited from York, Bradford, Leeds and Hull. At first, the deployment to Northern Ireland was intended simply to guard key installations in the province. There was a threat to installations in the province from the civil rights movement who were stirring up a lot of unrest in order to highlight a problem; and there was a problem. For the first three months however, I could not sense much of a threat.

Soldiers arrest a rioter

County Down was like a home from home and there was beautiful scenery, glorious beaches to train on, and plenty of local dances attended by girls who were often pleased to see British soldiers. It was really bizarre; it was all a bit of a phoney war at that time.

Later we moved further north to County Antrim, and by that stage the communist Republican movement had been hijacked by the IRA who saw an opportunity to stir trouble. The pot had been kept bubbling by them for many years, and they saw the opportunity to put their coals forward. As the violence escalated, we moved closer to Londonderry and on August 13, Prime Minister Harold Wilson called a Cabinet meeting, where the Home Secretary decided to deploy troops onto the streets of the province.

Only the night before we were sat on one side of the river watching Londonderry burning, and I think that it was then that we realised the seriousness of the situation. There was little fear at first, and when the troops moved in, on August 14, 1969, we stood on the streets holding the same banners we had used during the war in Aden two years earlier. They said 'Don't cross this line' in Arabic; can you believe that? It was the typical British Army method of using tactics from the previous war.

Both the loyalists and republicans seemed to welcome the troops and brought out cups of tea as they stood on the street. The loyalists saw us as on their side and the Catholics saw us as an unbiased organisation.

They could see that there was this unbiased organisation coming in to separate two communities and keep the peace. They welcomed us just as much as the other side, and if you have a difficult job to do it can be made a lot easier by people being nice and not throwing grenades at you; the hospitable atmosphere was not to last for long, however.

THE FIRST DAYS: 1969

Officer from a Welsh Regiment

These early days of troops on the streets became known as the 'honeymoon period'. Tea was brewed for the troops in huge quantities by ordinary people delighted we were there. A patrol of the Catholic Markets area of Belfast inevitably meant half a dozen stops for a drink and a chat, and several more for the loo. 'Community Relations' became the big Army occupation – organising trips to the sea for kids, dances for teenagers, or soccer matches with the local lads. And we all felt what a jolly good job we were doing.

I think we were aware of the political dimensions ... We all had a feeling there was injustice over housing, jobs, education and even justice. I think we certainly felt that we were on the side of the Catholics ... there was a huge amount of sympathy for them. That lasted a long time and it was probably the ham-fistedness of the politicians that put paid to that.

BELFAST 1969

Jim Parker, Light Infantry

3 LI was in Northern Ireland. The main body of troops was in a barracks in Belfast, we of Support Company were sent to HQ Northern Ireland, in Lisbon. We were billeted in the gymnasium, and if I remember we had to erect our own double bunk beds.

I know we spent a short time practicing 'Anti-Riot' drills as the battalion had done in Malaya. Then we were in open 4 tonne lorries driving into Belfast. We drove through streets littered with debris. Cheering people behind improvised barriers greeted us. Some threw cigarettes at us.

Support Company moved into the Church Hall on Crumlin Road. My first duty was to stand on the street across the road from the Church Hall. Pte Meston who had served in the Royal Marines, and was somewhat older than the rest of us partnered me. The general public was very glad to see us, and came up to speak and shake hands. Jim Meston would have none of it! When our officer came around he asked if we might move onto the roof the public toilet, which we did. Later, we moved onto the roof of the Fire Station, behind the toilet. Thus except for meals, and off duty sleeping I spent five days on the Fire Station roof. My combat trousers were ripped at the knees and backside from clambering about on the slate tiles.

One of the worst things a young soldier can do is 'fiddle' with his weapon. Jim Meston had to go down from the Fire Station roof for a meal or to the toilet. His personal weapon was a GPMG [General Purpose Machine Gun]. It was a weapon I had had very little to do with, other than basic training at Shrewsbury over a year before. Jim borrowed my rifle and left me with an unfamiliar gun. However, I remembered one thing about the GPMG, the safety catch could only be applied if the gun was cocked (and ready to fire). I fiddled and pushed the safety catch, and was surprised that it clicked on and off. I opened the top cover and allowed the ammunition belt to drop free. I

Belfast, 1969 (photo courtesy of Regimental Museum of The Royal Welsh)

checked the breach to ensure it was empty, and pulled the trigger and the working parts flew forward with a clang. I reloaded the ammo belt. When Jim returned I told him he had left the GPMG cocked. For the next seven or eight years he and I have argued this point. He has always denied he left me with a cocked weapon and I am convinced he did!

Much of the events that occurred on our first tour of the Belfast area have now blurred into several disconnected scenes in my mind some mixed up with the second tour in 1971.

'Granny' Grover heard I could draw and called me into his office. I was to go out with (I think) the Reconnaissance Platoon and draw what I could see. So, off we went in the middle of the night and plonked in the middle of nowhere. I was given an IWS [Individual Weapons Sight]. This was a night sight, through which it was possible to see in the dark. The vision through this device was green. I had never seen such a sight before and had never used one before. I could not make out anything notable, so I got into my sleeping bag and slept through the rest of the night until woken before dawn to make the return journey. Back at Company HQ I found out where I had spent the night, and borrowed a map. I orientated the map drew whatever was there. Then I handed the sketch it to 'Granny' who was 'over the moon' with the result.

Three or four of us were on duty on a wide road, as the evening drew on a young lady waved at us from her window a little distance away. We waved back. She remained there for a couple of hours. The next morning a little girl aged about 10 in school uniform left the house and waved at us and smiled as she walked past. I didn't know where to look. When our relief arrived, they all did so in a Land Rover. However, none of us could drive. In the end I took the wheel and drove the vehicle back to the Church Hall in first and second gear.

I had not intended to use the voices of people other than squaddies, but I received several e-mails from a lady who was present when Robert Curtis was killed (see 1971 also). Below are her words:

Doreen Gilchrist, Belfast

We used to feed the British soldiers at the corner of the street. One night our neighbours put money together in a collection and Roy and I went up to 'The Silver Key' fish & chip shop at the corner of Duncairn Gardens and Edlingham Street and bought a bundle of fish and chips for the boys. I have so many stories but this one is a bit of history and I suppose we never realised just how much until we got older.

LONDONDERRY 1969

Mike Heavens, 1st Glosters

I was given a railway warrant from Exeter to Londonderry and along with my kitbag and my rifle, I was given a replacement rifle for another Company member, and 5 rounds of ammunition which I was not allowed to load unless under fire! My journey to Liverpool was uneventful and few people took any notice of me but the boat trip to Belfast was a little uncomfortable under the intense scrutiny of many on the boat, perhaps it was the baggage labels, attached to the rifles through the bayonet fixing and muzzle flash hider, which fluttered in the breeze and announced my number, rank and name to all who cared to look.

I walked across to the train station after docking at Belfast, and after a short wait, got the train for Londonderry which travelled the coastline all around the North Shore, a beautiful if long trip.

On arrival at the Londonderry Rail Station I enquired as to the whereabouts of HMS *Sea Eagle* and having got directions from a very amiable if somewhat disinterested station master, I began the short walk up the hill through the Waterside and along the Belfast road until I spied the Naval Shore Station that was to become Ebrington Barracks. I nodded to the very bored sentry, who barely noticed me, and passed down the camp to the Quartermaster's department, who relieved me of the second rifle and arranged transport to my platoon deployed near Waterloo Place just outside the Bogside.

The Old Cash Stores near the City walls, had been firebombed during the summer riots and although the roof had been repaired and the windows boarded up, the wet, burnt wood smell, was still very strong, We were sleeping on the second floor where there was still a good portion of the floor usable and it had a rear courtyard where the vehicles could be taken off the main road, which ran close to the front doors. We had a stand to and sentry position in the now disused public urinals on Waterloo Place outside the shops there and although the urinals and W.C.s had been stripped out the smell was, how shall I put it, powerful! 4 guys slept there during their stag [period of duty] and 2 huddled around the braziers by the entrance. A presence on the ground was being maintained!

When not on sentry outside the store we patrolled, from Buncrana around to the Foyle South of Derry, the Donegal Border of the Republic. At this time our task was to reassure the Catholic population that we would defend them from further violence from their Protestant neighbours and the locals were very pleasant and tea and biscuit stops were frequent and looked forward to, and one or two of the guys played football for the local teams, one for the Bogside and another for the Creggan.

How times were to change!

During our border patrols we spent a lot of time up at the BBC transmitter station in the hills above Derry, using a small caravan as a guard post, and on occasions we even nipped down to the village of Muff across in the south, in full fighting order, to attend the local dance there, leaving a guy outside to watch the vehicles, as it didn't seem to matter much! The friendliness of the local catholic population impressed us all and they really seemed to want us there. Christmas morning 1969 I was awakened by a gentle shaking and a young schoolgirl, in her blue school uniform said in her lovely sing song accent ' Merry Xmas soldier, and I hope you go home to your family in safety' and I was given a present, wrapped in Christmas paper, of a pair of socks, one of the nicest Xmas presents I have ever received and then the girls sang a carol for us, whilst some very embarrassed squaddies looked on in awe.

I continued to serve in Londonderry until turned loose, on my pre-release course. In late January I was then sent on terminal leave and became a civvy (for almost 2 years!), but I never forgot the trusting and genuine smile of those school-girls and often wondered, what happened to them and where did we go wrong, to so soon change and lose all that warmth and trust? Finally, how would I have got from Exeter to Londonderry, just one year later? Certainly not like that trip!

It is worth noting that, just days before Mike Heavens' arrival in Londonderry an IRA member, Patrick Corry, was killed in an unrelated car crash. It was to become typical of the IRA at that time, just in the initial throes of tearing itself apart amidst the Official/Provisional split, to claim the incident as something else. The dead man it was claimed was a member of an ASU and therefore, on 'active service'. *Lost Lives* notes that one of the passengers in the car was a certain Gerry Adams.

SLR 7.62mm Standard British Army assault rifle

Early riot situations

THE BATTLE OF SHANKHILL ROAD

Jim Parker, Light Infantry

One day in October 1969 I discovered that I had two 7.62 mm rounds missing from my magazine. I knew this to be a very serious situation. In the Royal Engineers I knew this might have led me being court-martialled. I thought it best to inform my section commander. He shrugged his shoulders and said, 'We'll sort it somehow.'

That day or the next, on 11 October 1969, we were on one of those endless patrols and ran into a patrol of armed 'B' Specials, (the Northern Ireland part-time policemen). During a conversation with them I mentioned my problem and they indicated they might be able to assist. 'How many rounds do you want?' their leader asked, Taffy replied, 'Five will do. We could keep the other three as section 'spares' in case anyone lost their ammunition.'

That day there was incredible activity in Belfast, although I was not particularly aware of it at the time, the battalion was sent to ward off an advance by thousands of Protestants on the Catholic Unity Walk Flats.

I had been on a normal guard duty, and previously had seen my girlfriend. In all events I was very tired! I crawled into my sleeping bag on a camp bed in the Church Hall at the bottom of the Crumlin Road. When I was awoken I pushed my arms up through the top of my sleeping bag, and in doing so the zip slid down. I thought I was being called for my next stag, but soon realised this was something more important. Outside the Church Hall in the dark I climbed onto a 3 tonne lorry wearing a flak jacket carrying my rifle, wearing belt order webbing and steel helmet.

In this vehicle we, Support Company men, mostly of the Assault Pioneers, were driven through the night. I remember at one time we stopped and saw a group of men from the Mortar Platoon; one of them had blood on his face. We eventually arrived at Townsend Street where we clambered off the lorry. We understood there was a riot going on, and we might have to undertake the old Anti-Riot Drill we had practiced, on the streets of Belfast.

Were formed up into a 'block' some six, seven or eight wide and many deep. Those men with steel helmets such as myself were put in the front. An order was shouted 'Light Infantry, Quick March!' and we started off into the darkness. Then there were shouts and we were halted and turned about. The men without helmets were now at the front. In this large block we started to march back, and then wheeled around to the left, into a side street. At this point those in charge were instructed that the rioters were shooting down the street (in fact Shankhill Road) and we were not to proceed any further in a block. At the junction with the Shankhill Road alternative groups of men were sent across the road. Most of the Assault Pioneer Platoon lads were not sent across the road. We turned right onto the Shankhill Road, and I came under fire for the first time in my Army career.

We could hear missiles striking and bouncing down the road, which we assumed to be bullets. Many may in fact have been stones sent down the road by 'catapults' used by the rioters. The rioters used the bars of metal fences, and

More early riot situations

heavy elastic to propel missiles down the street. But we did not know that at the time. There was plenty of shooting going on.

All the way up the Shankhill, a newspaper cameraman was immediately behind me, as we ran from doorway to doorway – he often crashed into my back. I was very annoyed with him for getting in my way!

Whenever possible, I carried my rifle in such a way that the plastic butt (the part that fits into the shoulder when firing) was held over my private parts!

The word came down the line, where possible, to put any light out. One man on the far side of the road smashed his way into a small brightly lit shop. He went inside but found the light switch just inside the door. When he emerged he had an arm full of cigarette cartons. Some of these made their way across the road to us.

A Corporal from Recce Platoon near us fired up at the roof buildings opposite saying he had seen a sniper there. I doubt very much that he had!

In one side street an elderly woman wanted to come with us, reasoning that she would be safer 'with the soldiers'. We soon dissuaded her, telling her to go back into her house.

The newly devised 'Snatch Squads' were grabbing rioters and arresting them. This was being done further up the road and out of our sight. The snatch squads ran their captives down the road, and many of us swore and kicked out at the unfortunate prisoners as they were scurried along.

There had been apparently no arrangements to collect these captives, a so they were made to lie down in the middle of the road, near a crossroads. In the darkness one man rose to his feet and ran past us, into a side road. Soldiers were shouting out 'Stop or we'll fire!' Three soldiers ran after him, and then they stopped in a line. A Private of the Anti-Tank Platoon fired. The SLR made a loud 'Bang!' there followed the pattering of DMS boots and then 'Ugh!' The rioter had been shot in the lower back.

Stories came down the road, passed from soldier to soldier, of events out of our sight. Apparently our new Commanding Officer had been wounded and Lt Col 'Big John' had resumed command. A deputation from the rioters came forward to speak to Big John. They complained that members of his battalion were too rough. Big John removed his steel helmet and smacked the man over the head and said 'Like this!' A Major standing near Big John and thought he'd join in, and tried to kick the prone figure but missed and fell over.

With the coming of the dawn things began to quiet down. The RSM wearing a steel helmet, a tight pullover and baggy trousers strode back down the middle of the road. He stopped looked in my direction and shouted, 'What the f**k are you doing here?' I stood up and standing at attention and in my best parade ground voice replied, 'I'm supposed to be here, Sir! I'm in the Assault Pioneer Platoon!'

'Not you, c**t!' he snapped back 'That f**ker!' pointing at the reporter who had dogged me all the way up the street. The RSM ordered him away from the scene.

It started to get light, the alarm bells of a bank were ringing and word came down the street that we were to 'take to the high ground'. A group of us found our way into a school, and wandered around trying to find our way on to the roof. We had to break our way through a glass door, and then through a grey plastic 'bubble' in a corridor roof. We helped each other onto the flat roof.

From various buildings in the area searchlights flashed and we were frightened that our own people would fire upon us. It was by that time almost fully daylight. There was a helicopter flying overhead with a loudspeaker ordering the people to go into their houses.

A Private went over to the edge and looked down on the streets. There was a group of people standing outside their houses in the front garden. Keith started to shout at them, 'Get in doors!' It was evident to me they could not hear him. Keith was getting very annoyed and shouted again to the people to go in doors or he would shoot them. He cocked his SLR and was about to fire. I urged him not to fire pointing out that the group were not rioting and could not hear him.

When the headmaster came into his school in the morning, he looked sadly around at the destruction we had caused, but said little. He did offer that if we were still on the building roof at lunchtime we could have a cheap meal. A couple of us did take advantage of a school meal later.

Later with other men I went down onto the Shankhill Road where the CQMS [Company Quartermaster Sergeant] had set up a cookhouse in a building a few houses up from the school. As we arrived a TV crew were about to film those at the hot plate. I was very pleased with the thought of Mum and Dad seeing me on the national news. The camera began to roll when a cook lifting a container of boiling water and dropped it back onto the hot plate with a clang and scolding water splashed around! Although we at the front of the queue collected our food in our mess tins, we did not appear on the TV.

For that day's work Big John received the OBE, Pte James the George Medal, and Sgt Power the BEM. Twenty men of the battalion were wounded, fourteen of whom were admitted to hospital. Two civilians were killed that day. It is estimated some 1,000 rounds of small arms fire were fired and 200 petrol bombs thrown at British troops during the riots. The battalion is recorded as having ar-

Belfast, 1969 (photo courtesy of Regimental Museum of The Royal Welsh)

rested seventy rioters, fired 394 CS gas shells and 68 bullets. However, I know that should read 66 bullets, because I reported firing two shots to make up for my two missing rounds.

The following day, the first RUC officer to be killed during the troubles, 29 year old Victor Arbuckle was shot by Loyalist paramilitaries. The shooting took place in the Protestant Shankhill road area and he was the first RUC officer to be killed by 'political violence' since Constable William J. Hunter, who was shot in South Armagh in 1961.

On August 15, 1969, the day after the momentous first appearance of British troops onto the streets of Northern Ireland, a British soldier was killed. 20 year old Trooper Hugh McCabe of the Royal Irish Hussars was home on leave from his unit in Germany when rioting broke out in and around the Divis Street area of Belfast where his parents lived. Although there were suggestions in some quarters – discounted by the author – that McCabe was armed, these are denied by his Father, a former Second World War RAF Sergeant. He was shot on the balcony, the round entering his neck and he died very quickly afterwards. Speculation at the time further suggested that the 'B' Specials – whom several soldiers in this book claim were 'out of control' – may have been using some heavy calibre weapons in the area at the time. The .30 calibre weapons in use by this organisation were totally unsuitable for deployment in this urban setting.

Fully 18 months before the murder of Gunner Robert Curtis, a British soldier had been killed and, unofficially at least, before that fateful day in the New Lodge, others wearing the same uniform would be dead.

Two civilians were also shot during rioting; one of whom was a petrol bomber, the other being accidentally killed by fragments of a round which had broken up on impact with a wall. By an enormous coincidence, both men were related.

Chapter Three

1970

1970: A year of 170 bombings, 213 shootings and 2 RUC officers, 13 civilians and 10 terrorists killed

This was the year when an IRA 'own goal' killed 5 people, including the bomb handlers as well as 2 innocent children in the Creggan in Londonderry.

In this year, the Army shot and killed another petrol bomber in North Belfast and the UK realised that, in the words of a leading Ulster politician ' ... we are now at war with the IRA'.

In the June of this year, the IRA killed 7 Protestants in gun battles, mainly in the Ardoyne but all over Belfast.

In this year, soldiers converted a 19th-century stone mill into a fortress. Bessbrook Mill became the launching pad for helicopter-borne operations throughout South Armagh, a predominantly Catholic region midway between Belfast and Dublin known as 'bandit country'

NORTHERN IRELAND: 1970

Terry Friend, Royal Artillery

Our area was the Shankhill, Crumlin Road and all the filthy little ghettoes in between. Our destination was a deserted mill on the junction of Flax Street and Crumlin Road. The place was filthy and all the windows were smashed. It looked like a leftover derelict bomb-site from World War two and reeked of a damp odour like all empty buildings do. On the top floor, which was fairly high, we had a bird's eye view of some waste ground. To the left of it was the Ardoyne, a staunch republican stronghold, to the right was a Protestant council estate on higher ground.

It was whilst I was erecting my camp-bed and laying out my sleeping bag that one of the lads at the windows called out 'Hey, come and look at this!' We gathered and watched in amazement as a pitched battle between two gangs of youths took place on the waste ground. A continuous barrage of bricks and other such missiles was being hurled by both sides at each other. Eventually, they tired of their 'sport' and slinked off back to their respective ghettoes to lick their wounds and prepare for the next fray. This running battle was to continue spasmodically from time to time and eventually, we, the spectators, would tire of it. I returned to my camp-bed, stretched out and began reading a paperback novel.

From now until the end of the tour none of us would sleep without our clothes on. There were in fact, two forms of dress for sleeping in, both fully clothed but one without boots on. We also worked around the clock.

Two hours on, four hours off. During the four hours off you washed, shaved, showered (if you were lucky), ate your food, cleaned your weapon, and if you were really lucky, managed to get some kip in. Whilst you were on duty you were involved in three main activities; foot patrol, vehicle patrol or on stag at a sentry post in base camp. This was the routine when things were quiet. Bearing in mind also that we were all cramped in like sardines with no room to swing a cat in, there was the constant noise and disturbance, day and night, of people going on and off stag. Sleep became a rare and precious commodity, a luxury almost rather than a necessity. When things were bad, and they could get very bad, often for days at a time, you were lucky to get any sleep at all. It was quite a revelation to me, just how long the human frame could function without proper rest.

NORTHERN IRELAND, 1970

Barney Loughran, King's Own Scottish Borderers

During my Regiment's first tour of N.I. my company was based in Girdwood Park just of the Antrim road. One of our responsibilities was the policing of marches and setting up barriers to stop various factions disrupting the parades.

On one occasion a friend of mine whilst manning one of the barriers was approached by two locals demanding to be let through,' I'm sorry' my friend said, 'but I can't let you through until the parade has passed.' 'Look here,' said one,' I'm not one of your F—ing Fenians' 'Well I am' said my friend, 'and you are definitely not getting through.'

Mobile Patrol Londonderry
(photo courtesy of Eamon Melaugh)

At a VCP (vehicle checkpoint) in the Antrim Road, a car was stopped and the driver asked to get out and open his bonnet and boot by a weary Jock. 'Don't you know who I am?' said the car driver. 'Geese a clue said my friend, to which the driver replied 'I'm Gerry Fitt!' The tired and slightly ratty reply came back: 'I don't care if you are 'epileptic fit'; bonnet and boot please.'

BELFAST, 1970

Un-named squaddie

I was attached to one of the Infantry units at a police station; I used to drive them in, in Bedfords, [the Army's standard lorry] before it got too rough for soft-skinned vehicles. The Bedford was a workhorse but in them circumstances, they were just U.S.! [useless in Army-speak]

People know what happened over in the Bog – there was enough on telly and the papers – but I bet most of them don't know what conditions we lived under.

15 of us had to share a room, designed for 3 or 4 at most, and we had these horrible beds, stacked three high. Most of the lads were smokers anyway, and the ones that weren't – me included – soon became so! The air in there was permanently blue and when we were on duty, another 15 lads came in and slept there, and then we swapped over with them when we had done our F.P.s [foot patrols] for the day. It stank in there of cigs, sweaty socks and most of all, of B.O. When the Micks were rioting on the Falls Road or on the Divis, we were on 24 hour standby and in the end, we slept in our boots, some lads slept in their webbing or just loosened it a bit.

When you've got 15 squaddies fighting for space and washing facilities then you've got a recipe for trouble. There were enough conflict on the streets without it happening at Base as well. But, at the end of the day, on the street, where it mattered, we watched each other's backs.

The only things we kept clean in there were our SLR's cos' we knew that they would save our lives. Honestly, it were such a dump in there that had the RSM looked around, he would have had a heart attack and keeled over! When I think of all the bullshit from BT [basic training] and then think of all that shit, I used to think why they bothered! With all spit and polish I mean.

This soldier was attached to an infantry unit in Belfast in 1970/71.

'CABBAGE', BELFAST, 1970

Jim Parker, Light Infantry Soldier

He stood a massive six foot six tall, a West Country farmer's boy. The Company joke was that when he was a child, he had fallen out of his pram, and in error his mother had picked up and then brought up a cabbage. Hence his nickname of 'Cabbage'. In Germany he worked as a bouncer in the local strip joint, and in barracks was a disaster. He lost kit, looked scruffy, said the wrong things and was always in trouble.

A soldier takes aim through school windows
(photo courtesy of Eamon Melaugh)

On exercise and in Ireland he was a gem. Playing soldiers in Germany he carried the 84mm Anti Tank Gun as if it were a pistol. Once Cabbage was not with the 84 when we had to carry out an energetic withdrawal, and Taylor his No 2 had to lug the gun for a couple of miles. It nearly killed him. Cabbage caught up and picked up both the gun and Taylor who he carried for about a hundred yards.

On arrival in the Markets area of Belfast the local children took one look at him and called him 'Frankenstein'. Another of my section became 'Igor' and another 'Uncle Fester". Before long the kids of the Markets called my section 'The Addams Family'. Not only that, but as soon as 'Frankie' came around the corner they sang the Addams' Family theme tune 'De dadly dum, click-click! De dadly dum, click-click!'

Mums in the Markets told me that if the IRA fired at Frankie the kids would go mad! The Platoon and I talked about the situation and came to the conclusion that no harm was being done.

My section was on patrols one day when I was informed over the radio that a large group of women were making a protest on Cromac Street. They intended to disrupt traffic into the centre of Belfast. Intelligence had received early warning and traffic had been diverted. The women would be furious when they found they had been outdone. Therefore I was to keep well away from them. I didn't need a second telling.

The Markets area is but a quarter of a mile square, and we were advancing down a sidestreet when 300 very annoyed women appeared crossing before us. They stopped and turned to face us, then advanced up the side street.

As one, three hundred Irish ladies grinned and sang, 'De dadly dum, click-click! De dadly dum, click-click! ' They continued the tune repetitively. Cabbage, holding his SLR by the barrel conducted his chorus.

One stone was thrown from the back of the crowd, and I spoke quietly to Taylor to have his baton gun ready, just in case. As soon as he unslung the weapon, the crowd fled. Cabbage could be relied upon to carry heavy weights, arrest people and any task that required muscle.

On a bomb scare in Belfast city centre, we were told to stop all traffic, and pedestrians. Belfast people were used to bomb scares and often tried to make their way through the cordon. It turned out to be a real car bomb. After it had exploded and we were given the all clear Cabbage told me he had been offered ten pounds to allow a gentleman through. I asked him why he hadn't taken the money. Cabbage replied 'Cos you would have been angry with me!'

BELFAST: 1970

Dave, Royal Armoured Corps

I must delve back thirty seven years to a traumatic time for me that changed my later life. It is not easy to write down those memories from over three decades ago. The ghosts that have haunted me for all those years still return when I least expect them to, floating within my dreams so that once again I wake, screaming and sweat-covered, the reality of those times stark in my mind. The legacy of my service in Northern Ireland has been two complete breakdowns, and a malady that is now known as PTSD, Post Traumatic Stress Disorder.

My story starts in the summer of 1970, when, as a Trooper in an Armoured Regiment of the British Army, and the father of a weeks-old baby boy, I, with my Squadron, moved to Northern Ireland for a tour meant to last for just four months. Those four months were the beginning of a process that turned a twenty year old 'boy' into a thirty five year old man, mentally, over that short space.

We had collected some twenty plus Ferret Scout Cars from the Royal Armoured Corps depot at Bovington in Dorset, and what a sorry state they were in. They had been flogged to death in the twenty or so years since rolling out of the Daimler factory, battered, most with very poor engines. The Ferret had already been deemed a dead animal by the Army, ready for scrap, so little or no work had been done to them. All but two were Mk2s, in other words they had turrets, the Mk1 being turretless as originally designed. The turret was the home for an ancient.30cal Browning machine gun, of wartime vintage. All the ammunition for the Browning had been made in America. The Mk2 Ferret was very top heavy, the turret weighing in at around a ton, which made the whole thing rather unstable.

We embarked on the *Belfast Prince*, itself rather clapped out, for the eight hour trip over the Irish Sea. The bar was of course open, leading to many pints being quaffed, and many sore heads come the following day. Sleeping accommodation was the deck, or where you fell, depending on how much each man had quaffed. For me it was the deck, between three others, one who had really bad wind!

Soldiers stop for a 'wad' and 'char'
(photo courtesy of Eamon Melaugh)

The following morning found most of us stood by the ship's rail as we parted the mist into Belfast Loch, and saw for the first time what became for us the 'Devil's Lair', Belfast itself. The two great yellow cranes of Harland and Wolff emerged slowly into view, their bases encased in that great shipyard that had built the *Titanic, Oceanic*, then the great Cunard liners.

After docking, the Ferrets were driven off, those that would start, that is! We were met by some bods from the Ordinance, who kindly issued three rounds of ammunition each to us for our personal weapons, the Stirling Sub Machine Gun, whose magazine held thirty rounds, not three! If we had been 'jumped' on our final trip up to Aldergrove, where we were to be based, we couldn't have even defended ourselves, never mind defend anybody else! As we were a new unit, we didn't have the luxury of being shown around by the unit we were taking over from. It was just out of the dock gates, and on yer way!

Our billet was to be the old Sandes Soldiers' Home at the edge of Aldergrove Airport. The RAF had some hangars, offices and a cookhouse there. The Sandes Home itself was a prefabricated place consisting of two side by side cabins, more or less, with a third cabin over the top. Sergeants and above upstairs, the rest below, in one cabin. The bunks were three high, and in that space eighty of us lived, slept, cried, screamed at night, farted, and suffered.

We would be working three shifts over twenty four hours, so sleep was difficult, with men coming and going, kit being dropped etc. Our Ferrets were stored in a big hangar used by the Army Air Corps, who tended to look down on us somewhat, and the cookhouse was shared with the RAF Regiment airfield guards, who tended to look down on us a lot somewhat! It wasn't long before we started fighting them as well as the IRA. They were easier to beat!

The following day we were operational. Two huge cardboard boxes had arrived, with the logo 'Made in the USA' splashed over them. These boxes contained our 'Flak Jackets', all secondhand and very grubby, with such legend's as 'Smoke Pot' and 'Make Peace, Not War' written on them in biro. We found out that they had come from Vietnam. A few had bullet holes already in them, and big brown stains which we knew to be old blood. They must have dragged them off soldier's bodies to send them to us. 'Charming', we thought.

The next surprise of the morning was the issue of some broom handles and a saw. There were no riot batons for us, we were told, so make yer own. Our steel helmets disappeared next, for 'modifications' to be made. We didn't see them again for weeks. That time on the streets of Belfast was spent wearing just berets. Some nasty head wounds ensued as a result of that cock-up. At that time, the Police in Belfast were using vast amounts of CS gas, which meant that we spent most of that tour wearing our respirators. The trouble was that of course the gas penetrated most of our clothing and kit, which meant that when you took the mask off, the gas got to you at once.

Also, when wearing the gas mask for a while and you sweated, then the sweat built up inside the mask until a small lake came into view, and then you started to breathe sweat in. At that stage all you could do was to lift the mask away from your face at the bottom, letting the liquid run out, and letting the gas in! Not funny.

Our Troop was assigned to 2 Para, who were at that time based in a run-down cricket pavilion at a place called Paisley Park, one of the few green places I ever saw in Belfast. The Paras were at first insular towards us, all non-Paras are to them 'Crap Hats', but after the first few days they started to see the value of the Ferrets in putting up snap VCPs (check points) and blocking off streets where they where having a house search, so we did get on pretty well with them. Other 'postings' included the King's Regiment at Girdwood Park, and the Welsh at Henry Taggart Hall on the edge of the Ballymurphy Estate.

This last one was a toughie, with problems on the 'Murph' including snipers, and a girl pushing a pram, who used to whip a handgun from the waistband of her knickers and give the OP outside the hall four or five rounds on a daily basis! The Welsh lads didn't have the heart to shoot her, but I believe that she was shot by the Paras some time in the following year.

It was at this time that the order to shoot petrol bombers was issued. They were becoming a real menace to the foot patrols, ambushing them from the roof the flats in the Turf Lodge area, and also from Divis Flats amongst other places.

The petrol bombings did wind down a lot after the first couple of bombers were shot and killed, yet petrol bombs during a big riot were our worst enemy, only following the snipers on our fear list. Sugar was mixed with the petrol, or a strip of latex put into the bottle, or worst still paint. The effect of these additives was to make the burning fuel stick to you. We found that the only way to extinguish a burning soldier hit by one of these missiles was to use our standard issue fire extinguishers which were carried inside the Ferrets. These of course then became 'must have' items, so that ours were 'borrowed' very quickly, and therefore supplies soon dried up. I do remember that for the last few weeks of this tour we couldn't get replacements, and two soldiers were burnt very badly because of this non supply.

Recce Platoon, Divis Flats, 1970
(photo courtesy of Regimental Museum of The Royal Welsh)

Petrol in itself was a supply nightmare and a real shortage with the troops in Belfast. We used to race through the city at stupid speeds when traveling from Aldergrove to our allotted base-for-the-week, with cans of the stuff strapped onto the Ferrets, then offload it before we went out into the city proper. These supplies did not last long, and many was the time we were unable to patrol because of petrol shortage. The Ferrets in effect became our homes. We ate, slept sometimes, hid, and urinated in them. When out on the streets it might be fourteen or fifteen hours before you could once again get to a place of safety.

One such place was the Protestant area of Sandy Row, a Unionist enclave near to the city center. When a big riot was on-going on the Falls Rd, or Turf Lodge, or Andersonstown, we would break off during lulls and whizz around to Sandy Row, where we could park up and stretch our legs in complete safety, because it was guarded by fully armed members of the UDA or UVF! [Ulster Defence Association and Ulster Volunteer Force; both Loyalist paramilitaries] They would usher us in, shut their barricade and their wives would then brew up for us!! They scratched our backs, and we scratched theirs.

It was only a couple of years later that the troops started to give the Prod's agro, raiding their drinking clubs and giving them a hard time. We were just very grateful for their support during this period. If we had any ammunition short, they would supply us with 'buckshee' rounds. One guy I got really friendly with gave me an ancient Jap automatic pistol and ten rounds! I passed it on to another squaddie when we left at the end of the tour, but I did hear a story some years later about that gun, so it must have been passed along the line for ages!!

It was about this time that we first went into the Ardoyne area of the city. Mostly streets of terraced houses, back to back, just like where I had been brought up in Salford, the place was run down and stank. Ardoyne was later to become our main operational area, but now it had become the main fighting ground between the two religious factions. The burning of Brompton Park, a street in the area, one night had to be seen to be believed. Fifty odd houses on fire at once, it still makes me shudder. Butler Street, at the very top of the area, was where we first came under sustained sniper fire, and also our baptism with a new terror weapon, the nail bomb.

Packed into a Marvel Milk tin, or the like, was a quantity of explosive, and half a pound of nails. Unlike a petrol bomb, you couldn't see them coming, and the effects were deadly. I saw a young Marine hit with one, not funny. I often wonder what became of the lad. The snipers at this time were pretty inaccurate, thank goodness. A round from a high-powered rifle hit a wall inches from my head one evening, and to this day I carry bits of the bullet jacket in my head.

The mostly loyalist 'B' specials had just been disbanded, the RUC were unarmed, and went on strike for three days following the deaths of three of their number. They soon reappeared, however, but now armed to the teeth with a motley collection of rifles and shotguns. We were shot at again outside Holy Cross Church one night, at the top of the Crumlin Road. This time we retuned fire, but couldn't claim a hit.

Patrol on the Ardoyne, Belfast

A Ferret operating with another Regiment knocked down and killed a young boy one afternoon in Belfast, and as a result of the following riots, all armour was removed from the city. Instead we were given the job of country patrols from Aldergrove to Bushmills, through Larne, Ballycastle, Crumlin, Carrickfurgus, and back. This was mostly daytime stuff, and very welcome after Belfast.

To drive from Larne along the coast road to Ballycastle was indeed a wonder, with scenery the like of which I have never seen since. The Irish Sea crashes onto the rocks far below the road, and in the open Ferrets you could taste the spray. We would stop to search cars along here, or call into a village police station, or the brewery, or the distillery in Bushmills.

Death and mayhem seemed a thousand miles away. We would cover over one hundred miles in each patrol, and arrive back at base tired but happy, with glowing cheeks instead of the pallid faces we had been getting in the big city. Life was good ... But of course, this was the Army, and it must have been seen that we were 'having it off', because we then commenced night patrols over the same area.

Night-time was a different ball game, because the bomber and sniper were in his element in the dark. We did frequent car checks, my job being on 'point', object to stop a car thirty yards from the checkpoint, caution the driver, and then send him on in when there was a space. For this job I had an old paraffin lamp, with a dodgy wick.

One night we stopped on a long clear road, at about midnight, and put up a VCP. The Paraffin lamp had a cover on it that could shut off the light, or change the screen to clear, red or green. I kept the cover closed as a rule, so as not to become a target, until a car came, then I would move the screen to red. This night I lit the lamp, and slouched off up the road. I was tired, we all were, the night patrols and the strain of driving a Ferret in the blackness was getting the Troop drivers down. Alone with my thoughts, I suddenly saw a car approaching in the distance, and moved the cover to red. Waving the lamp from side to side, I realised that the car was not slowing down. I waved the bloody thing faster, but still no drop in speed. Now the headlights are on top of me, the squeal of brakes, the car was going too fast. All I could do was jump into the air, which I did, my legs straddling the bonnet of an old Morris Minor, and my head smacking the windscreen.

Blackness descended for what seemed an age, and I awoke to the screams of the car driver and his male friend as the rest of the Troop beat ten shades out of them! The impact had driven my cap badge into my head, leaving a mark that I still have to this day. However, after the incident, the lamp was examined ... It had gone out, sometime before the car arrived! Such was the shoddy kit we had to work with.

Another of our jobs at this time was escorting a big yellow lorry from the ICI explosives factory near Dundalk in the Republic, from the border crossing near Newry through to the Belfast quarries. This was very hairy and we always expected to be ambushed, but of course the IRA wasn't set up for operations like that in 1970. A spin-off was the fact that the stuff we were escorting was being used against us several weeks later, proved by the serial numbers on the empty gelignite cartons that the IRA would leave at the job.

We got a radio call one day that someone had tried to blow up an electricity pylon in a field outside Lurgan. When we got there, it was found that a charge had been placed around each of the four legs of a pylon carrying a lot of voltage. Two charges at one side had gone off, but the two charges on the adjacent legs had not ... the whole thing was swaying gently in the breeze! We just pulled out the detonators and left the rest to the EOD [bomb disposal] unit which would follow up. Early days ... we wouldn't be pulling tricks like that two years later, when the opposition got better trained.

Yet another job was checking the under-sea salt mines on the Antrim coast. A pointless exercise to my mind, as they were always short on the amount of explosives and detonators they were supposed to have and nothing was ever done about it! Detonators were highly prized by the IRA at this time. They could make their own explosives, but would have to rely on fuses, not very accurate, to set them off.

The IRA had started kidnapping people by now, as part of their campaign of terror. They were taking them onto the Black Mountain near Ligoniel and executing them. The bodies would be found by some poor sod going to work, reported, and our duty Troop would have to go out in the freezing dawn to 'guard' them until the RUC arrived. The RUC were never quick about this, and so it could be hours spent on that bloody mountain watching people who were too stiff by then and too dead to give a damn anyway. That was a bit gruesome. I won't go into detail, but these people had been left to die on the mountain after being shot in such a way as to make sure they suffered in a terrible way.

Things were hotting up again Belfast, and so the Ferrets were moved back in. My R&R, (rest and recuperation) four days had come up, and I flew home to Manchester to see my wife and son. A few days after returning, we had our first fatality. A Sergeant, who was a friend of mine, was killed in what was termed a 'road traffic accident' It wasn't, we all knew it, but the MOD did not want to announce a soldier killed in action, so there it stayed. [Believed to have been Sergeant Thomas McGahon. He is listed on the NIVA roll of honour but does not appear in any of the 'official' lists]. I had been promoted to Lance Corporal, local, unpaid, acting etc. Hardly worth it really, but it made my mother proud when I 'phoned her, so some good came out of it. We had been 'awarded' danger money because of our service in the Province ... 9d a day, about 4p in modern money!!! Phew, big spenders!

We now were mostly working in the Ardoyne area, house searches, car searches, riots, crap thrown from high buildings. The latest toy was to stretch cheese wire across the road at head height, so as to decapitate a Ferret commander. We retaliated with 'cheese cutters', lengths of angle-iron welded to the turrets in an upright position. Next phase was the opposition then plugged the cheese wire into the mains electricity ... Our cheese cutters were then shrouded in rubber! And so on; the battle of wits.

At a petrol station near the Divis Flats, Saturday afternoon was spent by the locals filling crates of milk bottles direct from the petrol pumps!! We stopped that one. They would spend all day humping flagstones up the flats to drop on us at night, but no one from Divis had a job, they were all on the dole! The soldiers were being taxed to pay their wages!

One day we were helping to block off part of the Ardoyne whilst the Paras did house searches. It was a big operation, with a large area shut off. We were using Dannet wire, coiled barbed wire, across the narrow streets. The local women, of course, were out in force, shouting, screaming, throwing dog shit and full babies' nappies at us, when one of the more vocal of the women suddenly screamed, clutched her chest, and collapsed across the Dannet wire! She had suffered a massive heart attack, and was dead! We all burst out laughing; it was so funny at the time. The Paras were all for taking her from behind where she lay, before she went cold! No wonder they hated us as they did. Much later, and on another tour, that incident was to become very tame, but that's a story that may never be told.

It was at this time that, 'officially' the first British Soldier to die in Northern Ireland was shot. [In February, 1971 on the Ardoyne] His name was Robert Curtis, from the Royal Artillery. I will never forget that night. After that it was no longer a game. We gave back what we got.

Dave was actually on duty on that night that the first British soldier was shot and killed. He and Doreen Gilchrist, who live a whole world away from each other, have so much in common.

Sergeant McGahon is noted on the NIVA roll of honour as dying on January 19 1971, several weeks before the-then Heath government admitted to the fact that a British soldier – officially the first – had been killed on active service in the Province. His name is not listed in McKittrick's *Lost Lives* and the author's e-mails to the Ministry of Defence have been, at the time of publication, unanswered.

BELFAST: 1970

Major David Smith, 15 (Scottish) Parachute Bn TAVR

I was posted as 2ic [second-in-command] of 15 Para to Northern Ireland and sent to 2 Para in order to gain information and experiences of internal security operations. I was posted to Patrol Company, which was stationed in the old Midlands Bakery in Snugville Street just off the Springfield Road.

The accommodation, I must confess, was fairly good but my bed, sadly, was situated under some rusty pipes so that when people walked on the floor above, a reasonable amount of rust was deposited on both myself and my bed. The OC – Major Derek Wilford – was later promoted to Lieutenant Colonel and eventually commanded the battalion in the Londonderry area. I became his understudy during my time with 2 Para and learned much from my mentor.

The Light Infantry was stationed adjacent to us and the border line between the two regiments was the Turf Lodge Road, with the LI operating in the Ardoyne and ourselves in the Shankhill, and the dividing road being their responsibility. On one occasion, the LI boys found themselves wedged between two groups of protestors in the New Lodge Road and Major Wilford and I discussed the situation before he asked me to go over with a platoon and see if we could help our fellow soldiers.

I left the platoon under cover of some houses and walked forward to assess the situation and I soon discovered that despite the mob and their precarious

Green Howards rescue a woman burned out of her house

position a young LI subaltern, showing a lot of good sense, was in control of the situation. I watched him grab a loud hailer and warn the crowds in no uncertain terms that if they didn't immediately disperse, he would order CS gas to be fired. The crowds ignored him and, true to his word, the gas canisters were duly fired, at random at them.

Out of the smoking mess, almost immediately an angry member of the mob came up to the LI soldiers and confronted them, no doubt choking back the CS effects; he found the platoon commander and in a loud Irish brogue rebuked him for firing the gas and informed him that they were Protestants and that the soldiers should be firing at the other group because they were Catholics! This outburst was indicative of the polarised thinking of many of the population at that time.

Since troops were never allowed outside the barracks except when on patrol, an Entertainments officer – Lieutenant Fieldhouse – was appointed to maintain morale and 'high spirits.' The CSM, Sandy Saunders, informed us that he was negotiating a bargain price for a piano, whereupon, one of the young officers told him that he was wasting his time because he had been around every man in the company and none of them could play the piano!

In true military fashion, however, the CSM's reply was rather typical of both that rank in general and the Army in particular: 'Don't worry about that sir; I'll detail somebody!' Suffice to say, the piano never appeared.

BELFAST: 1970

Major Dennis Gilpin, Royal Corps of Signals (TAVR)

One Sunday evening, I left the TA Centre in Belfast in the company of a female officer and it was in those dark days – quite literally, because all the streetlights were switched off. This was done to handicap snipers taking shots at soldiers, reducing their visibility (the squaddies had night-sights) but as all or most drivers just drove on dipped lights it was an eerie period in Belfast's life.

[A terrorist tactic at that time was to paint certain walls – outside pubs etc – in brilliant white in order that, on a night time, soldiers stood out and made better targets. Another tactic would be for drivers to suddenly put on their full beamed headlights and illuminate a foot patrol in the dark and thus light them up for a gunman. Nicky Curtis, MM, of the Green Howards recalls this happening in Upper Parliament Street in the Ardoyne; a threat to shoot them out soon deterred the motorist! By now, soldiers were beginning to recognise that, if a street suddenly went quiet or that children and adults would clear the streets, shots from a nearby gunman could be expected. After all, the IRA wouldn't wish to be seen to be shooting their own support base; that would come later.]

Just as I got close to the notoriously republican Short Strand area in east Belfast, I was forced to slow down as a group of armed men in hooded balaclavas crossed the road; although obviously up to no good, they just ignored us.

I had planned to drop my colleague off and then re-cross Belfast and drive to Antrim, some 20 miles away. We crossed the Albert Bridge and approached the Republican Markets area and the road was in total darkness. I spotted a movement in the dimly-lit road in front of me and thought that one person was crossing, but as I got closer, I saw that it was an entire mob and they were coming towards me. A survival instinct must have kicked in, because I slammed the car down into second gear and jammed my foot against the throttle and raced straight at them. The car was pummeled and I felt one or two solid thumps as I hit a few of them but I was through and took the corner into Ormeau Avenue on two wheels!

That night, the mob were hijacking all manner of vehicles and setting them ablaze to make burning barricades; a regular feature of Belfast nightlife. Had we stopped, then I doubt that we would have got out in one piece; the car would have been certainly taken. Had they seen the uniforms, it is unlikely that we would have survived! That incident was just one of many mentioned on that night's Ulster TV news.

Terry Friend, Royal Artillery

One day on a vehicle patrol we drove through a Protestant area called the Village. Everywhere were Union Jacks with red, white and blue bunting across the streets. It was what I would call a 'Coronation Street' area. Dismal terraced houses, no front gardens, like some poor North Country mining village. Even the kerb stones were painted red, white and blue; I thought it all looked pretty ridiculous. Scruffy youths lounged about in restless gangs on street corners and the atmosphere of hostility was so strong, you could almost taste it in the air.

THE BATTLE OF THE CRUMLIN ROAD, JUNE 26

Terry Friend, Royal Artillery

Then it happened, it erupted, the shit hit the fan and 145 Battery were right in the thick of it. The first riots started Friday night on June 26th. I spent most of that night at the top of a sandbagged tower, watching in amazement, at the junction of Leopold Street and Crumlin Road. There was a mob of about thirty, probably Protestants, ripping up kerb stones and paving slabs and hurling them at every vehicle that drove up the Crumlin Road. They were about 50 yards away from me. I rang through to control and mentioned it. The reply came back 'Do nothing.' I was flabbergasted. In the end, I just watched it all and decided that my main task would be to protect the guy below me on the front door. Eventually, in the morning, the yobs drifted off, back to bed no doubt. For me and the rest of the battery there was to be no such luxury.

After breakfast I spent most of the day in one of the sangars at the back. All day long the rioting went on. All the business premises on the Crumlin Road were burnt out, including garages. Palls of black smoke hung in the air over the city, giving it the appearance of a blitzed town from World War Two. To add to this atmosphere, the weather was bloody miserable as well. At my post at the rear of the premises I was overlooking a back alley and hemmed in by tall buildings so I didn't see much of anything. But I could hear it alright, for all day long there was the non-stop sound of C.S. gas being fired, plus pistol and rifle shots, and an almost continuous sound of the mobs as they rampaged up and down. The blokes were being shuttled back and forth for a quick snatch of grub, and then back outside again – their faces were drawn with fatigue.

The C.S. gas got so bad that at one point I had to don my respirator. At some time in the afternoon, a young mother and her pram came rushing into the back alley. The baby was screaming and [the baby] and the mother were crying from the effects of the gas.

I've often wondered about that baby, what a fucking awful world to be brought into. That baby is now an adult of 30-odd who has known nothing but hatred and fear all its life. That night was one of the longest I'll ever remember; I could hardly keep awake. Come the morning, we'd all gone for two days and nights without sleep. Sometime during the evening one of our attached Naval medics was shot in the face in his ambulance whilst attending to a civilian wounded. Later he was to be awarded the George Medal for his devotion to duty under adverse conditions.

In this month, June, to which Terry refers, 10 people were killed, as quite clearly, the descent into the maelstrom was under way. On June 26, two IRA members blew themselves up in an 'own goal' situation and a third died a week later from his injuries. Tragically, two young girls, daughters of one of the bombers, Thomas McCool, were also killed. These were Bernadette who was 9 and her little sister, 4 year old Carol. Five other civilians were killed either by the IRA or by other Republicans in this week, the first of the summer.

Chapter Four

1971

A year of 1,515 bombings, 1,756 shootings and 48 soldiers, 11 RUC officers, 61 civilians and 54 terrorists killed. This year also saw the deaths, for the first time in the present troubles of 2 Loyalist terrorists.

The year also saw, officially, the death of the first British soldier to die during the troubles. Gunner Rob Curtis of the R.A. was hit by machine gun fire along with five other soldiers and died in the New Lodge area one evening in February.

This year witnessed the terrible bombing of McGurk's Bar in North Street, Belfast, by the Loyalist terror group, the UVF, which killed 15 Catholics.

It saw the heroic death of Sergeant Michael Willets of the Parachute Regiment who was killed at Springfield Road RUC station as he deliberately sacrificed his own life in order to protect civilians from a bomb blast. Willets, the first soldier to be killed in Northern Ireland by a high explosive device (H.E.D.) was posthumously awarded the George Cross. Unbelievably, despite his heroism in saving civilian lives, his body was jeered at by crowds outside the RUC station as he was taken away in an ambulance.

It also witnessed the cold-blooded shooting at Ligoniel of three off-duty Scottish soldiers, lured to an ambush on the pretext of a party. The three young soldiers, two of them brothers and their cousin, were aged 17, 18 and 23.

Rob Curtis, officially the first soldier to be killed during the troubles

THE ARDOYNE: 1971

Corporal in the Green Howards

This was my first tour of the Province. The Battalion (Bn) had been over there for some time and the incident which comes to mind took place either on the day of, or the day after, Internment. I was over at the barracks in York, just sitting there, eating my tea, prior to leaving for the trip and I had watched the evening news and had heard that a soldier had been killed in the Ardoyne.

On the journey I had mixed emotions thinking about the guys from the Bn who had been killed in the short period of time that they had been in the Ardoyne. The word was that George Crozier had been killed earlier that same day.

I took a train to Liverpool, and then the ferry over to Belfast where I was met by some of our lads and taken by PIG straight to the Ardoyne area of Belfast. I already knew that a comrade – George Crozier- had been killed and that I was replacing him. [Pte Crozier was shot dead inside the very top part of the Flax Street Mill sangar on 23 August. He was hit in the head by a high velocity round fired from inside the Ardoyne area, possibly from the direction of Butler Street. See the account of the incident by Eddie Atkinson]

When I got there, I was given George's bed space and to my horror, I was given his bloodstained SLR !

I experienced a lot of highs and lows on that tour. Obviously, the lows included the killings of Malcolm Hatton, John Robinson, Peter Herrington and Peter Sharp.*

Even today, all these years later, I still can't put into words my feelings at the time of almost literally stepping into dead men's shoes.

The lows far outweighed the highs and one which readily springs to mind was when we were on lollipop patrol on Butler Street where the [Protestant] Crumlin Road meets the Ardoyne. We were shepherding the Catholic kids from the school at Holy Cross Church and keeping them away from the Protestant kids when we were ambushed.

One of the lads in my brick took a round to his stomach and he was a real mess. Thankfully, he survived, but he was casevaced out of the Province.

There was, of course, the 'high' of being on a Company op when we lifted Dutch Docherty and Martin Meehan, two known and wanted players. Whilst we were not all involved in the capture of these wanted IRA men, it did lift the spirit of the whole Bn.

Another incident which gives me a bit of a lift sometimes was a bit of mischief we got up to one Saturday night. There were a number of Catholic shebeens in the area, which were just shit-holes full of IRA men and their supporters and sympathizers. Anyway, one of the lads got a big A41 radio battery, some D10 wire and some Army tape and put it all together to look like a bomb!

About all that he didn't do was write the word 'bomb' on it! He placed this outside the shebeen, just as the music and festivities were getting into full flow. Of course, the place was evacuated because of the SD (suspect device) and an ATO [ammunition technical officer] man was called out to defuse it! The 'device' was made safe but it didn't half curtail the activities of the night!

Green Howards patrol the Ardoyne
(photo courtesy of Ray Rose)

*The Green Howards referred to were: Private Malcolm Hatton, killed on the Crumlin Road on August 9; Private John Robinson, also killed on the Crumlin Road, on August 14; Lance Corporal Peter Herrington, in the Ardoyne on September 17, and Private Peter Sharp at the junction of Chatham Street and Kerrera Street on October 1st.

The five Green Howards killed in a 7 week period earned the Regiment the unenviable – and somewhat disrespectful – nickname of 'Falling Plates'.

BELFAST, 1971

Pete Townend, Green Howards

We were out on patrol – had been since 2 am – it had been quiet with nothing much happening and were heading back in to base. There were 8 of us in my section (22 Charlie), all from 6 Platoon B Coy [company], 1st Btn Green Howards, including Kev, Matt, Tapper and Tommy. Weather was clear. About 5.55am we received a radio call, telling us to go and help cordon off an area at the junction of Jamieson and Flax Streets in the Ardoyne, where there was a suspected bomb planted in half a car tyre.

We arrived at the scene to find a section of 5 Platoon on the opposite side of Jamieson Street, lined up against the shops along that part of the street. 22 Charlie had come out onto the street from an alleyway opposite them. The armoured vehicle (commonly referred to as the PIG because of its snout-like shape) was standing at the edge of the alleyway, on the street. The back doors were open and the driver (Green) was sitting in the driver's seat. I positioned the section, and then waited for further instructions. I was informed by the driver that the radio at the back of the PIG was malfunctioning. I told Kev that I was going to have a look and see if I could get it to work. As I was checking the radio all hell broke loose ... it was about 6.05am on the 16th of September, 1971.

There were gunshots coming from behind us on Jamieson Street. I had been standing at the back of the vehicle when the shots rang out and I copped a hit in the back which spun me round, taking another bullet in the chest and another going through my right shoulder, clipping the side of my neck. I fell to the ground and could hear Kev [Blades] shouting 'Run now Pete' ... not knowing that I had been hit. I told him I couldn't move and I was aware of him kneeling over me shouting 'stay with me.'.

The next few minutes passed in a blur and then I was aware of being put in the armoured ambulance, and offered a cigarette. I then became aware of there being someone else in the ambulance, on the other side, accompanied by 3 lads. I found out later that it was Pete Herrington; he was the 2IC of the section across the road and he had been killed by the snipers as he was crossing the road to the PIG when we were checking the radio out.

I was taken to the hospital, I was sure the driver of the ambulance was Peter O'Rourke, and I can remember him cutting my flak jacket off when we were inside the hospital. I woke to find myself full of tubes and masks etc and the owner of a set of railway tracks from one side of my body to the other. My spleen had been removed, lung was punctured and ribs broken. Blood transfusions. Days passed; visits from some of the lads, family members; my fiancé had been flown in, as I wasn't expected to survive. After being in hospital in Belfast for 17 days I was transferred to Catterick Army Hospital and after a very short time I went home on leave to Middlesborough, travelling by train and arriving about midnight. My brother met me at the station and we then went straight to 'Blinkers' nightclub where I tried my best to give the Newcastle brown ale a good nudge!!! The next day I went to see Boro play ... think I was going to make it after all!

I got married on the day that the Green Howards were given the 'Freedom of the Town' 11th December 1971. Most of the lads were there for the big march through town and there was a mixture of happiness and sadness, thinking about Pete Herrington and George Crozier, yet enjoying the camaraderie that always was part of being with your mates. A whole lot of us went to 'Blinkers' that night, and spent most of the time splitting our sides at Nimrod and his constant stream of jokes.

One constant in the compiling of these accounts was the tenet among soldiers that the platoon was one's family and many ex-squaddies do not feel that civvies can understand the bond of the platoon and one's mates. The following is another view of the shooting of Pete Townend by one of his platoon comrades.

Sandy Shaw, Green Howards, Ardoyne area of Belfast

'PETE TOWNEND'

Private Kevin Blades, Green Howards

It began the night before the commencement of foot patrols; these FPs started at 01:00 and there followed 2 hour stints and we, unluckily, drew the 'dead hours' of 4–6 am [what the Gloster lads called the 'Star Trek' patrols]

On the first patrol out, which, I think, was 22 Charlie, the lads had only advanced about 200 yards from the Flax Street Mill, when a burst of Armalite automatic fire came from the Egg factory. As taught, the lads split up and one of them – MacMahon – actually fell over as they did so. The lads put the English language to good use and then they reorganised and started to pepper pot [rapid and constant firing] all over the place, but the sniper was long gone!

My team's call sign was 22 Alpha and we set off for our stint; apart from the fact that we were all knackered, all was quiet for the first hour-and-three-quarter. However, on the way back to base, we got a call to give one of the teams a hand, as they had come across a bomb in the road junction. When we arrived, Pete Townend went wild; the PIG doors were wide open – an inviting target – and the blokes were all bunched up, just inviting a gunman to take them out. And, to top it all, we had lost comms! An ATO was by the bomb, examining it and looking for ways to defuse it. Pete put us all in an alley, whilst he sorted everything else and made a call on their radio.

I was with him and we walked over to the PIG and we had just stopped short of the open doors when a burst of automatic came down the street, just missing the ATO who was working on the bomb, but it hit Pete, spinning him around, but tragically killing the other Pete (Herrington) and wounding the radio operator and the driver. The driver shouted that he had been hit in the eye and this sounded serious. Later on, we found out that he had two eyes tattooed on his arse cheeks and the round had gone through one of them.

[Private Peter Herrington was 26 and the father of three young children when he was killed at the junction of Flax Street and Brompton Park. The gunman fired almost 10 rounds at the troops and it was claimed that a group of civilians had covered him whilst he fired.]

When the whole thing was analysed, following Mack's fall after the first contact, he had, unbeknown to him, accidentally pulled the detonator out of the tyre bomb – wires led from it – and in a street full of rubbish and debris, no-one had noticed it. That day, the IRA was after 'the big one'; either a PIG full of squaddies or a foot patrol and the icing on the cake would have been the ATO man. [Whilst the IRA delighted in killing any member of the Security Forces, an ATO man or EOD bomb disposal man was considered a 'bonus' in their perverted eyes]

NORTHERN IRELAND OVERVIEW: 1971/2

Lt Colonel R.P. Mason 1, Royal Scots

The whole Northern Ireland bit had quite an interesting effect on the British Army and not just on the Infantry as it helped develop more professionalism than hitherto. There were vast benefits to the Infantry of course but to other Corps as well and the leadership opportunities and development of junior NCOs' responsibility were very evident.

The attitude to the wearing of uniform on and off duty changed dramatically, and not just for the obvious security implications – and there wasn't that noticeable dichotomy between military and civilian that there had been before: it was no longer safe to wear uniform whilst travelling off-duty and many soldiers, as the undercover war became more pronounced, even wore civvy clothes whilst on duty.

[The cowardly murder of Private William Davies of the RRW is a case in point; the 19 year old from the Swansea area was waiting for a train at Litchfield, Staffs with two other fellow squaddies when he was killed and his companions wounded by IRA gunmen.

In the author's youth and early teens it was a far from rare sight to see a soldier in battle dress, beret folded in his epaulette, proudly – and safely – wearing it in public.]

A colleague once said to me, one night in Belfast, 'It is so easy to spot a soldier in mufti; they look like Man at C&A, irrespective of the length of their hair!' Their bearing, I noted, was drilled into them from the first few minutes with a drill sergeant and never left them. What had become a common place sight, that of a man in uniform, soon was only seen in the garrison towns.

Each Battalion had its own Int section who wore civvies, grew their hair and even drove civvy cars. Our own QM did this when collecting rations for the men; it was the only safe way to do it!

The RUC's role also changed dramatically from the early 70s onwards; prior to this, they were second fiddle to the Army in everything they did, even to the extent of domestic matters. When I was a Captain, I was called out with some of the lads to a violent domestic argument somewhere in Belfast as the RUC wouldn't attend. As I went into the house, I saw a guy holding a big knife about to stab his terrified wife. I pulled and cocked my 9mm Browning and said quietly: 'Son, I wouldn't do that if I were you!' It worked and he put the knife down but that wasn't the point; we should never have been put into that position; it wasn't what we were trained to do. And, it wasn't until the second half of the 70s that RUC primacy came in.

Our role was never about domestic violence, missing cats, truanting kids etc, but the RUC couldn't handle it at the time because of the likelihood of political violence.

They became a more effective force and whilst before we were in charge and we did what was necessary, thereafter – and quite rightly – we had to discuss things with them. This did, however, make ops slightly more difficult.

Interestingly enough, until 1976, no Royal Scot was killed in Ireland; tragically, that changed when three were killed all at once. On March 31, Privates Roderick Bannon (25) John Pearson (23) and David Ferguson (20) were killed by an IRA landmine at Belleek. Sadly, they would lose a further four soldiers before Operation Banner finally ceased.

ARDOYNE: 1971

Nicky Curtis, MM, Green Howards

Through the fire, I looked at the mob of screaming red faces wobbling in the heat haze. The stench of fumes made me feel light-headed, but through the fire I noticed something. Although the front of the crowd was still bouncing with aggression – lobbing bricks and giving V-signs – there was a small pocket of calm at the back. A few noticeably older guys were exchanging words and nods and surveying the scene with some detachment. Something was relayed from the back and the mob, which had now swelled to over a hundred, started to advance.

There was a sudden loud crack. I looked around but we were all still there. This was a trick of the rioters: to set off bangers in imitation of gunshots in order to scare us or get us to react. There were only eight of us and we learned as quickly as they had had how warning shots over the head soon lose their power to shock. I sank the SLR into my shoulder and felt it buck as I sprayed a whole row of rooftops above the first advancing lines. The bullets hammered the slates apart and sent them spinning and smashing on to the people below. They scattered and backed off. It was unorthodox, but it sure as hell worked.

I radioed through and explained that this one was well organised. Within minutes, the back-up patrol had filed out of the mill, all tooled up with batons, visored helmets and the six-and-half-foot transparent shields used to form a wall.

By the time we'd been back to the mill to fetch our own and returned, the crowd had swelled to four hundred rioters while two cars engulfed in flames formed a barricade. The flames grew brighter as the sun went down.

ARDOYNE, 11TH MARCH 1971.

Private Eddie Atkinson, Green Howards

The headlines were that 3 Scots Soldiers had been murdered in Belfast. I read the article and recognized the name of Joe McCaig. He, along with his brother John and Dougie McCaughey (all of RHF) had been lured from a pub by girls and murdered by the IRA in Ligoniel, Belfast. I had been in the same company as Joe in I.J.L.B. Oswestry and we had only passed out from training in the December 1970. This was my first introduction to what lay ahead I thought 'Shit, this is serious stuff.'

'CPL JOHNNIE GOES ON FRONT LINE PATROL'

(Contemporary newspaper account, November 1971)

When we met Corporal Johnnie, he had only had about 5 hours sleep in the previous 24 because his battalion had had a hectic week of arms raids and arrests.

He was needle sharp for the foot patrol. He gave out code names and, after midnight, we were off into the grim, death-laden streets around Crumlin Road.

We flattened ourselves against walls and doorways, knelt anxiously beside deserted corner shops as cars were stopped and searched and drivers questioned.

Suspicious characters were lined up against railings and frisked for weapons. As we glide from street to street, few words are spoken. There is a sensation of fear as each man flattens against a doorway. Each could be a sitting duck for an unseen sniper in alleys and bushes. Then we make a 'lift' – two wanted men are picked up. First we wait in an alley for five minutes. 'This is to defeat the hen patrols' explained the Corporal. Hen patrols are the women who act as look outs, blow whistles and bang dustbin lids to warn the district that the PIGs are pouncing.

The house raided is in one of the endless lines of Ardoyne terraces. Why this house? 'Information received' replies the Corporal. It is 3:40 am. The corporal moves six men to the front of the house 'When its gunmen, you gotta give yourself some chance' he says.

The soldiers move straight through the house to the back, otherwise a fugitive could escape into the back alleys and through friendly houses; two other soldiers remain downstairs. The Corporal and the other two bound up stairs, bedroom doors open.

The wanted men are lying on beds – all dressed, shoes on, ready for flight. They are in custody before they are really awake.

At Hellfire corner, near the Crumlin Road, [a soldier] trains his weapon on a car with blinding headlights. The driver hastily douses his lights and swerves. 'Gunmen often blind us like that before opening fire' says a soldier.

The regiment has lost five men killed by snipers in recent weeks. We stopped near a school in the Ardoyne; 'See that hole in the school wall'. The soldier points to where a brick has been neatly chiseled out. 'A sniper shot four well-aimed bullets at us through there, luckily for us, he hit the PIG instead.'

The Corporal had a narrow escape from death recently. A sniper's bullet just missed him as he was sitting in a jeep, but severely wounded his friend.

There was also the tragic-comical side of life in the troubled Province, as these accounts, taken from IJLB's web site 'Pull Up a Sandbag' indicate:

Two of our guys on the beat came across two guys pushing a van and went over to help. They got it to the top of a street which was all down hill and had speed ramps recently installed. They told the driver to get in and they would push him. However, the driver would not get in as he pointed out the ramps but was assured that they would not damage the van. They told him to hurry up and get in as they had no more time to wait, but he still refused and when asked why he said 'There's a two hundred pound bomb in the back.' Apparently they had stopped to telephone a warning from a call box and the van would not start again.

In North Belfast a passer-by told a foot patrol that a man was acting suspiciously in a garden further up the street and when the patrol went into the garden a player was lying at the corner of the garden pointing a rifle through the hedge. They crept up on him and the corporal put the nozzle of the SLR to his cheek at which the player turned round and said 'I'm not waiting on you, I'm waiting on an RUC patrol' and calmly went into the aim again.

We stopped a van at a road stop and my mate opened the door to speak to the driver while I covered him. He noticed the sun visor above the driver was bulky and taped to the roof. Reaching up he pulled it and a pistol fell down onto the drivers lap and without blinking the driver said 'It's a plant'. We could hardly arrest him for laughing and even in court he continued to protest that we had set him up.

As I have already stated, I had not intended to use the voices of people other than squaddies, but I received an e-mail from a woman who was present when Robert Curtis was killed. She had been living on the border between the Shankhill and the Ardoyne when the squaddies first went in. Below are her words:

Doreen Gilchrist, Hillman Street, Belfast

I do not remember the date, or the day, but the shock has stayed with me. We had been at the corner talking to the soldiers and laughing with them. There had been as they called it 'sporadic gun-fire' all night over at Lodge Road, so we were actually standing at the corner of Lepper Street and Hillman Street, just a few doors up from my house.

The trouble seemed to get worse and the fighting along Lepper Street and in the New Lodge Road was getting bad. Up to that time it was just a lot of shouting, whistling, and stone throwing and of course a lot of petrol bombs, but it was streets away that night. Sometimes they came over from the New Lodge (which was a Roman Catholic area) and then from the 'Bay' (which was a Protestant area) and met up at the top of our corner fighting. It was terrifying.

This night at first did not seem much different from most nights and they were fighting with the Army in the New Lodge. It seemed to take a turn for the worse and my mum ordered us all into the house. We went up to the attic (third floor of a very small house) and we had a small tape recorder; it was the type that was portable about 10 inches long and 4 inches wide, with the buttons all along the bottom and a mike attached. We had only ever recorded ourselves singing Beatles, Stones and Small Faces songs and of course catching out your mum talking to neighbours and making them laugh at hearing themselves talking for the first time.

That night, however we put the mike out the skylight window. We couldn't see anything but the fighting was getting closer and louder. We did not realise just what we were about to tape. At first, on the tape, you can hear gunfire, and all the people in the street talking and the noise of the people fighting at the corner. Then a loud bang, screaming, shouting – you can distinctly hear a neighbour of ours at that time who was called Myrtle calling to her husband, 'Jimmy, Jimmy, get down Jimmy'. These were just our ordinary dads, and not troublemakers, who were talking to the soldiers at the time. It goes silent and then a burst of machine-gun fire. I was never so frightened in my life, and was so glad for the soldiers at the corner to save us and I prayed; there were soldiers out there the same age as me and Roy.

Often when there was shooting up and down the street the young soldiers used to lie in what we called our 'wee hall.' We had our front door, which was always open and then a wee hall and then a French door into the bigger hall. My Mum often cried and one night I remember her down on her stomach with the French door open when a very young soldier was lying down taking cover in our wee hall with his gun pointing up the street. She was pulling at his foot and begging him: 'Come in son, come in.' It is only in later years with my own family I realise the true heartache my mum had for these young boys, someone's son, someone's loved one across the sea, fighting in Ireland.

The night of the nail bomb and the machine gun fire was the night that the very first soldier ever to die in the Northern Ireland troubles was shot dead at the corner of our street. As I said, I did not remember the day or date but I always held that soldier in my heart and often talk about him and wonder about his family. I always remembered his last name was 'Curtis' and that his young wife was pregnant and had a baby girl in about August later that year.

He was with people who loved him and respected him for what he was doing. He was up around our corner and just before that had been laughing and joking with all of us young ones from Hillman Street. I don't know which one he was but I'm sure we would have fed him fish and chips. He would not have guessed that within the space of minutes he was going to be shot or die. It was just another day of 'the troubles' until that nail bomb and then the machine-gun fire.

We had to be protected by the army as we entered into the church, and while the service went on, the doors had to be closed as our church faced down the New Lodge Road. In our wedding photos you can see the IRA graffiti on the walls across the street. We lived with my Mum and Dad in 106 Hillman Street until

November 1971. I had just found out I was pregnant and our cars, my dad's, my brother's and ours had a union jack scraped into the paintwork, because we were Protestant and scraped also was 'Brits get out'.

Then we had six pounds of gelignite (apparently not made into a bomb) put at our back door to scare us. A soldier ran up the hall and into the kitchen shouting 'Get out, get out, there's jelly in the alley'. I hadn't got a clue what he meant but apparently the army called gelignite 'jelly'. We were taken over to the other side of the street and our Catholic friends and neighbours took us into their house for safety as the street had to be cleared. Two days later we got emergency housing in Comber, Co. Down.

On 2nd July 1971, Roy and I were married in Duncairn Presbyterian Church on the Antrim Road, we were eighteen and nineteen and had been childhood sweethearts. My daughter was born the next year (St. Patrick's day, 17/03/72) and my son was born in Sept 1978.

Private Robert Curtis of the Royal Artillery was in a group of soldiers hit by machine-gun fire on February 6 as they were involved in a firefight on the corner of Lepper Street and New Lodge Road. One of the other four, Private John Laurie, died of his wounds on February 15.

Robert Curtis, who was 20, was seen to fall and was thought by his comrades to be wounded but not seriously. One of his comrades put a lighted cigarette into his mouth and it was only when it failed to glow in the dark, that it was realised that he had been killed and his tragic place in the history of the troubles was assured.

Corporal in the Green Howards

We got wise to the tricks of the gunmen and their supporters. They had various signals to mark our movements. As we moved out on patrol, a spy on the corner would perhaps light a cigarette – then he would stub it out on the ground as a signal that we had turned into a certain street. They gave each other signals, such as rubbing their nose casually or they used handkerchiefs. [A practice later to be known as 'dicking' or being 'dicked']

Often they [the gunmen] would work in groups in the darkness and they would lie on a blanket in a street and fire at us. If a sniper was hit by one of our soldiers, his pals would quickly lift him bodily in the blanket, bullets, rifle and all and then whisk him away. Nothing would be found to give him away.

The shooting of Robert Curtis was seen as a milestone in the troubles in the same way as the shooting of a petrol bomber had been the previous year. The Army had very clearly warned that petrol bombers would be shot and when the first petrol bomber was killed – Daniel O'Hagan in North Belfast on July 31 1970 – the already precarious relationship with the Republican community would change, forever.

The following moving account is a reference to the accidental N.D. (negligent discharge) shooting of Private Kenneth Easthaugh on March 23 in the Ardoyne area of Belfast. Both of the soldiers in this tragic accident were approaching the end of this particular tour when this took place.

NEGLIGENT DISCHARGE; 4 VICTIMS – A STATISTIC OF NORTHERN IRELAND

Private 'S', Light Infantry

1971 was the year, I remembered it quite well, the incident of course. It had been my first tour in Northern Ireland and would never forget it. A Private in our battalion had been killed in an accident by a friend. I also remember a soldier who received 28 days for the accident whilst our Battalion was still in Plymouth. I always thought that this was a bit unfair, that a man who has caused the death of another soldier by an accidental discharge should do time in the guardroom.

I often wondered if the R.P.s [Regimental Police] cut him any slack or showed him any sympathy for his misfortune. Let's face, it if you kill someone by accident you have a big enough cross to carry without some dumb regimental copper screaming at you for 28 days. Some even enjoyed their role as Regimental Policemen. But there you go, I never did time. I only assume it was tough. But the memory of Private A. and Private Z. stayed with me ... I thought it was unfair that Private Z. did time yet at the same time, I always wondered why just 28 days for killing someone, why not 10 years for manslaughter or life for murder. It seemed unbalanced, the system, to me at least. What did I know?

It was 3 years later when I read the report. The report on the death of Private A. It was Confidential at the time, probably still is. How did I manage to read it? Well I had been posted away from the Battalion for 2 years and on my return I was posted to Bn HQ. On my first night back at the Battalion I was given the role of Duty Clerk. This meant staying in Bn HQ over night and waiting for a call to tell you that the Russians were coming, someone had died or whatever.

It was lying on the civilian typist's desk; I wonder tonight as I write this, why the typist's desk? Funny, I never gave it a thought before now. It was a confidential report. Anyway when I noticed the file and the name Private A. in the front temptation was too much. I sat at the desk and opened the file. It was full of official looking papers and reports; Special Investigation Branch (SIB) Statements from witnesses; notes from the Army Board of Enquiry etc. I was amazed that, after all those thoughts in 1971 mentioned above I was about to find out the truth.

Pte A. and Pte Z were in the back of a Land Rover in 1971. The Land Rover was soft skinned, not armoured – that is the back was covered with a canvas, with straps down the back holding it taut. At the scene of an incident the Land Rover stopped and Private A. jumped out. Immediately after Pte Z (the radio operator armed with an SMG – Sub Machine Gun) jumped out. As he did so the cocking handle of the SMG caught on the down strap of the Land Rover canvas, half cocked itself and discharged a round accidentally. This had happened because the safety catch was not in the safe position. The report went on 'The round hit Private A. at the base of his flak vest, travelled up his body and exited near the shoulder. Private A. died shortly after'. There it was; the story in detail that not many people knew about other than those with the authority to read the file.

I read on and wished that I had not opened the file. Private A's. wife lived in quarters in Plymouth and had given birth to a child whilst he was in Belfast and Private A never saw the child. I think I read this part 5 or 6 times with tears in my eyes. It was so moving. Being a father of a young child myself it caused me distress to even contemplate it. I put the file down and always remember trying to put it back in the exact position that I found it. Not that I was frightened that I would have been discovered reading it; I would not have. Well, it was just I felt I should not have picked the file up. I felt as if I had intruded into someone's grief and I had, I felt ashamed.

The top of this story states '4 Victims'. There are 4 victims in this short story:

Private A. He was killed unnecessarily

Private Z. Because he had to live with it. Was punished for not handling his weapon safely. A weapon which I might add was dangerous in any case. I myself bear a blued scar on the left hand little finger by mishandling the weapon and having an accidental discharge myself on the firing range during training.

Private A's wife, who was widowed at an early age.

and

Private A's child, who never knew her father.

The author is aware of the identity of the soldier involved, but supports Private 'S' in that he does not consider it in good taste or for the sake of his family to print his name.

Private Eddie Atkinson, Green Howards

The training we received for the Ardoyne tour of 1971 did not prepare us for what lay ahead. I can't remember how many times we practiced the box formation of riot control reading the Riot Act 'this is an illegal meeting, disperse or we will use force.' Oh yeah; right! As if they were going to take any notice of that load of bollocks.

My first night on the streets showed me it was a waste of time. I found myself on Butler Street with my back against a house wall with bricks and bottles raining down. The glass in a door to my right exploded and a window to my left [also] exploded; and then, I saw what appeared to be a cig flicked through the night sky. I soon found out it wasn't when it exploded! It was my first introduction to a nail bomb. A shout of 'Mount up, back on to the PIG.' We closed the back doors and set off round the corner. Bang, bang, bang: my introduction to a Thompson [sub machine gun and an early favourite of the IRA].

THAT TERRIBLE MISTY MORNING: LIGONIEL, 1971

Geoff Smith, ex 3LI

If my memory serves me well, I seem to remember that during the night that these young Jocks were murdered, 5 Platoon were crashed out to investigate a possible 'come on' shooting that had been reported in the Ligoniel area on the outskirts of Belfast. (I myself had asked to be returned to duty as a Rifleman for the Belfast Tour

Green Howards in North Belfast
(photo courtesy of Ray Rose)

of 71. I had been coerced into becoming a Company Clerk by some devious clerical type a few months before), and I was attached to Cpl Jack Garland's Section for the tour. We took over from 5 Platoon in the morning. It was a damp, misty morning and I believe 5 Platoon returned to Flax Street Mill for brekkies.

The area where the three young Jocks had been murdered was rural. Their bodies were in a narrow country lane that had a 3 foot high earth bank on either side. I seem to remember that it ran down to a main road from the village of Ligoniel and on either side of the road there were fields.

Initially we set about searching the whole of the Village, every house, every nook and cranny; I seem to remember that it was a dirty little place. Not a place one would want to die in or for. The scene of the murder was surreal; the lane dipped slightly about halfway down. On the earth bank on the left hand side as you walked down the lane, roughly in the middle of this small dip, there were neatly placed three pint beer glasses, partially full or empty, I never decided which. On the road itself a pool of blood, thick, congealed blood had formed, and in this blood was money ... the new coins which came out in 1971. The bodies had by this time been removed from the scene.

On talking to various members of the Civvy Police it was reckoned that there had been just two murderers. I was going to say at this point gunmen ... but these people were not gunmen or terrorists or freedom fighters they were just cold blooded, evil minded, 'bloody' murderers. Anyway, the police stated that they thought that two murderers had been involved because the two outside bodies had been shot in the back of the head and the middle body had been shot in the chest. The two in the head had been murdered first and the second had turned around before he had been shot and had been shot in the chest.

After a while a TV Crew turned up and, as I was young, a friend and I started messing around for the camera, dancing and laughing ... as you do. A very good friend of mine, Brian Chance said 'Knock it off; these blokes have been killed here'. This made me feel a bit silly for a moment but Jack Garland said 'No don't stop, let the bastards see it has not affected us' so I carried on for a bit longer ... childish or shock ... it was one of those times in your life when you look back and think 'that was a stupid thing to do' and worry about it forever.

About mid morning we set about searching the fields on either side of the road, on our hands and knees, looking for the rounds or something. Can't remember now. In fact I never worked out what we were looking for on the day. Probably an exercise in 'keeping the mind active.' After all this I can't remember what happened. Perhaps we returned to Flax Street or somewhere else. But I have never forgotten that day or the scene or the three young blokes.

It was after this that all under 18s were not allowed on the streets. I distinctly remember being relieved that my 18th Birthday had been but 3 weeks before ... I had missed permanent cookhouse fatigues for the rest of the tour by 3 weeks.

The murder of the three Scottish soldiers was in circumstances which can only be described as cold-blooded. The three young soldiers, two young brothers and their cousin, belonged to the Royal Highland Fusiliers. They were Fusilier John McCaig, at 17 the youngest soldier to be killed during the troubles, his 18 year old brother, Joseph and their cousin, Dougal McCaughey who was 23.

They were picked up, whilst off duty on the night of March 10, in Belfast city centre and offered a lift to a party. On the way to this fictitious party, the car stopped and the three young soldiers were offered a 'pee break'. As they did

Fusiliers in a Londonderry Sreet
(photo courtesy of Eamon Melaugh)

so, they were cold-bloodedly shot dead at the roadside and then their bodies abandoned. In one night, the number of British soldiers killed in Northern Ireland had doubled to 6.

One of the IRA gunmen reputed to have committed this atrocity was later killed by a British soldier. The Belfast coroner described the murder of the three young Scots as one of the ' ... vilest crimes heard of in living memory ...'

THE NIGHT OF INTERNMENT: BELFAST

Jim Foster, Green Howards

The fun and games really started the day that Internment was brought in; we were in the Ardoyne and SP company were stationed in Leopold Street just over Crumlin Road from Flax Street.

On the night of internment, I was Chuck Berry's PIG driver, and each section was given a selected house to go into in order to lift the bad guys. Chuck was given a house in Butler Street. Now, I should point out that he was 6ft plus whereas I'm 5ft 5 (and there were smaller guys than me, such as the little Joneses, the drummer boys and many more) I think that's why they called us the Yorkshire Ghurkhas! Anyhow, it was late and pitch black and anyone who says they didn't crap themselves that night are either brain dead or they were on a different planet to me. We arrived at our target, and Chuck said: 'Kick the door in !' I looked up at him in dismay as I picked myself up of the floor after bouncing off it. One of the lads whispered: 'Try the door knob !' We did so, and, yes it opened; Chuck was kind enough to tell me to check up the stairs which I did, using my SLR as an extension of my arms as by this time my arse had learnt how to clap.

On getting to the landing, the lady of the house came to the top of the stairs put the light on and told us he had gone! After that night things started to warm up. Later, on patrol on the Crumlin again, with me driving, we observed the bad boys building a bonfire just off Crumlin between Butler Street and Flax Street; Chuck ordered me move a pile of wood and stuff before they lit it. I put my foot down and the next thing I heard, was Chuck saying 'Right lads, rock backwards and forwards and get this PIG off the top of this bonfire or we'll be this year's hog roast if they light it!'

I was driving again and Chuck and all the section were sitting in the PIG on the Crumlin opposite Butler Street. Now, as luck would have it, we had recently put sandbags in the PIG to take the blast of any bombs to come our way. That night one did and it landed directly under us. The sandbags did work but the funny thing was Chuck and I could not get our weapons out of the front hatches and the Joneses were running around the vehicle like headless chickens. As I said earlier, these guys were smaller than me so the back of the vehicle was like a barnyard to them!

Chuck shouted to them to shoot, whereupon one of them did! The next thing you could hear from Butler Street was an enraged shout of "YOU MURDERING BASTARD!"

The Prods then started burning their own houses in Farringdon Gardens in the Ardoyne because they were been forced out by the bad guys; it was just like the OK Corral for a few days. I was still driving Chuck's section but he was on foot

Ardoyne seen from Flax Street Mill

somewhere in the Ardoyne. Hughie Macaulay and I were in the bus station in what used to be their rest room upstairs. Now the Prods, as I said earlier, were burning their houses by starting fires in the bedrooms and chopping the gas pipes downstairs and the final result was spectacular! Anyway, myself and Hughie were looking at the anti-tank platoon who were head down in Farringdon, using the gardens as cover, when we spotted a gunman open up on them. All we could see was the smoke from the barrel of the gunman so we fired about 10 rounds each as he ran across the road; he must have been about 300 yards away and we saw him go down and then someone crawled out to drag him in. But we couldn't say if we dropped him.

Just then, Joe Peacock, the Drum's platoon OC who we were driving, came in and started to shout; he called out to us 'What are you shooting at?' When we told him 'the bad guys', he said 'You wont hit them from here !' With that, a round whizzed over Joe's head; he took cover and said: 'Keep your heads down lads; I will see you later!'

Gun battles continued the rest of the night and later the next day and then, I think, the Paras came in to give us a break.

INTERNMENT: 1971

Major Eddie Bright, Royal Green Jackets

The relative calm that resulted from the initial aggressive stance taken by 1 RGJ at the start of the 1971 tour in the Falls Road area was starting to unravel. A similar pattern was emerging throughout the Province.

Despite the slowly rising tension in the Lower Falls area, the boss, Major Iain C-L was persuaded to take his well-deserved R & R and fly back to Germany for a couple of days. No sooner had he departed, in fact he was still airborne over the British mainland, when we were summoned by the Company Second in Command, Robin H-S to an O-Group [Orders group]. Apparently the RUC Special Branch had a tip-off that a well known IRA man was in the Long Bar in Leeson Street. As the Platoon Commander for this area, I was very sceptical that the Special Branch had any clue on what was happening in this area. Nevertheless, we were tasked to carry out a platoon raid on the Long Bar, a notorious drinking establishment in the heart of the Falls. As the resident 'authority' on the Lower Falls area, I offered my views on the consequences that would arise from our proposed action. The 2 i/c listened intently but the raid was ordered from on high and would go ahead regardless. It appeared rather coincidental that the boss was no sooner in the air when the raid was ordered.

The platoon briefing was conducted with a number of additional personnel joining us to boost the platoon strength, the Company Colour Sergeant Tony V was a useful addition. At over six four, he would be a good person to follow through the Long Bar front door. We discussed at length the best way to gain entry into what would be a very crowded noisy and hostile illegal drinking hole. With the other two platoons on standby, we duly hit the Long Bar with a degree of 'force with charm'. The result was as expected in the congested bar despite it being early afternoon. The violence erupted immediately we entered as the locals took exception to our 'social call' with a major confrontation developing in the streets either side of the Long Bar. Suffice to say, no IRA hierarchy were present but the perceived desired result was obtained – running riots throughout the area.

The screaming, threatening mobs that appear as soon as the slightest incident occurs never ceased to amaze me. One potentially nasty incident was defused when a baton gun was held to the head of a particularly obnoxious

More riots in Belfast

troublemaker who was threatening the life of a young RCT subaltern attached to the company. As the violent reaction spread throughout the area, the platoon withdrew as the standby platoons moved into positions to cover the move back to the Mill.

The return to mayhem in the streets hastened the return of the Company Commander who did not actually make it home for his R & R, being summoned at London Heathrow to turn around.

The rising excitement in Albert Street Mill was getting more evident as guards were placed on telephones to prevent anyone calling out, the riflemen beginning to realise that something big was in the air. Platoon Commanders and key attached personnel hurrying to the Company Commander's O Group further increased the awareness that what we had discussed at length was about to go down. Possibly the worst kept secret was about to happen, Internment – long expected but more especially so after the events of the previous week in Leeson Street. The raid on the Long Bar ignited the whole area, which was to be expected in what the locals considered a no-go bar.

As the Platoon Commander of the Reconnaissance Platoon, I attended the Internment briefing, Platoon Commanders, Special Branch from the mainland, local RUC officers and attached officers (from other units) rounded out the group. My platoon was to arrest the largest group of known IRA terrorists in the Lower Falls, a task eagerly accepted by the boys when I returned to brief the platoon.

The platoon was joined by a Scotland Yard Special Branch officer and another from the RUC Special Branch. The Scotland Yard guy certainly appeared to be relishing the opportunity to work with us on what was about to be a history-making event.

The Platoon moved quietly through the darkened streets in the early hours to our start line to wait the moment that was about to provoke a violent backlash throughout the province. H hour arrived and with both a degree of anxiety and an abundance of elation we moved in on the still sleeping Lower Falls community to take up the final positions close to our twelve hopefully unaware designated targets.

In true Green Jacket style, using our familiar charming and humorous technique honed over decades, we kicked in the doors to deliver a cheery good morning call to the unfortunates that still slept in their own beds rather than following the age old terrorist technique of changing locations regularly.

It would be an understatement to say the reaction from the quickly awoken populace was violent. As expected, it was swift and aggressive. We endeavoured to retain control of the fast disintegrating scene; women attacking riflemen with pots and pans as their criminal spouses were arrested adding further to the chaotic scenes; other households joined the affray creating bedlam as we dragged those arrested to the waiting vehicles to move to a temporary holding station. Even in such violent situations, it never ceased to amaze me how the lads refrained from striking back especially at the manic women despite suffering numerous physical attacks and sustaining a number of quite nasty injuries.

Eventually arriving in the holding centre, a local school, we quickly processed the arrested terrorists before embarking on what was about to be a violent journey across the city to Girdwood Park which had been set up as the Belfast processing centre.

Driving out of the school in armoured one ton vehicles, the scene as one wag remarked was more like Beirut than Belfast. We were immediately attacked with numerous percussion and petrol bombs thrown at and under the vehicles. The ear-splitting noise greatly magnified inside the steel-encased vehicles. The streets were alight with burning tyres and rioting mobs intent on gaining the release of the prisoners. The vehicle pitched and swayed as it was struck with incendiary devices, the driver focusing on keeping the armoured one tonner moving with the remainder of the convoy. The deafening noise added to the excitement with the boys still high on adrenalin. The journey to Girdwood Park will remain etched on the memories of the young rifleman as the treacherous route across the city was negotiated. Belfast looked like a major war zone; clouds of smoke filled the sky from burning cars and tyres, and was accompanied by small arms fire. Percussion and petrol bombs certainly added to a very bizarre scene for a UK city.

As we drove past the burning cars and through the black acrid smoke from the tyres, the scene should have been accompanied by the 1812 Overture. We now began to appreciate the fact that we were not alone in the early morning raids with military vehicles appearing from other parts of the city making their way to the same destination.

The arrival in Girdwood Park was greeted by what can only be described as a scene of organised chaos, vehicles arriving by the minute delivering their cargo of hardened Republican and Loyalist thugs from throughout the city before being led away by RMP [Royal Military Police] and RUC staff for processing.

Along with our group of arrested IRA criminals, we observed amongst them a number of very familiar faces being brought in for questioning. One or two of those familiar faces would go on to play a major role in the future of Northern Ireland, a possibility we would never have believed possible in 1971.

Eventually we arrived back at our company base in Albert Street Mill to a very different scene; the calmness inside the Mill was tranquillity itself. The realisation by many of the platoon, that they had played a part in a major event in Northern Ireland history, Internment, now began to sink in. The feeling was one of sheer satisfaction that at last the Government had acted firmly against the terrorists although time would judge if that was the best option to take.

We had, as a platoon, arrested some major Republican players who would now spend a considerable amount of time behind bars for their violent actions.

Meanwhile outside on the streets, the rioting was intensifying. A short debrief and a hastily-eaten meal were the only rewards for our early morning start before re-entering what was appearing to be a state of anarchy – a situation that we were not about to tolerate.

23RD AUGUST 1971

Private Eddie Atkinson, Green Howards

We were next on Guard duty and I was wandering around Flax Street mill when I was told to get my kit pronto and get up to the roof sangar. It was an hour or two early, and I didn't know what had happened.

The sangar was right on top of the mill and I walked into the room; in the corner was a ladder that led up to the sangar but, before I climbed the ladder I was told someone had just been shot up there. I didn't know at that time whom it was. I climbed the ladder and there was a girder that ran under the sangar which we used to put our hands on to help us climb up into it. I put my hand on the girder, and I felt something wet and cold; when I took my hand away it was covered in congealed blood; the blood of poor old George Crozier.

NORTHUMBERLAND MILL, BELFAST: 1971

Sergeant Roy Davies, RRW

Although the year as a whole was pretty bad, considering where we were based – Northumberland Mill near the Divis Street flats – it is pleasantly surprising to note that we only had one really serious incident during the few months we were there.

The pattern was that if there was a riot in the town, the mobs would come up the Divis and make for the flats. One of my jobs was to lead a 'snatch squad' and we would be held in reserve behind the front line of soldiers awaiting the order to go in and grab a ringleader or other trouble causer. On this particular day, I was told to grab a 'bloke in yellow'; the guys parted and in we dashed and got the 'bloke' and dragged 'him' back behind the lines. Only 'he' turned out to be an 18 stone woman and one of the roughest, ugliest women I have ever seen. She spat right into my face and called me an 'English bastard.' Boy did she insult me! I didn't mind the use of the word 'bastard' because my Mam and Dad were not married – they did later – but she called me 'English' and that made me angry. I shouted back at her 'I don't mind being called a bastard, I can't help that, but don't you ever call me English again!' I rapped her across the legs with my baton but an officer called out that there were cameras there and my Sergeant made me stop.

Straight after this, our Support Company pushed through us and pushed the mobs back to the flats, but as they reached the flats and the mobs disappeared, TVs, bricks, sofas, chairs and all sorts rained down on the lads. Of course all the lads underneath were hit by these huge heavy flying objects and quite a few were injured and I have never seen so many soldiers crying with pain.

NORTHERN IRELAND: 1971

Russ Slater, 17th/21st Lancers

Even in early 1971, it was not unusual for squaddies posted to Northern Ireland to visit local towns when off duty and go drinking. A young Scottish soldier, who had been out for a night's drinking, but was under eighteen years old, had been murdered, along with his elder brother, near Ligoniel. This caused outrage in the press, so the government at the time decided to send all soldiers under eighteen out of the Province.

Along with six other lads, I was sent to a camp near Salisbury and attached to another Royal Armoured Corps unit. Shortly after our arrival, this unit themselves were sent to Northern Ireland. Within weeks, this other unit had been involved in a nasty shooting near the border and one of their lads had been killed. After his

Reece Platoon, Divis Flats, 1971
(photo courtesy of Regimental Museum of The Royal Welsh)

burial in his hometown, a military service was held at this camp, which his family attended. I, along with the other lads from my Regiment was told to go and 'make up the numbers.' However, we were told to change our cap badges, as it was felt that ours, a skull and crossbones, would not be appropriate. When we arrived at the service, we found only a few members of this lad's Regiment there, one an officer, and none knew him all that well. After the service the family, naturally, wanted to talk to us about their son, thinking we were all close friends and members of his troop.

I was asked tearful questions to which I had no answer, so made them up. I remember the mother could see my obvious discomfort, and thinking it was because of her son, she put her arm around me and said 'Don't worry love, it's hard for all of us, but time will heal.' I felt so sorry for this brave mum; I wanted to say, 'Look, you don't understand; this is all bullshit!'

But I was only seventeen and out of my depth, so I said nothing.

The soldier whose funeral Russ attended was Corporal Ian Armstrong (32) of the 14th/20th Hussars who was killed on August 29 1971 near Crossmaglen. His two vehicle armoured patrol had accidentally crossed into the Irish Republic into the Sheelagh area and was attacked by a mob of Irish citizens. One vehicle was set alight – whilst the Garda and Irish Army did nothing – and one of the Ferret scout cars made it back over the border but had to stop for a puncture.

It was during repairs that an IRA ambush killed Ian Armstrong and badly wounded Trooper Ronald Ager; both the Garda Sichona and the Irish Army denied that they had refused to intervene.

ARDOYNE RIOT

Corporal Nicky Curtis, MM, Green Howards

At that point a guy who, I must admit, must have had some balls, found the bravado to advance the extra 10 yards needed to fling a petrol bomb close enough to hit us. The bottle seemed to disappear in the dark and suddenly it zipped out of the flames of the barricade and split open on the wall of shields. The shields danced back and split as a fire extinguisher was brought forward to douse the flames. One lad hopped around with his shins on fire until a fire blanket was wrapped around them. I heard a muffled cheer through the crackle and spit of burning cars.

Blakesey, Tapper [later to be sadly killed] and I swapped our larger shields for smaller portable ones, pulled out a baton each and got in position. This was what we'd trained for. The street was partially blocked by the cars but the open part was filling with the advancing mob. A rain of bricks clanked down on the helmets in front of us. One chunk ricocheted under a visor and split the lad's chin open. As he was passed back through the ranks we advanced like a Roman battle squad. I could see the ring-leader beckoning us on with one hand, a bottle topped with a flaming rag in the other. Now! The shields split. We belted through and out. The crowd spread. Most of them ran. A quick volley of bricks hit us from those who had dared to stand a second. Blood banged in my ears. Tapper shouted, 'Shit' as a brick hit. He stumbled and nearly fell, then caught up with a guy who turned and instinctively head butted him; the rioter knocked himself clean out on the helmet! The ring-leader spun to me, raised his arm, then tripped backwards and fell. The bottle landed intact and spun, flickering. I leaped over it and cracked him in the face with the arm shield as he rose. His nose liquidised against the hard plastic. I grabbed his shirt, which ripped open to the waist as he tore away and ran, bounced off a wall and disappeared. A whole crate of petrol bombs landed in the street and blew. I caught sight of people hanging like monkeys on the house roofs, lining up more.

We staggered back breathless, Tapper dragging his unconscious charge by the ankle. Blakesey was still out there, behind us, kicking a guy in the balls as another car was driven at speed at one of those already on fire, shunting it closer to us. Sparks flew off from the impact before the new car hit a lamppost and groaned. We all got back as a cheer erupted from behind the flames.

GLENGORMLY: 1971

Colonel Derek Parsley, Royal Artillery

In 1971, I was a Captain the 25th Field Regiment RA, and was posted to Belfast in the early July. We took over from the Welsh Guards at their base, an old factory in the northern Belfast district of Glengormly.

Member of the 'hen patrol' warns that soldiers are about
(photo courtest of Eamon Melaugh)

Our first morning there was to be remembered by all; we were having breakfast when we heard the rat-ta-tat of machine gun fire just outside. We all rushed out just in time to see our sentry on the gate, firing at a van zigzagging down the road. When we demanded an explanation of him, he replied that the van driver had thrown a package over our fence. We then summoned ATO (bomb-disposal unit) to come and investigate. ATO duly did so and then informed us that our 'bomb' was, in fact, the Sunday newspapers!

For a short time, our Battery was kept in reserve, but we were soon assigned to patrol the Falls Road area, a pretty tough Republican stronghold. I took it upon myself to help with this patrolling, simply because I wanted to become thoroughly familiar with the whole area; it was time well spent. I had at my disposal 3 troops [equivalent of a platoon in an infantry unit] each commanded by an officer with 3 sections of 8 soldiers commanded by a sergeant. Patrolling was an extremely diligent process since all were subject to sniper fire.

Later on we were called to operate a number of VCPs on the motorway between Belfast and Portadown. During this time, I had the chance to at times to follow some of the Protestant 'marches.' At first I was quite impressed – they all went off looking very smart in their black suits, bowler hats and orange sashes; then they reached a pub and in they all traipsed. Not quite so many continued the march, until they reached another pub and in they all traipsed, again; then the trouble began! The more they marched, the more they drank – and their behaviour reflected just that.

I had the chance to monitor one of these marches once and as I was travelling in my Land Rover, two small boys asked if they could look at our radio. I duly let them have a look, but asked how old they were. They were both about four years old; later I asked them where they lived and they pointed to what I knew was a Protestant area. I then pointed to a Catholic area and asked them who lived there; their answer was 'Them Fenian bastards!' What chance did they have to understand the sectarian divide?

In the beginning of August we were in the Ardoyne, helping the Green Howards who were having a spot of bother. That lasted for almost two days, during which we got little sleep. I was then summoned by my Battery Commander who told me that the CO wanted to see the pair of us. We were told that at precisely 3.00 am the following night, whatever we were doing, the whole battery was to drive to Girdwood Park, a barracks almost next door to Crumlin Goal. We were told that a policy of 'Internment' would commence that night.

So, at precisely 3.00 am we did just that and made our way to Girdwood Park. When we arrived we saw that a tunnel had been constructed linking our barracks to the gaol next door; those who were to be interned would be taken to Girdwood Park by our soldiers but immediately transferred to the goal where they would be subjected to a process known as 'deep interrogation.'

Internment was a completely new concept to almost everyone – and 'Deep Interrogation' is not at all a pleasant experience. Many people – and I must say this included me – did not like this and thought it improper. Most thought that it would do more to encourage terrorism than stop it. Fortunately, so many thought this way, including Amnesty International, that this concept lasted only a very few weeks. However, talking to some of the Military Policemen who did the interrogating, the amount of useful information they obtained was almost worth it.

Much later on, after several other jobs we had been assigned to, we were at an interface posted on Lenadoon Avenue when we were told that a rocket of some description had been fired at a building close by, injuring nobody. Apparently one soldier was heard to say 'Bit draughty in 'ere Sir, init!'

35 Battery now at the end of their tour lost no soldiers; the other two batteries were not quite so lucky. One had a soldier killed at a VCP, and another had an officer shot in the head and another soldier wounded. The officer was extremely lucky, since the bullet entered his head below the ear, travelled around his skull and exited just below the other ear; lucky fellow I thought!

The soldier killed is thought to be Gunner Clifford Loring (18) who died of his wounds on August 31, two days after being shot and badly wounded whist manning a VCP at Stockman's Lane, in the Andersonstown area. The round which ultimately killed the young Gunner from the Yorkshire area passed through the protective clothing of another soldier. Although 35 Battery lost no men, eleven members of the Royal Artillery were killed during the year.

FOOT PATROL: BELFAST: 1971

'Spanner', Royal Electrical & Mechanical Engineers

I was a soldier in REME attached to 25 RA. It was autumn, 1971 and we were billeted in a TA camp in Sunnyside, a Loyalist area but close to the Ardoyne. The Regiment manned two council houses which we had sandbagged up as an outpost.

Repairs finished for the day, I was ready for a rare bit of relaxation, maybe even a bit of sleep but then I spotted 'the skull' – our Battery Sergeant Major (BSM)- walking around collecting his men. I had done a few mobile patrols with him and, whilst not my usual duties, it got me out for a while. He looked at me 'Want in on this one, Spanner?'

I went over to see what was going on. Our REME clerk, 'big Rog' joined me and we listened in. There was information that a suspected bomb maker was in a house on the Ardoyne; the idea was to send a patrol in behind the house, through a park under cover of darkness and take a look. If seen, then the heavy mob would be called in to grab him; but if he tried to slip out the back then the patrol could nab him.

'Big Rog' went as radio man and we prepared ourselves for the patrol, ensuring we had nothing on us that would rattle or jingle; dressed in DPM combat suit, boots, belt with a single pouch for a spare mag and a field dressing, and all wearing our steel helmets. Rog and I were armed with Stirling SMGs, [9mm Sub Machine Guns] not really suitable for this job but we were able to swap them for SLR's with a couple of lads just back from mobile patrols who were going for a sleep. Rog got his radio and tested it. In those days, a radio to get you just a mile or two was a big, heavy pack.

To get to the park we would travel in open Land Rovers which had a driver, commander and six men in the back. We went up an unlit lane that ran between the rear of some prefabs and the park fence; we stopped, debussed and they left. The park was surrounded by a metal rail fence, with the bottom rail about six inches from the ground, and a top rail about four feet above with looped tubing forming the vertical rails and a decorative top. Some of these rails had been removed and we entered by the gap made, and crouched down behind a large bush for a final brief. I brought up the rear with Rog just ahead of me; the Lieutenant led off with the BSM close behind, and then single file, 3 paces between each man.

The ground was gently undulating, but with no embankments or ditches for cover we were in the open, with only the darkness to hide our approach. The lights of the Ardoyne seemed far away but provided a sense of direction. We soon found that the metal fence not only surrounded the park but divided it into large sections, so that gaps had to be found for us to pass through. At the second gap, Rog became stuck, and I tried to push him through, but only succeeded in making him more stuck. The man ahead, realising that Rog was not behind him, alerted the rest of the patrol and they all came back. Between them they pushed Rog back to my side, where he tumbled down.

A couple of the lads came through to help get the radio pack off his back, he was then able to pass through the fence and we passed the pack through to him and helped him to get it back on. We continued our trek but more care had to be taken to find larger gaps so that Rog and his radio could get through with no further delays.

The lights of the Ardoyne were getting nearer. Now the houses were clearly silhouetted by the street lamps and we soon reached the perimeter fence and we could identify the house of interest by a count back from the corner. There was a gap of about three metres with a small embankment going down to the back fences of the houses. That was where the Lt. wanted to be, right up to the garden fence. There was another gap just handy to our target so he tried to pass through but caught his ankle on the bottom rail, causing his head to come up sharply, his steel helmet hit the top rail and the fence rang out like the town hall clock striking one as he fell to the ground. Two of the lads went through to help him as the rest of us took up defensive positions. Lights came on at the rear of the houses, a couple of back doors opened and although no one came out, we were blown.

The Lt was helped back through the fence, his ankle hurting as much as his pride, but he said he could walk. Now we had to decide what to do; to go back through the park now it was known we were here, with no cover, would be an open invitation to anyone about who was armed to take pot shots at us. There was an alternative; a path between the houses lead out to the street. We could walk out that way and make for the two houses that formed the outpost. Rog would have to make contact to let them know we were coming. It was risky but we thought it was the last thing anyone would expect.

Going out to the street, we divided into two groups of four, one group each side of the street to give each other cover; I was now last man on the right hand side as we started our walk, expecting to meet trouble. Now, a strange thing happened: people were coming out of the houses to look at us, men, women and children. Whole families, but not with hostility as we expected, instead it was curiosity, we were asked, 'What are ye boys doing here?' several times, to which we answered, 'Just going for a walk, showing a friendly face,' which seemed to be accepted. We had expected stones, bricks, bottles and even worse, but were getting friendly curiosity, not even an insult was thrown. Eventually, we came to a 'T' junction on our right, and the lads on the left bracketed it. Then we crossed the open end steadily. On the opposite corner two women were out in the garden, dressed in loose, low cut blouses, tight skirts and dangly jewellery with lots of make up, 'Hello boys, what are youse doing here?' We explained and they offered us cups of tea at a quid each, which we declined, but they told us that we were always welcome!

This was unreal; this was the Ardoyne with a bad reputation for trouble and we were getting invites?

We continued our journey but then things started to change – no more people were coming out to see us. This made us ever more alert. People were staying indoors. Now we could see our objective, the sandbagged front of the post. It was a temptation to break into a run but that could be more dangerous so we held our pace. Now we could see rifle barrels pointing out from the lads in the outpost and soon we were in, all safe.

A call was put through to pick us up and now we were able to relax and make a brew, there was even dry rations and bread for snacks. Just a few days before I had driven a Humber APC PIG out here with rations and some lads for change over, now I was here waiting for pick up. It was a PIG that came for us; there was always a chance of danger when going from the post to the vehicle but nothing happened and we were taken back safely to camp for debrief.

We were later told that we were the first foot patrol through the Ardoyne since the Troubles began in '69. We had no reason to doubt that as the locals did seem surprised to see us.

We were not 'roughie toughies' or special forces, not even real infantry, just a bunch of Gunners with a paper shuffler and a spanner slinger, but when things went wrong, we followed SOP's and looked out for each other so we all got back safely and that is what really counts.

PIG PILE UP. BELFAST: 1971

Drummer Richard Nettleton, Grenadier Guards

Imagine a rapid response unit of six Humber PIGs as they raced through the streets of Belfast to attend a riot. Got the picture?

Now imagine what happens when the lead vehicle suddenly does an emergency stop ! Cue great cheers from the boyos ! The resulting chaos is that they all crash into each other and those doors which we all know the troops enter and exit through are in the back, were all buckled and bent and useless. Our response was somewhat dazed and a little tarnished that afternoon.

Had an IRA ambush been in place that day, I would not be relating this tale!

The PIG had several fatal flaws: it was vulnerable to the AP (armour-piercing) rounds which the IRA acquired from the USA, it was stuffy, it was slow, especially up some of the hills around the Ardoyne and the driver's view was extremely restricted.

Chapter Five

1972

This was by far the worst year of the troubles and never again would the deaths of soldiers, terrorists or the incidence of bombings and shootings ever reach these heights again.

It would witness 1,853 bombings, 10,564 shootings and the deaths of 129 soldiers, 17 RUC officers, 223 civilians and 98 terrorists. Indeed, the worst ever year for the deaths of civilians would peak at 224, four years later.

This year would see the appalling 'Bloody Friday' attacks when the IRA planted bombs in Belfast's bus depot. Some of the injuries were so horrific, that the death toll of 10 is only an approximation. The dead included 2 soldiers and 2 children.

Nine people, including an eight-year-old girl and two teenage boys, were killed and dozens were injured when three car bombs exploded without warning in the quiet village of Claudy, near Londonderry, in the north of the province, on July 31, 1972.

It would also witness the awful slaughter at the 'Abercorn Restaurant' in Donegal Street in Belfast which killed 4 civilians, 2 RUC officers and a soldier on March 20, that year.

Operation Motorman was carried out by British Army forces, with the operation starting at 4 am on 31 July 1972 to retake the no-go areas (i.e., areas controlled by the Privisional IRA) established in Belfast and Derry in the aftermath of internment the previous year. The operation used 27 infantry and two armoured battalions aided by 5,300 UDR men. The IRA did not attempt to hold their ground, as they lacked the necessary armaments and numbers for a direct confrontation with the army. The British Army employed an overwhelming force of 22,000 troops (roughly 4% of the whole British Army). By the end of the day there were no more no-go areas in Northern Ireland

On 21 September, the IRA shot dead 53 year old UDR Private Tommy Bullock in his living room and killed his wife as well.

This year also saw British Army strength (excluding UDR) reach its maximum number of 21,800 personnel deployed at any one time.

NORTHERN IRELAND, 1972
Un-named Officer, Light Infantry

I was a platoon commander in the Light Infantry in Northern Ireland.

My regiment, which was there in 1969, came to help the Irish people, to protect them against the Protestant extremists. But later, when we went again 1972, we found ourselves on the opposite side. We found ourselves being shot at an awful lot by the Irish Republican Army terrorists.

We lived in a couple of houses on the Crumlin Road, knocked in together. And we were really isolated. The only times we went out were on patrol, or when we went on to observation posts which were scattered around the area.

One of the days I remember particularly. We were involved in 'lollipop patrols'. These were patrols to separate the Catholic and Protestant children as they walked home from school, at about 3.30 to 4 o'clock in the afternoon. This particular area was on the Crumlin Road. One area was Protestant; one side was Catholic; and we would be setting up a position, looking into the area.

Now one day, my platoon was there. We were being stoned by quite a large number of children – more so than we would normally expect, and clearly they were trying to draw us into the area. Just at that moment in time, a camera crew came up the Crumlin Road and positioned itself on the pavement. I went over and said to them: 'Sorry, you can't film here until you have permission from the headquarters.' And I pointed them towards the headquarters down the road.

At the same time, the Corporal shouted to me. 'Sir', he said, 'the children are starting to clear.' Now, this meant to us that a gunman was going to come out and start firing at us. So I immediately turned round, ran back, told my soldiers to take cover and we cocked our weapons.

Two shots from a high-velocity Armalite rifle were fired; they caught one of my soldiers in the arm and the upper thigh. It was my corporal who got hit. He went down, and immediately I could see that he had been hit in the main artery in his leg, and blood was pouring.

I ordered immediately two soldiers to get round him – two people I knew had first aid experience – to stop the blood. But very quickly the blood had already made a trail down the road. I could see that he was losing pints as the seconds ticked by.

I called up the crash crew immediately, but they didn't come straight away, and I was getting a bit frantic at this point. There was no sense in following up the gunman, because we couldn't see him. We didn't fire any rounds back, because we weren't sure what they were going to be firing at. The most important thing was to get the soldier into the hospital as soon as possible.

I felt really devastated at the time that I had not done enough to protect my soldier from the shooting. But I found that they didn't blame me for it. At the end of the day, our regiment, which was there for four months in 1972, lost five soldiers killed and 25 were seriously wounded. It was a very, very bad time for the security forces. It was the worst year, in fact, for security force deaths in the whole of the history of the province.

It was the start-up, really, of the IRA campaign against the Army being there, and I think that we were quite green. We didn't know how to deal with the situations, and we were very vulnerable. And I think later on we learnt more about not overreacting. That was the important thing: not to overreact, not to fire back when you didn't know where the gunman was – so that you didn't embitter the population.

At the end of the day, it took a number of years for the British Army to become more policeman-like, and to be more considerate to the population. The trouble is with the Army; if you put it into a civilian situation, they can sometimes act like they do in a battlefield, and that is the difficulty. Training is that you fire back immediately you're fired upon. And you cannot do that in Northern Ireland. You cannot do that with civilians around and children around.

The five Light Infantry soldiers to which this officer refers were Private Richard Jones (21), Sergeant Arthur Whitelock (24), Private Ronald Rowe (21) and Private Thomas Rudman who was 20. Private Tommy Stoker's death is recorded elsewhere in this chapter.

SUNDAY 30 JANUARY 1972
Major Andrew Macdonald, 1 King's Own Border Rgt

Back then, I was a young platoon commander – a Lieutenant – in Burma Company of my Battalion, and based at Ballykinler on Province Reserve. Each of the Battalion's three companies had one platoon each supplied with PIGs – 4 wheeled lightly armoured and very cumbersome vehicles that were called PIGs, we presumed because they looked like them. The other two platoons travelled in 4 tonners. Because of this, the platoon with the PIGs considered themselves very special (or lucky). In the early hours of what we would later call 'Bloody Sunday', we were deployed to help units in the Londonderry area as they had experienced severe problems with increased rioting and were concerned about the security of the base during the planned march.

In the very early hours of Sunday, 30 January, I was called in to see our Company commander, then Major Joe Milburn. He said to me: 'I've got a job for you; you're going to reinforce a Guards company in Bligh's Lane in the Creggan!' Joy!

We prepped ourselves and off we went, arriving at Bligh's Lane base in the early hours of the morning. As our PIGs pulled into the base, we were greeted and I was taken to see the Guards' company commander. I should point out that at this early stage of the conflict in NI, many of the bases were hastily constructed by the Sappers and comprised of wriggly tin with breeze block watchtowers and reinforced areas.

I reported to the OC and he said: 'I'm really glad that you're here; how many men have you got?' I replied: 'Sixteen men – and me, Sir!' He just looked aghast at me and I recall he uttered an expletive that preceded 'I was expecting a platoon! Do you know what's happening today? They're planning the biggest march we've ever seen and we're on the route!'

We settled into the base for a short rest and then later, we were shown our deployment positions. The task in hand was to be able to reinforce any part of the Base perimeter in case of attack by the crowd.

It was almost dawn and the weather was cold, dry and clear that day, if I recall correctly. The crowd began marching down the road past the base towards the centre of Londonderry. There were thousands of them almost brushing against the walls as they marched on. We all sensed that this day was not going to go well and that it was a confrontation in the making; even before the events of that day unfolded in the city centre.

I was in the yard at my deployment position. Suddenly, we heard a 'thump, thump, thump' which everybody immediately recognised as shooting. The sound was especially familiar to the guys who had been on the ground for the past several months – the tell-tale sound of a Thompson sub machine gun is unmistakable. We knew, whatever later unfolded – and we all watched the tragic events on the television in the base – that it wasn't our Army that started the firing that day.

Even today, over 35 years since the tragic events which took place in Londonderry on January 30, 1972, the controversy rages on. The Parachute Regiment maintain that they were fired upon first and the IRA claims that the Paras started the shooting. To the neutral, the doubt will always be there, but given the track record of the IRA and their avowed campaign to shoot and bomb their way to the conference table, there will be an equal number who believe the Paras.

What is, however, certain, is that 13 people were killed in Londonderry on that day and that statistic will never change. One of the dead, Gerald Donaghy, is named as an IRA member by *Lost Lives*. Amidst the turmoil and controversy of that day, one death has been sadly overlooked and overshadowed. That very same day, Major Robin Alers-Hankey, of the Royal Green Jackets, died of his wounds four months after being shot by the IRA whilst providing cover for firemen fighting a blaze in the city.

The following month, six more soldiers were killed, including Parachute Padre Gerry Weston who died in the Aldershot Officers' Mess along with six other civilian workers.

CASTLEDILLON TO LONDONDERRY: 1972

Corporal Tom Clarke, RCT

I was sent out in the late part of 1971 with 60 RCT and stayed there until the following March; I started with 1 Para at Castle barracks, Holywood but ended up in a real mud hole at Castledillon with the Royal Engineers.

The place where 4 of us RCT lads was sent was in the grounds of an old asylum which backed on to a lake; it was only a small lake, mind, but everywhere was mud and more mud. In this mud bath we had outbreaks of scabies and no doubt, trench foot. We had a dummy by the door – occasionally, we would stick a fag in its mouth – just to fool snipers and every day we would alter its stance to make it seem a little realistic. We were never fired at there so we can only assume that it fooled nobody.

The 'love affair' between the local people and ourselves hadn't quite broken down and we still were given the odd cups of tea and biscuits, even around the early part of 1972. We worked on the construction of a prison at Warrenpoint, and at this time the 'Kesh was still an airstrip and nothing much more than that. Then, one weekend, late in the January, the top boys got wind of a very big Civil Rights demo which was being held in Londonderry. We bussed the Paras up there before retiring to a motor park in the city and waited for further orders.

We really had no idea that it was going to kick off, but as we stood around our PIGS and Bedfords, we knew something was happening by the sounds coming from where the Paras were confronting rioters and gunmen. Then, all of a sudden, we began receiving incoming rounds – 5 or 6 at that time – and we dived inside the PIGs or whatever cover we could find, and we could hear the rounds clanging off the outsides. We listened to the chatter on the RT [radio transmitter], and from the noise on the radio waves, we knew that something major was happening.

Not until later, did we learn that it was, in fact, the events of 'Bloody Sunday' unfolding right there not a million miles from where we were.

LURGAN: 1972

Major Dennis Gilpin, Royal Corps of Signals (TAVR)

One night, the UDR commander, Major Frank Jones, in his own private car, but wearing his uniform, was out visiting his patrols. Several IRA men followed him, overtook him and riddled his car with bullets from a Thompson. His car was hit ten times and although one of the rounds missed his nose by millimeters, he was unscratched; needless to say, he never wore his uniform in his car after that.

We were never targeted deliberately [7 TAVR soldiers were killed during the troubles] as we were not perceived as a threat to the IRA, but there were incidents involving our members. A Lance Corporal from Lurgan TAC, who was a postie in normal life, was shot very early one morning on his postal rounds. I visited him in hospital where he was being guarded by an armed, plain-clothed policeman as they felt he would be targeted again. When he left the hospital, he left Northern Ireland completely and was even escorted by the SF [Security Forces] to the boat to England!

When the UDR moved into Lurgan TAC [T.A. Centre] we got to know some of the officers and SNCOs socially. There was a young Second Lieutenant in the UDR and he was in a 'mixed' marriage; he was a Protestant and his young wife was a Catholic. Every day, he would drive into a Catholic area and collect his child from his Mother-in-Law's house. One afternoon, he was shot dead in front of his shocked family by the IRA, apparently considered a legitimate target. I'm sure that they later boasted about killing him but I doubt that they added that it was done in front of his defenceless family in cold blood.

[This young officer who was considered a 'legitimate target' for going into a Republican area, was 2nd Lt. Irwin Long from Lurgan. He was shot on Lake Street and, despite being rushed to hospital, died an hour after the shooting from his wound. In 1993 his daughter was married and had no father to give her away.]

We often had visitors from the regular army and they joined us for social visits; one morning after such an occasion the evening before, I was telephoned at work and informed that the guest of the night before, a Warrant Officer in bomb disposal had been killed by an IRA booby trap.

This soldier was 28 year old Sergeant Roy Hills of the RAOC who was killed when he was examining a mortar bomb, left at the firing scene by the IRA which was thought to be booby-trapped. The IRA had fired 2 mortar bombs at an Army base in Lurgan.

ARDOYNE, 1972

Pete Reid, Light Infantry

Ardoyne 1972.We were on an outpost at Fort Ash, when 'A' Coy rang to say one of their Saracens had hit a dog, and killed it. From the details of the address, the owners lived in the Alliances, in the Proddy side. I rang the owners, and they appeared to be quite elderly and very shocked. No recriminations, but they asked if we found another dog, would we give it to them? 'Sure! No sweat!' I chirped back happily, and put the phone down.

Two days later, Lt Chris 'D' led a patrol in from Old Park Police Station, for a social visit. Tagging on to the end of the patrol (this often happened) was a dog. The perfect dog. A pretty little black and white puppy. Pup was friendly, but rather grubby, and so into the bath he went, out, dried, and into a Land Rover for immediate delivery.

There were two Proddies, an elderly ex-WW2 soldier called Pops, and the other was a very pretty lady whose name I forget. They were both very friendly to us. Anyway, they heard about the incident, and told us the pup was well settled in, and its new owners were over the moon; job well done!

12 days later we were rotated back to Fort Ash. We'd just settled in, and sorted the stags, when the phone rang.

'Is yers the Lieutenant who gave us the dog?'

'Yes!"

'Well, will yers take him away?'

'Why? – I heard you were happy with him'

'Well, the focker had worms so bad, he's daid.'

End of 8 Platoon's diplomatic reputation.

LENADOON, 72–73

By a then Corporal in the Green Howards

Our Bn was posted out again to Northern Ireland, in the October of 1972. We were involved in mainly intelligence gathering; this meant a 3 week cycle of ops/patrolling/ camp duties.

The ops were mainly on the top of the high-rise flats in Lenadoon; the big ones and on top of them we built sangars with General Purpose Machine Guns (GPMG) covering all outlooks. On one particular incident, we had a fully loaded GPMG overlooking some garages. We had observed that someone had neatly chiseled out some of the air bricks in the garage wall to give them a good shooting point, a good field of fire.

[This tactic was so aptly and tragically demonstrated later the same year in the Oldpark Road in North Belfast. 20 year old Ronald Kitchen of the RCT was killed by the IRA when the gunman shot him through a hole made by removing a brick.]

This one night, we observed someone acting suspiciously and we got ready for action. Now, the GPMG was bagged up and on tripods and set for sf [sustained fire, i.e. set to fire on fixed lines by means of a bolt] and all we had to do was squeeze the trigger! Anyway, we fired and the dozens of rounds hitting this wall caused it to explode and fall down! Whoever was in there had a bloody lucky escape because under all the debris there was no sign of him! The funny thing was, our OC whose idea it was, had a lot of explaining to do to the garage owner.

We had to keep meticulous logs and sometimes of the most trivial of occurrences. For example, we had to note what time the milkman came on a morning, which house he went to and how many pints he left at each house. Doing that helped us to spot patterns. If a house always had 2 pints and then suddenly, they started having 10 or 20, for example, it was a sure sign that that there were more people staying there than normal and that would make us suspicious.

There was a lake behind the Lenadoon estate from where we could observe many of the houses and note the goings on. We lay many a night – often for stags of 7 hours – freezing in the frost so we might set up ambushes or even prevent one of theirs.

When we went in to lift one of the players, we generally did the 4 am knock so as to catch them unawares. Obviously if we charged in with a PIG or a Sarra [Saracen Armoured Vehicle] and made a noise then hen patrols would soon hear and out would come the dustbin lids and everyone would be aware of our presence.

So, what we'd do, is to pre-position the Saracen outside the perimeter and then walk in quietly and then hit the door of the house where we were making the lift. We identified the suspect and arrested him and then called the Saracen in. Unfortunately, the bloody thing wouldn't start and people were starting to wake up around the area. Thinking on one foot, I quickly ascertained that the suspect was a driver and that he had a car parked outside. The four of us quickly bundled ourselves and him into the car and we made him drive to our HQ! Needless to say, I got a real bollacking for that!

The Green Howards or XIX as they like to be known, lost only one man on that tour, Private Raymond 'Tapper' Hall, who was 22, shot at Newtownards Road in Belfast on March 5, 1973. As I was told when interviewing, it was one too many!

ARDOYNE CONTACT

Corporal Nicky Curtis, MM, Green Howards

My unit's call sign was 22 Alpha. We got a reputation. Everyone seemed to know us. The commanders back at base listened in on the radio frequencies for our call sign. They knew that when we went out, more likely than not, we'd end up in a gun battle. They weren't the only ones listening in. So were the Provos. They also wanted to know when we were out so they could come and meet us.

After months of confrontation, now the days of walking out of the mill and into nothing more than a leisurely stroll (or even a normal riot) were over. More often than not, we'd walk into an ambush as soon as we hit the street. We'd leave one at a time, covering each other as we did. An alleyway about half way up Flax Street, about five hundred yards away was a favourite hide-out for gunmen. Invariably, shots would ring out and we'd skirmish towards them. 'Skirmishing' was the practice of moving forward gradually, one man advancing whilst the others laid down covering fire. The ambushes happened mostly at night and, as we'd already shot out nearly all the street lights during previous attacks, in almost complete darkness.

We'd hear the familiar crack-bang-thump. The 'crack' was the noise of the bullet breaking the sound barrier (usually just as it passed you), the 'bang' was the actual gun-shot and the 'thump' was the bullet hitting the wall beside or behind you. The crack and thump told you nothing, except that you must be still alive to hear them. There would be no barrel-flash; that only happens in the movies, so the 'bang' was the only thing we had to pinpoint the gunman's position. The gunshots seemed to carry through the night over the whole of Belfast. I knew the sound would cause radios to be flicked on back at Command HQ as they listened in. We'd open with our call sign, '22 Alpha' and then 'Contact! Wait Out!' meaning enemy contact made, wait for further reports. News of our contact would make its way from the company commander, Major Rocket, to the lieutenant-colonel of the regiment, Ronnie Eccles and from him to the top boy, Frank Kitson, 39 Brigade commander. And Command were always greedy for information. Even as we were in the middle of a fire fight our radio would crackle with '22 Alpha. What's your sit-rep?' – meaning situation report. So, here we were, trying not to get our heads shot off and they'd expect us to take a break and give them an update. My usual response to this madness was to tell Austin to switch off the damn radio. By the time it was all over, with the gunman usually darting off to hide, we'd switch back on to hear the chain-of-command in a panic. I'd say 'Sorry, sir. We must have been in a dead-spot.' This was an area that blanked out transmission. At least it allowed us to get on with the business of not getting topped.

A Green Howards VCP nets an illegal gun
(photo courtesy of Jim Foster)

FLAX STREET MILL, CRUMLIN ROAD, 1972
Private, (RRW)

I remember when we lost our 1st in Flax St Mill, Belfast, John Hillman. I was up in that OP a few days later and the IRA opened up. Corporal X, [said] have a look to see if you can see where them shots are coming from. 'Sir if you want to know, you take a look.'

There used to be 3 of us up there, 2 downstairs, and 1 up in the OP, where John got it. No-one was allowed up there for a while. We had to go up and move a dummy around.

We used to shoot marbles with our catapults at the IRA Club below us, it had a lovely tin roof, I think it was all tin. See the buggers run when we used to fire at it.

The dead soldier referred to here, Private John Hillman, was shot in the O.P. in the Flax Street Mill and died of his wounds on May 18.

FLAX STREET MILL, ARDOYNE: 1972
Major Allan Harrhy, RRW

I had been away from the Bn and I returned as a Sergeant in the April or May of 1972 and was sent to Signal platoon at the Flax Street mill. Even today, my memories of the place are mixed; I thought that it was an amazing place, rather like what I expect the 'Alamo' to have been like. In the mill at that time, was HQ Company (of which I was part) and 'C' Company which was the rifle company.

I remember poor John Hillman who was in my company very well; a nice lad who was the sports storeman. As I said, he was a lovely little fella, very helpful, very friendly young soldier and he was allocated the roof sangar. This position was very exposed and 1972 was a very nasty year and the Ardoyne was an exceptionally dangerous place and people manning sangars had to be very careful.

[IRA snipers would have their rifles mounted on bipods and fixed on the observation slit, ready to fire in an instant the moment they saw the movement of a soldier's head]

I can't be sure, but he may have stuck his head out of the observation slit just to get a better view of something. [See the following account by Roy Davies] He was hit in the head by a shot fired by an IRA sniper but not killed outright. I heard 2, maybe 3 shots from where I was, down in the mill below where John was; it wasn't unusual to hear incoming rounds. Then there was a shout that someone had been shot and you go cold inside wondering which of your comrades has been hit. We had a good medical team which would 'crash out' a casualty to the RVH [Royal Victoria Hospital] in double quick time.

As I said, poor John had been hit in the face, but he didn't die outright and during the evening, we were informed that he was in a bad way but was hanging in; he hung on for 3 days and then we were told that he had, sadly, died from his awful wound.

John Hillman was 29 and was married with 2 young children and his wife was pregnant at the time. He was wounded by a shot fired from inside the Ardoyne on May 15; he died on May 18 of his wounds.

The remainder of the tour was conducted in some very warm weather, to the backdrop of constant gun battles and the radio air waves were clogged up by shouts of 'Contact – Wait – Out.' Firefights broke out not only all over our personal TAOR [Tactical Area of Responsibility] but all over Belfast as well. We just had one small part of the city, in the Ardoyne and Crumlin Road areas and it was insane, so imagine that multiplied several times.

During that time, the Bn lost 6 men; all killed in a period of just two months. This excludes our neighbours, the Royal Anglians, Royal Artillery, King's Regiment and the Paras and all or nearly all of them lost men during this dreadful period. They will all remain my memory, but the one lad who does stand out was the RCT lad who was attached to us; he was a big lad, about 6' 2" and dad to twin daughters. Peter Heppenstall was his name and he was shot on a foot patrol with us on July 14. Not a nice time for the Battalion.

In addition to Private John Hillman and Lance Corporal Peter Heppenstall, the Royal Regiment of Wales lost four more men in what was the worst period for them in the whole Northern Ireland campaign. On June 12, Private Alan Giles (18) died of his wounds having been shot the previous day in a gun battle in Alliance Avenue on the Ardoyne. Just 7 days later, Private Bryan Soden who was 21 and married with 2 children was shot in the head and fatally wounded in the Ardoyne by an IRA gunman using armour-piercing rounds. And then in a terrible 2 days period for the Welsh lads, on July 13, Private David Meeke (24) was shot and killed at Hooker Street and on the next day Heppenstall was killed and Private John Williams (22) was shot and killed in Alliance Avenue having been lured into an ambush by an explosion.

ARDOYNE: 1972
Sergeant Roy Davies, RRW

I had been sent over by my CO over to the Flax Street Mill in the Ardoyne to carry out a couple of jobs. However, as we approached, we heard several shots being fired; maybe 3 or 4 and we raced up to the gate. As we arrived, we saw poor John Hillman being brought out after he had been badly wounded in the head and he looked in a bad way. I went inside and asked what had happened and apparently some kids had been throwing stones at the roof top sangar and John had called out to them to stop. As he put his head out of the slot, an IRA sniper who had been waiting in an empty house opposite took his chance and shot the poor lad.

At Finniston School, we often put a dummy with a fag in its mouth up there in the top sangar in order to at least maintain the illusion that we were watching them, but whether or not it fooled the IRA, I will never know. Funnily enough, you know, we rarely used the word 'sangar' we tended to call them the 'butts' and the one around the back was called the 'looney bin.'

Later on that same day, as we were driving back (with Lance Corporal Rosser) we were fired at from the 'Bone area and at least 5 rounds hit the Land Rover from our left. I swerved and then glanced over and saw Rosser in the passenger foot well and I thought that he was dead. Then he called out that he was ok and we tried to drive out of the situation but we were hindered by all the ruts and bumps in the road [to slow down vehicles] and we could not get half as much speed as we desired!

In the April, we had another casualty, one of our lads, Private Cooper, was shot and very badly wounded. He was outside the Finniston School in the Protestant section and we considered this safe, but quite unintentionally, he walked around the corner and into the view of people on the Bone. He was hit instantly- at least 3 times- and fell wounded in full view of me as I was only 10–15 yards away. The other lads dragged him past my position and down a ramp into the Company first aid room. I know that he lived – because I saw the letter that was sent to the OC about his injuries – but I didn't see him again.

The sectarianism was just plain nasty and I remember seeing the local Protestant school caretaker take exception to something a young Catholic girl had said and he calmly walked over to her and smashed her in the face with a brick; pretty little thing she was as well. Anyway, a mob from the Bone area found out and came in their dozens and they would have killed him but he got out of the country and was never seen again.

On one occasion, we were driving through the Ardoyne in a PIG and the IRA had gotten hold of their first APs (armour-piercing bullets) and attacked the vehicle. Of course the APs went straight through the skin and badly wounded one of the lads inside. After that we got Saracens.

There was one final story from that tour and it just about sums up the mentality of some officers. One night a lad was up in the 'Butts' and he was playing his radio and an officer – who shall remain nameless – didn't like having his sleep disturbed. As a consequence, the radio was 'charged' and put on 'trial' and found guilty and it was jailed in a cage at Finniston School for three weeks!

PTE D.A. MEEKE AGED 24 YRS 13 JULY 1972

Arfon Williams, Royal Regiment of Wales

The loss of a friend and comrade is the most stressful, unhappy and traumatic experience that we will face in life. Bereavement is the price we all must pay for the joy of being a friend and having a friend and losing a friend. It is impossible to avoid such pain but it is an outstanding feature of human spirit that allows us at these times to remember that joy and to celebrate the memories.

But after all this time I can and will not forgive the murdering, cowardly thugs, who took the lives of my friends

Rest in Peace, all who fell.

The later killing of Private Richard Sinclair who was only 18, of the Queen's Regiment on October 31st, was the eleventh such death in the Ardoyne area of Belfast. 6 killings the year before saw the emergence of the Ardoyne district as a very dangerous place for British soldiers.

ARDOYNE: 1972

'Buzzy', Light Infantry

In 1972, I was a member of 7 Platoon, 'B' Company part of the 1st Battalion Light Infantry, serving in the Ardoyne area of Belfast. My platoon was sent to check out an area where whole ranks of houses were burn out.

I was a member of the Company search team; myself and a few other blokes had to go thought these derelict properties. As I entered one building I immediately smelt marzipan; we'd been warned that some explosive smelled like marzipan so I was on my guard.

Being very careful, I went into the lounge where there was a sideboard. I opened one door and was just about to open the other when I spotted a wire. I called Sgt Smith (who later won the Military Medal) and he looked over my shoulder and told me to sit down and not to move an inch. He thought the bomb might be light sensitive or attached to the door, and didn't want to disturb anything.

I was petrified but sat there for over two hours within inches of a bomb waiting for the ATO to arrive; I was shitting myself!

When ATO arrived he left his boots outside and came in wearing slippers! Perhaps it was to lessen any sound that might activate the bomb. He asked me what I had seen and I showed him. It took him 20 minutes to cut the wires then he took off his slippers and told me I could go. I was a lucky man!

THE LOWER FALLS – CLONARD 1972

Mike Heavens, 1st Glosters

I decided to re-enlist after almost 2 years outside (diesel fitter in Bristol) one rainy morning in February. I arrived at the Army Recruiting Office in Bristol mid-morning of the 3rd of February and there was my ex Platoon Sergeant, now Colour Sergeant recruiter, who welcomed me in with the words 'Now is a really good time to re-enlist as they're taking anyone back due to the strain of Northern Ireland!'

The wife was most unimpressed by all this but, by train and boat, I arrived at Belfast Docks on the Sunday evening to be picked up by a team kitted out for war in a 1 ton Humber APC affectionately know as PIG One, which, I'm sure, the British Army had ditched some 10 years ago. It was with much mirth at my stupidity in re-enlisting that I was conveyed through the Victorian streets of Belfast's Lower Falls to my new home on the Green Line known as North Howard Street Mill. As I dismounted from the PIG, there were many cam-creamed, blackened faces from my past grinning at me, with that piss-taking mockery, only a squaddie can portray with just a smile or look!

5 floors up a winding staircase similar in steepness to the Eifel Tower, I arrived sweating and puffing at 7 Platoon's billet to be welcomed by the sight of row upon row of double-bunked steel beds and lockers in lines reminiscent of Guardsmen on parade. I was back and with B Company this time. The mill was like many others that were taken over during the 'troubles', it was home to a rifle company who lived on the top floor, all the walls were a soft pulp wood type of compound, all the

troops slept in rooms by platoons and all the washrooms were giant affairs with lines of wash basin and showers and loos and urinals like some giant prison. There was constant noise from the group coming off, the group going out being briefed, bombing up, and servicing the vehicles and radios and a thousand and one other things to check before you went out the gate into 'Indian Country.'

Then there was the group on guards and duties, the sentry by the gate in Sangar one, the sentry up on the roof in the Roof Sangar which stared down the Falls Road and across the top of the Flats, the Divis Flats that is, the dixi bashers, spud peelers and loo washers all lived in the perpetual gloom of a place with all the windows bricked and sandbagged up and with the constant 24 hour noise level of Concorde on the runway. It took some getting used to, but we all did.

That next day was spent getting used to the base, briefings and getting more kit. Flak jackets that smelled of their previous owners and had more blood groups written on them than laundry markers, batons and shields, leg protectors and baton guns along with 5 rubber bullets the size and shape of a rather large willy and which all disappeared from the road after a riot action. Where did they all go? Rumour had it that every bedroom in the Falls, Clonard and the 'Murph had at least one on the window ledge.

The day had not started well that early March morning. 'D' Company had been RPG'd on Leeson Street in a Saracen doing a 'taxi' run. As usual the back doors were open and as they came off the Grosvenor Road and headed up Leeson Street a 'Boyo' had leapt out of a doorway and sprayed the road behind them. The rounds struck all around the vehicle and, trapped in the back, you can just swear or kiss your arse goodbye, whichever is your inclination. Then the RPG man had run into the road and fired. The round could be seen tracking up the road with its trail of white smoke, in the typical RPG fashion and it had deviated very slightly at the last second and instead of coming through the back door and kissing all the lads goodbye, had struck the right rear tyre, ricocheted off into the shop alongside, demolishing the rickety front and badly wounding a man and his son.

By the time the 'Sarra' had screeched to a halt, the gunmen were gone and all that was left to do was help the wounded civvies and give a fire team a little run around chasing shadows. At least it stretched their cramped legs. We were the 'immediate minus' team, fully dressed – bombed up and sat in the PIG ready to go. Our task was to shut off the Falls at the Divis street junction and do flash VCPs (stop everything basically and jam up the roads so vehicle escapes were impossible). It proved as fruitless as it usually was. Just as we were packing up there was a giant explosion just down the Falls Road near the Clonard Street junction, SITREP [situation report] to Zero(Command) and we were off.

2 minutes later we arrived at a scene of total devastation. Where 3 houses once stood, was a dirty great rubble-filled hole and smoke and dust everywhere. The road was almost blocked with house bricks, roof tiles and timber and there was a guy half-buried on the far side of the street opposite, his head covered in blood. We turned to and began scrabbling with the rest of the residents looking for survivors whilst another team looked after the injured guy, who turned out to be a local Provo we were keeping an eye on but was just low pond life in the scheme. The rest of the Company was turned out by the OC and after 4 hours the search was called off after we had cleared the road and pulled all the various body parts out we could find.

I had found a foot and ankle along with part of a calf muscle neatly trimmed off as if with a knife and the trainer was hardly marked. All the body parts were given to the local priest and the locals asked to identify anything that they could. Tony Lewis, a local nasty, was identified by a local married woman whose man was in the 'Kesh', by his underwear which was still attached to a large part of his torso. This led to some smutty remarks from the troops and a glare from the priest.

It appeared that three of them, with the fourth on watch by the opposite house, were preparing a bomb for the city centre when someone did something wrong. We had been after Lewis for some time in connection with the city bombings and the death of these 3 did not get much sympathy from us and although the nationalist press had a spread on the 'heroes', we just struck him off the ' lift on sight' list and the tour went on.

Next day little Ned Buck lost 2 toes when a round passed through the trousers of the guy in front and struck him in the boot. And that same day Mickey Bailey was accidentally shot by one of our own as the patrol came back from a long one.

'Tiredness kills' goes the slogan but Mickey survived the chest wound and after 6 months in hospital went home to Bristol and a life on the social, because he'll never work again. Everyone loses in a combat zone but the tour dragged on to its inevitable conclusion and after 3 months back in Minden we began training for the next tour!

[The incident which Mike Heavens refers to, the IRA 'own goal' on Clonard Street, took place on March 9 of that year. Also killed were fellow-IRA members Sean Johnston, Gerard Crossan and Thomas McCann]

UDR VCP: 1972

Officer, 1, Royal Scots

I had been down near the border with the Republic in South Armagh and I was wisely driving in a civilian car and wearing civvy clothes, although I was armed with my PPW [personal protection weapon]. As I approached Belfast, I saw a huge queue of cars at what transpired to be a VCP manned by the local unit of the UDR.

I inched closer and closer to the checkpoint and had no intention of announcing to the whole world that I was a British officer and got my ID card handy in order that I could – surreptitiously, of course – show it to the soldier who approached my car. I showed it to him, whereupon, he stamped loudly to attention and gave me the biggest salute ever !

OPERATION MOTORMAN, LONDONDERRY: 1972

Lt-Colonel R.P. Mason, 1, Royal Scots

We were in Belfast on the night before Motorman [the British Army operation to end the IRA/UDA no-go areas scattered throughout Northern Ireland] which took place on July 31, 1972. In the very early hours of the morning, we set off in Battal-

Belfast during 'Operation Motorman'
(photo courtesy of Eamon Melaugh)

ion convoy, having been ordered to an RV (rendezvous) point of Drumnahoe just outside Londonderry. We were all tense, nervous and excited and it was quite like I imagine the night before D-Day was for the troops who stormed the Normandy beaches, although on nothing like so grand a scale.

We settled into a disused factory and men were everywhere cleaning weapons, chatting, smoking nervously, some sleeping and there were lots of little 'O' groups [orders] scattered all over the place had 500 men readied themselves. It really was an amazing night/morning and as 2IC for 'C' company I much to prepare in order for the task ahead; the pre-op performance was utterly fascinating.

Then it was 'go' and into the Creggan we went; the FUP [forming up point] was in a farmyard and, separated by a field, the school through which we would advance. As we prepared to advance, some bright spark from Int observed quite a few spots where turf had been removed from the field and declared that we were facing a 'mine field' and that we should delay. There was, of course, a totally innocent explanation, as a local householder – probably one of the few with a pride of pride in his garden – had cut up the turf to improve his lawn !

Off we went, through the 'minefield' and burst through the fence surrounding the school and straight on into the Creggan.

After all the hype and the prep and the nerves, the whole thing was much of a non-event; the day went quieter than expected and though the mobs were out in force with bricks and bottles thrown as we used the armoured vehicles with their front-mounted ploughs to forcibly remove the many barricades, we had no seri-

Londonderry during 'Operation Motorman'
(photo courtesy of Eamon Melaugh)

ous casualties. One IRA was shot that day somewhere in our area, though I am unsure as to by which Regiment.

On that day, the IRA, aware of the massive presence of the Army wisely decided to stand by and lick their wounds in order to continue the terror war on another day. One IRA member – Seamus Bradley – was killed that day and another civilian was also sadly killed in what appears to be a tragic shooting accident. By the end of the day, Motorman was a success and there was nowhere in the entire Province which was closed to either the Army or the RUC.

MARKETS AREA, BELFAST: 1972

Jim Parker, Light Infantry

Whilst in the Markets, a car, presumably full of Protestants, stopped at the end of a street and fired two shots into the predominantly Catholic area of the Markets. One Private – well trained – quickly reported that one shot had hit the wall above his head. 'Where did the other go?' Piggy hopping around holding his ankle replied 'In my fucking foot!'

There were several jokes about Piggy being shot in the trotter and having saved his own bacon. But my favourite was the Battalion Newsletter headline which read: Cpl Dick was shot in the Foot, or was it Cpl Foot who was shot in the Dick?'

SHOOT TO KILL?

Rifleman, Royal Green Jackets

There was a lot of criticism in the papers that we saw about our shoot-to-kill policy. We talked about this a lot, amongst ourselves and we were confused, because we were in a life and death situation and when we shot, we shot to stop the man with a gun or a man with a nail bomb. Of course we shot to kill; we aimed at the biggest target, the geezer's chest just as we had been trained to do.

A woman said to me when I was home on leave 'Why don't you shoot at their legs and wound them ?' I said 'Mrs, this ain't Hollywood, it's not a film, and it's us or them.' I was expecting her to advise us to shoot their weapons out of their hands ! I mean, how many POWs did the IRA take ? I'll tell you something else; once when we shot this geezer, our medic tried like hell to save his life, pumping his chest and trying to make him breathe. I couldn't see the IRA doing that!

THE COMPANY SEARCH TEAM

Jim Parker, 3 Light Infantry

I was in charge of a search in the Ardoyne. The family consisted of a homely 'Mum' a couple of teenage kids and 'Dad'. He looked like the typical waster, whom you wouldn't trust one inch. As the search went ahead, the family was put in one room, whilst the head of the house 'Dad' accompanied me, and could watch the soldier searching. I opened a door to find an airing cupboard crammed with towels and bed sheets. I slipped my hand in between the snowy white towels and my fingers touches something. I grasped the object and pulled out a fist-sized wad of notes. The find was probably the wife's savings for Christmas, carefully hidden away from Dad. His eyes lit up as I handed it over to him. No doubt he never mentioned it to Mum, who in turn would have assumed we had found and stolen her nest egg.

Five o'clock one morning, my search team, an arrest team and an RUC copper knocked on the door of a particular house. The man of the house was arrested for murder and taken away. With him gone, I conducted a search of the house. The woman being the head of the house accompanied me and the search progressed. 'Do you think he'll be back for his dinner?' she asked me. I was incredulous; if my spouse had been arrested for murder I would assume I'd not see her again for weeks!

As it turned out hubby was home in plenty of time for his midday meal.

I searched or at least led the searches of two of the filthiest living quarters I have ever seen. One was a house in the Markets. When we arrived there were no adults. The bare upstairs bedroom floors had holes in them through to the ground floor and covered in faeces. In one unlit, unheated bedroom was a filthy bed in which slept four or five fully clothed filthy toddlers.

The pleasant Protestant gentleman of one house had served in the British Army. He was very chatty and relaxed. We found Army training pamphlets in his loft. 'What do you expect?' he grinned, 'I did twelve years in the Skins.' There were photographs of him in uniform in the kitchen. By which time the search was all but complete. One of my lads went to open a drawer by the sink. The man laughed and said, 'That doesn't open!' and my soldier moved on. I stepped forward put my hand under the drawer and slip it open to reveal two pistols. One was an air pistol and the other I believe was a starting pistol.

A CLOSE SHAVE FOR WORKMAN: 1972

Private Ernie Taylor, Green Howards

During our time in Belfast, we were sent out to the city centre, after a car bomb had gone off, in a Land Rover. This vehicle had a silly bar on the back which you could hold onto or rest your weapon on and I was watching the street when I heard a round go off. I cocked my SLR and I saw a man with what appeared to be a gun in his hand.

I brought my rifle into the aim position, got him in my sights and squeezed the trigger; nothing happened; misfire. I squeezed again and nothing; there's a guy in front of me with a weapon and I can't shoot him. Then, thank God, I looked again, and the 'gunman' is a worker putting up some wooden boards, with a nail gun after some IRA bomb damage. The sodding noise all sounds the same; what a lucky lad he was and I was even luckier as I wouldn't have wanted to live with that on my conscience. The actual round which jammed didn't even get into the chamber and I had to pull the bloody thing out with my fingers.

So many emotions went through my mind; what if I had killed an innocent man? What if he had been a gunman and I was sitting there, staring at the business end of his weapon and my own was useless?

BELFAST AGAIN: 1972

Major Mick Sullivan, Prince of Wales' Own Regiment of Yorkshire

Shortly after Bloody Sunday, in 1972, as a young Corporal, I was posted to Belfast and found Northern Ireland to be a changed place. First came the riots, then the stones, followed by the bricks, the petrol bombs and eventually, the sniping. It got worse and worse.

Having been away from Northern Ireland and left it in relative peace, we came back to complete chaos following Bloody Sunday. Things had escalated and moved on; watching your colleagues being badly injured and killed brings you back to earth very quickly. There were no cups of tea this time. Soldiers were burned by petrol bombs, hurt in riots or shot at by snipers. There would be riots every night and you had bricks and bottles raining down on you. I never did feel frightened, but the adrenalin kept the fright away.

By now, the IRA had stirred up the Catholic minority to believe the Army was just a tool of the British Government, which was appeasing the loyalist majority, and they thought the Army was not tough enough on the Catholics, and they were reacting. They were saying 'we've got muscles as well. This is our country and we have a right to live here and we're going to riot as well.'

The horrific things I saw, such as children being killed or injured in car bomb attacks, will never leave me, but, it was part of my job. One joins the Army in order to soldier. You don't wish for conflicts but at the same time that's what you join for. It seems very macho, but it's a lot more sensitive than that. It's doing the job that you joined to do in a professional way.

The Army's role was to keep the peace so the politicians could thrash out a solution. And we did that, with professionalism, for 38 years.

TURF LODGE, NOVEMBER 7TH 1972

Rifleman Kevin Stevens 1 RGJ

You just know when you wake up the day is not going to go as planned and Tuesday 7th November 1972 was definitely going to end up in that category! My company, 'A' Company, of the 1st Bn, Royal Green Jackets, were billeted in St Teresa's Parochial Hall next to the-then incomplete Fort Monagh just up from Andersonstown and looking up the Monagh Road past the Granshas, a very upmarket part of Belfast, to Turf Lodge.

The accommodation in St Teresa's was spartan to say the least but we now had just 10 days to go. After 4 hectic months, since arriving in the July as part of Op 'Motorman', we were pretty well seasoned troops and of course we had the experience of our senior members from earlier tours in '71 and before, to fall back upon. Although we had been unfortunate to lose Dave Card early in the tour to a sniper's bullet we had not had too many injuries otherwise and nobody wanted to add himself to the list.

We had been stood down for the morning, having been out until the early hours but when the call came for a section to cover a two hour patrol naturally we' 'willingly' volunteered. The section who were supposed to be covering the

Looking out over Turf Lodge

lunchtime patrol were late coming down from Green 1 (a hilltop lookout post) and wouldn't be back in time; therefore callsign 12B would have to cover it, and so we prepared ourselves for an 11.30hrs departure.

The weather that day was surprisingly mild with blues skies, fluffy clouds and it certainly didn't feel like November. However it had been raining earlier on and there were a few puddles around. The significance of these puddles will become clearer a little later on. I was by far the junior member of the section which was led by L/Cpl Lionel Hitchcock with Rifleman Dickie Adams bringing up the rear as tail-end Charlie. Sadly both these great people are now no longer alive. I was behind the section commander carrying the Larkspur A41 radio, a great lump of a thing with the range of about 2 baked bean tins connected by a short piece of string, and you could lose the signal back to base if a car drove by. It was totally unsuited to urban conditions but it was all we had. The days of the Clansman and Pye walkie-talkies were a little way off yet. I also suspect that it was not because of my clear Oxford accent but because I was, after all, the 'nig' of the section that I got the radio. A 'nig' in Green Jacket terms is a brand new, fresh out of the box, keen-to-go soldier – me?? Well at least I could hear what was going on all the time.

We bomb burst out of the gates of Fort Monagh and quickly took up our patrol pattern ensuring we were well spaced for the dangerous part of the outbound patrol across the open area between the fort and Turf Lodge itself. We were comforted by the fact we were also covered by the three sangars as we made our way across the road and headed for the corner of the Granshas nearest to the Turf Lodge. This particular corner was one of the local firing points for the IRA who took almost daily pops at the fort and I had come under fire myself from there on least two occasions in the previous 4 months. It would have been great if we could have sited an OP (observation post) there but there was absolutely nowhere to put one. In the end, we had to put up with the shots always seemingly coming from that area. This day though, it was unoccupied, not even an empty case to take back and hand over to the RUC.

Having negotiated this particular hurdle we made our way around the Granshas for 30 minutes or so then headed up into Turf Lodge itself. Turf Lodge is not like other areas of Belfast such as the Lower Falls; these are not 2-up 2-down terraces with postcard sized back gardens and a door onto the street. Turf Lodge was a lot more modern that that and was a combination of flats, short terraces and semi-detached houses with gardens back and front. It was not a particularly well kept area but at least it was a little more open. This was a mixed blessing of course as it meant the players could now take pops at us from between houses but from several blocks away. Again I had been involved in a couple of 'contacts' on the estate in this way.

So far I have painted the area as all bad but in truth a lot of the people there were quite friendly as much as they could be, given the-then political climate. The estate was very much ruled by the Official IRA or 'stickies' as they were called and any trouble tended to come in from outside, from areas such as the Ballymurphy. We even had a couple of places we could get a sneaky cup of tea depending on the time of day. It was towards one of these we were heading in a roundabout way. After patrolling to about 12.45hrs we made our way to a flat of a well known female malcontent, someone who would abuse us roundly if she were to meet us on the street. As we adopted an all-round defence strategy, Lionel knocked on the door and when it was answered, announced the fact we were going to search her flat, naturally we got abuse thrown at us but she didn't argue too much and in went half of the section. There then followed five minutes of noise and swearing before the first four came out and relieved us while we carried on the search. In we went and continued the search, well actually whilst one of us clattered around a bit and while the woman swore at us loudly we enjoyed a cup of tea. The lady in question was one of our tea stops and also gave us a little information on the side but appearances had to be kept up!

We left the dwelling about 13.10hrs to patrol back slowly to base. It was at this time I noticed how quiet the estate had gone. People were not to be seen anywhere which seemed very odd, not even a dog was on the streets and as anyone who has served in Belfast or any other urban area in Northern Ireland will tell you dogs are not exactly a soldier's best friend and I am sure they are trained to bite anything with an English accent, the dogs in Turf Lodge were no exception but at least they wagged their tails when biting you!

The area was so quiet that I called it in to base and informed them that in my considered opinion something was up. The Ops Room agreed with me and asked us to pay special attention to the school off to our right about 300 yards on the way back in as this again was another regular firing point.

Down the Monagh Road we came, everyone very much on their toes by now as we had all got the same eerie feeling, never walking in straight lines, constantly turning around to look behind them, eyes in the backs of their heads, well spaced with an extra eye on the school. As we came within 50 yards of the fort we heaved

Turf Lodge riot

a collective sigh of relief, job nearly done for a few more hours then there in front of me – a puddle !! Now the one thing I have so far not mentioned was that I had managed to get a kit exchange and amongst that kit was a brand new pair of boots, well there was no way I was going to get them wet so I stepped out to my left to avoid the puddle whilst at the same time turning back around to look again back up the road towards Turf Lodge.

Suddenly I found myself not only completing that turn but another one before I recovered my balance. I realised at that point I had been shot mainly on account of the fact there were now rounds flying in all directions (a second one took off most of the aerial not that I noticed at the time). It is at this time that the strangest things cross your mind, in my case and I remember it quite clearly is the fact I did not want to jump over the nearby bank into relative safety but into a large area of stinging nettles!! I therefore ran additional 5yds or so and jumped over into a clear area instead. Strangely enough at this time there was absolutely no pain whatsoever but my arms felt very, very hot. The pain came much later when I finally woke up in hospital.

First IA (immediate action) is to send a contact report which I did trying as best I could to describe what was going on. As a rifleman with only one arm I was out of the picture for returning fire but the rest of the lads having spotted where it was coming from (just near the Granshas firing point – again) were putting down 'the good news' large. Now it started to get exciting. Lionel decided on a full blown section attack across the open area – probably the first and only time this has happened in Belfast. He called for me but I had to explain I was now a little more occupied with watching the red stuff coming out of me. The injury was only to my upper arm but as the round was a 5.56mm from an Armalite rifle (as I found out later) the damage was severe and most of the blood vessels were ruptured, the bone had been splintered, tendons ripped apart and there was, as the doctors put it, a lot of muscle wastage. Lionel did the sensible thing in my opinion and got on with winning the firefight. There was not a lot he could do for me at that moment without perhaps losing more men.

Some 2 or 3 minutes into the contact HQ started asking for any casualties, naturally I replied 'no', before realising that might not be the correct answer so informed them that in fact there was one and gave them my butt number. Suddenly there were people coming at me from all directions; the first being 'A' Company medic; no weapon just a first aid bag. To be honest I had by now lost an awful lot of interest in what was going on around me probably in direct proportion to the amount of blood I had lost. I was actually feeling quite relaxed about the whole thing by now as pictures taken at the time show.

A Saracen arrived complete with the Regimental doctor and he started to fix me up prior to my move to Musgrave Park Hospital. Soon I was on a stretcher being lifted back up the bank and into the Saracen, however I refused to lay down with the result I ended up with a head injury as well, not this time from a bullet but from banging my head on the frame of the door !

On arrival in hospital I was rushed into theatre where much to my disgust my boot laces were cut and the new boots thrown into a plastic bag, my jacket was eased off me and my tee shirt cut off me, again all thrown into the plastic bag.

Turf Lodge riot

What happened to my trousers I cannot remember, as at this point someone stuck a needle into me and I floated off into the land of dreams.

My final thought though was 'What a silly way to end the day!'

Kevin refers to Lance Corporal David Card who was 21 and from Portsmouth who was shot and killed by an IRA sniper on August near Bearnagh Drive in Andersonstown. His comrades desperately tried to save him but were pinned down by heavy enemy fire.

Anonymous Private, Royal Green Jackets

Our Sergeant, generally no more than a couple of years older than us, would tell [him] to 'fuck off' before proceeding to give us the info we might need over the next maybe 3, but generally 5 or 6 hours, e.g. known 'players' (IRA men sought for a variety of reasons), whom we needed to pick up and, through Company or sometimes Bn intelligence we knew had sneaked back to the shit-holes they had lived in before going on the run from us, just to see their ancient Mammy, one last time. Sometimes it would be to assist a green bottle [RUC] contingent who were serving court papers for ordinary criminals, but even these soon took on political dimensions, as the populace of the Lower Falls would come out en-masse, to hurl bricks, bits of metal, bottles or Irish cocktails (plagarised from the generic term Molotov) or whatever they could lay their grimy hands on. We might be picking up some scumbag (or toe-rag as the cockney lads in my coy were wont to call them) for theft, drunkenness or whatever but the sight of our uniforms, steel helmets, rifles and riot shields would immediately raise their status in the eyes of the locals into 'brave urban guerillas' and the trouble would begin.

I should point out that Divis Street is dominated by a huge multistorey block of Council flats – all occupied by Catholic families in a rat-ridden, filthy, almost monolithic tower – and is best analogised as a multi-level cesspit ('I didn't know that they could stack shit so high' was a comment I heard on several tours) and was a prime location for Provie gunmen to snipe at us and for the locals to report, from their vantage point, our patrol movements on the streets below.

Springfield Road leads eastwards towards a huge crossroads. The Falls Road was to the right, Grosvenor Road straight on and to the left Divis Street, opposite the Vic (Royal Victoria Hospital) was Dunville Park.

The flats had been the scene of the murder of a squaddie from another mob who was shot dead by a sniper located on one of the upper floors – cheered on, no doubt, by the people who populated this sewer of a building sometime in the January of this year and was a site most ex-Belfast squaddies still hold a feeling for of awe, which is half-way between dread and repulsion.* The rifle used in this murder, was, I believe, later recovered from a dead Provo, slotted by another Regiment.

As we raced out from our 'home' there would still be people about and some would shy away from us, wishing to avoid trouble from us, but, more importantly for them, to avoid being caught in the crossfire of an explosion or of incoming rounds aimed in our direction. Sometimes, fuelled by pints of Guinness and McCaffreys, or whatever illegal 'hooch' ('poteen', pronounced 'putcheen', they called it over there) they had been imbibing at whatever illegal shebeen they frequented. These shebeens, illegal drinking dens, were rarely raided, especially the Protestant ones as the green bottles themselves would drink there.

We would move at a fair pace along the Springfield Road, and then we would see the Vic to our right and over on the left Dunville Park and our pace would quicken; 15 men on the left of the road and 15 on the right, with the lead man wetting himself and the back marker on both sides of the street, both alternatively walking backwards and then the correct way, ever watchful for a gunman coming out of the dark shadows of a midden or an alleyway after we had passed.

We became ever more alert, ever more vigilant and many lads flicked off their safety catches, and, illegally with their SLR's already cocked (i.e. a 7.62 mm full metal jacket up the spout) were now ready for action. The streets are – or certainly, were – all black terracing, rows of about 12 or more houses at a time, all back-to-backs, with no gardens, punctuated by alleyways and middens which contained their outside lavvies (toilets) and their dustbins. Lots of rubbish in the street, the odd burned-out car, bricks etc, the flotsam and jetsam of an urban conflict. Some of the houses were boarded up, some obviously fire-damaged, but nearly every one, almost without exception, had a brightly polished red front door step. On every gable end, there would be some Republican graffiti, some crude and roughly done, some very artistic and well painted. 'Brits out !' was a popular one as was 'We stand by the IRA' and 'Don't ball lick the Brits ! Fight 'em' another popular one was Death to touts !' (a tout was a spy) and many had the Irish tricolour (illegal, of course, in the north) or a balaclava-wearing gunmen resplendent with revolver (or 'short' as we – and they – called them – a rifle was a 'long').

Soon, we would be noticed, and women, mostly fat and scruffy with head scarves concealing their rollers, would come out and tell us to 'fuck orf' and then they would grow in number and then begin shouting and soon their men folk (anything from aged 7 to 70) would join them and begin hurling abuse and the odd missile, which we learned to dodge (some lads had metal gaiters to protect their shins from bricks etc) with a growing agility and soon out would come the dustbin lids, which they hammered, seemingly in unison on the roads, as they alerted people in other streets – and, *ipso facto*, the player [IRA member or members] we might be seeking – and possibly gunmen as well.

When we had forced our way through to our objective, quite a crowd would have built up and another platoon from our company, lurking in some back street or other, would be called in by our RT man (radio) in order to help us. Eventually, we found the house and without ceremony, we would kick in the door, three men upstairs, three downstairs (these houses were of the two rooms-up, one-down variety) whilst the rest of the platoon, or platoons if we needed the reserves in, formed a protective semi-circle outside the front – and only – door, keeping the growing mob at bay, or at least in range of a quickly executed rifle-butt to the face. It wasn't pretty, but we had a job to do and we didn't want to go home in coffins.

*Thought to be Corporal Ian Bramley of the Glosters, shot on Hastings Street, near the Divis Street flats on February 1st of that year.

"You ain't getting through us, boys!"

LONDONDERRY, 1972

Lance-Corporal Hogg, Scots Guards

To our horror, yet another night's beauty sleep was ruined (by now we need as much as possible). There was a special operation to do and this time we were after some really big fish. The Rossville flats were sealed and in went the arrest team. This time we got him but were disappointed not to find anything else in the house.

L/cpl Speed and L/cpl Hatton's sections teamed up together to do a VCP. In the course of this they arrested someone for identification and were immediately confronted with a mini-riot.

SCOTS GUARD

Hard times for IRA

Since we last went to press, quite a lot has happened, but thankfully, apart from a brush with the Derry Young Hooligans, who were seen off by L/Cpl Buist and a pot-shot at our post in the Rossville flats which made Guardsman Steven duck a bit sharpish, our area has been calm. Nevertheless, the opposition have been feeling the pinch, and along with the other companies we have been instrumental in rounding up a few wanted men. All three platoons have been involved in early morning lift operations and not to be left out of it, callsign 49 spotted a wanted man on the street and swiftly put him in the bag.

Guardsman Jim Mackenzie, Scots Guards
(photo courtesy of Jim Mackenzie)

Only one early morning raid drew a blank, but 13 Platoon made up for it by discovering in their search of the house some very interesting documents and a quantity of acid. The acid was tested with some panache by pouring a little of it on a kitchen brush. Most of the brush disappeared in a hiss of steam like something out of 'Doctor Who.' Most of the panache disappeared too and a certain amount of 'no-you-carry-it-back' followed.

DIVIS STREET: 1972

Driver Ken Haslam, Royal Corps of Transport

I joined the army in May 1971, and, on finishing my training I was sent to Germany, 9 Squadron, 10 Regiment RCT. My first tour of NI was in July 1972, and I was attached to 2nd Bn Royal Anglians, in Albert St Mill, over looked by Divis Flats.

At first it was ok as there was a truce, but this didn't last long, and the shooting went on; about the 17th July (a Tuesday) I was on foot patrol with the section to which I was attached; we left the location and went to Collingtree Road about 2 mins away. When we arrived the officer and someone else went into one of the houses and the rest of us took up our defensive positions and waited. However, as we did so, a gunman opened up on us and I was the unlucky one and was shot in the leg and foot. I fired one round from my SLR at the shape in the window from where the round had been fired and then fell.

At first it didn't hurt, but when I tried to stand up I saw the blood running down the wall, and put my hand over the wound to try and stop the bleeding. Within seconds my hand was by covered in blood, I shouted to the guys that I had been shot and put my hand up. However, when they saw this, they came over to me and started to put a field dressing on my hand ! I asked them what they were doing, and shouted: 'it's my leg that I'm shot in.' I was taken to the R.V.H. but they didn't want me to stay there so I was taken to Musgrove Park hospital. After my first op and I was in my bed coming round I saw 3 people standing there.

One was my SSM [Squadron Sergeant Major] and the other 2 were S.I.B. (Investigations) and their first question to me was: 'Why did you do it?' (meaning shoot my self) I was horrified and retorted: 'I didn't !' and they then left, never to be seen again.

After all of my convalescence and sick leave I was sent back to my unit in BAOR [British Army of the Rhine] but to my surprise on getting back to camp on the Friday, I was told that I was going back to NIon the following Monday. This was so I could get my 30 days in, which as a soldier to qualify for the GSM for active service. But to my horror I was to find out that I was not going to get my medal because the 30 days had to be consecutive, not split.

There was a nice postscript to this; I got my GSM on the next tour.

---

* GSM: General Service Medal. This is awarded to all soldiers who serve 30 consecutive days on Active Service.

LONDONDERRY 1972

Scots Guard (from *Rose & Thistle*)

We have had one further tragedy within the company. Lance Sergeant MacKay who was attached, to the Recce platoon, who was fatally shot whilst on Land Rover patrol on October 28. Everything was so sudden, so out of keeping with the events at the time and so immediately tragic. However, the depths of despair were at once replaced by a sense of urgency and increased drive, and not one member of this company will ever forget the debts that are still owed by the dregs of Derry.

The whole of November has been quiet. Patrolling, ambushing and observation have been carried on increasingly day after day and night after night. The vigilance has been rewarded with an almost complete withdrawal of open hostility. The moderate people are now more friendly, the hostile quiet and we are all desperately hoping that a sense of real living, decency and balanced thoughts is now almost beginning to form the basis of a new look community.

'Luckiest Man in Northern Ireland'

On 5th September about mid-afternoon, a 'G' company patrol commanded by a Lieutenant Erskine-Crum was moving along Cable Street. Guardsman Spinks was the rear man of the patrol and as he turned into Drumcliffe Avenue, a single shot rang out. The bullet, a Garron armour-piercing round hit Guardsman Spinks

Guardsman Spinks: 'the luckiest man in Northern Ireland'

in the middle of his back and he was thrown about 5 yards along the pavement. His injuries, however, amounted to only bruising and shock, for the bullet had struck the Federal Riot Gun slung over his back and fragmented on contact with his flak jacket. Within 24 hours he was back out on patrol again – with a new riot gun and new flak jacket.

SPRINGFIELD ROAD BOMB: 1972
Paddy Lenaghan, King's Regiment

I was with Bn HQ, stationed in Springfield Road police station; I was a member of support coy, anti-tank platoon. The support personnel at Springfield road were tasked with, among other things, foot patrols in the surrounding streets, manning the OPs [Observation Posts] on the roof and at the main entrance into the police station.

In hindsight and with the passing of time we should have been very worried about our deployment; anyone who claims that they were not scared in Belfast has never been there! I have spoken to Aussies who served in Vietnam and I was able to say that at least their enemy was Asian; ours wore the same clothes, drove the same cars, shopped in same shops, and used the same money. It was not until they opened their mouths that they were different and even then you still did not know if the person was a Catholic or a Prod; we could have been patrolling in any city on the mainland.

If my memory serves me correctly, 30 May began on a high note; one of our patrols had arrested a group of young people in the process of robbing a supermarket or shop (we needed morale to be raised as at this time we had lost two members of the Bn, Corporal Allan Buckley who was shot on the 13th and Kingsman Hanley on the 23rd, both in the Ballymurphy area.

[The soldiers Paddy refers to are Alan Buckley (22) who was shot dead on the Whiterock Road, on the Ballymurphy estate on 13 May, 1972. He was married with one small child. Just 8 days later, Kingsman Eustace Hanley (20) was shot and killed by the IRA whilst guarding troops who were removing barricades in Springhill Avenue on the Ballymurphy Estate.]

If I recall correctly, there were workmen in the police station carrying out repairs; this has to be remembered in light of later events. I had been told that I was to take out a foot patrol that night, and was given the time of the patrol and the personnel. I am not clear of the time the patrol left, or of any item of great importance occurring during it, or indeed the duration; thankfully at this time we were lucky. We wondered just how many more to complete before our tour ended. I seem to remember that the unit we took over from was a Jock regiment that had suffered casualties just prior to completing their tour.

We had completed our patrol, and we went through the unloading procedure, handed in our mags and I gave my verbal report. I know for sure that at one point I made my way down past the police locker rooms to the dining area where the last reel of a film was still running. Now, to enter the dining area, you had to pass through two glass security-type doors with thickish glass wire running thru them, and as you enter the dining area there was a type of tuck shop run by an Asian. The film was still running and I don't remember how long I

Life goes on for this Belfast resident

waited, before the film ended, but it did. The person showing the film had left the rewinding machine at the last location he had shown the film so he had to rewind the film using the projector. Some people commenced leaving the dining area to go to the rooms upstairs to watch the news. I was standing with my back to the glass doors still with my SLR and still wearing my flak jacket and as people were leaving to go upstairs to watch TV, I bummed a cig' and saw Marcel Doglay playing on the small pool table and I could hear voices from the kitchen – cooks or their helpers getting late meals ready; I saw someone with a lit cig' and asked them for a light

I remember hearing a loud crack (on joining the Australian army I became an engineer, have taken part in many demolition practices, and I am now pretty sure what an explosive demolition sounds like) the like of which I had ever encountered. I heard the crack and the next thing I can really remember was laying on the floor; my mouth seemed full of dirt or dust, my eyes seemed full of sand, and it was foggy and there were papers floating in the air. I could hear someone screaming; I could hear what today you would call a car alarm but could not see my rifle and I seemed to be laying on a pile of concrete rubble. I tried to raise myself up but my left hand hurt; like the pain you will get if you kick a rock in bare feet and also my left thigh ached amongst the noise I have described; I clearly remember someone's voice saying 'I can smell gas.' I was on my knees when I heard the comment and I yelled 'For fuck's sake, get me out of here.' I was completely disorientated and where there had been a wall off to my right there was nothing.

I could see vehicles with their bonnets up, and all this fog and paper floating around, the screaming, the alarm going, I seem to remember trying to find my rifle with my right hand as for some reason my left hand was now starting to give me pain, I looked at my left hand, which I had to raise it up to my face and saw that the ring finger was laying at a funny angle; there was a lot of blood in my palm and I grabbed my left wrist and squeezed it. I do not know how long all of the above had taken but there I was, in the middle of I do not know what; shit in my mouth and eyes and what felt like blood dripping down my face and my finger on my left hand playing silly buggers. Then someone – I cannot remember his name – helped me to my feet. I remember telling him to find my rifle and him saying 'Fuck it.' He led me into what I would call the reception room and I then saw the source of the screaming; a woman was behind the counter, she had both hands in her hair and was pulling her hair and screaming, and a big policeman came in to the room and hit her, she stopped screaming.

The M.O. Major Cramer carried out a quick assessment of the ones in the room, and as more people were brought in, checked the injuries; he told me I had a broken finger and would be back at work soon. I don't remember seeing Marcel Doglay, whom I had last seen as I was getting a light. We were then told that ambulances had arrived but we had to wait as a crowd of locals had gathered outside and were attempting to force entry, and prevent ambulances from leaving. The CO came down the stairs with the Adjutant, buckling on his pistol belt as he passed me. On arrival at RVH, [Royal Victoria Hospital] we were met by medical staff and other nurses were also attending to patients; they were so calm about everything, no yelling or panic; quietly professional. The next thing I recall is waking up and seated on my right hand side was one of the mortar platoon corporals, complete with nine milimetre pistol sitting at my side and I asked him what the fuck happened; he believed a bomb had gone off in the police locker room. I asked how the rest of the boys were and that's when he said Marcel didn't make it.

[Kingsman Marcel Doglay (28) was killed in the explosion at Springfield Road police station. He was married with 4 children and it was noted at the time that mobs of people jeered as his body was removed in the ambulance.]

We were airlifted to a hospital in London where I discovered that my left hand had taken the force of the blast. Flying objects, probably glass, had caused a deep injury to my hand and managed to shatter the bones in my ring finger. Iit had been pinned in the initial op, but it was later amputated. My wife was given a rail warrant to visit me and the kids were being looked after back in Weeton camp by the chief clerk's wife. Whilst in hospital the Queen Mum, who was Col-in-Chief of the Regiment, visited all the injured from NI who were gathered in one ward, she actually spoke to me, nice lady.

I was going to sign on for another 3 years and I went to see the Colonel who enquired how I was and could I grip well with my left hand, (I got into the Aussie army, fired weapons etc) but do you know 35 years later I still cannot completely close my left hand, although my remaining fingers do close together.

I did find out that my wife was visited by a Staff Sergeant and a Priest and that she was convinced that I was dead!

I am glad that I survived that tour of Northern Ireland, but I would never be the same person (beside losing my finger) I now admit I was not the same person and drinking became a way of life; binge drinking it would be called now.

Then I joined the Australian Army and served a full term, but that's another story.

That 1972 tour was one which produced further losses for the proud men of the King's Regiment; in addition to the aforementioned losses, they lost Kingsman James Jones (18), Kingsman Brian Thomas (20), Kingsman Rennie Layfield (24) and Kingsman Roy Christopher (20) in a 5 week period.

PIPER SAVES THE DAY AT NEWRY: 1972
Private Stephen Burke, 1st Argyll & Sutherland Highlanders

Between July and November, 1972, I was on a four month tour with the Argyll & Sutherland Highlanders serving with the anti-tank platoon in Support Company. We were stationed at the UDR barracks in Newry, Co Down.

One day, whilst I was on camp guard duty, a large and very hostile crowd began to gather outside the front gates; quite what they were complaining about I don't know, but they were chanting and banging on the metal gates. Things were beginning to get pretty serious and at any moment, I was expecting to be sent outside in order to disperse them. However, our OC, Major David Thomson, MC, (later to become a General) was a very shrewd leader and, instead of sending out his troops, he ordered the Pipe-Major up to the gates, with his bagpipes ! The Pipe-Major paraded up and down the barracks playing his pipes and before long, the protestors were singing along and dancing to the tunes !

After a while, peace was restored once again as they all walked off, and I have always admired the way Major Thomson handled that difficult situation. His imaginative, innovative and passive methods were an inspiration to us all and I am sure that it helped form bonds with the disaffected community.

LURGAN: 1972
Major Mick Low, Gordon Highlanders

This tour was a mixture of urban work in Lurgan and surrounding towns with some rural patrolling eastwards towards Banbridge.

One night when on the peace line between the two communities in Lurgan, a toe-rag opened up on us with a Thomson sub-machine gun, and we all dived into doorways and other fire positions. I checked on the Jocks to see that all was well, but 'Smithy' from Aberdeen was standing in the middle of the street. I shouted to him to get into a fire position, to which he replied, 'Sarge, I cannae, because youse have a' the good anes.' We all just cracked into fits of laughter.

On one rural patrol to Donaghcloney, we had a piper with us and he played a few tunes for the proddies. The OC then took a call from some Nationalist councillor and we had to go back the next night for the piper to play a few tunes for them. After one episode with the newly formed UDA, I had some rather harsh words with one of their thugs. Next thing I knew was the UDA had placed a sum of £500 on my head, dead or alive.

Usually when we entered one Nationalist estate, we were met by one old woman who was rather dirty and unwashed. The language was equally as dirty towards us Brits. We then sent a special patrol to her house and left her with 24 bars of soap with instructions to her, 'Wash your mouth out when you next take a shower.' My final thoughts of that first tour in Ulster were how quickly we all had to adapt to situations that blew up out of nothing.

LONDONDERRY: 1972

Mike Morgan, 1st Bn Grenadier Guards

My first tour of Northern Ireland was at the tender age of 18 years old; serving for 4 months November 1972 through to March 1973 in the Creggan Estate Londonderry.

We were billeted in a place called the Essex factory on Bligh's Lane which is just above the area of the Bogside. The initial training for the tour was carried out in Munster in Germany with riot control and patrolling techniques. My first patrol was initially only for a 2 hour duration around the Creggan Estate during which I can say, I was very nervous. The section I was in consisted of a total of seven men and, for my sins, I was given the task of 'tail-end Charlie.' During this patrol we were involved in a riot and a shooting; the riot was dealt with by using rubber bullets and gas canisters but we never caught the gunman; luckily no one in the section was injured.

During the tour, riots and shooting were a regular occurrence and one that sticks in my mind, was a normal patrol down Creggan Broadway where we were met with a crowd of around two thousand rioters. The Broadway had lots of roads leading off it, and as we patrolled past, crowds emerged from every one of them and by the time we reached the end of it, we were met with this hostile crowd who immediately started throwing everything at us. The only thing we could do at that time was to try and contain them and the only way we could do this was to fire rubber bullets and gas canisters at them. We called for back up and ended up being on the ground for a total of 5 hours, firing a total of approx 50 rubber bullets and around 10 gas canisters to disperse the crowd.

During the tour we also found caches of weapons ammunition and explosives so all in all, a productive time.

A second tour from March 1974 through to August 1974 mirrored the first tour with riots and shootings but I felt more confident as my previous tour experience came into play. Both tours were carried out with no loss of life to the Regiment and I was proud to serve with the 1st Battalion the Grenadier Guards. I served another 4 tours of Ireland with the famous 1st Battalion, the Gloucestershire Regiment.

My personal feelings were why this conflict ever took place and why were we there patrolling places that belonged in the UK? However I was there to do a job irrespective of my political feelings and in one way I really enjoyed all the challenges I was given and being only 18 at the time it made me quite proud I was doing something for my country.

The reaction of the people in Londonderry especially was to give as much trouble to the British ' invading Army' as they could; if you had one- to- ones with a lot of the people, sometimes they could be quite nice and would not blame you for being in their country, but next minute they were abusing and throwing stones at you.

The younger generation just grew up with it and did not know any difference (very good shots with stones though).The only thing I can say about the Bogside was it was probably twinned with Dodge City or Beirut, and remember taking Frankie Howerd and 'Pan's People' down to Belfast for a CSE show and we had to travel through the top end of the Bogside. We were in the old Saracens, and got caught in a mini riot by some youngsters from the Bogside; the next thing I knew, Frankie Howerd was out of the Saracen and chasing the kids. I managed to restrain Frankie and get him down to Belfast for his show. He could not believe it when I told him that kids rioting was a normal thing for us to handle.

LONDONDERRY: 1972
Colonel Derek Parsley, Royal Artillery

We were posted to Northern Ireland for a second tour, but this time to Londonderry. By this time, Northern Ireland had become a problem area and we went in the latter months of 1972.

My job this time was to run the Public Relations desk and our first problem presented itself even before we arrived. On the ferry, we were instructed by the Captain that all weapons must be handed in to the armoury before sailing. Though we were unable to reverse this order, I ordered all soldiers who were able to conceal some sort of weapon that they should do so.

My job was a trifle boring, but for one incident which I will always remember. During the afternoon of November 30, I was asked whether I would allow my photographer, Gunner Paul Jackson, to take a photo of what was thought to be a bomb in a local supermarket. I agreed but insisted that he must be in an armoured vehicle. The vehicle moved to the site of the supermarket and Gunner Jackson began to take shots through the slit in the armour. Tragically, the bomb exploded and the camera went straight through his head and killed him.

This unmitigated act of sheer terrorism affected me a great deal. Ireland was not at that time my favourite place. I found it difficult, when I attended the funeral, to try and tell his family why this sort of thing could happen in a society such as ours. I am still no wiser.

Paul Jackson (21) was killed when shrapnel from the blast at Long's Supermarket on the Strand Road entered the armoured vehicle. He was married with 2 children who lived in the Leeds area.

OBITUARY FROM THE *ROSE AND THISTLE*
By Lieutenant A.G.B.I. Cheape

L/Sgt McKay's sudden and tragic death on Saturday 28th October shocked and stunned us all. He was travelling in a Land Rover up Bishop Street Without, when a single shot mortally wounded him in the head.

L/Sgt McKay was a popular and experienced section commander and since joining the Battalion in November 1965, had served almost exclusively with the

Recce Platoon. To his parents, his wife Dot and to his two young children, we extend our very deepest sympathy. He is greatly missed by us all.

BELFAST: 1971/2
Marine Brian Bounsell

The Royal Marines did over 41 tours over there, in Northern Ireland and have earned their place in history with fifteen killed in action. My first tour was in 1970 with the Ardoyne snatch squads. Some people were still quiet to start with, but that soon changed when we started arresting the main men. Mind, they must have had a good laugh at us with aluminium shields that bent around your arm when hit by a house brick.

On my second tour that was different altogether; we were deployed to Girwood Barracks in the New Lodge in 1972. What a change from the first tour; loaded weapons as soon as you got ashore – from then on, 'one up the spout'. This next bit might bring a smile to the faces of any ex-Paras; we were told that some of the prisoners in the Crumlin Road jail had rioted and taken prison officers hostage, and that we were to get them out, which we did after a bit of a battle. The ringleader of the rioters was serving life for stabbing a Para in a pub on the Falls Road and we found out which he was and when we got him, gave him a real sorting out.

One day, the mobs found out that we had an OP on the top floor above a funeral parlour and the bastards set fire to it. Even when the fire brigade turned up, they stoned the bloody thing.

One day, I came so close to being shot – that pleasure was just around the corner in the future anyway – and that was after we got the call for assistance in the New Lodge area. Now, anyone who knows the New Lodge Road/Antrim Road junction knows that there is a dog-leg there and you have to cross over in order to look down it. As I reached it, I went down onto one knee and as I did, the sniper had to shift his aim and instead of a bullet in the head, all I got was a face full of brick dust as the round impacted right near my face.

Next came another landmark event in Belfast's history, 'bloody Friday', and on that day we were tasked to help Felix [bomb disposal] which was normally a bit of a cushy number. However, as soon as we got there, the calls began coming in and our guy defused six bombs that day; the bravest man I ever met.

[July 21, 1972, is a day which will long live in infamy as one of the blackest days in the tragic history of the troubles; forever known as 'bloody Friday.' The IRA set off 20 car bombs, killing 9 people and injuring 130 on a Friday afternoon with the streets crammed with shoppers; a day of utter chaos, confusion, panic and violent death. People were literally fleeing from one explosion right into the mouth of the next.

The IRA bombs killed two soldiers – Driver Stephen Cooper (19) of the RCT and Sergeant Philip Price (27) of the Welsh Guards and an RUC Sergeant, Robert Gibson. They also killed 6 civilians, including three teenagers and managed to kill two of the very community they claimed to defend.]

The last incident I remember before my own shooting was a device which we found on the Sydneham bypass. Felix went down to inspect it but in the meantime had us get the 'Charlie G' [Carl Gustav anti-tank rocket] ready to blast the device. However, when he came back, he looked a worried man and told us that it was a 500lb bomb and that had we detonated it, we would have all been wiped out.

On Operation 'Motorman' we took the barricades down in the morning and then they put them back up that night. I was getting a right bollocking from my Corporal when the bastards opened fire and they hit both of us; the pain was excruciating and that was the end of my tour for the moment.

I spent a week in the RVH and then two weeks in Musgrave Park, before being flown to Northolt where a Sea King helicopter took me to RNH Plymouth where I was another three weeks as an in-patient. Then a further two weeks pyhsio and back to the New Lodge to finish my tour. My troop sergeant who was more seriously wounded than me made a full recovery and now lives in Canada.

On July 29, a young soldier, Tommy Stoker, who lived in East Ardsley, the author's home village, was manning an OP in Berwick Road in the Ardoyne area of Belfast. He was a Private in the Light Infantry and had only been with the company in Belfast for 2 days, although he had quickly made some friends there.

Whilst making some adjustments to his SLR a comrade in an adjoining room accidentally fired one round which hit Tommy in the back. His obituary in the *The Bugle Sounds'* (Light Infantry), kindly supplied to the author by the Regimental Association, reads:

'Pte. Tommy Stoker died of his wounds in the Royal Victoria Hospital, Belfast on 19th September, after a courageous struggle of more than a month and a half following his injury on 29th July, shortly after his arrival in Belfast. He will be deeply missed by the many friends he made in his company during his few months in the battalion. We send our sincere condolences to his parents, Mr and Mrs. Stoker of East Ardsley, Yorkshire.'

Tommy was one of three soldiers killed by the phenomenon known as 'friendly fire' in the space of approximately 8 weeks. The other two were Private Ronald Rowe, 21, from Tommy Stoker's battalion, killed on the Ardoyne, on August 28 and the first Royal Marine fatality in Northern Ireland, Robert Cutting, 18, of 45 Commando. He was shot and killed in a mix-up between two Royal Marine patrols on September 3rd in the New Lodge area.

In the same month as Tommy Stoker was wounded, a series of fierce firefights occurred during the day and night of the 14th, in the Belfast area. Over 6,000 rounds were expended at the end of which, 4 soldiers, 2 innocent civilians and 3 IRA gunmen had been killed. Scores were injured during the exchanges which were widespread over the city. The range of Army regiments involved is aptly demonstrated by the units to which the dead soldiers belonged to. The four dead soldiers were: Robert Williams-Wynn (14th/20th Hussars), Kenneth Cranham (Royal Fusiliers), Peter Heppenstall (RCT) and John Williams (Royal Regiment of Wales)

The Light Infantry continued to take casualties and 11 days after Tommy Stoker died of his wounds in the RVH, 20 year old Thomas Rudman of the 1st Battalion was shot and killed by the IRA in the Ardoyne area. Some 12 months or so before this tragedy, his brother John had also been killed by the IRA in the Dungannon area.

The author, by now no longer a serving soldier, had watched, tragically be-mused at the mounting toll of dead British soldiers. Although this year's grim tally would be halved 12 months later and decrease thereafter as the Army's tactics evolved and the naïvety which typified the first years on the streets was eradicated, deaths had occurred at a rate of over 2 per week! The IRA – and any other psycho-path with a rifle – were shooting soldiers with a seeming impunity; the tragic bemusement became a resigned frustration.

Photo essay

David Barzilay

Looking through hundreds of photographs to provide a photographic essay for this book brought back memories of over eight years spent in Northern Ireland as a reporter on the *Belfast Telegraph*, a correspondent for Independent Radio News and Northern Ireland correspondent of the *London Evening Standard* - memories of gun battles, bombs, murders, human tragedy and humour but above all the troops from dozens of battalions who served there for months of duty and then returned home, only to be called upon again and again when the need arose.

Some of the stories seem unbelievable now, but I know that the soldiers, who experienced the same sort of things that I did, and have now been given the chance to tell their own stories, will appreciate some of these memories and anecdotes.

A chance telephone call from a photographer called Peter Woodard, who was working for the *Daily Express* in Ulster, saw me travelling to Londonderry for a weekend break with my old colleague. It ended up with us covering one of the first civil rights marches to be attacked by Protestants and which turned into a full-blown riot.

It was obvious that it wasn't going to end there and in February 1969 I joined the *Belfast Telegraph*. It wasn't long before I was given the task of liaising with the army and looking for military stories.

As the situation got worse, the resident battalions stationed around the Province realised that they were going to be drawn into the conflict and that they would need help from elsewhere.

By August 1969 attacks between Protestant and Catholic communities were becoming commonplace and law and order broke down completely, with dozens of buildings set on fire in Belfast. I remember walking up the Falls Road and seeing general-purpose machine guns mounted on hastily-constructed sandbagged emplacements. Streets leading into the area were cordoned off by reels of barbed wire and on every corner stood a soldier with a fixed bayonet.

The Roman Catholic community who came onto the streets offering tea and sandwiches saw these soldiers as saviours. It wasn't to last. Behind the barricades on both sides attitudes hardened. The Ulster Volunteer Force called for new members and already some members of the Official IRA thought that not enough was being done to protect the Catholic community and take the fight to the British - after all it was their troops that had now set up more permanent positions all over the Province.

In the middle of all of this was the ordinary soldier and more and more I found that it was their story that I was writing about. They were stuck in the middle, having to deal with situations from both communities. They couldn't understand being targeted by people who only weeks before had bought them tea and sandwiches and by people who proclaimed that they supported the Crown.

I remember being with the 2nd Battalion, the Parachute Regiment as they came under intense fire on the Shankhill Road and listening to the Colonel of the Regiment, Mike Gray, saying that they might be waving Union Jacks but as long as his soldiers were coming under fire he would hit back hard - and he did. He persuaded me to walk with him up the Shankhill Road, kicking over buckets of water that had been put outside houses so that rioters could wrap their faces in damp clothes to save themselves from the worst of the CS gas.

It was one of the first of many incidents that I was personally involved in. They are too numerous to mention here but a few spring to mind …

… An explosion outside the former Grand Central Hotel in Belfast where a van bomb had been left. Soldiers in sandbagged emplacements either side of the building stayed at their posts. The bomb went off, wrecking the front of the building. As the smoke cleared a gunner from the RHA emerged from behind the sandbags laughing. 'What's the joke?' I said 'Well, in the gunners we often fire the guns but we never get to see the end result,' he replied.

On another occasion I was travelling with the 14th/20th Lancers on the way back from Londonderry to Belfast where an inspection of the Troop, which consisted of a Saladin, Saracen, and a three-tonner, was to take place. Travelling through a small town near Antrim the troops were attacked not by gunmen but by dozens of children throwing paint pots that they had stolen from a local decorators store. At the end of it, the Troop looked like 'multi-coloured swap shop'.

There were many serious and tragic incidents, like finding the body of a murdered UDR soldier on a border road, seeing bomb disposal officers that I had spent time with being blown apart, seeing soldiers coming under attack all the time in a situation where it was often impossible for them to identify their enemy. It was a privilege to report on their activity.

David Barzilay
March 2008

All images in this section © David Barzilay

A Ferret armoured car and one-ton Humber (PIG) carry out
a roadblock on a street off the Falls Road, Belfast 1972.

In 1969, when rioting was at its height, soldiers had to take rest whenever and wherever they could.

A Falls Road resident decides to leave before the curfew is imposed, 1970.

Just one of the hundreds of street murals used by the IRA to let everyone know whose territory they were entering. The same occurred in Protestant areas, where they were put up by organisations like the UVF (Ulster Volunteer Force), 1971.

Protestant paramilitaries in a show of strength in Belfast, 1972.

In the early days curious children often surrounded soldiers, 1970.

Incendiary devices were used very successfully by the Provisional IRA
to cause havoc in built-up areas.

An air observer sits in the door of a Wessex helicopter as it flies over the M1 motorway, 1971.

Republican sympathisers demonstrate against the Paras and internment, 1972.

A soldier from the Royal Regiment of Fusiliers on patrol in Belfast
is watched by small child, c 1970.

The Royal Regiment of Fusiliers had to deal with many explosions on their 'patch' including the blowing up of the local Co Op, Belfast, March 1972.

A member of the Royal Scots Dragoon Guards takes time out, 1971.

The early beginnings of the 'Peace Line' which separated
Roman Catholic and Protestant housing estates in Belfast.

A Protestant paramilitary at pains to disguise his identity.
Mirror specs were all the rage at the time!

Dozens of unapproved roads criss-cross the Ulster border and it was impossible
to patrol them all. They were the favourite route for bringing vehicles
into Northern Ireland often packed with guns or explosives.

A Protestant supporter returns from a march, 1971.

Lough Neagh, the largest freshwater lake in the United Kingdom was often
patrolled by the Royal Marines, who successfully stopped gunrunners
using a variety of small craft, 1972

On patrol in South Armagh – Bandit Country

The Army Air Corps flew constantly to provide intelligence, c 1970.

A Wessex helicopter on patrol in Bandit Country, South Armagh, 1971.

A senior officer flies in to inspect unapproved road closures in
South Armagh, 1975.

South Armagh – 'Bandit Country' from the observation slit in a
Saracen armoured vehicle, 1971.

The IRA's propaganda machine was always at work – even down to putting mini posters on this tourist sign, which was the first one that visitors encountered when they travelled over the border into Northern Ireland near Newry, 1971.

Police stations near the border quite often came under attack and frequently had an armoured presence.

A little light relief. Many battalions had pin-ups who visited troops throughout the Province.

A Royal Regiment of Fusiliers soldier in an ambush situation on the outskirts of Belfast, 1975.

Members of the Royal Scots prepare to search Catholic homes
in the Duncairn Gardens area of the city.

Chapter Six

1973

A year of 1,520 bombings, 5,018 shootings and the deaths of 66 soldiers, 13 RUC officers, 129 civilians and 42 terrorists.

This year would see 5 soldiers killed by an IRA car bomb on May 19 at Knock-na-Moe Castle Hotel, Omagh.

The following month, the IRA would kill 6 civilians with another car bomb, this time in Railway Street, Coleraine.

It also saw, for the first time in the current conflict, the death of a soldier on the mainland, when Captain Ronald Wilkinson of the RAOC was killed whilst defusing an IRA bomb in Edgbaston, Birmingham in late September.

In this year, the IRA used women to lure off-duty soldiers to a party on the Antrim Road, Belfast and then shot three dead and seriously wounded a fourth.

It saw also the awful deaths of RUC men Mervyn Wilson and David Dorsett, killed by a booby-trapped car in Londonderry as they were going off duty.

View of Belfast from OP

AFTER THE SHOOTING. 1973

Rifleman Kevin Stevens, Royal Green Jackets

It was two days before I recalled anything after the shooting, and I was to spend a month in Musgrave Park, possibly the finest hospital in the world for injuries of the nature we tended to pick up in Northern Ireland and I have the greatest respect for the men and women both civil and military who looked after us so very well. I was in a small ward of just four beds, though there were several wards, three of us were from various regiments and were 'war wounded', the other was in fact another Green Jacket from the 3rd Battalion who had been admitted suffering a rather nasty boil in an area making it very difficult to sit down.

During my time there I had about six operations as the surgeons slowly put my arm back together and I became a little resistant to the knock-out drug which they would put in my hand every 3 or 4 days. I became so sure I could beat the drug if only for a short period of time that I actually bet the doctor (an Australian on secondment) that I could make it from 10 down to zero before going under. The wager was struck, a bottle of brandy and 200 duty free cigarettes. Not only did I beat his count I confirmed I had beaten it before going out like a light. When I awoke there was the bottle and cigarettes on the side; I liked that particular doctor!

In the December I was flown by Wessex helicopter then Andover aircraft to Northolt just outside London for onward transfer to the Royal Herbert Hospital, another military hospital in Woolwich, London. What a contrast in styles; Musgrave Park was a friendly hospital where you felt appreciated for the job you had been doing. The Royal Herbert staff generally speaking really didn't care (though there were some notable exceptions), you were just a number to them and the deputy matron was a proper dragon. A Major by rank but whom, we were sure, had been trained by Hitler himself.

An example of the attitude displayed was that we were expected to stand to attention by the sides of our beds (self-made of course; proper corners and the sheet turned just so much) ready for her daily inspection at 0900hrs. I had a problem with this – my final operation before leaving Musgrave Park had been to have skin taken from my left leg and grafted on to my left arm. For whatever reason the dressing on my leg had not been changed for several days and it had now gone crispy and dried to the leg itself, it was therefore very painful and I couldn't put any pressure on the leg at all. So I was laying smartly to attention on my bed when the dragon entered. 'What's your injury?' she barked at me. I tried to explain especially about the problems I was having with my leg but she wasn't listening. 'Then there is no excuse not to be standing by your bed, get up NOW!'

I wriggled off the bed, and stood to attention or as best I could, the pain in my leg hit me, I fell over and re-broke my arm which by now was slowly healing. Add one more operation to the list! I was excused standing up after that ! The funniest part of this was that the deputy matron ordered that I should be issued crutches to move about with ... . So there I was one leg with a big bandage on (now changed) and one arm in a plaster cast and sling I was expected to somehow grip two crutches. I never did get the hang of it. Having got a feel for the hospital I sought out one of the lads who had come across the week before me to see what the score was. He put me in touch with the escape committee.

Several of the more adventurous inmates had discovered that by sneaking out after the 1900hrs bed check through the boiler house they could get out of the hospital and down to the local pub, the Brook at the bottom of Shooters Hill. I put my name down for the escape party and the following night sallied forth in a tracksuit concealing my prison – er, hospital – pyjamas to the pub, where I was shocked to see amongst the clientele several of our nurses and doctors. I was informed that there was an unwritten and unbroken rule that in the pub we didn't know each other and a blind eye was turned as long as we didn't get caught coming or going. We never did.

On February 7th 1973, three months to the day after being shot, I was discharged and returned to the Rifle Depot in Winchester to await posting back to my unit in Celle Germany. On 7th March I flew to Hanover and was picked up by transport to return to my unit where I was placed on light duties until the July when I was returned to full duties – just in time for another tour in Belfast, the Lower Falls this time though.

JULY, 1973: BELFAST

Bernie Homer, 1 Glosters

Our welcome was to be greeted with a riot in the first week in the Markets area of Belfast. Our reply was to fire the whole Battalion's issue of baton rounds for a 4 month tour, in the first week.

BRITISH ARMY SNIPER: LONDONDERRY, 1973

Warrant Officer Haydn Davies, Royal Regiment of Wales

It was on a late hot afternoon in August 1973. I had been tasked the previous evening from my unit at Ballykinler to report to the Royal Fusiliers in the area of the city wall above the Bogside in Derry.

I arrived about 4pm and reported to the Royal Fusiliers and started to set up a sniper hide on the ramparts of the wall. Sniper hides are difficult in an urban situation, so concealment from fire was the best we could achieve, and sooner or later we would be seen. To solve this problem we moved our position from time to time along the wall.

The City wall area had a brick building behind it called the 'Masonic'. This building housed the platoon of Fusiliers, a jolly lot who were quite fed up of bricks being hit out of the wall by rifle fire and showering down on them within and outside the building. The soldiers were particularly annoyed because their dining hall was inside on the upper floor where most bullets struck and they constantly got brick chunks in their food. They had been receiving the aimed rifle fire for some days previously. My task was to: 'Observe the situation, locate the sniper and return fire for effect'.

I positioned myself and my fellow sniper, Pte Swannick on the city wall. The wall was a high stone structure with a drop of about forty feet down onto a sloping grass bank. The bank sloped right down to the Bogside Inn, which was

British Army Sniper: Londonderry, 1973 (photo courtesy of Haydn Davies)

situated 200 metres below us on the part of the main residential area of the Bogside facing our position.

We chose a sniper hide on the wall near to the Walker Memorial. The memorial had been destroyed by explosion some time recently. The top of the wall was castellated along its whole length. Behind the top of the wall were ramparts that allowed walking along its safe side. The height from the rampart floor to the top of the wall on our side was about four feet, which allowed ample movement. Camouflage nets were draped over the wall. Observation was achieved through the gaps in the castellation, using the camouflage nets for cover and relying on 'trapped shadow' behind, to prevent silhouette. In all it was a comfortable task with complete freedom of movement. The Fusiliers behind us meant we had no local security problem; a cushy number, we could even brew tea.

We set up and prepared our 'optics', loaded and sat and observed and waited. We positioned ourselves about 10 metres apart. Swannick was an excellent rifle shot. He was renowned for his shooting skill in the Regiment. He was a quiet Monmouthshire man and as steady as they come. I loved to watch him fire on the range, especially at longer ranges. It was as if the rifle grew out of his shoulder, there was no visible bodily movement as the shot was discharged.

A large element of urban sniping is to get to know the pattern of life in front of you. Who lives where; who comes and goes at certain times; who works where, and at what time they leave for work and return home again. The milkman, the postman, people coming and going. It all makes a big picture. An important fact was to watch the reaction of certain people, male and female to the approach of Army foot patrols. Some ignored them. Some hid behind walls and corners, some turned and ran. Others would throw a rock over a house at the patrol, believing that they were unseen in the act.

I was not convinced that the sniping, as was firmly believed, was from the Bogside Inn. It couldn't be. There was no cover, no covered escape route and certainly no unobserved firing positions there. Also it was too public and wide open. I liked the wiry Irish and they were too clever to use that place. For planning yes, but not for the action!

About six pm that second evening two shots came at us from a great distance away and went some feet overhead. The shots came from the area of the edge of The Creggan, about 600 metres away or perhaps from Cable Street. The 'crack and thump' give us that indication of distance. It was the IRA testing a rifle perhaps? 'Why waste rounds when there are Brits about!'

Later at about 7pm I was using my rifle telescope and moving my observation from window to window, searching the lower and upper windows of the houses and flats in front of us. The Bogside had gone quiet, which was unusual for a summer evening. I saw some faces looking from different windows and looking in our direction. I saw in two houses that the occupants were using binoculars. I moved to another castellation on the wall and continued my scan of the area. Something sinister was being planned in front of us.

Some minutes later I saw a young girl, walking hurriedly towards a block of flats to my front. It was a hot night and she was wearing a heavy thick check long coat. She walked awkwardly and in my opinion she was carrying a rifle. Her right arm was locked in carry position in her coat, after some steps she would adjust her carriage of the rifle. She was of small physique and whatever she carried, it was heavy for her. She ran the last few steps to the flats, opened the swing doors and went inside. In all this time I was discussing with Swannick and that I would do the shooting while he observed in case this was a 'set-up' for someone bigger about.

The girl and two youths appeared in an open window of a living room on the second floor, distance was about 200 metres. The two skinny youths were quite young and would have had little experience of what they were up to otherwise I would not be on to them.

The three disappeared from view. I went with my telescopic sight from window to window on the same level. All eight or so windows were open, most with curtains which were closed or partially open. Once I saw the girl come forward in a window. She was standing alone and looking directly up at our position, she was without her coat. She turned her head as if speaking to someone. I thought that they were probably waiting for a target.

Suddenly a high velocity shot rang out and hit our position. A near miss! I did not see which window it came from. I kept my rifle on the flats and waited, my sights moving from window to window. I thought there would certainly be a second shot.

Then I saw the girl appear at the entrance door on the lower floor. She had her coat on again and obviously carrying the rifle. She stood for some seconds and looked directly up at our location. I placed the pointer of my rifle telescope scope right on her breast, just below her throat. I saw a young face with dark hair, a slight girl, a pretty face. I took the first pressure on the trigger and stalled as she looked up towards me. She was like a hunted animal, her head moving sharply in several directions!

Suddenly she started to run to her right towards the Bogside Inn and then away from me in a straight line. I placed the rifle telescope on her back and took the first pressure again, an easy target; ... I couldn't do it!

As she ran I fired two shots, the first a deliberate shot aimed one metre to her left and the second shot a deliberate one metre to her right. The noise of incoming rounds of high velocity so near must have been horrific to her.

I saw her run behind a wall about three hundred metres away. She must have been in a state of shock. A young lieutenant of the Fusiliers talked a foot patrol onto her position by radio. She was found and taken into the base, where I believe she was charged with the offence of carrying arms.

For my part, I felt that I had failed as a soldier in my duty. At first I was sorry that I had let her go to carry arms again. I cared little about my reputation as a sniper. I cared more that I felt it was not an entirely military target; a young teenage girl perhaps not yet seventeen.

For missing the target, I was called to account by my commanding officer; as a father of two young girls I took it on the chin and made no reply as his ravings went on for some minutes. There followed a long silence, both of us standing face to face in his office. His six foot figure towered over me. He kept repeating, 'you missed!' you missed!' I made no reply, as he glared at me. I felt he was trying to decipher what I was thinking. Then after another pause he quietly said. 'Go back to your company and polish up your bloody sniper skills.'

As time went on I became glad I'd let her go. Some months later when Pte Swannick was killed at Ballykinler and later more of my friends were killed in the county of Armagh, I thought deeply about the incident and regretted my actions. Now over thirty years later and in different times and with a welcome peace in Ireland, I am truly quite happy with my choice of action. It was a moral issue not a military one. Only the man on the spot has the right to make such choices.

The young girl came from Ivy Terrace in the Bogside. If she reads this narrative or another of her contemporaries reads it, then I am sure she will know exactly who she is! I hope now that the girl is a happy mother of children. I often wonder if she thinks of that August afternoon in 1973 and does she ever realise that my bad shooting was completely intentional; having seen her face and small feminine figure magnified to three times magnification ... I just could not do it!

Private Michael Swannick who was only 20 and a soldier in the DERR was killed on October 28, the following year. Along with a comrade Alan Coughlan of the RWF, he was caught in the blast of a van bomb placed at Ballykinler Army camp by the IRA. 30 others were injured by the bomb, placed deliberately outside the soldiers' rest area.

Warrant Officer Hadyn Davies, RRW added:

Though both Swannick and Coughlan were badged RWF I think you will find that they were both RRW. They were both nice lads but Swannick who I knew much better was a 'cracking' lad, quiet and unassuming, the type this country needs most. His passing was most unfair to all.

ULSTER: 1973

Private Ken Donovan, RRW

I was given an 18 month posting to Northern Ireland in 1973 and we were first located at Palace Barracks at Hollywood, just north of Belfast; the majority of our
duties were to back up some of the many regiments in the province which had
been overstretched. My major emotions were of frustration; I had heard so much
from guys who had been on earlier tours and it was the fear of the unknown.
Some of the guys lied, some exaggerated and I was frustrated as I had no idea exactly what I had let myself in for. As it panned out, it wasn't as daunting as I
thought that it would although it took me a few weeks to realise this.

The majority of my time was spent in Belfast city centre, searching people
who were trying to bring in weapons and bomb-making materials which could
cause extensive damage to civilian life and buildings. This was a tedious job but it
had to be done in order to deny the paramilitaries any access to the immediate
town centre. We also carried out extensive VCPs in and around the City; this was
to restrict access and movement of arms. We carried out foot patrols in all areas
of Belfast from the Shankhill Road, the Ardoyne, Divis flats, Andersonstown and
the Turf Lodge to name but a few.

The people on the street were different depending on where they were; not
too bad in the City centre where some would talk to us and others would ignore
us. You could tell the difference between Protestants and Catholics, by the

Ken Donovan (RRW) on foot patrol
(photo courtesy of Ken Donovan)

clothes they wore, by their attitudes and even by which segment gate they entered the centre.

At one stage, we were sent to Londonderry's Ebrington Barracks to help out the RRF and we were detailed to guard the Craigavon Bridge which was a major link to the Bogside. Now and then, you would get a sniper take a few shots from the Waterside district but luckily never when I was on duty. Once we were sent to Clady village – just 4 of us – to guard the RUC station there; it was so small, that I think only one officer and his family lived in the station. Other duties included manning the sangars at Maggilligan Prison and patrolling the perimeter wire and, as this wasn't enough, monitoring the visitors for arms and other contraband.

The Bn was also deployed to County Fermanagh to operate border patrols as the IRA were using small country lanes to ferry arms and ammunition from the South. In order to try and stop this, the R.E. blew up some of the roads, preventing vehicle access and making the IRA's job much harder. One of our tasks was to make hides near these roads and stay under cover for 2 to 3 days and longer, monitoring and logging all movements from either side of the border. We relayed this back to HQ and from there to Intelligence. We were able to watch all the local players and neither they nor the villagers and farmers ever knew of our presence.

Back in Belfast and foot patrols; a typical one on, say the Short Strand or Ballymacarret in East Belfast would go like this. We would enter the street in ones and twos, with the sangar gate slightly ajar; one man across the road to secure the position and then another to the side and then another and then move up the street. All this routine would be worked out beforehand and we never took the same routes. All of the FPs [foot patrols] would have a 'tail-end Charlie' who would walk backwards and the next man who would often turn and keep an eye on him. Two or three other bricks would be out at the same time and all communications would be by hand. One thing which we never did was to use our names as they could be used against us by the locals to trick us.

The lengths of patrols could vary, but they were generally 30–45 minutes at a time. We would try to be friendly, especially to the kids but all we got back was verbal abuse – 'Fuck off, ye Brit bastards' was a common one. They got to recognise our cap badges and once that they saw that we were Welsh, they would call us 'sheep-shaggers.'

Back in Belfast, we invariably had run-ins with the local youths and adults usually during house and body searches on known IRA members; part of our brief was to assist the RUC in arrests.

On Sunday, April 21, intelligence came through that there was a bit of a march and trouble could escalate. It did so and 'C' Company was deployed to the Divis flats where there wasn't an awful lot going on, and just as it was getting boring, it all kicked off. A few bricks and some verbal and then the yobs wanted to march down Divis Street and our instructions were to halt their progress.

That is when 8 Platoon earned their coin so to speak; you name it, they threw it at us. We held them off as they rioted for 3 to 4 hours and as it was such a hot day, I must have sweated off a couple of pounds in weight. We were soaked in sweat but we had to focus on the job in hand. Personally, I must have fired 30 baton rounds or more that day and I was one of only two baton gunners. In one of the side streets, we had two other platoons hiding and ready to go in with their

Ken Donovan (RRW) on foot patrol
(photo courtesy of Ken Donovan)

snatch squads. As soon as we got the call that a snatch squad was going in, we stopped firing baton rounds until they had grabbed a 'body' and then we would start again; it was all so well timed.

The following day, some miles further to the south of Ken Donovan's violent exertions, the IRA abducted 18 year Mohammed Abdul Khalid, from his car near Crossmaglen. They riddled his body with up to 30 bullets. His heinous crime? He served tea at the British Army base and his father was the camp barber.

SOUTH ARMAGH: 1973

Russ Slater, 17th/21st Lancers

Our year-long tour in 1973 saw us supporting the resident battalion, 2 Para, in South Armagh. The British Army, RUC and UDR losses in this area were high, and the now-common term 'Bandit Country' was earning its reputation. In the previous twelve weeks, nine soldiers had been killed, two from our own regiment. This meant long hours, non-stop patrolling, endless operations and trying to stay switched-on.

During one such operation, our Saracen pulled into an RUC station for a quick tea and fag stop. It was about midnight, so the police station was fairly empty. The five of us went into the kitchen to put the kettle on, took off our flak vests, webbing, and sat at a small table in the middle of the room. A few seconds

RRW on border crossing duty
(photo courtesy of Ken Donovan)

later, three very drunk plainclothes RUC detectives came in. The second one staggered into my chair, kicked out at my SLR, which was leaning against my leg, and sent it clattering to the floor, with the words 'Get this crap out of my way, youse English bastard.' I jumped up, raging mad, my parents insulted and my weapon no longer zeroed.

'English bastard? I'm only here cos you lot are fucking useless!'

The drunken policeman grabbed a knife from the kitchen top and lunged at my stomach. A mate quicker than me swung his rifle butt and smashed the bloke in the mouth, blood and teeth going all over the place. He went down, and my mate's SLR was then pointed at the other two. 'Get him out of here.' The two coppers did as ordered, but the hate and animosity was easy to see.

There were no repercussions and nobody complained; half of my family is Irish but this was the only time in NI that I seriously thought: 'What the fuck am I doing here?'

THE FALLS (AGAIN) TOUR 1973

Sergeant Mike Heavens, April–July, B Company 1 Glosters

The advance party of the Command element flew from RAF Gutersloh to Belfast's Aldergrove Airport and we were back! The trip from the airport was made, as usual, in the Makralon armoured 4 tonner (armoured – what a laugh!) This box-on-wheels resembled an old guards van that you used to see on the railways but it lets in less air and light and has 20 or so squaddies packed in the back. It is fronted in the convoy by a Ferret Scout Car (when available), but more usually by a PIG (Armoured 1 ton for the use of) and reared [at the rear] by a Saracen bought back from the Saudis. This was after it was discovered that the Provo's had RPG's and knew how to use them and we didn't have anything not tracked and small enough for the narrow streets of Belfast; since they had all been sold off to the Saudis by some enterprising Staff Officer and Civil Servant grouping! This grouping has done (and continues to do) more damage to the British Army's ability than any other factor known in the MOD.

In between this hired/snatched-back, motley group, were the baggage trucks and their guard, who had no armour but as they are of the Quartermasters staff are either invulnerable or dispensable depending on your point of view! Our convoy was met at the entrance to and escorted into The Broadway, at Celtic Park. This old storehouse for the RVH (Royal Victoria Hospital) was fairly run-down but had been sandbagged and breeze blocked with gay abandon by the Royal Engineers and at least looked the part. The RGJ [Royal Green Jackets] were, for some reason, extremely pleased to see the advance party and insisted on a tour that very day!

We had groped our way around the dingy interior seeing section sleep rooms, section briefing rooms, section stand to rooms – I won't go on, I'm sure you get the picture, and arrived at the roof sangar. This was a monster sandbag emplacement of huge proportions that dominated the roof area and looked out over Celtic Park and Rodney/St James and up to the Rocks, a group of Victorian-style terraced houses opposite the junction of Donegal Road and the Falls.

As we gathered there on this, our first day, and before the main body had even packed to leave Germany, we could see a Saracen negotiating the chicane of dragon's teeth across Ivy Street that calmed traffic before it got to the mill

RRW on border crossing duty
(photo courtesy of Ken Donovan)

entrance. It had gotten only halfway into this series of 'S' bends when there was an explosion from the large derelict factory some 50 metres away and we could clearly see the RPG man as he let fly; immediately he turned and ran into the wrecked factory – a burst of small arms fire rattled against the Sarra's side from a gunman plainly visible at the other end of the Match Factory.

He then gave a final squirt in our direction, the rounds flew way over our heads and he disappeared too. Our briefer, apart from relaying the info to the ops room via the intercom, seemed surprisingly unimpressed by this but it definitely had the opposite effect on the 3 section commanders from 1 GLOSTERS! 'Welcome to Belfast' was the laconic statement and we continued the tour.

The Saracen, less a few scudge marks on the paint and hole in one of the dragon's teeth on the road, was undamaged. The RCT driver was, I'm told, ordered to change his underwear immediately on arrival in the base! The Broadway was our base for only a few weeks as the change in Orbat [order of battle] NI was underway. Longer tours with larger areas meant fewer tours, or so it was sold to us, and the Rodney/Broadway went to the Whiterock unit and we doubled up with our 'D' Company in the Lower Falls which, it had been decided, needed dominating!

Albert Street Mill sits brooding beside the Divis Flats and is a huge reminder of the old textile industry of the Victorian era in Belfast. This was our new home which we shared with 'A' Company and sundry other engineers, Truckees and fitters of various badges; a hive of activity day and night, it hummed with noise as well as smells.

The choggy's shop in Albert Street, was a non-stop provider of everything from polish to egg banjos and writing and reading material to sweets, and 'Ram Jam Butty' (no one knew his real name I'm sure) was all smiles and Pakistani business know-how and must have left there a rich man. Mind you he earned it. A married man with 5 children, left behind in Pakistan, he lived at the back of his shop on the 2nd floor and was at the beck and call of the 24 hour business of soldiering in Belfast. He went and got all his own stock totally unguarded and took his risks, monetarily as well as physically, with the same amiable smile. Monetarily, because he ran a tick book in an area of some 300 soldiers all intent on ripping the choggy's off. 'Donald Duck' and 'Mickey Mouse' were common soldier's names there but many an errant squaddie was caught out by the final muster before leaving, when the CSM paraded the Coy, and the choggy walked the ranks demanding his payment from Mr 'Richard Head' and co!

Contacts such as shooting incidents were common, as were booby traps and 4 of A Company guy's were hit in the Divis by a booby trap in an electrics box – 2 died and the other two were badly wounded, one of whom was a mate of mine, Ray Peart, the Section Commander. Blinded for life he eventually went on to represent Great Britain at the Paraplegic Olympics and he still attends reunions to this day. I went horseriding with him some 3 years later when I was an instructor with the TA in the city where he lives.

Patrolling was done now in what were called multiples. These consisted of at least 3 teams with the other company group being out somewhere else in the patch with the 'whippets' doing a rotation around the whole. Whippets were the nickname of the Ferret Scout Cars used as back-up in the harder areas and manned by the Cavalry, who were a very good bunch of lads. Despite this, casualties there were, but it was all part of this strange life we led. Sometimes we got lucky. A patrol from 'D' Coy got ambushed in a back alley in the reservation, at 50 yards range, by a Thompson. The lead man was the platoon commander who took 8 rounds to his chest and one in his arm – the flak jacket stopped all the chest strikes but his arm was badly damaged. Immediately behind him little Paddy 'X' who got just one round but this tore through his guts and he was lucky to live.

The IRA had gotten to targeting the lead man because he was usually the commander so we changed our tactics and put a scout out front. With true squaddie sick humour he quickly became known as the 'bullet catcher'. This and the 'tail-end Charlie' were the two dodgiest patrol places. Walking backwards became an art form! As we finished off our tour and counted our blessings the Light Infantry who had taken over from us in the Broadway, had, despite our warnings, gone into the Match Factory, that derelict factory used on our first day for a hit against the Saracen; it was booby trapped and 2 died, such is the small margin by which one soldier lives and another dies.

Minden never looked so good; we patched up our wounded, remembered our dead and got on with the next event, as squaddies have from time immemorial.

The incident to which Mike Heavens refers, took place on May 13 when Corporal Thomas Taylor of the LI was killed and Private John Gaskell died of his wounds the following day.

It was a bad year for the Light Infantry, as they lost three more soldiers before the year was out. Private Reginald Roberts was killed on his 25th birthday on the Ballymurphy Estate, Lance Corporal Richard Miller was shot and killed near the RVH and Private Stephen Hall was killed at Crossmaglen. By the end of this decade, the overworked RVH had become the world's leading specialists in the treatment of gunshot wounds.

LISBURN: 1973

Corporal Tom Clarke, RCT

I was given a residential (30 months) posting to the Province and deployed to HQNI at the Lisburn garrison and detailed to be the personal driver to the Deputy Commander, Colonel Cubis.

Now, Colonel Cubis – of whom, more in a moment – was an interesting guy; he was with Colonel Carne and the 'Glorious Glosters' at the battle of Imjin Hill in the Korean War. He lost his hand in battle there and had a variety of three very interesting false hands. Depending upon which one he used, I knew what kind of a day I was in for as his driver. If it was the gloved fist then I was in for an easy day as it would be just meetings; if he wore the hook, it would be a mundane day and if he wore his knife, then it was going to be a hard one!

On one occasion, we were deployed to Stormont where the 'sponge' protest was on. Apparently, someone in the British government had called the Stormont lot 'spongers' and the Ulster Unionists had all turned up with pieces of sponge in their lapels and created a bit if havoc. Paisley was there and he kicked off and I had the pleasure of watching a few big, burly Redcaps escort him out of the Stormont building.

I was once ordered to drive for the Brigade Commander who was in a foul mood before he went in for his meeting and an even fouler mood as he came out of it towards the car surrounded by red-faced officers as he continued to harangue them. I should point out here, that he had an anti-abduction device fitted which would give a severe electric shock to anyone who tried to get in at him. He had just grabbed the door handle and my knee – accidentally, I promise you – just nudged the switch and made the device live. Of course the shock ran up his arm and the bodyguard grabbed him and he got the shock as well and then, just to compound things, the radio man grabbed him too and all three were being electrocuted at the same time. In no time a rather amused audience had gathered and they didn't look too sympathetic.

Funnily enough, they never asked me to drive for them again.

LONDONDERRY: TWO FINGERS UP AT THE IRA

Pete Guild

My 2nd tour in 73 was to a factory in Londonderry in Bligh's Lane. As the majority of the Regiment was billeted in the factory we were the lucky ones who got the bomb-proof caravans!!!!!

Lt John Quinton Adams (left), Major Nigel Roberts (right)
(photo courtesy of Regimental Museum of The Royal Welsh)

On arrival we had to draw bedding etc from stores and take it to our respective 'van.' At that precise moment a gunman opened fire on us from the roof of a nearby school. We, to say the least, were startled, until that is our armourer realised that the guy was firing a Thompson Sub Machine gun at us.

Well, he then proceeded to go to the most open space in the factory and started giving the gunman the fingers. That was enough for the rest of us and we all rushed out and were dancing and giving lewd/rude gestures to the guy. Apparently our armourer realized that his weapon could not reach us and so decided to show this act of bravado. The gunman was jumping up and down with rage at the sight of us all laughing. I still laugh to this day about it, although Bligh's Lane had a few other nasty moments too.

LOWER FALLS ROAD/DIVIS STREET, 1973

Bill Jackson, 1 Glosters

In '73, as the battalion was about halfway through its tour of 'OP Banner' in the Lower Falls, A Company was in Albert Street mill and instead of our own drivers; we had R.C.T personnel.

Anyway, on this one particular day I think we had a troop from 12 Squadron R.C.T. This day the Squadron commander along with the Squadron Sergeant Major (SSM) arrived and he saw the state of the vehicle (in manky condition) which was no fault of the R.C.T guys. Mind you, this officer was a right tit head and hadn't a clue what was going on. He probably still thought that we were still using blank rounds out there on the streets! He ripped into the drivers about the state of the vehicles; in fact 'filthy fucking shit pits' was the technical term he used.

They never learn anyway and this troop of R.C.T drivers (poor bastards; I felt really sorry for them) got a parting shot from the S.S.M. He said in a very sarcastic way 'I will be back tomorrow to inspect all the vehicles. 'Yeah, right!' was my first thought. Earth to Sergeant Major: wake up!

'A' Company had a cordon and search to do the following day along with the R.E search team and all the vehicles were needed. So that day the R.C.T lads worked like Trojans, to at least paint them all nice and shiny green; ooooohhhhhhhhhh lovely! Stupid buggers – nice shiny vehicles going to the Divis flats and Lower Falls! Anyway, at 6 o'clock, the cordon and search in and around Divis went in. All the PIGs and Saracens were used, having just been nicely panted in shiny green. Oooooooohhhhhhhhhhhh lovely!

But the Squadron Commander of the R.C.T knows best; after all he's the boss! I am still thinking: 'he's a tit head!' The cordon was in place and the mobile patrol and foot patrols were in place just before the R.E. search team started doing their stuff. The tenants of Divis flats got a bit hostile as they always did, on the sight of seeing us. Anyway, about 5 hours later and the search finished and the rioting had stopped; Then after that, it was more like running battles with the locals yobs and the vehicles rolled back into Albert Street mill and, who should be there to greet us? It was the Squadron commander and the Squadron Sgt Major!

As we came to a stop and got out to unload our weapons, some lad from 2 Platoon started singing: ' ... we can sing a rainbow ... ' and laughing hysterically, as most of the newly painted shiny green vehicles were covered in all kinds of

Major Brian Hanley (left) – trouble in Lower Falls Road
(photo courtesy of Regimental Museum of The Royal Welsh)

paint; red, yellow, blue, white, and a bag of sand paint remover. Bricks, dirt, glass, cans, bottles and any thing else that could be thrown at us! The rest of us fell about with laughter at the state of our newly painted shiny green vehicles and the look on the R.C.T. lad's faces was a pure picture and to cap it all off, our platoon commander said to this Major: 'Nice paint job!' We Glosters are very sympathetic! What a day; it was so funny.

TURF LODGE, BELFAST

Rifleman

One evening, on foot patrol, we were cutting through an alleyway trying to get up behind a couple of players we wanted to lift for questioning. We had a lance-jack up front – in later tours this soldier would be known as the bullet catcher – and he cut through a ginnell and tripped a wire strung about 6 inches off the ground.

The bastards had put some H.E. [high explosive] inside a Heinz baked beans can and the blast took his right foot clean off. When the smoke had cleared, we saw him – most of us took a few seconds to regain our composure – lying on the ground, white-faced, even in the gloom, looking at where his foot had been, just moaning, almost sobbing.

Later that night, a couple of the Boyos from the area threw some rocks at us. Did they pick the wrong time to do that ! At least three of them were searching for their own testicles in the street afterwards!

LONDONDERRY FISH & CHIPS SHOP: 1973
RSM Haydn Davies attached 1 DERR

A mobile patrol dropped me and two others off on the waste ground a few hundred metres in front of the Bogside Inn; it was an 'observation task.' Our position was to be on the flat roof a busy fish and chip shop which was about two hundred metres on the Rothvil Flats side of the Inn. We got onto the 'chippy' roof from a darkened car park to its rear. It was a most bitterly cold night, and we had got very cold waiting for over an hour to make sure we were not observed and to manoeuvre ourselves into position. Once on the roof I crawled forward and found a nice vantage point. I was lucky in that there was a very large extractor fan of about one foot in diameter which blew hot air from the fryers below over the whole length of my body.

After a few hours of uneventful OP work it was time to withdraw, and I started crawling to make my way back to the rear of the concrete roof. I tapped each of the other two as I crawled past them. I only got incoherent grunts from them. I tapped them again and got nothing only more grunts. They were virtually frozen stiff. I had to drag them in turn back to the large extractor fan and stay another ten minutes listening to their groans of delight while the hot air blew on them to get them warmed up.

I silently reprimanded myself for being so thoughtless, however we were there to look for Martin McGuiness who apparently liked his fish and chips; he was a wanted man at the time.

Grenadier Guards on foot patrol in Belfast (photo courtesy of Richard Nettleton)

SANDY ROW INCIDENT: 1973

Corporal Tom Clarke, RCT

One day, I was driving the Colonel back from a meeting and we came down to the exit of the M1 Motorway at Sandy Row in a long wheelbase Land Rover with myself, the Colonel, bodyguard and 2 Royal Pioneer Corps (RPC) sharpshooters.

Just as I hit the bottom of the road, a guy jumped up without warning from my left and I could see, even in that split second, that he had a Thompson and he opened up a burst at us. I heard the cracks and then saw the smoke and hit the brakes, swerved, went through 180 degree and stopped. One of the rounds hit the rear nearside wheel arch. Then, one of the Pioneer lads shouted 'He's dropped his gun, sir and he's running; what shall I do?' The Colonel ordered, 'Take him down' and the lad fired just one round from his SLR – the range was about 60 feet – and down the man went, pretty much dead straight away.

We called in the contact and within 5 minutes, we had a helicopter, RUC men and other units and we had taken a defensive position around our vehicle. Later, we were debriefed and then interviewed by RMPS [Royal Military Police] and SIB and that was the end of the matter.

We were involved again, later in the tour, this time during the UWC [Ulster Workers Council] strike which crippled Northern Ireland, and as usual, Colonel Cubis was in the thick of it. We received word that a few Catholic lads were holed up in the Harland & Wolff shipyard during the strike and that they feared for their lives.

I'm sure that their Protestant workmates would have been fine, but the UDA and the ones behind the UWC strike didn't take prisoners. The Colonel negotiated entry and we found the 5 terrified lads and bundled them into the back of the Land Rover and got them away to safety.

Bernie Homer, 1 GLOSTERS

When I joined the Glosters in 1973 in Minden, I found out that the section I was posted to had just lost 2 guys killed due to an explosion a few months earlier in the Divis flats and 2 guys wounded. I didn't realise at the time I was a war casualty replacement along with my fellow sprog, Bob. We were kids amongst men who had been under fire. The other guy with me was a long-term mate called Bob Massiah, and he was posted to the platoon. The other two casualties were Ray Peart and Andy King. Ray was blinded for life; Andy soldiered on for a while longer in the Bn.

The soldiers, to whom Bernie is referring, were killed by a bomb at the flats; Privates Geoffrey Breakwell and Christopher Brady, on July 17th.

They were killed after a routine search of the Divis Street flats when a booby-trapped fuse box exploded. Two other soldiers were injured – one seriously and a resident of the flats was also hurt. The IRA 'claimed' responsibility. Although, several of the newspapers, in defiance of the terror group, worded it differently and reported that the IRA 'admitted' responsibility.

The following account, also from an ex-Gloster, confirms the tragedy of the Divis on that day.

Bill Jackson, Glosters

On the 1973 tour, my best mate Geoff Breakwell got blown up in the Divis flats along with Chris Brady and the section commander was completely blinded and the 2 I.C. was blinded in one eye. This happened in July 73 as the battalion had just 2 weeks left in Ireland.

Like I said, he was my best mate; on the day it happened ATO [Ammunition Technical Officer] was doing some kind of demonstration in Albert Street and we and the rest of the section were on a mobile patrol around Albert Street and the area of Sandy Row in a PIG. We were coming back to base when we heard the explosion and took it to be ATO doing a demonstration.

Then over the radio, we were informed of a bomb blast in Divis flats. 'A' had just been going via link 5 and caught the full blast of the bomb; an old mattress had been placed in that link in the morning, because one of our other patrols had seen it in there and moved it to take a look and found nothing but it got reported as suspicious. However, just as the patrol got there it was set off.

OMAGH: 1973/74
Keith, Blues & Royals

This was an accompanied 18 tour months in Omagh. We left Liverpool for our tour which started in May 1973. My wife was due to give birth any day, and my other daughter was just 2 years old. The crossing was not bad for May.

We arrived as part of the advance party on a dry May morning from Liverpool on the *Ulster Queen*, a ship I was soon to come to know very well, the same as her sister ship. The first thing that made us sit up and take notice was the warning about where you could park your car. This was not about yellow lines etc. This was about ATOs blowing your car up if you parked in an illegal zone.

We made our way down the gangplank on to Belfast dock. Coaches painted in Ulster bus colours plus Bedfords were waiting to pick us up. Plus the covert vans with lads in the back as escorts. This was now becoming real. It came even more real as pistols and SMGs were passed out among some of the lads. The wives were getting worried and the kids thought' wow we're off to war' or some other tale whizzed around their heads.

We left Belfast heading north to the M2. Yes, the long way around but safer than the normal route. The countryside went by as we made our way to our new home. We arrived at our new home just by St Lucida Barracks, the former Ireland Brigade training depot that had been robbed of weapons in 1955 by the IRA.

The first few days flew; I took over the dept I was in. This was an admin duty but I knew I would soon be on patrols etc once my wife had given birth. Omagh had been quiet, allowing the new troops to think that life was not as bad as the Army had told us. We were lying in bed talking, and my wife turned to me and said 'It's quiet here' and before the last word was out her mouth there was an almighty bang. I turned to her and said 'You and your big mouth.' We laughed, not because it was funny but more out of fear thinking, 'well, the war has started'. Little did I know it was going to hit home.

A few days before, I had seen Pip Cox, a Corporal of Horse from the Blues and Royals. I had known Pip from my Mounted Squadron days. He was my outgoing troop 3 bar [Sergeant] as I arrived. He was now a Pilot in the Army Air Corps. He had also been in Osnabruck.

We had a quick hello as he came down the hangar 'I will try and get you a flight' he said, before dashing off. He was off on a recce.

The following morning after the bang I give it little thought beside 'must find where and what'. I met a young Air Trooper on the gate and asked him had he seen Pip that morning and was told that he was on an early flight. 'That's life' I thought, 'we [can] meet up over the coming weeks'.

As I was walking to my Dept I was given a call from across the way. I noted a Sqn NCO grabbing hold of as many people as he could. As I walked across he was talking to another person. He yells back 'You're still on your own mate?' I replied yes. 'That's ok; forget it.' I was later told that I had known one of the people up at the 'Knock Na Moe' castle. I had been up by the 'Knock Na Moe' 2 days before at Mrs. Kelly's stable asking about safe areas to buy stores that I would need. The Knock Na Moe had been given a good recommendation for good food as it was a safe place to eat.

I made my way back to work not giving it another thought. This was until lunchtime. I lived just across the bridge so I made my way home for lunch. I was hungry after a long morning. I had just finished eating when the news came on. There [had been] a bomb in Omagh last night that killed four soldiers while a fifth was in hospital fighting for his life. They named the dead and I heard the rank of Cpl of Horse. I knew who it was and my head spun and my belly made noises that would wake the dead. I rushed upstairs, just making the toilet. My wife had followed me as she too, had heard the news. A black cloud came over me. I couldn't get my head around it. This was the first time I had known someone killed because of the troubles; it was not to be my last.

That night after work, I walked home slowly. I met a lad from the outgoing regiment; he was really down. I asked 'What's up mate?' He told me he had been up all day at the' Knock Na Moe.' I told him I knew Pip and thanked him. He smiled as he knew what I meant. He walked on a few doors and his wife was at the door; she gave him hell as his dinner was burnt. 'You said you would be home early tonight.' He lost his cool and shouted at her. She shouted more and slammed the door in his face. He sat on the edge of the walkway. I joined him. We talked. I think his wife was in the kitchen. We were talking about Knock Na Moe. She came out, she said 'You were picking up those poor sod's bodies?' 'Yes, love' he said. Tears flowed. Both went in together and peace returned to his household.

I made my way home still feeling the pain. A few days later my wife was taken into hospital. I was told to phone at half six which I did. As I was asking about my wife, I heard her voice asking 'Is that my husband?' and was told 'yes' by the nurses. 'Tell him to ring back later". Her voice vanished. I asked what was up, and was told. 'Your wife has been rushed in to the delivery room; she's having the baby.'

I called later to find out that my son was born a few minutes after I called at six thirty. This lifted my heart after the last few sad few days that had gone before.

The incident at 'Knock Na Moe' to which Keith refers, was an IRA car bomb placed outside a pub, on May 18, which killed 5 soldiers. 4 of the soldiers were attached to the Army Air Corps, including Keith's friend, Barry 'Pip' Cox of the Blues and Royals who was 28. The three others attached to the A.A.C. were Arthur Place (29) of the Prince of Wales' Own, Royal Marine Derek Reed (28) and Sheridan Young (26) of the Royal Military Police.

A fifth soldier, 25 year old Sergeant Frederick Drake of the 'Skins' (5th Inniskilling Dragoon Guards) died of his wounds 16 days later in hospital. The IRA later claimed that the device was timed so as to only kill soldiers, but, had it detonated just 5 minutes later, when dozens of people were leaving the dance hall and restaurant, the death toll would have been appalling.

Within military circles, there is a consensus that, not only were the IRA – as usual – lying about the timings of the bomb, but that they hit upon a target of 5 soldiers purely by accident. It is believed that one of the 5 men purchased the car from an RUC officer and that the number was known to IRA intelligence. When the car was spotted outside the Knock Na Moe, IRA operatives recognised the plate as known RUC and booby-trapped it thinking that they were targeting policemen and not soldiers.

One thing is for certain, whatever the veracity of the theory, there was a marked decline in the sale of used RUC cars to squaddies.

In a year when tragedy was on the front page of the newspapers on a daily basis, it was thought that little could shock a general public – and Government, apparently – any further, already inured to continuing atrocities. That was to change with the killing of 19 year old Private Gary Barlow of the Queen's Lancashire Regiment (QLR).

Gary was on foot patrol in the Lower Falls area of Belfast when he was separated from the rest of his comrades and was immediately surrounded by a gang of women from the area who forcibly removed his SLR. He was then held there and – according to some accounts from women who tried to rescue him – became distraught and called out for his Mother. An IRA gunman was sent for – apparently the same age as Gary – who then cold-bloodedly shot him in the head from point-blank range after he had been pushed into a garage.

OMAGH

Keith, Blues and Royals

I heard that Bryan Criddle had been awarded the BEM and was going to be posted to Cyprus in August and was to be a Sergeant.

About a week afterwards, I was in the UDR bar when in walked a number of Dog Troop, including Bryan and his good lady. There was much drinking that night as it was to raise a glass or 6 to Bryan's BEM and posting as a Sgt.

I can still recall hearing in camp that Bryan had been hurt while searching for a bomb which was set off by remote control near Clogher in Co Tyrone. I heard that the Troop leader had stayed with him and he kept asking about his dog Jason. He was rushed to Musgrave Park hospital but sadly died a few days later and his dog, Jason had to be put down as he took a lot of the blast.

It was 2 months since Pip had been killed and it was hurting; now it was two people that the IRA had killed that I knew. I found out some 10 years later that Bryan's wife had remarried, and, if I recall correctly, she was younger than Bryan.

The next person to be killed, Staff Sgt Ron Beckett, was not someone whom I knew very well. He was aged 37, and in the RAOC. He died as he dragged a 20 lb bomb from a post office in the border village of Tullyhommon. The bomb had been left by two carloads of IRA men. I knew that he was our ATO and a brave man. To lose an ATO does hurt as we know he was the target; he never knew who the enemy was but they knew him.

Life was sad; we had not been in the posting for 4 months and the number of people I had known who had been killed was rising.

I wished that November 1974 – the end of the tour – was just a day away but it was not. The only thing I could wish for was a safe run up to Xmas and beyond.

If I thought 1974 was going to be a better year I was only living in a dream world. That is for another time.

Bryan Criddle was 34 and a dog-handler in the RAVC (Royal Army Vetenary Corps) as well as an ATO; he was fatally injured by the blast from a milk churn bomb and died of his wounds 5 days later on July 22, 1973.

LISANELLY, JUNE 1973

RTR's *First Edition*

Three terrorists, members of the Provisional IRA, were killed instantly when their car, carrying a bomb exploded a mile from Lisanelly Camp on Monday, June 25. The three men were in a green BMC 1100 car and it is believed that two of them were priming the bomb in the back when it exploded prematurely on the main Gortin-Omagh Road. The car disintegrated when the 50 lb bomb exploded.

Two of the bodies were mutilated and parts of the car and pieces of the bodies littered the adjoining fields. The explosion happened on an open stretch of road and no one else was injured.

After the blast, Corporal Barney Moran and members of 2 Troop, 'A' Squadron sealed off the area surrounding the scene and stood guard as experts examined the wreckage. The bomb was obviously intended for a target in Omagh [thought to have been the Army base at Lisanelly] and whilst we deplored the loss of life, it was fortunate the only victims of the bomb were those who showed a callous disregard for the lives of others.

The three terrorists were Sean Loughran, Dermot Crowley and Patrick Carty. Carty was widely considered responsible for the murder of a UDR corporal some weeks earlier.

Castlereagh - an 'own goal' as an IRA bomb explodes prematurely
(photo courtesy of Pat Moir)

BELLEEK, JULY 15, 1973
RTR's *First Edition*

Following a tip-off by telephone, a road mine-clearing operation was mounted on the Ballynaghra-Trigannon Road east of Belleek, Co Fermanagh, which resulted in the capture of two members of the Provisional IRA and the discovery of a 180lb bomb.

The first tip-off was received on the Friday morning and was followed by further calls over the next two days. Suspecting a possible ambush, Major David Lewis, OC of 'A' squadron, based in the area, decided not to act too quickly, planning to put in an operation later. L/Cpl Taylor – on OP duty – noticed two men acting suspiciously in the area and the operation was brought forward.

A Royal Engineers search team from 11 Field Squadron was flown in by helicopter; included was Corporal Bryan Criddle [tragically killed just 3 days later] and his sniffer dog, 'Jason'. VCPs were set up on the approach roads, commanded by two Lieutenants, Hine and Jackson, and the aerial ops were commanded by a Major Lewis.

Sections of the Assault Troop provided covering fire and flank protection to the search teams as an inspection of the roads and culverts was made. As the search progressed, electrical wire was found leading from the high ground, along a stream bed towards the road. Then a command detonator was found along with some discarded crisp packets indicating that someone had lain there for a period of time.

Just then, two men were seen running towards the distant hills and three of the soldiers gave chase. The two men disappeared from view and as the search for them went on, one of the soldiers – Corporal Hepworth – almost tripped over a man's legs sticking out from the undergrowth. They quickly overpowered the man and his comrade who was also hiding and an assault rifle was grabbed. Both men were dressed identically in green combat jackets and black trousers.

The ATO – Staff Sgt. Ronald Beckett – compelled one of the pair to follow the command wire down the hillside to a culvert. He discovered 180 lbs of H.E. in several plastic bin-liners and the Staff Sgt made one of the terrorists defuse his own bomb!

The following month, Beckett, like his comrade, Bryan Criddle, would also lose his life at Pettigo on the border with the Republic.

Raymond 'Tapper' Hall was killed on the 1973 tour when he was shot in the back by so-called 'Loyalists' in Welland Street, Belfast as they protested about the internment of Protestants. He was aged just 22 and died of his wounds on March 5, some 4 weeks after he was shot. The following tributes to him are paid by his mates in the Green Howards.

Anti-internment March. Lt Nick Evans (right)
(photo courtesy of Regimental Museum of The Royal Welsh)

ARDOYNE, 1973: 'TAPPER HALL'

Private Kev Blades, Green Howards

'Tapper' was a hell of a lad and he was one of my best mates; as a soldier, he would follow an order to the letter.

When one of the lads got a full mag pinched during a club search, a Lieutenant marched in and stopped the bandbox and ordered the mag to be thrown outside. If it was done within 10 minutes, there would be no questions asked; if it wasn't, the doors would be slammed shut and CS gas would be thrown inside. He was a bastard, but the lads would follow him anywhere. He told Tapper and me that no one was allowed out.

'Tapper' said 'Hang on here, Kev', went off and came back with two dildo guns [so-called because the baton rounds were dildo-shaped]. After 10 minutes or so, two gobby blokes came to the door and tried to get out; two rounds of 'dildos' however soon changed their minds. Within 5 minutes a man and a woman tried to do the same and we changed their minds with a repeat performance with the dildos! I looked at 'Tapper' and he repeated that no one was to come out. Inside the club, all the people inside were singing hymns which quite amused us. Two more hymns followed and then the door opened slightly and someone slid the mag out.

And, away we walked with no questions asked!

THE DEATH OF 'TAPPER' HALL

Pete Townend, Green Howards

Tapper was in my platoon (6) in B Coy; a tall, lanky lad, a bit of a larrikin at times, but he was a good-hearted lad, reliable and trustworthy, even if he did tap everybody for a fag … (hence the name 'Tapper') All in all, a good mate; and anyone who says otherwise can argue with me.

We went on a lot of skirmishes during tours of NI and during that time I never had any doubt of his ability to back me, or anybody, whatever the situation required. He never questioned orders, just got on with the job at hand. One day one of us had to go to another company as a driver/operator so I decided that Tapper and I would flip a coin for the job. He lost the toss and went off to do what he had to do. It was during this assignment that Tapper took 2 bullets, seriously wounding him. His Dad came over to be with him while he was in hospital and I remember being called into the canteen to meet him. We had a good talk about Tapper, and I was at least able to tell him that his son was a good lad, one to be proud of. Such a sad way to meet a mate's father. I saw Tapper in hospital a couple of times but he was to die shortly afterwards from his injuries.

THE FAMILY IN OMAGH

Keith, Blues & Royals

Having your family with you, when you are on active service, can cause problems especially when you have kids. As many ex-servicemen know, kids who have a father in the Army see any soldier in uniform as Dad when they are at that younger age. So when I was on patrol in Omagh I would warn my wife so she could miss shopping in the town that day and thus prevent my kids from seeing me. One other reason was to make sure my daughter did not become a target.

My first trip out was to Rockwood near Castlederg, a former hotel which I have heard has now been brought back to life in a new role. The Squadron and an RE's [Royal Engineers] Squadron were closing a number of border crossings with the Republic and so I was tasked to command the last old-type Saracen ambulance up to Rockwood. It was a quite trip, but happily, we were never called on.

THE KILLING OF AN ATO MAN (FROM RTR'S *FIRST EDITION*)

Pettigo, Co Fermanagh

Eight armed IRA members raided the border village of Pettigo in late August, taking hostages and lining them up outside the customs post there. They then blew up the post and a nearby garage and shot and wounded a 13 year old boy and soon afterwards, S/Sergeant Ronald Beckett of the RAOC was killed defusing a suspect device.

The armed men drove into the village from the Irish Republic and immediately seized and lined up hostages – including women and children – and asked their names and religion; at the same time, other terrorists were placing suspect devices. When one of the hostages, in giving his name., inadvertently identified himself as a member of the UDR, and was threatened, he knocked the pistol in the

Soldiers at North Howard Street Mill, Belfast

hand of a terrorist and the shot went high. Another shot was fired as he ran away and then a 13 year old boy was hit in the arm, and later taken to hospital. The UDR man managed to reach his house and grabbed his SMG, returned and opened fire on the IRA gunmen who fled the scene and escaped over the nearby border. Within a few seconds, the bomb detonated and the customs post was destroyed, with the people escaping injury.

Very quickly, both RTR [Royal Tank Regiment] men and RUC officers were on the scene where they were informed that there was a suspect device inside the village's post office. Ronald Beckett inspected the device and then tried to detonate it with a controlled explosion; tragically, when he went back to inspect it further, it detonated and he was instantly killed.

ENEMY IN THE MIDST: 1973

Major Dennis Gilpin, Royal Corps of Signals (TAVR)

I was working full-time and then carrying out my duties with the TA at weekends. By now, security was paramount and we were all concerned that wearing British Army uniform even if only on a weekend, made us legitimate targets in the perverted logic of the IRA.

I was very suspicious of a guy I worked with, whom I shall just call 'Terry' who was involved in odd incidents from time to time, involving the Army and his cars. About a year after we had started sharing an office together, he told me that he was going off for a week's holiday in the Republic but he never returned to work on schedule. Later on during the same day of his planned return, we were told that he had been arrested by the SF and that he was in Long Kesh prison also known as the 'Maze.' [Long Kesh was a maximum security prison where convicted terrorists – Republican and Loyalist alike – were kept in 'H' blocks]

He had shared my office for an entire year and he knew that I was in the TAVR but thankfully, I had always been aware of the risk of passing on any information that might have been useful to a terrorist so I didn't speak of my hobby outside my immediate circle of trusted colleagues. That was part of my training. I never saw 'Terry' again.

Another colleague in the TA who had a narrow escape was one Lieutenant Murphy who was stopped in an IRA VCP and had a revolver stuck into his face by gunmen. This was early one morning on the edge of a notorious Republican area. He feigned a weak smile at the gunman who simply shouted 'Out' at him and, as they only wanted his car – which he never saw again – he wasn't questioned or searched!

At the end of this series of interviews with Major Gilpin, the author looked at the SF deaths and found 7 – a comparatively low number – of the soldiers killed during the troubles were members of the TAVR. Whilst killings of TA personnel were comparatively rare, the following members died as a consequence of their uniform:

Sergeant James Fleming, attached to the RCT was shot off-duty by the IRA, together with two Protestant friends – one of whom later died – and their car set alight by their killers. This incident took place on 9 July, 1972 in the Grosvenor Road area of Belfast.

On 21 October, 1974, Ranger Samuel Gibson attached to the RIR was abducted from his home in the Ardoyne area of Belfast and shot. A member of the North Irish Militia, he ran a laundry round, and was taken by the IRA as he made his last call of the day.

On June 30, 1976, Colonel Oliver Eaton of the TA was killed by the IRA at his place of work on the Springfield Road, Belfast. Colonel Eaton was also a member of the Police Authority and a prominent businessman in Northern Ireland.

On 19 April, 1979, a Cadet Force Captain, Paul Rodgers visiting from England on a liaison tour with the Royal Anglians, was shot by the IRA in Belfast.

The INLA killed part-time Sergeant Major Hugh McGinn 3 days after Christmas, 1980. He was attached to the RIR and was shot dead at his home in Armagh City.

On 9 May, 1984, an IRA UVBT killed Corporal Trevor May who was attached to the RIR; the bomb was attached to his car which was parked outside the telephone exchange where he worked in Newry, Co Down.

Finally, on October 9, 1989, Lance Corporal Thomas Gibson, an ambulance driver attached to the RCT, was shot by the IRA as he waited in his car in the centre of Kilrea. He was the last of the 7 (known) TAVR members killed as a consequence of the troubles.

CASTLEDERG INCIDENT: 1973

Blues & Royals Soldier

One event which still gives me nightmares today took place whilst out on patrol in Castlederg during which, we had been given the task of doing roving VCP and people checks in the area. We were told no other UDR, RUC or unit patrol would be in the area.

This was good enough information as this would let us know no other armed patrols were on the patch and that any armed men would be fair game. We were jus entering a part of the centre of Castlederg; I had the Bren and knew my role was to cover the patrol. I spotted a shop's side entrance for cars which led to garages at the rear. There was a small pillar which I guess was from the days of horse drawn wagons which provided me with some cover and where I could see down the lane.

It was dark, and from approximately 30 yards, I spotted someone coming towards us so I kept my eye on him as he got closer. Then, I thought 'bloody hell, he has got a gun.' Then I noted others behind him. I called on the RT to confirm with the boss that we were the only ones out and he replied in the affirmative, and that we may have strange company. I waited until they were near enough that I could shout and they could hear me.

The yellow card flashed in my mind as I went into automatic gunner switch-on mode. I shouted but they kept moving forward and I shouted out aloud again as per Guards Depot drill. But still they kept on walking towards me. I moved my left hand forward towards the cocking handle and then after one more shout I cannot recall my thoughts. As I shouted I know that I said under my breath 'for God's sake, stop.'

The lead man took two more steps; why I do not know and I was pulling back slowly when he stopped. I carried out the drills and the first person came towards me 'What the fuck are you doing out here?' Breathlessly, he explained to me that they had thought that we might need back up and the rest of the patrol came in and was checked.

They do not know how close they came to death that night in Castlederg.

BLAIR'S YARD AND STORMONT: 1973

Major Ken Draycott, RRW

By this tour, I was a Colour Sergeant in the Signals platoon, and we were sent as Resident Bn to Palace barracks; on a residence tour, you are not often flogged to death and a lot of the temporary tour battalions tend to get all the dirty work.

When we arrived, I was on a 24 hour call in Ops in TAC HQ and we inherited an old removal-style van which had been set up and furnished as a complete ops unit. We called this the 'gin palace' and it was fitted with radios, mains, phone terminals, masts and sockets. When a situation occurred, we moved this van, lock, stock and barrel and would nick electric and phone supplies wherever we landed. During the Ulster Workers Council (UWC) strike we were deployed to Blair's yard and as we were parked up, the RSM demanded that every man have his hair cut and detailed the Bn barber to plug his electric shaver into our sockets !

We were later deployed down the home of the Northern Ireland Government at Stormont and we performed various guard and security duties, including being dug-in, in bushes and on the palatial lawns. One day, whilst a huge and controversial debate was raging inside, I decided to visit the 'Gents'. As I stood there at the urinals, relieving myself, a leading Unionist politician, Brian Faulkner walked in and he looked over at me. He smiled and said, 'In 30 minutes, the Northern Ireland Government will collapse".

I duly reported this to my boss who reported it to his boss and all the way up the line to the GOC [General Officer Commanding] and sure enough, the Northern Ireland Government collapsed

The final incident which I can recall on this tour took place when 'Black Mac' – so called on account of a bad facial injury which marred his good looks – was put in charge of community relations. He informed us that he had arranged a darts match against the locals and the night of the big game arrived. Then in walked a disparate looking bunch of thugs; the type you wouldn't wish to meet in a dark alley. They were the local Loyalist paramilitaries and at the end of the evening, we were handed a plaque inscribed 'From the Red Hand Commandos.'

The Red Hand was a Protestant terror group every bit as ruthless as the IRA.

Chapter Seven

1974

A year of 1,383 bombings, 3,206 shootings and the deaths of 56 soldiers, 15 RUC officers, 145 civilians and 22 terrorists.

The figures of the soldiers killed that year would have undoubtedly have been lower had it not been for two tragic incidents as the IRA intensified their attacks against troops on the mainland.

On February 4, nine soldiers and one of their wives and two small children were killed when a bomb planted aboard an Army coach exploded on the M62 motorway near Huddersfield. On board were 2 members of the Royal Artillery, 3 Signallers from the RCS and four soldiers from the RRF.

On October 5, later that year, at a pub in Guilford, known to be frequented by off-duty Army personnel, a bomb killed 2 Guardsmen from the Scots Guards and the first two Women's Royal Army Corps soldiers to lose their lives as a consequence of the troubles. The bomb, planted in the 'Horse & Groom' public house also killed a civilian (a young plasterer named Paul Craig) and injured over 60 others. A further device was planted in the nearby 'Seven Stars', another pub popular with off-duty soldiers, but it was thankfully evacuated before detonation.

In May of the same year, the UVF launched a month of madness in which their bombs killed 39 civilians, including 26 in the Irish republic.

YORKSHIRE: 1974

Mo Norton, sister of Bombardier Terence Griffin, R. A.

Terence ('Griff' as he was known by his friends) spent his last weekend on leave at our family home in Bolton with his friend Len. They had a happy weekend together with us all.

Just after midnight my father heard a newsflash on the radio that there had been an explosion on a coach but very little information was forthcoming at this stage. We waited all day for news; we kept listening to the news bulletins on the television hoping and praying that he would be safe. We were continuously ringing the telephone number that was given out but they could not tell us if Terence had survived.

After waiting over 17 long and arduous hours we were finally told that Terence had died. 12 people in total, 2 of them little children, including a whole family, were killed and many more injured. To say we were devastated would be an understatement. We were all totally heartbroken. My lovely Mum and Dad and my two sisters were so completely overwhelmed and distraught with grief. We each have had to deal with our grief in our own personal way, but I will never, ever forget 4th February 1974 and what effect it has had personally on my life.

189

A few years ago I took part in the Legacy Project's Needs Analysis which was working towards identifying what support needs I and others had. I have since become involved with the Legacy Project at the Peace Centre in Warrington. These last couple of years I have been to Ireland, both in the North as well as the South many times and met with other people who have been affected by the Northern Ireland Troubles and who are involved in peace and reconciliation. It is so very humbling to hear some of the heart-wrenching stories of those whose lives have been devastated by terrorism but have found ways of turning their experiences around and are now actively involved working towards peace and reconciliation.

On February 4, 1974, a coach chartered for use by soldiers and their families set off from Manchester headed for North Yorkshire. A member or members of the IRA placed a large explosive device in the luggage hold of the coach. When the device detonated as the coach drove along the M62 close to Huddersfield, eleven people were killed and a twelfth died 3 days later.

Paul Reid (17), and Leslie Walsh (19) of the Royal Signals; Leonard Godden (22), and Terence Griffin (24) of the Royal Artillery; Michael Waugh (22) Guards; John Hines (22), James McShane (29) and Stephen Walley (19) of the Royal Regiment of Fusiliers were all killed.

Killed with his Fusilier comrades was 23 year old Clifford Houghton along with his family; Linda Houghton (23) and their two young children Lee (5) and Robert (2).

This cowardly attack which did not advance the cause of Irish nationalism one bit, served to warn every member of the Armed forces and their families that there were no longer any 'safe' places on the mainland; the terrorists were very decidedly among us by this stage.

BALLYMURPHY ESTATE: 1974

Private 'Sadger' 1st Cheshires

I served with the Cheshires on the 1974 tour and the Ballymurphy estate was one of our regular patrol areas; it was a shit hole and we called it the 'Murph. We would often patrol through the back gardens and see what we could spot through the dirty back windows.

On this one occasion, one of the bastards set a dog on me; a bloody big one and it snarled and leapt at me, sinking its fangs into my leg; it hurt like nobody's business and I ended up having five stitches in it. There was a plus side, however, and I ended up with 2 days on my bunk, recovering. The unfortunate thing was that all the other lads took the piss because they were scared of being shot and bombed and there was me, having a rest because of a bloody dog bite !

Whilst we were there, we came across this graffiti and it read 'Cheshire bastards out.' With a bit of covering up and cleverly adding on words, we changed it to 'Cheshires are outstanding' – I'll bet the locals were chuffed !

The Ballymurphy Estate is located on the far western side of Belfast, sandwiched between Springmartin to the north and the Loyalist Shankhill, with Andersonstown to the south and easy links to the Falls and Milltown. It is a sweeping area of council housing in a totally Catholic area and is a hot bed of Republicanism.

To the soldiers who were stationed there at Henry Taggart or who patrolled those hostile streets, it will be forever known as the 'Murph. During the troubles, at least 14 soldiers were killed there, with the King's losing 4 men, the Duke of Wellington's losing 2, eight years apart; the place also saw the killings of two Light Infantry men.

The Cheshires lost Corporal D.A. Smith who died of his wounds on July 4, 1974 during Sadger's tour, after he was wounded by a sniper on the 'Murph. Corporal Smith who was 26 and from Lancashire was wounded 3 times in a firefight with the IRA.

BACK TO BELFAST: 1974

Bill Jackson, 1 Glosters

1974 found the Battalion back in Belfast, only this time 'A' Company were not in the Lower Falls like we all expected but split into 3 platoon locations.

1 Platoon was in Albert Street Mill; 2 Platoon were in the Gas Works, Upper Markets and 3 Platoon in the Mission Hall, in the Lower Markets. Number 2 and 3 Platoon's TAOR [tactical area of responsibility] was the Markets area while 1 Platoon had Donegal Pass and some of the Sandy Row area up to the Belfast Hospital.

The first week started off incident free and we just had the odd V.C.P and foot Patrol; nothing major. That was, until the first Saturday of the month. 11 Charley (my section) was doing a normal mobile check in and around Donegal Pass, when it came over the radio that a car with explosives in it was in the Lower Markets by 3 Platoon's Mission Hall. Apparently, it had been stopped by one of 3 Platoon's sections during a VCP. The driver jumped out and told the patrol that he had been stopped by 3 masked men a few miles away and a cardboard box had been placed on the back seat and was told to drive it to the Mission Hall and just leave it there and go.

The balloon went up and the Mission Hall's Sangar and most of the building was evacuated. Our section commander asked if he could help, to which he received the answer 'yes'. He was told to help cordon off the area around the car as Felix and the ATO's guys were on their way. Just then, Felix passed us at a rate of knots, so we followed them out to the area of the Mission Hall and we jumped out of the 2 Land Rovers. 'No PIG?' said a lad from 3 Platoon, 'No,' we replied, 'We're hard bastards!' Then Ted, the commander said:' Bullets bounce right off us!'

'Yeah, right', I thought; 'that's one theory I don't want to put to the test!' and walked over to 3 Platoon's commander, and asked him 'where did he want us?' Now I must tell you this; 3 Platoon's commander was not a happy chap; in fact he was a right miserable twat at the best of times, and all this car bomb stuff really pissed him off.

VCP in Belfast

As Ted approached him, this officer said 'Don't you salute officers?' in the most obnoxious way. To which he replied: 'Ok but some twat with a gun will kill you!' 'Good idea, Ted; salute him', some bright spark shouted! 'Salute! Salute the c*** and be quick!'

Needless to say, this Rupert started to jump up and down like a raving lunatic right in the middle of the Markets; what a prat! We were told to look after the ATO guys, but meanwhile, the owner of the car came to talk to my mate and myself and asked 'What will happen to my car?' we replied: 'Oh, its more than likely to get blown to fucking bits; but don't worry, we'll be ok back here!'

The poor owner started crying, explaining he'd only picked it up that morning; it was a brand new, from the forecourt, Austin 1800. Poor sod; anyway wheel barrow trundled up and blew the side window out of the rear door and then put some explosive in this back seat, next to the box and blew it up! Just the right amount to raise the roof; as the fire brigade was putting out the fire, the box turned out to have a house brick in and with some wires coming out of it.

Poor bastard! And just to add insult to injury, he was told he'd save a fucking fortune on petrol! Never mind; shit happens and we left him crying his eyes out sitting in the gutter.

THE ARDOYNE

Soldier, Royal Corps of Signals

I served in Northern Ireland as a member of the Royal Signals attached to 20 Medium Regt Royal Artillery. In 1974, whilst we were there, we were searching a house in the Ardoyne Area of Belfast; we had a R.A [Royal Artillery] Captain in charge of us.

The house we were searching had a gas leak, and the Officer informed us (as if we had lost all our sense of smell) of the leak, and that he would keep watch outside; presumably to make sure that no-one tried to blow us up!

During the search, he stood in the doorway and lit a cigarette, thus blowing us up! I have never trusted R.A. officers since.

ON THE BORDER: 1974

Keith, Blues & Royals

We received reports that there would be – imminently – a large demonstration by people from the north and south in protest against border closures. So we travelled each weekend down to St Angelo to police them. Nothing happened for the first two weeks and then on the third we were waiting, ready to move. Those of you who remember will recall that, back in the 70s, Sunday morning TV was barely in existence and so we were just watching an 'Open University' programme and nodding off. The programme ended and was followed by a church service featuring a deaf choir. One of the lads said 'I bet they sing with sign language.' When the service started the choir stood up and did, indeed use the sign language. We fell to the floor in fits of laughter. One lad stood up and said that it wasn't funny and, of course, he was right but somehow all the waiting and all the time wasted was forgotten and the moment brought smiles to our faces; I know soldiers acting like kids is nothing new, but it helped us.

A few hours later we were called out and off we went with other troops. When we got there a small event was going on but there wasn't much trouble. We had been told to remove our kidney pouches which contained our mess tins, but a few hours later we were upset when they brought out dinner; stew could be eaten, as we could put that on bread but rice pudding was impossible.

August had come around and the months were slowly ticking away, and this time found us back on the borders. It was rumoured that a local gang was planning a bomb in the south which they would bring over the border. Accordingly, we set OPs around the closed crossing, and on the first night I noted what looked like a man waving some people to move towards us. We were right on the border with the Republic just a stone throw away. I gave the other lads a push, keeping an eye on this person. He had not moved for a while, but every now and then what looked another arm popped up. One of the lads moved along the side and noted he had not moved also, and we kept an eye on this for the rest of the night.

As day light crept over the land, we noted that the 'arm' was a broken young tree and the second was a bull's horn which had been rubbing the tree. As we preparing to get back to look around, the air waves were broken by another team next crossing up from us.

A car with two men had crossed from the south and it had parked up and the other team had been watching it for about five mins when they were joined by another car from the north. One man was pushed out while the other was helping the other crew put what looked a milk churn into the back of the second car. While this was going on the team told base that they had all the men in the sights and had noted that the other man was sitting on the ground away from the others.

We were told to watch and hold our fire and we were saying 'go on you fool: shoot' but we later realized that they were had been correct in their drills. What had been happening was that our mobile back-up team had moved to the crossing to help arrest the bombers. The size of the bomb seized – and made safe – was about 400lb which would have severely damaged the local town.

DIVIS STREET, BELFAST: 1974

Soldier, 1 GLOSTERS

We used to have a system called 'Star Trek' patrol and in this the command element and corps attached, would do the 'dog' watch hours.

One night in the early hours the OC went out with the CSM along with a detachment of Company signallers, Chefs, CQMS Staff and the medic when they were ambushed near the Divis Flats. The Chef was the lead man – known as the 'Bullet Catcher'- and he caught one straight in the throat. As the chaos of the follow-up and all took place, the medic ran over to this poor unfortunate ACC[Army Catering Corps chef, who was now turning deep blue as the wound had swelled up his throat and cut off his airway. This medic, only a Lance Corporal, calmly took apart his Bic Biro, he then cut a hole in the now very still cook's throat, and using the empty plastic tube of the pen as a tracheotomy (and I don't care how you spell that) he inserted it into the hole he had cut, blew into this Biro tube and then sucked and spat out the frothy blood.

The chef survived after a mad dash to the RVH and still attends reunions with this very large scar on his throat. Contrary to some views, he was also a good chef!

A DARK NIGHT IN CO TYRONE, 1974

Keith, Blues and Royals

I was on a covert op one night and was lying down in a field. I could taste the gun oil in my mouth and I can remember seeing some men walking towards me with guns in their hands, coming into our space.

I called command and informed them that gunmen were approaching and asked if there were any of our patrols out there. The answer came back 'No. All clear'. I looked back to where they were and shouted out to them but got no answer back; my hands were shaking as I levelled my weapon at them. Just one more shout, I thought and then I will open fire. I counted 6 in all and could see the man at the rear. I was thinking about the lives I would take, and shouted one final time.

They stopped and I thought 'Thank God!' as I replaced the safety catch. There was a yell and then one man stepped forward as I instructed him and then I recognised his face. He was talking but I couldn't catch the words as my heart was beating so loudly and then all 6 men were in the alley way and they were safe.

I still think of that night and often wake in a sweat, feeling cold, remembering how I almost killed 6 men. The fear and the hurt never goes away as I think of that incident in Co Tyrone.

BILL JACKSON, 1 GLOSTERS
Belfast

I was on my first tour in Ireland and was based at Albert Street Mill with the rest of A Company. Also there was Felix the ATO bomb disposal guy. We had 3 states of patrolling; State 1: that was foot patrols in and around Divis Flats. State 2 which was mobiles in and around Sandy Row Q.R.F. [Quick Reaction Force], and the dogsbody patrol. This could be escort duties, i.e. picking up vehicles from Lisburn, helping out at Tac HQ and doing the hotpot run, which is closing a number barriers in and around Belfast. Finally, state 3 which was like a rest time; staff from personnel, admin, cookhouse duties etc.

Number 1 Platoon was on state 2; each section swapped around and did 8 hours at each task. Well this particular time, it was 11C's turn to go on dogsbody patrol. As it was near 6 o'clock, it was time to get ready to go out on hotpot. This time it would end very differently to how it normally ended.

The last two barriers to be closed were one at the foot of the bridge going into Sandy Row and the one on the junction of Durham Road and Grosvenor Road. This particular night, the Sandy Row barrier had just been closed and the one at Grosvenor Road was in the process of being closed, when this car came from nowhere and tried to get through! Fortunately, the soldier that was closing the barrier was a bit quicker and sent the barrier straight through the car's windscreen.

The rest of the platoon was having something to eat in the cook house at the time and when we all heard what had happened we all, to a man, shouted 'It's got to be Harris!' When the section came back in, the person involved was indeed Harris!

When asked why he had done that his reply was: 'The barrier gets closed at 6 clock and he wasn't about to get past me, so I pushed the barrier shut, which went straight through into the windscreen of the car and nearly took the drivers head off!'

When we pressed him further, Harris replied: 'That's his fault; he was driving the car and he could have braked!' That was life in Belfast!

KEITH, BLUES & ROYALS
Omagh, 1973/74

On the 9th Aug 1973, the Married Quarters (MQ) in Omagh was bombed by the IRA, making it the first garrison in N Ireland to have its MQs attacked in this manner.

The local IRA in Carrickmore halted a postman in his van on his rounds, and forced him to drive his van into the garrison with a 400lbs bomb on board. Why was this not stopped and searched as it entered the MSQ area? The answer is simple; the Royal Mail is not allowed to be interfered with, and the IRA knew this.

There had been no warning given and at that time of day during school holidays, under normal circumstances, the toll would have been worse had not many families been away on leave. At 0920 hours the bomb went off in Alexander Road. The number of people injured was 16 women and children; mainly injured by flying glass. 3 had to be taken to hospital but were able to return home later that day. Amongst those taken to the hospital was a mum-to-be. Two MQs were damaged, but fortunately, the families were away. The main area of damage was up to 200 yards.

This was not to be the last time in my tour that the Quarters in Omagh were hit by bombs, but it would be nearly 8 months later before that happened again.

Our return to Omagh was greeted by a bomb on the 12th in Omagh town centre; what a welcome back! In the first week of February there was another bomb in the town centre; and we quickly realized that a pattern was being set for 1974. It did not stop there, and on the 9th there was an attack with incendiaries. Several shops, including the paint suppliers, were hit and the whole town was badly affected. Then the Crown Office got it and March came and life got no better.

It was while walking his dog that Major Farrell was murdered. He had served in the Royal Inniskilling Fusiliers in Burma and had been working in the Omagh ACIO and he was a real gentleman who would say 'good morning' as he passed you with his dog (a German hunting dog) and you were always greeted warmly.

[Major Donald Farrell was a retired Army officer who was working in the Careers office; whilst parking his car at the village of Glebe near Omagh, he was shot 5 times by a Republican organisation. His badly wounded dog was put down by a soldier who arrived on the scene with a patrol]

It was starting to warm up, Spring had arrived and then came the month of May; just 6 months to the tour's end, but no one said it out loud. This particular month started off sadly with lost of Eva Martin at the Deanery; she was the first Green Finch [female UDR] to be killed. There was an attack on the building Eva was working in and she was making her way to safety down the stairs when an RPG 7 was fired at the building. This hit the area of the stairwell that Eva was on and she was sadly killed. She was found by her husband Richard who was in the same unit. Eva was a local school teacher, whom I had never met but from what others told me she was a lovely woman.

This was the beginning of a bad month but we did not know it then.

Keith refers to 28 year old Eva Martin, a UDR soldier and the first UDR female to be killed in the troubles. It is believed that almost 40 IRA members were used in the attack on the base at Clogher and they used a number of cars to clog up the surrounding roads, greatly exacerbating the post-attack chaos.

In relation to the attack on the MQs at the camp in Omagh, the IRA must have known that only women and children would have been around at the time of day (9:20 am) the device exploded. Many in the RTR felt at the time that it was a desperate attempt for publicity after a period of reverse.

TOUR 4 – THE LOWER FALLS (WHAT AGAIN ?) 1974
Sergeant Mike Heavens, 1st Glosters

1 Glosters were warned off for a Belfast Operation Banner Tour, centred on the Lower Falls again, from August to December 1974.

I went on the advance party once again but this time found myself in the Markets area, not that you could notice much difference between there and the

Lower Falls – same sullen faces, mean dirty streets, murals of the 'heroes' and graffiti everywhere. You could tell where the one area stopped and another began as the curb stones went from orange, white and green to red, white and blue, whilst the tricolour fluttered on these lamp posts but the union flag flew from those! We had only been there a couple of weeks when my platoon commander was knocked down and injured during a VCP op next to the Ulster TV building. Road traffic accidents, of various sorts, caused more casualties than the troubles ever did! Alone in the Gasworks in the Markets area of Belfast, what more could a young Platoon Sergeant ask for. In the main wall of the gasworks at a height of about 35 feet there was a hole and behind that hole on scaffolding was the Sangar known as 'the Klondike', it was very close to the local pub (you could watch all the doors or roads to it) and it looked straight down the main road into Belfast city centre from the south of the city.

The locals did not like this and the day after a call sign found an arms cache in Essex street they let us know their displeasure! That night 'Lofty' Painter from Birmingham was the Sangar sentry and he was supposed to be bright eyed and bushy tailed alert, but he was having a crafty fag and keeping his hands warm whilst peering through the observation slit, so one of the local stickies (because this area of the Markets was Official IRA and there had been several skirmishes to keep it that way), took aim at the glow and gave him a good part of a mag of M1 Carbine rounds! 4 of these rounds came through the observation slit removing Lofty's beret and turning his underwear smelly! Luckily for him that was the extent of his injuries as he had flung himself backwards off of the stool he was sitting on and ended up in an ignominious heap, whilst the dust settled on his head and the smell of burnt cordite and shattered brickwork pervaded the air.

It was the Provos turn next and they left a car bomb outside the Sangar up against the base wall. ATO got to it before it functioned but in disrupting it, part of the device initiated and Havelock House (Ulster TV) had a good spattering of debris and lost a fair bit of glass, but the Klondike survived.

The Prods too were active and one evening a group of 4 in a car deliberately ran into a group of [Catholic] teenagers standing on the corner of Essex Street mowing down two of them; unfortunately for them the car stalled, a mob gathered and they were severely beaten. We got there real quick, rescued the two that were out on the road getting a kicking and whilst they were put into the PIG with a guard, we then had to wade through a very hostile mob to get to the other two still in the car and getting a severe going over. Under a barrage of missiles, clubs and fists, we got these guys out of the car and into the close-by mission, this being a local Christian charity and here the lovely staff, despite their political beliefs, gave these people some first aid, whilst we barricaded the front and back doors until the RUC arrived and got them away.

I was pleased to see later that they got 10 years for this offence and the two kids recovered completely; the locals gave us a certain amount of grudging (very grudging) respect for a while after. About this time the powers that be had another TAOR [Tactical area of responsibility] change and the Gasworks was abandoned to its fate. We went to the Unity Flats and Tiger Bay area and after a short while, the gasworks was attacked and bombed by the Provos, but the unit doing the raid cocked it up and destroyed themselves as well as a giant

Tear gas in Londonderry

gasometer. This simply collapsed in on itself into the water-filled safety area. The IRA ASU though, lost 2 men when the device functioned early, one so badly taken apart by his own blast that his torso was found high up on the remaining gantry.

The tour staggered on to its inevitable end with the usual long hours of knackering duties, troubled sleep time and short bursts of high excitement and after what seemed an eternity, it was back to Minden.

Thankfully, Mike's regiment, the Glosters lost no men on that tour, but during their 5 months on the Falls, in the Anderstown area (to the west of where the Glosters were) an Irish Guards soldier, Guardsman Samuel Murphy, was murdered off duty visiting his mother in Bernagh Drive in the November.

This was also the year in which the 1,000th victim of the troubles was killed. On January 21, in the Bogside area of Londonderry, Sergeant John Haughey was killed by an IRA booby trap. The next milestone of 2,000 would be reached only 49 months later.

BELFAST: JULY 21, 1974
Geoff Smith, Light Infantry

It was dark, not raining, at least as far as I can remember, I had been standing around the Ops Room when we got a slidex message in from one of the covert

OPs. They had heard shots in a derelict house not far from them. They could not assist who had been shot because they would have compromised themselves. The OC and 2IC, with their escorts, crashed out with the standby platoon. I was in 2IC's crew that night. Really I was in whoever's crew it was that needed me.

We drove out of the company base, Mullhouse, and into the Distillery area of Belfast, This was a run down, dirty, almost completely derelict area. Practically all the windows had been blocked up. It was a dull place, terraced houses, corners, and back lanes, dark. We stopped in a street; I think it was Arundel Street off Grosvenor Road, opposite what was the junction of Cullingtree Road that ran through the Falls area.

We then did a brief search of the suspected house that the shots had come from. Eventually we found him. The body. The human being whose life had just been snuffed out. The OC and 2IC walked into a house and came back out shortly afterwards and said there was a body in the passage. Someone, I cannot remember now, possibly the OC (he was a good man the OC, one of the best) took me to the house entrance and shone his torch to the very end. I looked along the line of the torch. My eyes focused on an empty passageway, you know the long passages you used to get in downstairs terraced houses. The walls had paper hanging off, I seem to remember maybe a door off to the left halfway down and what I imagined was a corner off to the left at the very end, possibly into a living room. The floor was not a floor, just joists running left to right and what looked like a void of darkness beneath them. I took all this in, in an instance. Then suddenly I realised I had been looking at the body all the time. I somehow had taken the whole scene in two separate images within my mind's eye.

The body was lying at the far end of the passage, I seem to remember, crumpled up in a face-down position. It was straddled across the end three or four floor joists. It was wearing a pair of green trousers that looked slightly flared at the bottom, brown shoes that looked soldier polished and a car coat, a short mid-thigh thing that was brown with cheap vinyl edging. Someone said 'He's dead, shot in the head.' The torch went out and I backed away from the door and stood by the Land Rover.

Then the van arrived. I honestly can't remember if there was a policeman there or not. There probably was, but I just can't recall. The van ... that bloody van, black. It was, I am sure, a Morris van, the type that was used extensively by delivery drivers in the late 60s and early 70s. You must remember, the steering wheel was almost forward of the windscreen and parallel to the ground; the engine was between the driver's seat and passenger's seat. It has stayed in my mind ever since ... the van and oh yes! that bloody stretcher.

The stretcher was white or cream. I was not sure in the darkness, I would say white. What is your idea of a stretcher? Two wooden poles with canvass stretched between. We have all seen them. That's my idea of a stretcher. But not this stretcher. Not this bloody stretcher. It was metal, yes metal. A metal frame, a metal frame that has steel mesh instead of canvass. I looked at it as it was carried past me into the passageway of the house. I knew what I would feel when that bloody stretcher came past the next time. I did feel what I thought I was going to feel. Revulsion, sickness in the pit of my stomach. My God, could they not even take this body away decently on a proper stretcher? Like they would at a road traffic accident. Why not? this was a human being; this was once a living thing. Why on this bloody stretcher?

They opened the back doors of the van and for me, pushed the bloody stretcher in far too fast to be respectful. Like something in the butcher's shop, it was a nothing to them, those horrible men who tossed that bloody stretcher into the back of that van. Someone said 'That's another one for the meat wagon.' Then I understood ... it was a piece of meat. They slammed the doors and drove off. Just like that. It was nothing to them, just another job; they had probably got used to it living and working in that horrible place.

After a while a man in plain clothes walked up to where the OC. 2IC myself and someone else were standing and said 'He had been shot twice in the head, once in the back with a trussion at the front and once in the front with a trussion at the back.' I pondered what this word trussion was and the OC told me it was where the bullet had stopped but failed to come out; simply a lump. We all went back to base.

Later, not much later I had been informed that the body was that of a soldier – an ex-Royal Green Jacket who had recently married his Belfast girlfriend. He had been in a bar in the Markets area of Belfast and had been kidnapped, taken to the house and shot. But I can't remember his face; perhaps I never actually saw his face ... all I can remember is that Bloody Stretcher.

[Brian Shaw was 21 and had, as the soldier quoted above says, been in the Royal Green Jackets and had served three tours with Regiment in Northern Ireland. He was abducted and murdered by the IRA after his marriage to a local girl and was on his honeymoon back in her native city. Picked up by the IRA in the Cornmarket area, he was taken to a disused house in Arundel Street and then murdered.]

We were doing a mobile patrol in and around Dougal Pass and we were in Land Rovers. These were the days before we were stopped from using Rovers.

[The Land Rover was the beast of burden for the Army and the mainstay of its transport, but it was no match for RPGs or HE devices as it was too soft-skinned].

It was a Saturday and a nice sunny day and it must have been about the end of August or the beginning of September. We had not long got to the pass from Albert Street Mill, and, as we were going down, I think, Elm Street, the incident happened. We were near the bottom, when there was a loud pop and the Rover started to swerve all over the road. Ted managed to get the Rover he was driving, stopped and we all jumped out thinking it was a contact [i.e. an incoming round] only to find it was a puncture!

Well, if you could have seen it; 10 hairy-arsed solders running around like idiots and a Land Rover with a flat tyre! It was like 'Clowns 'r us'! Worse was to follow, as the breakdown kit was no bloody good; the only thing that worked was the wheel brace. So one bloke loosened the wheel nuts and then 4 of us had to lift one side of the Rover! We managed to take the wheel off then some daft prat said all we need is a contact and we're fucked!

Now, Ted being Ted who was our section commander at the time thought it was very funny and he grabbed a baton and slammed it on the roof the vehicle. We nearly shit ourselves; one lad ran away and one nearly pissed himself; and the other went the colour of boiled shit and the rest of the section fell about in fits of laughter!

One of the lads asked why he did it and he told us that seemed like a good idea at the time and went off laughing his head off!

We put the wheel back on the Rover and carried on with our patrol; just another fun filled day for 11 Charley!

THE CHIP SHOP OP

Major Andrew Macdonald, 1 King's Own Border Rgt

The Chip Shop OP is so called because for 21 days we ran an operation to maintain a covert Observation Post (OP) in the derelict roof space above a chip shop on the Falls Road in Belfast during the height of the troubles but a period that included the so-called cease fire in 1974.

I was an experienced platoon commander stationed with my company in the Lower Falls in Belfast. Much of that part of the city was run down and undergoing redevelopment and there was considerable potential for hiding out in OPs in old buildings. Much of our intelligence was gained through watching and photographing from these locations.

I had an additional responsibility as company OP officer. The job was important because every unit had to produce a detailed report at the end of its patrol which provided information on, amongst other things, sightings and incidents, the state of buildings. The aim was to maintain an updated log of possible OP sites.

Typically, we'd occupy an OP with four men for 2–3 days until we had sufficient information (photographic, usually) on the target house, person or people, or until we were compromised (local children were sent into derelicts to check out for lurking Army patrols).

One day, I was summonsed by the Battalion Intelligence Officer who called me into a private office in the base (Mullhouse – an old disused mill). A man was ushered into the room. I thought he was a tramp but he introduced himself as 'John' and much I later found out that he'd been living locally, under cover. He was an early version of the plain clothes surveillance operators. How he did this I'll never know to this day – brave man.

He told me that I had a job to do which was to find a place from where we could observe and photograph the XXX centre (too politically sensitive to put onto paper but they're highly respectable now!). They (the Intelligence people) needed photographic evidence of the comings and goings from the building. It later transpired that, amongst other things, this location was used as a staging point for the transfer of bombs which would then be carried into the city centre to feed the bombing campaign (at its height in the mid 70s).

I told John that I knew the place well and that there was no place from where we could carry out any covert surveillance. He told me how important it was and to go and have another look and find somewhere.

The target building bordered our inter-company boundary, so I asked my colleagues in our sister company whether they knew whether we could do this from their side of the road. They said, no chance etc. I was not convinced and knew I had to look myself. As crossing the boundaries is a sensitive matter in the parochial world of the military, I asked to go and see for myself with one of their patrols.

These sorts of recces take place in the very small hours. Over the next two weeks on several outings we searched for somewhere to use. I pushed very hard to investigate every possible solution and hey presto, on the third of these recces (I think), we discovered that by entering over a back wall using two sets of ladders and balancing like alley cats, we could gain access to the roof void above the unused upper floor above a Fish and Chip shop. We got in there to check out the angles and found that a viewing hole just under the eaves already existed (bricks loosened and removed) which was probably from an Army operation years previously (so much for up-to-date records).

Two weeks later we mounted the operation and maintained it for 21 days during which we changed teams 4 times. Time and space precludes me going into the comical goings on to get the daily film and micro-tape recordings out to the passing patrols, the changeover antics, as well as the disposal of human waste. Say no more! Indeed, how and why the OP was compromised just 6 hours before it was due to be pulled out is another story in itself and is best told by those who were in the OP at the time!

Whatever, the end results were startling.

Suffice to say that whilst we did not know who we were looking at, except that most of the 'faces' all had code words and some we knew from our local knowledge, we do know that the Int guys identified many senior terrorists from that operation. Our work provided photographic evidence that became invaluable in the intelligence war. Of additional importance was that they (the terrorists) really had no idea how long the OP had been watching them for and what evidence we had gained – much uncertainty in their ranks.

The operation had many flaws in its procedures and operating systems – there had been no proper training for this sort of thing pre-tour and the kit issued was not designed for such operations. However, the operation contributed to the formation of formal training and establishment of systems and processes that eventually led to 'close observation' units that became deployed as the norm in future operations province-wide.

IRA CAPTIVES

Corporal, Light Infantry

There were several vehicles, armoured PIGs, in the car park outside Flax Mill, Belfast. Each held about ten squaddies; an infantry section. I can't remember now if we were all there because we were about to go out on an operation, or if we had just returned.

A radio message came over the air that a patrol in the Ardoyne area had spotted and arrested two wanted men. It was suggested that they might even hold positions of importance in the local Irish Republican Army. Possibly company commanders, quartermasters or even known snipers!

A PIG swung into the car park and as the back doors were opened two men in civilian clothes tumbled out the back. Three or four of the parked PIGs disgorged soldiers who ran towards the civvies and boots and firsts were thrown. Young men in my Section whooped with elation, but I prevented them from leaving the vehicle.

Within seconds some thirty to forty soldiers had surrounded the boys on the ground, some kicks and punches were thrown. Two or three officers ran out from the Mill shouting and waving the crowd away.

One of the officers noticed that my section was still aboard our vehicle, and brought the two terrified young boys in and their escorts across to me. I was ordered to take them to TAC HQ (or wherever arrested men were to be taken).

The two 'terrorists' were very young, no more than seventeen. Their trouser legs, in the fashion of the Belfast youth, only reached down to their calves, and their jackets looked too small.

On arrival the intelligence people came rushing out to greet us. They looked in the back of the PIG. Their faces dropped. 'Who the f**k are they?' The reception committee was furious, 'Take 'em back, and drop them off where you found them!' I was told.

We drove into the Ardoyne and the two boys, still shaken by their ordeal in the car park, climbed out of the PIG and stood hands in pockets glaring at us as we drove off.

If they hadn't been IRA sympathisers before, they were now!

Later whilst on leave I overheard some people talking in a pub in Gravesend in Kent about the Vietnam 'My Lai Incident.' They condemned the American soldiers and added British soldiers would never act like that!

When I related to the civilians what I had seen in the Flax Street Mill car park a few weeks earlier they didn't believe me. The landlord was so angry with me he asked me to leave the building!

Bernie Homer, 1 Glosters

1974 ... We were carrying out a search operation in, I believe, the Mulhouse area, searching whole streets. I was in the back garden of a house, with two of my mates providing cover for the search team, where an old lady lived. She came out with 3 cups of tea for us. I remember saying 'thank you' to her and she promptly put her finger to her lips and told us not to say it too loud.

We immediately knew why she had said that and I felt really sad that she was afraid to be thanked in case someone overheard. That, I'm afraid, is the saddest piece of memory I know; she was an old lady who was a human being, whatever the people were around her.

I felt saddish because my family are Irish and I am proud of that, and my grandfather fought for the IRA in 1916. But I am English, born and bred and also proud of that. But I was a Gloster and that counted more than anything, I was protecting my mates/friends.

BALLYMACARRET, BELFAST 1974
Haydn Davies, CSM Support Company RRW

A hugely fat girl whose language was very extreme used to abuse the front gate Sangar sentry whenever she passed the company position. She was mostly ignored but eventually she hit on a tactic that put the whole company right up in arms. She stopped the bad language and abuse, and started to whistle the theme from 'Dad's Army' at us. This was far more than the boys could stand. The girl had now declared total war. She would stand facing the big tin security gates with her hands on her oversized hips and whistle the tune very professionally and loudly from beginning to end.

One late afternoon while I was in the upper Sangar, I saw her approach and commence her routine for the benefit of the sentry in the Sangar below. She was halfway through her act when I saw a very young Welsh Soldier with rage written all over his face run from the Sangar side gate which was to her rear. He ran up behind her and forcibly put his size seven army boot most firmly into her big fat arse and somewhat lifted her off the ground with the force. He disappeared very quickly back through the gate, the company honour now being fully restored.

What the kicker did not know was that he was captured on the perimeter CCTV. No action was taken against him, but we had great chuckles in the Ops room watching secret re-runs.

GEOFF SMITH, LIGHT INFANTRY

Belfast, 1974

[The sauna] had been opened just a few days. I had never had one in my life but had heard about how cleansing they were. The sauna of course: the one in Albert Street Mill. We heard that Geordie Dee the QM had one installed at the Mill, and, it was open to all ... too good to miss this opportunity but, who do I get to go with me and, how do I get there? After asking a few questions in the right ears, namely B Company commander's ears, I was given the ok. So I started my hunt for a driver and an escort for the journey to Albert Street Mill. I managed to find them all within the space of a few minutes without too much persuasion and bother. Guff was the driver, Katy Boyle and Bob Hutch from 5 Platoon the escorts. Dead easy really – we all wanted to try the sauna. So I grabbed a radio and we all headed into the vehicle park to get a Land Rover. I jumped in the front, Guff jumped in to the driver's seat whilst Katy and Bob jumped on the tailgate and away we went.

Bob Guffick was Coy HQ and was a cheerful Hartlepuddlean who during the 74 tour went around Mullhouse singing Abba's song *Waterloo* but replaced Waterloo with Hartlepool. Katy Boyle and Bob Hutchinson were excellent soldiers always talked to people with respect and knew their business as soldiers. I had a lot of respect for them both.

Anyway, we got to Albert Street ok and got into the sauna. It was brilliant. I marvelled at this thing in the middle of the floor full of hot stones I took great pleasure in dropping a mug of water on it from time to time. It was very relaxing. Then it was time to go.

We loaded up and started back to Mulhouse in the Distillery Area. This journey required us to pass through the worst area in Belfast. The Lower Falls. ('B' Company were having a hard time of it. Shootings, Weapons Finds Riots, you name it, 'B' Company had to deal with it). When we were driving along Cullingtree Road, which ran across to the Lower Falls area and on to Grosvenor Road, we had just passed what I think was the junction of Leeson Street when suddenly from out of the darkness leading into a back lane, I saw a brilliant light arcing towards me, the Land Rover and everyone else on board. This brilliant light was just like a sparkler, you know, when you throw a sparkler through the air how it keeps sparkling and draws an imaginary light trail behind it. That's how it was. A sparkler had been tossed at us by some appreciating Roman Catholic cheering us on our way ... I think not. In a fleeting moment I imagined it as a sparkler – nothing else crossed my mind. It was a sparkler ... what else could it be? This sparkler landed right in front of the Land Rover more or less in line with my seat. And, we drove right over it.

All of a sudden all hell broke loose from behind me ... 'Blast Bomb' was shouted in perfect unison by Katy and Bob riding shotgun on the tailgate and a mad scramble as both clambered into the armoured rear of the Land Rover. Then it went off ... 'Boom.' Then in a flash of seconds a number of things happened. Katy and Bob got back on the tail gate and someone shouted 'Hot Pursuit' which was brave of them, I felt myself being forced back into the back of my seat as I started speaking into the handset of my radio 'Contact, wait, out, Blast Bomb Thrown in Cullingtree Road. Blast Bomb Thrown in Cullingtree Road, Blast Bomb Thrown in Cullingtree Road'. Like some rambling idiot. I was thrown into the back of my seat not through any bomb blast but by Guff putting his foot down and going hell for leather past the back lane and across Grosvenor Road – without looking left or right.

Anyway, I was starting to worry at this point as to where some form of backup was coming from. I had heard no response to my radio message. I had fully expected that all of' 'B Company and the SAS were on their way to bring us all back safely. But nothing. Suddenly we were back at the base. I jumped off the Land Rover and ran to the Ops room, where Major Nich and the crash out platoon commander were looking at the Ops Map and talking about a bomb blast they had heard. I shouted out 'It was thrown at us in Cullingtree Road. Did you not hear my radio message ?' 'No' replied Major Nich and without looking for a response from me said 'Why did you not do a hot pursuit ?'

Major Nich walked away from the Ops Room map and was starting to strap his pistol on and as he walked past me he said, out of earshot of everyone else in the Ops room 'TRY PRESSING YOUR MIC SWITCH NEXT TIME YOU SEND A CONTACT REPORT.' ... Boy did I feel stupid ...

I am thankful for three things on that night; the first, was that we had taken an armoured Land Rover and not the open-topped one. The second was that I had two really professional soldiers as escorts who knew their business and thirdly that I had Guff as driver who had the presence of mind to put his foot down and get us all away from a possible ambush AND that he did so without giving me the chance to even consider doing a 'Hot Pursuit.'

THE BOMB AND UWC STRIKE: 1974

Soldier, Blues & Royals

You always remember important events, as though they only happened yesterday or even just a few hours ago. The sounds, the colours and smells; that is what the night of the 9th May 1974 is to me. It started like any other night; children to put to bed and then settle down for a few hours peace.

It was about 9 when our dog Sue wanted to go out. She had been on heat and it was to be her first round around the field where there were loads of rabbits. She had not been out long when I heard her yelp, so I went to the front door to call her and see what was up. One of the guys from the ACIO was coming along the walk way. He said to me 'Keith; I think we have a suspect device outside the office. Can you go around this area warning people?' I told the wife to get the kids up and move across to our friend's house. While she was doing that I went around warning people, and the reason why I moved my family to our friends was we were only 80 meters from the car and we were facing it.

It was around midnight when the RUC officers started shouting 'Get out! Get out!' I was at the front door and started to shout as well just in case some people hadn't heard them. It was a second but it seemed longer; I looked in to see my daughter getting off the chair when, 'bang' she was half way between the door and the chair and she was running as fast as her little 3 year old legs could make her. I turned for one final look and she was being followed by dust, wood and glass. I was trying to putting my body between myself and any glass, wood etc and my 1 year old son. This all happened in seconds and I thought 'no Lord; please look after her, please.'

This scene has given me many nightmares over the years. Waking up sweating. I looked down the hall way but she was not there. I panicked and then I saw her under the stairs with my wife and friends. My heart stopped beating quite so fast. Were they ok? I went in, trampling over broken glass and could see that my daughter was crying, but a hug and kind words helped her. My wife was ok. She wanted to see how our home was. That was not allowed at that point but after what seemed a lifetime we were allowed to go and check, get a few things and make our way over to the UDR barracks.

I went across; all the windows had gone and in our kitchen my bike had been thrown across the room. All the army cups, plates and glassware had been blown out of the cupboard and smashed.

The stairs were moving side to side and at the top, the bedroom wall was leaning outwards. In our living room, the new curtains looked like shredded nets and the wall was learning in. There was a part of the car embedded in the wall; I remember that it was part of the axle. The carpet had been battered and on parts you could see the burns and yet another new item now damaged. Items were gone from the window sill and there were dozens of plates broken that had once hung on the wall.

As I reached the top of the stairs, I could smell a mixture of Chanel 19 and my aftershaves, which did not mix well with my wife's perfumes. The floorboards near the window were herringbone shaped; all raised and touching each other. Our bed was covered in car bits. The curtains like those downstairs were now like netting. The front rooms away from the bomb were ok and the children's' room was soon to become the family bedroom, while the repair work took place; but for now very little damage.

I had only been in the house a 10 minutes when the call was put out that they thought there might be another bomb So I left and we moved across to the UDR camp where we able to get a hot drink. I cannot recall how long we were in there, but I do remember dawn coming up when they allowed us to return to our homes. My mate David and I walked around to where the bomb had gone off; you could still smell and it was just like being in a WW2 film just after the Blitz.

When we got back we checked my neighbour's home as he was away visiting his wife's family in another part of N Ireland. As we walked in we noticed the sword which had hung on one wall was stuck in another wall. We removed and put it on a chair. We did not see any car parts as he was to the side of me and the other block of maisonettes saved him from a lot of damage. We went upstairs we walked in the master bedroom, where, to our front was the baby cot and right in the middle was a large pieces of glass were the baby would have lain. When he returned I was telling him that we did not hear his wife come up the stairs. She heard me telling him she screamed. It took a few seconds to clam her down.

The DOE started on the work right away, but the problem was that while we were getting our homes sorted out, the Ulster Workers Council was bringing Belfast and then N Ireland to a stop on the Wednesday, 15 May 1974. It was just 5 days after the bomb, windows were in some and in others they were still boarded up. We were still sleeping in the kid's bedroom, but the problem we faced was loss of electricity, and we did not have gas. We went into Omagh and there were almost no camping stoves to be had and all I managed was a single burner. The UDR came to the rescue by allowing the wives to use the kitchens which was a great help.

After a while, we had full electricity again and the coalman knocked at the door, as we had been told we could refit the coal fires a few days earlier. It would mean we would be warm again and he said he would return on Friday for the cash; he did not and we were told that he was warned off by the UWC strikers.

A few days later it was over; the workmen returned next day and got on with repairing the homes. May was over and the strike had lasted 2 weeks.

BELFAST FIRE, 1974

Ernie Taylor, 3 LI

It was the middle of the afternoon, and we were in a side street next to the Mission; 3 Section had been called out as there was a huge fire. One of the guys, Cabbage, grabbed a fire extinguisher (I think it was him) and we all we all ran down the street and went to the front door and could see that, outside the house, there was loads of smoke. We couldn't get in, and so we broke a window and could see that there were kids inside.

We had the extinguisher, but the frigging thing was totally U.S., but we used it up anyway. We couldn't do anything at the front so we went to the back; I think it was Jim [Jim Parker, Corporal] who sent us round. I can't remember the order anymore, but there was Benny, Corporal Jim, 'Cabbage' and me, and the only thing that has stuck with me, is what we found.

The Fire Brigade was there and water was everywhere, but that's not what upset me; the stupid father had nailed the back door shut ! The kids couldn't get out but the stupid xxxx was happy because he was on holiday in the 'Kesh [Long Kesh Internment Camp]

We had to carry his poor babies out; we carried a 2 year old boy and his four old sister from the back kitchen where they had been hiding under the kitchen sink next to the fucking door and the taps were on.

The doctor has been at me to rest because I'm getting flashbacks from something that I thought I had dealt with over thirty years ago; I still can't get rid of the smell, even to this day. I think that they've got a posh name for what troubles me these days; anyway, I was taken back to Minden, Germany where I saw the nut doctor. I thought that I was fine, even though I kept disappearing and throwing wobblies; anyway, they kept me in there for a while, and then shipped me to the depot and immediately told me to hand in my kit; all of my kit! They didn't leave me a pair of skiddies or a suitcase, and then I was out; discharged; temperamentally unsuited; whatever that means !

They gave me a train ticket home and that was it; years later, I had to go down to the Recruitment office to demand my GSM !

And I still can't get those kids off my mind, as if it wasn't bad enough that we couldn't get in to save them.

Corporal Jim Parker was also involved in the incident and he writes:

With regards to the story by Ernie Taylor; he was in my section. I remember the incident, he and Cabbage (Frankenstein) went around the back, and I was at the front. I knew Cabbage carried the bodies out, but had forgotten that Taylor did it too.

The fire was caused by a colour TV setting fire (this happened on two occasions, which I know of). The back lanes of those houses were absolutely filthy; the father or mother had nailed the door shut to stop the kiddies going out there. Ernie talks of two Jims, that was me, and Jimmy Lister, a Private, my lead scout. I never at any time entered the house. I was at the front of the house, in a very Republican area. I thought only big Pte Steve Pearce, (aka Cabbage and Frankenstein) went around the back. Because he was such a huge guy he was used for various jobs, like arresting people. Whilst on the cordon a woman brought us tea, the neighbours warned her against doing so but she replied to the effect, 'They are helping us, I don't care!'

AFTER THE UWC STRIKE
Soldier, Blues & Royals

Some lads had been tasked to another area to help during the UWC (Ulster Workers Council, a Protestant organization) strike. A local well-known family had spotted our new boys (the older hands among us knew how to handle these people) and gave them hell for the few days that they were there.

It was on the last night and some of the newer lads who had been verbally and mentally roughed up thought 'we are going to get our own back on this lot.' So one of them asked if there were any broken plates or broken cups which no one wanted and was given a few. That night, the last patrol took place and so out went the cups etc. As they came near the house of the family with the biggest mouths, they stopped, got the tray out with the cups and walked up to the front door making as much nose as he could. Making no effort whatsoever to keep his voice low he said to the man who answered the door: 'Thank you for the brew; the cakes your wife got us were spot on.' And off they went. The next morning, as they left the area, they went past the house. The father was sitting on the step with a bruised face and all their windows were smashed. Their kids were sitting by their dad as all their neighbours were standing around and cursing them.

Revenge was sweet!

OBITUARY OF PTE WAYNE ROBERT SMITH QGM

From Geoff Smith, Light Infantry

In March 1974 he moved with B Coy to the Lower Falls area of Belfast stationed in Mulhouse Company Base. On 13 May 1974 he was a member of a patrol in Distillery Street when his patrol came under fire.

Wayne saw a child standing in the road in the line of fire and dashed out into the shooting and bundled the child into a doorway out of harm's way. For his coolness and courage he was awarded the Queen's Gallantry Medal.

CREGGAN ESTATE, LONDONDERRY: 1974

Chas Hawley, 1st Bn Grenadier Guards

It was the 27th May 1974, and we were just relaxing listening to 'Band on the Run' in the comfort of our superb digs at 'Piggery Ridge' on the hill at Creggan Heights. Always amused me; what a great easy target we really were, stuck on top of the hill. We had only been there a week, and the top of a sangar was blown off.

Anyway, off we popped with my four man patrol led by my great leader 'Rompers' (I was just eighteen and two months at the time). About an hour into the patrol, the camp had been shot at with, thankfully no casualties, just a couple of shots at a returning Land Rover; we moved to the back of the shops on Central Drive.

Rompers and Harry at the front of the patrol were then approached by two young girls and a boy. A few words were exchanged and Rompers asked all to open up their coats. This they did and they were then sent on their way. They were then greeted by Gary and me, 'tail-end Charlie.'

I then asked them to open up their coats, and they pleasantly informed me that this they had just done. I then told them to try again and also to take their hands out of their pockets; this they did and duly dropped an Armalite, .38 pistol, clip of ammo and a comb. They were all searched and immediately placed on the deck, spread-eagled. Looking up, I could see Rompers and Harry, totally unaware what was going on and still tabbing down the street. That was funny.

We did shout to him and he then got on the radio (Pye set) and soon reinforcements arrived at our location. By this time, a crowd had gathered, as we had caused a bit of a commotion and 'Armalite Harry' (some irate IRA commander) was wondering were his gear was.

Major Manners arrived, cracking Coy Commander; this was 3 Company's first find and spirits were high. One of the girls asked the Major if she could put her coat back on and he nodded, but also told her, 'Try to run and this guy will shoot you.' That remark did sink in and reinforced that this place was vile. Then it was back to the camp, made a statement and back to the room and 'Sailor Sam-Band on the Run.'

Rosemary Fisher, John Joseph Fisher and Bernadette Campbell were all arrested by myself and received 3 years each; they were all sixteen.

DIVIS STREET: 1974

Sergeant John Silkstone, RAMC (attached Glosters)

Our time in Northern Ireland was spent at the police station opposite Divis Flats; the Flats were a social housing complex built on the edge of West Belfast's Catholic area, near the city centre. The Army occupied the two top floors of Divis Tower as their surveillance centre, because of its commanding overview of Belfast City.

One day the alarm sounded, and the ambulance, which was a converted Saracen, sped out of the gate – to collide with a VW Beatle. The driver stopped, and I told him to get going as a police officer had been injured in a blast down town. On our return, the local police stated that they were charging the driver for leaving the scene of an accident. I informed them of the facts, and that it was one of their own who had been injured, but they would not relent. The following afternoon, there was a march in the street. It was usual for the marchers to throw bottles of paint and paint stripper over the wall into the police parking area as they went by. The police began to move their cars from the police compound to park them in the ambulance compound, which was at the rear of the station. I

A new sport: stoning a Saracen
(photo courtesy of Eamon Melaugh)

quickly shut the gate to our compound to stop them entering. In the discussion that followed, I informed the police officers that, as my driver was being charged for an offence when he was just helping one of their comrades who had been injured, I was not going to be charged for helping more than twenty of them by allowing their cars to be parked in the safety of our compound. The charge against my driver was dropped and I opened the gate.

One evening the alarm sounded; by the time the ambulance was ready to leave the location the doctor had still not appeared, so I went off to the accident without him. The casualty turned out to be a civilian who had been hit by a car, and by the shape of his right leg it was obviously broken. He refused to allow us to treat him, and so we waited until the civil ambulance arrived to take him to the hospital.

After splinting his leg, they placed him on a stretcher – but, while placing him in the ambulance, one of the ambulance men slipped, throwing the patient off the stretcher and onto the floor.

On our return to base, the doctor was waiting. He informed me that he had been on the telephone, and by the time he'd got from the back of the building to the medical centre I had gone. A couple of evenings later, the same type of incident happened again; once more I left without the doctor, who was taking a shower at the time.

The third time the alarm went off, we ran out of the medical centre. As I ran to the ambulance, I was wondering if the doctor would make it this time. As I dived into the rear of the vehicle, there was the doctor lying on a stretcher reading a book. Looking over the top of the book he said, 'You're not leaving me behind this time, Sergeant Silkstone.' I gave him ten out of ten for initiative.

While visiting one of the locations the RCT driver and I were walking past one of the walls when a bomb went off on the other side. The area was strewn with

Divis Flats (photo courtesy of Regimental Museum of The Royal Welsh)

pieces of brick and rubble, and the driver and I were knocked to the floor. I was not injured, but I was disorientated – and there was a terrible ringing in my ears which lasted for about three days. The driver was hit by a piece of flying masonry, and thankfully his flak jacket saved him from serious injury. After being seen by the military doctors at Musgrave Park Hospital, we were both allowed back to camp.

The thing that angered me about Northern Ireland was that the other lads and I had to pay to be there. Living in Germany, we had overseas allowance; when posted to Northern Ireland, this allowance was stopped. So in effect your pay was reduced for defending your country against terrorism and helping the police to perform their duty.

Back in West Germany, one day we had just sat down to Sunday lunch when a car backfired; within a split second I was under the table, with visions in my head of the bomb incident back in Belfast. I will never forget the look of horror on Jan's face as I climbed out from under the table. It then hit home how much she'd worried about my safety while I was away in Northern Ireland. I expect all wives worry about their husbands in such circumstances, but while performing my duty I needed my wits about me and couldn't afford to think about the wife worrying back home. That may sound hard and cruel, but self preservation is a fact of life.

Chapter Eight

1975

A year of 691 bombings, 1,803 shootings and the deaths of 20 soldiers, 11 RUC officers, 196 civilians and 20 terrorists.

This year also saw the loss of the first policewoman during the current troubles, when Mildred Ann Harrison was killed by a bomb whilst on foot patrol in Co. Down.

In the August, the IRA displayed its classic sectarianism by making a gun and bomb attack on the 'Bayardo' bar in the Protestant Shankhill Road. 4 innocent Protestants with no paramilitary links were killed and 60 were injured.

It also witnessed, on April 12, the UVF make a gun and bomb attack on the 'Strand Bar' in Belfast's Short Strand area which killed 6. This was, apparently a retaliatory attack for a Republican attack on the 'Mountainview Tavern' on the Shankhill Road, Belfast which left 5 dead, exactly a week earlier.

In this year, the UVF staged a fake UDR roadblock and stopped a bus carrying a group of musicians returning from the Republic, the Miami Showband bus. They loaded a bomb on board, intending to detonate it later to make it look as if the band was transporting bombs. However it went off prematurely killing 2 of the UVF men. The others panicked and shot dead 3 of the band members. 'Miami Showband Massacre.'

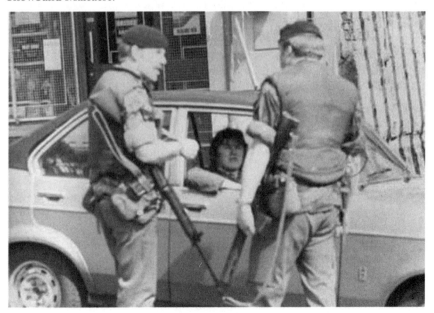

VCP in Belfast

213

SOUTH ARMAGH, 1975

Sergeant 'O', Green Howards

This was my fourth tour and we were posted to what was called the 'bandit country' of South Armagh. I was in the Signals platoon and amongst my duties was putting together code words to use on the RT. For example, 'Domino' meant the death of one of our own and 'Winged' meant a wounding.

17 July, 1975

We were down for an op at XMG and the night before, we had an 'O' group [Orders] and I sat down next to the Company OC for the XMG [Crossmaglen] area, Major Peter Willis. The following day, the day of the op, I was duty radio operator from 7 am onwards and I had to monitor all radio traffic. The actual op was at Bessbrook Mill and I sat down and had breakfast with Gus Garside who was the ATO and Sergeant McCarter, the R.E.'s Search team man. On the way there, I also had a chat with Corporal Brown of the RAOC who was going on the op with the other 3 lads I mentioned at a bridge called Ford's Cross.

The op was in full flow when a large IED [improvised explosive device] detonated and all 4 of those lads were killed. Then, the words 'Domino' and 'Winged' came over the RT and although, initially, they didn't affect me, it was only later that the words had a full impact on me.

Later that day, I was invited to help bring in the 4 bodies of my comrades from the helicopter – I declined.

The four men killed that day were Major Peter Willis, Green Howards, W.O. Edward Garside and Corporal Calvert Brown both of the RAOC and Sergeant Robert McCarter, Royal Engineers. The IRA had planted a bomb underneath the bridge.

LURGAN INCIDENT: 1975

Mick O' Day, 12 Intelligence

I was now away from the Scots Guards and working with Brigade and this one particular incident took place in a village near Lurgan. Intelligence (Int) had received a tip-off that weapons had been hidden in a boarded up house and the local squaddies had put in a covert op in order to recce the house just in case – as it turned out – that it was an IRA 'come on' and our lives were at risk. We obviously took the warning seriously, that there might be weapons there but it was pointless rushing in and getting ourselves blown up.

Tragically, a local girl who had previously lived in this now boarded-up house when she was younger had innocently approached the rear of the house with a friend and had prised open a few boards and climbed in through a window. Intent on showing off her old stomping ground, she had played about in the rooms for a while and then she opened a wall cupboard – probably a fuse box or something like that – mounted at head height. Clearly the device was designed to detonate and take off some squaddie's head.

The explosion killed her instanttly, decapitating the poor kid. The soldiers rushed over and found her body and her friend, distraught but unharmed. The incident was sent up to Int and I went along take photographs of the crime scene. I was presented by a shocking sight; her head had been thrown across the room and bounced off the opposite wall whilst her body had fallen right at the point of the blast. What struck me was how little blood there was, so instantly had she been killed; cauterised by the sudden heat and force.

How did I feel about it ? I felt sad but detached as it was my job and I just put myself into another dimension and simply elevated myself above the terrible sight. You just get the job done; you get to the stage where you just take the pictures and don't even think about it.

The darkroom, where you are alone and developing the pictures, is where you realise the horror of what you have just photographed.

THE MURDER OF A SOLDIER

Steve Atkinson, Royal Corps of Transport

In the 1970s I was posted to 17 Port Regt RCT as a Seaman B3. It was here that I met a Sergeant (name now forgotten), who was to be my first 'Skipper.' His family was from Northern Ireland and he was Navigator A1 and the Coxswain in charge of Work Boat 05.

Anyway, one morning Sgt 'X', received a message from 51 Squadron's OC or SSM, although I wasn't privy obviously to the details as I had only worked for him

The Battalion Ops Room. Captain Andrew de Lukas-Lessner (IO), Cpl (now Major) Mike Hooley, Major Ian Hywel-Jones MC (2i/c), Pete James. (photo courtesy of Regimental Museum of The Royal Welsh)

Border stand-off: Squaddies meet the Garda

for a couple of months. The message, apparently, referred to one of his relatives, over in Ulster who might have been his sister and she was very ill and wasn't expected to get well. Sgt 'X' was granted compassionate leave to go home and see to his family crisis; time dulls the memory, but I think he received this on a Friday morning.

On the Friday evening he was on the Liverpool/Belfast Ferry, but he never arrived at the family home. He was most likely picked up by the IRA, probably bundled into a car and he was found the following afternoon in a back garden or small field, in Belfast; he had been shot and murdered.

He is buried at Marchwood Church's small cemetery near Southampton (St John Apostle) and the funeral – which I attended – was a semi-military affair with all relevant persons attending also – CO, OC, RSM, etc.

The author spoke with the vicar of the church in question who was not at the church at the time, arriving in 1987. After some checking, the vicar was able to provide the following details: Sergeant Phillip Herbert (43) of 17 RCT was buried at the church on February 3, 1976. It is unlikely that this was the person to whom Steve Atkinson refers.

COOKSTOWN: 1975

Sergeant Major Haydn Davies, Royal Regiment of Wales

I was friends with a gentleman named Allan Harrhy of the RRW and I was visiting him in Cookstown one day while I was the Bn RSM. I suggested that his blokes should have haircuts. He asked 'who will cut it?' and I suggested that we got the barber up in the main street to call in and do it. I went out on foot patrol with him and called in at the barber's shop. Allan said to the little, aged Irish barber 'Would you like to come into the fort and cut the boys hair'? The barber thought for a moment and said. 'I'll come to the fort and I'll bring my razor, but it will not be their hair I will be cutting; I'll cut their f*****g throats'

BELFAST

Jim Parker, Light Infantry

During a tour of Belfast, my Section Second in Command was busted to Private and moved. His replacement was a Lance Corporal, who I'll call 'Bob'. He came from another company.

Quite soon after, my section was on vehicle patrol. A large battalion operation was in progress and we were in an area unknown to us. I was in the front passenger seat next to the RCT driver. The remainder of the blokes were in the back of the PIG.

We passed a crossroads and I spotted a crowd of people in the street to the left. Immediately after petrol bombs exploded near the PIG. I realised that I had seen the bomber, I ordered the drive to halt and jumped out of the cab and shouted for the section to follow me!

I sprinted back to the crossroads and there in the middle of the road was a man with an unlit petrol bomb in his right hand ready to throw. Our Yellow Cards (orders for opening fire) specifically allowed us legally to shoot and kill a person throwing a petrol bomb. I knelt down and aimed at the chest of the bomber. I also realised I was on my own. Where was my Section? I wanted a witness. I had no problems with shooting the bomber but I wanted a witness.

There was a clanking as one of my blokes ran up and I shouted for him to kneel beside me. 'That bloke is the petrol bomber!' I shouted and nodded to the bomber.

However, between the bomber, and me there now stood a woman holding a baby. The bomber was walking backwards down the street, the woman holding out the baby as if offering it to me as a gift. She walked backward too. After what seemed like hours my section arrived and I started to advance down the street. The bomber had reached the next junction and fled out of sight. The woman nestling the baby stood in the middle of the road smiling!

Callsign 3 ordered me to another location, and wouldn't listen to my request to be allowed to destroy the petrol bombs clustered in doorways in that street.

Later I discovered Bob was following SOPs of his former company and would not allow anyone to leave the PIG without his helmet (he was quite right). This resulted in what to me was the long delay in them following me.

BALLYMURPHY ESTATE/ SPRINGFIELD ROAD: 1975
Lt-Colonel R.P.Mason, 1 Royal Scots

A would-be IRA volunteer by the name of Sean Mckenna came to our attention in 1975 and he clearly was very keen to join their ranks. As part of his initiation test he was to launch an attack on the RUC station on Springfield Road which was very close to the Ballymurphy Estate in West Belfast.

His first mission, apparently, was to lob a blast bomb over the high fence of the Springfield Road police station and into the compound beyond. He lobbed the device, but, lacking the power to clear the high fence, it bounced back off the top and into his hands where he duly caught it – some sort of instinct no doubt – and it detonated! Henceforth, he was known as 'Fingers' Mckenna.

BELFAST, 1974/5
Private Marcus Lapsa, Royal Regiment of Wales

I served in Northern Ireland from 1/3/74 to 13/5/75 with the Royal Regiment of Wales, it was an eighteen month posting and we were in Palace Barracks, Hollywood, just outside Belfast.

We worked an 8 day week that consisted of two days on duty, two days off, two days 48 hours standby, two days 24 hour standby; at least, that was the theory, but as an extra duty as a regiment we took over the running of an east Belfast base (Ballymacarrot). This included the Short Strand area.

As I was only seventeen when the Regiment moved to Belfast, I did not do the full tour of eighteen months. There was a directive at the time that all soldiers had to be at least eighteen (this was because a couple of seventeen year old soldiers had been shot). I was eighteen on the 22/2/74 and on the 1/3/74 I was shipped to Belfast. I had two weeks CQB [Close Quarters Battle] training at Ballymena and then joined my Regiment.

As a young soldier I do not mind admitting that I was pretty scared at first, particularly as missing 4 months of the tour left me catching up as the other lads were fairly confident. I remember one of my first WRAC patrol's in the city centre (this is where you would have two soldiers and a WRAC [Women's Royal Army Corps] so you could stop and search people within the City Centre). It started off ok, stopping various people, most of who were polite and just went along with their day's shopping.

I saw this picture of beauty walking down the street towards us. She was approx 17 to 19, with long flowing hair and really stunning with a mini skirt on. I smiled and winked and said 'Good morning.' I will remember her reply until the day I die; she looked at me in horror and said 'Away to fuck, ye British bastard' I can remember this so clearly and at the time I thought how could God be so cruel giving a stunning beauty such a vile gob!

When we were patrolling Ballymacarrot it was a long haul, with two hours on and four off. We used to go out in four man patrols, and there was not a worse time to patrol than Sunday afternoon. I can remember a time when the sun was out, the doors were open and the music from 'Top of the Pops' was blaring out. I shouted across to Bez (Tyron Beswick) 'Give us some bass, Bez', and then the four of us were walking down the street in full patrol gear, playing air guitars with our rifles for the whole song!

I can't describe the looks we got from the civvies, but at least it broke the monotony especially when we started dancing to Mud's 'Tiger Feet'

One day, whilst on patrol in East Belfast we heard shots being fired, and as I was radio controller at the time I called in with our call sign and the standard 'CONTACT. WAIT. OUT." We then heard a bomb blast and again I called it in, and we were told it was from the Short Strand. We were only a couple of streets away, and when we got there the Strand Bar was a mess. All that was left was a pile of bricks with debris everywhere. The adrenaline was pumping and we waded straight in to try and clear things and pull people out, not even thinking about gas mains or anything.

I remember us all just putting our rifles in a pile and working with the locals to do what we could. I don't remember how many lives were lost; possibly five or six, but I do remember saying 'I've found someone!' and pulling some bricks away and seeing a leg. Someone more experienced said 'Don't bother there; help over here, it's just a leg !' The image of the leg with a burnt patch on the stocking was a reminder that this was some fucked up place to be in.

When more of the Company arrived, we were sent back on patrol, with a bollocking for leaving our rifles in a pile although they were all still there.

The next day on patrol, the locals were talking to us, which was a big step forward, or so we thought. Then the IRA killed over 20 kids in a series of pub bombings in Birmingham. The day after that all we got from the local lads were chants of 'Birmingham, Birmingham', and it did not take long to get back to normal! As a Regiment we had been very active all around the province; being involved with various things, marches riots etc. The worst time for us was in October, 1974, when the Maze prison was torn apart by rioting and the Loyalist prisoners burnt down their blocks. We were one of the first in and it was a total mess; no rifles were allowed, just riot gear, and when we got control, there was a standoff just outside the compounds. Then we were put into the compounds and had to stand as a show of strength; we were in there for an hour and then we were outside for another hour (we were not allowed to sit)

This went on for ages as the prisoners were making demands and saying if they were not met they were going to break out at a specific time. This kept the tension constant. During the day, this standoff involved us standing all the time whilst they were lazing around; we were absolutely knackered because after this, we then had to do patrols all through the night on a 2 hours on; 4 hours off.

We knew this was going to go on for a few days so as we were Welsh, we would patrol and sing to keep them awake so they were as tired as us. Then a call came over the radio that the trouble was starting again as there was a terrible noise coming from one of the compounds. There was a call over the radio from the guards, saying 'not to worry, as it was only the Taffs singing.'

Strand Bar was attributed to the UVF (12th April 1975) and the riots at the Maze prison were on 16th October 1974.

BELFAST

Soldier, Light Infantry

It was nearly over. Almost 4 months had passed since we had arrived. It was all nearly over. The guards, the patrols, the escorts, the fights and squabbles that come with 4 months of living in each other's sleeping bags practically. Yes it was nearly over.

I had spent a couple of days getting the Company nominal roll in order for TAC HQ so that flights could be allocated to all the Company. It was very important I did not miss anyone off the nominal roll. It had to be checked and rechecked and typed up again if wrong. There was none of your computers in those days. It was always three copies and if they were wrong you could just not cut and paste or delete with the simple click of a key. It all had to be done again. Finally it was complete and nobody was left off. I had checked it a million times with the CSM.

We set off for TAC HQ in Hastings Street. Me, my escort who were the O.C.'s Crew, an RCT Driver and the nominal roll. All tucked up together in a lovely safe and solid PIG.

We left the Distillery and drove up Grosvenor Road and turned right at the main junction onto the Falls Road. We had to use a PIG as no soft-skinned vehicles were allowed down the Falls Road. The Falls Road was prime sniper territory.

The Falls that day had that 'there's something not quite right' feel about it. Lots of yobs standing on corners. We could see them as soon as we turned into it. Bob, who was normally O.C.'s Driver, was sitting next to me on the vehicle at the rear door. As soon as we turned into the Falls Road and saw the yobs he closed the back door of the PIG and opened the window in the back door; a wise decision as it turned out.

As we drove along the Falls and came up to a junction opposite Lesson Street a crowd of youths moved into the main street which slowed the PIG down. At this point everyone had their weapons at the ready, even the nominal roll had been discarded to the floor of the vehicle. Suddenly a youth of about 18 years of age ran from one of the side streets and launched himself at the back of the PIG. He managed to grab the top and hang onto the back of the vehicle. He was looking directly into the back of it through the port hole on the back door and he was grinning.

I then witnessed a very cool and unhurried action on the part of Bob. He calmly uttered a few words, which I can not remember now, but something like 'Oh no you don't' he did not swear as I and others would have done. He then unslung his baton gun, poked it through the porthole and shot the yob straight in the face ...

The yob screamed and dropped onto the road; someone shouted for the driver to 'get the 'F**k out of it' and away we sped around the corner on our way to TAC HQ.

Bob sat back down and said 'F**k did you see that. Right in the face.'

I understood Bob's attitude that day. A few weeks earlier, in practically the same spot we had been out with the OC to visit the spot were one of our lads had been shot in the thigh and almost died. Bob was driving a Land Rover without a door and as we passed a junction, I think Leeson Street, someone had thrown a half house brick which had caught Bob on the side of the head. He brought the Land Rover to a halt, and he was visibly dazed. The OC ordered everyone out and to take cover and he told me to get Bob out and into cover, which I did by dragging him out of the driver's seat and behind the vehicle to give him time to recover.

When backup arrived the scene at the junction was getting a bit hairy. A yob was snatched and the OC told me to arrest him ... big mistake, I ended up having to go to court in Belfast as a witness for him to get a £10 fine.

THE ARREST OF JIM PINKEY, BELFAST
Jim Parker 3 Light Infantry

7 Platoon, stationed in Belfast, received instructions to bring in George Pinkey. My Platoon Commander gave me the address and sent me off with my section to make the arrest. The Pinkey family was very large and were familiar to us. There were three or four robust brothers. As we were preparing to leave the Mission Hall another section commander, told me he had seen George Pinkey walking towards his house.

The Pinkey brood lived in a three storey terraced house not too far from the Platoon Base and my crew were due for our break. I walked straight up to the front door, without sending someone around the back as per Standing Operational Orders.

I wrapped on the door and almost immediately Mrs Pinkey, a large motherly-type lady, flung the door open and asked without preamble, 'Which one do you want, but?' (Belfast people end every sentence with the word 'but'). I answered 'George.'

Car bomb explodes in Belfast

City Centre security cordon in Londonderry
(photo courtesy of Eamon Melaugh)

'George!" she shouted over her shoulder, 'George, they've come to arrest you, but. Come down here!' I heard a muffled reply from above.

'He's not here, but,' she said, 'He's at the pub, but!' and named an establishment a few streets away. I swore under my breath, knowing I had buggered up my job. He may have escaped out the back door by now, or hidden somewhere in the house. 'Sorry Mrs Pinkey,' I gritted my teeth angry with myself, 'but I'll have to come in and make a search for him!'

The lady pulled a face and as she followed me up the stairs repeated that George was in such and such a pub. I made a quick search for George Pinkey, and then went back to the Mission Hall with my tail between my legs. The Lieutenant quite rightly was angry with me for not surrounding the building, as I should have done. We were both convinced George had escaped out the back.

I was pretty fed up with myself, and knew it would take a long time to live that one down. About eleven o'clock just after closing time, the bell at the front of the Mission Hall was rung. There in the dark stood George Pinkey. 'Me Mam, said you wanted me, but!' he exclaimed through the wire fence.

Someone went to ring the Intelligence Section. On his return he said, 'Can you come back tomorrow morning?' 'Sure, what time do you want me to come, but?'

1975/6 RESIDENT BATTALION IN PALACE BARRACKS, HOLYWOOD

Bernard Loughran, King's Own Scottish Borderers

A member of the Battalion community relations team was visiting a particularly strong Protestant area and an even stronger Protestant club. Knowing that CR team members visited all kinds of government departments [one of the leaders] enquired as to whether there was any possibility of the club getting a grant to do some renovation that was required. 'I doubt it very much, after all you are a strong sectarian organisation.'

'No, we are not!' came the reply, 'any Protestant can join.'

Another time on a visit to another strong Protestant area, I had with me a friend of Polish extraction with a very Polish name.

'Who's your friend?' said the local, I introduced him with his nickname and was asked what was his second name was. 'Don't worry about it' I said. 'What's his second name?' much more forcefully this time. 'You probably wouldn't be able to pronounce it anyway as it is Polish' I replied.

'Polish? Polish? I've never met a Protestant Pole in my life.'

On the mainland, RAOC soldier Roger Goad (40) was killed attempting to defuse a bomb in a shop on Church Street, Kensington, London.

Chapter Nine

1976

A year of 1,428 bombings, 1,908 shootings and the deaths of 29 soldiers, 23 RUC officers, 224 civilians (the worst year for deaths) and 21 terrorists.

Eugene Reavey's three brothers, aged 24, 22 and 17, were shot dead in their home at Whitecross in South Armagh by the UVF in this year; another family – the O'Dowds – lost three of their family members. In retaliation, the so-called Republican Action Force made a gun and bomb attack which killed 10 civilian workers when their mini-bus was attacked at Bessbrook, South Armagh, an incident thereafter known as 'the Kingsmills massacre'.

In October of this year two R.A. soldiers, Gunners Anthony Abbott and Maurice Murphy, were checking out a deliberately abandoned car and were lured into an IRA ambush and shot. The car, involved in an accident earlier, had been left on Oakfield Street on the Ardoyne. Gunner Murphy died at the scene and his comrade died of his wounds, just under a month later. Three other members of the patrol were also wounded.

There were 2 separate machine-gun attacks on Catholic bars by the UVF in Belfast and Antrim which left 11 civilians dead.

GLENNANE: 1976. THE MURDER OF THE REAVEY BROTHERS
WO1 Haydn Davies (RRW) RSM 2 UDR

I had been home for a few days of Christmas leave and just arrived back at work at Gough Barracks Armagh, it was early evening 4th January 1976. The CO put his head through my office door and said. 'What are you up to RSM?' 'I'm going to Glennane Sir!' I replied. 'I'm going there too, ride with me' said the CO.

I got myself ready and thought 'Bloody hell.' I hated riding in that stupid staff car, such an obvious soft target. I changed my pistol at the armoury for an SMG and a full magazine of 30 rounds. We drove off into the misty cold Armagh night, the CO, myself and the female Greenfinch driver and my driver who came as additional escort. The female driver was a blond 'little cracker' from the Bessbrook area; a little consolation on a dismal night.

Halfway through the journey we started to pick up radio traffic of a shooting incident close to Glennane at Whitecross just outside the base and on our route. Three dead was mentioned and the RUC were at the scene. We drove into Whitecross over the crossroads and down into a lane and down into the muddy yard of the house were we had been directed on the radio. Two police Land Rovers were parked in the dark yard, all the lights were on in the house. The police moved about in a respectful silence. 'No need to go in' whispered a policeman 'Just look through the window; it's a bloody awful sight' I looked and saw the shot up bodies of two dark haired young men,

Armoured Land Rover

teenagers. Blood spattered the wall above one of them. A wounded third man was being attended to upstairs. He sounded to be in the most terrible agony.

An older woman arrived back at the cottage and was spoken to by a policeman. She tried to rush to the house, but was stopped from entering. She then let out an immediate howling sound of the most dreadful grief, it continued on for some minutes and then she collapsed, she came to, and the grief started again. She was forcibly but kindly escorted away to a neighbour's place some distance away.

I stood by a police Land Rover and spoke with the attractive blonde Greenfinch driver. My words to her were. 'Jesus Christ! Just imagine rearing those boys to see them come to this.' She made no immediate reply and then said quietly 'Good enough for the likes of those.' Before I could reply to her, my driver, himself a Catholic, squeezed my arm to keep quiet. My chemical attraction for her died on the spot.

On arrival back at Gough barracks I made a written report of her words. I felt she should be sacked. The next morning I gave the report to the Adjutant and explained to him what she had said. He took the letter. He didn't read it but merely placed it into his in-tray without comment. I heard no more of it for a while then about a week later the Training Major (Light Infantry) came into my office and sat down. He started to speak to me in sort of parables without hitting any subject. It became obvious that he had been told to speak to me, but he was making a hash of it. After a silence he said. 'RSM, don't become involved in Irish politics, leave it alone or you will be the loser' He left my office, and as I sat in thought! I just thought, 'What a hopeless situation!'

The three Reavey brothers were: John (24), Brian (22) and 17 year old Martin who died of his injuries 26 days later in hospital. The killings were claimed by the UVF and the bloodletting was not finished there. At nearby Ballduggan, three members of the O'Dowd family were attacked at a get-together and the UVF added three more bloody murders to their tally.

KINGSMILLS MASSACRE: 1976
WO1 Haydn Davies (RRW) RSM 2 UDR

Just a few days into the New Year 1976 I was at B Company 2 UDR location at Glennane, just a few miles from Bessbrook. It was early evening and I was in the Ops room planning with the CSM the patrol programme. The base was in an isolated area on a small hillock surrounded by a high metal fence with a barbed wire top and was situated alongside a country road in the remote Armagh countryside; most dangerous when you consider the singular route to enter and leave the base. Coming and going was a hairy experience.

I was just about to pack up and leave when suddenly a loud series of automatic shooting commenced some distance away. Although, at first I thought it was the 25m range and thought no more of it, running feet and shouting of orders told me otherwise.

Orders were shouted from outside the Ops room to get the 'Crash out' vehicles out into the night, and to move to the direction of the shooting. I jumped into my covert vehicle with my driver and followed the two Land Rovers out of the base and up the road. The patrol vehicles seemed to know what direction to head in. We headed past White Cross where the night before the Reavey boys had been murdered in their isolated home.

After some minutes we came to a roadblock, or what appeared to be a roadblock; regular army vehicles had just arrived, and as we got there, police vehicles pulled in behind us. Some twenty metres in front of us a brown minibus was parked in the road with its lights off. In the lights of the army vehicles parked on the other side of the minibus I could see about a dozen bodies lying in the road. In the glare of the headlights I could see steam rising from the bodies forming an awful haze; soldiers were moving between the bodies with torches looking for signs of life; one was found alive but it was thought he would not live.

Our two Land Rovers formed a vehicle check point a hundred metres back down the road to keep traffic away, though not many people moved about Armagh at that time of night. Very soon, I drove back quite sickened, to Glenanne base.

I sat in the Ops room with the Company commander Major Adams, a tall, good affable man and totally impartial to both sides of the community, and with Sergeant Major Dalgliesh. We listened to the brigade and local battalion nets. Figures were given out as ten civilians dead, one critical and some missing. The missing appeared later, some had either made other arrangements to travel that particular night, and one had been weeded out as Catholic and sent away from the scene by the assailants.

Such is the closeness of the community that the Glenanne company of part-time soldiers knew the identity of the occupants of the minibus and speculation was rife as to who was working that night and who may have been on 'day off' and possibly missed the carnage. A phone call from the local police station gave us the list of casualties. All of them were well known to the assembly in the ops room.

CSM Dalgliesh suddenly asked. 'Where is McConville? ' 'He is in No 3 Sangar Sir' said the radio operator and the CSM responded: 'His brother is on the list' said the CSM. 'Where is he? He should have been relieved over an hour ago? Go and bring him here' said Major Adams to the radio operator. 'No, I had better go and fetch him' said the CSM.

Some minutes later McConville came into the Ops room with the CSM. And just looked at us all in silence. Before Major Adams could speak McConville said quietly. 'I know Sir, I heard it on the intercom' a pause then he said. 'I had better get home.' He stayed in the sangar because, as he told us later that he could not quite face the truth regarding his brother.

Over a week later I called in to Bessbrook Police station and walked around the minibus which was parked up on waste ground. It was peppered like a colander. Human hair; blood; and parts of flesh and bone were stuck to the sides of the vehicle. Some of the occupant's belongings, lunch boxes etc were still in the vehicle. No one would go near it. I was told a few days later that the vehicle was taken onto waste ground and burnt out.

In 1992 the Glenanne base was blown from the face of the earth by the biggest bomb ever used in the troubles.

This appalling tragedy, forever to be known as the 'Kingsmills massacre' was carried out, most likely by the IRA, but claiming to be the 'Republican action group.' It was said to be a direct retaliation for the murders by the UVF of the three Reavey brothers and, on the same night (January 4) of three members of the O'Dowd family.

The men, 10 Protestants and one Catholic, worked in a nearby town and were returning home by their regular minibus when they were stopped at Whitecross by masked gunmen. Each in turn was asked his religion and the one Catholic was told to run away. The gunmen then opened fire with machine guns and 10 were killed but an eleventh, though hit 17 times, somehow survived to tell the tale.

This meant that, within 5 days of the New Year 17 men had been killed in sectarian attacks and an 18th, injured on Christmas Day in a separate incident, died of their injuries on that same day.

Jim Parker, Light Infantry

In one Protestant area we regularly patrolled in Belfast, soldiers were frequently invited in for 'a cuppa.' Perhaps in hindsight it was stupid, if not dangerous. There were regular shootings and incidents and we carried our gas masks and CS gas grenades besides our usual armoury of Self Loading Rifles and Baton Guns. I don't think we carried our helmets too, but I'm not sure now.

There were nine or ten men in my section. My Second in Command was Geoff Lucas. As we strolled down a leafy avenue a middle-aged motherly woman came out of her house and invited us in for a cuppa. I conferred briefly with Geoff and agreed to go in, leaving a couple of blokes outside.

228 A LONG LONG WAR

I led the remaining eight blokes into the hallway of the terraced house. It was a small house, the staircase was to the right and I saw the feet of another, elderly, woman making her way down as I passed into the living room.

The living room was homely, very tiny and warm. I had to make my way through the furniture, then around the back of a sofa, and then turn back on myself to get to the seats around the coal fire. Dressed in combat kit, flak jacket, wearing webbing and carrying weapons made movement very awkward.

Meanwhile, Geoff Lucas was the last to enter the house, and the elderly woman had reached the bottom of the stairs. She held out her hand to Geoff, who reciprocated. The woman snatched his hand and bent forward and bit him! Geoff was stunned! She then calmly reached her hand out to Pte Mortimer in front of Geoff who drew his hand back in self-defence.

Mortimer and Geoff passed a message up the line of soldiers like Chinese whispers. 'She bit Geoff! That woman bit Geoff! Geoff got bit by the old woman!' Eight of the Light Infantry's finest, armed to the teeth, were now jammed into a small stiflingly hot sitting room, terrified of an old woman aged about 70. The old woman came into the room, with that strange glint in her eyes possessed by some unfortunate mentally disabled folk. She grinned and offered her hand out to eight cringing squaddies.

The middle-aged woman who had invited us into her home appeared from the kitchen with a tray of cups and a teapot. She put them down and smiled affec-tionately at the other woman and said 'Oh, that's Mary,' she vaguely made a mo-tion by the side of her head, to indicate mental disorder, 'She likes soldiers!'

BELFAST
Soldier, Light Infantry

Whilst in Belfast as a Section Commander, I was given the task of attempting to capture a wanted Irish Republican Army terrorist. The general idea was that my section would be dropped off from a vehicle and creep forward in the dark across a wide stretch of open ground. From there we could observe the front door of a public house. Part of my section under my second in command, Bob, would cover our rear.

The usual preparations were made, and I remember that we wore socks over our DMS boots [standard issue], to lessen the sound of our approach. I carried an IWS (Individual Weapon Sight) attached to my Self Loading Rifle. This and the IWS made for a rather heavy but not uncomfortable weight. This IWS caught whatever light in the sky and the result was a magnified green tinted view. I collected two batteries, one as a spare for the IWS, before leaving base. I also carried a Pye radio with an earpiece, and would be on the Company net contact with not only Company HQ, but also Bob, who too, carried a radio.

The armoured PIG slowed down a stopped long enough for my section to scramble out the back. We could then hear the vehicle quite clearly drive all the way back to the Mill. It struck me; the whole of Belfast could hear the PIG and would have heard us dismount.

We crept through the dark and Bob and his group dropped off at the prearranged spot and my little group crawled as quietly as possible forward

Soldiers dug in on border watch

across open groups. The grass beneath us was short and cropped like a lawn. Our objective, the public house said to be frequented by prominent members of the IRA, had a doorman who spoke to all who entered.

We settled in for a long wait, feeling safe with Bob fifty yards to our rear. The snatch squad and I lay facing the pub. The plan was, when I recognised a wanted person, we would leap to our feet rush forward about thirty yards and arrest the culprit.

After a very short time I ran into three problems. Firstly, I could not remember what the main IRA target looked like. His image had completely gone from my mind's eye. Secondly on looking through the IWS sight I could not with the best will in the world distinguish between one person and another, even if I could recognise a wanted person! Thirdly despite the extra clothing I had put on for this operation, I was bloody freezing!

I had anticipated laying in this ambush for about four hours, but within minutes my teeth were chattering with cold. After fifteen minutes I was shivering and feeling very depressed. At regular and short intervals, I switched on the IWS to watch the pub door.

Three shadowy figures approached the pub and I observed they were women. My IWS went blank. I tested the switch, to find it was 'on'. Swearing under my breath I removed the battery from its housing and then replaced it, but to no avail. I had drawn up two fresh batteries, perhaps the CQMS had issued me with a duff one by mistake. I struggled to remove the spare battery from the breast pocket of my combat jacket, beneath my flak jacket. On replacing the battery my IWS sprang into life and I could observe shadowy green figures moving about at the entrance of the pub. I was very cold.

Taking great care I whispered and explained to my snatch team what had happened to the IWS. We lay on the ice-cold ground, and listened to snatches of conversation from the pub. Although I could not distinguish one patron from another at least I could observe.

It crossed my mind that if I were to claim to see a wanted man, we could dash forward and just grab anyone! The colder I became the more that idea became an inviting prospect. My feet were like blocks of ice and my ears burned with cold. I struggled on and watched the security doorman – then the IWS went blank! Again I checked the on/off switch but it would not come to life. I went through the same procedure as before changing batteries. The IWS flickered into life for a few seconds and went off again. Apparently these batteries were affected by the cold.

I had been in touch with Call Sign 3 (Company HQ) throughout the first dreadful hour. I realised that no one there would believe that my IWS batteries had gone flat due to cold. I would be accused of not ensuring I had spares. As tears caused by the agony of cold trickled down my cheeks I decided to let them know of my tactical problem.

'Hello 3, this is 31B!' I whispered into the microphone, 'My IWS has packed in, permission to return to base?' I realised I should not have asked for permission to bug out so soon. Inevitably the watch keeper in his snug warm operations room would not or could not sanction the cancellation of this operation.

I was bloody freezing, and by that time quite frankly didn't care two hoots about capturing some Godforsaken IRA yob! The idea of bugging out had captured my imagination!

My mind tried to weigh up the options of selecting the next person to approach the pub for arrest. For a period of perhaps five minutes (ten hours it felt like) no one appeared. What was the point of remaining when I couldn't see any people due to having no working IWS? It also dawned on me that both my legs were stiff with cold, and there was a possibility that I would be unable to stand up, let alone run forward and make an arrest. This was a common phenomenon that most infantry soldiers have encountered after laying for a long period in an ambush position. I could only guess that the other member of my ambush crew were in the same plight as me. Low groans and muttering caused me to believe they too were suffering.

Whispering into the radio I asked Call Sign 3 for permission to bug out as I had no IWS and was unable to identify any targets. After asking for the second or third time, they graciously informed me that I should wait ten minutes and then withdraw. Ten minutes! That was an eternity! Using field signals I indicated to my group we were moving back to Bob's position immediately. Having lain motionless in one position for about two hours our legs wouldn't work! As we started to crawl back with pains like exaggerated pins and needles attacked our calves and thighs. I could here the groans of my crew above my own.

As we approached Bob's position he challenged us, and I answered quickly, because I had bugged out too early, Bob might think we were IRA creeping up on him! Bob was in a sheltered hollow and was amazed at our condition. Some of my blokes were crying with the pain their legs and the cold.

It was that night I learned I was not and never would be SAS material!

THE DEATH OF A GREENFINCH: ARMAGH 1976
RSM Haydn Davies, Royal Regiment of Wales

Jean Leggett was a lance corporal 'greenfinch' (female UDR) in 'A' Company 2 UDR. I saw quite a lot of her as she came and went most evenings when she reported to collect her flak jacket and signals kit to accompany the men as a signaller in the mobile patrol vehicles. She was an English girl from Hereford; a jovial sort, and whenever there was a burst of laughter from a group of people Jean was mostly in the middle of it with some joke she had cracked. She was an exceptional 'greenfinch' and conscientious. Always ready to do one of the many courses available to better her self. She was a good signaller; clear and very concise on the air.

One evening as the patrols were forming up to go out, she put her head of dark curly hair around my office door and said ' Good evening, RSM Sir, It is part of my therapy to tell as many people as possible that I have given up smoking.' I suggested she put it out over her radio. She laughed and left.

Two hours later I went down the corridor from my office and entered a very silent depressed Ops Room. As I did so, I could feel that something serious had happened. The Ops officer took me to one side and said. 'A' Company mobile has been ambushed out at Middletown, one dead and one wounded, we don't know who it is yet' I left to await the news and returned to my office, these occasions meant long nights for us all. Ten minutes later the Ops officer together with the 2ic The Earl of Caladen came into my office; together they told me that the fatal casualty was Jean Leggett. It was planned that the Earl and I should go and tell Jean's husband, who was Colour Sergeant Leggett of the Irish Guards. This was a task that I did not relish and we left in the Earl's private car and for some reason he was carrying a large bottle of whiskey.

Colour Sergeant Leggett was a Regular soldier attached to the Battalion, the only others were the Training Major, the Co and me. The 2IC and I drove to the 'Clump' 'a sort of covert small group of semi-secure married quarters where the Leggetts lived. It got its name from a large group of mature trees at the summit of the small hillock above the quarters. Dreading the task I knocked at the door; both of us stood in the dark as the quiet voice of Colour Sgt Leggett verbally identified us from the darkness within. You just did not open doors in Armagh without the drills of checking who was there. The door opened and we stepped inside and into the lighted living room. I think he knew that something was wrong. Then the 2ic said 'There has been a shooting' Then after a pause. 'There has been a fatality, I am afraid it is your wife.' The 2ic immediately thrust the bottle of whiskey into my hand and left. Then began a very long night; poor old Leggett, I could say little to help him. Uncontrollable tears rolled down his face and didn't stop for many hours. 'Where are your two children' I asked. 'Upstairs in bed' he replied. It was decided to let them sleep until morning.

We sat for many hours until daybreak and the tears rolled all night. He used an army towel to stem the flow, but on it went. He smoked one cigarette after the other without a break between. I was a non-smoker but I wanted to ask him for a cigarette. I had a most terrible urge to smoke with him; I tried to make useless conversation while he kept asking 'Why! Why?' 'Where is she, what have they done with her, where is she now?' 'Who is looking after her?' he asked that last question a hundred times. I felt useless as I replied each time something like 'she will be in good hands that is for sure'

Eventually – and after tens of cups of tea – he fell asleep on the settee. I put a blanket over him. By now it was about 6 or 6.30am and I left the house to go and knock on the doors of the local quarters in turn and tell them of what had happened. Some of them knew already. A Welsh girl married to the Bn chief clerk went upstairs to collect the children. Others went to console Colour Sgt Leggett. One woman went completely hysterical! But thank God for good women at a time like this.

I went down to the barracks and saw a crowed of UDR soldiers standing around the Land Rover in which the patrol was ambushed. No one had cleaned up the blood of Jean and the other wounded girl. They were all standing looking at the spectacle, so I ordered its cleaning and as this was being organised, the Training Major came on the scene and went completely ballistic with the MT staff for allowing spectators in the area of the vehicle.

We had a service for Jean on a cold and wet morning a few days later on the square in Gough barracks. The whole platoon of 'greenfinches' broke ranks and cried on each other's shoulders and consoled each other. We sang 'Amazing Grace' and saw Jean off as best we could.

Just as an aside the wounded girl with Jean was awarded the MBE, it was well deserved. She got it for good work in looking after Jean before she died at the scene, and for maintaining good communications during the incident. Some of the UDR girls were much more versatile and quite often more use than some of the men, this was a well known spoken fact amongst the regulars attached to the UDR.

Lance Corporal Gillian J.B. Leggett, who was 33, was shot and killed in an IRA ambush on the Armagh to Middletown Road on April 6, 1976; she was the second female UDR member to be killed during the troubles.

BELFAST: 1976

Steve Atkinson, Gordon Highlanders

In 1976 I transferred/rebadged to the 1st Btn Gordon Highlanders and joined them whilst they were doing their 18 month tour of duty at Palace Bks, Belfast; I was posted in to A Company as a member of Alpha Section of 11 Platoon.

In the marching season of 1976 Belfast was a busy place for the Gordons; one 'event' was a march which had the purpose of placing a tricolour on the main council offices in Belfast. This march was to be diverted away in Castle St, Belfast. 'A' Company was tasked to be the first to meet the marchers, and we formed the 'baseline' and close support, with Major Kennedy in command; all the world's media were present, and the mood of the marchers was ugly.

There was of course a full-on 'riot', and during this a Lieutenant from the Argyll & Sutherland Highlanders took it upon himself to charge into the mob alone. He was grabbed and given a fairly bad beating by the crowd before he was

Army armoured car

rescued by a 'snatch' squad; this in full view of the media. I should add that we, the Gordons, had a Platoon of the Argylls attached to us for this 18 month tour as we were understrength.

During this tour, there are a number of events which stand out in my mind, for example, a member of the Gordons, whilst relieving the Royal Marines at 'Fort Monagh' in the Turf Lodge was shot twice and injured by a cook serving there during a meal time. The reasons behind this incident were never made clear, at least not to me.

One of our officers was shot through the back by a sniper, nicking his aorta, but, before he passed out he himself, bravely called in the 'Contact' report and tasked the relevant assistance to come and help, including 'Starlight', the Medevac helicopter. Happily, he was back to duty in a few months. At around the same time, one Jock from the company was severely injured when an IED [improvised explosive device] was detonated, throwing him across to the other side of the street in the Ballymurphy; sadly, he never returned to duty as his injuries were too severe.

In the summer of 1976, a civilian worker at Palace Barracks had his family taken hostage during the night, his car was fitted with about 50lb of explosive, and he was told to drive to work. Fortunately, at the gate, an alert sentry noticed his 'uneasy stress' and questioned him. He told the sentry about the situation and was ordered to park the car on the other side of the road, adjacent to the main gate and run back to the guardroom. I'm pleased to report that the QRF had time to block both carriageways of the road and the immediate area was made safe before the bomb detonated a short time later. Damage was caused but thanks to the sentry's quick thinking, there were no casualties.

LONDONDERRY: 1976

Corporal Rocky Evershed, Royal Engineers

My story starts back in 1976, when I was a Corporal in the Royal Engineers, attached to RELO (Royal Engineers Liaison Office). We were a team of a Sergeant as I/C, myself as 21/C, one RCT Driver and 3 general Sappers. Our job was, regardless of time, to remove barricades, repair fences, and ensure all checkpoints were adequately protected. On one particular occasion we were called out at 2am, in the morning, to deal with a fence that had been ripped down by IRA sympathisers.

We duly went out, and found that the fence was over an arch (gate) from the Catholic side of the city, to the Protestant side. Anyway, we got stuck in and made the repairs, and returned to our base. The time now was approx 0600 hrs. It is worth mentioning at this point, that whenever RELO got called out, on their return, the bar would always open for relaxation. On this particular morning, we entered camp, and four of us decided we needed a drink to unwind, before jumping into our pits. Sgt 'X' decided that he wanted a quick wash and brush up first, and that he would meet us in the bar about 20 minutes later.

Consequently, the 4 of us settled down to our first drink, when all of a sudden we heard an ear splitting roar. 'That was f*****g close' I said, but didn't think any more of it, until about 5 minutes later, when an orderly from the Sgt's Mess came running in, and said that the Sgt's Mess had been 'blown up.' We immediately went down to the Mess to see if there was anything we could do and to our horror half of the Mess was missing!

We hung around all night, and the next day, and we were eventually told what had happened. On our return from the 'shout', Sgt 'X' went back to his room to refresh himself. On sitting on the bed, to remove his boots, unbeknown to him, there was a 20lb pressure bomb in a paint tin, placed underneath his bed. (The decorators had been in the Mess some 3 weeks already) As soon as he sat on the bed, the booby trap detonated and he was killed instantly. This was such a sorrowful night; we'd come to expect that we were prime targets, but 'In your own bed.' How could it have it have happened; how had it been allowed to happen?

I didn't have the answer to those questions; all I know is I lost a friend, and a bloody good NCO that night. Later, as second in command of the troop, I was ordered to identify the body, the Sergeant. Y'know, never has it felt so good to disobey an order, and tell the reviewing officer, that if he wanted identification, to do it himself. I was not about to spill the contents of my stomach, for all to see. The RCT Driver eventually identified the body, and later, I was privileged to be asked, by the family, to attend the funeral.

That's it; life is NOT a bed of roses, and I quite often think 'If things had only been different.'

Rocky later gave me permission to use the murdered soldier's name; he was Sergeant David Evans (28) a married soldier with 2 children from the Wiltshire area. A second device was also found under another soldier's bed but thankfully, it failed to detonate.

BELFAST: 1976

Major Mick Low, Gordon Highlanders

Our name for this tour was very quickly established as 'Rentajock', and on some weeks, we were working in excess of 120 hours. I was also the Company Search Advisor with one of my sections as the search team. Early morning calls became routine, which was not very nice trying to retain a family life as well.

A four day cycle was supposed to be the operational requirement. Day one: 40 minutes notice to move anywhere in the Province. As often as not we were in downtown Belfast assisting the 6 month tour units. Day two saw us at 2 hours notice to move, mainly Belfast and UDR Bns in Belfast and Antrim. Day three was spent on Guards and duties with my platoon scattered to the four winds guarding key points. The other platoons spent their day guarding our own camp and carrying out fatigues.

One Saturday we were providing support in the form of patrolling the Clonards, a particularly nasty little area off Springfield Road and it just happened to be the Grand National day. Well, we all know the Irish love horse racing. At the time of the off, we huckled all the boyos out of the Bookies shop on Kashmir road. They were going berserk at missing the race as we 'P' checked them all. After about 45 minutes we let them back in, they were absolutely steaming mad. To crown it all, I popped my head in the door and asked who won the race. 'Ya wee Scotch Bastard' was heard as we gleefully left the area. Jocks 2- Boyos 0.

British Army sniper keeps alert

BALLYKELLY 1976 – 1978
Mick, 1 Glosters

We were deployed to the old RAF base at Ballykelly where they had previously flown Shackletons for Coastal Command.

Situated about midway between Coleraine in the east and Londonderry in the west and within a stone's throw of the Northern Ireland coast alongside the main Belfast Highway which passed its front gate, it was ideally situated for a resident infantry unit base. 2 companies were out in the TAOR, one in County Londonderry, centred on Kilrea and the other in South Tyrone and centred on Dungannon; there were also lots of smaller unit bases and it was a very busy time out there for your 6 weeks rotation.

Operations went on in a similar fashion to other tours, with search ops – VCPs and reconnaissance a daily and routine affair. There were Eagle VCPs (airborne in a Wessex or Puma or Lynx or Scout, swooping down on a vehicle in a lonely area of moor or mountain) flying out of Kilrea. We spent a lot of time perfecting these techniques and in this, we much preferred the Navy flyers who would go almost anywhere and do almost anything asked, whilst the RAF stuck, very much, to the strict interpretation of the rules and the task was second best.

The wide open spaces of the hills and mountains around south county 'Derry were much used by the Provos for transit – weapons caches and training, but finding them was a needle in a haystack task in this type of country. However, sometimes we got lucky, and after a team had bumped an ASU [IRA active service unit] near Maghera [Glenshane Pass] we were called in to do the follow up.

One squaddie* had died and another was hit seriously, but in the firefight, at a range of just a few metres, they had hit one and the blood trail from the contact point was a foot wide and 25 metre's long, until it suddenly stopped. After close examination you could clearly see where he had used grass and moss to stuff into the wound and stop the bleeding, but a faint trail was still visible and it led up the hill to a large thicket of trees and gorse. 2 of the guys went in and after a shout and the clicking of cocked weapons and safety catches; there came another cry of 'OK I give in.' It was a known player, Frankie Hughes!

Frankie Hughes had been wanted for some time after the killing of several UDR soldiers by UVBT [under vehicle booby trap] and shootings. He was carrying a chromed .38 revolver, which was removed by the SB officer and the large and bloody hole in his side, made by the SLR round, had been stuffed with a jay cloth as well as grass and moss. He was taken away and after interviews, he went into the Kesh but the saving of his life was a waste of time because he starved himself to death later as one of the hunger strikers.

We also spent much time lying up under hedgerows watching the houses of UDR men suspected of being on the hit list, as well as huddled up in ditches and manure heaps watching houses and likely hide areas; we would use standard VCP ops to seal a large area and search the vehicles within it or we would do a planned route clearance op to another location, to ensure no culvert bomb awaited a unit vehicle somewhere along the route. There were also call outs to assist in 'Derry City and the occasional 'tight ring piece' time awaiting a call out to an incident or riot or suspected device or something similar; life was never dull.

During the UK firemens' strike we were sent down to assist 10 UDR in Belfast in giving cover to the Green Goddess crews; at this time there was a bombing campaign going on with attacks on businesses in the city centre, but this had been so well sealed that they began targeting the routes to it. This night we were called out of Musgrave Park (the caravan park at the back of the hospital) where we were living, to an IED device that a warning call to the BBC said was on the Lisburn Road near the Village area; we duly arrived, deployed and began searching the various shop fronts.

During this phase I came across a plastic bag attached to the shopfront grill by a butcher's hook through the handle. Now you would think that, after all these tours and with that much experience, I would click alert but I still pulled the bag open to look inside. The petrol can had a mortar round taped to it and a wrist watch timer as well as the usual parkway timer and semtex ball with detonator! I let it down slowly and walked very 'tight-cheeked' to the Land Rover, which I then pulled back 50 metres and yelled to the guys to clear all the houses from this junction outwards. We hadn't been going 5 minutes when it detonated and a giant hand threw me into a wall and then tried to push me through it; a large bolt stuck out of the back of the calf my right leg and I was totally deaf.

The ensuing fire was ginormous, so I pushed the cordon farther out and ATO cleared the route in, to allow the Green Goddess boys to get started on doing their thing. At the same time I tried find out where the rest of my platoon were and more importantly, how they were. 'Chin' Humphries, the acting platoon sergeant got back to me and shouted out his SITREP – we had 3 guys wounded by the blast and me deaf and limping. I was doing the SITREP back to Zero when a young motorcyclist tried to rush his way through the cordon. The fire hoses all

Another day, another Belfast riot

Another Belfast riot

over the road threw him off the bike which then careered on into my guys manning the checkpoint and taking out 3 of them, one very seriously.

'Chin' had a somewhat violent discussion with the youth until he was led away; we had been quite seriously thumped and this left us very thin on the ground but we coped! Some 3 days later, we went back to Ballykelly just in time for Xmas, leaving 5 of our guys recovering in Musgrave Park (Mlitary Wing). My hearing came back in time for the Sergeants' Mess Christmas Ball and the rollicking I was getting from the wife.

We had handed the TAOR over to 1st Cheshires and [sometime later] a bomb in the local pub at Ballykelly village killed a number of them, but how this was allowed to happen we will probably never know, but for us the area was out of bounds as a natural and high risk target – maybe, in relaxing the rules to normalise an area, the risks too have to be taken but it was ever thus in the province!

[* The soldier who was killed at Glenshane is thought to have been Lance Corporal David Jones of the Parachute Regiment.]

The incident to which Mike is referring was the attack at the Droppin' Well public house which killed 17 people when it was attacked by INLA terrorists on December 7, 1982.

CROSSMAGLEN: 1976
Corporal Tom Clarke, RCT

This was an action-packed tour and so much happened during these months, that I'm not even sure where to start. We were sent down to XMG and were attached to 2 Para and when they shipped home, 40 Commando Royal Marines took over. We were supposed to be driving Saracens, but none of the boys liked them, vulnerable as they were to the IRA culvert bombs and we rarely did anything other than ensure that they were fuelled, armed and ready to go if they had changed their minds.

XMG – as anyone who was there will tell you – was a hell-hole and I guess that we shouldn't have been surprised when we dropped in by helicopter and the two RCT guys we were replacing jumped on with barely a few words. There was barely a backwards glance and they looked so glad to be out. Our sleeping accommodation was basic to say the least and the only things in there apart from an old bunk bed and a couple of mattresses, were 2 Browning .50 cals, eight spare barrels and 5,000 rounds of ammunition.

Before we flew in, we had been warned that the posting was a 'dry out' one and that there would be no booze and birds and music and then, to our surprise, on arrival, we were told that a disco was planned. This was to be on the Saturday night and quite a lot of helicopters began landing and bringing in what we thought was loads of booze and then 15 women were flown in. We thought 'Yes!'

North Armagh (photo courtesy of Regimental Museum of The Royal Welsh)

but they were put into combats and webbing and put onto the next chopper as though they were going out on patrol. All through Friday and into Saturday, patrol activity increased at an incredible rate. By evening, there was only 6 of us left in the base and it was then that we were told that it was a 'come on' to the IRA and we hoped that they would think that our guard was down for the festivities and try and 'bounce' us.

So, all night, we shouted and sang and threw empty booze bottles over the compound walls and made a real racket. The IRA stayed away, but the next morning, the good people of XMG came to the camp to complain about the noise!

There was an attempt by the IRA to cause us some grief one night and they did this under the guise of a drunken fight outside the camp. Two guys got out of a taxi, apparently drunk and had a spot of fisticuffs which soon broke up and they dispersed. Some time later, a patrol came back in and reported what looked like an army-issue torch outside the gate. The guard commander went out and managed to loop a bit of string around it without handling it, fed the string out as he walked backwards and got behind a metal fence and then tugged. Boom! Another detonation but no casualties.

THE CASE OF THE DAMAGED DRESSES

Major Andrew Macdonald, King's Own Border Rgt

It was during the period which later became known as 'Marie Drumm's long hot summer'. A Sinn Fein activist, she promised that she would shut down the whole of west Belfast and, as posterity has recorded, we prevented her from doing that. Once she had announced her determination to disrupt our part of the city my old CO, Joe Milburn, made it plain that we would prevent her from achieving her objectives.

At the time, ourselves and some Jocks had control of Turf Lodge, Lenadoon, Glassmullan in Andersonstown, Fort Whiterock and Henry Taggart on the 'Murph.

The incident which I am about to relate was when the Mobile patrol and the Recce platoon were based at the Glassmullan camp. A gunman had taken a few unsuccessful shots at one of my patrols and, although none of the lads had been hit, soldiers take great exception to being shot at – it annoys them just a little – and, on catching sight of the fleeing gunman, immediately gave chase. They opened fire and a couple of rounds went wide and hit the upper floor of a local house before one of the lads hit the gunman in the leg and down he went. The soldiers were using, of course, 7.62mm rounds in their SLRs [muzzle velocity 823 metres per second] and the impact almost took the unfortunate gunman's leg off. Very badly wounded, he hobbled to the nearest house and burst in and locked the door behind him.

My soldiers needed no invitation and crashed in through the door, disarmed him and dragged him out without ceremony and off he was whisked.

We did apologise to the lady of the house and told her that we would make good any damages and she was, surprisingly fine about the whole incident. Later that day, there was a polite knock at the gate to our base, and she was taken to see the boss and presented him with a rather large bill, including the door which had been kicked off its hinges and considerable damage to her clothes. Naturally, the boss queried the latter and so he accompanied the complainant back to her house to inspect aforementioned damaged clothing.

She took him up to her bedroom – chaperoned no doubt by a squad of young soldiers – and showed him a bullet hole in the wardrobe; she then opened it and showed him 9 or 10 dresses all with an identical entry and exit 'wound' in exactly the same spot in every one of her dresses! A stunning day for community relations.

MORE BELFAST

Jim Parker 3 Light Infantry

I used to drill it into my section that although I conducted most searches and stopped most people whilst they guarded me, they should not hesitate to stop and search if they thought it necessary to do so. Pte Wills, generally speaking a quiet young man who spent most of his spare time writing letters home to his wife, went off with another section and the Intelligence Sergeant Curly Cusworth.

On his return he told me with great delight how he had stopped a young man walking down the street carrying a plastic guitar case. The young man immediately dropped the case, and then from there on professed to have never seen it in his life before. The case contained two Armalite rifles, an M1 rifle, a .38 revolver and an amount of ammunition. I was very pleased for Pte Wills. However, his name was never mentioned in any of the reports printed later about the incident.

Typical squaddie humour, cartoon of the period (courtesy of Roy Davies)

I finally made some sense of the origins of the eponymously named 'Borucki sangar' in XMG. I have seen it spelled Berucki, Barucci et al and no two persons seem to agree. He was 19 and a member of 3 Para.

A former Parachute Regiment soldier wrote:

He was killed by an RCIED [remote controlled] in XMG on August 8, 1976 when a parcel on the back of a bicycle was detonated by an IRA terrorist. He wasn't suspicious as he knew the man to whom the bike belonged.

THE KILLING OF JAMES BORUCKI: 1976

Corporal Tom Clarke, RCT

This incident took place on August 8, 1976. I knew the lad reasonably well and we always chatted; on the day he was killed, I was in the choggy eating a wad when he came in and we got chatting. He knew that I was pretty bored stuck inside the compound day after day and he asked me if I fancied doing his stint on the next patrol out. I said that I would and off he went to see his CSM in order to clear it with him.

A few minutes later, he came back and said that request had been turned down and off he went with the rest of his patrol; a three brick strength. I should point out to you that SOPS [standard operating procedures] for returning to base at XMG was to approach with one guy on defensive position on the wall to watch the stick through. He would cover the patrol and then they would cover him coming back.

Another Belfast riot

A couple of hours later, I was sitting in the Ops room with the 2ic and watching the patrol come back on CCTV. We watched James – the last man in – and as he walked past a black pushbike, there was a loud bang and then a plume of smoke and the lad was gone. James was killed instantly by what turned out to be an IRA remote-controlled bomb. Poor lad. I can't say that I knew him really well, but he was a nice lad, enjoyed having a chat with him when we had time and he was always ready with a smile. I think that the IRA booby trapped that bike because they knew we wouldn't be suspicious about it.

ANDERSONSTOWN: 1976

Perry Lusher, King's Own Border Regiment

I was checking out Belfast on 'Google Earth' recently and could not find any familiar landmarks such as the Amity Flats near Shankhill Road, or the old police station where my company was based for four months during the winter of 1974/75, even the sniper paradise of the circular housing estate Ballymurphy eluded me!

I was born in Blackpool, England and emigrated with my family to Canada when I was nine. There were several reasons why I ended up in the British Army but the main one was my desire to drop out of high school where I was going nowhere fast. I enlisted back in Blackpool as soon as I turned seventeen and began my first tour of Northern Ireland almost two years later. One of my reasons for joining the King's Own Royal Border Rgt was that, at the time they were just completing an eighteen month tour over there and weren't due to go back for a couple of years.

As I mentioned, my company were to keep an eye on the Unity Flats area and Lower Shankhill Road as far as I can remember. A lot of bombings were going on around that time but I seem to remember a brief ceasefire about halfway through the tour. We were the first outfit to escort two-man RUC patrols back into the Flats. This took some balls on their part although they never went near the hardcore Republican areas like the Ballymurphy, where we ended up on my second tour the summer of the following year. That deployment was far more eventful with eight of our guys wounded as far as I can remember. The I.R.A. had managed to get a shipment of Armalites from the States into the country and there were a few of them being put to use in the 'Murph. It's just occurred to me, I can't recall if they were military M16s or civilian semi-auto M15s, but I recall the night they opened up on one of our patrols inside the local lumberyard, hearing automatic gunfire.

The patrol had been sent in as somebody had been tossing Molotov cocktails into the Protestant-owned yard; my section was just outside and we were trying to knock out a nearby street light with rocks, when a couple of gunmen opened up from the top of the nearby apartment building. I think that we all shot the lamps out at the same time before turning our SLR's and emptying the rest of our mags on the building. The poor people inside must have been terrified and ducking under their beds; fortunately nobody was injured including our guys.

But we weren't always so lucky; one night one of our patrols went inside a Republican bar to look for suspects when things got ugly and the guys got jumped and they had to fight their way out. It was in that incident in the club that an Alsatian was let loose by the opposition and got a baton round down its throat.

One of my mates who was there said he actually fired into the crowd. When the standby platoon arrived, the corporal in charge was fired on from a nearby hill and seriously wounded. I think that incident actually made the news, but most of what went on in that area went unreported, which in retrospect was probably more to do with the government keeping a lid on the situation than a shortage of press.

Another incident that a patrol from our Recce Company was involved with in the Andersonstown area actually sparked the big peace movement that year.

Borucki sangar in Crossmaglen

The incident which Perry refers to was the shooting of an IRA gunman, Daniel Lennon on August 10, 1976 following a car chase through Andersonstown. The car in which Lennon was trying to escape then hit three children who were walking with their mother, killing them. As a consequence of the tragic deaths of the Maguire children, Joanne (8), John (2) and baby Andrew, two local women founded the Peace Group which became internationally famous. The children's mother, Anne Maguire was very badly injured in the accident and committed suicide 41 months later.

The casualty figures for 1976 were further swollen by a RTA whilst soldiers were being driven to the airport for a flight home on leave. On March 13, an Army vehicle collided with a lorry and the following four men were killed: Gunner James Reynolds (RA) Corporal Douglas Whitfield and Sergeant Michael Peacock (both RAOC) and Signalman David Roberts (Royal Corps of Signals).

Chapter Ten

1977

A year of 1,143 bombings, 1,081 shootings and the deaths of 29 soldiers, 14 RUC officers, 59 civilians and 10 terrorists.

A two month killing spree by the IRA, targeting off-duty UDR soldiers, left 5 dead including a female UDR Private, Margaret Hearst. She was shot in her parents' garden at Doolgary, Armagh. By the year's end, 13 UDR personnel had been killed, all, without exception, off-duty and often in or near their homes. For a UDR soldier, the morning routine had become a thorough under-vehicle inspection.

BELFAST: 1977. TWO VIEWS OF THE DEATH OF A SOLDIER

Rifleman David John Hallam, Royal Green Jackets

I served with 1st Battalion the Royal Green Jackets. I was sixteen when I signed up and was nineteen by the time I was walking the streets of Belfast; it was 1977, the Queen's Silver Jubilee.

I remember that it was a long three days and nights – we only got about six to eight hours sleep the whole three days. Then, the shit hit the fan, as rioting broke out and one riot went on in the New Lodge Road for about twelve hours; our riot shields were breaking under the weight of the rocks and iron bars which were raining down on us.

At that point, the order came over the net that we should use baton guns because we were now getting petrol bombs thrown at us. We had PIGS three abreast across down the street and from a good vantage point, you could see the ring leaders. At this point, we moved down in block formation with two of us as the snatch squad and, as we got close the front row opened and the pair of us ran into the rioters and grabbed the one we wanted and took him back to the formation. We then moved back to the PIGS and our only worry was that gunmen could be in the crowd – which sometimes happened.

Things calmed down and a few days went by, though everyone was still tired. However, the boys in Recce platoon who were in their OP needed their mail and rations and so after a bit of a discussion, Billy Smith took it out, but on his way back just off the Antrim Road and only 100 yards or so from the front gate, an IRA gunman was waiting. He opened up from a window and fired three rounds at Billy; he was hit twice in the back and once in his head. The wound in his face was so big, it took seven field dressings to fill the hole and the poor lad took thirty minutes to die.

I remember the Land Rover coming through the gates with blood pissing off the floor and some of the boys had to go out with buckets of water and brooms to wash the blood off the street. Everybody in the company was getting ready to go out on the streets to find the killer and we were all deeply upset and pissed off.

246

Belfast kids stone a Green Jacket patrol (courtesy of Dave Hallam)

However, before anyone could get to the front gate, the company commander doubled the guard and ordered us all to stay in the base.

We had to carry on as normal and the next day we went out on patrol and there was some sort of party going on in the streets and the boyos were all singing, mockingly and insultingly: 'one nil, one nil.' We knew what they meant. We stopped everyone we came across; getting names, doing checks and telling them 'OK fuck off' when we had finished with them. However, as bad luck would have it, I stopped this particular bloke and held him by the collar of his coat, demanding his name, which he gave me; so we did a name check and it came back ok. We told him to 'piss off', but a few seconds later it came over the radio the awful words: 'correction; wanted for the shooting of Billy Smith!'

Oh fuck! We ran the way he had gone, but no luck; he had gone! Luckily, about a week later the boys got the bastard.

The tour went on with the same type of shit; sadly, we came back home, one less that time. Billy's wife was due to have a baby two weeks later; this is something I will never forget.

GIRDWOOD PARK, BELFAST: 1977

David Smith, Royal Green Jackets

Corporal William (Billy) Smith was shot and mortally wounded on the night of the 31st August 1977 at approximately 21.00. He was serving in the Recce Platoon 1st Battalion Royal Green Jackets based in Girdwood Park Belfast. Billy and three others were returning from Unity flats in a short wheel based Land Rover; as it turned into Kinnard Place, off the Antrim road (opposite Gerry Fitt's house) 3 shots rang out.

I was inside Girdwood Park having a coffee before going out on a foot patrol and we immediately switched on our (Pye sets) radios. We heard a voice say 'Contact, sunray; call sign 60 alpha mortally wounded.'

Cpl Billy Smith had been hit twice, once in the shoulder, and once in the head but sadly, he was beyond help and died shortly afterwards. 5 Platoon 'B' Company, 1RGJ immediately cordoned off the whole block of houses and shops opposite and waited most of the night. I spent the night in a doorway while we waited for the search teams and police to finish their work. When we eventually moved back into camp, myself and Lee Griffin were told to clear up the remains of Corporal Smith which were on the road and which covered a wide area. I went into camp and got a bucket of hot water and washed it over the road and down the drain. I thought at the time, 'this is not a very respectful way of disposing of another British soldier'; it was surreal.

I remember a girl coming down the footpath, with a smile on her face. What I said removed it quickly; it was something along the lines of, 'you'll get this f****g broom around your head.'

The perpetrator, Paul Baker, who lived in Upper Meadow Street, was arrested some weeks later and the weapons were recovered from a search of 25 Pilot Street, Belfast. The weapon was recovered from a 'tip off' but I can't be absolutely positive; I recall the Light Infantry lifted him in their area (Ballymurphy). They were going to bring him back to Girdwood Park, to us but he begged them to take him to North Queen Street RUC station.

Corporal Smith, who was 29 and from the Liverpool area was shot by a gunman – later jailed for a double murder – in Kinnard Street, New Lodge on August 31, 1977.

Green Howards graffiti (photo courtesy of Jim Foster)

ROYAL VICTORIA HOSPITAL, BELFAST: 1977

Lance Corporal 'Tiny' Rose – 2 Royal Anglian Regiment

I served in Northern Ireland, January–May 1977 and was stationed in the Royal Victoria Hospital, Belfast as part of the intelligence unit, visiting the casualty department to see gunshot wound patients or anyone else who might be of interest. Funnily enough I should not have done this tour of duty but was assured that I was being sent on a safe job!

On 26 May 1977, mid-day, I was walking along the corridor in the hospital to collect lunches, and thought it strange that the corridor was empty at this time of day as it was usually busy with people going back and forwards for lunch. I passed an open door, checked and there was nobody about outside and was about 15 metres past the door; the next thing I knew was that I was being shot at. As the first shot hit me in the left shoulder, it sent me tumbling to the ground and spun me round so that I was looking at the person shooting. Whereupon he fired 2 more shots at me, one of which hit me in the left leg, near the hip joint and the third one hit me on the right side ending close to the spine.

Each shot felt as though I had been kicked in the balls and the two which hit me after I had gone onto the deck actually lifted my body off the ground. The pain was terrible.

As I fell to the floor the gunman was still shooting at me, and I tried to fire my Browning 9 mm but it had jumped out the holster and was laid under me. When I got the weapon in my hand and went to fire, all I got was 'click' and realised that the mag had jumped out with the impact of hitting the floor. By the time I had resolved the problem with one hand – as my left side was useless – the gunman had fled out the door, leaving a knife on the floor and rounds of live ammunition. After I was removed from the scene, several further bullets were removed from the wall.

I was taken to the operating theatre, but stopped on the way to speak to my wife on the phone. Whilst in the operating theatre, they decided to clean the wounds and leave them open. On the following Tuesday I was transferred to the military hospital where I was taken to theatre once again for the wounds to be checked over and stitched up. The bullets were not removed as they decided it was too risky to remove as one could possibly leave me paralysed and the other would leave me impotent. To this day the bullets are still in me and in the last 3 years I have gone from being 30% to 60% disabled and getting worse every day.

My wife, June, was at first told that I had been stabbed and she was in a state of shock and confusion. Later, she would be speaking to my CO and she told me the following account. 'It's not nice when the CO comes to your bedside and says 'I'm pleased it was your husband who was shot.' It was only many months afterwards I realised that what he meant was that Tiny lived because he is 6' 6", a smaller man would have been dead as the bullet through his shoulder would have gone through the head and the one in his spine would have hit the heart area.'

The funny side of things was when my partner came to the casualty department to take my weapon from me and instead of ejecting the magazine, he ejected all the rounds into the sink and they had to get a plumber in to retrieve the ammo.

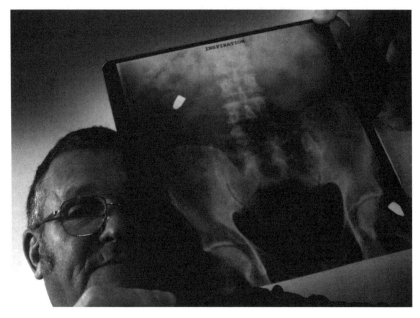

'Tiny' Rose holding up an x-ray showing injuries that still scar him today (photo courtesy of Mike Day, www.ijlb.com)

I was transferred to Queen Elizabeth Military Hospital in Woolwich where I stayed until suitably fit to return to my quarter in Gillingham, Kent. I was back and forward to hospital for a year and medically discharged on 7 August 1978 with no help or guidance as to what would be my life in Civvy Street.

FERMANAGH BOMBS: 1977
Cpl Richard Peacocke, 321 EOD

I joined the RAOC's 321 EOD Detachment at Omagh, Co. Fermanagh on 11th December 1976. The team was led by Sgt Martin 'Wally' Walsh and I was to be his 'No.2' as an Ammunition Technician Corporal. We had a Signalman attached and were protected by a team of 9th/12th Lancers (9/12 L) soldiers under the command of a Corporal.

Wally and I were old friends as he and I had graduated from the Army School of Ammunition at Central Ammunition Depot Bramley together in 1974 – the 1973A AT Course, for afficionadoes – and had done quite a bit of EOD training already, though not with the new Wheelbarrow robots or proper bomb suits. He had transferred over as a full Corporal from the Royal Military Police and was promoted to Sergeant before me. Thus, he was 'No 1' or Operator – FELIX, I think, was still just a call sign then – and I was his No 2.

The day I arrived at Omagh, the team were up-country in rural Fermanagh or Tyrone dealing with yet another dozen firebombs, and didn't get back until very late that night. Early the next day, I had a quick tour of the equipment stuffed into the back of an armoured Ford Transit van, as it was then, and we set off on a series of EOD tasks that were to span the next few weeks.

We were treading on dangerous ground. The accepted opinion had been that Tyrone-Fermanagh were IRA QM [supplies] areas and so not hot spots... hmmm? This didn't seem to be the case, as Wally's team had been at it solidly for some time before I got there, and certainly didn't stop just because I had arrived!

I had already lost two close colleagues to the violence there. Doug Whitfield had died in a car crash on the way home and Cpl 'Cal' Brown had been blown up alongside WO Gus Garside in a gap in a hedge at Ford's Cross in Armagh on 17th July 1975 – just 18 months before – so we were all on our mettle.

[ATO Edward Garside (34) and Asst ATO Calvert Brown were both killed in an IRA bomb explosion at Ford's Cross, Forkhill on July 17, 1975. They were killed alongside Major Peter Willis (37) of the Green Howards and Sergeant Samuel McCarter of the Royal Engineers. Please see the 1975 chapter for an account of this.]

In the next month, we dealt with several sets of dozens of small cassette case firebombs – they always came in dozens like oysters – a handful of parcels and boxes, some typical-looking bombs (one with a clock on top and battery underneath), and a couple of car bombs.

Often we were escorted by the armoured recce vehicles of 9/12L [9th/12th Lancers], and the sight of a Fox armoured car with a flat tyre being raised on a bottle jack while the undergrowth all around bristled with Lancers at the 'ready' is not one a young man easily forgets – nor the rocket-like flight of the jack down the road when the driver just backed off it to save time!

At one urban car bomb I was sent around the corner to check on the report of another bomb, when this second device went off – 'initiated', as we used to say. As I was just around the corner from it I was blown off my feet, skidded on the

EOD on the long walk

back of my Flak jacket down the wet street, and slid straight under a Saracen armoured car, only stopping when my EOD helmet caught under the rear differential casing and nearly pulled my head off!

A Lancer jumped out and pulled me clear, and I ran around the corner. A small device had initiated in the doorway of an electrical goods shop. A large redheaded RUC Constable was standing in the doorway across the narrow street from it looking rather shocked and probably wondering why he was still alive. He was holding his cocked Sterling Sub-machine gun at the high port across his chest and was stock-still staring at the hole in the wall across the road from his post. Next to him was a large shard of windowpane stabbed into the door behind him and still quivering. I asked him if he was okay and he said yes, but he couldn't move because he was covered in broken glass. I let the firemen deal with him – and told him he was a lucky sod.

A second car bomb we dealt with was in the middle of the night in Castledillon or Castlederg or some such small town – I don't recall, as there were so many bombs and so many towns. Our Wheelbarrow [robot to inspect and destroy explosive devices] went forward and delivered an opening charge, then broke down yet again. Wally was forced into a series of manual approaches under the close scrutiny of the locals: the town was a straight road with houses along it and the RUC/Army cordon was in but visually open along its length. Wally was tired and, being a soldier first and a technician second (as one should be), he got pissed off and cut a corner or two on his Render Safe Procedures (RSPs).

Wally had a cold that was blocking his sense of smell and stopping him sleeping, so he didn't catch the scent of CO-OP Mix coming of the partially-disrupted device; we could smell it, but his tiredness and cold had made him grumpy and I

IRA culvert bombs (photo courtesy of Mike Tomassen)

don't think he really believed us. We wanted to 'soak' the thing – to leave it for a while – until the road could be cleared of civvies and morning came, but he disagreed and stood stubbornly on his superior rank. He then made the RSP errors.

He made a series of manual approaches – he walked up to the car – without his EOD suit on. He disrupted the TPU – the Timing and Power Unit – and used the hook'n'line to drag two milk churns from the boot. He then squatted on them and used a mallet to knock the churn lids off; and then emptied the explosives out. All this happened under the gaze of the locals and anyone else who wanted to watch and film it.

It all ended happily that night, but we castigated him severely when back in private (which he took well), and also had no idea of the horror to come from this set of macho-inspired mistakes caused by tiredness and illness. We should have reported him to the Boss but he seemed chastened and we thought the lesson learned. Don't misunderstand me – he was an excellent and experienced EOD Operator, a good soldier, and a great Team Leader, but he was tired and poorly that night. What we didn't know was that he had been watched and filmed by the PIRA.

Now, the next part is hard to explain and impossible to understand. We were getting a bit of rest as the Boyos took a break from their incendiary attacks over Christmas. The whole area of operations had gone quiet and we crept peacefully into January 1977, when I started to feel very, very uneasy indeed. It was late at night, and cold and frosty. A full haloed moon shone down from a clear sky. The whole barracks was bathed in a weird silver-grey light. I felt strangely that someone was watching my every move, and I just couldn't sleep. I had to do something, but what?

I knocked on the door of the telephone operator and asked her if there had been any reports that evening of anything going on. She was wide awake and felt the tension too, but said all was quiet except that the Duty Sergeant had asked her the same question, and the Dog Section had phoned to apologise as their dogs were restless and barking. I started to believe that something was wrong.

Two days later we got a call about a bomb having been laid in the night at a post office on the Eire-Fermanagh border, at Newtownbutler on the Clones road. This is still a major border crossing and any disruption there is commercially and politically serious, so Wally and 'Sasquatch', the area's Royal Engineer Search Advisor, devised a planned approach and RSP to clear the blockage as soon as possible. The plan called for me to command the team alongside an RE road clearing effort to rendezvous with Wally and his escort, who were to ride in to the site by helicopter with the Heli-EOD kit as an emergency back-up.

Early on the morning of 9th January 1977 we set off from the barracks in armoured convoy while Wally and his escort went to the helipad to await their chopper. Not long after we set off from our start line, they flew low over us and on to the bombsite. As we crawled along the two miles to the scene behind RE soldiers sweating under the weight of mine detection equipment, the sky cleared and the sun blazed down on us low on the horizon – a beautiful frosty winter's day. We were all reasonably relaxed when there was a thump in the distance, and I started to feel sick. The Battalion Net crackled open with a 'contact wait out' report followed quickly by 'Felix Down', and Sasquatch came sprinting down the line of vehicles from his halted search teams to confer with me as to what to do.

Overlooking the Ardoyne area of Belfast (courtesy of Dave Hallam)

I was by now really worried about a 'Come-on' follow-up attack – Gus and Cal had only been killed 18 months before – so we agreed to continue the clearance plan under his command to get safely to the scene, which was only a short way ahead anyway. As we moved forward again, helicopters flew over us at high speed and very low – the various OCs and COs arriving at speed.

Our convoy finally entered the cordoned area around the post office and our Signalman erected a comprehensive ECM [electronic counter measure] screen. The RE Searchers and Sasquatch fanned out and searched the area, and I had the job of handing over a shocked team to the EOD Captain investigating what had gone wrong.

We found out much later that Wally had been filmed at the previous car bomb and been seen sitting on the milk churn with his hammer. He had been watched as he had attacked the device by hand, and a trap had been laid. When he had arrived by helicopter at the scene, he had been told that the device was contained in a milk churn, and that it had malfunctioned the night before and been soaking ever since inside a tight cordon. He had then decided to ignore his carefully conceived plan and re-enact his previous RSP errors, those same errors he had been filmed doing a week or two before.

He decided perversely to approach the device without ECM cover, his combined team, or his remote vehicle, and wearing only a Flak jacket and beret for protection. He attached his hook'n'line and toppled the milk churn out of the shop entrance. He walked up to it and sat astride the churn. He reached inside.

Fred, his close protection NCO from the 9/12L then said he shouted over that he could see wires and a clock but couldn't make heads or tails of it. Fred wisely took cover behind a low wall 25 yards away as he saw Wally reach into the open neck of the churn. As he ducked down, he felt a concussion and a noise so loud he couldn't hear it; and when he looked again Wally and the churn were gone and a puff of grey smoke was drifting across the border in the bright sunlight, and the frayed end of the hook'n'line was lying near him in the road.

An extremely brave and highly intelligent man, an old friend, a good soldier, a loved son and brother, and an honoured father and husband died before he reached 30 years old through a foolish error – but arguably that's how we were all going in those days so long ago.

The follow-up revealed his Browning side-arm in the snow some distance away. I took charge of it, and had to clean bits of Wally off it into a corner sink full of warm soapy water. I defrosted it and found it was loaded and ready with a round missing; it had cocked and fired in the explosion. The missing round became a focus and worried me for some time until the forensic scientists found the spent case.

Sergeant Martin Walsh who was 28 and who lived in Hereford was killed on January 9, 1977 by an IRA booby trap at Newtownbutler, Co Fermanagh. He was married with 2 children and a very popular member of his team.

BELFAST: 1977
Steve Atkinson, Gordon Highlanders

1977 was not an especially happy year for the Bn, because on August 28, L/Cpl Jack Marshall, from 'D' Company, was shot and killed by a sniper whilst on foot

Back alley in Ardoyne area of Belfast (courtesy of Dave Hallam)

patrol in the Ardoyne. After this, two 'Jocks' from the Gordons, were killed in an RTA along with two RUC officers who were both severely injured.

[Lance Corporal Jack Marshall, who was 25, was the father of a young child, died shortly after being shot by an IRA sniper in the Brompton Park area of the Ardoyne. He was from the Dundee area and died in the RVH in Belfast. In the same incident a local child was also injured in the shooting but recovered.]

In the summer, the firemen went on strike, and we covered this by providing firefighters and close escort for this period; 6 weeks in all, there were no serious incidents involving us during this period other than fires and fatalities from fires. During this time I personally was a close escort for those acting as firefighters; we operated from Flax St Mill. I recall that every fire we attended, we needed to put a long crowbar into the fire hydrant cover, tie a piece of line around the top, clear the area and open the hydrant cover by pulling on the line; this was in case the fire was an ambush and the hydrant cover booby trapped.

One young 'Royal Scot', Private 'X' who attached to us, lost control of himself, and attempted to shoot the other members of his section, in the accommodation block at Palace Barracks. He was detained in the guardroom but committed suicide by choking himself to death during the night; this if I remember rightly was early autumn '77.

[The author is aware of this unfortunate soldier's name but has been asked to withhold it.]

In that autumn, the now infamous destruction of the La Mon Hotel disco happened; terrorists, believed to be the IRA, placed an IED in a fire extinguisher filled with petrol. I think 14 or 15 young people were burned to death, and many more injured.

[On February 17, 1978, twelve people, including seven women, were burned to death when the IRA placed a firebomb at the La Mon house, a bar and club situated outside Belfast. Even to those hardened by the sights of atrocities during the troubles this was regarded as one of the most sickening events of the period 1969–98. Newspaper reports of the time report that most of the bodies were burned beyond recognition. A pious statement from the IRA apologised for the fact that the warning they gave the RUC was inadequate; they did however, refuse to accept criticism other than from the relatives and friends of the dead and their own followers. Another empty gesture from the men of violence.]

On a lighter note, after a minor contact incident where a sniper shot and missed him, 2nd Lieutenant Pearson forgot that he had one round 'up the spout', (chambered), and accidentally shot himself in the foot with his SLR, whilst resting the muzzle on his boot. He was back on duty in a couple of months. One of our Sergeants, Mick Kelbie, stepped on a large IED; he was lucky in that only the detonator went off.

One serious incident comes to mind though, during our Belfast tour, in 1977. Two Royal Artillery lads were killed in the Belfast City Centre, from a M60 MG, fired from an elevated position outside the city. Royal Artillery, Military Police and those types of 'non infantry' soldiers were given the city centre as their 'patch' as it was deemed 'slightly safer' than the more hostile areas that the Infantry or Royal Marines would cover. The latter areas would include the Turf Lodge, Ballymurphy estate, Whiterock, the Ardoyne and the Lower Falls area.

BELFAST 1977

Jim Parker 3 Light Infantry

Following Standard Operational Procedures on or about 23 June the Platoon Commander and his three section commanders; me, Jimmy Robinson, and another Cpl who I cannot place, flew off to Belfast to spend a few days with the 2nd Battalion The Royal Anglian Regiment (affectionately called the 'Angle Irons') who we were to relieve. Our area of responsibility altered a bit from theirs, but it was similar.

More and more Light Infantrymen arrived and 3LI drivers, many of whom were familiar with the area, drove vehicles on administrative runs. The Angle Iron Corporal came to me, 'Jim,' he said quietly, 'I've just seen vehicles driven by your blokes leaving the mill and turning right!' He continued, 'That way leads straight onto the Falls Road; it's a perfect ambush site!' I agreed with him.

I remember the briefing for my section's first patrol. A briefing by the Platoon Commander or the Platoon Sergeant always preceded all patrols. Each patrol was to be carefully pre-planned including the route to be taken.

Reece Platoon, Divis Flats
(photo courtesy of Regimental Museum of The Royal Welsh)

The Platoon Sergeant came to brief me and with the section gathered around a map. With a chinagraph pencil he began to draw our intended route. 'Sergeant, can I have a word ... ' he looked up, 'What?' I wanted to speak to him in private. 'What the f**k is it Cpl Parker? Spit it out!' he snapped.

'That area is no longer part of ours; it's in another Company's area now!' I explained, and one of my lads sniggered. If looks could kill the Sergeant's expression would have dropped me stone dead. 'Right,' he started again, 'You'll patrol these streets,' he looked up at me, 'If that's alright with Cpl Parker?' 'Those buildings don't exist anymore Sergeant,' I explained, 'The whole area is flattened.' There were a few loud sniggers, and a deadly glare from him.

About the same time soon after the Platoon's arrival our Platoon Commander, wanted to reconnoiter a site close to the Divis Flats. An area, I had known well two years before, as did my driver. We were to travel in two Land Rovers, my vehicle following his. 'Have you got a map, Cpl Parker?' he queried. 'No, sir,' I grinned 'I know this place like the back of my hand!' 'You need a map, Cpl Parker, go and get it!' 'But, sir ... ' 'Go and get your map, Cpl Parker!' the little pipsqueak insisted.

From the section I heard muffled sniggers. I had to make my way up three flights of stairs to collect a map I had no need of. I returned from my trip and deliberately stuffed the unwanted map up the back of my flak jacket.

The place we were intending to visit (although Booth had not told me so) was a former Company position, which was to be guarded on rotation by 'C' Company sections. The weather was bright and sunny and my vehicle followed the other Rover. The Lieutenant's driver took several wrong turns; many streets were blocked off for security reasons. So it was not an easy task for someone new to the area. The young officer, after driving around for a while stopped his vehicle within full view of the Divis Flats (an IRA stronghold). Clutching his map he ran back to me and said, 'Where are we Corporal Parker? Show me on the map.' More sniggers.

I noticed at the Mill, that most of our vehicles, because it was more convenient, drove out of the main gate and turned right. Onto the junction with the Falls Road exactly which the Royal Anglian Corporal had warned was dangerous.

My section had gathered in the briefing room in preparation for a foot patrol. Once again I tried to take the Sergeant to one side to speak to him, but as usual he wanted me to speak in front of the lads. I said to him that the Angle Irons had warned me about vehicles leaving the Mill and turning right into a potential ambush area. The Company Commander walked into the room at that time. The Sergeant called over to him, and said something like:

'Sir! Cpl Parker thinks that vehicles shouldn't turn right on leaving the main gate, because the Angle Irons said so!' his voice dripped with sarcasm. The Company Commander spoke to me in a most patronising tone, 'Corporal Parker, you get on with your job and leave transport routes to others who know what they are doing!' Or words to that effect. My section was having a great time watching me squirm.

The nine sections, from the three Platoons in the Company, guarded the ex-Company location I spoke of earlier on rotation. We soon discovered it was a nightmare to guard properly. All the NCOs made comments about how potentially dangerous it might be. Cpl Jesse James, the holder of the George

Borucki sangar, Crossmaglen (photo courtest of Mike Day, www.ijlb.com)

Medal at one time, wrote an eight-page report, which he passed on to the Company Commander.

My section was at this position near Divis Flats when an ambush occurred in North Howard Street on 19 June 1977 – a Land Rover with Lieutenant Colonel John Hemsley and the battalion's Padre and a 4 tonne with soldier passengers was fired upon by three snipers as they drove into North Howard Street from the Falls Road, exactly where the Angle Iron Corporal had predicted.

Two soldiers, Pte Richard Turnbull aged 18 from Guisborough, Yorkshire and Pte Michael Harrison aged 19 from Dinnington near Sheffield were killed outright. The CO, Rev David Hewitt and the CO's driver L/Cpl Georgeson were wounded.

One of the uninjured passengers in the 4 tonne was a Private Stockley, who told me later, he heard shots and turned to speak to the man on his left and saw a 'rose' growing on his forehead!

I was informed by fellow Corporals, that the OC refused to allow them to conduct a 'follow up', as we had practiced, because, 'someone might get hurt.' Until that day, 3 LI had the lowest casualty rate of any major British unit whilst on a tour of Ulster.

Although it was sometime later in the tour, a hand-thrown bomb exploded in the perimeter of the section guarded Company near Divis Flats, and we Corporals were proved to be right yet again.

Both the C.O. Lieutenant Colonel John Hemsley and Padre Hewitt had only been in the Province for 2 days, prior to the IRA ambush at North Howard Street.

THE QUEEN COMES TO BELFAST

Jim Parker 3 Light Infantry

Her Majesty the Queen's visit to Northern Ireland, and the Anniversary of Internment coincided; we were involved with riots and demonstrations. Strangely I can remember very little about those exciting times. One day I had to go with my PIG to TAC HQ, where there was a minor riot outside the main gate. I asked an officer if we might delay our departure until the row had quietened down. But he'd not hear of it. Leaving the HQ battened down, with our protective metal windows up, the driver was unable to see clearly, hit and knocked over the brick gatepost! This was shown on TV that night!

There were heavy riots when the Queen visited Belfast. A soldier was leaning across the bonnet of an armoured PIG firing his baton gun at the large hostile crowed. To operate the gun the soldier raised his visor. A missile, one of many thrown that day, smashed on the bonnet. A chunk of grey concrete bounced and went down his throat. Within seconds he was chocking. Literally chocking to death. Jimmy Robinson who was taking cover behind the same vehicle, realised something was wrong. He made straight for the distressed soldier and grabbed his neck and wriggled his hands about until the object shot out of the lad's mouth. I watched this all happen helplessly from about twenty yards away. Jimmy, I believe, saved the man's life.

Chapter 11

1978

A year of 748 bombings, 755 shootings, and 21 soldiers, 10 RUC officers, 43 civilians and 10 terrorists killed.

This year also saw the incendiary bombing by the IRA of the La Mon Restaurant near Belfast which burned alive 12 civilians. It also saw the first shooting down of an Army helicopter at Bessbrook, killing Lt Col Iain Corden-Lloyd, of the 2nd Battalion, Royal Green Jackets.

On June 21 that year, the Army shot dead 3 IRA gunmen as they prepared to rob a Post Office at Ballysillan in Belfast. Sadly, an innocent civilian was killed in the cross fire.

Green Jackets in Belfast (courtesy of Dave Hallam)

Green Jackets in Belfast (photo courtesy of Dave Hallam)

PERSONAL RECOLLECTION: BELFAST 1978–1980.

Martin 'Starsy' Starsmore, 1st Battalion, The Green Howards

I was a serving soldier with the 1st Btn Green Howards for eight and a half years. I served in the Province on an 18 month tour which was horrendous at times. In those days you were at risk of a contact every time you left the camp gates; most times we travelled to our ops in unmarked Sherpa vans.

We did our ops in the city centre segment gates, the Ardoyne, the Markets, Divis flats and the Shankhill Road area; we also did operations all over the province, including convoy patrols in Armagh escorting post office vans.

I arrived in the province as an 18 year old with no experience on the streets; I had to do a series of N.I. training before being allowed on the streets. Within my first few months of being in the Province, I saw a lot of things that would turn people's stomachs. For instance, one day out on patrol in the Ardoyne area, a young girl came running round the corner been chased by another female wielding a bread knife. She plunged the knife into the girl's back, but she survived; we later found out it was the girl's mother.

Another time out on patrol in our Land Rover going down a back alley, we got a call on the storno [radio], telling us to stop where we were, as another patrol from another Regiment had been coming from the other side of the alley, when the squaddie standing up in the Land Rover got some cheese wire lodged in his forehead. He was ok, but that's what they used to do, to decapitate you.

I was on duty in an op when a guy came outside the op shouting: 'I have been shot! Help me', but we wouldn't go down because that's what they used to do, try and get you to come out so you walk out into a trap; anyhow the chap had been shot in the stomach, but it was down to sectarian killings.

Green Howard (photo courtesy of Jimmy Foster)

Another instance occurred when I was on duty on a segment gate in the city centre – a woman came through with some hand mufflers on, when she was asked to remove them she pulled out a 9mm pistol and shot the civilian searcher in the leg. There was another incident when I was on duty at Crumlin Road prison, where a prisoner had been getting escorted through the tunnel from the courthouse to the prison, when he pulled out a blade and sliced the officer's throat. Lord Mountbatten was blown up on my tour; we went to Warrenpoint when the Paras were blown up by the hay-bale trailer.

The only one that I still get flashbacks of is, when we were out on routine foot patrol in the Markets area of Belfast, when we stopped to do a pub check. Now, the pubs were surrounded in metal cages and cameras everywhere, and all the walls painted white nearby. I was stood about 13ft away from the main door of the pub, crouched down behind the corner of the wall, when a soldier from another Regiment (which I would like to be kept anonymous), stood against the white wall. I told him to come away but it was too late! I heard the crack and seen the lad slump and slide down the wall; he had been shot in the head. We could not do anything; he was dead, but you can imagine the panic, 'Where is the gunman? Can anyone see?' We called all the necessary call signs and got the area secure and safe.

For me people don't look on Northern Ireland as a war, but from my experiences I would strongly disagree, as every day for 18 months was spent wondering whether you were going to see the end of your tour. Obviously I was one of the lucky ones, but my heart and condolences go out to all that lost their lives for a lost cause.

PORTADOWN: 1978

Mick O'Day, 12 Intelligence

I had now been in Northern Ireland for three years as Brigade photographer and by this stage I was responsible for photographic training and technical advice in the South Armagh area. I was nearing the end of an extended tour and was based near the 'Coach' at Bainbridge at Mahon Barracks. Bainbridge was one of the 'safe' havens in the Province and the IRA didn't bother us there; it was very much a Proddie town.

I was in the 'Coach' one night getting pissed – as usual – and I was eyeing up this really beautiful girl but lacked the courage to ask her to have a drink. Cursing myself, I left and then decided to go for it, but to my surprise, she then approached me, chatted me up; Christmas and Birthday all rolled into one ! The name of this beauty was Shioban Sxxxxxxxx and, whilst alarm bells should have started ringing, I was clearly thinking with another part of my anatomy; that and the beer, dimmed my natural military caution. I started dating her – she was a Catholic girl who lived on a farm near Lurgan – and saw her several times.

On the third or fourth date, I picked her up – she obviously knew that I was a Brit, but assumed with the long hair etc that I was a civvy – and we drove to the cinema in my very un-military sports car. We parked up, and as we did, three yobboes stood in front of the car in a very threatening manner. I quickly pulled out my personal protection weapon, a Walther PPK, cocked it and positioned it

Funeral at Portadown (photo courtesy of Mike Day, www.ijlb.com)

Royal Green Jackets on rural duties (photo courtesy of Dave Hallam)

between my legs, at which point she went ballistic but then wasn't the time for explanations. The three stared at us and then walked away and, against my better judgement, we went inside the cinema. At this point, I had no idea if they were ogling her, the car or just trying to intimidate me but decided to take the risk.

We only stayed 15 minutes and then left and to my consternation, saw that they had followed us out and got into their car as we got into ours. I drove Shioban home – in absolute silence – down the winding country roads to her farm and then set off for home myself. Just as I got to the end of the long farm track, I noticed that they had pulled their car across my path and that there was no way through and I was forced to a stop about 2 metres from them. One of them was out of the car and in his arms was a Thompson Sub machine gun or it might have been an AK47, but my mind was concentrating on staying alive rather than identifying weapons! He strode up to my car and stuck the firearm through the window and said to me in a real Lurgan accent 'I don't know who ye are, boy, but if ye come back, we'll fuckin' shoot ye.'

What saved my life was the fact that I didn't open my mouth because had he heard my British accent, he would have assumed undercover soldier and that would have been it! Then they pulled out of my way and drove off and I did the same. Later on, back at base, I did an immediate check on Shioban Sxxxxxxx and found out that she was the girlfriend of a major player who was in the 'Kesh for murdering RUC and squaddies. I had picked up and was sleeping with major 'slot' material but my excuse was that I was mesmerised by her beauty.

I had had a very lucky escape and made sure that I never risked my life again.

Roy Davies (RRW) inspects bullet holes in PIG (photo courtesy of Roy Davies)

ARMAGH: 1978
Sergeant Roy Davies, RRW

I had been made up to Sergeant by this tour and my brother Hadyn was now an RSM and we were both in Armagh at the same time.

I was in charge of a VCP one day, and we stopped a car which had two blokes in it, both wearing big coats. I asked them where they were going and one of them unbuttoned his coat and showed me his RUC uniform. Now, apparently, he was the top or one of the top policemen in the country and he demanded that I let him go. Really, he could have been anyone and I wasn't happy with his explanation so I asked him where his hat was and he told me, angrily that it was in the boot. I told him to get out and show me and he refused and I shouted loudly to one of the lads to cock his rifle and point it at the man, which he did so.

Finally, I got on the radio and he took it from me and spoke at length to my CO and complained bitterly about my conduct. Eventually, he handed me back the radio as I was having another look at his vehicle and the CO gave me a real bollocking and ordered me back to the base in Armagh city. I was put on CO's orders; my punishment? Banned from future VCP duty, which pleased me no end, I can tell you.

Mike Heakin, later RSM 1 RRW, killed by the IRA at Ostend 13 August 1988 (photo courtesy of Regimental Museum of The Royal Welsh)

BELFAST: 1978
Steve, UDR

There are some events that, whether we were involved in them or not, are burned into our memories for many reasons.

I was literally just off the Liverpool boat after some leave, and was on my way to catch the bus from Oxford Street, when I noticed a pair of stripped-down half-tonners from 4RTR go past – the guys in the back had their weapons in the aim position, scanning as they drove down the street; I knew then that something bad had happened recently.

This was when the segment gates were still in operation in the City Centre – as my bus made its way through the streets I saw other well 'switched-on' Rover crews at traffic lights around town.

It was only when I got back that I heard the sorry story.

On March 3, 1978, on what is traditionally known as 'rag day', at least four IRA terrorists dressed in fancy dress mingled with students who were in all manner of attire as they collected money for various charities. In the city centre that day in Lower Donegal Street, close to the site of an earlier IRA atrocity at the Abercorn restaurant, civilian searcher Norma Spence (25) was on duty and nearby Trooper James Nowasad (21) of the Royal Tank regiment.

Belfast was systematically destroyed

The detritus of urban warfare

The detritus of urban warfare

Apparently, the young soldier was smiling at the merriment and was then shot by the gunmen; Norma tried to run away but they ran after her, shooting her three times and killing her.

Chapter Twelve

1979

A year of 624 bombings, 728 shootings and the deaths of 48 soldiers, 14 RUC officers, 48 civilians and 3 terrorists.

It was also the year of Warrenpoint! On a terrible day in August of that year, on the same day as Lord Louis Mountbatten was murdered by the IRA, a total of 18 British soldiers lost their lives in a bombing ambush. On August 27, 16 men of 2 Para and 2 men from the Queen's Own Highlanders were killed there; it would be the worst single day for loss of soldiers' lives during the troubles. It would also be the worst day's loss of soldiers' lives for the British Army since the Aden mutiny in June, 1967.

A sad loss, later that year was of a Warrenpoint survivor, Private Peter Grundy of the Parachute Regiment who was killed by an IRA bomb at Forkhill, 9 days before Christmas.

NEW LODGE, BELFAST: 1979
Stephen Griffiths, 1st Battalion the Green Howards

I first joined the Battalion in Berlin on a two year posting, and then in June 1978 we were told we were going in for an 18 month tour of Northern Ireland. I had a short leave at home then travelled down to Liverpool on the overnight ferry to Belfast.

On arriving at Belfast I didn't really know what to expect and very soon, we shot round the outskirts of Belfast and on our way to camp at R.A.F. Aldergrove where we were the first Battalion to do an 18 month tour. On arriving at camp, we were very quickly sorted out by the admin block people, and handed our flak jackets, batons, and riot gear. Then it was all go!

I then started the long haul of walking the streets of Belfast in areas such as the New Lodge, Ardoyne, and, of course, the City centre. Like most units on active service, your day is split up into different times such as 2 hours on immediate, and then 10 minute. Then comes all the rest camp duties, ops room, sangars, gate duty; the list is endless and tiring. Like many others, I was only 18 when I landed in Ulster and raring to go.

The first couple of weeks were very quiet and not a lot was happening; that was all to change! We had riots, contacts, kneecappings, bombs and robberies; as I said before, the list was endless! It seemed like a big game at first, going out to riots, giving protection to the R.U.C, checking people, VCPs, house searches and the like.

Later, I was stood down at North Queen street police station having a drink and a burger in the choggy shop waiting for my next patrol. I was talking to Cpl Jim Burney from the 1st Battalion the King's Own Border Rgt, who was just going out on patrol. He said to me 'See you in a couple of hours! Get them pool balls set up.'

270

Ever vigilant – a squaddie stands watch

It never happened ! He had just 2 weeks to the end of his tour when he was hit in the chest by a sniper. BASTARDS! That's when it hit me; the short time I had known him, I had found him a great bloke and morale booster. R.I.P.Jim.

So as they say: 'stag on.' More street patrols in the pissing down rain, 10 till 12 midnight then get back to camp to try and dry out. And back out at 4 in the morning – still pissing it down- Oh, God, I wish was at home; still 16 months to go. Anyway as time moved on, we members of 'B' Company, or at least the selected few, became Spotter platoon, which was to take us all over Belfast in various locations and OPs. The work we did was quite interesting, using all the specialist equipment cameras etc. And most of all, being able to keep in touch with the patrols on the ground and to direct them to any suspicious circumstances.

I would just like to fit in that during my time in the Ops, seeing and hearing lots of things, there is one thing that sticks in my mind. It was a Sunday night about 9.30pm, and it was quiet and then a car came towards our OP; it went past us and went down a street on our blind side. About twenty seconds later, I heard a burst of three to five rounds being fired and then the sound of screeching wheels; it wasn't hard to imagine what had happened. However, I remained silent on the radio and then another OP in the area said '30A, was that a contact?' I replied that I wasn't quite sure, knowing full well that it was and giving the gunmen's car a head start out of the area.

Then after two minutes a crowd of people came from the public house screaming: 'Get help, you bastards; someone has just been shot! '

Bandit country! Locals look on

It was only then did I break radio silence, and then within two minutes the area was flooded with security forces. If only I had had acted quicker, that car – probably from some Loyalist organisation – could have been caught! Who knows, or maybe I was thinking of Jim?

27 year old Corporal James Burney who was from the Lake District was shot by the IRA at Baltic Avenue off the Antrim Road just 6 days before Christmas, 1978. The round which killed him also wounded another soldier.

TURF LODGE: 1979

Kingsman George Prosser, King's Regiment

I was 18 years old and this was my first tour of the Province and I went out having been frightened for some time at the prospect of being there. I had spoken to other Kingsmen, especially those who had been on the infamous 1972 tour when seven of our lads had been killed. This was the May of 1979 and in the previous month, four soldiers had been killed just in West Belfast.

On April 5, two lads from the Blues & Royals, Anthony Thornett and Anthony Dykes, were shot and killed in an ambush at RUC, Andersonstown after the IRA had held a family hostage to carry out the attack. Just 6 days later, in a carbon-copy attack, the IRA had killed two of our lads on the 'Murph. Kingsman Christopher Shanley being killed and Stephen Rumble losing his fight for life 8 days later. I was a member of the Search team and had been involved in follow-up operations in both incidents; it brings your own mortality home to you when you get this close.

The incident to which George refers took place on April 11, 1979. IRA gunmen holed up in a house in Glenalina Crescent on the Ballymurphy estate and attacked a King's Saracen. Kingsman Christopher Shanley (21) was killed and Lance Corporal Stephen Rumble (19) very seriously injured. Christopher was single and came from the Liverpool area.

Eight days later, Stephen lost his fight for life and died of the wounds sustained in the attack on the Ballymurphy estate. He was also from Liverpool and was married with a pregnant wife. Having had the honour and privilege of meeting both his widow Karen, and daughter Stevie, the author can attest to not only the incredible nature of this soldier but to the lasting legacy he left.

George Prosser:

As I said, I was frightened but so busy and so involved that you can only really focus on your job; you don't have time to worry about your future. Anyway, the tour was coming to an end and despite the loss of Chris and Steve, Colchester and some home leave was tantalisingly close. We had been getting so many 'red hot tips' from our Int boys; we had tips about weapons or known players and we even had a tip off about Gerry Adams; all were fruitless and time wasters. Then we received news that some radio transmitters had been stolen and that they might be smuggled into the area for use by the IRA during the hours of darkness. We had previously spent many nights holed up on the Turf Lodge [separated from the 'Murph by the length of the Whiterock Road] trying to intercept the couriers without success.

Wednesday May 9 started well; sunny and bright. My patrol (23 Bravo) was briefed for a routine patrol; nothing out of the ordinary and off we moved. Enroute for the Turf Lodge, we encountered another patrol (23 Alpha) who covered us as we crossed and we reciprocated and then we advanced into the estate. As I walked through Ardmonagh Gardens, I chatted with two guys from the other patrol and we reached the 'Disco Block' (where the local youngsters had music parties) and noted the patrol commander and another guy were on the top floor for a vantage point. We then headed for our position near the tallest flats in the area and a haven for IRA snipers.

It was easy for a gunman to squeeze off a shot and then disappear into the surrounding with no chance of capture. Myself and another guy went to the top floor where we could see over the entire estate. It was calm and we chatted for about 15 minutes, covering our arcs of fire and then suddenly, there was a huge bang. I saw smoke coming from a large hole in the roof of the 'Disco block' and I recall a great sense of disbelief where everything stopped and I didn't know what had hit me; this is shock. Confusion was overcome by an order from the patrol commander to follow him and we raced down four flights of steps, cocking our weapons as we ran.

At the rear of the building, as we ran through an alleyway, we were warned that we were in full view of the 'Murph and a secondary attack – used with great effect by the IRA – could occur. In Ardmonagh Gardens there was chaos and confusion as other patrols poured in and I got down on my belly in one of the gardens faced out towards Whiterock Road, making myself as small as possible. By now, people were flooding out of their houses and there was another bang; I jumped as I knew it was a shot but had no idea where it had come from; my heart was pounding. Things calmed a little as snap searches were being made and we heard that someone had been killed and any door not opened immediately was kicked in. All the flats were empty apart from one in which a couple were sitting.

They were unwelcoming but they knew from our mood that we weren't going anywhere until we had searched it. New began to filter through that one named guy had been killed but we were not told that it was Andy Webster; a little later it was confirmed and I went into complete denial; it was such a hammer blow but I had to accept that there was nothing I could do about it.

Back at Ardmonagh Gardens a Saracen ambulance was there and there were people milling about, including lots of children which struck me as odd; many of them were shocked and crying. Then we realised that the IRA had launched a bomb attack whilst a 'Save the Children' playgroup was taking place; yes, the IRA had detonated a bomb as the children attended a nursery class! It beggars belief that the IRA who claimed to have the interests of local people at heart could carry out such a callous attack.

This was not the first nor last time the IRA would display its complete disregard for human life – any kind of human life – and on February 25, 1973, a little boy, was wounded and died. William Gallagher,who was 9, whilst playing in his own back garden in the Creggan estate in Londonderry triggered a trip wire fixed to a bomb intended for soldiers; he died later in hospital. The IRA callously tried to blame the Army for deliberately triggering the device. Earlier, children were hurt near the Divis Street flats in Belfast when they were caught in a blast which killed a Gloster soldier.

Kingsman Prosser

The terrorists had waited until Andy was in full view of the top window and then detonated the explosives; he never stood a chance and lying just outside the entrance to the flats was Andrew's rifle. Another lad had been injured but we knew no more than that.

A young lady then came over to me – in her early 20s – and she sobbed as she put her arms around me; she said 'I am so sorry that the young lad has been killed.' I put my arm around and led her to the safety of her home and she asked: 'Why is all this going on?' I urged her to go inside and replied 'I don't know.' I realised that her sorrow proved to me that what we were doing was welcomed by some, at least and what she did was courageous considering the repercussion of her actions from the other locals.

One local man came out and was seen to be smirking and there was something about his demeanour which just didn't seem right and he was arrested. Two youths began gloating about Andy's death which was both

Andy Webster, King's Regt – killed in action on the Turf Lodge 19 May, 1979 (photo courtesy of George Prosser)

despicable and very foolish as our emotions were running very, very highly and people can lose control at such times.

After an hour or two, we returned to Fort Monagh and, as we expected, the atmosphere was one of great sadness and a feeling of emptiness hung over the place. Words cannot describe the scenes that I witnessed inside the platoon accommodation; many lads were in tears, others either stood or sat in silence trying to make sense of it all. Nobody knew quite what to say so few words were exchanged and members of other platoons seemed embarrassed to say anything for fear of causing distress; I suppose that I would have felt the same.

The other injured soldier was in the RVH and physically at least, he would recover; psychologically, who knew? Can anyone experience what he had and not be affected? He had survived, apparently, because as the explosion occurred, he was standing under a stairwell and was protected from the full force of the blast; he was lucky, because had the bomb gone off just a few seconds later, he too would have been killed.

We had to go out again on patrol that evening and we were very subdued at the briefing as we were told to be professional and let the locals see that we could still perform to the highest level despite what had happened. Clear instructions as to avoid confrontation with the locals were given irrespective of provocation as that showed our discipline. The only recollections I have of the journey back to Turf Lodge are that it was very quiet and except for a small group of kids, it was like a ghost town. Whether or not they stayed indoors deliberately, I honestly couldn't say, but it was a wise decision on their part and it ensured that there was no further incident.

After only 15 minutes of that patrol we were ordered back to camp; I am not entirely sure as to why, but it was felt that there was a very strange atmosphere and maybe the commander on the ground felt that there might be another attack with more casualties.

One thing I would like to say was that every man of the regiment involved in the events of that day behaved impeccably and they were a credit to that regiment.

Andrew Webster was single, aged 20 and came from Merseyside. His parents first heard that a soldier had been killed shortly before an Army families' officer broke the news to them of Andy's death. The author met Nell, Andy's mother, during the course of research for this book and can attest to her courage and dignity.

BELLEEK: 1979

Mick O'Day, HQ 3 Infantry Brigade

Belleek is very close to the border and a lot of shit went on, down there. On one particular occasion, a Republican march was being organised by Sinn Fein and as ever, we knew that PIRA would be around so we'd be watching.

[The IRA were past masters at laying just over the border on the Republic side, sniping at SF targets and remote detonating explosive devices which they had planted on the Northern side.]

We drove into the RUC station there on a photographic op to see which players we could spot and we found two Special Branch (SB) from the RUC in attendance who took command of the op. No planning, no preparation, no discussion, the four of us in my car just drove out of the gates and a the few metres from the station to the 'T' junction then sat with our stills and video kit waiting. My mucker and I just looked at each other in disbelief, we both thought that the entire thing was a fiasco so far – anyone who might be interested – had seen us drive out of the fortified RUC compound, down the road and then stop! Who were we trying to fool? We were sitting ducks.

As the march got near us, as expected, all sorts of bricks and bottles and shit came raining down on the car; the video man got a great movie of a man hurling a brick and the brick arcing through the air and crashing through the rear windscreen! Of course, we immediately drove back to the RUC station fortunately only a few seconds drive away; the mob knew exactly who we were; it was so amateurish. Lucky for us, they were only chucking bricks and bottles.

So there we were, sitting in the compound, car wrecked and the licence plate now known to the IRA – for all the jokes about the Irish, their intelligence was spot on – and we were in trouble. We put in a request for air-evacuation to Portadown but we were refused. Fortunately for us, the IRA are not always that quick to react – they put a lot of effort into making sure they could strike, then run away to safety (IRA … I Ran Away) so they planned their ops thoroughly to reduce the risks. So we set off, half expecting the worst, tails between our legs in a battered, windowless car which had just been pelted by a mob because it had been sitting by the roadside, with four guys in it, two of whom were waving big lenses around and pointing them at the marchers. No mistaking who we were; this op had broken all the rules.

We were armed of course but not heavily armed. As we drove off down a long single track road – too narrow to turn the car around on – we saw a car parked at the side a few hundred metres away and four men moving with what appeared to be 'longs' (rifles). They disappeared into the woods by the road and naturally we thought that maybe, we were about to be attacked, so my mate opened the sun roof and stood on the passenger seat, head out, weapon cocked ready to open or return fire on these men.

We drove very fast and at what was, we thought, the very last moment, saw that the men were all armed with ... fishing rods ! They never did find out just how close they came to being on the other end of a hail of 9mm and departing this earth that day.

COALISLAND: 1979

Major Allan Harrhy, RRW

This was a very interesting tour and the Bn spent 6 months in the area around Coalisland although on one occasion, I came close to meeting my Maker sooner than I had planned.

Whilst on foot patrol in the town, it was brought to our attention by a civvy that there was a suspicious looking package tied to the window sill of a nearby bank. We checked his story and it was correct, so, true to our training, we evacuated the area and threw a cordon around several surrounding streets and I looked at the package through my binoculars and confirmed that it was very likely to be a bomb. I radioed for the ATO and also the RUC and received instructions that the former was on his way.

I got the message back that ATO was on his way and the route he would take and I needed to let the patrol know this and then I made what was nearly a fatal mistake. Instead of going behind the shops to see the rest of the cordon, I decided to avoid all the mud and the puddles and instead walked past the bank – on the opposite side of the street, of course – and the suspect package. As I got directly opposite and just 20 feet away, I heard the timing device go (just like an egg-timer sounding) and I dived into the doorway right next to me and it exploded! It shattered all the windows around me and set fire to the bank and a huge chunk of metal whizzed past where my head would have been and straight through the window of the doorway. My ears were ringing and I was dazed and I couldn't believe that I was alive.

Despite this incredible ringing in my ears, I heard my radio burst into life and I will never forget, to my dying day, what was being shouted. It was Lance Corporal Murphy and he called 'The Colour Sergeant is dead, he's been killed!' I quickly got on the radio and explained that rumours of my death had been greatly exaggerated.

THE FUNERAL OF ANDY WEBSTER: 18 MAY, 1979
Kingsman George Prosser, King's Regiment

Lance Corporal Webster was buried with full military honours in the grounds of Christ Church, Moreton on the 18 May, 1979 after a service in which literally hundreds of people had attended. Not just his family and friends but many former colleagues from the Regiment and some veterans of the 1972 tour. As a mark of respect many local people lined the route as Moreton said farewell to one of its sons. Sadly most of his colleagues were unable to attend due to operational commitments. We did, however, have a short service in his honour at Fort Monagh.

He was finally laid to rest in the grave with his elder brother who had died two years previously aged just 26.

As a little postscript to this, some time later when I was out on leave I was shopping with a relative and a car backfired and I ran into the doorway of a British Home Stores to take cover. At witnessing this, my female companion was astonished at my behaviour and so too were other shoppers nearby. There again, they did not know the situation I had just come from; had they done so, they might have been a bit more understanding. I was like a coiled spring and still nervous and had not had time to completely unwind.

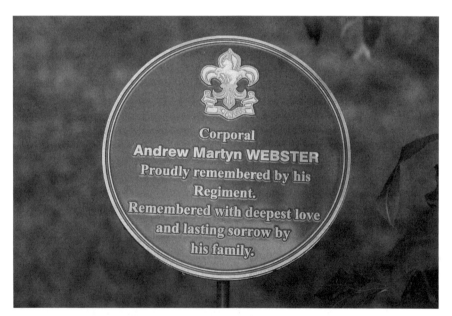

Memorial to Andy Webster (photo courtesy of George Prosser)

PADDY LARKIN, 2 LIGHT INFANTRY

Belfast, 1978–79

Whilst stationed at North Howard Street Mill we frequently visited my area for a cuppa before commencing our patrol. I was born and bred in Springmartin and still had friends and relations there.

I left Belfast to join the LI as my neighbour had married a chap from 1LI. I was previously in 10 UDR at Girwood. I can remember to this day how sometimes people in Springhill Ave used to shout but when they realised that I really did know them, they shut up with the shock.

I was sent away as a child with Catholics from Springhill Ave to Holland for 3 weeks so I got to know quite a few of them. My Dad drove a black taxi on the Shankhill road and he used to have the Light Infantry plaque on his dash board until I saw it and removed it.

He lived up at the top of Ardoyne Road and he drove a black taxi up and down the Shankhill. He had been stopped so many times by 2LI that he came to the Mill to complain. I was sent to the front gate sangar to take the complaint.

My dad and his girlfriend where there but as they had not seen me for such a long time they did not recognise me. He started to complain about him being stopped and his taxi being searched so often. He used to have a LI plaque on his dash but it disappeared and he wanted it back. I informed him that it was not his and he should not have had it.

He tried to tell me that his son had given it to him as he was in the LI. I then told him that he did not and that I knew that he had taken it from his mother's house who was my guardian all my life. He then realised who he was talking to and told his girlfriend to get in the taxi and drove off and I have not heard from him or seen him again.

Henry Taggard Memorial has closed down and has been pulled down. Springhill has totally changed; all those grotty houses have gone and been replaced with newer grotty ones.

A DAWN RAID ON SPRINGFIELD ROAD, 1979

Squaddie, Infantry Regiment

Without exception, the houses stank of cabbage, onions and piss! I once kicked over a bucket of such liquid in a 4 a.m. raid and still remember the way that the ammonia stung my eyes instantly! There were kitchen areas – usually a corner, curtained off – and then shabby furniture, on which the overspill kids slept (six or seven people might occupy the upper two bedrooms) and every room was dominated by a picture of Jesus and, or the Virgin Mary and Catholic bibles aplenty.

One constant was that, even that early in the morning, whenever a crowd gathered – without exception, minor (and sometimes major) riots would break out, often spreading beyond our FP area into other adjoining areas where other regiments might be patrolling. We returned the Irish cocktails, nail bombs, broken glass, paving stones and the like with CS, baton rounds (rubber bullets) and our expertly trained snatch squads and, when the need arose, we returned Provo gunfire with 7.62mm rounds.

Sometimes we got the player – more than often, they had fled – and sometimes we got some petty thief for the green bottles and as we threw him in the back of a PIG (Patrol Infantry Group; an armoured vehicle) he would cry out 'Up the Provos!' when in actual fact, they were as much as an enemy to him as we were!

ARMAGH: 1979

Major Mick Low, Gordon Highlanders

I was now a shiny bum, but determined to support the Jocks on the ground as best as I could. A tour that took an eternity to pass as very little happened in our area of responsibility.

However I couldn't let the opportunity pass without reference to the sentry box in Drumadd Barracks. It was a rainy day and one of the Jocks on duty was inside the box, when a helicopter came into land on the helipad. The box was blown over with the Jock still inside. The poor guy could not get out as the opening was towards the ground. Talk about a long stag.

My lasting memory was on the day that Lord Mountbatten was murdered in Co Sligo and the Parachute Regiment and our fellow Highlanders lost many men at Warrenpoint.

THE DEATH OF A UDR MAN: 1979

RSM Haydn Davies, 2 UDR

I was posted as RSM of the 2nd Bn of the Ulster Defence Regiment in Armagh City. While I was there I befriended Lance Corporal Tom Armstrong, he was the gamekeeper to The Earl of Caledon on his estate near to the Irish border at Middleton. Caledon estate was a large and beautiful wooded country estate where deer and wildlife ran wild.

The present Earl was second in command of the battalion and the son of the late Earl Alexander of Tunis. Tom was 65 and over-age to serve in the UDR, but a few white lies were told to allow him to serve and look after the security of the estate while guarding the battalion second in command. Tom was armed with a service rifle and a personal protection weapon, a small .22 pistol.

Tom was certainly out on a limb, he was often alone by day and night. Being right on the border his life was positively under threat. We all feared for his safety. The estate had been attacked recently, and UDR members had been killed locally. Tom actually lived on the Irish border with the back door of his cottage virtually in the south. I visited his house several times and found it quite unnerving. We had his chimney fitted with night marker flares. In the event of attack he could pull a cord and the flares would shoot skywards. A British army infantry company was situated at a border check-point about one mile away.

Some nights I spent some hours with Tom on the battlement roof of the Estate house at Caledon. I once introduced him to the 'Starlight scope' which

Squaddie takes a breather in bandit country

allowed vision at night, Tom thought it quite magic but thought it would never replace his 'eyes and ears' for knowing what went on around and about the estate. As we packed up to leave on these evenings Tom would place his rifle in the Earl's arms room and lock it up with a chain lock. Several times I said to Tom. 'Why don't you take your rifle home with you?' His answer was always the same. 'When they come for me there will be too many of them'

They came for Tom on the 13th of April 1979. The estimation is that there were between three and six of them. Tom was ambushed in his little van on the way home after feeding stock at the estate during early morning. He died at the scene from multiple gunshot wounds.

I attended Tom's funeral with a heavy heart; he was most certainly one of the world's nice fellows, gone! I recalled his stories of how he would heat the greenhouse each spring time and always produce new potatoes on St Patrick's Day for the Earl's lunch. Also how he thought he knew who bombed the main Caledon house, and that he would 'Have a word with him one day'

As I stood at the graveside, I looked out over the countryside and saw three castles: One a medieval motte and bailey affair, the other a 17th century castle, still occupied. A little distance away was the third: A British army tinned and sandbagged fort! I looked at all three defensive sites dating over ten centuries, all situated within a kilometre square. I realised then, that dear old Tom was far from being the last to suffer a violent death hereabouts.

Thomas Armstrong was actually 64 and he was murdered by the IRA on Corr Road, Tynan and was the oldest serving UDR soldier to be killed. He was killed on

Good Friday, having been shot 15 times. It is reported that the funeral of this man who was due to retire one week later, was attended by over 1,000 people from both sides of the border. Yet again the IRA had killed simply for the sake of it, for no political or military gain whatsoever; yet again they had selected a soft target.

COALISLAND: 1979

Major Allan Harrhy, RRW

One morning, like pretty much any other, I was absorbed in the routine of the Ops room at Coalisland when I was shaken by the sound and vibrations of an enormous explosion and I do mean ENORMOUS! The whole police station was rocked.

The target, however, was not us and we kitted up and 'crashed out' of the station in the direction of the explosion and as we hit the road with our Land Rovers, we saw an ambulance with its blue flashing light and in the absence of any accurate sit reps we decided to follow it. It travelled towards Washing Bay, which for us was an area which we respected enough to patrol on foot. It was, however, regularly mobile-patrolled by the UDR and my first thoughts were that a UDR patrol had been ambushed and blown to pieces, judging by the sound of the explosion.

Suddenly, the ambulance swerved to the left and screeched to a halt and we naturally did likewise. As we jumped out, we saw an enormous bomb crater 10' deep and as wide as the road; it stank of H.E. and just about everything else. But of casualties or wrecked vehicles, there were no signs whatsoever. We started to search the entire area and saw on the hilltop two figures legging it away from the

Squaddie in Northumberland Street area of Belfast

top. We didn't bother to open fire as they were too far away and we weren't sure if they were the bombers or just innocent civilians. So, we slogged up the hill and found the firing point very quickly, marked by a large sheet of plastic on which they had lain to keep dry.

We found the command wire leading to this gully at the top of the hill and the device was very simple with an ordinary domestic bell-push being the triggering device. Because we had gotten there so quickly, they had not had the chance to remove any of the evidence. ATO later confirmed that it was a milk churn packed with explosives and hidden by the road and that it was probably aimed at hitting a UDR patrol due later. It seems that the would-be bombers had gotten bored and were playing about with the bell-push and had triggered the device prematurely.

DUNGANNON: 1979

Major Ken Draycott, RRW

By now, I was Company Sergeant Major of Support Company and the Bn was posted to Dungannon and all 4 of the companies were split. We were due there on December 30 in time to relieve the Jocks from the Scots Guards who wanted to be home in time for Hogmanay. We were due to sail from Liverpool, but the weather was terrible and the ship's skipper refused to sail. This would have led to a riot among the Jocks over in NI had we not relieved them and eventually and grudgingly, the skipper sailed and so bad were the seas that there was barely a man on board who wasn't violently sick.

The big thing when we arrived at Dungannon was searching, searching and more searching; it was the ethos of the time. Our RSM – Haydn Davies – was the Bn Search Advisor and I had 3 search teams under me. We searched at local level once a week; up at 3:30 am and r.v. [rendezvous] at 6 in the area in question. We would be given our maps and our task and off we would go; looking for IRA arms caches and the like.

I was also responsible for 'hot searches' (immediate aftermath of incidents etc) and I used the 'Winthrop' theory. Captain Winthrop (RGJ, I think) theorised that the IRA, if they had hidden arms or explosives wouldn't rely on the simple 'Treasure Island' method of hiding trove. Their methods would be simpler, but nonetheless, effective; in that, they would find an area and then find something which stood out and use that. If, for example, they were using – as they often did – a graveyard, they would select a distinctive headstone and use that as a marker. I put this to the test one day and whilst searching a graveyard at Dungannon, spotted a pink marble headstone, and, sure enough, we made a find right by it. We called out the sneaky beakys to stake out the place and our job was done; well done in fact.

In truth, we didn't have that many great finds in the Company and we always suspected that the RUC Special Branch kept all the good tip-offs to themselves.

One particular day – market day in Dungannon – I was in the Ops room when a young Second Lieutenant by the name of Marshall, a likeable but naïve young platoon commander came on the radio. He told us that they had discovered a suspect package inside a horse box in the market place. The last words I heard were 'We are advancing to have a look ... ' when all of a sudden

Royal Green Jacket with IWS on his SLR
(photo courtesy of Dave Hallam)

there was a huge explosion and the room shook and no further words came from the radio. A couple of seconds later, there was a whoosh and then a crash right next to us and I dashed outside to see a huge but charred horsebox wheel had flown through the air and landed in the yard. We could see the smoke and the, suddenly, the radio crackled into life again and I hear the immortal words of the young officer, Marshall, ' I can now confirm that it was a bomb.'

We had a bloke called Morris 61 and he was our token Englishman; the only one in the entire Bn. Nice lad but unfit and overweight and he was the Company commander's driver and photographer. Anyway, we heard that some of the Army top brass and the Secretary of State for Northern Ireland, Roy Mason were coming in by helicopter for a visit. His estimated time of arrival was midday and all our officers including the CO would be there at the square to meet him and his entourage.

The Company commander grabbed Morris 61, told him to get his camera and be on the square 15 minutes before arrival and to make sure when Mason landed that a photograph of him together with the leading politician in the Province was secured. By now, the snow had started to fall and by midday, it was like a blizzard and was really starting to pile up. It was well past 12 when we were informed by radio that the flight had been called off. The blizzard continued and then, suddenly, at 12:20 a bedraggled Morris 61, resembling a snowman burst into the Ops room shouting: 'What fucking time is this Roy Castle coming?'

Republican march at Dungannon (photo courtesy of Mike Day, www.ijlb.com)

COALISLAND: 1979
Steve Atkinson, Gordon Highlanders

In the Summer/Autumn of 1979 we again found ourselves in Northern Ireland; this time the Battalion was split up into small units to serve a 4 month tour in Tyrone. By this time I was in the Drums & Pipes and we were tasked to operate from the police station in Coalisland; we were Platoon strength, with a handful of RUC officers, and from the Drums & Pipes perspective, this was to be an eventful tour.

During our tour, a large IED was detonated in Dungannon town centre; I think there was one minor military injury. Lord Mountbatten was murdered whilst fishing, after an IED had been placed in his small boat by the IRA; the craft exploded in the water off Mullagmore, Co Sligo; three other people including his 14 year old grandson were also killed. On the very same day, the Warrenpoint ambush took place; this was a well planned and executed ambush.

[Sixteen members of the Parachute Regiment were killed – the Regiment's worst ever post-war casualty toll – and two members of the Queen's Own High-landers were killed alongside their Para comrades. A civilian, Michael Hudson from London, was also killed in the crossfire as a post-explosion firefight with the IRA took place.]

One night during a mobile patrol (I was one of our section's 2 drivers) we were driving in Coalisland; as we turned right into Annagher Road from Stewartstown Road, to head up to Monagh Park, I was just centering the steering wheel when gunmen opened fire; this was around 22:00.

The two gunmen opened fire on my Land Rover from above and behind. They were behind a low wall at the top of an embankment, and the range was about 100 yards. There were multiple strikes to the Land Rover and I stopped and we debussed; hurriedly, I got out of the passenger side as rounds were striking the road on the offside. L/Cpl 'X', who was top cover with a GPMG received a small piece of bullet shrapnel to his left upper cheek and the splinter went through the glass of his spectacles as he was dismounting, As I stopped my vehicle, Private Davie Laurie, who was driving the second vehicle was turning right and the two gunmen diverted their attention to his Land Rover, which he brought to stop some 30 yards in front of mine. By this time I was already returning fire, and, though it seemed longer, the whole incident lasted about 10/15 seconds or so; one of my 'brick' received a small sliver of shrapnel in the back of his calf muscle, but there no other injuries. The Land Rover, however did not do so well, because the gunmen were firing 'wild' and not aiming right, so the rounds were bouncing of the road; one went up into the rear differential, one went clean through the front offside radio antennae at its base, a clean hole which left the antennae still upright, and a few more bounced of the 'Makralon' light armour of the vehicle.

I tried, unsuccessfully to shoot out a street light that I had mistakenly stopped under, with a couple of rounds, but had to return fire in a different direction almost immediately. Both gunmen got away, and there were no serious injuries, but both Land Rovers were in 'workshops' in Armagh for about 7 days and we got them back then.

L/Cpl 'X' received about £750.00 and a new pair of glasses for his injury. I think he bought a 'double keyboard' electric organ with his compensation.

The whole incident took place around 2200 hrs, and was a close call. But for the amateur shooting of the two gunmen, it could have been worse. I would add that all of us were using tracer for the first two and last but one in our magazines; the first tracers were used to identify the target, and the last but one, to avoid having to count the rounds. Amongst the 4 persons in each 'brick' we carried 80 7.62 rounds per SLR, 1 M79 grenade launcher with 5 HE rounds, 1 FRG 'riot gun' with 5/10 25 'grain rounds and 1 GPMG with 200 rounds. IWS night sights were optional, and occasionally, depending on the type of patrol, Browning 9mm worn 'outside' over the flak jacket shoulder or belt holsters.

1979: ON ATTACHMENT TO 3 UDR BALLYKINLER

Bernard Loughran

During the time when Earl Mountbatten of Burma was murdered and many members of 2 Para and Queen's Own Highlanders killed at Warrenpoint, I was driving through Castlewellan from a point west of the town where a culvert bomb killed members of 3 UDR.

A stroll in the country, Crossmaglen

I saw a large group of children resplendent in their school uniforms watching us drive past and as we did so they all looked at us and laughed, quite obviously because people had been killed.

For some reason the image of those callous laughing children is as vivid today as it was nearly 30 years ago.

The incident to which Bernard refers took place on January 6 1980 at Burren, near Castlewellan. Three of his comrades, Privates James Cochran and Richard Wilson (both 21) and Robert Smyth, who was only 18, were killed by an IRA bomb.

This meant that in just 6 days of the New Year, Army losses had already reached 5, as two Paras had been killed, a few days earlier, in a friendly fire incident near Forkhill.

DUNGANNON: 1979

Steve Atkinson, Gordon Highlanders

One evening I was about to set off en-route to Dungannon on a 'Ration and Mail' [the Army-speak for delivery service]. As I drove out of the Police station at Coalisland, a single gunman opened fire at my vehicle from a building site, where a church was being built, from about 60/70 yards, with an automatic weapon. I immediately reversed back into the Police yard, and came to an abrupt stop; I then ran to the entrance and returned fire. L/Cpl Veno Harper also returned fire with his GPMG. Fortunately the gunman's fire was erratic and all his rounds went very 'high. Our ACC cook was thrown out of the back of my Land Rover, due to my rapid reverse and sudden stop, and landed in a small pile of building sand in the Police station's yard. Whilst I returned fire, the main gate was closed by the sentry, and we spent about 20 seconds getting ready, and then stormed out of the station and across the road into the church building site, and conducted a 'hot' follow up of the area; no one was injured, and again to our displeasure, the gunman escaped.

That evening we carried out a Night Lurk Patrol of the area, but turned up nothing, and did the ration and mail thing the next morning. I think had I had the M79 to hand, I would have used a round or 2 into the building site, but as these things happen in a very few seconds, there is no time; besides the M79 was for use in rural areas, not urban locations.

The Police station at Coalisland was a very small one, situated on a corner, looking out on the three roads that pass through this village. In the outlying rural area was the home of 'Bernadette McAliskey' (Devlin), whom I once stopped on a VCP and found her to be polite and co-operative.

At the Police station we were billeted in 3 'Portacabins', 8 of us in each one, small cramped and close, but as the endless round of patrolling, guarding and 'sangar' duties never seemed to end all that happened in these 'small boxes' was sleep.

The 4 months tour that the Gordons did in the autumn/winter of 1979 didn't see any other serious terrorist casualties amongst our number, but I am sure that other incidents and contacts occurred during my time in the province.

Army base in Crossmaglen (photo courtesy of Tom Clarke)

Chapter Thirteen

1980

A year of 402 bombings, 642 shootings and the deaths of 17 soldiers, 9 RUC officers, 45 civilians and 5 terrorists.

It witnessed the cowardly ambush of Corporal Owen McQuade of the Argyll & Sutherland Highlanders, shot and killed outside Altnagevin hospital in Londonderry as he waited to collect a colleague.

It also saw a chilling new tactic by the IRA when, on February 16, Colonel Mark Coe, R.E. was shot whilst off-duty in Bielefeld, West Germany. He would be the first of 8 British personnel killed on the European continent. The IRA's European ASUs targeted British service personnel in Holland, Belgium and Germany over a 10 year period.

CROSSMAGLEN, 1980

Major Andrew Macdonald, OC Arnhem Company, 1 King's Own Border Rgt

XMG is the Soldiers' abbreviation for Crossmaglen – arguably the most dangerous part of Northern Ireland in which to serve.

XMG is a small town situated in the so-called 'Bandit Country' of South Armagh. During the 70s and through to the 90s, it featured in the many very serious incidents involving death and wounding of soldiers and members of the

Army base in Crossmaglen (photo courtesy of Tom Clarke)

Andrew MacDonald, Crossmaglen (photo courtesy of Andrew MacDonald)

security forces. It had a fearsome reputation and a four month tour there was a time you'd remember. It has to be said that the current tours in Afghanistan and Baghdad (longer and in worse conditions) are considerably harder, I believe.

My job as a young 28 year old Company Commander (rank of Major) was to run the base and all the attendant operations for the four month tour. We had 120 men under our command and a 25 km border with the Irish Republic into which we were not allowed to pursue fleeing terrorists.

The base was heavily fortified, including from the threat of mortars. There was no vehicle movement – everything went in and out by helicopter – and patrolling in the town of XMG was highly dangerous especially as it had six exit roads, 3 leading directly to the Border less than 3–5 miles away.

Every unit that occupied XMG for a tour knew that it faced a major challenge. Whilst the task was technically 'to support the civil power', there was no civil power activity so much of the job was about staying alive and taking the fight to the enemy who were, in the main, smugglers and gangsters taking advantage of the lawless nature of the area to benefit from scams that took advantage of EU regulations (cross border agricultural carousel crime, fuel scams etc). Police and customs activity was sporadic and had to be supported by large numbers of Army in support.

In a four month tour there is not enough time to put in place a strategy but long enough to get hit badly by the enemy as soon as they recognises your weaknesses. And if they don't get you, they get the next lot.

You had to be both defensive and offensive. But without intelligence, going onto the offensive is pointless work and the British have been good at counter-insurgency because they've paid careful attention to his aspect. The problem as always was shortage of real intelligence.

We had an intelligence section that was not hugely effective; the Special Branch and SAS operations were based on specific high level intelligence that was their preserve. In the middle there was nothing.

However, on the morning of 15th March, we took our second fatal casualty and I decided to act decisively – I had all the intelligence I needed now. The shooting was from a churchyard and the escape was straight across the border – they'd have been drinking and laughing in a pub in Dundalk within 30 minutes. So, we went onto the offensive.

The Concession Road ran across our territory. This was a road that cut across the bottom end of the County of South Armagh thus providing a shortcut for motorists travelling from Monaghan to Dundalk (this, a staunchly republican town where the Mountbatten murderers planned their operation). Control of the Concession Road's two unmanned crossing points (designated H29 and H31) was something of a right that the local PIRA organisation felt that they had; they seemed to be free to mount illegal checkpoints whenever they liked and then melt way across the border. To deny this 'shortcut' would have been hugely inconvenient and would also demonstrate hat PIRA were not in charge. This we did, but it gets better.

They became angry that we controlled 'their area' and began to attack our checkpoints which were well dug-in with machine gun support (yes, this was technically the UK). After skirmishes, they gave up trying. We then moved up a gear by putting 'weak' forces on the ground to draw them out. Behind these weak positions were concealed reinforcements and reaction forces. On one particular occasion, a large party of gunmen attacked a disused farm which we'd occupied but unknown to them we'd concealed a heavy machine gun post (GPMG SF) on the hill overlooking the farm under cover of darkness the night before. The firefight lasted for 30 minutes and I had to re-supply the position at dusk with additional ammunition by helicopter (scary but fun). We don't know how many we killed as you cannot pursue over the Border for fear of creating an international incident through the incursion.

There were several incidents like this when were establishing control of the concession road and they were all one-sided affairs. After the big one, they never attacked us in force again.

When it was time to handover to the next company coming in – traditionally the most dangerous part of a tour – we secured reinforcements and created a ring

Captain, King's Own Border Regt, Crossmaglen
(photo courtesy of Andrew MacDonald)

The enemy; IRA gunmen pose for photographers

of fortifications around XMG effectively controlling every road in and out of the town. We called this 'Strongpoint.' For the first time in years, we were able to patrol in the town in safety and allow the police to arrest car tax dodgers, collect unpaid fines and go about the normal duties of the civil power. We left with no further incidents.

We felt that we settled some of the outstanding imbalance on the account for the two young soldiers we'd lost even if we didn't actually collect the skulls of those who been shooting and bombing us. Knowing we'd taken it to the enemy was the most important bit for the soldiers who'd worked hard to do their duty unquestioningly.

I hope that I had established for future commanders in XMG several important operating lessons and tactics. We were able to feed back into the pre-tour training organisation additional experience and realistic lessons not previously taught to incoming units. Several of my soldiers were decorated for their courage – and most of them went there as boys but came back as men.

I learnt that it's easy when it's going well – the important bit about leadership and management is what you do when the shit hits the fan and people look at you to hold your nerve and stand up and deliver.

None of this mentions the role the soldiers, NCOs and young officers played in helping me as commander to recover from the early setbacks on that tour. I include in this the CO who was 100% supportive throughout. They were outstanding.

RAF SAC Nigel Crosby at Aldergrove, 1980

I left school at 16 and joined the Army in the summer of 1976 – the Coldstream Guards Training in Pirbright; I passed out and transferred from the Army to the RAF in 1979. I trained at Cosford in telecommunications / radio/telephone.

Patrol kit, South Armagh

When I finished my training I was told that I had an overseas posting 'Yes' I thought then they told me RAF Aldergrove; 'Where is that I asked?' Northern Ireland for 2 years, I was told.

I had no idea where to go. I found my way to an arrival counter where I signed in and was told to go to the first Sherpa van outside (note: only the military drove Sherpa vans at that time). We then went to Aldergrove Down and passed the first checkpoint 'C for Charlie', which was manned by the RAF Regiment and passed all the other checkpoints manned by RAF police.

In the Phoenix Club (NAAFI) I met 4 guys from 39 Inf Brigade down in Bessbrook Mill in South Armagh; they had flown up in the daily Wessex helicopter from 72 Sqn (we did the radio ground to air/air to ground from our base)

These lads had come up to collect a new Land Rover and to drive it back down to Bessbrook; we spent the night listening to what life was like for them down there in Bandit Country. They told us that we were having it easy up here, compared to them. Anyhow we spent the night drinking and joking, and they looked quite happy; they left in the morning at approx 10:00.a.m.

I was working that day when we had a 'flash message' saying that a Beer Keg bomb had been detonated by the roadside killing 2 and injuring 2 In an Army Land Rover. A Wessex was dispatched to ferry the wounded and bodies to Musgrave Park Military Wing; we did not know at the time that these were the same chaps we had spent the night drinking with (I thought they said they were from 42 or 45 Commando).

VCP, Northern Ireland

Chapter Fourteen

1981

A year of 578 bombings, 1,142 shootings and the deaths of 23 soldiers, 21 RUC officers, 52 civilians and 5 terrorists.

The numbers of RUC fatalities rose that year, partly as a result of the IRA's use of a landmine in Co. Tyrone, which killed 4 officers. In addition, 12 UDR soldiers were killed, as the IRA deliberately targeted them whilst they were off-duty. These included L/Cpl Ronnie Graham who was shot and killed whilst delivering coal in Lisnaskea, Fermanagh.

UDR Private Cecil Graham was shot at Doonagh and was one of three brothers killed by the IRA.

May 19 of this year was a day of tragedy for the Royal Green Jackets, losing Riflemen Michael Bagshaw, Andrew Gavin, John King and Lance Corporal Grenville Winston and their RCT Driver, Paul Bulman, killed by an IRA landmine at Camlough Lake in Armagh.

THE 'CROSS'. 1981

Rifleman John Moore, Royal Green Jackets

The 1981 PIRA hunger strikes had just started and a group of Republican prisoners were fasting to death. A deadly battle with the British Government and the Prime Minister, Mrs Thatcher, ensued and she was determined not to compromise or concede to their five demands. It was very tense on all sides of the political divide and the British Army, as usual, was in the middle of it.

On a cold winter's day in March our troop ship, the *Sir Lancelot*, left Liverpool and sailed towards Belfast. Many hours later a convoy of coaches greeted us at the Belfast docks and transported my battalion, 1st Royal Green Jackets, to the Maze prison from where we were flown by chopper to our final destination – Bessbrook Mill, South Armagh. As a rifleman just about to turn nineteen, I was excited yet full of nervous apprehension – this was my first tour of duty in Northern Ireland. My very first glimpse of my new home appeared through heavy cloud and mist as the Wessex engines changed pitch and clattered steadily towards Bessbrook. The sprawling Mill was formerly a nineteenth century linen factory and surrounded by attractive countryside and rolling green hills.

My company, 'C' Company, designated Patrol Company ('Rent-A- Company' or 'Go Anywhere Company') for the South Armagh tour, was lucky to be based in the relative safety of Bessbrook. Bessbrook Mill along with its incredibly busy heli-pad (nicknamed 'Bessbrook International' by locals) hid behind enormous panels of grey corrugated iron limiting the vision of any foe and giving a small amount of protection from the odd terrorist throwing something nasty our way. A heavily protected guard room was situated by the main gate and the huts accommodating soldiers acting as the Quick Reaction Force were always active. Our rabbit warren-like accommodation block near the top floor had luckily been modernised. The spacious rooms were clean, comfortable and usually had only four or five men sleeping in each. The armoury was also situated near our rooms. At the far end of our lines lived our telly accompanied by a brand new video recorder that was paid for equally by all the lads in the company. The TV was actually housed in a windowless briefing room and although relatively small it was surprising how many lads could pack in there once our sergeant spread the word that he had acquired a decent porno film or even the latest Hollywood action movie.

Although we were mainly based in Bessbrook along with a few hundred other troops we often had to work from other bases dotted around South Armagh, including Crossmaglen. British soldiers knew Crossmaglen as 'XMG' and the locals called it 'Cross'. XMG, a staunchly republican town, snuggled in a pocket of Northern Ireland enclosed on three sides by the Irish Republic and was considered by British troops to be the most dangerous and hostile posting in the Province, a town firmly fixed in the psyche of the British Army.

The scruffy bleak town, comprising only a thousand or so people, had already earned a legendary reputation. The six roads leading towards the centre of XMG terminated at the chief dominating feature of the town – the Market Square. The Square fronted by small drab houses and businesses was reputedly the largest of its kind in Ireland, overlooked constantly by an army observation post named Borucki Sangar in tribute to an unfortunate soldier from 3 Para who had been killed at that exact spot by an IRA bomb in 1976. At the western end of the Square stood an intimidating statue erected by the IRA in memory of their members who had died for their cause.

Towards the edge of this hard and gritty town a secondary school and housing estate had sprung-up, many of the unkempt properties and fences festooned with British taunts and IRA slogans. The narrow streets and roads were lined by leaning telegraph poles many topped with tatty Irish tricolours and black ragged old flags fluttering in the fierce wind declaring allegiance to the Republic and support for the hunger strikers. The base, always called 'barracks' by the locals, was situated near the centre of town. It was sandbagged and built with tremendously thick walls to lessen the effect from bomb blast damage and gunfire. In addition to these defences ugly looking anti-rocket wire, cameras and mortar protection surrounded the base. The actual camp, consisting of a police station, operations area, briefing room, living-accommodation, cookhouse, gym and helicopter pad was about the size of a football pitch: the RUC posted there were charged with maintaining law and order always policed the area with the backup and strong presence of an army patrol. Originally, it was just an old police station housing local officers but it had developed to accommodate over a hundred soldiers and policemen in cramped and sometimes filthy conditions. Living there was hell and during our tour a team of engineers worked twenty-four hours a day trying to improve and extend the camp creating even more noise and layers of thick mud; the whole place reeked of sweaty bodies, stale air and rotting rubbish. At least the food was good and plentiful; amazing considering the limited space the cooks had to work in.

The Bunkhouse accommodation was long and narrow with up to eighteen men in each uncomfortable room, most of the rooms covered in posters and pictures of naked women forming a crude type of wallpaper. The squaddies were blatantly reminded of what they could be missing at home but at least the wallpaper brightened up their surroundings and gave the blokes some comfort. It was amazing how the soldiers endured the intolerable tobacco smoke-filled environment and got along with each other in the claustrophobic rooms with bunks in three tiers. Punch-ups rarely took place and much of the stress and tension was lost to exercise on the multi-gym equipment.

I was chuffed at only having to go to XMG every now and then, able to escape the constant threat of attack and the awful conditions of the camp in that frontier town. The occasional times we stayed overnight in XMG we were housed in a leaky empty attic section of the building that was being constructed and using the outside portacabins, a poor excuse for loos and showers. The XMG barracks' only lifelines were the helicopters flying in the stores and men and flying out armed patrols and heaps of refuse and waste, army vehicles had long been banned from actually travelling to the town unless in a huge armed convoy.

Conditions in XMG had to be experienced to be believed and added to this was the stress of taking a bullet or being blown up, an enormous pressure for many young soldiers who were barely old enough to vote for the politicians that had sent them there. At one time, soldiers were even banned from being outside or sitting in the sun because of the real threat from a mortar attack. Soldiering in the town was a lonely business and turning every corner tinged with menace; we were almost like ghosts in a movie, walking through a scene hardly interacting with the normal environment. No locals would talk to us, almost ignoring squaddies, and would only half-answer direct questions usually with a sarcastic wry reply, never giving anything important away. It was all part the game and we all knew the rules. The entire atmosphere was filled with fear and mistrust and we could feel we were being scrutinized from a distance on each and every patrol, hatred-filled people slowly drawing their plans against us or just waiting for an opportunity to snipe at or bomb anyone wearing a British uniform.

There was a real risk that a bullet or bomb would suddenly end our lives but we were more fearful of being horribly maimed or blinded for the rest of our days and created willing pacts and promises with each other: some swore that if a colleague or friend wanted to be 'put out of their misery' or spared from future disfigurement or brain injury after an IRA attack then their mates should shoot them – on the spot. Many of the promises were undertaken whilst drinking heavily but some guys really meant it and probably would have carried-out the deed if necessary but as far as I was aware no one ever actually had to shoot their mate!

Our training teams in England had taught us semi-urban patrol techniques for XMG and their teaching standards were high. The first rule to remember when leaving the camp was to always burst out of the place fast like a bomb exploding in all directions (a tactic developed to make us harder to attack) and only regrouping after a few minutes and ready to continue with the patrol. Communicating with each other on the streets was predominantly made using sign language and a mixture of nods, winks and rifle movements. We were drilled in the way to move along the streets in multiple patrols, usually two soldiers on the left and right at the front and the other two at the rear – always alert and ready to react to gunfire from any direction, at any time. When our patrols stopped in the street individually we tried to keep moving, performing an action called 'ballooning' bobbing around like a balloon in the wind ducking and weaving to make ourselves difficult targets to shoot, our eyes always scanning rooftops and windows for snipers. It was weird and visually strange to watch but it worked and the more body movements performed the safer and less vulnerable we felt. Working in small close-knit teams we instinctively knew what each other were doing or thinking, relying on complete trust of every member of the patrol to do their job well and watching each others' backs. We had learnt what to look for when on patrol and treated anything out of the ordinary with great suspicion. Standing by a vehicle with no one inside it was also a total no-no; the IRA were fond of placing explosives in innocuous-looking cars and blowing them up when squaddies got in range.

Good patrolling skills, the ability to remain alert and a degree of fitness were also demanded if we didn't want to get hit but often when it came down to it, luck, or bad luck was the main determining factor in whether we went home in one piece or not. After every patrol there was a tremendous sense of relief that we had got back to camp and able to unwind and rest, although we could never properly relax in South Armagh. The most basic of pleasures were demanded by all soldiers and after cleaning our weapons we nearly always dived towards the strategically placed urn for making tea!

There were a considerable number of 'contacts' in and around XMG especially during the first few weeks of the tour. On one occasion, gunmen managed to slip into the outskirts of the town and occupied a house, holding the residents at gunpoint until they could effect a sniping attack on the next patrol that came along. Two riflemen and a sergeant, who had been to Ulster on numerous tours, were hit but in all three cases their lives were saved by the flak jackets they were wearing. In mid March another fortunate rifleman who survived a machine-gun attack in the countryside outside XMG returned to camp totally unscathed but with a war story of a lifetime: a bullet had passed straight through his water bottle attached to his belt only inches away from his wedding tackle. He later had to be treated for shock after taking out his bottle to make a brew and realising just how close he had come to being shot, an extremely lucky man.

As we continued our tour the Republican hunger strikes gained momentum and support making our time in this turbulent patch even more violent and tense than usual. On 19 May callsign 42F – a Saracen carrying four Green Jackets and an RCT driver – were instantly killed by a huge landmine explosion near Bessbrook. They were the second of a two vehicle patrol ruthlessly ambushed by the IRA with the simple push of a button. I was sent as part of a large group of soldiers to form a cordon around the site of the attack. After many hours as we returned to Bessbrook a group of young lads bricked us and chanted the popular Queen tune 'Another one bites the dust.' We were outraged by their taunts and wanted to take out our revenge on them – they were lucky our corporals stopped us.

A month later my company were tasked to spend nearly two weeks camped on Slieve Gullion based on the fringe of an evergreen forest with a suitable landing spot for helicopters close by. We made our new base really secure and put a number of machine gun posts on the slopes with awesome firepower and clear views of the country below. In addition to this we protected the camp with various electronic detection devices and trip flares should anyone dare try and reach us at night. The work from our country base was still hard and dangerous – snap vehicle check points, frequent searches, OPs and long foot patrols always protected by patrolling in multiply bricks (satelliting). We were away from much of the pressure and were even allowed to have our telly and precious video up there with us, powered by a generator.

With only a couple of weeks before our four month tour was due to end our platoon were given one big final operation. Intelligence suggested that IRA units were mounting illegal vehicle checkpoints along the border – we were to stop them. We were transported from Bessbrook in 'Q' vans to a spot south of XMG near the border and from there we patrolled to our various given locations in the dark to setup covert OPs. Our brick, three men, chose a derelict van in a scrap yard about 150 metres from the border to watch and listen for IRA activity. Conditions in the van were cramped – during the day we sweltered and at night it got pretty chilly. On 16 July, on the third night of our mission, as dusk approached I took the stag position. Moments later our hide was raked by heavy automatic gunfire from across the Irish border. Terrorists had discovered our patrol and used an M60 and Armalite rifles to counter-ambush us; the IRA unit were later thought to be about 6–8 strong. My brick commander, L/Cpl Gavin Dean (Deano), was immediately struck by two bullets. I returned fire using two weapons. During the short but intense fire fight I was hit in the upper spine by a high velocity bullet instantly paralysing me from the chest down. The other member of our brick was slightly injured but managed to walk out of the yard and was flown by chopper to Musgrave Park Hospital, Belfast, along with Deano and me both on stretchers. The contact occurred only ten days before we were to be reunited with our families at home.

As we reached hospital Deano died, aged just twenty-one.

I was very seriously ill and the next day my parents were taken to Belfast to see me. I was then flown to London to begin a lengthy period of recovery in QEMH, Woolwich. During the first few days on Intensive Care, as I was upside down on a special bed, I was told that Deano – my friend – had died. The news hit me hard.

The treatment and care at QEMH was excellent – it had to be as I was to spend almost eleven months as a patient there followed by nearly eight months at JSMRU, Chessington. During this time the Falklands War had come and gone resulting in hundreds of injured servicemen joining me for treatment and intense physiotherapy. Although being in any hospital is unpleasant, my time at both units was made bearable but still an unforgettably tough experience. The camaraderie and military spirit was surprisingly good and there was always an element of competition with my peers but as long as I could compete with the soldiers from the Paras (my regiment's old adversary) I was happy. I met one particular Para and I suppose by rights we should have 'kicked off' (fight) but we became friends – besides I couldn't use my legs and he had none to kick off with!

Being presented with my first wheelchair was like attending a funeral on Christmas day. The excitement of opening a present and taking off the wrapping paper mixed with the sadness and terror of having to sit in the grotesque thing. I soon learnt to live with my chair and over time realized it had become my new best friend. In mid May 1983 I was medically discharged from the army, a poignant day in my life as I had to face civvy street as an incomplete paraplegic. I had to adapt and overcome on my own – a sudden shock after being looked after so well in the military system. I always think of that fateful night on the border and remember Deano and his family.

I had left Ireland but Ireland has never left me.

Gavin Dean, who was only 21, died of his wounds in a Belfast hospital the day after being wounded; from Rainham in Kent, he had been involved in a fierce firefight with the IRA. It is alleged that the terrorists used a heavy M60 machine gun and at least four other weapons in the attack.

NORTHERN IRELAND: 1981

Rifleman 'C' Royal Green Jackets

We all hated the camera crews and journos with a vengeance. Unlike today when the press and TV are 'embedded' with forward units in Iraq etc, in those days they used to roam at will and seemed to turn up whenever trouble was brewing. Whether or not they listened in on our RT or not, I haven't a clue but if they didn't, they had an uncanny knack of knowing just where trouble was.

The Yanks were always the worst, but the Krauts ran them a pretty close second; the former were always in our faces and calling us 'boys' and our officers – no matter what their actual rank was – 'lootenant' or even 'General' ! One of our officers told him that he was a Captain but in any case, it was pronounced 'Left-tenant'· NOT 'Loo-tenant'!

MAGHERA: 1981

Steve, Ulster Defence Regiment

Allan Clarke was a full-time member of 5UDR. On Saturday 12th September he was walking up Hall Street in Maghera after visiting the local bookies' office, as was his habit.

A car passed him and then sped away, leaving Allan lying on the pavement. He had been shot three times and swiftly lost consciousness. He died shortly after as a result of his wounds.

His funeral was held two days later, and one of the pallbearers was his neighbour and friend John Proctor, a member of the RUC Reserve. Later that day John went to the Mid-Ulster Hospital in Magherafelt, to visit his wife who had recently given birth to a son.

As John left the Maternity ward, he was shot and killed in the car park, by the same team who had killed his friend barely two days earlier.

The boys of bomb disposal

321 EXPLOSIVE ORDNANCE DISPOSAL (EOD) COMPANY, 1981

Major 'MT', Royal Army Ordnance Corps, Senior Army Technical Officer (SATO)

321 EOD Company was responsible for bomb disposal in the Province, and I commanded it from July '81 to March '82. Although I was OC I was usually referred to as SATO. Five hunger strikers died during July and August, and there was increased terrorist activity in reaction to each death. During September six more began hunger strike and the IRA kept up a high level of activity, even after the strike ended on the 3rd of October. As a result there was rarely a day during '81 when some part of the Company was not involved in operations, and some days when most of it was. The Nationalist areas all put up hundreds of black flags on lamp posts. I found this quite useful, as you instantly knew you were entering an area in which you had to be extra vigilant.

During '81 the Company Headquarters and a rural team were based in Lisburn at HQNI [Head Quarters, Northern Ireland], as was the Chief Ammunition Technical Officer (CATO), a Lieutenant Colonel. Three Sections, each commanded by a captain, were deployed throughout the province in support of the local infantry units. The Belfast Section had 3 city teams. The Londonderry Section, covering the north of the Province, had an armoured team in Londonderry, the remainder being rural. The Dungannon Section covered the south of the Province with rural teams. Its teams in Omagh and Bessbrook also had an air-portable capability.

Each Team was commanded by either the Section Captain or a Senior NCO. For ease of reference during operations all team leaders were usually called ATOs. The 2i/c was the Team 'Number two', usually a Corporal AT, who operated the wheelbarrow, prepared any explosive equipment the ATO needed for his next approach to the bomb, and dreamed of the day when he'd have enough experience and rank to command a team. Each Team had a 'bleep.' The rural

Teams also had a driver, who helped with everything, but whose main role at an incident was to help the Team commander get into the bomb suit, which was difficult to do alone. The City Teams usually totaled about fifteen.

The fact that the Teams were necessarily widespread meant that most of them were effectively on call 24 hours a day.

Transport for the city Teams was all armoured, typically a Saracen and three or four PIGs, whilst the rural Teams had two Makralon reinforced Ford Transits. All Teams had two wheelbarrows (7/2), and some Teams had remotely operated Eager Beavers, based on the widely used military forklift truck.

By '81, as a result of hard-bought experience, both the technical and operational response to the bomb threat in the Province had become quite sophisticated. From the Company's point of view our pre-ops training was rigorous and relevant, our equipment was effective, soldier-proof and soldier friendly, and our operating procedures covered most likely eventualities. We had good relations with the Royal Engineer Search Teams that we regularly worked with during the approach to remotely initiated bombs. The infantry officers commanding the cordons we needed around us, to guard our backs while we deal with the task in hand, understood how we worked, and kept us free of interruption. The REME Workshops in Belfast repaired all our equipment, and treated it as a high priority.

Like all unit commanders in the Province I made many decisions a day, some good, some in hindsight I'd rather gloss over. To me the biggest decision during my tour was made within days of arriving in the Province, and immediately after I took over. We received a warning of a car bomb in Market Street, Lisburn, via the Samaritans. The Lisburn Team was deployed and I and 'Geordie', my driver, got into the only car available, which had no siren or blue light (our own car was still being prepared for us). By the time we got close enough to see the Team's location, in a little side street, the traffic had jammed up. With no light or siren the other drivers were not about to give us priority. Fortunately there were two 'Meter Maids' near by, who were only too keen to help get us through the traffic. The Team was well placed, out of line sight from the suspect car, but fairly close, because there was really no where else to work from.

The ATO had already deployed the team's only wheelbarrow (the other was in Workshops), and had placed a spotter on the other side of the road behind some low, very substantial, concrete flower pots. (the cameras on the 'barrow were ok close up, but it was often difficult to see if you were abreast of the target, and a spotter helped with this). As the 'Barrow approached the car it started to rain, and the 'Barrow stalled. With no other 'barrow the ATO immediately volunteered to make a manual approach (i.e. walk in and deal with it). I was tempted to agree. But because I'd heard that warnings via the Samaritans were usually right, I refused to let him, and we dragged the 'Barrow back by it's umbilical cord. The number two quickly sorted the problem, and got the 'Barrow back down to the car. I moved to the edge of the corner we were sheltering behind, and peeped round it to watch the attack.

The number two shotgunned the boot, and as it flew open it revealed two beer kegs. I moved my head back round the corner to talk to the ATO and there was an almighty roar as the bomb exploded. I saw something flash past at about head height, (it was the remains of the 'Barrow) and immediately ran for the back of the nearest open Transit Van. So did the rest of the team and the RUC liaison officers. I suspect we were all thinking the same thing, 'what goes up comes down.'

We listened to the 'crash bang tinkle' as debris fell on and around it. Once silence reigned we all immediately thought about the spotter, and ran out into the road. He was still prone behind the flower holders. Eventually he took the binoculars from his eyes and turned his head towards us. I noticed that his forehead was covered in dust, leaving an almost perfect imprint of the binoculars. All he said was 'Bloody Hell'. (I met the ATO again, years later, during the Foot and Mouth Outbreak in Devon. We chattered like magpies and laughed till we almost cried).

Some days always stick in your mind. The 20th of August 1981 sticks in mine. It was a glorious sunny day, and my first task for the day was to brief the media on a large recent explosives find. I was to meet up with them at the Belfast Section location. On my way out of barracks I dropped into the local Brigade HQ, to chat to the Operations Room staff and see what was happening. As we talked a suspect car was reported near the end of the M1, and the Ops staff decided to send a city team out to it. I don't know why, but I felt uneasy about this, and had the Lisburn Team deployed instead. Geordie and I then drove into Belfast.

There was an open area just next to the Belfast Section Control Room, where the explosives had been laid out. I had just started to brief the press when the Control Room staff called me in. They had suddenly got four suspect vehicles to deal with. As we discussed which Teams we should send a further three or four more were reported. I knew immediately that we were facing a disruption day, and that the traffic in Belfast was going to come to a standstill. In the end more than a dozen cars and trucks required our attention, and although it was unlikely that they all contained bombs, each one had to be treated as if it did. It was obvious that to clear them quickly, and get life back to normal, I would need to call in several of the rural teams.

This all took time to arrange, and even more time to deploy Teams through the stalled traffic. Driving along pavements became the order of the day. By midday we had six or seven Teams deployed, and there were no more reports of suspect vehicles. So I decided to visit the Teams. We loaded the car with sandwiches and drinks and set off. It was truly surreal squeezing our way through all the stalled traffic, or drifting gently along the pavement past the pubs and shops, with the light on and the siren sounding. There was an almost carnival atmosphere, as lots of people had congregated on the pavements in front of the pubs drinking in the sun. There was even some music and Irish dancing.

Of course there was the usual 'deadly' side to it all. The Belfast Captain dealt with a booby trapped van near the Albert Bridge, and one of the trucks caused a lot of concern before it was found to be a hoax.

The last job of the day, at about 20.00 hours, was with the Lisburn Team, who had started the whole thing off in the morning. They were faced with a very large bread truck, parked across the road, suspiciously close to what looked from a distance like a small culvert. After proving that the culvert and the cab of the truck were no threat we decided to blow open the locked back door. The ATO thought a quarter of a pound of PE [plastic explosive] would do the job. I, wrongly, suggested half a pound. When the charge exploded all the aluminium cladding of the body work ended up wrapped around the cab. It looked as if the truck was wearing a ruff, and we were confronted by row after row of neatly stacked loaves. Even SATO's are fallible! I then remembered that I had forgotten to complete briefing the press.

As the weather changed from high summer into autumn the EOD work did not slacken, and the IRA continued to ring the changes in the type of attack they used.

It is worth noting that the IRA sometimes warned the local populace of an imminent bomb attack on Security Forces and that many householders once warned, would open their windows. This would reduce some peripheral blast damage and reduce the incidence of deadly shards of flying glass.

BELFAST 1981

Fusilier, 'A' Coy, 1 RWF

The abandoned box van's engine was still running. The driver's door was open. We watched as two RUC 'Hotspurs' pulled up behind it. A few bobbies got out and walked to the back of the Box Van. Our boss shouted to them to keep back, as we were getting a check done on the key holder (to see if the van had been reported stolen) He said: 'ATO's been tasked.'

The RUC Officers were clearly under pressure to get the incident dealt with and the highways cleared for traffic. They ignored our boss's instructions and continued to approach the vehicle. A couple of them opened the rear shutters, and climbed inside. I can remember looking around for combat indicators that this van may go bang. I saw a couple of kids sitting on an electric junction box, about 5 metres from the van, I relaxed slightly.

The search of the rear of the van was now complete, 2 RUC Officers walked around to the driver's side of the vehicle. Myself and the other 7 members of the patrol watched in horror as an RUC Officer climbed into the van via the driver's door, placing his knees on the seat. I can recall saying to my mate, words to the effect that 'No way could I do that'and then the inevitable; an almighty explosion, amplified by the surrounding buildings. Everything seemed to slow down; I watched the bonnet of the vehicle and other debris float down to the ground. It felt like an age. Then ... a brief period of silence, only broken by our Colour Sergeant patrol commander shouting 'Get fucking down there.' Surprisingly the kids had gone.

We ran the 30–40 metres to the scene ... terrible ... 4 or 5 RUC Officers injured; we disarmed a couple of them. Two of them were critical (one died). We were trying to stop the bleeding, but all we had were field dressings, it was impossible. We were trying to help them and still protect them and ourselves, there were only 8 of us. It seemed like an age before reinforcements arrived, although it was probably about 5–7 minutes max. I can remember during this short period, local mothers doing the school run, some with pushchairs. They were laughing and cat-calling, that really impacted on me. One of these lads was dying, and it was all being played out in front of this hateful audience.

Wreckage of RUC patrol car after IRA landmine explosion
(photo courtesy of Tom Clarke)

Later that day, my brick were all sat in our room, watching Gloria Hunniford recount the horror of that day on the early evening BBC Ulster News. None of us relished the thought of another patrol, then the squeak of the corridor door swinging open, and the unmistakable sound of our C/Sgt's boots clumping down the corridor ... He sticks his head round the door and says: '10 minutes boys, in the briefing room ... anti-robbery patrol, up the Turf.' He knew best, like falling off a bike, you've just got to get back on. It sounds glib now, but at that time, that's how I dealt with it. The memory of that day will stay with me forever.

MAY 1981

RAF SAC Nigel Crosby, Aldergrove, 1981

Bobby Sands had died that day after his hunger strike and we had decided on a night out; this was classic bad timing!

Going were myself and a lad from Comms Flight (SAC Alan 'Geordie' Allenson) telephone operator Cpl Wally Allcock, who was my Boss, SAC Brian Jarvis, SAC David Fowler, SAC Gerry King and few others from Engineering Sqn along with their boss Flt Dean and 2 civilians who worked in the Communications. The Driver was Ricci Ricardo (that's what we knew him as), a retired RAF Chap who lived in Antrim and worked on the Telephone Exchange. We had been on a jolly to Bushmills Whiskey Distillery up at Port Stewart; on our

Another view of the wreckage (photo courtesy of Tom Clarke)

return we took the civilians home to Newtownards on the outskirts of Belfast and dropped them off.

We were all a little happy, 'merry', and thought nothing of having a sing-a-long in the back as the Sherpa van drove back in town with us singing and joking. We then turned a corner in the centre and then, crunch: Ricci had hit a car parked across the street. We drove straight into a full scale riot emanating from a side street. The Sherpa stopped; we stopped singing and started to shout at Ricci 'What a wanker!' Within seconds (seemed like minutes) the whole world changed with the noise of bricks, bottles, and dustbin lids hitting the van sounding like thunder.

It rained bricks and glass; Paddy had stopped chucking at the Army lads and turned their full attention to us. Allan was hit full on the right side of his face with half a Charlie (half a house brick) which knocked him clean out.

The Army lads who were not 50 yards away could see this unfolding and drove a PIG straight up to the back door. Allan was shipped over first followed by the rest off us jumping across and lying in heap drunk in the road.

This was the most scared I had ever been but it would not be the last.

TWINBROOK, BELFAST: HUNGER STRIKES 1981

Fusilier, 'A' Coy, 1 RWF

The afternoon before the local council elections in 1981, the company was deployed from RUC, Woodburn to protect some of the polling stations. These elections were being contested to the backdrop of violence and anger precipitated in the main by the hunger strikes. Our multiple drew the short straw, and were given a secondary school in Twinbrook to look after. Now, under normal circumstances this would have been a cushy post, but unfortunately though for 3 Platoon's 'A' multiple, this was the home of Bobby Sands. He was already dead and it would be fair to say that local feelings were running high, especially as Francis Hughes, another IRA hunger striker had died the day before.

We took over the school, which was a typical large glassed 2 storey building, surrounded by railings. Within half an hour the local rent-a-mob had started to gather outside, and our boss, an experienced Colour Sgt, had posted us in different upstairs classrooms and entry points with orders to prevent anyone gaining access. Then the bricks started coming our way, which was no problem, because after 3 months of this, I was well versed in the art of the 'squaddie two step and duck.' This went on for a little while, and then the crowd decided to up the ante, and started placing blankets over the railings. Shit; this meant we couldn't see them, or what they were doing behind them. We soon found out, as the first of hundreds of petrol bombs which would come our way that evening began to rain down on us, from over the fence. We responded with plastic, and this was really how the night continued.

By about 9 or 10pm, the attacks on the school had reached their peak. The crowd was well organised and determined, but so were we. The school looked like a scene from a war zone with all the window glass smashed. Small fires had broken out throughout the classrooms, after petrol ignited on curtains, which we were quickly putting out. The baying mob outside, by now well reinforced, were entering the school grounds, as they conducted little forays. We were responding with baton rounds, and small snatch patrols, and caught a few of the rioters, though it would be fair to say we were struggling to contain it. I think we only numbered about 12–15 men.

During this period of time, I can remember looking across the Twinbrook estate, from the upstairs classroom and seeing a couple of Land Rovers from the RRF, making their way to our location, in order to reinforce us. I can recall one of my mates shouting 'here they come', and then I saw the Makralon Land Rovers engulfed in a multi-petrol bomb attack; obviously they had been ambushed, and this was serious. The guys deployed to protect themselves, and tragically a young girl from the estate was killed by a baton round; what a waste of a young life and even we hardened squaddies were gutted. Listening to the radio comms on my brick commander's radio, as the tragedy unfolded, it affected us all.

The girl who tragically died as a result of that accident was 14 year old Julie Livingstone of West Belfast.

NORTH HOWARD STREET MILL: 1981

Major Allan Harrhy, RRW

We were the 'spearhead' battalion and deployed to Northern Ireland as a consequence of the hunger strike which was gripping the whole Province as convicted

IRA men were starving themselves to death. By now, I had been made up to CSM and we were at the Howard Street Mill in Belfast.

The mill was jampacked with soldiers from several units and we had 2 Companies RRW, one Company RWF and a Company of the Royal Scots. My Company was given an area of the Springfield Road and we had one month of constant riots; I don't mean 'occasionally', I mean every single day! As each hunger striker died, the old biddies would be out on the streets, banging their dustbin lids and mobs would swarm out, armed with bricks, bottles, rocks and soon the petrol bombers would appear.

It was really horrendous, really frightening for me as well as for the younger, inexperienced soldiers. The riots were huge and unbelievable, ugly mobs of people consumed by hatred and venom and who just wanted to kill us. They threw petrol bombs, acid bombs (very, very nasty), homemade grenades, empty bottles, paving stones, anything at all that they could get their hands on. We replied with baton rounds and on one occasion, we returned live rounds when we came under fire from a gunman. These riots would continue until the early hours and then they would retire, shagged out – like us – to their beds for a few hours sleep and then ready to restart in a few hours time.

Between May 5, 1981 and the death of Bobby Sands, the first IRA hunger striker to die and August 20 when the tenth and final hunger striker – Michael Devine – died, several thousand soldiers were injured in the accompanying riots and gun battles. However 8 soldiers – including five Royal Green Jackets, one RCT and one UDR soldier – and five RUC officers were killed in this horrible three and a half month period.

NORTHERN IRELAND

Private, Green Howards

We were manning a VCP one day and we pulled a car in which Gerry Adams was travelling.

I was the chat up man and my job was to speak to him whilst my oppo talked to the driver and went to do a plate check over the RT. Well, I tried to speak to him just to pass the time of day, but just got a sullen silence and he wouldn't even look at me.

I persisted and all I got was a gob full of sewer words; what today, we would call industrial language. The more I smiled and chatted to him, the filthier the language got. So, just to wind him up a bit more, I said something like 'Ok, Gerry, if you won't co-operate with me, I'll just have to radio your details in.' He swore a bit more and I got onto the RT to base and gave them his details to do a name check.

There was a pause, the net was silent and then a burst of laughter broke out! Then all I could hear was 'Happy birthday to you; happy birthday to you. Happy birthday, dear Gerry, happy birthday to you.'

It was the bastard's birthday that very day! His face went purple with rage and he gave me a few parting swearwords as his mate drove him off.

BELLEEK: 1981

Major 'MT', Royal Army Ordnance Corps, SATO

There were mortar trucks in Bessbrook, Belleek and Letterkenny. The one in Bessbrook failed to fire its mortars. In typically paranoid SATO mode I wondered if it was a come-on, and booby trapped for the ATO follow up, but it had simply failed to fire. At Belleek, with the Omagh ATO, we had visits during the job from the General and some of the HQNI Operations Room staff. I enjoyed showing them what really happened on the ground, rather than briefing them in HQNI. (Belleek was also the first time I wore "Aunty Vi's" cardigan. I had told "Vi" I would be standing about a lot and needed something warm to wear. I asked for something in green, thinking about camouflage. It was green alright, a very pale luminous green. It might as well have had a sign on it saying 'shoot me.') On the truck at Letterkenny the mortar bombs exploded spectacularly, and reduced the vehicle to a set of wheels and a buckled cab.

Remotely initiated bombs, often in culverts, continued to be a problem. However the one near Rosslea, dealt with by the Omagh ATO, had its funny side. As we searched our way towards the bomb, which was right against the border, the Irish carried out a sweep on their side. We met up with them, just before starting the final approach, and they told us they had found two terrorists dozing under a tree at the firing point.

The usual steady stream of suspect cars, explosive finds and hoaxes continued unabated.

There were a string of under-car bombs aimed at the RUC during October, sadly with all too many of them being successful. However the Lisburn Team successfully defused one in Warrenpoint that had been attached to the car outside Newry RUC station. The fortunate RUC driver had obviously got into it very soon after the bomb had been laid, and reached Warrenpoint to pick up his wife from work before it armed. After we had cleared it he told me she had spotted it and virtually dragged him out of the car. He must have left in a hurry because when we arrived the engine was running, and the lights and radio were still on!!

There were car bombs. There was one in Dungannon at the end of October. The Captain had been on R and R, and arrived back just as the suspect car was reported. He immediately took over from his temporary R and R replacement and was driven out to the scene in his civvies. Nobody was going to have one of 'his' bombs.

The Captain from Londonderry defused a 1,000 pound bomb near Strabane in November. The firing point was across the Foyle in the Republic. As far as I can remember this was the largest bomb yet during my tour, and it was quite some sight.

Then towards the end of November the tempo started to slacken until it was possible to relax a bit. It didn't stop, but it certainly became easier to cope. We used to joke about the IRA being on winter R and R in Spain. Christmas, apart from the Belleek mortar truck on the 23rd, was fairly peaceful, and the Team reporting over to Girdwood for stand-by during Christmas day left base with carols blaring out and streamers and balloons blowing in the wind from the radio aerials.

Chapter Fifteen

1982

A year of 368 bombings, 547 shootings and the deaths of 39 soldiers, 12 RUC officers, 50 civilians and 7 terrorists.

Although more soldiers were killed that year, a factor increased by the Royal Parks' bombings in London, the reduced number of bombings and shootings in the Province was a reflection of the Security Force's ability to find arms and explosives caches.

On July 20 of that year, on the south carriageway of Hyde Park, 4 soldiers of the Blues & Royals (and 7 of their horses) were killed by an IRA bomb. Just 2 hours later, a bomb exploded underneath the band of the Royal Green Jackets whilst playing to an audience in Regent's Park; 7 Green Jackets were killed.

It was in this year, that the 'Droppin' Well' public house in Ballykelly was the scene of a terrible outrage, with 17 people killed. 8 soldiers from the Cheshires were killed; these were Privates Stephen Smith (24), Clinton Collins (20), David Murray (18), Neil Williams (18), and three Lance Corporals: Philip McDonough (26), Stephen Bagshaw (21) and David Wilson-Stitt (27) Two ACC Privates were killed, Terence Adams (20) and Paul Delaney (18) and a Light Infantry Corporal – David Salthouse, who was 23.

The bomb, planted by the INLA, also killed 6 innocent civilians: Patricia Cooke (21), Ruth Dixon (24), Alan Callaghan and Valerie McIntyre – who were both only 17 – Angela Hoole (19) and Claire Watt, who was 25.

BELFAST: 1982
Lance Corporal Steven Horvath, RAMC

The RSM informed me that that I was off to Northern Ireland for my first tour of duty. My pleas that I could not be sent as I was still only 17 years of age fell on deaf ears and resulted in me yet again bleeding. 'Fuck off and go and see the chief clerk to sort out your NIRT training dates, you're off to lovely Belfast.' These were the last words I heard the RSM scream at me as I marched like fuck out of his office before I got another kicking!

Within two weeks I had landed at Aldergrove airport. En-route to the FST (Field Surgical Team) at the MWMPH (Mil Wing Musgrave Park Hospital), I foolishly kept checking for snipers in the trees and bushes expecting to see some daft old sod with an Armalite or M6o sticking out like a sore thumb blatting the living fuck out of me. The FST at MPH is the place any injured military person is brought to be patched up, if possible, by the wide array of RAMC and QA nursing staff. The first day was not only a big learning curve but was also my initiation into the FST. As a field medic when the RSM had told me I was coming to Ireland I thought, 'Fuck yeah; get out on the streets in a brick with the lads and do my bit for Queen & Country'. That was not the case, it was a case of Taffy being stuck in military operating theatre with the rest of the REMFs (Rear Echelon Mother Fuckers) as us a field medics referred to the rest of the RAMC, because us 'Field Medics' are trained for and meant to be up at the shitty end of the fun with the lads on the streets. That's what we are trained for.

Amongst the more serious aspects of the job were the constant reminders of why we were there, the continuous influx of seriously injured and horrifically maimed and disfigured fellow service personnel.

Although an unknown face, anyone who was casevaced through the doors of the FST was still our brother. It was during these times that the medic in each of us truly switched on, as we pulled out all the stops, irrespective of our own lack of sleep or rest to repair our fellow soldiers who for no other reason than 'They were there at the time,' became another victim and statistic of the troubles.

No amount of training and videos can prepare you for the sight and sounds of yet another British casualty who had fallen foul of terrorist rounds and/or bombs. Once in the operating theatre their screaming sometimes dwindled with the increasing pain-killing injections, or as sometimes was the case, their lives just ebbed away with us helpless to stop it as their injuries were so horrific and severe there was literally nothing we could do but try and ease the pain as they slipped away from us.

Every day we faced the scenario of severe injuries and maiming, and all too frequently we were so helpless to stop our colleagues and brothers from dying in front of us. The sounds and screams are always there in my mind, as are the smells of burnt and melted combats fused as one with a soldier's skin and organs, which are obviously part of our job that we experienced.

Unfortunately we weren't as successful in saving as many as we hoped, it is then the regret and guilt hits you like a 200 mph steam train, but to dwell on this takes away your focus from the job in hand. You have to try and move on and do better for the next brother or sister coming through the doors.

At times we felt we were losing the war but every now and then rejoiced at the battles we won either direct or indirectly.

Two memorable incidents were the Loyalist shootings of Bernadette Devlin and the dirty protests and hunger strikes of people like Bobby Sands and his fellow inmates.

I recall when we heard the news over the net that Bernadette Devlin had been shot by Loyalist terrorists we shouted for joy. Personally by this time my attitude and opinions were such that the loss of any Republican supporter/campaigner would be met with rejoicing and yet another few pints.

I remember at the time of the shooting of Devlin and her husband I was overcome with grief and pain, not for the pain and suffering those two were experiencing, but knowing the fact that as a member of the RAMC, it was a fellow RAMC Doctor that saved the bitch's life. One minute her fellow terrorists are killing us, next thing it was us saving their lousy fucking lives. But there you go, we all took the oath to save life, and that is one of the things that makes us the best army in the world.

Yet another incident that brought us some light relief were the hunger strikes and dirty protests of early 1981 in the Kesh.

The thought of people like Bobby Sands and his fellow muppets wallowing in their own crap-smeared cells starving themselves to death during the protest, only served to give us a small reason to celebrate. At least they were inside and not on the streets killing us, there was enough of that going on already. When Bobby Sands died God did we celebrate! 'Die you Fenian bastards!' I thought, and 'good fucking riddance to bad blood.' I soon came to regret my thoughts. As more hunger strikers died the backlash for the lads on the streets was brought home in a familiar style. More shootings and bombings.

As a veteran of the 'troubles' as they are sometimes so nonchalantly called, I look back on my time in Northern Ireland and say 'troubles, my arse.' It was all-out fucking war with an unseen enemy.

To the brothers/sisters who came through our doors and lived to tell the tale and return home I say this: Well done in surviving and thank you for giving me the strength and confidence to make myself a better medic and ultimately a better person. To the brothers and sisters who fought so valiantly, but sadly lost the fight of their life. I am truly sorry that I amongst others will not able to help you win the fight.

During my time in Belfast in '81 I had broken my teeth on the blood, guts, broken bones and ruined lives at the hands of our arch-enemy, the terrorists who constantly strove to rid Ulster of us.

Major 'MT', Royal Army Ordnance Corps, SATO

The new year came in, and right up until I left in March, it all began to slowly wind up again. It didn't reach the level of the previous summer, but it still had its moments. On 5th February the ATO from Bessbrook also defused a 1,000 pounder, in Camlough, in an operation lasting nearly 24 hours. A little later I joined him for a night operation to clear a hijacked truck and a 100 pound bomb on the Belfast to Dublin road at Killeen. It happened on the eve of the England v Ireland Rugby match! We managed to clear it by 02.00hours on the Saturday morning.

In the last couple of days of my tour there was a car bomb in Lurgan. The RUC managed to arrest the driver at gun point as he got out of the car. As they handcuffed him he ' ... suggested they leave quickly' as he had armed the bomb, and the clock was ticking. So we had a good idea of how long we had to stop it. The ATO and I arrived together, and estimated that we just had time to make one approach to the car. The team prepared the 'Barrow and the Number two started to drive it forward when disaster struck. A crucial actuator snapped, the top hamper fell forward, and the 'Barrow was useless. There was no time to prepare the other, so the Team improvised, found a length of rope and tied the hamper roughly in place. At the car, the number two shotgunned the rear window and extended the boom, which fitted neatly into the space available (how lucky can you get)? After the Maxi-candles had been fired we waited anxiously until about 10 minutes after we knew the bomb should have exploded. The Team all joined hands and played 'ring' o roses' in the street to celebrate (A nice way to end your tour!)

From a strictly personal point of view there were two incidents that affected Geordie and I that I will never forget.

Ambush patrol (photo courtesy of David Roalfe)

A week or so after the disruption day we attended a clear-up operation near the border. Two members of the RUC had been killed by a culvert bomb. The operation finished. The helicopters came in and extracted the military. The RUC liaison officers drove away in convoy. I stayed on for about twenty minutes, getting photographs of the incident area. Then we drove off.

We were travelling along a very straight, narrow lane when I suddenly saw that ahead of us there was a man in civilian clothes with a rifle. There was a vehicle just behind him half blocking the lane. We both had the same thought, our private nightmare, that we'd run into an illegal IRA VCP. The lane was too narrow to turn round, so there was no alternative but to drive on. Geordie gave me his 9mm and I put it on my lap under a map. (My little Walther was excellent for concealment, but I always felt you'd have to hold it against someone's head to kill him). I said 'Drive up to him. When we stop and he gets close enough I'll have a go at him.' Just as we came to a stop an RUC officer in uniform stepped out from behind the vehicle!! It transpired that they were involved in the same operation, but had not yet been stood down.

To travel around the Province freely both CATO and I and our drivers were always covert. There was always the threat of running into an illegal VCP, but I felt the greatest risk was of being mistaken for terrorists by our own side. I can't remember the exact date, but I think it was November. There had been a very successful but lengthy operation in Londonderry, so it was about midnight when we started back to Belfast. We had all the forensic from the bombs in the boot, and one of the Londonderry Team who was going on R and R in the back, so we looked pretty tail heavy. As usual we were not hanging about.

As we got to Magherafelt we had to slow down for a sharp right hand bend in the road. As we approached the corner small silver objects started to glisten in the headlights beam. When we got round the corner there was a tractor and trailer blocking the road, and we could see even more little silver objects on either side of the road. It was the RUC, and the silver objects were their cap badges. I said very quietly 'Sit still. They are all looking for an excuse to open fire.' After a very sweaty three or four minutes one of them approached the car, and we were able to persuade him we were Army. Somewhere along our dash back to Belfast we had been reported as a suspect car bomb, and they had reacted very quickly to set up the road block. When I'd stopped shaking I was quite impressed.

My enduring memory of commanding 321 is of the feeling of pride and anxiety every time I had to watch another young, determined ATO walk down the road alone to sort out 'his' bomb. Yes, if it was possible he'd have used every remote tactic he could to disrupt the bomb. If it was a car he'd have sent the wheelbarrow up and Maxi-candled and shotgunned it. Yes, I'd have given him the best advice I could. But in the end he always had to walk up alone and finish the job. There was always the threat that something new might be waiting him, or a second well hidden device was near by, or that there was a booby trap.

They were great guys.

A BABY IS BORN IN LONDONDERRY: 1982

Lance Corporal Steve Horvath, RAMC

From time to time we would have to take casualties to the A&E dept in Derry. Any time we did this there were always three of us in the ambulance, a driver, an escort and myself, all of us armed with 'Shorts' or 9mm Browning pistols and 1 SLR. The fact that these were our ambulances didn't get past the evil eyes of the local IRA sympathisers in a small village between Ballykelly and Londonderry called Greysteel.

Greysteel had for many years been a local hotspot and sanctuary for PIRA members and their supporters. Needless to say we are often faced with running the gauntlet of the brickings and even shots at the ambulance during our runs to the hospital. There were one or two occasions whereby we literally had to ram our way through an illegal vehicle checkpoint or IVCP as they were pretty frequent on the A2 between Ballykelly and Derry.

One of our boys whose wife was pregnant and due to drop at any time, called me out to his quarters as his wife was just about to give birth. So we collected his wife and him and proceeded on our run down to the local hospital from the married quarters. So there I was in the back in the ambulance up to my wrists in blood and broken waters trying to deliver the baby that was desperately trying to make its entrance to the world, when all of a sudden our driver shouted 'IVCP' [Illegal Vehicle Checkpoint] and slammed on the brakes.

Most of the time if we encountered an IVCP we would be stopped and let through. However this night was different. Having pulled up, my driver and escort were questioned at length about the patient and me in the back in the ambulance. The three of us had our 9mm's ready just in case when all of a sudden the back doors flew open and I was ordered out of the back of the

Beechmounts, West Belfast (photo courtesy of Andy Carr)

ambulance by some scrawny twat who couldn't have been more than 17years old. Rapidly showing him my blood soaked hands and wrists I explained in my best queens English, 'Fuck off you boggy cxxx, if I leave now this baby and mother will die.'

As he began to move closer and point his weapon at me I leapt back to the open door, my right-hand instinctively reached in between the patient's legs where I had hidden my weapon and retrieved my 9mm. Before he realised what was happening I had my left-hand squeezing the life out of his throat, whilst the 9mm barrel had been forced into the bastard's gob, smashing some of his teeth in the process. In an incredibly calm and quiet voice (my ring piece and rest of my body was crapping itself), I whispered in his ear: 'You have 3 seconds to tell the pricks at the front of this vehicle that all's ok here otherwise you'll be sharing Bobby Sands shit smeared cell in hell!!!' Instinctively he yelled as I released my throat group just enough for him to shout out: 'It's okay!! Fuck all here, let them through.' I let go, he let go, as I slammed the ambulance doors and yelled: 'Fucking move – get us out of here.' Ten minutes later I had delivered a beautifully healthy girl, mum and baby fine and I was a relieved man.

'Job done boys, let's go home.' As it was nearly 4am by the time we started on our way back to the camp, my driver, my escort and I had discussed the incident and decided we would keep our mouths shut about it as we couldn't be bothered with all the bullshit and paperwork and SIB interviews that would follow from an imminent investigation as a result of the incident, so from that moment on we never discussed it again.

6TH DECEMBER 1982, THE BOMBING OF THE DROPPIN' WELL PUBLIC HOUSE, BALLYKELLY BY THE I.N.L.A.

Lance Corporal Steve Horvath, RAMC (attached Cheshire Regiment)

Prior to reading the following extracts I wish to inform the reader that there are some recollections of the Droppin' Well Public House bombing at Ballykelly in Dec '82. Therefore should the reader have any knowledge or know anyone from this incident then you may find this part of the book upsetting or traumatic, and please put the book down. It is not my intention to cause any pain or suffering to the reader in any way. The following story is a compilation of some of my darkest and fondest memories of my time whilst serving with the 1st Bn 22nd Cheshire Regt.

Not far outside the main gates of Shackleton Barracks was a very nice village pub called the Droppin' Well, in squaddie lingo our local haunt. The locals were a pleasant lot who welcomed us with open arms. Above the pub were a series of shops, my memory fails to recall what they were but I think one was a hair salon and the rest I cannot remember.

From the time I arrived in Ballykelly the Droppin' Well had become our watering hole. On occasions we had our fair share of altercations with some of the sympathisers who would travel up from Greysteel to give us some grief. On one particular night, one of our lads took a serious kicking for no apparent reason outside the pub. Needless to say the next night a huge number of us made a late-night visit to Greysteel and executed our revenge on the local men with such aggression and violence that we made it clear: — 'Screw with one of us you screw with all of us.'

On patrol, Warrenpoint (photo courtesy of David Roalfe)

Cheshire Regiment prepare for patrol in Belfast

We'd already had several bomb threats at the pub and on these occasions the commanding officer would put the pub out of bounds until such time as the Intel deemed it safe for us to venture back in. Naturally we were extremely cautious and weary once we stepped outside the gates of camp, though somehow we were relaxed within the village of Ballykelly, after all, we weren't in central Belfast, Londonderry or 'Bandit Country' as South Armagh was known. To all intense purposes we were in the middle of a quiet non-hostile friendly community.

Much of what happened during the event of the night of 6th December '82 is still locked up in the dark recesses of my brain. Some time maybe the memories will come to the fore and I will hopefully then be able to put them into perspective

6th Dec '82 was a typically nondescript day in Ballykelly with the normal routine activities happening during the day. The evening's activities had been focused on chilling out in the NAAFI and then over to the pub.

The atmosphere within the Droppin' Well was one of a relaxed environment, both civilian and military alike enjoying each other's company. My memory of the few hours before the event, and much of the immediate aftermath refused to release themselves. I think I remember the shopping complex came down on top of us; just seconds before the explosion I'd moved away from the pillars, which I now know were taken out, bringing the complex down on top of us all.

Being near the external walls of the pub I was lucky to escape with minor cuts and bruises and able to get myself out of the rubble. What seemed to be hours passed by, in fact it was only a matter of seconds or minutes when our lads started arriving, followed by the emergency services. My first instinct was obviously to try and find Avril as she was in trapped in the collapsed pub and shopping complex. Looking at the state of the place and the devastation around I could not get back in. My paramedic instinct naturally tried to take over, but there was so much emotion, fear, anger and tears that my brain went into some sort of overload as I started trying to dig my way through the rubble. For what appeared to be an eternity I then sat there in total disbelief that this could happen to 'our pub'.

Once our lads arrived from the med centre laden with emergency med kit and we got to work. This is what all my military medical training had been designed for, to get in and do the job, and get the lads and lasses out alive. I remember one casualty our MO was having a crap time with, trying to get a drip into the man's arm. The MO shouted for me to get the cut-down kit so that we could open his veins up to get a drip in. As he shouted I noticed that the young lad was pissing blood from both his shattered legs like a fucking river.

'Fuck the cut-down kit', I told the MO, 'cut his fucking jeans off and get me more bags of Hartman's solution'. As I was screaming at the doc, I dropped like a fucking stone onto the lad's right thigh with my kneecap straight into the crease of his groin an attempt to stop the femoral artery pissing out more blood.

Almost simultaneously I had cut the end off the drip tube, ripped what was left of his jeans from his backside area and rammed the drip tube some 5/6 inches up his arse. His screaming and fighting during this was making me feel as if I was going to puke, never mind the poor bugger's life I was trying to save.

(By pumping fluids up his arse, it would get into his system faster than if we had tried a cut-down as he would have bled out by the time we managed to get a drip in his arms.) 'Get me more bags' I yelled to the doc, 'unless you want him to fucking die on me.'

To this day I do not know who it was I worked on, but all I do know is that my methods, which were not in any training manual, did in fact save the lad's life. As a result of my actions, my Medical Officer tried to get me court- martialled for my unorthodox method of getting fluids into the dying soldier. As it turned out the MO was bollocked and told not to be a c***.

To be totally honest, the remainder of the night and most of the next day are a blank in my memory banks. For the next four days and four nights I think I managed all of about four or six hours restless sleep, pushing and pushing every second, picking up the pieces of our torn and shattered lives the best we could. It was a time of blind and somehow controlled panic, filled with emergency treatment, recriminations, regret and stunned silence as the thought of something of this magnitude could happen in 'our' sleepy village of Ballykelly.

Within a week of the bombings I was sent as cover medic to our border position at Auchnacloy to provide medical backup for the resident company of some 120 men. The next month saw me treating countless numbers of distressed and hurt broken young and old soldiers. It was totally unavoidable and inevitable that I went into a status of total emotional and psychological shut down. The responsibility to care for a company of broken men who had suffered an unimaginable loss of friends, family, brothers and trusted colleagues rested on my shoulders as the company medic, counsellor, therapist and makeshift priest.

Droppin' Well, 6 December 1982 (photo courtesy of Ronnie Gamble)

Life in Ballykelly was never the same for both our civilian friends and families and our own military community. There remained a sense of disbelief and cautious awareness by us all. The scars of 6th December 1982 will stay with many of us for all our lives. People have been affected in many different ways by the horrific events of that night in December 1982.

Some, myself included, have not realised just how much they have been affected until many years later. However we must at least try to reflect, and remember our fallen friends, and keep the memories and ultimate sacrifice they paid at the forefront of our thoughts. By keeping their memories alive we're able to not only honour our fallen comrades, but to somehow help the remainder of us still suffering, to somehow heal ourselves and come to terms with our losses and pains.

Steve 'Taffy' Horvath has since 2004 been classified as a 'Disabled War Veteran'. He was diagnosed with 'Severe Chronic complex PTSD' (Post Traumatic Stress Disorder).

Since 1982, he has suffered nightmares, flashbacks, panic attacks, major anxiety attacks, and major fear and paranoia episodes. During some of his nightmares he ends up patrolling his garden and surrounding areas, checking for the IRA/INLA attacks. He sometimes ends up jumping out of his bedroom window during one particular nightmare that takes him back to being inside the Droppin' Well. His brain tells him the pub will blow up in 5 minutes so he has to escape out of the window in order to avoid the 'explosion' that his brain tells him is going to happen. He has had a number of suicide attempts to try and end the daily and nightly hell he relives everyday with his memories of Ballykelly.

Chapter Sixteen

1983

A year of 410 bombings, 424 shootings and the deaths of 15 soldiers, 19 RUC officers, 37 civilians and 7 terrorists, including, for the first time in 3 years, a member of the Loyalists.

In this year, William Doyle, a County Court judge, was shot dead by members of the IRA as he left mass at a Catholic church in south Belfast. The IRA also exploded a land mine in Tyrone killing four members of the Ulster Defence Regiment (this was the highest casualty rate suffered by the UDR in a single incident).

The week before Christmas, in this year, 40 year old lance Corporal Brown Mckeown, UDR, was shot dead in front of his son at Magherafelt.

MACRORY PARK 1ST MAY 1983

Private Tim Castle, Light Infantry

8 Platoon, Coy HQ, and an attached Support Platoon from the D&D in Ballykinler on Brigade reserve were deployed to Macrory Park police post. This was situated opposite the City Cemetery on the Whiterock Road wedged in amongst some back-to-back housing known as the Brittons. We had a round of patrolling for three days, camp duties for 3 days (which meant 8 hours rotating round stagging on in the sangars and gate sentry, and Red 1 section, which was the crash team on 2 minutes notice to move. This meant you ate, drank and slept dressed with your INIBA (improved Northern Ireland Body Armour) on under your combat jacket for 8 hours at a time, you then rotated onto fatigues for 8 hours, which if at night meant you could get a couple of hours of sleep.

The first task I had was with Red 1 so I expected a couple of uncomfortable hours kip. Not so; we were crashed to Fort Whiterock on the Springfield Road to get batteries for the watch keeper who was the Coy 2 I/C, and I thought this could be a real pain for the next two months! I remember doing 'Lurks' in the City Cemetery where we would hide and watch for illegal activities, 'G' would use it as an opportunity to letch and generally perv' at the underage drinkers, glue sniffers and shaggers getting up to no good. I was amazed that this was the first time I had stayed put in a graveyard after dark without being scared witless; I put this down to the SLR and 20 rounds of 'ball' [ammunition] I carried!

Of the four of us in the team, only 'G' and Rosie had been here before. We now occupied a TAOR (Tactical Area of Responsibility) with our Company that a Bn had covered the previous tour in 1978. I thought this is going to be hard work. Stagging on was seriously dull and not enlivened by the Coy 2 I/C demanding that we record the vehicle details of every car that passed the camp. There were so many you couldn't write a tenth of them down.

There was one particularly nasty period when the Provisional IRA decided to shut the city down. They planted one bomb in a transit van and let it off. They also put another 8 hijacked vans around nearby to make the Bomb disposal guys' lives harder. The patrols' platoon ended up on a cordon for 16 hours including the fatigues and Red 1 section. Only the guard section was left in place and we stagged on for 16 hours straight. I was so tired I can't even remember if I stayed awake or not! That night we became patrols' platoon and even the Platoon Cdr fell asleep giving a briefing. I remember walking along the Beechmounts and waking up around the corner on the floor having walked into a lamp post.

'G' did his best for us and when we stagged on into the small hours he would buzz our sangars on the intercom and give us a quiz, 10 questions on military subjects or the latest members of the top 60 players' list. He would come around with a flask and check your answers; it gave you a lift and helped keep you awake. Most of the sangars were covered by CCTV and almost unnecessary; it was a real pity to spend a scorching hot summer with cam cream on whilst your mates were on the beach. After about a month they withdrew all the cam cream, which was made by Max Factor and apparently gave you skin cancer. It certainly gave you zits!

The unit chippy turned up to nail face veils over each sangar window. Occasionally the cooks, bottle washers and CQMS store men would do a stag so we could make up an additional patrol. The storeman was a complete pain and he used to put the window shutter grease around the eye pieces of the binoculars so you got a free pair of Panda eyes. How he was never filled in I'll never know.

Culvert bomb (photo courtesy of Ronnie Gamble)

N Edwards (facing) top cover (photo courtesy of N Edwards)

The other platoons were based at Fort Whiterock, the Company CO with another ops room, a rifle platoon doing Red 2 the 10 minute standby section, 1 section on sangars and ops room runner and 1 section providing additional patrolling manpower. The RUC station at New Barnsley held 2 more platoons doing a similar role to Macrory Park but covering the Springmartins, Corry's wood yard and the lovely Ballymurphy estate. The tour started with 8 Platoon and the attached D&Ds at Macrory, 9 Platoon at Fort Whiterock and 7 Platoon and Recce Platoon at New Barnsley. After 2 months we were to rotate.

PRIVATE TIM CASTLE, LIGHT INFANTRY
The Murder of Geoff Curtis

I was on Red 1 on the day after the 1983 elections and the results were starting to come in on Breakfast TV. I was asleep and was shaken awake to run into the back of the PIG. Red 1 consisted of a PIG and Piglet (Armoured Land Rover). We crashed out of the gates to the Bull Ring, the notorious central area of the Ballymurphy estate, and were briefed by 'G' on the way, 'There has been an incident and Starlight has been called.' 'Starlight' – the unit medical officer – was based in our camp and went round in a 6 wheeled Saracen. We had let him out of the gate in front of us!

We bumped around for about 3 minutes and piled out at the scene of a bombing just as the RMO was covering the body of Geoff Curtis with a blanket. Geoff had been third man in the 31L patrol call sign. The IRA were out to score a policeman or two on the day that Maggie won the election, a way of saying we haven't gone away and we haven't forgiven the Government for the hunger strikers' deaths. We must have been seconds behind the RMO yet there was nothing to be done. A few months earlier the INLA had tried to kill a policeman on patrol with a bomb, it went wrong and a local child was killed. The INLA were thrown out of the Divis flats where this occurred. The IRA didn't want the same thing to happen.

Geoff's patrol had two policeman at the front and Second Lieutenant Will Tricks behind; Geoff then crossed the Bull Ring and headed off up Glenalina Road. There was a lamp post behind a brick wall and a command detonated IED was hidden here with the lamp post as an aiming mark. Sadly for Geoff the two policemen decided to talk to a very young child, and the IRA must have seen this from their firing point and held off. By the time it was safe for them to fire the patrol had moved and Geoff was level with the bomb. He was killed instantly and 2 others were wounded and his family and friends hurt beyond comprehension forever!

Despite a vigorous follow-up and several arrests, no one has ever been charged with his murder. About an hour later whilst I was still in the cordon I looked through a front window of a house to see myself debussing within 5 minutes of the blast. It turns out that the news crews were warned of an incident at The Ballymurphy yet none of them chose to warn us. I hate the press to this day!

N Edwards knocking out Monday night's Coronation Street with his White Sifter!
(photo courtesy of N Edwards)

North Howard Street Mill (photo courtesy of Andy Carr)

Private Geoff Curtis was 20 and was killed by the device – a 15lb bomb – and two other soldiers and the two RUC men were wounded. Curtis was from the Grimsby area and seconds before the device exploded, one of the RUC had actually shouted a warning to him. He was a very popular soldier with his many comrades in the Light Infantry.

Interestingly enough, complaints against the mass media were a fairly common thread throughout the interview process; comments ranged from 'How did the bastards also know when and where and incident was going to happen?' to the oft-repeated 'The bastards were always in the bloody way!'

Private Castle continues:

Later on in August, the Supergrass events took place. Robert Lean, who was reputedly the QM for West Belfast and thus in a position to name names, was lifted. As with most terrorists he squealed, as I suspect they had plenty on him and were willing to send him down for a long time. He turned Queen's Evidence and thus the Supergrass lifts were born.

We were sat in the briefing room at New Barnsley when Mr Burton briefed us, and, as with all British Army briefings we were given a thorough background into the op. The vehicles and escorts to lift the suspects on the list were coming into our patch from out of town. We would have to secure the lift targets and hand them over for processing. Each call sign was given a target address. We had one in Whitecliff Parade. The wheels were to meet us as soon as we secured the site but prior to actually lifting the player. We surrounded the target house and 'G' called in to 'Zero' that we were ready and could we have an ETA for the wheels. 'Zero' was Captain Schermoully and he was at Macrory Park controlling the op.

He replied that the wheels were there and we should get to the right address. The wheels were actually in Whitecliff Crescent, the road behind, but that didn't matter as the 2i/c was in charge so he was right. This was bad news for the wheels as they were very exposed to trouble there! The women had woken up and were bashing bin lids on the pavement!

Eventually 'G' lost patience and said; 'Let's go!' I ran at the door blocking the alleyway separating the two houses, and launched a flying kick at the door for my boots to go through. I landed on my backside, all the locals burst out laughing especially when the gate opened outwards! In the event he wasn't there but we lifted a huge amount of baddies from the area as a whole. Lean reneged on his statements before going to court and most of the players walked free.

Chapter Seventeen

1984

A year of 258 bombings, 334 shootings and the deaths of 19 soldiers, 8 RUC officers, 25 civilians (the lowest number in the 15 years since the violence had intensified) and 11 terrorists.

It was another bad year for the UDR, as the IRA again targeted them, killing 9 plus a TA soldier attached to the R.I.R. In all but three of the killings, the men were either at work or on their way home from their full-time jobs.

BELFAST: 1984

'Sneaky Beaky' (Undercover Soldier)

As a former member of the 'green slime', I was attached to a plainclothes unit in the Belfast area, as a member of support staff. I had a mostly desk-driven job and completed many mundane hours of collation work. On very rare occasions, a handful of staff in support roles were allowed to accompany a plain clothes officer into West Belfast, to see the Republican areas we heard about on a daily basis.

This was a great opportunity to be able to see these hardliner areas, wearing civvies, in the company of an experienced plainclothes soldier. I left our base very excited, but slightly nervous at the prospect. We eventually entered the 'West' and I was driven around the estates and shown the places of interest from over the years. Whilst chatting away with my colleague we pulled up at Kelly's Corner, the junction of Whiterock and Springfield Road, which had been and still was a hot spot for the area. My colleague said "Why don't you have a go on foot" and directed me to purchase something from the Spar on Whiterock Road. I initially protested, but my colleague reached over opened my door and all but bundled me out of the car.

As he drove off and I started to walk in the direction of the shop, my legs felt like jelly. Despite my best effort at wearing 'plainclothes' I felt as though everyone around me could see a sign above my head saying 'squaddie'. I walked past the Sinn Fein prisoner's visitor centre and approached the shop. I immediately saw two local PIRA players standing in the doorway, virtually blocking the door, deep in conversation, with another group of boys standing a few feet away, looking about in every direction. I'd already committed myself to entering the shop and didn't want to raise suspicion by veering away.

I could barely breathe as I squeezed past the two PIRA players and entered the shop; both stopped their conversation and looked at me as I entered. I walked up the first aisle and picked up the first item, a packet of biscuits, which I could see. As I reached out my hand I prayed to God that no-one could see me, as my hand was shaking so badly I nearly dropped the packet.

View from Sangar, Victor 2, Buncranna Road (photo courtesy of N Edwards)

I made my way to the till and thought,'Shit, what if the girl on the till asks me something?' The boys in the doorway were only feet away. Fortunately she was nattering away to her mate and after muttering 'thanks' in my best Belfast accent I negotiated the boys in the door way again.

As I walked away my colleague rolled up and collected me. I can't describe the relief I felt in getting back into that car, with my colleague laughing at the state I was in.

Sadly, after our return to base, the unit OC found out about my jaunt on foot and my colleague received a right bollocking. On reflection my colleague provided with me with the highlight of my tour and an insight into another operational world. I still have the biscuit wrapper as a memento, bearing the label 'The Spar, Whiterock Road'

NORTHERN IRELAND: 1984

Soldier, 11 UDR

My platoon was guarding a power station which was my first experience of static guard duty after passing out from my recruits' cadre. Anyhow myself and another recruit, Joe, were tasked together to stag for 2 hours in the sangar at the gates after dark. Things were mindnumbing until without warning a rock hit the side of the sangar, quickly followed by several more. Looking out I noticed several shadowy figures slip behind the electric board vehicles parked within the complex. Seeing my opportunity I slipped out of the sangar reassuring Joe on my departure.

Quickly I made my SLR safe removing the magazine as I approached the vehicles and stepping quickly round a van I quickly cocked my weapon and challenged the figures that happened to be from my platoon and were attempting to scare the new members of the platoon. However the tables had been turned and needless to say the incident was never spoken about again apart from calls to fetch the brown corduroys in times of strife.

Joe didn't enjoy this experience and left soon afterwards. I stayed on for 10 years, reaching the rank of sergeant and eventually commanding the platoon.

On a more sombre note in 1984 I formed part of the burial party for a friend and member of the platoon who had been murdered at his work, shot in the back of his head. All the while carrying his coffin I expected him to knock the side and surprise me declaring it all to be a joke. Unfortunately this was not the case and his body still remains in the grave within 2–3 miles of where he was shot.

In addition my 2 friends shot were both called David; the second funeral I spoke about – Davey- was shot arriving to his work and knocked off his motorbike with a shotgun blast. Whereupon the second gunman ran over and shot him several times with a pistol as he lay helpless on the ground. The first of my friends was made to kneel on the ground and executed with a shot to the back of the head.

Once again in 1984 I carried the coffin of a friend and colleague, which was televised by the local Ulster Television. As the escort party, myself included, marched up to the waiting hearse the camera zoomed straight onto my face meaning next day at work, in Belfast, I repeatedly had to rebuff the stories about my 'secret identity'. So much about personnel security when clearly it had been breached without my help.

RUC Springfield Road front sangar (photo courtesy of Andy Carr)

Back of Rosville Flats in the Bogside (photo courtesy of N Edwards)

The UDR members mentioned in the above account are known to be Private David Montgomery, who was shot by the IRA at his works, at Moira on the Airport Road on March 8 and Private David Chambers who was shot by the IRA as he arrived for work, at Dollingstown on June 4 of that year.

Free Derry wall, Bogside (photo courtesy of Andy Carr)

Chapter Eighteen

1985

A year of 251 bombings, 237 shootings and the deaths of 6 soldiers, 23 RUC officers, 20 civilians and 4 terrorists.

It was a particularly bad year for the RUC with the year's tragically high total swollen by the IRA's use of a mortar bomb on a police station in Newry, Co. Down, which killed 9 officers, including 2 policewomen. This was the highest number of RUC lives lost in a single year since the commencement of the troubles.

Although soldiers' deaths were down, with only two Regular troops killed, of the six soldiers who lost their lives in the continuing struggle with terrorism, four were members of the UDR. One has to balance the reduction with the previously mentioned appalling loss of twenty three RUC officers.

Not only were four UDR soldiers killed, but one of the civilian deaths was a deliberately targeted former UDR man. On February 24, Douglas McElhinney was shot by the INLA at a friend's house in Londonderry, just four days before the IRA mortar attack on the station at Newry.

During the course of the year, four serving UDR would be killed by the IRA. These were B.E.M. winner, Private Jimmy Graham (39), one of three brothers murdered by terrorists, killed as he drove into a primary school in Fermanagh to collect school children. Almost 4 weeks later, Private Trevor Harkness (36) was killed by an IRA bomb whilst on foot patrol in Pomeroy. The IRA waited until the following autumn before they murdered Sergeant Bobby Boyd (55); he was shot dead outside his home in Londonderry. The final UDR death that year was Captain Gordon Hanna (46) who was murdered by the IRA using an under-vehicle booby trap on November 29.

The bulk of this chapter is dedicated to the soldiers of the Ulster Defence Regiment and I am indebted to Ronnie Gamble for the following accounts (see bibliography).

BATTALION HQ, NORTHERN IRELAND: 1985
Corporal, E Coy 5UDR

Battalion Headquarters staff were very fond of using the numbers game. They believed the only way to fight terrorism was to go out on the road and stop as many cars or people as you could on any night. You would leave a patrol briefing at the start of the night with the phrase, 'I want you to stop 100 cars tonight' ringing in your ears. The platoon used to get very angry at this dumb request. The patrols were no longer being selective, pre-emptive and pro-active. The patrols were simply out to stop many innocent people by playing the numbers game.

All this was done to satisfy some smug Base Rat who would produce the impressive figures at a conference the following day. We ended up stopping ordi-

Top cover West Belfast (photo courtesy of Andy Carr)

nary people of all persuasions. We felt that we were criminalising the general public by employing these tactics. It was the wrong way to win hearts and minds.

BELFAST 'BOMB': 1985
Sgt Richard Peacocke, 321 EOD

We got called to a city centre suspect car at midnight. When we got there, we found the police surrounding a cleared area behind a row of shops with, at its centre, an old red car with its driver door wide open and engine ticking over. We dismounted and prepared to send in the Wheelbarrow, though I was concerned about the engine running in the car. The police told me a young man had been seen to screech it in, jump out, and run away. But why leave the engine running? They didn't know. It was odd. Bombers were generally tidier people than that.

The Wheelbarrow rumbled out, all charged up to blow this threat off its wheels – there was no way I wanted it driving at the cordon after I attacked it – and it got half-way there when a panicky reedy Belfast voice called from the cordon that it was his car. A lad carrying a pile of ten or so pizza boxes approached us shamefacedly and said he was the person who had left it there, and could he have it back please as he had to deliver these pizzas before they went cold? We let him go to the car once I had made my weapons safe, and he sped off for all the world like 'Starsky & Hutch.'

MAGHERAFELT: 1985

Platoon Commander, E Coy 5UDR

When I was a PC platoon commander in Magherafelt I was awarded the MBE for both my leadership and the operational successes my platoon had at that time. I was a qualified Unit Search Adviser and on one memorable occasion I personally found a sniper rifle while I was deploying my platoon on a search operation. This was a joint RUC and UDR operation, a follow up to a shooting incident the night before. Both search units stopped for a break at midday then the RUC left the area and we decided to continue with the search in the area already covered by the police. We had already found many items, which led me to believe there was something more to be found in the area. The finds included sets of rubber gloves and balaclavas that had been discarded by the terrorists in their haste to escape from their ambush position.

As I jumped over a fence to continue the search I saw a shiny object in the undergrowth. On closer inspection it turned out to be the scope still attached to the sniper rifle.

On another occasion I organized a follow-up search after a patrol had found two rifles in the Maghera area. This uncovered a holdall. On first inspection it was seen to contain sets of rubber gloves so I called forward the SOCO (Scenes of Crime Officer) and he started to collect the evidence for forensic examination. As he emptied the bag he suddenly froze. The bag also contained half a block of Semtex with a detonator, battery and a clock attached. We had to clear the area and task in the ATO (Ammunition Technical Officer) to deal with the device.

SWATRAGH VILLAGE: 1985

Dog Handler, E Coy 5UDR

The Garvagh detachment saw action against terrorists on many occasions. I was part of a multiple patrol in a Shortland armoured car approaching Swatragh village one night from Garvagh. The other part of our patrol reacted so fast to a 'shoot and scoot attack' that we managed to catch one of the gunmen hiding behind the Rafters Bar in Swatragh within minutes of the attack.

Some of the experiences were memorable for the horror of the situation. Later on in my military career I became a search dog handler. I will always remember the search I had to conduct in Swatragh village. That was after a Land Rover patrol had been ambushed from the children's playground on the Swatragh Bridge. The Republican terrorists had used an RPG rocket and it had hit one of the patrol vehicles. I spent the day picking up body parts that the dog had indicated before we recovered the patrol weapons. The smell of the man's body was very strong.

IRA gunman poses on a street for publicity purposes

SOUTH DERRY: 1985
Corporal, E Coy 5 UDR

On one occasion I was part of a foot patrol going through a village in South Derry. I tried the door handles of all the businesses as I walked up the street. I found the door open at one of the local bars. My patrol commander was not happy with this situation especially when he found that the back door was also open. We woke the bar manager and informed him about the situation. He of course promised to sack the bar staff for their security lapse.

At that time it was common practice for the PIRA to inform the business owners to leave the front and back doors open in order to perform a 'Shoot and Scoot' attack on the army patrols. This was particularly true for attacks against mobile patrols. After the second Land Rover of the patrol passed, two gunmen would come out of the premises and kneel on the road to shoot off a full magazine between the two red taillights of the rear Land Rover. With at least three people in the back of the vehicle there was always the chance of a kill.

DIVIS STREET FLATS: 1985
Sgt Richard Peacocke, 321 EOD

We got called to the Divis Flats, an infamous area of Belfast. A command bomb had detonated and killed the Corporal of a patrol passing a corner of the flats. We

Divis patrol (photo courtesy of Andy Carr)

needed to investigate and check for further devices. It was a real mess, with water and crap and bits of rubble everywhere. Somebody had gone to a lot of trouble laying in a command wire down a drainpipe and across a lot of space to attach one end to a bloody great mine and the other end to a battery pack, still sitting beneath the back window of a flat two floors up. There had to have been collusion as the firer could not have seen the target and the kids in a nearby school had been kept out of the near end of the playground during the attack.

Mao Tse Tung described the situation perfectly in his dictum that the guerrilla fighter is like a fish in the water, the water being the general population. Without the water, the fish dies. Without the fear and collusion of the people of the Divis Flats and the school, the Corporal would not have died. Such was his fate – and their guilt to this day.

The soldier killed in that IRA bomb blast which could so easily have killed children as well was Lance Corporal Anthony Dacre (25) of the King's Own Border Regiment. He was patrolling the Divis Street flats area on March 27, 1985 when the device exploded; he was married with 2 young children and came from Essex.

To this day, the controversy rages about the IRA's callous attack with no regard for children's' lives and it was thought at the time, that the pupils in the nearby school were kept inside because of the cold weather. There are those in the S.F. who believe that the school was 'instructed' by the IRA to keep the children inside.

Divis Flats, West Belfast (photo courtesy of Andy Carr)

Cpl Brownlow, E Coy 5UDR

In the interests of maintaining the personal security of E Company veterans I have been precluded from discussing many of the incidents that resulted in the capture and imprisonment of many Loyalist and Republican terrorists. It has also been impossible to recount the number of bravery awards and presentations these soldiers received without compromising their personal security.

UDR personnel were phenomenally brave. Despite the fact they were deliberately targeted by Republican terrorists for murder, this small select band of volunteers enrolled into the Regiment and remained with the Regiment for long periods of loyal service.

Throughout the 22 years of the UDR's existence only three percent of those eligible to join ever made the effort. It would be wrong to condemn outright the 97 per cent eligible people for their failure to join the UDR. Because the off-duty soldier relaxing at home was an easy target, most of these murders were carried out in front of their children and partners. In many cases in County Londonderry the murders included the children and partners of the UDR soldiers.

Despite the constant expectation of being the next to be murdered the part-time soldiers often did an ordinary job through the day and reported in for duty in the evenings and weekends. They were easy prey for the murderers as they went about their daily business. They were easy prey after spending the night protecting the whole community and returning home, alone and unprotected, to be shot in the back.

The Permanent Cadre soldiers were difficult targets for the terrorist murderer because of their long duties and fragmented family life. But they were vulnerable at certain times.

I can't say that I noticed any great change in the attitudes of friends and neighbours towards me after I had joined the Regiment. We tried to keep things as low-key as possible but it was hard to hide the fact that you were a part-time soldier, because in those early days you went to and from duties dressed in uniform and it's not exactly easy to hide a rifle.

Lt Col Hamill, 5UDR

The off-duty threat of an under-vehicle booby trap was something we had to live with. All soldiers took this threat very seriously and our vigilance paid off on a number of occasions. Very, very rarely did I ever get into my car without at least checking underneath and frequently much more thoroughly. Personal security issues when off-duty were paramount for us all. We spent a lot of time training soldiers to be vigilant when off duty.

CO LONDONDERRY: 1985
Soldier, UDR

Once on returning to base after a stint on patrols the Platoon Sergeant told me to report to the OC. The OC said to me, 'I believe you visit Altnagelvin Hospital,' I told them that I did and that I had an uncle there who was terminally ill.

He said, 'As from this minute you will not go back into Altnagelvin Hospital. I'm not being a bastard, but it's for your own good. There are at least three Republican units operating from that area that we know about.'

I obeyed his order. I never saw my uncle again. When he died I didn't even get to his funeral as I was away doing border patrols again.

SINN FEIN OFFICES: 1985
Sgt Richard Peacocke, 321 EOD

We were called out – again, at midnight – to a blast incendiary bomb hung on the grille of the window of the local Sinn Fein office. A NI blast incendiary was a vicious and nasty device. It consisted of a gallon or so of liquid fuel – usually petrol – in a plastic bottle, attached to a TPU and half a pound of explosives in a metal case. The result of one of these beasties going off is a hail of shrapnel followed by a blast and a large and rolling ball of flame. Nasty. So we shifted ourselves.

Now, at that time it was well known that Sinn Fein was the political wing of the IRA, but EOD teams curried no truck with such political distinctions and we responded without fear or favour to try to protect the population from the fanatics. Much the same as now, I guess.

We arrived at the scene and, sure enough, there was a typical PIRA BI hanging by a wire clothes hanger from the grille of the office window. Also there was the local RUC Special Branch – which was unusual, to say the least. They asked if I would 'blow the bomb into the building' but I told them to 'fuck off home' – they didn't.

I rolled out Wheelbarrow and my No 2 drove it so as to position Pigstick (one of our more effective weapons) to attack the TPU, and then shotgun to open the bottle, if need be, afterwards. I gave the order to fire and the device disappeared in a cloud of smoke off the TV screen. A perfect hit, we found it lying beneath the window in small pieces – with no fuel at all anywhere to be seen. In fact, we could discern no explosives either. Odd. Could this have been a 'come-on' gone wrong? But, then, why was RUC SB there? I pondered, and while I was pondering a beefy RUC Constable affected an entrance into the offices by smashing the padlock on the door. The RUC SB officers swarmed forward with cries of, 'We'll check to see if they have put another one inside!' and, by the time we got there, they had the office files out and all over the desks copying everything they could.

What could we do? We had been set up as patsies by the RUC and, as we were in support of the civil power, could do nothing but collect the bits of the hoax bomb they had obviously laid and go back to base to report the matter.

Not all the call-outs were for terrorist devices or hoaxes. One lady called us because her husband had died of old age or something, and she had found a grenade in the loft among his wartime souvenirs. How, you may ask, does someone forget they have a live Mills Bomb in the loft? Well, folk are funny sometimes, and they obviously had.

We turned up – but, in Belfast in those days, turning up itself was a big deal – and took the grenade away. It was a live one but perfectly safe and in good condition. The sad, tearful and lonely old lady gave us sugary sponge cake and Soda bread with lashings of Irish butter, washed down with a lovely cup of tea. We wished her well and gave her a hug for her loss. Sometimes the job was really worth doing.

Chapter Nineteen

1986

A year of 275 bombings, 392 shootings and the deaths of 12 soldiers, 12 RUC officers, 33 civilians and 4 terrorists. 7 of the soldiers were UDR members with the IRA using booby-trapped car bombs either outside the part-time soldiers' houses or places of work.

The remaining 5 included the sad loss of 2 young privates of the Royal Anglian regiment, killed by a landmine at Glassdrummond near Crossmaglen.

Of the 12 RUC officers killed, 6 were deliberately targeted whilst off-duty, a tactic the IRA employed with devastating success against members of the UDR.

DIVIS STREET: 1986

Lieutenant Colonel G.P. Moss, King's Own Borderers

I was a young Lieutenant at the time, commanding 'Milan' platoon and our TAOR was both north and west Belfast and around the Ardoyne, New Lodge, Unity flats and the Divis. We were on a mobile patrol with 2 RGJ in the area of the notorious Divis Street flats when we came under attack. A lone IRA sniper positioned on

The cornerstone of Unity Flats. RSM Tony Ryan, Lt Col Robin Godwin-Austen (CO),
Major David Bromham (2i/c)
(photo courtesy of Regimental Museum of the Royal Welsh)

one of the upper walkways had fired one round at a Green Jacket, unfortunately hitting him. He was very quickly spotted and legged it immediately, but as he ran into open view, a sharp-eyed soldier spotted him and fired one round at him from his SLR – which I might add, had no optic sight – and missed him by only a few inches. The round impacted on a metal railing and unfortunately for us, the gunman then disappeared.

The Green Jacket wounded was called Peterson, but I am pleased to note that he survived the shooting; what also pleased me was the reaction from the RGJ; they were first class. We had a cracking seven weeks with the 'Black mafia' and then three further good weeks with the Welsh Guards.

S. ARMAGH 1986
Warrant Officer, Coldstream Guards

We deployed into Newry after the IRA assassinated 3 RUC men from Corry Square; the IRA men became known as the 'Newry Butchers' because they walked out of a Butcher's shop and gunned down 3 RUC men in broad daylight. The RUC 'went on strike' and refused to patrol until the military were bought back in to Newry. The Recce of 2 Bn Coldstream Gds were responsible for the whole area for 4 months.

Corry Square RUC Stn 1986. Goldstream Guards Recce brought into 'police' the town after PIRA assassinated three RUC men in the town. The RUC refused to work unless the military came back. PIRA dressed as butchers hence the name for the incident became 'The Newry Butchers' (photo courtesy of Barry Crane)

I did some overt searches of houses in the Derrybegs and quite often found dog shit and used sanitary towels placed under beds and in drawers to p**s off squaddies.

We raided a house in the town where we suspected a nurse was selling drugs stolen from the Daisy Hill Hospital; at about 0400hrs we went in with the RUC and found a bloke covered in shit and gibbering. When he saw us he started laughing and was immensely relieved; he thought we were the IRA coming to kill him.

We also did a raid on the Gypsy camp down by the bottom end of town; a load of 45 gallon oil drums full of Poteen were taken back to the Police station. We had not drunk for a number of months and were invited to 'Take a wee dram' by the SB officers who obviously knew what would happen. We only just managed to patrol back to Corry Square and even then a number of the Patrol had to sit down in bus stops en route.

STRAND ROAD POLICE STATION: 1986

Barry Hughes, Royal Welch Fusiliers

We were attached to 1 Royal Anglian Regiment (Vikings), undertaking a tour of duty of Derry in 1986; our platoon was carrying out satellite patrols of Strand Road police station. It was a three brick operation with two bricks on the ground and one in reserve on standby in Strand Rd Police Station.

Barry Hughes, 1986 (photo courtesy of B Hughes)

Entering the Bogside on patrol (photo courtesy of B Hughes)

The evening patrols went as normal; first out was Paul Hubbuck from Haverfordwest the other brick commander; my brick was on the ground working to a flexible patrol plan moving along adjacent streets in support of each other changing direction and routes as seemed fit according to the situation and the feel for the ground/local activity.

We patrolled for a while and lay up in rapid hides to observe the ground and support movement of our other brick whilst moving through vulnerable ground. Information was received later from RUC intelligence that during our patrol, a relative of the daughter of an occupant in a street adjacent to Strand Road police station (opposite to the side we had started to patrol along) called at her parents house only to find a the door open. Calling out to her parents – who had been taken to a rear upstairs room by 5 men – and getting no response she was very concerned. Unknown to her they were armed with rifles, light machine guns and grenade launchers.

As the lady came in the house she noticed the men and ran out screaming for help; the terrorists then aborted their planned attack on a British patrol; i.e. us.

Now we were either very lucky that we chose a different route to start with as other times this street would have been taken, plus lucky as the lady chose to visit her parents this night? I prefer to think it was a mixture of both our professional patrol plan and a lot of luck. The firepower they posed with their advantageous fire positions, plus the element of surprise, mean that no doubt we would have sustained heavy losses that evening had we walked into this IRA ambush.

The following are lucky to be here today: Cpl B Hughes, LCpl Mayor, Fusilier Vale, Fusilier Camplin, Cpl P Hubbuck, Fusilier Bylthing, L/Cpl Pritchard, and Fusilier Thomas 08.

Royal Welch Fusiliers tea up! Shantallow area, Derry (photo courtesy of B Hughes)

Following this attempted attack, some weeks later Strand Road Police station sustained a grenade rocket attack during an IED operation on a School in the Shantallow. Later whilst both bricks patrolled the Waterside, area we came under attack from a radio-controlled IED; we reported the incident and later a fire point was identified but the device had been removed. This attack was prevented due to our technical ability at the time.

We knew that we were getting close to either catching someone, or at least their equipment. We carried out many ops during our tour and that was without the locals knowing we were on the ground; that was a feat in itsself. But our tour came to and end and gratefully we all made it out safely; oddly I enjoyed this tour but it was a shame that after all our work we didn't catch the terrorists.

However one week into the new Regiment's tour, they carried out similar operations in the area, and we had advised them to use a rapid hide (O.P.) and they caught 4 guys in a car with guns and equipment.

THE ARDOYNE: 1986
Lieutenant Colonel G.P.Moss, King's Own Borderers.

A prominent player, one Martin Mehan – whom I probably shouldn't name, but I will – had been arrested by the battalion (before my time) in 1979 and jailed for possession of firearms, receiving 6 – 8 years. He was released from the Maze in 1986, along with 4 or 5 other IRA men and they returned straight to the Ardoyne, which had been relatively quiet for a number of years. With, however, such an influx of so many hardened players at one time, that was bound to change. Mehan and his men really – and very quickly – changed the entire complexion of the place.

Shortly after their arrival, a Royal Corps of Signals (TAVR) soldier was snatched by Ardoyne hoods – one of whom was thought to be Mehan – and smuggled into a safe house. These guys were not overly bright and probably thought –as they found military I.D. on him – that he was a regular soldier. However, very quickly, through RUC sources – we managed to identify Girdwood Park as the place that they were holding the kidnapped TA man. An operation was very quickly put together with the SAS, RUC Special Branch and ourselves planning to storm the safe house and rescue the man. The outer cordon was massive – Battalion strength – around the Ardoyne and then the inner cordon closed in on the actual house.

The IRA cell holding the man must have gotten wind of the op and split up, leaving the badly beaten and bound man in the house. Mehan himself jumped over a wall and smack into the hands of Milan platoon! Thus it is our proud platoon boast that we nabbed the bastard twice ! Bn morale was sky high after such an amazing op and I am pleased to report that the TA man recovered from his ordeal pretty quickly.

DONAGH, SOUTH FERMANAGH: 1986

Corporal Ian Jones, 3 LI

We were on the South Fermanagh border with the Irish Republic, operating from the RUC station at Lisnaskea. Tuesday 20th May 1986 was another day on border duties; except that it was local Election Day and we were required to carry out route clearance patrols of the routes by which the ballot boxes would be travelling. This meant an early morning briefing.

I had two changes to my usual 8 man section patrol; my Platoon Sergeant, Dave Wilson and the Company Clerk, whose name escapes me. This point plays on my mind even to this day because, as you will read later, I owe him so much. This meant that I could give my 2IC and one of my section lads a day off; a decision they were probably later grateful for. Our route was from Rosslea RUC Station and then head towards the A34, finally, back to Lisnaskea, passing through the village of Donagh.

I was very aware that Donagh was a major Republican area, and also aware of intelligence reports suggesting that the tricolour was flying there, with an IED at the base of its flagpole. As a result of this, I requested that a Royal Engineer Search Team (REST as we called them) was attached to my patrol; this request was denied. I then asked for a Royal Engineer Search Advisor (RESA), but was again refused. The reason was that our route would not take us near the position of the flagpole.

I did however have Electronic Counter Measure equipment in my patrol consisting of a Fast Chimp and two Jokers. These were the latest ECM devices to prevent remote controlled detonation of bombs. Both pieces of equipment worked on crystals. The Fast Chimp was fitted with both red and blue crystals, and the jokers had a red in one and a blue in the other. With these pieces of equipment there was reassurance that all would be ok.

I was also aware that an hour prior to my patrol passing through Donagh, a dual RUC and UDR patrol would have passed through the village, so if anything was going to happen, I was of the opinion that it would happen to them. That might sound selfish but every soldier felt the same; if it happens to someone else (not a mate) then it isn't happening to me.

The patrol passed very uneventfully until about 4/5 miles outside of Donagh, when we came across the RUC/UDR patrol sitting around in a lay-by having a fag break. I was livid; they should have passed through the village at least an hour before us, but here they were, still some miles short and all sitting around in a big group as if it was a Sunday outing. Don't get me wrong; I had great admiration for the men and woman of both the UDR and the RUC. Doing the job they volunteered to do, and knowing the dangers they faced for doing it, needed real courage.

Not wanting to cause a situation or confrontation, I informed the patrol commander that my patrol would clear the remainder of the route, and that they could return to barracks. A route clearance patrol had a unique structure to it: two men, 20 to 30 yards in the fields to either side of the road and 50 yards ahead, so that they could possibly come across detonation cable, leading from a firing point to explosives hidden by the roadside. There were then two hedgerow men, again one each side of the road in the field, but close to the hedge. My mate Jessy James was the left hand hedge man, and he was carrying the Fast Chimp. That left Dave Wilson and me as the road men; rank does have its privileges.

As we reached the outskirts of Donagh we were met by a convoy of vehicles heading towards us. Suddenly, Irish music started to blare out of loud speakers mounted on the front vehicle. I can't remember exactly how many vehicles there were, but as they passed I noticed that in one of the vehicles, sat Gerry Adams and Martin McGuiness. As the vehicles passed, the occupants of all the vehicles glared and snarled at us, but Adams and McGuiness just blanked us, staring straight ahead. As the vehicles passed through us I heard a voice shout something in Gaelic, I doubt it was of a friendly nature.

We carried on, and as I came around the bend on the edge of the village, I saw two young males, no more than 17 years old, sitting on a low brick wall on the 'Y' bend of the road. As soon as they saw me they got up and walked in my direction. I felt very uneasy and shouted at everyone in my patrol to be cautious. They were about 17years old; about 5'10" of normal build. They walked straight towards and passed Dave and myself, but they never even looked at us; just stared straight ahead and kept walking. After they had passed us I heard one say to the other, 'Murdering bastards aren't we.' Perhaps we should have stopped them, but we continued on our patrol. After all, we should not have been in harm's way, according to the intelligence.

However, this made me more edgy, and I told the two field teams to go to ground and hold covering positions. I brought the two hedge men onto the road and with Jessy across and behind me, I slowly moved forward. My Intention was to secure the junction, before moving through it and away. As I moved forward, I could see the Y junction, with the road on the right leading further into the village;

the road on the left which was the one we would be taking leading to the A34, Lisnaskea Road. Just prior to this on the left, was a small road which led up to some houses. On the corner of this road, nearest me was an unoccupied stone cottage and across from that were the village pub, Post Office and store.

I decided to take up cover behind a small grass mound, which was at the far corner of the cottage. To this day I cannot explain why, but as I approached the cottage I felt uneasy; I started to turn away from the cottage, but somehow, time seemed to pass in slow motion. It was the same feeling I had had when attending a car bomb in Omagh town centre some months earlier which had exploded whilst we were still setting up our cordon.

As I began to turn my body, I heard Jessy shout; I turned my head, then suddenly I felt a shock wave hit me. It was like a punch from Mike Tyson. I found myself looking directly at the pub across the road, where I could see Jessy looking back at me. Then strangely, the pub started spinning in front of me. At the time, I remember thinking: 'what the hell's going on', but obviously, it was me doing the summersault, not the pub. Then the noise of the explosion hit me; it was like hundreds of people crumpling crisp packets in my ears. It's the weirdest feeling and if you have never been in a bomb blast, you can't imagine what happens. However, if you have been in a blast, it is one of the hardest things to explain, without people who read your story thinking that it is a load of made-up rubbish. Then nothing; no light, no sound, no movement.

It was like being in a deep dark void, floating weightlessly. I remember thinking how peaceful everything was. I had forgotten where I was, who I was and what I had been doing moments before. There was no pain; nothing. It was like I was the void; I was the dark endless space.

I have read many things about the afterlife and out-of-body experiences, and like many others, have just thought it a load of nonsense. Since this day I have had an open mind.

I can only say what I saw; but whilst in this void, a light appeared; very small at first but slowly getting larger and larger, as though it was coming towards me. It could have been just a result of the explosion, but this light didn't appear to be any ordinary light. It was hazy around the edges and was a brilliant white. As the light came closer, I started to hear scratching sounds.

It seemed like an age, but was probably in fact seconds, or minutes and the scratching got louder and louder. Suddenly, the bright hazy light seemed to vanish in the distance, to be replaced by the sound of voices shouting. I could feel the pressure of my body and the pressure of being buried. Then the pressure of being buried was lifted, as I heard the lads clearing the rubble that lay around me. It was a fine, warm day and I could feel the heat on my face, but could not open my eyes. How had I seen the light, I don't know, and have no explanation, but it is something that I have often thought about.

Despite all the shouting and hurrying which I could hear going on around me, I felt totally at peace; in no pain and seemingly untroubled. I became aware of my breathing, but I could sense that it was through my neck rather than my mouth. Then I heard the voice of the Company Clerk, who had only been allowed to come out with us, because it was deemed a low risk patrol.

WoIIR Gamble waiting for a lift to Clady PVCP
(photo courtesy of Ronnie Gamble)

Like I said at the beginning, I feel annoyed that I can't remember the name of the man who dug me out of the rubble, who gave me what first aid he could, and who stayed with me, talking any rubbish he could think of to keep me conscious. However, there was a moment, when I had the opportunity to remind him, but this was at a later date. Dave Wilson, who had taken command of the patrol, shouted at him to enquire how I was. I can still remember to this day his immortal words: 'Half his fucking face is missing.' But, despite this, it seemed to have no effect on my state of mind; calmness prevailed over me.

I have no concept of time surrounding the events of the afternoon, apart from the fact that when I was later given back my Army watch, some months later, the time had stopped at 12:50pm. I lay there in the road for what seemed like hours until I heard the sound of a helicopter. I was drifting in and out of consciousness so often that I don't remember much, but one feeling I had was that of flying. I know that I was actually inside the helicopter, but the sensation was one of being perched on the skid pads.

And then nothing; the next three weeks passed without a single memory.

Ian Jones' experience in the aftermath of this explosion will be told in a later volume.

Landing at Clady PVCP (photo courtesy of Ronnie Gamble)

WOII R Gamble at Clady PVCP manning the console
(photo courtesy of Ronnie Gamble)

THE CLADY CAR BOMB: 1986

Platoon Commander E Coy 5UDR

I remember one terrorist attack very clearly. This happened at Clady Permanent Vehicle Check Point (PVCP) on the Co. Tyrone/Donegal border. That was a weird day. For example, the security specialists came in that day to check out the CCTV system and ensure that all the cameras and monitors were in working order. I was in command of the PVCP for that period. My job was to rotate the soldiers around the various posts and operate the PVCP from the central console.

I was checking through the vehicles and as normal the RMPs and an RUC officer were standing out on the road checking the traffic. The RUC officer shouted in, 'There's a guy out here saying that there is a bomb out here'. I immediately checked the CCTV monitors and the car was not visible. It had been parked on the only blind spot in the whole PVCP. I shouted out, 'Is that guy drunk or joking?' and the RUC replied, 'I think he is serious.' So I hit the alarm and verified the situation was for real by physically checking the car and checking the registration.

By that time the men had all paraded with all their kit for a 'Bug Out'. But this was for real and they were deployed to their cordon points on the perimeter of the base. We had to stop anyone or any vehicle from coming into the PVCP as well as securing our own safety. The Garda secured the opposite side of the bridge.

No sooner had we evacuated the PVCP than the bomb went off. It was only at that time we discovered that the cordon points were too close to the bomb. Every cordon point was showered with shrapnel and bricks from the explosion. After

Above and overleaf:
Clady photos show the devastation created in the middle of Clady village by the May bomb. All the photos were taken in June before the repairs started.
(photos courtesy of Ronnie Gamble)

the explosion we returned to the PVCP. It was a total mess. We were hungry because the bomb had been parked just as we were organizing the evening meal. Every time we tried to use the cooker the rings would overheat and explode. That was not something we wanted, more explosions. We ended up eating cereals whilst the rings continued to explode, not a very relaxing situation.

We spent the rest of the night at the location controlling the traffic, without any washing facilities, food or back-up to relieve us. The following morning the normal changeover with another platoon took place and we walked to the pick-up point to be airlifted back to Ballykelly by helicopter. We were in the air for ten minutes when the loadmaster looked back at us and shouted, 'We're ditching, a bird has hit the rotor blade!' The pilot managed to get the chopper into Omagh

The Battery sign on HQ, Fort George RUC Shantallow
(photo courtesy of N Edwards)

base. We then had to wait there until a new rotor blade was fitted to the helicopter before we were able to finish our journey.

At Ballykelly the patrol had to be debriefed on the bombing incident before we could make our way back home. The bomb went off at approximately 6pm and over eighteen hours passed before we eventually reached our homes.

Clady, a small frontier village in County Tyrone, was hit by a 500lb IRA bomb on Saturday, May 3, 1986. As the newspapers of the time reported, it was only by some miracle that no-one was injured in the blast which devastated the tiny village. The attack, aimed at an SF base, destroyed a petrol station and a pub.

FORT GEORGE, LONDONDERRY: 1986

Corporal Mike 'Squeak' Edwards 81, Royal Regiment of Wales

Our tour began in September 1986 and went through to January 1987; we were based at Fort George, Londonderry.

This was my fourth tour of the Province; we had been in Londonderry for about 2 months and were quite used to the area and the shit that came with it. I can honestly say on some of the patrols we carried out that we wondered if we would come back in one piece; we used to say for a joke to our colleagues, if we didn't come back 'you can have our radio or our monies which are under the pillow'; it made us feel a little better.

Each patrol we carried out in our area was so demanding and mind draining as the whole area of Londonderry had so many supporters and sympathisers. Indeed, we had so many players in our area that when we stopped and questioned them they would make it so difficult and awkward for us. I remember in the Brandywell area I stopped this player and just asked him where he lived (which I knew) and he came back with the longest name you could imagine. I asked him if he could spell it for me, he came back ' ... you thick English Bastard ... ' I informed him that I was Welsh and I asked if he could spell where I lived; he replied yes. So I told him I lived in a small town called Ystrad Mynach; his face was a picture.

On November 4 we were called to the briefing room by our Plt Commander Dai Richards, and were informed that we would be carrying out a combined foot and mobile patrol in the Waterside area. We would begin our patrol at 1900hrs and be back in camp by 2200hrs. My call Sign was Yankee 44 and my 2ic's call sign was Yankee 44 Alpha; we would meet outside the Ops room ready to move at 1845hrs.

We carried out our kit and radio checks and made ready to mount our vehicles and then set off for the Waterside area. It was a pleasant clear night and we were in good sprits. We had to cross a large double decker bridge called Derry Bridge; once over, we would be on a dual carriageway about 300–400 metres long with open spaces to the right and to the left. I looked to the front of me and moving down the road on the opposite side was a large white van. As it came down the hill it turned into a small car park, which I knew would be too small for this type of vehicle, and I shouted to my top cover that we would be making a stop and checking this vehicle out; I also informed my 2ic of my intentions.

We travelled up the carriageway, turned right at the top and came down onto the opposite side; my call sign stopped on the entrance of the car park and took up various positions; my 2ic stopped behind me and did the same. I moved

Fort George 1986: Mike Camplin and Barry Hughes
(photo courtesy of Cpl B Hughes)

towards the van which was straight in front of us, with a member of my crew. I could not see anyone in the driver's side or passenger's side which made me very apprehensive and cautious. I stopped about three yards from the front of the vehicle and informed a crew member to have his hand ready to cock his weapon if anything were to happen. At this time we were all aware that we could be in a very dangerous situation.

I moved to the driver's side of the vehicle and banged on the door, and, just like magic a person shot up in the seat, which startled me a bit. I shouted to this person to lower the window, he leaned out of the window and said 'Can I help you?' I said 'Yes; why are you sitting in this van in this car park?' He replied 'I am waiting for my girlfriend who works in the Police station.' I informed him that I needed to see some ID and I would be checking out his details.

I moved away from the van; however, aware of the danger, I made sure I could see him, and sent his details and the vehicle's details to my Ops room; within a couple of seconds I was informed 'no trace.' As I moved back to the driver, he was leaning back in his seat and it appeared he was speaking to some one in the back. I told my crew member that we would be looking in the back and to make sure he was ready for anything that may happen. I asked the driver to get out of the van and to open the back doors; he appeared nervous and didn't want to do this and said it would be a waste of time. I told him again more forcefully to 'open up the back or be arrested.' He climbed down from his seat and moved very slowly towards the back and I could sense that something was about to kick off. The driver placed his left hand onto the handle and on opening the door he tried to move out of the way but I placed the barrel of my weapon under his arm pit and said if anything were to happen now he would be the first to go. He moved back in front of me and opened the door, on looking inside I couldn't see anything so I told the driver to open the other door. On doing this, I saw that there were two men sitting on the wheel arch wearing hooded tops and plastic gloves. I can't explain to you how I felt on seeing two men with rifles and a large holdall full of ammo; what a catch! My emotions were all over the place; I was happy, sad and relieved all at once. The driver had a black woollen hat on and I reached up and pulled it down over his face; that image will stay with me forever. We moved the three men to the side of the van and our military training just kicked in. QRF were deployed and everyone came to the scene; it was mayhem and we had an extra surprise on checking the front of the van where we found a 9mm pistol with extended magazine of 19 rounds and one in the breech and a two-way radio. Later, our Int boys decided that the ASU were planning to shoot up a police station or an RUC mobile.

I am grateful for the two teams I commanded that night and the roles they all played in putting away a top Active Service Unit for 12 years.

NORTHERN IRELAND, 1986
Private Tim Castle, Light Infantry

I was out on the ground at the time in an OP watching a road junction for a vehicle. The live op was only a few days old; we were inserted by a couple of cars and tabbed up a hill to a position already selected for our trigger OP. A trigger OP is one where you watch an area for a particular person and vehicle; report it in thus triggering other call signs to take over. After OP routine of 2 on stag, 2 on sentry, 2 on admin/kip and 2 on sleep we were alerted by a contact report over the net. We stood to, gathered up our monkeys and parrots and made ready to leave.

Later that evening we were extracted and briefed on what had happened. The Boss (OC COP) was driving an unmarked Ford Escort estate doing live letter drops to an OP. He had a lovely lad called Kevin Jones in the car riding shotgun. Both were armed. As with all COP tasks we were operating in an Out of Bounds Area (OOB) and didn't expect to see any other security force patrols. The Boss was driving towards the OOB which was demarcated by a river in a small village. Approaching the bridge over the river the Boss and Jonah saw a car across the road and an armed man in dark clothing run across the road ahead. The Boss who using his great driving skills executed a handbrake turn and drove the car back as fast as possible to the nearest SF base, Castlewellan RUC Station.

The car forming the road block followed, both were moving very fast so the boss raced down the funnel of the RUC station towards the gate sangar and seeing the car behind him realised it must be a DMSU type unit that had strayed. He pulled up and leapt out with both arms in the air right in front of the gate screaming 'Security Forces; don't shoot!' Jonah piled out but drew his 9mm pistol. The unmarked RUC car stopped and 4 policemen debussed pointing revolvers and rifles. The cars were nose to tail. The part-time reservist constable in the rear nearside seat was armed with a Ruger Mini 14 rifle 5.56mm.

He opened fire at Jonah who, realising that he needed to put his hands up, was trying to do so whilst not pointing his 9mm at anyone. The Peeler fired 9 times at very close range. 2 rounds hit the car, 6 rounds hit the sangar and one hit Jonah in the right arm just above his elbow. The round travelled up his humorous bone shattering it and exiting vertically at the side of his shoulder. This caused the pistol to involuntarily discharge into the floor next to Jonahs feet. He was an unlucky soul having had more than his fair share of scrapes in the short time he served.

About 2 years of very painful treatment ensued in which they rebuilt his arm but the nerves were so shattered that he had to relearn how to hold a pen or a beer glass.

I believe the Police Authority for NI settled out of court for somewhere in the region of £100k. I hope he has spent wisely but knowing Jonah he's in as much bother now as then! There was no doubt the usual enquiry, I think we came out of it reasonably well but NIPG was disbanded, moved to the NITAT team in the UK and rebranded.

FAT CORPORAL SAVES THE DAY. DRUMAKAVELL: 1986

Lieutenant Colonel G.P. Moss, King's Own Borderers

A few months later, we handed over our sector to the Scots Guards and we headed south to Crossmaglen (XMG). This was at a time when the 'Golf Towers' were being erected (we were in G20 Drumakavell) and sangars in use. We were to relieve a unit of the Prince of Wales' Own and we soon discovered that the night before, they had seen some serious action.

They had dug slit trenches in front of the partially-built towers and sangars which were only 300 metres from the border with the Republic. Manning these sandbagged trenches was a POW multiple commanded by a junior sergeant, equipped with night-sights but nothing more deadly than an old Bren which was magazine-fed and held only 30 rounds. Suddenly, they were attacked by a large force of the IRA who had sneaked across the border and numbered 12–15 terrorists; the attacking force was very well armed with SF (sustained fire) machine guns, tracer rounds and nightsights. Their firepower was quite awesome but though heavy, was quite indiscriminate and the POW returned fire as best they could and though no hits were confirmed, there were several bloodstains found the next morning in the IRA firing point.

Two of the POW night sights (one IWS and one optic) were hit by IRA gunfire and while it was considered a couple of lucky shots at the time, it was felt afterwards that it was just excellent marksmanship using state-of-the-art equipment. At this point, a rather rotund – I would describe him as well-fed – Lance Corporal who had been in charge of the inadequate Bren gun, leapt out of the well sandbagged trench into the open, ran towards the IRA FP and put down a withering hail of lead – albeit having to change the mags every few seconds – and dispersed the attackers.

Though the IRA sharpshooters possessed excellent equipment, put down some fierce fire and seemed to have the upper hand, they were deterred and ultimately dispersed by the rotund NCO who totally distracted them with his brave, but foolhardy, actions.

During the rest of that tour, we had a lot of near-misses and we had, sadly, one fatality (Tony Dacre, who was killed 3 weeks into the tour before we left Belfast) during a time when we were working with the Royal Highland Fusiliers. He was killed by an IRA bomb. I knew his younger brother well, but I didn't know Tony personally.

Anthony Dacre was 25 and he was killed at the Divis Street flats on March 27, 1985 by a remote-detonated bomb placed in an old shed and set off as his foot patrol passed by. Children were observed playing in the area at the time but the IRA still detonated the device.

FORT GEORGE: 1986

Corporal Barry Hughes, Royal Welch Fusiliers

The story I have is about a man called Paddy who worked for us at Fort George; he was a family man from the Shantallow who was employed in the main kitchen. He had worked there for years like many others and he was unlucky enough to live in the Shantallow.

In 1986, Paddy had had a few warnings from the Provisional IRA, 'informing' him of his error in working for the Army, but instead of punishment they decided to use him as a human bomb delivery service. It was 1.20am when Paddy turned up at the front gate in his brand new car bought with his hard-earned cash; the gate man recognised Paddy and opened the gate, although he must have thought that it was an unusual hour to come to work. The poor man was totally distraught; he was shouting 'There's a bomb in me car and they have my wife and family hostage.' There were tears running down his face and he was apologising all the time and totally scared; the camp was stood -to and ATO tasked.

I was part of the outer cordon group and deployed around the camp given various tasks, with the protection of ATO being one. The bomb disposal man duly arrived and started his task, probing the suspected IED with the help of his Robot. He fired two shots into the device, messing up Paddy's car a little in the process but the main device failed to go off, and further examinations found that someone had failed to fit the detonator. After some more searching around, none was found.

Lucky for us and Paddy (as 200lb of explosives did arrive) although someone ended up with more parts than they started with; no Irish jokes please. End of op and back to bed!

Some weeks passed and nothing further happened; then we were tasked to Victor six on the Creggan/Strabane route where another IED had been delivered. The road was out of bounds due to a suspect car being conveniently parked on the access road. So we were deployed by motor launch down the river Foyle passing under the Craigavon Bridge and being spat on by all the yobs!

Fort George 1986: Yanto Evans and Barry Hughes
(photo courtesy Cpl B Hughes)

Arriving at the river's edge we then faced a tab of some 4ks uphill in thick jackets; God it was hot in July. We arrived at the VCP (Victor 6) and set about putting in the cordon.

What happened here was that a man in his van was stopped on his way to Victor 6 by some members of a nationalist group and told to deliver a barrel packed with explosives, which he did as he had no choice in the matter. He arrived there quite annoyed and as the van was his livelihood and he did not want to lose it he picked the bomb up and placed it on the ground; it is amazing as his next job should have been in Heaven!

Well, ATO was tasked arrived and dealt with the device and no detonation that day either. So back to the boats, under the bridge and yes, we ended up, covered in yob gob!

There were some funny moments, however, like the time I was on plainclothes duty and being asked for directions in the Ardoyne, radio under seat; being checked for weapons when entering a shop and the look of shock when the guy found one, and finally, going into the bookies in the Waterside to collect my winnings fully armed up and escorted by my 4 man brick!

Photo essay

Paul Crispin

It was always a dream of mine to be a photo-journalist (still is), my most admired photographer being Don McCullin. So on one of my tours of N.I. I was lucky enough to have a certain amount of free movement among the troops on tour there. This is a small example of those photos I took between 1986 and 1987.

With the whole collection I tried to show what it was like to be a British soldier serving in N.I. in the late 1980s. How they patrolled the streets seven days a week 24 hours a day; how they interacted with the poor long-suffering people of the community and how they coped with the constant threat of death every second of their time there.

It is not my intension – nor was it at the time – to take political sides, nor be judgmental of a situation that has its roots deeply embedded in a turbulent and often bloody history, I was looking more into the role and character of the individual. I was very keen to show the detachment a soldier needs to remain neutral in a job that wouldn't always allow it. This neutrality often portrayed the soldier as a machine – I was after the individual; the human element.

The children in the photos you are about to see are now the adults of today; the adults that are shaping a new Northern Ireland, a Northern Ireland of peace and prosperity once more.

My only regrets about my tours of N.I are that assimilations of the situation are being re-enacted around the world to day; how many 'Northern Ireland children' are there suffering in the world as the children of yesterday had? How long must we wait before they are the adults of tomorrow and why do we have to make them suffer so? Will the world ever learn from the troubles in Northern Ireland?

My only wish when viewing these photos is that you view with an open mind and a neutral heart so that you can understand them with a 'soldier's eye view' and see the character of the person behind the uniform who was just trying to do his job.

Technical Info

Most of the photos were taken with my trusty and brilliant Nikon F1 and any lens I could borrow from the stores. The film was also mostly Ilford HP5. The negatives were scanned using a Canoscan 8000F.

Paul Crispin

Note: Unless stated otherwise, all photographs were taken in Belfast 1986

The Terraced Houses   This photo shows a view of the terraced houses that were typical of the poorer areas. Built in the Victorian age to house the workers of the docks and mills, a lot became derelict and were a safe hiding place for many a terrorist.

The Danger Point   The exit and entry to the satellite camps were considered a dangerous part of the patrol. The camp guards, operations staff and patrols had to synchronize with each other so as not to leave the troops too long in the 'killing zone'. These satellite camps usually housed a company of soldiers, complete with vehicles, administration staff and equipment. The camps constantly needed to be updated and modified to keep ahead of the threat, hence the corrugated sheets you see that are for mortar and sniper protection.

Protect the Little Children
"Even children follow'd with endearing wile,
And pluck'd his gown, to share the good man's smile"

Oliver Goldsmith

The children of Belfast were something special. Through all the hardships, hate and sectarianism their innocence and fun were often a source of hope to the soldiers patrolling there.

Nowhere to Shop   Most of the local shopping precincts, the heart of any community, were no longer used. Their owners, tired of the danger and intimidation, had long gone. With their windows boarded up and adorned with the local faction's graffiti, the mothers of the area therefore had to travel downtown to do their weekly shopping.

Poverty the Noose   This photograph was taken in the Divis Flats – thankfully pulled down now – one of the most deprived areas of Belfast and a breeding ground for future terrorists. I took the photograph just after I had finished searching a flat and was taking a break from the stench of fouled nappies and human dirt. I suddenly realised that we had no 'resident' backup and heard footsteps coming up the stairs. Luckily it was a section of soldiers sent to assist. He was relived as well when I exchanged my 9mm for my trusty Nikon F1!

"Poverty is a noose that strangles humility and breeds disrespect for God and man."

American Indian Proverb, Sioux.

Loyalist Murals   The 'Red Hand of Ulster' in the middle of this mural, and in most of the murals, is predominantly a Loyalist symbol but is also used by Republicans as well, and is one of the only symbols used by both factions. Legend has it that two chieftains were racing across the water to claim the land. In a bid to lay first claim, one of the chieftains chopped off his right hand and threw it ashore. Not the most peaceful way to start a nation

Kneecap Alley   This was taken in a particularly dodgy area in West Belfast. The alley was known for the 'kneecapping' ('punishment' shooting or beating) of local alleged criminals by the paramilitary group controlling the area. These soldiers are securing the area for the SOCO (Scene of Crime Officer) after another ruffian was given some rough justice the evening before.

PIG on Standby Two 'PIGs' on standby in a Republican area. You can tell it's a Republican area because of the mural on the wall. These areas were considered high risk, so extra precautions were needed.

Down the Sights As close as I could get to looking down the sights of an SLR. This was taken at the site of a suspected bomb. Often these were hoaxes just to keep the troops busy. Sometimes they were 'come-ons' where the terrorists would ambush the soldiers as they arrived at the scene, so extra caution was needed in these situations.

Let the Riots Begin   Riot control relies heavily on the team holding together. The NCOs (Non Commissioned Officers) are not there to push the troops on but more to hold them together. It can be quite frightening knowing that there is only a thin piece of plastic between you and the madding crowd.

Baton Down This is the baton gun that fires the dreaded (if you're on the wrong side) plastic bullets. This was taken just before the riots that happened on the first anniversary of the signing of the Anglo-Irish Agreement.

Orders Confirmed   A 'brick' commander keeps lookout with his radio operator nearby.

Alert in Belfast   Before a British soldier could go on tour in Northern Ireland he needed to complete a four month specialised training course. This course covered policing, patrolling, close-quarter combat, fitness, politics, first-aid, more fitness and then some more fitness, just to make sure. He, with all the other members of his regiment, were then tested by command to see if they could cope with the unique difficulties faced by soldiers on tour in Northern Ireland.

Back and Sides   The mobiles always had two men on lookout – one looking back and the other to the sides and front.

Over Exposure   The open countryside of Belfast, apart from being beautiful, could also be an ideal sniper location. The soldier had to be extra cautious when exposed.

Roger That   Officers as young as 22 to 23 were normally in charge of platoons, about 35 men, and were often just out of basic training themselves. They were usually guided by their platoon sergeants who had, as was often the case, a number of Northern Ireland tours under their belts. Here a young second lieutenant is radioing his orders to his platoon.

The Loneliest Job in the World   This has to be one of the most stressful, frightening and bravest jobs in the world – Bomb Disposal. The area is cordoned off and made as safe as possible. Then these guys have to approach the bomb not knowing whether it's a remote device, how it's constructed nor what size it is. He needs to think like the bomb maker to outsmart him; one mistake and it's his last. To me, these men are the bravest on the planet.

The White Butt   Soldiers would stick white pads on the butts of their rifles
(SLR) so they could jot down any relevant information given to them at the
intelligence brief before they went out on patrol. This information could be car
registration numbers, suspected terrorists, or call signs. Also note that the
cocking handle of the SLR was always flipped out should the weapon need
loading in a hurry. Believe me, the nanosecond makes a difference.

Is my shirt ready?   The RUC question a local laundrette owner, probably whether or not his shirt is ready.

Thoughts of Home
> "And that each day is like a year,
> A year whose days are long."
>   Oscar Wilde

Some days just dragged on and on. 12–14 hour patrols were the norm rather than the exception and thoughts of home and safety were never far from the soldiers' minds.

Chapter Twenty

1987

A year of 293 bombings, 674 shootings and the deaths of 11 soldiers, 16 RUC officers, 54 civilians and 32 terrorists.

It was a year which saw a crowd of, mostly, civilians buried in rubble from a building, collapsed by a bomb, at the war memorial, Enniskillen, during a WW1/WW2 Remembrance Day ceremony. 1 RUC reservist officer and 10 civilians were killed by the IRA on the 'Poppy Day Massacre.' 10 years later, Gerry Adams of Sinn Fein, 'apologised' for the attack.

It was also the year in which an undercover SAS team shot dead an 8 man IRA gun and bomb squad near Loughall RUC station; tragically, a passing and innocent civilian was killed in the crossfire.

An IRA ASU attacked an Army barracks in Rheindallen in West Germany, injuring 30, including West German officers and their wives and 4 British personnel.

ENNISKILLEN AND THE UDR TOUR 1987–1989
RSM, Ulster Defence Regiment

My wife and I left for a posting to 4 UDR in Enniskillen, County Fermanagh.

It was my first tour in the County of Fermanagh and whilst I thought South Armagh had a rugged beauty, Fermanagh is gorgeous with a wild scenery of lakes and hills not surpassed anywhere except perhaps, by the Mourne. 4 UDR had been badly hit by the attacks on its personnel, especially in the border area from upper Lough Erne around to Belleek and for its soldiers, it was so very difficult to live and work in a community where some of your neighbours, had such a strongly held political view point that they were quite prepared to kill for it and therefore, hiding and securing you and your families' identity and whereabouts, became very necessary but almost impossible and so you therefore, are an easy target.

Despite this it was still well recruited and consisted of 4 part-time rifle companies at various locations throughout County Fermanagh and a permanent cadre of E Company and TAC HQ which were based on the old American Second World War Airfield known as St Angelo. Flat and overlooked by hills, it was a natural and easy target and had been mortared on a number of occasions and so sported overhead and side walls of concrete over the inhabited areas, and was known as Op Widgeon, so typical of the 'temporary' nature of many camps in the province. Under all this protection were the accommodation and offices complex which had been portacabins, in another life, and so things were pretty cramped to say the least. The camp was surrounded by 9 foot high breeze block walls, topped off with barbed wire and it was entered at one end via a manned guardroom and helipad area, into a camp which, of necessity, was long and thin to allow it to sit

Colin Haslem Kirkpatrick (Ziggy) . One of the few British soldiers to be abducted by the IRA and survive (photo courtesy of Ronnie Gamble)

on the old concreted area of the runway. There were cameras everywhere, to allow the duty personnel to view all areas not visible to the naked eye.

It had too, all the facilities (if somewhat crude) to allow for as normal a military life as could be possible and the Fermanagh folk know how to have a bit of a 'crack' or to you and me 'a good time' and we did – frequently. What made that tour the easiest to do and the best to have taken part in were those amazing people of Fermanagh. Under constant threat and working long hours especially the part-timers whose day, militarily, began AFTER a full day's graft at their civilian employment, they retained a remarkable ability to be warm and sociable and nothing seemed to get them down.

Operations down there were almost all rural with only Enniskillen providing any real urban conurbation. There was also a very long stretch of a very leaky border with the Republic and although the legal crossings had manned checkpoints, the illegal ones, including many of the 'tanked' ones, still let a constant flow of traffic through. A large patrol of 1 DERR, under op con, were tasked to watch a newly tanked crossing point and in the early light of dawn suddenly found themselves under heavy and sustained machine gun fire from the south from an annoyed IRA unit who wanted to move the tank before the cement set. No casualties but a lot ammo expended on both sides.

The crossing stayed blocked for only a short time after they left! The families of the UDR also served with lots of father, son and daughter and even, on occasions, mum too in service mode; the risks were all accepted as part-and-parcel of life here. A part-time Corporal in B Company who was also a farmer, attended a farm auction down near Derrylin and when his business was concluded returned to his car and as he opened the door a UVBT detonated, badly injuring him in both legs and hips. The report as it progressed was being handled by his daughter, a signaller in the Bn Ops room until she got relief to go home to her mother.

He sadly died of his wounds and although the military funeral was very uplifting and all that the family had asked for, it seemed small recompense for such a waste of a valuable human life. This waste of life was never more graphically demonstrated than the two lovers ambushed in their car as they arrived home late one evening. They lived on the road between Irvinestown and Belleek and were due to be married soon, they had nothing to do with the SF but an ASU got its target wrong and they died in a hail of AK 47 rounds before they even got out of the car in their own driveway. The site was pitiful to view afterwards and even squaddies, hardened to all this, had lumps in their throats.

There too, were sad occasions that defied logic. The Assistant Adjutant Vera, a blonde and very pretty lady, went on leave to Portugal, along with her sister who was a serving RUC officer. The night of their arrival, tired and worn out from their months of duty and the travelling to get to Portugal, they went to bed early and they did not wake up. The hot water boiler was defective and carbon monoxide leaked into their chalet and by the morning, they were both dead. That funeral too, was a real difficult occasion. Stresses and strains are felt by everyone in the SF or its family, but when you realise that most of these people lived and breathed whilst carrying a firearm and then stress can take you into a region not normally visited.

The cookhouse was run by a very amiable and competent chef who also had a sideline, run by him and his wife, of a fish and chip van that toured the local area. Unknown to us they had been having marriage difficulties and she suddenly left him. One night several days later, he laid in wait for her near Irvinestown and, as the van pulled up he shot her dead with his personal protection weapon, a 9mm Browning Automatic, he then calmly turned himself in, saying almost nothing to this day and sadly accepted his fate. I had to give evidence at his trial and he sat through this in total and abject misery saying nothing, disputing nothing and offering nothing, his life sentence just added to the sadness of it all and I firmly expect him not to live through his sentence but it's the kids who will have lost all.

I had arrived in the August and my first real military parade was to be the Remembrance Day parade in November. That day dawned and the parade assembled down by the river car park and whilst it sorted itself out into Company groups and order of march etc, the Pipes and Drums arrived wearing their rain capes and the CO, perhaps annoyed that rest of the parade didn't have these, ordered them to change and parade like the rest of the Battalion. The march was then to proceed toward Enniskillen town centre and its War Memorial Monument; bands playing and bayonets fixed behind the skirl of the pipes and rattle of the drums, always a dazzling show and a heart-stopper.

The parade was well on its way when there was a giant explosion from the War Memorial area, and all pretence of military movement was abandoned in the rush to help and whilst the scene of carnage has been well documented it is difficult to convey the rage felt at the death of these civilians who came to watch a Remembrance Day Parade and the sheer stupidity of a group that thought that this type of event could change anything in the way that they demanded.

The Community Centre had a Bingo night the night before and 'someone unknown' packed the rear wall of the store room which backed onto the road, connected up a video clock timer and left it to do its job.

The Prince of Wales and Lady Di arrived a few days later to lift spirits and their walk around and sit and chat sessions were not only much appreciated but also did much to lessen the pain and the impact that such a trauma leaves behind. Had the parade not been delayed by that innocuous event of the rain capes, the slaughter would have been so much worse. Our tour was to produce many more events and incidents but when we left in early autumn 1989 it was with much regret and with many fond memories that we returned to the mainland. I was then to go to the other side of Northern Ireland Operations, the training for them and a posting to NITAT.

This soldier uses the words ' … defied belief … ' and it is so easy to see what motivated that comment. On that November day in 1987, the insanity of the IRA's campaign was there, plain and simple, for all the watching world to see. No doubt the event was cheered on in Irish-American bars in New York and Boston and Chicago where Irish-Americans from 10 generations back raised a glass or two to the 'boys back home'.

There were 11 people killed; only one, an RUC reservist, was connected with the Security Forces. The dead were: William Mullan (74) and his wife, Nessie (73), Kitchener Johnston (71) and his wife, Nessie (62), Wesley Armstrong (62) and his wife, Bertha (55) and his brother, Edward (52), John Megaw (67), Alberta

Enniskillen, November 1987 (photo courtesy of Mike Heavens)

Quinton (72), Samuel Gault (49) and the youngest victim, Marie Wilson, who was just 20 years old.

DEATH OF A RUC MAN: 1987
L/Cpl 'B', Royal Signals

It was around midnight that the tasking bell rang. We were tasked out to Enniskillen; the tasking was brief, High Street, scene of an explosion. Kit on, side-arms drawn from the weapons locker, hanger doors up, start the vans and wait for the boss to come down to the shack.

We did our usual and flicked the blues on as we approached the camp gates so they would have them open for us to pile straight through and we swung right to go through the town. If I can remember the route it was Omagh, Fintona, Dromore, Irvinestown and on to Enniskillen.

We approached the cordoned area and began to set up our ICP within the cordon while the boss went off to get a brief. We Bleeps did our wiggly amp stuff and the No. 2 started getting his kit together.

The boss came back and began to relate his briefing to us; his eyes told most of the incident details. RUC patrol had been subjected to a bomb attack, one fatality, two injuries, 'start your tasks please gents.' No one spoke, the situation didn't allow it. I rigged my kit, pulled the van into the best position and started my sweeps. After around twenty-five minutes I finished and reported the all-clear to the boss. He decided to skip the wheelbarrow and go for a manual; after all, the ambulance crews and every other man and his dog and been through there.

After he cleared the scene the boss handed the scene over to NIFSL [Northern Ireland Forensic Science Laboratory] who in turn asked for his assistance to screen the scene for evidence. They had surmised that the device was an RCIED (Radio Controlled Improvised Explosive Device) and wanted the boss, No.2 and myself to assist in tying to separate any potential parts of the device from the nearby shop debris. This was to be more challenging than it first seemed as the shop in question was a toyshop, the front of which was loaded with remote controlled toys, fluffy toys with battery packs, wires and switches etc!

We must have been on our hands and knees for around an hour when it started to rain. I had a handful of bags and every piece we picked up was examined for potential. If it was a 'no', it went in one bag; the 'yes's' went into another bag. As I examined the pieces, I wiped them with my gloved had to check for markings and deposited them, wiped my hands on my combats and started again. I think we called clear from the incident at around 04:30 hours and made our weary way back to camp.

Once back, the batteries in all the kit were replaced with fresh, the old topped up and put on trickle charge, cup of tea, kit off, crash and hope to God that the beauty in the dream was still at the bar (although probably somewhat half-cut by now!).

The following morning I stirred for first works, showered and grabbed my combats from the door of the wardrobe, pulled them up my legs and starred in horror. They were pure red. From the knees to the waist. Where I had been kneeling and wiping my gloved hands, where it had rained, I couldn't move, speak or do anything. After what seemed a lifetime, I pulled them off, marched them to the washer and put them on a boil wash. While they were in the machine, I jumped into the shower and scrubbed myself clean again. That memory has stayed with me to this day, 21 years and I can see it as if I was in the shack, pulling on those very combats. Constable Ivan Crawford is someone who I never met in life, but his death was the first (but not the last) time that the true price of sacrifice was made clear to me.

The RUC officer, to whom this soldier refers, was a Reserve Constable who worked in the motor repair trade as his full-time job. He was on a routine foot patrol in the High Street when the device – in a litter bin – detonated. He was 49 years old.

DEATH OF A MATE. BELLEEK: 1987

Rifleman Mike Hewlett, Royal Green Jackets

My regiment, 1st Battalion the Royal Green Jackets, was based in Osnabruck, West Germany. I had been serving about a year and a half, and we were off on a major two week exercise when, without warning, it was called off and we were told to return to camp.

Initially WUDR were expected to dress in skirts for their duties. Some senior officers expressed the opinion that this would clearly identify the women and thus prevent them from being killed by republican terrorists. Bad idea, the terrorists used 'shoot and scoot' tactics into the backs of Land Rovers as they were going away from them. All they had to do was shoot between the two taillights and they would hit something, skirts or trousers, it did not matter. (photo courtesy of Ronnie Gamble)

The CO was there and he informed us: 'When we return from our break we start N.I. training, and then straight after the training we start a 4 month tour.'

We only spent one day riot training as I remember, but then this was the mid eighties not the seventies. The majority of the training was focused on attacks from snipers and bombs.

My company, 'B' Company were destined for Co.Fermanagh. Twenty years on, I remember it was here that I noticed the mood change. Not a lot of conversation, as for most of us it was our first tour; like the majority of us, I had grown up as a kid through the seventies when Northern Ireland was at the forefront of news bulletins. Riots and bombs were commonplace and another soldier's life taken; scary place to be.

After a short wait in the hangar we were led to a Chinook which took us to our next destination, St Angelo camp. It was here that a lot of our kit was put into storage and we were issued with live rounds; then it was on to a Lynx and to our final destination, Belleek. If I remember correctly we were on something like a two week turn around, meaning we would return to Belleek about half way through our tour. But for now this was where our four months started.The helicopter landed in a field not far from the police station and we didn't see anything of the town and before we knew it we were in the police station: our home for the next few weeks. We had taken over from the Marines and most of them had gone; just a few remained for the handover.

Mike Hewlett on the right with two collegues preparing to go out on patrol in Belleek (photo courtesy of Mike Hewlett)

The routine ahead of us was 8 hours patrolling the streets, 8 hours on QRF and sentry duty followed by 8 hours sleep. Being in Fermanagh meant there was going to be plenty of rural patrols ahead of us. Our preparation for this tour was taken very seriously; we were all extremely fit. In Osnabruck Huey (LCpl Hewitt) took us out as a platoon on a gruelling run to start the day.

Time came to go out on our first patrol on the streets of Belleek, which was a fairly small town, famous for its pottery. A map of the town was studied as our section commander and 2ic explained where we were going to patrol. The section commander (Junior) led a four man team (brick) and L/Cpl CZ the other half of the section. The idea was for us to be patrolling different areas but knowing each other's exact position at all times. Kit on, load rifles and make our way to the gate. If most soldiers are honest, they will admit that the first time you leave the station is quite a scary experience. It definitely made my heart race the very first time I patrolled the streets of Ireland. We were in and out on patrol many times from many different police stations but twenty years on I still remember going through those gates on the first patrol.

The entrance and exit to any station in any town can be a vulnerable place, so as the gates open we ran out at staggered intervals, and then formed up as a brick into a patrolling formation watching each other's backs at all times, and being completely aware of every thing around us. As we slowed up and started patrolling the heartbeat started to slow, which started beating faster as soon as those gates opened. We got to the end of the road from the police station, where a junction led into the main high street of Belleek. This was a vulnerable place, and getting from the small side road leading from the police station onto the high street was visible from the south – an ideal position for a sniper and judging by the bullet holes in the signpost on that corner, they had had a good go at slotting a squaddie there before. We ran into the high street across this vulnerable area visible from the south and again formed up into formation and carried on patrolling.

People young and old were going about their normal daily business, just like any town back home really. We didn't stay out long on that first patrol, but it was good to get it out the way and we could now settle down and get on with the job in hand. Throughout the next eight hours we were in and out, no set pattern; sometimes patrolling for twenty minutes and some times a couple of hours. After every patrol we would have a debrief, which was good as it helped keep us on our toes. Fermanagh in the mid eighties was no war zone, but you had to remember that anything at any time could happen. Those first eight hours patrolling the streets went without incident; just getting a feel for things and getting to know what each member of our brick was doing without too much conversation.

It was on July 19 1987, and my section had just finished our eight hour stint patrolling; we had eight hours on QRF (quick reaction force) next. It was quite early in the day and there were a few of us chatting in the backyard of Belleek station. I remember Huey was swinging from a metal staircase in very good mood, as he had just phoned his wife and been told he was going to be a dad. After a bit of silly chatter we left for our beds and left the next section to take over patrolling. Because we were on QRF, we could have a lie down but you had to keep your kit on, including your boots. Our section of eight men was split in to

Heli-pad, St Angelo Camp (photo courtesy of Mike Hewlett)

two rooms, four men (brick) in each room. My room consisted of Junior (section commander), Stacy (the crazy yank), Nobby and myself.

All off a sudden the place just seemed to erupt and I could hear lots of commotion, but above all, I heard Sergeant (Simmo) shouting 'CONTACT.' We jumped up, threw our flak jackets on (bullet proof vests) grabbed our weapons and ran to the gate, and dashed down the road towards the high street. We knew at this stage that there was a man down, but just couldn't believe that it was one of our own. We reached the end of the road and my platoon commander (the boss, Cornell) was there, and quickly explained the situation. As you came down the sidestreet from the police station and met the high street, there was a bridge in front that led to the south. Heading down the street, I quickly established that the casualty lying on the floor in front of a hotel was Huey. There were a few lads around Huey giving him medical attention and I sprinted across the street and took up position outside the hotel giving cover to those attending to him.

He had been hit by a single shot to the head by a sniper from across the border, and although I knew that the person who committed this crime had long gone, I could not take chances. I continually observed the hill side across the border for signs of any movement. At the same time residents of the hotel were trying to leave; holidaymakers, some with children who were quite stressed with what they had just witnessed. I abruptly shouted to them to get back inside. Essentially the whole area had become a crime scene; no vehicles could be moved.

At this point Huey was still alive, and we had convinced ourselves that he would pull through. The next thing I heard was the thud of a Lynx helicopter in the distance, and then suddenly it came into sight; roaring down the high street towards me at some speed and then disappeared out of my view over the top of the hotel. Then it came hovering back into view and dropped straight down in the high street, which was an amazing bit of flying for which the pilot should be commended. Huey was taken away on that Lynx, sadly the last time we saw him. He died on the way to hospital; a very sad day. I am sure I can say on behalf of my platoon at that time that Thomas Hewitt will always be missed, and that not many days pass without me thinking of that day when a great man's life was lost because of the troubles of N.I.

21 year old Lance Corporal Thomas Hewitt, who was from Cumbria, was shot and killed on 19 July, 1987 whilst on foot patrol in Belleek. He had only been in the area for a few days and was shot from the Republic, although the Irish authorities denied this. One senior British Army officer said at the time that the IRA had expert knowledge of the area and could attack almost at will; the alternative he said was to stop street patrolling completely. Lance Corporal Hewitt left a pregnant widow.

BELLEEK: 1987
L/Cpl 'B', Royal Signals

Another tasking with ATO was to clear a suspect device outside of a shop in Belleek. Being a border area town, we were to be flown in with all our kit. The flight would take 3 trips. One for my kit, and 2 for the tractor units and wheelbarrow etc.

The flight out of Omagh to Belleek in itself was pretty uneventful, I sat close to the door getting a good look over the peaceful countryside wondering if there

RUC Rosemount SF Base (photo courtesy of N Edwards)

was some kind of dividing line that said, 'town here, so you can fight, countryside here no fighting please!' Anyway, the Wessex dropped my kit and then landed to the side to let me off, it was always a bit nervewracking because although we always landed inside an infantry cordon, you never got to see anyone.

So I lifted the lid, started the generator and switched my kit on. Now, with all the flashing lights and stuff, we had a cover which we pulled over us to block out the daylight and enable us to see clearly so I was happily buried under this working away when I was tapped on the shoulder.

'Not now mate, give me 5 minutes' I called. Another tap, 'Come on mate leave it out, I need to finish this.'

I was then nudged, now nudging me really hacks me off and I started shouting, turning and pulling the ground sheet off me.

'For f**ks sake you arse, I said I'm f*****g bus ... '

I never finished the word busy as I came face to face with a bloody big cow! Scared the crap out of me, I hadn't seen them in the corner of the field we'd landed in, but I could imagine all the grunts laughing their bollocks off at me!

FERMANAGH: 1987

L/Cpl 'B', Royal Signals

Probably the biggest job that I was personally involved with during my time with ATO was the mortaring of RUC Kinawley in Fermanagh. We were tasked mid-morning following the attack on the station; at that time, we had no idea of the scale. I'll apologise now if there are any omissions here, but this is the first time I've put something like this down in writing and the events took place 20 years ago.

We had two bosses at that time, WO2 'G' was on his way home following the completion of his tour, SSGT 'S' was the incoming ATO. S/SGT 'S' was athletic and learning to fly, so when a Gazelle was sent for them so that they could overfly the site prior to commencing ops he was, needless to say, a happy bunny. The remainder of the team, well, we had to make our way to site in the vehicles and meet the two bosses on site.

The cordon was massive and the first point of note was that the majority of the houses, bungalows and shops all had their windows open, so this was not a surprise attack, at least not to the locals anyway. The second was the good spirit of the infantry and fuzz, it appears that the camera operator had seen the long dark shapes of the mortar's incoming and hit the mortar alarm which gave everybody chance to get under some form of cover. We set up our ICP in the middle of the street and found ourselves looking at a tractor with a rather large hay bale sat on the back of it.

The two bosses appeared, both of them ashen-faced and looking decidedly sick. What they related to us was sort of funny, but not, but there again the British soldier's sense of humour is well known for not being strictly PC and in fact, it is the basis I think of what got all of us through these times in our lives. The flight from our camp in Omagh to Kinawley was uneventful and offered a good view of the countryside and the chance for the new boss to get a glance at his new area. Once over Kinawley, they surveyed the damage and identified what they thought to be one or two unexploded MK10 mortars. As they were hovering for a better look, the Gazelle lost its downdraft and dropped, the pilot reckons, about 200ft! The pilot managed to catch the aircraft, but so bad was the incident, the pilot conceded that he thought that they had all just brought their ticket to the never-ending gig!!!

So, with all members of the team present and in one piece (so to speak) we set to work, wheelbarrow unloaded, set up, sent out, bleep sweeps completed, all clear, wheelbarrow deployed on the firing circuits and successful, it was time for the boss's manual approach. The bleep mobile was positioned and started its work and shortly after, the boss went down and had a look at the situation. Before too much prodding and poking was done, the boss decided that he wanted to get the tractor moved a vehicle length to discount the possibility of booby traps so he took the tow rope down and hitched it up to the tractor. Once he had cleared the area and got back to the ICP, I hooked the other end to the tow eye on my Transit and got into the cab.

Starting the engine I gave the 3.5 litre V6 Rover engine a damn good tickling, put her in reverse and gently took up the slack until I could feel the weight. I stuck my foot a good way down and dropped the clutch. The damn thing stalled! Never mind, a bit red-faced but none the less unfazed, I restarted the engine, gunned it a bit more and started to pull. Tons of revs, bit of tyre smoke and the acrid smell of a burning clutch but the beast at the end of the rope was having none of it and hadn't moved a millimetre. I tried and retried to get the thing to move but it was having none of it and after 20 minutes and a nose full of clutch smoke, we gave it up as a bad idea.

The boss went back down for another look and spent a large amount of time gently moving the hay back from the top, looking for the launch tubes that had sent the mortars on their way. Eventually, he uncovered the tops of nine tubes, all with signs of firing, all of them empty. There were one or two unexploded mortars in the derelict house adjacent to the station, but in no way had enough damage to the RUC station been caused to account for the other seven, we had a problem. The two bosses decided that as it was getting late and dark, the best idea would be to keep the cordon in place, go back to camp to get fed, replenish the vehicles and to call HQ for some advice and hopefully, some assistance, and that's what we did. Two points to note. You really felt part of an EOD team because everyone was involved and knew what was happening. Secondly, you were never afraid to ask for help, it was not a sign of weakness but if you didn't know it or were unsure, there was always someone who did know it or had the right advice and they were only a radio or telephone call away.

The next day, bright and early, well it wasn't bright when we got up, in fact it was damn cold, but bright when we arrived with a dusting of frost around, we made ready to start the next day. Reinforcements in the shape of SATO (Senior ATO) and two instructors from the mainland had turned up. Work continued on the tractor and hay bale and a RIC flight had been booked for that morning, the results to be expressed straight to site for deliberation.

After a couple of hours work, the bosses between them had uncovered the nine mortar tubes. They had been welded into a steel frame which was hooked onto the hydraulic hitch of the tractor. The tractor would have just looked like it was moving hay around but once parked, the frame lowered to the ground to make the frame ridged and give a stable firing platform, and hence the reason why we were unable to move the thing the day before.

Once the tractor was cleared, we all assembled for some 'happy snaps' and split up to complete the remaining tasks. Myself and the No. 2 took a walk down to the Police station and started searching through the rubble and the building in an effort to locate any unexploded mortars whilst we awaited the outcome of the RIC flight. We couldn't find a thing, but the damage caused by the few that found their target was extensive and God only knows what would have happened if all nine mortars had found their target and exploded.

By the time we had walked back to the ICP, the RIC results were available for scrutiny and we all poured over the panoramic photographs looking for the tell tale stick like objects and located 3 of them in the derelict house and another couple kicking around. A discussion took place to identify the quickest and safest means of dealing with the little sods and then the well oiled machine kicked into action. Given the fact that we were in mid-handover, SATO was down and 2 instructors from the mainland, any outsider would have thought that we had all worked together for a very long time.

Hooks and lines were rigged, weapons primed and made ready for positioning and everybody got ready to start work on making safe the IEDs. It was decided not to notify the locals of the impending weapons firing that was to take place (more like mini explosions really), if we ended up shattering a few windows – what the hell! Charges were placed on the beams of the old roof the derelict house to cut them and bring the mortars down to ground level; charges were also placed on those on the lower ground area. Lines were attached to each in turn so that we could hopefully pull them out of the derelict house and into the open street. Once everyone was safely back in the ICP, the No. 2 barked out his warnings and fired each charge in turn and then we waited and left the mortars to soak for a period of time.

The plan had worked and all the lines pulled. The mortar from the roof area was pulled out across the street and half way up a lamp post until it struck the pulley. With three of us on the rope, we pulled it up and dropped it down a dozen or so times to make sure that nothing untoward was going to happen and then pulled the others out.

The two bosses, SATO and one of the mainland instructors went to look at the IEDs in the derelict house, the other instructor tapped me on the shoulder and said to grab an adjustable spanner and follow him as he picked up a clear plastic bag. We waltzed up the road to the MK10a that was still in one piece and hanging from the lamp post and between us, we untied it and carried it around behind an 8' brick wall and out of sight of the ICP and ground troops. He indicated for me to sit on the ground and laid the mortar across my lap, 'Just open that up' he said and without another thought, I undid the nuts on the top of the mortar and gently eased out the cordite that would have fired the main charge. Once out we put the plastic back over the open end of the mortar, upended it and emptied out the main charge of home made explosives. The instructor picked up the end cap and plastic bag and I threw the mortar over my shoulder and grinning madly, we walked back down to the ICP.

We cleared the site around 6pm that evening on the second day. The explosives bagged to go back with us ready for collection, everything else bagged for the forensic guys to try and gather some evidence from, this was probably, if my memory is right, the only 2 day job that we did (our detachment that is) during my time with 3 2 1 EOD.

The job, at the time was one of the biggest mortar attacks the province had seen, hence the appearance of the training team from the mainland. We were told that once all the incident reports etc were in; they would make this incident a part of the special to theatre training, something that we had all gone through. It made us feel just that little bit special for a few minutes to know that we had been a part of something that was thought to have been that big a deal, after that little session of self appreciation, once we started the next job, it faded away to become 'just another job.'

Chapter Twenty-One

1988

A year of 466 bombings, 537 shootings and the deaths of 33 soldiers, 6 RUC officers, 45 civilians and 8 terrorists.

This was the year in which millions of people witnessed, live on television, the abducting, beating and eventual murder of two soldiers. Corporals David Howes and Derek Wood, both of the Royal Corps of Signals (RCS), had accidentally strayed into the funeral procession of Catholics killed at the earlier funeral of 3 IRA terrorists, who had been shot dead by the SAS in Gibraltar.

The year witnessed the first RAF fatalities, as 3 Airmen were killed whilst off duty in Nieuw Bergan, Holland and Roermond in West Germany. It saw also the Royal Navy's only fatality, when Lieutenant Alan Shields of the Navy recruiting office was killed in Belfast, when a bomb was detonated under his car.

It was also the year in which an IRA bomb was placed under an Army lorry, and 6 soldiers returning from a charity fun run were killed. The fatalities affected 3 Regiments with 4 Soldiers from the RCS, a Green Howard and an RAOC Lance-Corporal.

In January, UDR Captain Timothy Armstrong was murdered as he walked with his fiancé along Ormeau Road in South Belfast.

On November 23rd of this year a 67 year old man and his 13 year old grand-daughter were killed by an IRA bomb intended for the RUC; Barney Lavery and Emma Donnelley became the 3,000th and 3,001st victims of the troubles. Yet another milestone had been reached in this tragedy.

LONDONDERRY: 1988

David Hardy, Light Infantry

I was the top cover, rear-facing, on a piglet (an armoured Land Rover) and on a routine mobile patrol one night in the city; absolutely pitch black and we were driving under a pedestrian walkway. Suddenly, the lad facing forward shouted 'Duck!' and as I ducked down a huge paving slab hurtled through the air from the bridge (about 5 metres above us) and shattered on the road, missing me by a foot or so. One or two mph slower and myself and my fellow top cover would have been killed in an instant. It looked a huge thing, so God knows how many of them it took to lift the bloody thing over the railing.

On another night, we were driving through an estate in a Republican area. As we turned a corner we could see, ahead of us, two Ulster buses, burning furiously away, with a mob of about 50+ civvies, young and old, male and female. It looked like they were dancing all around the flames, waving and shouting; almost like a full-scale riot.

PIGs on patrol, Belfast

There was a patch of green, maybe a quarter of a mile away and we wisely decided to stay back, just circling this patch of land whilst we kept our eyes on the mob. We radioed the sitrep through and then just had to bide our time. We trained our gats (SA80s) on them as we peered through our firing slots, but they knew that we wouldn't fire live rounds at unarmed civilians. Then, they began to advance on us to try and surround us, so we had to keep our eyes to the front and rear; behind us were ginnells and alleyways from which they could sneak up on us.

There was only the one vehicle – a four man brick with a full-screw in charge of us and nothing appeared to be coming to reinforce us. Then the Corporal said:' Stick one in the chamber [of the baton gun] and stick it out of the turret.' As soon as they saw this appear, they knew that we meant business and began to back off. [This was a sure sign that IRA gunmen were not in attendance, as one of their prime tactics was to use the rioting mobs as cover, then fire at the soldiers as the crowd parted to allow the shot to be made. In this instance the mob backed off, which was evidence of no gunmen in attendance.] Just then, the RUC and the fire service arrived; the fire service had to have an armed RUC escort whatever the situation was, and we were able to back off; another routine mobile patrol !

Just as an aside, they quickly learned that whereas we wouldn't use live ammo on them unless we knew that firearms would be used against us, they also knew that we wouldn't hesitate to use baton rounds when we were threatened.

David was terribly injured in the August of this year; see his account of the Ballygawley coach bombing later in this chapter.

ANDERSONSTOWN FOOT PATROL: 1988

Private David Creese, 1st Glosters

We were newly arrived in the Province from Germany and we were stationed in quite a soft area; Shackleton Barracks. It is near the town of Limavady not far from the northern coastline of Co Londonderry. My company was told on first parade that we would all be deployed into the local countryside on a two day patrol, as part of our familiarization of the area and would be introduced to the local civilian population. Patrolling down the hedge-rowed lanes, across fields and through small coppices and woods with the odd V.C.P thrown in for good measure, the two days passed in a flash. I thought that the countryside was very much the same as any other area in Great Britain.

We had barely been back in barracks 5 minutes when we were told that we were off to Belfast for 'Operation Delivery.' Three dead IRA terrorists were being brought back to N.I. from Gibraltar in body bags after being shot by the SAS. I was happy to take part in this deployment as morale was high, and we had three less terrorists to worry about; a good result if you are a serving soldier knowing you are what they call a legitimate target. We were mobilized to Belfast; deploying to the outskirts of the city and then moved to Fort Whiterock in heavily armoured vehicles. Once we had been briefed on the local area and timings of patrols, we prepared for the first one; fourteen hours of patrolling, and constantly changing fire positions. This would be the first of five such patrols.

Team picture taken next to the mortor base plate during clearance ops following the
mortoring of RUC Kinawley in 1987
(photo courtesy of Andrew Bennett)

At 13:00 we were by the gates ready to leave. Fort Whiterock is situated on the edge of Turf Lodge, a housing estate that does not have a particularly good name, and one which sounds pretty uninviting to anyone, especially a teenager wearing a camouflaged uniform and hated by all Republicans. As the large steel gates opened we exited the base. A winding access road flanked by wriggly tin shielding us from sniper fire, led down onto the estate. When we reached the end of the driveway we burst out from the fort; 'hard targeting' right and left. I remember gazing in awe at the housing estate looming over us, and for a fraction of a second losing sight of my fire team. I quickly had to think in which direction we had to go at the start of the patrol, once we had broken cover from the fort. Several fire teams had left the base at the same time saturating the estate with troops, which made it twice as difficult to locate your own team. I looked around again only to find I was actually with my team all along (panic over), and only just out of formation. We started making our way through the Lodge into new Andersonstown, moving along the streets and taking up fire positions near gateways and doorways, squatting down and looking through the SUSAT sights on our SA80s.

You have a real tendency to wish the hours away. As we entered a no through road, several children were in the street and greeted us with their own friendly style; a mixture of foul- mouthed obscenities and a handful of stones. My team leader, the second man in the staggered patrol formation, was suddenly pelted by a green tennis ball. It hit him on the left side of his neck, and at the pace the ball was travelling it must have hurt like hell. All the children laughed out loud cheering at such a well aimed shot, and all I could think of at that time was 'welcome to Belfast and one hour down thirteen to go.' As we were patrolling through New Andersonstown, a report of small arms fire came across the radio. The shots were not aimed at any patrol, but to signal the 'Gibraltar three' are back on home soil, and every ones' senses are heightened as all sorts of feelings rushed through our minds.

The team commander used hand signals to move out, and we continued. Soon we were in Andersonstown and then onto the Falls Road (a name I had heard a thousand times on the news during my childhood). Now I was here myself in full combats with 'cam cream' on my face and a rifle in my hands. We were only on the Falls Road for about 200 metres then back into the housing estate. It was now about 16:00 and we were in the street where Mairead Farrell (one of the three IRA members killed in Gib) lived, and as we patrolled along the street in the direction of her house, a small boy aged about 3 years old stood in his underpants in the middle of his garden watching us. The patrol stopped and we all took up fire positions in gateways; one of our team was in the gateway of the little boy's garden when suddenly the young boy shouts 'get out of my f**king garden you black b*stard', in a strong northern Irish accent. The reason he had called us black b*stards was because we were all wearing cam cream on our faces and not because of our race or creed. The evening drew on and darkness fell. With so many troops on the ground, we patrolled around the same areas for most of the fourteen hour patrol. At about 2200hrs, we had moved back up to New Andersonstown near a small block of shops, where a group of youths had been hanging around and causing a bit of a disturbance. There was a large alleyway to the rear of the shops, and one of the teams had secured the area. By now the group had disbursed and was nowhere to be seen. The team in the alleyway had found a crate of petrol bombs. One member of the team decided it would be a laugh to throw one (not lit), but what he didn't realise, was that the platoon Sergeant was on the other side of the wall and the bottle just missed him!

The next thing we knew the Sergeant was on the radio calling it in, and before long, other teams were joining us looking for a bit of aggro. Soon things died down and we were on the move again into Andersonstown. The straps on my white sifter were digging into my shoulders even through my bullet proof vest. The patrol ended at about 0300hrs; back at Fort Whiterock, knackered and glad to see my sleeping bag.

FERMANAGH: 1988

L/Cpl 'B' Royal Signals

Probably the biggest job that I was personally involved with during my time with ATO was the mortaring of RUC Kinawley in Fermanagh. We were tasked mid morning following the attack on the station. At that time, we had no idea of the scale. I'll apologise now if there are any omissions here, but this is the first time I've put something like this down in writing, and the events took place 20 years ago.

We had two bosses at that time: WO2 'G' was on his way home following the completion of his tour: SSGT S was the incoming ATO. SSGT 'S' was athletic and learning to fly, so when a Gazelle was sent for them so that they could over-fly the site prior to commencing op's, he was, needless to say, a happy bunny. The remainder of the team? Well, we had to make our way to the site in vehicles and meet the two bosses there.

The cordon was massive and the first point of note was that the majority of the houses, bungalows and shops all had their windows open. This would indicate that it was not a surprise attack [a tactic to reduce damage from broken glass], at least not to the locals anyway. The second was the good spirit of the infantry and fuzz; it appeared that the camera operator had seen the long dark shapes of the mortars incoming and hit the mortar alarm, which gave everybody a chance to get under some form of cover. We set up our ICP in the middle of the street and found ourselves looking at a tractor with a rather large hay bale sat on the back of it.

The two bosses appeared, both of them ashen faced and looking decidedly sick. What they related to us was sort of funny, but not, but there again the British Soldier's sense of humour is well known for not being strictly PC and in fact, it is the basis I think of what got all of us through these times in our lives. The flight from our camp in Omagh to Kinawley was uneventful and offered a good view of the countryside, and the chance for the new boss to get a glance at his new area. Once over Kinawley, they surveyed the damage and identified what they thought to be one or two unexploded MK10 mortars. As they were hovering for a better look, the Gazelle lost it's down draft and dropped, the pilot reckons, about 200ft! The pilot managed to catch the aircraft, but so bad was the incident, the pilot conceded that he thought that they had all just bought their ticket to the never ending gig!!!

Bogside (photo courtesy of N Edwards)

So, with all members of the team present and in one piece (so to speak) we set to work: wheelbarrow unloaded, set up, sent out: bleep sweeps completed, all clear: wheelbarrow deployed on the firing circuits and successful: it was time for the boss's manual approach. The bleep mobile was positioned and started its work and shortly after, the boss went down and had a look at the situation. Before too much prodding and poking was done, the boss decided that he wanted to get the tractor moved a vehicle length to discount the possibility of booby traps. So he took the tow rope down and hitched it up to the tractor. Once he had cleared the area and got back to the ICP, I hooked the other end to the tow eye on my Transit and got into the cab.

Starting the engine I gave the 3.5 litre V6 Rover engine a damn good tickling, put her in reverse and gently took up the slack until I could feel the weight. I stuck my foot a good way down and dropped the clutch. The damn thing stalled! Never mind, a bit red faced but none the less unfazed, I restarted the engine, gunned it a bit more and started to pull. Ton's of revs, a bit of tyre smoke and the acrid smell of a burning clutch but the beast at the end of the rope was having none of it, and hadn't moved a millimetre. I tried and retried to get the thing to move but it was still having none of it, so after 20 minutes and a nose full of clutch smoke, we gave it up as a bad idea.

The boss went back down for another look and spent a large amount of time gently moving the hay back from the top, looking for the launch tubes that had sent the mortars on their way. Eventually, he uncovered the tops of nine tubes, all with signs of firing, all of them empty. There were one or two unexploded mortar's in the derelict house adjacent to the station, but in no way had enough damage to the RUC station been caused to account for the other seven- we had a problem. The two bosses decided that as it was getting late and dark, the best idea would be to keep the cordon in place, go back to camp to get fed, replenish the vehicles and to call HQ for some advice, and hopefully some assistance, and that's what we did. Two points to note. You really felt part of an EOD team because everyone was involved and knew what was happening. Secondly, you were never afraid to ask for help, it was not a sign of weakness but if you didn't know it or were unsure, there was always someone who did know it or had the right advice and they were only a radio or telephone call away.

The next day, bright and early, well it wasn't bright when we got up, in fact it was damned cold, but bright when we arrived with a dusting of frost around; we made ready to start the next day. Reinforcements in the shape of SATO (Senior ATO) and two instructors from the mainland had turned up. Work continued on the tractor and hay bale and a RIC flight had been booked for that morning, the results to be expressed straight to site for deliberation.

After a couple of hours work, the bosses between them had uncovered the nine mortar tubes. They had been welded into a steel frame which was hooked onto the hydraulic hitch of the tractor. The tractor would have just looked like it was moving hay around but once parked, the frame lowered to the ground to make the frame ridged and give a stable firing platform, and hence the reason why we were unable to move the thing the day before.

Once the tractor was cleared, we all assembled for some 'happy snaps' and split up to complete the remaining tasks. Myself and the No. 2 took a walk down to the Police station and started searching through the rubble and building in an effort to locate any unexploded mortars, whilst we awaited the outcome of the RIC flight. We couldn't find a thing, but the damage caused by the few that found their target was extensive and God only knows what would have happened if all nine mortars had found their targets and exploded.

By the time we had walked back to the ICP, the RIC results were available for scrutiny, and we all pored over the panoramic photographs looking for the tell-tale stick-like objects, locating 3 of them in the derelict house and another couple kicking around. A discussion took place to identify the quickest and safest means of dealing with the little sods, and then the well- oiled machine kicked into action. Given the fact that we were in mid-handover, SATO was down and 2 instructors from the mainland, any outsider would have thought that we had all worked together for a very long time.

Hooks and lines were rigged, weapons primed and made ready for positioning and everybody got ready to start work on making safe the IEDs. It was decided not to notify the locals of the impending weapons firing that was to take place (more like mini explosions really), if we ended up shattering a few windows – what the hell! Charges were placed on the beams of the old roof the derelict house to cut them and bring the mortars down to ground level; charges were also placed on those on the lower ground area. Lines were attached to each in turn so that we could hopefully pull them out of the derelict house and into the open street. Once everyone was safely back in the ICP, the No. 2 barked out his warnings and fired each charge in turn and then we waited and left the mortars to soak for a period of time.

The plan had worked and all the lines pulled. The mortar from the roof area was pulled out across the street and half way up a lamp post until it struck the pulley. With three of us on the rope, we pulled it up and dropped it down a dozen or so times to make sure that nothing untoward was going to happen and then pulled the others out.

The two bosses, SATO and one of the mainland instructors went to look at the IEDs in the derelict house. The other instructor tapped me on the shoulder and said to grab an adjustable spanner and follow him as he picked up a clear plastic bag. We waltzed up the road to the MK10a that was still in one piece and hanging from the lamp post. Between us, we untied it and carried it around behind an 8 foot brick wall and out of sight of the ICP and ground troops. He indicated for me to sit on the ground and laid the mortar across my lap, 'Just open that up' he said, and without another thought, I undid the nuts on the top of the mortar and gently eased out the cordite that would have fired the main charge. Once out, we put the plastic bag over the open end of the mortar, upended it and emptied out the main charge of home made explosives. The instructor picked up the end cap and plastic bag and I threw the mortar over my shoulder and, grinning madly, we walked back down to the ICP.

We cleared the site around 6pm that evening on the second day: the explosives bagged to go back with us ready for collection: everything else bagged for the forensic guys to try and gather some evidence from. This was probably, if my memory is right, the only 2-day job that we did (our detachment that is) during my time with 321 EOD.

The job, at the time, was one of the biggest mortar attacks the province had seen, hence the appearance of the training team from the mainland. We were told that once all the incident reports etc were in; they would make this incident a part of the special-to-theatre training, something that we had all gone through. It

Grenadier VCP patrol (photo courtesy of David Roalfe)

made us feel just that little bit special for a few minutes, knowing that we had been a part of something that was thought to have been that big a deal. After that little session of self appreciation, once we started the next job, it faded away to become 'just another job.'

UNDER FIRE: LISNASKEA 1988
David Hardy, Light Infantry

I was moved to another company and we were sent to man PVCPs on the border with the Republic. I was on the 12 hour night shift – 6pm to 6am – which was pretty boring because it was pitch-black, but it was, I must admit, pretty relaxing.

One night, just as we went on, a car was stopped at our checkpoint near Lisnakea; I was inside the armoured sangar, typing in the car's details – or would have been because I never finished it – when there was a huge bang. It was like being inside a church bell whilst it was being rung! Someone came up from behind and shouted 'We're being shot at!' The idea, I reckon, was to get us all outside into the open and then spray us with automatic fire. At the commotion, the car drove off in a hurry.

What we didn't know was, that the bang was in fact the second shot, and the first, which had flown over the top of us, we never heard. There was a lad at the front and the first round went over his head, as I said, but the second embedded itself in the sangar wall at chest height, narrowly missing him. Suddenly and automatically, all our training kicked in and we went into autopilot, grabbing our gats (weapons) and dashing outside. We left by two different exits so as to confuse the gunman (or gunmen); one squaddie stayed inside and the rest of us, heavily armed, pegged up the road to investigate.

We searched for a while, but couldn't find anything or anyone in all that darkened farmland which surrounded us. We went back inside the sangar and, as we unloaded our weapons, I suddenly felt physically sick as the adrenaline kicked in. I just thought inwardly: 'Fucking hell – we were lucky, especially the lad on the front!'

A team came out, investigated, and found the FP. At the same time they discovered a crossing point on the border which our engineers had previously dug up. The IRA had filled the crater in, a bit at a time, over a period of weeks without us even noticing, and they had used this to make their getaway back over to the southern part. Even if we had found the FP and seen the gunmen, we could not have followed.

I should have gone to sleep on the 1st of January and stayed that way until December 31st, as this was a bad year.

SOUTH ARMAGH, 1988
Private Tim Castle, Light Infantry

Our Call Sign – AM43G – had a few interesting jobs; we were tasked with getting photographs of a known player in Fermanagh. He was well aware of the Army's effort in surveillance, and had cleared back all the hedges from his farmhouse for about a 400 to 500 yard radius. We had just been issued with a Nikkor 2000mil mirror lens for the Nikon FM cameras. This thing was a beast and filled the SAS Bergens with which we were issued. Gerry Brayne carried it wrapped up in his sleeping bag. There wasn't any room to carry a tripod for it, so we took some sandbags and used those. It came with a 4 by 40 telescope sight on the side, as the field of view was tiny. You set up the sandbags on the edge of the ditch (always ditches!), lined up on your target using the scope, and then attached a camera body to the rear of the lens. For this job we shared Gerry's load of signalling kit between us. I carried a GPMG despite us being trained for the LMG on the previous COP.

During that OP we had seen him, at last light, go out into a field and place an object that looked like a pistol in a hole in the ground. This he did every evening. So, after seeking permission, on our last night we did a quick search for his hide. We marked the spot with an IR torch from the OP, and Benny with Gerry, sneaked into the field using night sights to follow the IR beam. They found the hide and the alleged pistol, the tension was unbelievable. I lay tightly wrapped around the butt of my GPMG ready to give covering fire should it all go wrong. Benny and Gerry appeared smiling like Cheshire cats. It was a stop cock to water the cattle troughs and he had been carrying a tap in his hand!

The player concerned had no idea we were there, and we ended up with some great pics of this man, and just about everyone that visited his isolated farm for the next week. Following our return to camp, the contact sheets were printed in

Dunville Park, opposite RVH West Belfast (courtesy of Andy Carr)

time for a debrief. We wrote the patrol report, and received a big pat on the back from the Boss for getting pics of such good quality without him knowing. The platoon's reputation was rising at Brigade!

We started to get more planned ambush jobs, including one up near Magherafelt. This was a job to take out the attack team assembling a Mk 10 mortar. We were tasked to provide the QRF, as another team had the actual ambush site. We spent a fruitless 10 days inside a UDR base waiting for the off. Nothing happened, and the ambush team was withdrawn. There were lots of jobs like the ones above including some which were our apprenticeship in the Province.

One such task was a close protection job for a UDR man whom Intelligence believed was under threat; jobs like this allowed us out to play with some more exotic weapons.

We were increasingly deployed further away from the Battalion TAOR, and before the year was out we were deployed to Crossmaglen. The set up had been that the ARB (Armagh Roulement Bn) had responsibility for this area. It was then realised that regardless of how good the ARB COP and local platoons were, they needed a real continuity set up. In my first tour we had company NCOs attached at each location from the nearest 2 year Bn. They were Intelligence section lads and, whilst good at their job, weren't trained for COP work. We were tasked to provide a permanent Officer/SNCO, and at least 2 teams in Crossmaglen. This meant that, with leave and courses taken into account, the lads could expect to spend 10 days out of 30 in the 'Cross'. The role was meant to be shared with the ARB COP and the Resident Bn COP from Ballykinler.

The Ballykinler Bn was the RWF and we were soon so stretched, that we ended up manning Borucki Sangar as mixed teams. We also patrolled the town during periods when other agencies put it OOB.

During this period the ARB changed from the Royal Hampshires (crap accom and food) to the Queen's (a bit better). The Queen's deployed as the first Bn to have the new L85A1 rifle, or SA80 to the world. We converted during this period but held onto all our stock of older weapons for jobs that might need them.

The Boss set a challenge. He pinned up, in the COP ops room, a big sheet of pictures of people with no name or trace seen that year so far in the town square. It paid off, and within 2 weeks there wasn't a face from the list unnamed. The ARB COP ended up being deployed to Fermanagh and worked a patch that we had handed over to the Royal Artillery on Op 'Cara Cara'.

This was a bit of a pain for the next unit in, which was, I think, 42 Commando. Some of their Close Observation Troop had been detached from Poole for operational experience, and definitely didn't want to do boring Fermanagh. Brigade relented and the 'Bootnecks' eventually came under our direction at XMG.

The Marines without a doubt looked after us very well and fed us far too much! Some of the married lads were seen carting Bergens full of steak to the helipad for a weekend BBQ. The ARB had its HQ at the famous Bessbrook Mill. When the Marines were there almost all of their light admin tasks were done by WRNs [Women's Royal Navy]. I was impressed to say the least. We moved in and set up an ops room for all COP work in the new 3 Brigade border area. I was left to my own devices for weeks on end as Benny had returned to the UK to start skiing training. The team was almost broken up and used to infill vacancies on jobs as required.

Preparing for a three day border patrol, S. Armagh 1986 (2 Coldstream Guards Recce Plt.) (photo courtesy of Barry Crane)

At roughly the same time the PIRA had deployed a nasty new weapon known as VISA [Vehicle Incendiary South Armagh]; this was basically a car with explosives packed around a full fuel tank. It was detonated by remote control. This meant that we would deploy en masse to Bessbrook and set out from there. Luckily during my time they didn't manage to use it on us. We were meant to patrol normally having made everywhere OOB. Human figure 11's springs to mind.

The Marines left, and I think the Paras were due in, but at some point the Scots Guards took over at Bessbrook. South Armagh got so busy that all the reserve companies from all 3 Brigades were deployed at the same time.

I was left spare on an op again so I pulled ARFLO [Airborne Reaction Force Liaison Officer.] This meant that I took command of a section of troops from whoever was unfortunate enough, and even their officers had to ask before doing anything. Luckily S. Armagh was a helmet area and we wore no badges of rank. I got away with all sorts!

Jimmy Benfold, Light Infantry

While commanding a PVCP on the border, the OC brought along some visitors, a Canadian General and a Pakistani General. Whilst showing them around and briefing them, the Pakistani General, with a straight face, asked me where the minefields were situated. I looked at the OC and the OC returned the look; the pair of us were struggling so much not to laugh. When I told this General that we didn't have any, he was shocked. He could just not comprehend that the border was not closed and protected by minefields. As they were leaving the Canadian General gave me a wink and a shake of the head as if to say 'what a plonker.'

Would life have been easier with minefields? I suspect PIRA would have had mine clearing teams trained and looked to turn them on us

LONDONDERRY 1988

Captain, the Green Howards

I went back to Ireland for the sixth time during this year; little realizing that it would be my final tour. It was my first time in the Province for 12 years, having the Bn going to the Aldergrove area in 1978–80.

I had been promoted to Captain and was Ops officer to one of the Rifle Companies. I did, however, from time to time, actually command the company when it went out on ops in the Londonderry area.

It was not unusual on this tour – as resident Battalion in Londonderry – to have on a fairly regular basis, sightings of 2 of the top men in the Republican movement, Martin McGuinness and Gerry Adams with their henchmen or other 'associates'

It was always felt that these two guys, although passing themselves off as Sinn Fein, were still players so far as the IRA were concerned. But it always appeared that the powers-that-be had made them untouchable.

The Green Howards lost only one man on that tour, Corporal 'Silver' Metcalfe, who was killed by an IRA bomb with 5 others when returning from a charity fun run at Lisburn.

GIBRALTAR FUNERAL: 1988

Private David Creese, 1st Glosters

The following day and once again we prepared for another fourteen hour patrol over the same streets, but when you patrol the same streets for such long hours, day after day, you eventually become complacent; now nearly 20 years later I can look back and know that that was exactly what we had become. Two days later in the early hours of the morning of the third patrol, our multiple of twelve men crammed into a garden at the rear of a house in Andersonstown. The garden was surrounded by high fences and was not really overlooked. We stayed in the garden for approximately twenty minutes, with two men guarding the entrance to the garden and ten hairy arsed squaddies lying flat on their backs either gazing at the stars or with their eyes shut. Looking back on that moment it was foolish and careless, but then again when you're chin-strapped, it's a risk you are willing to take even if it is for a short period of rest.

When we left the garden we made our way back down to the Falls Road and into a heavily fortified RUC station near Milltown cemetery. Inside the compound we were briefed on a new task. The funerals of the Gib 3 were to be held in Milltown cemetery the following morning. It was our job to search it for any devices, as a well-placed bomb in such a large pro-IRA funeral would cause untold devastation, and that would be too good a target for Loyalist paramilitary groups to pass up. In our multiple of twelve men only three or four of us were search-trained and part of the unit search team. As we swept our way from the main gates to the rear of the graveyard, we searched around the gravestones and onto the freshly dug holes where the coffins would be lowered some hours later. The cemetery was clear of devices and we made our way back to Fort Whiterock.

Finally, we were in the safety of the Fort once again, and we unloaded our weapons. I was looking forward to getting in my gonk [sleep] bag as the funerals would be taking place within the next ten hours, and we would not be going out on patrol until the funerals were over. When I got up that morning we heard reports of an attack on the mourners. A man had entered the cemetery from the direction of the M1 motorway, had thrown hand grenades and used small arms fire on the people there. That man was Michael Stone and the attack has been well documented; it is also one of the moments in time that you can tell people where you were and what you were doing when it happened.

I recall going into a dark and smoke-filled room in Fort Whiterock which was being used as a NAAFI. The room was full of guys stood around watching a TV news report on the attack; all we could do was stand and stare. We were not going to be sent down to the cemetery or the surrounding streets. The chaos of the attack was bewildering and putting troops on the streets would have caused a riot so it was a case of stand back and see what happens.

Michael Stone killed 3 people that day and injured approximately 60 people (men, women and children). During the attack his pistol jammed and he was set upon by a crowd of mourners. Stone received a brutal and savage assault by the baying mob and was lucky to survive; fortunately for him the RUC intervened. One of the mourners who died that day was Kevin Brady a member of the IRA. His funeral was held 3 days later, which led to the corporal killings. By this time my 5 days in Belfast were over, yet my 2 year tour had only just begun.

On March 16, a huge IRA funeral was held at Milltown cemetery in west Belfast for the three IRA members killed in Gibraltar by the SAS, 10 days earlier. The massive cemetery which includes a Republican plot is sandwiched between the Turf Lodge and the Ballymurphy estate; slightly further south is Andersonstown; in essence three huge Catholic areas and hotbeds of Republicanism.

At that funeral a lone UFF gunman, Michael Stone, launched an apparent one-man gun and grenade attack on the mourners, which included a heavy IRA presence. Stone killed three people that day, including two innocent civilians and an IRA member. The funeral of the three dead men was to be held on March 19.

That day was a Saturday; millions observing the funeral on TV news programmes watched as a silver car driving towards the cortege was suddenly forced to stop, and its attempt to reverse out of the situation was foiled as it found itself hemmed in by several black cabs. At first, no-one seemed to understand what was happening, and then a huge mob of mostly men converged on the car, which was seen to have two occupants; one of them, the author noted perversely at the time, appeared to be wearing one of the Don Zapata moustaches then fashionable.

The mob then charged at the car and one of the occupants pulled a pistol, partially climbed out and fired it over the roof. The crowd then scattered in panic. They came back, and some armed with iron bars and even a step ladder, smashed their way into the car dragging the two occupants out and began severely beating them. The two men were seen to be bundled into black cabs and there the TV footage stopped.

Eyewitness accounts state that the men were stripped to their underwear and socks – possibly during the course of the savage beating – and, appallingly, one man had one of his eyes gouged out. Their bodies were thrown over a high wall into waste ground at Penny Lane where they were then killed by an IRA gunman; all this was observed and videoed by an Army surveillance helicopter.

The two men were Corporal Derek Wood (24) who had been in the country for some time and Corporal David Howes (23) who had only been in the Province for a week; both men belonged to the Royal Corps of Signals. Why or how they stumbled onto an IRA funeral at such a heightened time of tension, following the Michael Stone killings has yet to be officially explained. Following conversations with several senior soldiers who were close to the situation – all of whom refused, naturally, to be quoted – one can speculate that there were three possible explanations.

The first theory – and this was the most suggested cause by senior officers – was that Corporal Wood, the more experienced, certainly in terms of the Northern Ireland situation was simply showing off to his less experienced colleague. Another theory suggested was the converse of this and that the lesser experienced soldier was egging on his Ulster-wise colleague to take him into the 'hot spots.'

A third, less likely suggestion was that the two men were on undercover work and trying to get information on known players who would almost certainly – irrespective of the danger of being seen in public – come out for the second most high profile funeral in the area in the space of just 3 days. Did the pair have photographic or surveillance equipment in the car? Doubtful. If this had been the case, wouldn't the IRA or Sinn Fein have had a field day in producing that equipment? They would then have tried to placate the watching world, following that terrible lynching of the two soldiers by claiming that the Army had shown supreme disrespect. The Army had the surveillance helicopters with their incredible, state of the art technology with which to identify and isolate players in the crowd and doubtless, the 'sneaky-beakys' would have been nearby with their telephoto lens and video cameras. Why then would the mission have been a spying trip? If it was, it was indeed amateurish.

Whatever their motives – and the inexplicable reason as to why they didn't try and shoot their way out of the crisis – only a few very senior and high-ranking officers and the two poor soldiers themselves will ever know. The former either didn't know or will never reveal why and the latter cannot.

Republican black cab in which the two Signals Corporals were abducted before being
murdered in Penny Lane, Belfast

THE KILLINGS OF THE CORPORALS: 1988

Lieutenant Colonel G.P. Moss, King's Own Borderers

I have to stress that I didn't witness the terrible murders of Corporals Derek Wood or David Howes, but I watched the surveillance video of that dreadful incident and talked to those who witnessed the whole thing and I can relate it to you as much as I am allowed to.

Most of the world witnessed the events of that day, March 19, 1988 and I do not propose to go over ground which your readers are already aware of. After the two men had been beaten almost to the point of death, their barely-conscious bodies were thrown over a wall onto waste ground at Penny Lane, Milltown. Two IRA gunmen – known to me and still alive and at large but I cannot give you their names – had been called in to do the hit once that awful mob had finished with those two poor lads. The guns used in the attack had been brought in by the Republican black taxis and were smuggled to the two men.

The surveillance helicopter now came down to about 80 feet [there is an unconfirmed report that the rear gunner is heard requesting permission to open fire with his GPMG but none is forthcoming] and the two IRA men, already identified at that stage, put their jackets to cover their heads and faces. One gunman shoots the first man – lying unconscious and helpless – in the head and the helicopter comes down even lower. At this stage, the second badly hurt Corporal is seen fighting like a demon as he fights to save his life and at this

Memorial to Derek Wood – murdered by the IRA, Penny Lane, Belfast

moment gunman 'X' shoots him in the head. The second gunman then calmly shoots both men twice even though they are at this stage probably already dead.

The men then split up and one is seen getting into a red Ford Sierra and is driven away from the scene with the helicopter in pursuit into the St James area. Within minutes it arrives at a garage workshop and drives inside and the helicopter pilot tried to call in a mobile patrol onto the position. Suddenly, the garage doors are flung open and two red Ford Sierras speed out and shoot off in opposite directions; the pilot has the agonising choice of only being able to chase one. As posterity has recorded, he chased the wrong one.

It has long been considered in intelligence circles that the two car plot was a well planned and executed ploy by the IRA; not that the murders of the two Corporals was anything but random and tragic ill-luck, but rather, in the event of needing to throw a helicopter off the scent.

AFTER THE FUNERAL KILLINGS: 1988

WO1 Phil Gilbert, 1 Scots (Formerly 1 Royal Scots)

The following information will be known by those who read the daily newspaper accounts pertaining to Northern Ireland (NI) during 'The Troubles'.

The following account covers a mere 5 days of an enjoyable, yet challenging, career. A snapshot of my time serving in the British Army, on a tour of duty in NI, which was to be one of many. Wrong place, right time? Or right place, wrong time?

I was three-quarters of the way through a four month tour of West Belfast; a Cpl in A Company, then 1st Battalion The Royal Scots (The Royal Regiment) which today is known to all as 1 Scots (The Royal Regiment of Scotland). We were stationed at Fort Whiterock at the top of the Turf Lodge estate in West Belfast. It was a busy time with lots of direct and indirect incidents throughout the Battalion Tactical Area of Responsibility (TAOR). Moreover, we were also the first Regiment in NI with the newly issued SA80 rifle.

On Sunday 6 March 1988 three individuals, who we were told were Irish Republican Army (IRA) members, were shot dead by undercover members of the Special Air Service (SAS) in Gibraltar. It was reported, by eyewitnesses, that no warning shots were given. As I understand, the incident occurred because the British government believed that a bomb was about to be detonated. Whilst I do not claim to know the exact facts surrounding this incident, I do know that this incident resulted in intense controversy and a chain of events which, not only led to more deaths in the forthcoming weeks, but due to my army career were also to have an impact on me personally.

The rights and wrongs meant nothing to me at the time; I was only twenty five years old, a Team Commander, responsible for three other team members and part of a multiple of twelve men.

On our Patrol's cycle, which usually lasted two to three days, I was tasked to provide part of a cordon around the home of one of the deceased individuals. This was intended to deter a 'show of strength' by the Irish Republican Army (IRA) when the cortège arrived back from Gibraltar. We positioned ourselves in a cordon around a house half-way up the Turf Lodge Estate in a mundane 'twelve on, twelve off' scenario. We settled into the routine with no problem at all. Twelve hours over, relief in place and so on and so forth. This was not to last. A volunteer of the IRA, who had allegedly been engaged in harassing our Fort with sporadic fire earlier in the week, decided to take on one of the Teams providing the protective cordon. To cut a long story short, this individual was killed through the bravery of one of my colleagues, a Team Commander, who assessed the danger and dealt with the individual mentioned with total unselfish disregard for his own safety. Consequently, he was decorated with a 'Mention in Dispatches' on March 14, 1988.

We continued patrolling in Anderstown and around Fort Whiterock in order to prevent mortar attacks. On March 16, the routine was suddenly interrupted by a Loyalist gunman disrupting the IRA funeral in Milltown cemetery; more were to be left injured or dead, an unwelcome escalation in a very tense period. This also meant some attention from the local residents who were, understandably, directing their attention at us both verbally and physically.

We then moved from Patrols to 'Blues', to form part of a joint patrol with the-then Royal Ulster Constabulary (RUC). We were familiar with our role within the joint 'Blues' patrol, and enjoyed both the hospitality of the RUC Woodburn canteen and the way of life. Our settling-in period was to be shortlived. On the 19th of March, we were at the gate inside RUC Woodburn waiting to deploy. The funeral cortège of one of the Milltown Loyalist killings [by paramilitary Michael Stone] was interrupted by two individuals who approached the cortège head-on in a silver VW Passat. A Lynx helicopter above relayed a football-like commentary of the events on the Anderstown Road. We all sat quietly; speechless and helpless, within the confines of our armoured Land Rover. Was this an audacious Loyalist attack like three days before?

Having endured the professional commentary from the Lynx pilots (which, with hindsight, we could have done without) we were ordered to move to Penny Lane, a barren piece of ground at the back of the shops off the Anderstown Road. On arrival, I stepped out of the vehicle and was confronted by two motionless individuals lying on their backs in the open wasteland; they were clothed in just their underwear and socks, and a car was alight 50m away; it was burning furiously. A priest was giving the last rites; he then moved on.

I checked for a pulse on both of the bodies, unaware of their identity. They were both dead. The sight of the bodies didn't unnerve me, as they looked so peaceful. My thoughts at that time were of anger but I still had a job to do. I covered them up with blankets from my vehicle. After a while, the Fire Service arrived and extinguished the fire and it was then that a chill went down my spine; an armoured plate was identified behind the driver's seat. These were our guys ... and I will never forget this incident.

To forget them would mean that their sacrifice was in vain.

The two soldiers killed in this shocking incident as stated earlier belonged to the Royal Corps of Signals and why they had strayed into such a sensitive situation has, as I wrote earlier, has never been satisfactorily explained. Their murder by a baying mob sickened the watching world and marked a new low in the savagery of Northern Ireland.

BALLYGAWLEY, 1988

David Hardy, Light Infantry

I left the UK around lunchtime to arrive in Ireland one hour later, but we were driven backwards and forwards from airport to airport picking up soldiers; some flights were late, some delayed, and so we finally left Belfast International around 11.30pm or 23.30 hours.

Just as we were about to leave the airport, I can remember this guy standing outside the bus looking at me and as he did so he pulled his finger across his throat, you know when you see it on telly when they give the sign to behead some one, that sign or motion? I thought about that every day since: IF ONLY, I had gotten off, told someone, confronted him and asked him why, but if only me auntie had bal** she would have been my uncle.

So I lay across the seats, my feet on the seats at the other side of the bus, my head was vibrating on the window, so I pulled my leather biker's jacket over it to stop the vibration and dozed off.

The terrorists made a mistake that night; they got their calculations wrong – just a bit. I am pleased that they did as I might not be here to tell you about it. Remember the equation Time= Distance= Speed – well that's the one that they got wrong.

The bus had already passed the bomb, (which, by the way was two fertilizer bags filled with semtex) all 200lb of it; they just laid them on the road side and put a little dirt on top to cover them up. They had used a telegraph pole as a marker; when the bus reached it they would detonate the bomb; the bus will be doing about 40mph, so what you do is put the bomb just after the pole so by the time the bus gets to the pole and you react and push the button the bus will just be past the pole itself, right where the bomb is. Wrong! The bus driver knew that the lads just wanted to get back to barracks and get their heads down, as they were cream crackered from hanging about all day, so he was speeding and the bus was well past the bomb by the time they set it off.

I had just done the explosives course so I could have levelled Durham Cathedral with 50 lb. You see, semtex needs a resistance; ok put a lb on the living room floor and set it off, and the result will be a scorched carpet maybe a broken window. Now stuff the same lb in to a tin with a screw top and cram it somewhere; get the picture?

It was a beautiful summer's night with a full moon; was it hell! It was August, cold and raining as I lay there face down, I was on the verge pointing towards the ditch. I only know this because I was at an angle and my head was lower than my body.

As I lay there, my vision started to come back and my brain started to kick in; like your PC when you first start it, it takes a little time to run through the various programs before you can start to do ' out with it.

My instinct was to get up to find out what had happened, but my body was telling me otherwise, these extra joints seemed to come from nowhere, my legs lay at a funny angle but there was no pain, then I heard crying moaning and groaning- it sickened me to the gut. It went through me like someone scratching their nails down the black board; I never want to hear that again as long as I live.

As I lay there wondering why I could not stand up, this huge bright white light came from nowhere, it was so bright that it should have hurt you eyes but it didn't. As the light started to get brighter, this overwhelming feeling came over me of peace, calm and not a care in the world, (it was the most beautiful feeling that I have ever had). I believe it was death staring me in the face and if that was death I no longer fear it. I could no longer hear the sounds of the rain or the lads crying. All of a sudden this guy walked straight out of the light, I was not scared or worried he just said 'everything is going to be all right', the words seeming to fill the air around me. I could not see his face but I knew it was a guy. I could see his arms, legs, body and head but like a mist or fog where his face was. All that I can remember saying was 'what do you mean every thing is going to be f****** all right, just help me get up' then with that everything went black again.

This next bit is based on what I have been told, whether by my parents, nurses, doctors, surgeons or what I have read in my medical notes.

I was taken to hospital in the back of a Range Rover by a local, and I thank him/her for it, we are not talking on the back seat here, we are saying the back seat the back-like boot and tail gate down.

On arriving at Dungannon or Duncannon hospital, they said there was nothing that they could do for me here and that I needed to go to the Royal Victoria Infirmary in Belfast, this is about 50 mile or so away. I think I was airlifted but not sure. With that they splinted, bandaged, gave fluids and I was on my way. In my records I was in and out of consciousness, laughing and joking with the nurses as you do, then my pupils went full blown, they thought that I had a massive seizure but no one knows.

Meanwhile, my parents were at home in bed. My dad got up the next morning to go to work, and as he was having breakfast he listened to the radio and heard what was going on, but they were not giving details. He told my mam, but they thought that they would have heard something by now, so at around 7.00am he went to work.

At work he was still very worried that no details had been given yet, and could not concentrate on his work so the boss sent him home. Ten minutes after arriving home, at around 12.00 noon, a police car pulled up outside the house. Knocking on the door they said,' are you Mr and Mrs Hardy? Your son David has been injured; you have fifteen minutes to pack a bag; you're going to the airport.'

Now my mam and dad had never flown before and had booked a holiday to Florida, my mam was worried about flying but when she landed in NI she had never given it a second thought.

As they sped along the A1M to Newcastle Airport, clocking 100+ mph they got to the airport, no passports; never thought about them, straight on to the tarmac and on to the plane, but they had to go to Heathrow or Gatwick. Cannot remember if they held the plane there until they arrived, then they set off to NI. They were met by an Officer that said that he was my Platoon Commander or knew me anyway, and then off to the hospital.

List of David's Injuries:

Left thigh broken in 2 places. This caused a rupture in the femoral artery; they had to take a lump of vein from my right leg to use as a sort of bandage.
Left shin and calf bone shattered with bone loss (1 inch shorter in this leg)
Left ankle rebuilt.
Left calf missing (had to replace it with muscle taken from stomach free flap abdominal only, got a 3 pack!)
Right shin and calf bone broken in 3 places.
Both left & right legs heavily skin grafted.
8 ribs broken.
Left fore arm broken.
Left upper arm broken.
Collapsed lungs (needed ventilating.)
Bleeding of the brain (three holes in the head to relieve pressure) (subdural haemorrhaging?)
3/4 blind in left eye.

21 pints of blood in one 11 hour operation taken out of theatre for 2 hours, then back in, 7 pints of blood in the next 14 hour op.

I was called a polytraumatized person. That means you had one if not several injuries of which at least one was life threatening!

Ok – in the hospital, my mother was shown to where I was in I.C.U. The security was tight, very tight. There were 2 RUC lads at the door at all times, all IDs had to be shown to get in, doctors, surgeons and nursing staff. When my mother first saw me she nearly fainted. Metal, bandages, wires, tubes. You name it, it was sticking out. She told me that she could just see my face, every thing else was covered. As she removed my ring, the one she got me for my 18th, my whole body started to swell my head went to the size of a football and my scrotum (ball sack) stared to swell under the sheet. At this time she says bells and buzzers started to go off.

The days passed, though the daily hospital routine was a logistical nightmare. It took six or more nurses to change the sheets every three days as the bed was full of dead skin and stained. Dressings were painful to change too as they had to be eased off, and even though I was on pain relief I could still feel them working. They gave me gas at these times though, and it made me float around the room. It was not only the dressings of course, all 24 pins and frames holding my legs together had to be cleaned every day. I felt a bit like a well-polished car. I realised by now the importance of changing the dressings daily, as I could smell the results! Things got better over the weeks, and I managed to joke that maggots might be cheaper than dressings!

I remember one nurse giving me a bed bath, which I looked forward to because I smelled, and she covered a sponge with foam and whacked me straight in the jewels. That woke me up I can tell you! I also had to have my teeth cleaned for me as I couldn't bend my arms, so I made that a goal, to be able to move them. It took about two weeks, but I did it in the end.

I think that's what got me through it, setting little goals as I progressed. I never had any doubt that I would never walk again. I just thought I would be up and about in a couple of weeks, though my weeks were longer than anyone else's. That's because I was out for so long, and time meant nothing really.

The nurses were brilliant though, and I thank them.

8 soldiers from the 1st Battalion, the Light Infantry were killed and 27 injured, including David Hardy, in that landmine attack at Curr near Ballygawley roundabout, County Tyrone, on August 20th, while travelling back by coach to base in Omagh from the International Airport at Aldergrove.

By some miracle, David survived.

The men killed in the IRA bomb attack – all Privates – were: Blair Bishop (19), Jason Burfitt (19), Peter Bullock (21), Richard Greener (21), Alexander Lewis (18), Mark Norsworthy (18), Stephen Wilkinson (18) and Jason Winter who was 19.

Mrs Rachel Hardy

Just before the incident – about a week before – I was at the local hospital and they had arranged a Tarot card reading and I was getting some funny looks and funny questions from the reader. She said that she saw me surrounded by men! I didn't think any more about it, but a week later, I was in Musgrave Park, Belfast surrounded by loads of men!

I remember the date so well; it was Friday 19 August and I had missed saying goodbye to David and giving him a hug before he went back to Ireland after his leave. I felt restless all night and woke in the early hours with a really bad headache [David's Light Infantry coach was hit by an IRA landmine at 12:20 am]. At 8:15 am, the phone rang and it was my husband Arnie, who had gone off to work early in his van; he had been listening to the radio and had some news about a bus in Ireland. He asked me to put the TV on and I saw what had happened to David. I started to cry and David's brother Alan who was 17 at the time and also a soldier, told me not to worry. But I said to him 'Come and look at the state of this bus' as the first pictures unfolded of the wreckage.

There was no contact telephone number or anything, and I was shocked and hysterical and I remember picking up the phone and calling the Operator. I was in tears and told her what had happened and that I desperately needed to speak to someone in the Army. She was lovely, promising to find out and phone me back, which, shortly afterwards she did, giving me a number which I instantly rang. I managed to speak to someone in the Army and explained who I was; I was greeted by a barrage of questions about his age, destination and even my Mother's maiden name! I now understand the need for security as there are some very sick people about. [Interestingly and poignantly, one of the badly wounded soldiers managed to crawl to a telephone box and made several calls for help but was not believed initially].

They told me that David was on the bus and that he was 'stable.' I didn't even know what stable meant at the time! It was now 8:30 am and I phoned my daughter Angela's workplace, and asked them to drive her home as I didn't want her driving; in the meantime, Arnie had returned home. As soon as she walked in, she immediately asked 'Is it our David?' The morning wore on with no further news and then, at 1pm, two uniformed policemen arrived at the door and informed us that we had 15 minutes to pack our bags as they were taking us to Newcastle airport. Off we roared, sirens sounding, blue lights flashing, reaching speeds of 140 mph, although they did, at one stage, have to stop for petrol!

We had been due to fly to Florida the next week anyway – neither of us had ever flown before – and we were doubly nervous. An Army officer met us and showed us great sympathy and he took us to the plane, which had been delayed just for us. We flew to Heathrow as there were no direct flights to Belfast that day and even the Heathrow flight was delayed for us. We landed in Ireland and were taken by a member of staff who escorted us to the arrivals area; it was there that I got chatting to a person whom I took to be a policeman, but within seconds, a Light Infantry captain, by the name of Baker, dressed in civvies came over to us. He recognised Arnie as they looked alike and we were driven to a place in Belfast where other anxious families were gathered, waiting for news of their loved ones.

This was now some 14 hours since the news of the attack, and almost 22 hours since the landmine exploded. I now know that the delay was, certainly in our case, because it was still 'touch and go' for David. An RUC officer later told me that he had been with David when he arrived at the hospital, and that he didn't think that he would live. After that, a plainclothes soldier took us to Musgrave Park RUC station, and then we were bundled into an armoured RUC vehicle full of armed officers and an Army escort, and rushed to the Royal Victoria Hospital. When we arrived, we were surrounded by these armed police and marched down a corridor with people moving out of our way and into ICU. I didn't recognise David until a nurse pulled me back and took me to his bed, when

I saw the state that he was in, my legs just buckled [the author was shown a serious of photographs of David 3 weeks afterwards and his injuries, even at that stage were horrific].

His body – normally lean and athletic as he was in the battalion ski team – had expanded due to the effects of the explosion. He was on a ventilator and under a 24 hour armed guard. He was on this deliberately, as he was put in to a coma because the sheer pain would have killed him. After about 2 and a half weeks we were called in, as they were going to attempt to wake him a little, just enough to ask one or two simple questions, or even to see if he could recognise us. He had a massive bruise on the back of the neck, and had had a large clot removed from inside his skull via 3 burr holes; this was also to relieve pressure within the skull itself, so they wanted to know if there was any brain damage. They told us to prepare for the worst because of the injuries; they started to step the medication that they were giving him down, and over a period of time he suddenly opened his eyes a little, he looked at me and said 'What are you doing here? (At this point I was relieved, to a degree, that he knew who I was, and that he knew where he was and that we should not be there, but he was still nowhere near out of the woods) I've just left!' He thought that he had just left England for N.I., so had no comprehension that he had been in a coma for over two weeks. To him it was as if he had blinked and no time had gone at all, this had him confused a little; he then looked at me again and said: 'Oh, yes; the wheel came off the bus!' at which point they put him back to sleep for a few more weeks as the pain was still an issue.

During the 5 weeks I spent in Belfast, there were loads of explosions and the RUC had to block off a lot of roads. We couldn't see David every day, and there was one 48 hour period where we couldn't get through because of bombed buses and burned-out cars, and then there were shift change problems and getting the armed driver to get to us. When we did see him, I was very concerned because his legs were smelling, which might have been gangrene. They were in such a state that I was worried about amputation; as I knew that David would rather have died than lose his legs. Later on, more details of the explosion emerged, and because the landmine had detonated near a village, the noise had been heard and the villagers came out to help using their car headlights to light up the scene. Also, because it was raining, the flames had been doused pretty quickly. It later transpired that behind the Light Infantry coach, there had been another one carrying an Orange Order marching band, and that they were probably the IRA's intended target. All the men in the second coach helped pull the survivors out of the mangled ruins, even though I will probably never meet them I cannot thank them and anyone else enough, not just for saving David, but for saving many lives that dreadful night.

He was later moved out of the ICU, and I didn't feel that he was safe because the security was not as tight. During my time there, a hospital porter passed by and sniggered and said out aloud: 'Eight-nil.' Fortunately for him, I didn't understand the insult at the time until an RUC officer explained it to me. David was still very seriously ill when they helicoptered him to Woolwich hospital in London.

Time has healed a little bit, but I still feel bitter about the whole thing.

Later on, the Army sent me a box with all his personal possessions in it, a lot of it was bloodstained. What crossed my mind, was that, had he died, this would have been all that I had left of him.

Having met David and Rachel personally, I can attest to the poignancy and emotional heartbreak this family suffered and the above interview is a tribute to his fantastic family.

Just 2 days later, the first Royal Navy fatality of the troubles, Lieutenant Alan Shields, 45, a Navy recruiting officer was killed when the IRA booby-trapped his car as he drove to his home in Bangor, Co Down.

Just 12 days after that appalling attack on the Light Infantry's bus, three members of the IRA were killed in an ambush by the SAS at Drumnakilly. The IRA had gone with the intention of murdering an off-duty UDR man at his job, but found themselves on the receiving end of the attack.

OSTENDE, BELGIUM: 1988

Major Allan Harrhy, RRW

By this year, I was a Captain and Families' Officer at the Battalion and, whilst this incident takes place away from Northern Ireland, it is nevertheless directly connected with it, and I would like to pay a tribute to my friend RSM Richard Heakin. In fact, he was a very close pal of mine and I still feel very bitter about his murder.

The Bn had been posted back to the UK and a lot of the families had flown, with their ultimate destination being Warminster. Richard was driving the family car home from Germany where he had been based. He reached Ostende and was heading for the ferry terminal and he was stopped at some traffic lights. Two IRA terrorists were sitting on a bench near the lights. They spotted his distinctive BAOR number plates and these two cowardly killers calmly walked forward and shot him dead. These cowards had been sitting just waiting for an opportunity to kill anyone in a British car with Army number plates. Poor Richard was simply in the wrong place at the wrong time.

Just the night before, I had met his wife and their two young children (9 and 7) off the flight at Luton; as families' Officer and because they were late in, I had met them and helped them and their luggage into a hotel for the night. I travelled back to Warminster and was met immediately upon my arrival and informed of Richard's murder. Because he was my friend, I volunteered to drive back to Luton and pass on the awful news to his family.

I had to wake them at 5 am and tell a distraught woman that her husband and the kiddies' dad had been murdered by the IRA. That was the most horrible moment of my life.

For the life of me, I cannot see how the killing of an unarmed man, going home on leave, whilst waiting at traffic lights, can further the cause of Irish Nationalism in any shape of form.

North Armagh (photo courtesy of Regimental Museum of The Royal Welsh)

Richard Heakin's murderers were never caught and few eyewitnesses could agree on the descriptions of the killers. The British Government immediately scrapped the distinctive Army number plates. An IRA spokesman representing the murderers warned that any member of the Crown forces was subject to attack wherever they were.

BENBURB: 23 NOVEMBER 1988
Private David Creese, 1st Glosters

We had just returned to Dungannon SF Base after a foot patrol; it was the end of our operational day and we were looking forward to some downtime. The base stood on the top of a small hill, near the outskirts of the town, and we were stationed there in company strength for between 6 to 8 weeks at a time; our accommodation was one of 7 portacabins containing 11 bunks, so as you can imagine there was not very much room for us with all our kit, but then again it was only there for us to sleep in and we did not get very much of that.

As we were sorting out our kit, we heard a loud rumbling sound in the distance. We all suspected the noise was a bomb, but we all continued with what we were doing. Only two minutes or so had passed, when suddenly the ops room runner burst in through the door, and told us to get our kit back on and assemble on the helipad. A van bomb had gone off outside Benburb R.U.C station about 8 miles from our location. We all boarded the Wessex helicopter, and flew to Benburb. During the flight the adrenalin was pumping through our veins as we prepared for the unknown. The flight did not take long, and we were there in minutes.

We touched down in a field about 200 metres from the R.U.C station, jumped out from the Wessex, took up fire positions on the ground until the chopper left, and then advanced towards the station. Once we had reached the road, we cordoned off the area. The road was strewn with debris from the explosion, all of the houses near the station had had their windows shattered, and their curtains were flapping in the wind. At the time of the explosion 2 people had been passing the station and were killed instantly – a young girl (Emma Donnelly) and her grandfather (Bernard Laverty aged 67). The force of the explosion had thrown their bodies into the field opposite the R.U.C station, and the bodies had to be recovered by 2 volunteers. It was the one and only time in my army career where I was given a choice whether to do a task or not. A number of us stood silent, then 2 guys stepped forward and said they would do it. When the job was done, they came back and told us what they had seen and done.

I can now say to be truthfully honest; I am glad that I do not have to live with those memories.

The two victims were driving past the RUC station at Benburb when the van, hijacked earlier, exploded, killing them both instantly. The IRA – as usual – claimed to have given an adequate warning which the police deny. In killing a well-known Catholic and an equally innocent young schoolgirl they committed yet another atrocity against the community they claimed to defend. Emma Donnelly was only 13 years old.

NEW BARNSLEY, 1988
Private Tim Castle, Light Infantry

ATO features again during our final weeks in New Barnsley, Cookie, he of the 'come on' shooting in the Beechmounts, managed to find another command wire IED. This time it was in a hedge on Divismore Way almost on the outside of the estate. I can't remember exactly whether the command wire was found before or after the bomb, but there was a few days gap and neither was found together. Cookie, I believe, nearly lay on top of the beer keg. We put in a cordon and ATO was tasked. A very nice man, but sadly he seemed to forget to tell the locals that he was about to fire a disruptor charge. Either that or because he was using the new CLC, a mini hayrick charge on a roll, the blast was something else and destroyed lots of windows in the area!

Our team had to attend court during this period as we were witnesses to an arrest made by the RUC DMSU [Divisional Mobile Search Unit]. I also was warned as an arresting soldier that I would be back for court eventually.

Belfast Magistrates court is a strange place; soldiers in mufti trying not to look like soldiers mingling with the families, and in some cases the actual people they had arrested. All in all a very surreal experience, but a chance to be driven through Belfast City centre to see what we were trying to keep in one piece.

The funny bit was, the escort we were given was armed with a 9mm pistol. We all went to the gents for a wiz before being called to court. As the escort walked back up to our court through the lobby his jacket was caught between his pistol and his back. Yes, just about everyone saw it! Mind you we were left alone from then!

Sadly less than a year later Cookie was deafened almost completely at Sennelager ranges during field firing, and this scruffy little likeable Yorkshireman was medically discharged.

Chapter Twenty-Two

1989

A year of 427 bombings, 566 shootings and the deaths of 21 soldiers, 9 RUC officers, 37 civilians and 2 terrorists.

On 22 September that year, the IRA planted a bomb at the Royal Marines School of Music in Deal, Kent and killed 11 Marine musicians.

This year saw the distressing sight of an off-duty RAF Corporal, Islania Maheshkumar, shot and killed along with his baby daughter at Wildenrath in West Germany. The IRA 'apologised' for its mistake.

It also saw the loss of three young Paras, as their vehicle was destroyed by an IRA landmine, at Mayobridge in Armagh.

A new tactic by the IRA was unveiled at a border checkpoint at Fermanagh; not only did they use guns and grenades, but also a home-made flamethrower. Two members of the King's Own Scottish Borderers were killed in this incident a few weeks before Christmas and another was seriously injured as up to 12 terrorists made this mass attack.

ANDERSONSTOWN ROBBERY: 1989

Lance Corporal 'Ossie' Osbourne, Queen's Regiment

I was a newly promoted L/Cpl and it was a time when the IRA was still in full force. I was with the 2nd Battalion the Queen's Regiment in West Belfast. The Company was based in Fort Whiterock close to the Turf Lodge and Ballymurphy estates; I have to admit it was a very exciting tour; scary at times but always a buzz. It was during a joint RUC/Army Patrol through the Turf from Fort Whiterock to Old Andersonstown RUC station.

I went firm with my team outside a newsagents waiting to be called into the Police Station by the boss. My ex-partner had just given birth to my eldest son and I noticed a football in the shop window. I am ashamed to admit it, but I started to daydream a little and I imagined my son playing with the football at home in our garden. Suddenly I got the call over the radio to move into the RUC station and I instructed the lads to double in, which we did. As soon as we got in to the Police Station we were fast-balled (deployed) back out to a street just a few yards from where I had gone firm only 2 minutes earlier. I held the team in their positions and waited for further instructions.

After about 30 minutes the lads and I were getting a little pissed off, we did not know why we were moved back out so quickly and had no idea how long we were going to have to stay out! I saw an RUC Officer standing by the newsagent where I had been day dreaming just a short while earlier. I approached him and asked him what was happening.

'You will not believe it,' he replied 'this place has just been robbed and one of you lot were standing outside as it happened!'

'Oh, really,' I said, and slunk away feeling a little stupid!

It turned out that two lads had held up the newsagent with a pistol; they demanded all the fags and the cash in the till. As the owner was about to start loading the 'swag' into a bag I appeared in the window and scared the crap out them. I had been too busy daydreaming and did not see a thing, even though I looked straight at them. Once I left, the two robbers fled with only 200 cigs to their name.

My chance of medals and fame was missed, all because of a football.

As a matter of thought, I was recently in Iraq and was part of a foot patrol in Al Amarah. It was my first time on patrol there, and I have to admit to being a little nervous. Before we moved out, I remember the feelings I had were exactly the same as the ones I had just before I moved out of Fort Whiterock, West Belfast for the first time. Different tours, different locations, different enemy, 18 years apart, but the same strong feelings of nerves and the unknown. It was strange how I recognised the feelings even with the two events being so far apart.

On that 1988/89 tour, the Queen's lost one man: Corporal Alexander Bannister who died on August 8, shot by an IRA sniper at New Barnsley, 24 days earlier. Corporal Bannister was just 21 and came from Kent.

AN INCIDENT NEAR EDERNEY – ALMOST!

Mike H. RSM, 4 UDR

In the Province, for all sorts of obvious reasons, the most innocent of activities can be misunderstood or appear to be sinister and such an incident took place between Ederney and Pettigoe in County Fermanagh in 1989.

My wife, Sandie, and I were attached to 4 UDR and during our two years with the Battalion had made many friends and enjoyed a good social life despite the troubles. This particular day we were off to some friends for dinner; they ran a farm between Ederney and Pettigoe near the South West Border with the Republic. He was also a SNCO with the Regiment and so a natural target and had therefore briefed me on the route to take, places to look out for and the final approach etc – all things with which you became quite used to and familiar with.

As we sped down the long lake shore road that runs between Irvinestown and Belleek I spotted a figure who had suddenly popped up from behind a large, high hedgerow of Leylandii, running alongside a house about 100 metres distant. I grabbed my PPW and tried to stuff my very protesting and wriggling wife into the foot well, whilst I steered the car with my knees and raised the weapon to fire as we sped by, a manoeuvre not to be done without a desperate need. As we drew alongside this hedgerow, I prepared to fire and the figure reappeared and as I began pressing the trigger and concentrated on keeping my wife from forcing herself into the line of fire, the hedge trimmer that he was using became very obvious, at that point I nearly lost all! My wife forced herself skywards protesting

South Armagh: a lucky escape for members of C Company, 3rd Battalion the Queen's Regiment. Two Land Rovers were targeted by a 500lb bomb detonated by command wire, hidden in a derelict building. The fact that they were driving erratically put the terrorists off! There were no serious injuries. (Photos courtesy of Darren Croucher)

very loudly as the car commenced to swerve quite violently and I then dropped the pistol!

The next 100 yards were a blur of angry wife, very wobbly driver and desperate attempts to stay on the road and it was probably some 400 metres later that I felt I had enough control and could avoid the flailing arms of my really pissed-off wife, that I stopped to explain and cool her ruffled feathers whilst I mopped my sweating brow.

The severe lack of sympathy that I got from our hosts, and my wife, over dinner, only added to my embarrassment but the amusement at least calmed the situation in my adrenalin-filled underwear, and it could have been so very tragic for all concerned, if I had fired when the urge told me to! All is sometimes not what it appears in the combat zone and collateral damage is rarely acceptable!

The thin gossamer thread of fate which spared the unsuspecting gardener's life could, so capriciously, have taken another person's existence. Only two years earlier, in the same area where Mike had almost killed accidentally, 39 year old UDR Corporal James Oldman was shot by the IRA as he arrived at work.

NORTHERN IRELAND: 1988/9

Lieutenant Colonel G.P.Moss, King's Own Borderers

During the course of these years, I was posted to HQNI and had the opportunity to observe and understand a change in IRA tactics. For example, just two ASUs both operating independently of the other and being generally unaware of their respective members and organisation committed the bulk of murders and attacks in 1988 and 1989.

We had by and large pinned down both these two units of the IRA and although they were responsible for possibly 30 of the 38 military and police deaths, the figures were down on previous years. Some of the killings of SF personnel were of the random, opportunistic nature, where a squaddie or RUC man might present an unpredicted but nonetheless, unmissable target.

In the case of both the Lisburn bomb attack and the appalling tragedy of the Ballygawley coach attack where 8 Light Infantry boys were killed returning home from leave, a third ASU had crept under the radar. This third element was entirely unexpected but had catastrophic consequences. In this year, one man alone had been responsible for over 20 Army and RUC deaths.

That man was known to us at the time and is still known to us but for some reason, he was untouchable; today he lives a 'respectable' life.

Chapter Twenty-Three

1990

A year of 310 bombings, 559 shootings and the deaths of 15 soldiers, 12 RUC officers, 45 civilians and 4 terrorists.

This year saw the deaths of 5 soldiers and an Army civilian worker when the IRA bombed an Army checkpoint at Coshquin, Donegal, a border crossing near Londonderry. This involved the IRA's first use of the proxy bomb when a 42 year old man, Patsy Gillespie was forced to drive a bomb in his own vehicle to the checkpoint being manned by soldiers of the King's Regiment. This act was described by the Catholic Bishop of Londonderry as 'crossing a new threshold of evil' and marked a new low in the history of the troubles.

It witnessed the murder of Queen's soldier Sergeant Charles Chapman outside the Army Careers office in Wembley, London, with an I.E.D. planted under a minibus. The IRA murdered Private William Davies of the RRW on a railway platform in Staffordshire and then ventured back on to the continent to kill Major Mike Dillon-Lee of the R.A. in Dortmund, West Germany.

The IRA murdered 2 Australian tourists in May near an Army camp in Holland mistaking them for off duty soldiers.

It was also another year in which off-duty UDR men were targeted and by the end of this year, 8 had been killed.

BALLYKELLY: 1990

Kingsman Jason Hughes, 1 King's Regiment

Life as a Kingsman in Ballykelly was a myriad of weeks away in varying parts of the country with short spells in camp before the next deployment. A good thing really as the buildings were old Second World War huts with a tendency to flood at the merest sight of rain. A little unfortunate considering the climatic conditions of our country. As all soldiers will tell you time away means more money for drink on your return providing you are single of course, so no one seemed to mind too much and it was what you came here for anyway.

I remember arriving in the province on the Hercules, being flown straight into the camp, unsure of what lay ahead; on reflection the training prior to arrival as much as preparing you for the job in hand, has you wound-up like a top and suspecting everyone of being a terrorist. This would take several months to dull the edge of fear and suspicion, the reality of meeting these people on the street and having to talk to them whilst knowing the horrific acts of violence they were suspected of committing was quite something else. It has always been a little difficult even to the end, understanding why there never seemed to be enough evidence to put these people away.

Start of tour; raring to go!

The most horrific incident by far to happen during our time here was the human bomb on the checkpoint in Londonderry known as V2 where five of our lads were killed along with the driver of the car. Whilst not being actually involved in the bombing it highlighted the best and worst extremes of the country. My story of the incident is from just after the explosion happened.

My platoon was working out of Coalisland police station on that fateful night; I remember the call coming over the radio that the bomb had gone off and there had been casualties, although the number was not disclosed at this point. We were told to move to an HLZ [meaning either a hot landing zone or more commonly a helicopter landing zone] and get ready to move back to Ballykelly as we were to be redeployed as cordon troops. The return was done in almost silence; the anger was evident but kept simmering below the surface.

Within a short period of time we had taken up cordon positions around the perimeter of the explosion and I say this loosely as the area that debris had been thrown was so huge. The proximity of the checkpoint to a housing estate had also meant that almost every window in the estate had been blown in; how no residents had been killed was a complete surprise. [17 civilians were injured and 25 homes badly damaged which shows the contempt the IRA had for people who were nominally at least, their supporters.]

From our position at a road junction a short distance away the carnage was very evident, and the job we had was to keep people away from the scene and then go out on patrol in case of further attacks. It was later that day the names of those killed were released, and it was then that I found out my room mate from Berlin – our previous location prior to here – as well as a friend I had gone through training with had both been killed. It made the next two weeks we spent living on a street corner very hard indeed. Due to operational commitments we never even got to the funerals and that is something that has lived with me all these years.

The only bright point to come out of this dark time was the local people and the compassion they showed to us which was completely unexpected, they fed us and kept us in coffee for the complete length of time we were resident there. This was the first time I began to see that the place may have a brighter future.

The incident to which Jason refers – and mentioned in the chapter preamble – took place at a PVCP in Buncrana Road, Coshquin outside Londonderry on 24 October, 1990. The Provisional IRA used a 'proxy bomb' for the first time when they abducted and held hostage the family of a local man Patsy Gillespie. He was tied into the car and told to drive to the PVCP or his family would all be killed. Patsy was 42 and worked on an Army base in the area and it is thought that the IRA used this to sickeningly justify their appalling actions.

The bomb detonated as the van arrived at the checkpoint and despite bravely shouting out a warning to the soldiers, the bomb detonated and Patsy and five soldiers of the King's Regiment – recruited from the Lancashire/Cheshire area – were killed. Seconds after the explosion, IRA gunmen opened fire on the devastated position from the Republic side of the border.

The soldiers were: Kingsman Stephen Beacham (20) from Warrington; Lance Corporal Stephen Burrows (30) from Blackpool; Kingsman Vincent Scott (21) from Liverpool who was in his final few weeks in the Army; Kingsman David

Memorial to Patsy Gillespie, killed by IRA proxy bomb which also killed 5 Kingsmen at Coshquin (photo courtesy of George Prosser)

RCT soldiers, Belfast (photo courtesy of Phil Morris)

Sweeney (19) from Widnes and Kingsman Paul Worrall who was 23 and from Runcorn.

Patsy Gillespie was a 42 year old man who lived at Galliagh near Shantallow and worked on the Fort George base. He was married with three children and a testimony must be paid to his bravery in trying to warn the soldiers who were manning the VCP. The IRA clearly developed the concept of the suicide bomber in their usual well-planned, meticulously cowardly way.

Three soldiers' children and Mr Gillespie's three children were left fatherless by the outrage.

BELFAST & LOCALITY 1988 –90

Paul, UDR

I served with the Royal Irish Regiment, formerly known as the Ulster Defence Regiment (UDR), for two years and three months between 1988 and 1990, predominantly in Belfast and the surrounding area, as well as tours on the border region. Our main aims were to deter the transport of munitions and disrupt terrorism within the province in support of the Royal Ulster Constabulary.

I was nineteen years old and I had just completed high school in a different country. My main reason for joining the UDR was to gain experience in a disciplined organisation, with a view to joining the police. It seemed terribly exciting to be on active service being so young (naïve!) I must state that I did not come from a Loyalist family. I had strong sentiments about 'the Troubles' of my homeland, but that was that, I simply wanted stable employment with a view to building a future for me and my country.

I never came under 'contact', i.e. army parlance for coming under fire, but I did see and get involved in some rather violent encounters, especially against our 'occupying force' by Republicans and their sympathisers.

On one occasion, whilst patrolling the Markets area of Belfast, our armoured Land Rover was hit with what appeared to be a full bottle of wine, given the nature of the small explosion, what was splashed and the amount of shattered glass on my clothing. I remember chuckling to myself thinking that given the area of our patrol it must have been a cheap bottle of plonk, as opposed to any sort of vintage. Anyway, missile throwing was the usual method of provoking our units. As a result, our vehicle slowed down and we decided to alight in order to investigate. In retrospect, it may have been wiser to drive on, as this may have been our opposition lining up for a fatal attack. However, when you have such a young group of men together, it is difficult not to be excitable and test one's curiosity. Paul, my close friend and respected work colleague, and I got out by opening the rather heavy armour plated rear door and walked in the direction of the assailant. Immediately, several terraced house front doors opened and men, women and children moved briskly in our direction. My Non-Commissioned Officer (NCO), Sam, and the driver, 'Meatloaf', were still within the vehicle. My initial thought was 'we are the law abiding force' and will stand our ground. I

Back of a PIG, Belfast

know – absolutely full of bravado with little practical experience of these type of events, not having been long out of basic training at Ballykinler! Unfortunately, Paul had his SA80 rifle barrel grabbed by the main culprit; therefore, a potentially dangerous scenario was erupting.

Through sheer fear, I immediately cocked my weapon in readiness to fire and screamed at the man holding Paul's weapon to desist. It is very strange what goes through one's thoughts in these awkward, potentially life-threatening times. I recollected that the aggressor was a man aged late thirties to early forties with a thick dark moustache, dark hair, and scruffy light shirt and faded jeans, and that he really should be doing something more positive than throwing bottles of wine and jostling young soldier's equipment. The look of defiance in his eyes was something I shall never forget. I knew that his intentions at that stage were very dangerous. Paul then also cocked his rifle, which gave us a split second of time to run in the direction of our vehicle. After locking the door and driving off, I remember thanking the 'Divine Being' for allowing me and my chums to withdraw from the situation unhurt.

On another occasion, I had coincidentally taken the night off for personal reasons. I was subsequently made aware that our patrol had been attacked. The circumstances were that the next morning on my return to duty I was informed that our armoured patrol in the same Markets area of Belfast had been hit by a handheld explosive device, which resembled a torpedo. My colleagues nurtured the same 'dark' sense of humour that soldiers sometimes attain and presumed that the device was a fake. You see, the local youth found it hilarious to throw similar looking weighted cardboard objects at the military and police vehicles. Upon examination by the bomb squad, it was confirmed to contain an amount of Semtex or Czech industrial explosive, commonly used by our enemy, the Irish Republican Army (IRA) and had the potential of killing the whole patrol. The Officer in Command purchased a crate of the 'best' champagne to show his empathy with the troops!

Whilst on a static guard duty at the main entrance to Belfast city centre on Bridge Street, I noticed a small group of men and women coming past our location. One of the men was shouting derogatory comments at our patrol and was holding something in his right hand. Fearing that he may try and throw a missile, I approached him running. He immediately called me the usual term of 'endearment': 'Brit Bastard!' I always found this to be very ironic, as the person normally using the terminology was a fellow Northern Irishman. I enquired as to what he was holding in his hand. He became more aggressive. By this stage, I was surrounded by the group, who were screaming and shouting. I distinctly recollect looking back at the NCO in charge on that night. I cannot remember his name, but he was temporarily in charge of my brick (four man army patrol), who was a rather chubby fellow with a pencil moustache and an accent that was from just outside Belfast. As I caught his eye, he looked frightened and looked away. I may have expected cowardice or lack of authority from senior commissioned officers (forgive me but I have experience of this!), but from my peers this was too much! I remember swearing at him and the remainder of my colleagues and demanded that they come to my aid. By that stage the man with the item in his hand tried to grab at my chest area with the opposite hand. I was unsure of his actual intention, but my response, whilst forceful and aggressive, seemed necessary in the circumstances. I head butted him in the face. One must keep in mind that I was sporting an issued Kevlar army helmet with attached visor. The man did not collapse, but covered his facial area with his left hand. He was frogmarched away by his peers, who were now silent. Was I ever proud of this incident? No. It taught me how quickly a situation may escalate and not to step into a situation without the appropriate support. I never did find out what was in the man's right hand!

Whilst completing my short service with this regiment at Girdwood, Palace and Ladas Drive barracks I never actually realised just how much danger I had been in until about six months after I had left. I heard from a news report that a Private Brian Lawrence had been targeted by IRA members and shot near his home address in north Belfast. Not only was he a friend and a popular member in our company, he was a husband and father.

Private Brian Lawrence who was 34, was parking a car at the tyre and exhaust shop where he worked, on June 17, 1991. Gunmen in a stolen car fired at him a dozen times and he was hit seven times and died. The IRA were believed to have been behind this cowardly attack.

BALLYGAWLEY ROAD: 1990

Kingsman Jason Hughes, 1 King's Regiment

I would like to deal with another moment of true horror which I experienced during the two years that thankfully didn't end up in another body going into the ground.

Our platoon was patrolling the fields just outside Omagh on the infamous Ballygawley road, used by drivers trying to turn their cars into airplanes judging by the speed they travelled at. We had been tasked to rat trap the road. That is, to stop all traffic on specific intelligence that a terrorist unit was travelling along it. With great haste we made it to the road but it was pitch black, and, using all the lamps we had at the time we set up GPMGs at both ends in order to stop all traffic. How long we had been there my memory escapes me, but me and Shaun were in the road to stop the cars and question the occupants. Then two cars came around the corner some distance away and our hearts began to hammer; the engine noise of a car accelerating towards you isn't one that goes away in a hurry, and in what seemed an age we both began to move towards the road's edge, knowing the car wasn't going to stop.

The next sequence happened in a split second but I turned around on reaching the edge of the road and heard a bang as the car clipped Shaun and hurled him onto the side then went on down the road. It only stopped just beyond the last man on our checkpoint, who we later found had cocked the machine gun and was taking up the pressure on the trigger only to see brake lights blink at the last moment. The man in a hurry who had caused the accident had no idea how close he came to leaving the planet.

Shaun at this point, was lying at the roadside still awake but unable to feel anything below the waist, and the darkness disguised the blood loss and the

Aftermath of IRA attack on a rural RUC station

extent of his injuries even from those who were trying to treat him. But we knew it was very bad. The helicopter was called and came with great haste, and the courage of the pilots to land on a road at night with wires close by was extraordinary; the medic on the chopper saved his life three times on the journey to the hospital.

We however were lifted back to Dungannon our base of the time, given a cup of tea, wrote statements to record the event and sent to wash the blood off our hands, then it was back to business as usual.

Chapter Twenty-Four

1991

A year of 604 bombings, 499 shootings, 13 soldiers, 6 RUC officers, 71 civilians and 20 terrorists killed.

8 of the fatalities suffered by the Army in this year were members of the UDR. 4 were killed at Glennane when a lorry bomb was rolled down a hill into the barracks where it exploded with devastating effect.

In the June, an off-duty Para, Tony Harrison was murdered as he visited his fiancé in East Belfast.

In the same month, an IRA ASU was ambushed by the SAS – all 3 terrorists were killed – at Coagh in Co Tyrone.

The year would also witness the murder of Coldstream Guards Corporal Simon Ware at Carrickovady blown up by a 300lb IRA booby trap; the following moving account is by his brother.

Corporal Dan Ware, Royal Green Jackets

In August 1991 I was the second in command of my section of eight soldiers. My responsibility lay with the command of a team of four but in the absence of the section commander, then I would take over the reins of the command of the eight man section. The Company was based at a small security force base called Rockwood, situated about three miles south east of the County Tyrone town of Castlederg. A small security force base nestled beside the large River Derg, secluded from view by the rural features of natural habitation, though it was no secret location as it had been there for many years. Apart from the Ops Company we formed part of it was also the home of the local Ulster Defence Regiment Company who used it as patrol base. Surrounded by large cover from view screens and overlooked by tall observation towers, it was the life and soul of the battalion Ops Company. The operations room, intelligence cell and offices were contained separately, as too was the accommodation, rest areas and cookhouse. I would often forget to realize that I was with my battalion only 50 miles or so from Simon's battalion just doing the same job.

It was 06:30 on Saturday 17th August 1991. The QRF commander, Cpl 'Frank,' woke the whole Company quickly as another incident had occurred on our company area. The quiet Saturday morning was now woken by the assertiveness of troops and commanders rallying around rushing to deploy to yet another terrorist incident. A small handheld coffee jar grenade had been thrown at the house of an off-duty UDR soldier in Castlederg, and had failed to detonate. The Mark 15 'coffee jar' grenade was a fairly new type of device at the time currently being used by PIRA. It was first introduced on 25 May 1991 when a

Corporal D Ware, Royal Green Jackets (photo courtesy of Darren Ware)

soldier was killed in an explosion within North Howard Street Mill in Belfast when the device was thrown over a wall and detonated inside the security force base.

Back at Rockwood the Company was getting dressed and sorting out our kit, making sure we had all that was necessary, as we did not know how long we would be deployed for, but no doubt most of the day. I was a section second-in-command in A Company, 2 Platoon. It was a really professional company and there was a good bunch of experienced and keen soldiers of all ranks who always got on with the task, and morale was pretty high. Like many incidents before and after, things went smoothly and that reflected in the professionalism of everyone, backed up by the OC having said that he had confidence in us.

Back at Rockwood there was no time for breakfast; other agency troops and police had put a loose cordon around the bomb scene and were waiting the arrival of further troops and the ATO. The semi-detached house was on the left side of the Castlefinn Road, just on the edge of town on the road that leads to the border of Eire, which was only about a mile away. The terrorist may have used that road as an escape route or merely mingled back in the small town as if nothing had happened. Rockwood was about three miles from the bomb scene and was too close for a helicopter deployment meaning the troops either walked or were dropped off by vehicle. By the time a helicopter was arranged to fly from Omagh, pick up at Rockwood and then drop off outside Castlederg we could have walked it.

We arrived at the scene having been briefed and received a quick set of orders and I briefly spoke to an RUC officer who didn't have much to say about what had happened. I got on with my section's task. Mark was the section commander and our simple task was to satellite patrol around the inner cordon to provide protection for troops at the scene and to dominate the ground to the east of the cordon. I initially passed the time of day with Dave G briefly on a quiet street on an estate behind the police station; a predominantly Protestant estate that was quiet and gave us no problems. We both had the same idea that we were going to have a long day ahead just patrolling until the ATO had made the bomb safe, a task that we were used to. We'd done it before and no doubt would do it many more times and fortunately it was a dry and sunny day. Unbeknown to me at the time, my day was probably going to be the longest, a day that will remain clear to me.

I heard over the company radio net a message from the Adjutant to the Company Commander to ring him on the secure telephone. The Adjutant, of all people, why would he want to speak to the OC in the middle of an operation? He was based at Battalion Headquarters in Omagh and would have no involvement in the incident we were dealing with. I pulled a face to myself, as it was unusual for that to be transmitted, particularly in the middle of an incident and miles from battalion headquarters. The company commander had asked if it could wait but was clearly told no and I recall the distinct reply from the Ops officer of 'No, it's urgent' The OC made straight to Castlederg RUC station. Even he admitted later that his mind started to race, and he detected something was wrong. The Adjutant told the OC what had happened, and he now had the grim task of telling me, one that he did not look forward to.

Some of us on the clearance operation assumed that there had been another incident, possibly at our other company location at Strabane. A short time passed and the company commander called the platoon sergeant, Martin H, on the radio: 'I need a call sign to assist with another task, you have Foxtrot Two One Delta with you; I need to use them.'

Foxtrot Two One Delta was my call sign and I was told by the company commander to return to Castlederg police station with my team. I walked along the main road, grinning at other troops who would be staying a bit longer on the clearance operation, knowing that I was probably going to get a better responsible job. But it felt odd that the OC was only using one team, as the minimum was two. It wouldn't be long before that grin was to be wiped off my face.

We arrived at Castlederg police station and were met by the company commander and the CSM, Jamie H. My team and I were ushered into a Land Rover and we made the short journey by road back to Rockwood escorted by the QRF. I asked the OC what the job was, but he insisted he briefed me in his office on return.

The Land Rover came to an abrupt halt outside the company operations room. The OC jumped out first, grabbed me and as he began to lead me up the stairs to the ops room I heard the CSM tell my team in a firm voice to get out and go with him. As I followed the OC up the stairs the Company Second-in-Command came to the top of the stairs near the ops room and said to the OC: 'I've booked the helicopter for half past eleven.' I looked at my watch and it wasn't long to go and I thought that this must be a good job.

The OC ushered me into his office and told me to sit down. There was something not right in his demeanour or his face and he said those immortal words that I will never forget: 'There's no easy way to say this, but your brother was killed by an IED in South Armagh this morning.' I said 'No.' Everything just fell apart; there was a pause of disbelief. I dropped to a sofa armchair and just burst out crying uncontrollably. The OC was emotional too and he had to leave the office. He was gutted too and he knew it would be a body blow that I did not deserve. He'd told me in a professional manner and didn't hesitate. His priority was to get me back to Rockwood and out of the Province pronto. I sat there still fully kitted up with my body armour, webbing and weapon and plenty of ammunition, just constantly crying to myself, in disbelief, not believing that Simon had been killed and I felt detached as I had lost a big part of my life; I no longer had the brother I looked up to, the only one. I looked up to Simon in many ways but most importantly because he was older and more experienced than me and I respected him for being older. I respected him for having joined the army and giving me the influence, courage and support to do the same and follow in his footsteps.

I had even attempted to join the Coldstream Guards but was rejected for my lack of height. Simon gave me the encouragement to continue in my attempt to join the army and I settled for a career I landed with. Simon and I were not just brothers but good mates too. We had gone through a lot together, the divorce of our parents and our separation that followed when I was eleven and Simon was thirteen. We supported each other and made sure we were OK. By the time we met up together in secondary school we had our own friends but would still look

Cpl Simon Ware, Coldstream Guards and Cpl Darren Ware, Royal Green Jackets.
(Photo courtesy of Darren Ware)

out for each other. When we met up on leave for a beer we would look after each other and reminisce. On the 17th August 1991 that opportunity, that routine and that friendship was taken away from me – a blow that I felt extremely hard to accept and take in. Over the years the Northern Ireland development has turned many corners, but for this journey it came to a place that could never be turned back. If only those that dealt with it could imagine what they were doing to take away somebody so close, somebody who was a friend and a positive influence.

The CSM came in straight away and took my weapon and webbing off me. Perhaps he was thinking safety in mind. After all, I had just been told that the IRA had murdered my brother and I had a weapon and 120 rounds of ammunition on me. The OC came back into the room and I began to ask so many questions, questions that he did not know the answers to as it had only happened an hour or so before so he didn't know much. He had been told by the Adjutant that Simon had been killed instantly by a landmine and little remained of his body. With all good intentions, with a helicopter in bound from Omagh, the OC just wanted to get me out. He had tasked the CSM to fix my extraction out, which he did flawlessly. I remember the CSM telling me that I was earmarked for six weeks off, but of course if I needed more time then it was there. He had told me that the helicopter would fly me straight to London Heathrow where I would then be met and driven home. I didn't want to do that, as I needed to get back to Omagh to pack some kit, get out of my combats. He said that would be OK and that he would have to liaise with the pilot but my time would be short.

Somebody took me from the Ops room to my accommodation, I couldn't remember, there was so much going on in my head. The powers that be had obviously decided I was not to be left alone – can't blame them really. I remember going into my room that I had shared with the rest of my section. My other three team members that had come from Castlederg with me were all sat on the same bed on the left side of the room, dumbstruck and speechless with straight faces. They must have been thinking, 'shit, what do we say?' My bags had been packed for me and I left the room and walked along the corridor, led by the CSM towards the helipad. The platoon commander, only a young 2nd Lieutenant and young in service, met me outside the room and he gave me a manly hug of condolence but couldn't say much else. I told him to make sure that the lads get back and to look after the platoon. The CSM led me to the helipad and soon after, I heard the distinctive hum of the helicopter in bound. The sight of the helicopter became bigger and bigger until the Wessex was lowering to land on the helipad, in the field adjacent to the SF base, surrounded by large oak trees which afforded a limited amount of cover from view. The wide and fast flowing River Derg rushed by. It was the most welcoming sound and sight at the end of every patrol, knowing it was coming to pick you up and take you back to your patrol base to get cleaned up and to enjoy some creature comforts until your next cold and wet patrol. The CSM had a few words with me on the helipad as the chopper approached. It was not the same as a CSM to Corporal work-related chat – it was a manly sympathetic one offering me support and comfort. The CSM was strict and thorough in his job and a lot of people were shy of him. It was clear where you stood – it was either black or white, and as long as you did your job and duties properly and professionally and didn't step out of line you were alright. The type of typically-portrayed Sergeant Major that you wanted really. He told me how gutted he and the OC were and how every one else would be when word soon spread through the battalion. The Company and the command structure did all they could to help. The thoughts of the OC were that they couldn't linger for too long. Everyone felt for me on a personal loss but for operational reasons, had to move on.

I boarded the Wessex, which flew me to Omagh. The door gunner handed me a pair of ear defenders for the journey. It felt strange for me to be in a helicopter on my own as I was so used to getting in one with the rest of my multiple. As it took off from the helipad, the door gunner, in the normal routine manner in the kneeling position held the large machine gun and observed the area around as the helicopter reached a safe height. He then half-closed the door as it flew of towards Omagh. I recall just looking out of the door, flying over the beautiful countryside of Northern Ireland, the waters, the flush green fields, forests and hedgerows only bloodied again by the death of another soldier in the fight against terrorism.

I was politely told that the helicopter had to go very soon. I got out of my uniform, throwing it on my room floor, got changed into my civvies and threw a load of stuff into a bag. I left my room in a right state but I didn't care. It was a short flight to Belfast airport, where I then boarded a domestic passenger flight to Heathrow. I don't recall being ushered anywhere at the airport. It was only an hour or so flight to London; I just sat there in my seat just wandering what and why and surrounded by people going about their normal business.

Once I had collected my bag I was led to a waiting unmarked military vehicle, which had been dispatched from Wellington Barracks to drive me home to Holt, Norfolk. It must have been the driver's most dreadful journey; having to sit next to someone who he had never met before whose brother had just been murdered, for a two hour car journey. I remember every half hour the radio news reporting a Coldstream Guardsman being killed in South Armagh – another victim of The Troubles. News of the incident had been reported very soon. At 9.50am the first TV crew arrived at the scene of the explosion, and by 10am the first news bulletin reported a bomb in South Armagh. The second bulletin at 11am reported that a Guardsman had been killed. Every time the news was broadcast the driver would turn the volume down but I told him it was alright to leave it as it was and listen to it; after all I had a lot more to cope with ahead.

He dropped me off at mum's house in Holt, and left soon after. I did consider the offer of a brew and something to eat but he agreed with me that the atmosphere was not going to be good and he chose the easy option to leave.

Simon's company commander, Christopher, was in the UK assisting in the training of the battalion who were to take over Simon's battalion. He was at Stanford, a military training area in Norfolk. Christopher learnt of the tragedy from the CO by phone and was then sent to break the news to mum. He told me about that time, how he had the dreadful responsibility of breaking the news. He knew it needed careful handling for fear of saying the wrong thing or adding to the distress. Christopher knocked on the door at around 12 o'clock, and believed that as soon as the door opened, she knew before he could say anything. Although shocked, he says that she was brave. He then stayed for about an hour and a half talking through Simon's job and the facts that he knew. Christopher was able to tell mum that Simon would have felt no pain and from information passed to him, the bomb would have killed him instantly. Christopher felt that this gave her some comfort, and having completed his task, he left the house.

I don't recall the initial few hours but all the family were there and all just asking questions to one and all. They would look to me for the answers and help. I couldn't answer them at this early stage as I only knew as much as them. I reassured them, that being in the job that I was, then I would be able to find out. I was determined to.

We spent the rest of that day and night at home. The phone did not stop ringing, people were visiting and the television and radio was on constantly, awaiting every available news bulletin for updates. It was like I was gathering evidence. I remember the main late evening news at the time when the first pictures of the scene were transmitted on ITV. I saw the taped-off cordon sites and a large wooded area. I initially thought to myself 'why had they been in the wood?' but it was easy for me to criticise though. I was not the patrol commander, I didn't know the area; they could have been doing a routine patrol task in the wood for all I knew. The news reporter then reported a landmine explosion in excess of 250lb. I couldn't believe it, my early thoughts were maybe 50lb. Mum asked me what injuries Simon would have inflicted. I had to be honest and say that if he were in close proximity of the device then his body probably would not be found. Her teacup and saucer smashed all over the floor. The family wanted answers and so did I, so I had to be honest from the start.

Simon was 22 years old when he was killed. He had served in the Coldstream Guards for five years and was from the Regiment's Second Battalion. On March 9th 1991, two days after his wedding, he deployed to Northern Ireland on his second tour. On Thursday 15th August 1991 he had formed part of a three team multiple tasked on a three day patrol of South Armagh in the Newtownhamilton area. Amongst other tasks they were ordered to try to locate a montage of 96 terrorist photographs that had been lost ten days earlier by another patrol. The area had obviously been over-patrolled. At 0730 hrs on Saturday 17th August the patrol had left their night time lie-up position a mile away and moved off to a helicopter pick-up point in a field north of Carrickovady Wood, close to the Newtown Road. Their extraction was due at 0820hrs.

At 0800hrs the patrol Sergeant's team – with Simon as the third man – entered a fire break in the wood and followed it through to a distinctive bend. As Simon exited the left bend an explosion erupted only feet away killing him instantly and completely destroying his body. The patrol having reacted to the attack frantically searched the location for Simon. There was no hope of finding him. In the two day follow up search operation his body was never found, only parts of his body were found amongst the blood stained trees. Only the barrel of his GPMG was located mangled and bent, parts of blood stained equipment and small parts of him that remained were found. The largest part that was found, his left lower arm, was located outside of the wood 330 feet away. His wedding ring was still intact; it was only five months old.

I have no bad feelings for the people of Northern Ireland or its countryside, but pure hatred for those terrorists that murdered my brother.

CROSSMAGLEN: 1991

Carol Richards (formerly Carol Ware)

Lance Corporal Simon Ware murdered by the IRA 17th August

Darren lost his one and only brother and best friend on that day and I can't imagine how he must have felt, and to continue to see out his tour of duty after must have been very hard. He was very brave and I know Simon would have been very proud of him, as we all were.

I lost my husband that day, he was my best friend too, and my soulmate. I lost my mum to cancer the previous year and without Simon's love and support I don't know how I would have coped, I didn't know then that only one year later I would lose him too. The worst 2 years of my life! And also the best if that makes sense (because I was with Simon).

Only a few months before our wedding Simon got the news that the 1st Battalion were being posted to Germany, I had just started a new job so wasn't keen on the idea of being in Germany for 2 years, so Simon put in for a transfer to the 2nd Battalion, so that we could be together in England. Not long after the transfer he was given the news that the 2nd Battalion was doing a 6 month tour of Northern Ireland, leaving 2 days after our wedding. I was gutted! But also relieved as we then heard that the 1st Battalion were going into Iraq for the 1st Gulf War; 'far more dangerous' I thought; it didn't occur to me that Simon wouldn't came back.

I made friends with a couple of the girls in the quarters, one girl's husband was in Iraq and the other girl who lived opposite had a husband serving in Northern Ireland with Simon. We used to keep each other going, we bought telephone extension leads so we could take our phones into each others flats in case one of the lads phoned, we couldn't risk missing a call. We deliberately avoided listening to news bulletins, it was easier to be oblivious, we had girly nights in, shared meals etc, you just don't think about the worst happening because you can't get through it otherwise.

The families' officer, Keith Robinson, arranged a couple of trips for the wives; the first was an assault course and barbecue at Pirbright barracks. It was a great fun day and a big morale boost. The second trip was a day trip to France, that day was Saturday 17th August 1991 – forever engraved in my mind and heart, a day I shall never be able to forget.

We left very early about 6 am – a great bunch of girls off for a day out, we were having a fantastic time a really good laugh all the time, not knowing what had happened. During the ferry trip home the families' officer disappeared for what seemed a long time. When he reappeared he gave some story about there being a problem with the coach driver. One of the wives later told me that she had sussed that something was badly wrong and tried to ask him about it, he more or less confirmed it without speaking out loud but told her she wasn't to say anything. He made the decision to keep quiet until we got back to Dover which as I recall was another couple of hours away. The trip home was the first time that the army had been able to get word to the families' officer about what had happened (no mobile phones in those days).

I've no idea how he must have felt having to pretend to have a good time all the while knowing what awaited me at Dover, but understandably he felt it would not be right to tell me on the ferry.

When we got to Dover one of my friends was taken off the coach first, I didn't know why at the time, but Keith (F.O) wanted to ask her how well she knew me as he was worried about how to tell me and who should be with me when I was told. Another of the wives on the coach was someone I had known during my nurse training so she was called off the coach too, then I was led off by Keith. Coming towards me were two WPCs and a man in a suit. I was completely bewildered, I thought I was about to be arrested for bringing back too many fags and too much booze but I hadn't bought any more than anyone else so I couldn't understand why I had been singled out.

I was taken into a sort of toilet block ante room, and then this man in the suit who introduced himself as the regimental adjutant told me that Simon had been killed. I screamed. I've never screamed before, at least not in any kind of emotional way, then I just cried and cried, the adjutant sat on the floor with his head in his hands not knowing what to say, he looked about the same age as Simon, the two WPCs were crying, and the friend who had come in with me was swearing, ironically she was a protestant girl from Northern Ireland.

Myself and two friends were taken by car to my brothers in Hertfordshire, we stopped at services en route, and unbeknown to the driver we had stopped at the same services as the coach with the rest of the wives on. I remember walking in to the restaurant area and seeing their faces, they were all completely devastated; they obviously felt for me while at the same time relieved it wasn't them.

I spent a sleepless night at my brother's who then took me home to the home I should have been sharing with my husband. We had actually only spent one week together there when he was home for R 'n R, I remember the morning he went back to Ireland, he stood in the bedroom doorway and told me he loved me, little did I know I wouldn't see him again. I spoke to him the Wednesday before he died, he told me he was on operations and wouldn't be able to talk to me until Saturday. When he signed off he told me he loved me just as he always did, but then he added 'remember I'll always love you'. I will never forget it because it was almost as if he knew he wasn't coming back and that was the last time I heard his voice.

I went to Heathrow to meet his body being brought home, I was completely unprepared to see his coffin draped in the union flag emerge from the hold, and it was taken to a waiting hearse. I went to the hearse and placed a red rose on the coffin, I said goodbye to him in my head, I wanted to say goodbye out loud but I couldn't speak. Everyone said I was really brave but I didn't feel very brave I felt as though my heart had been ripped out.

The funeral was at the Guards chapel, the same place that we were married. How different an atmosphere walking behind his coffin to how it had been only months before. I was overwhelmed by the amount of people that were there, a fitting tribute to a truly wonderful person.

Although time has moved on and I have had happy times since I still think about Simon a lot and every time another soldier dies and I see a union flag-draped coffin my heart breaks for that soldier's family.

Remembrance Day parade has held more significance for me in the last 16 years than it did before even though as a former sea cadet I have attended remembrance day parades every year since I was 14, the last post didn't make me cry then but I cry every time I hear it now.

If there can be any consolation it is that Simon died doing the job he loved. He was a wonderful husband, son, brother and friend and is still very much missed.

S ARMAGH 1991

Warrant Officer, Grenadier Guards

The Recce Plt deployed on a 6 month COP tour and were employed on covert observation of a senior Army Council [IRA] member. We were the first team to get video of Thomas 'Slab' Murphy holding a weapon; it would not have stood up in court as he would have claimed it was a toy. The ASU were rehearsing an attack and all our video was quickly extracted back to Portadown SB HQ. A few days later the IRA bombed a village (Glenanne?) back to the Stone Age. It was never rebuilt.

I was in an OP when LCpl Simon Ware [Coldstream Guards; see account elsewhere by his brother, Darren] was murdered in the woods to the south of Newtownhamilton (NTH). Even though we were at least 20kms away the poncho on the OP still rattled. The multiple Commander was absolutely monging it due to extreme shock and eventually had to be instructed by the Drill Sergeant over the net to get the guys in 3 ranks in order to see who was missing. A sad day. It was during this tour that the Anti-Tank Platoon were able to get 900+ rounds returned in a single contact near Cullyhanna; at the time it was the most rounds returned. It was only by bad luck that a 66mm Attack Rocket was not fired; as the Commander tried to open it the strap got caught and it would not fully extend!

At the time we had an OP going in to monitor a rocket hide in the southern part of Newry; I did the map and air photo studies as we had to cross a thin stretch of water. I surmised that it was about 15 ft and we set about preparing for a river crossing. We had the pool at Aldergrove closed down and we were issued with immersion suits to practice kit stowage etc. Come the night of the job we were covertly dropped off near to Newry Town FC where we then made our way down to the water's edge; as we neared the edge it became apparent that I had ballsed up the study and had not taken into account that the water was tidal. What I had presumed to be 15ft was in fact 20+ft and a surging torrent. One of the lads dived in to attempt the crossing and got swept away towards Warrenpoint, nearly into Southern Irish waters. We had to call the vans back in and attempt to do a rescue of our knackered team member, who did not even have the energy to curse us.

At one stage we had to send a COP team up to Route 11 which overlooked Bessbrook and was generally manned by the Royal Artillery; they were on leave and therefore a Coldstream Multiple were standing in. As my COP team were on target I was chatting to the multiple Commander who was a friend. Suddenly there were a number of muffled explosions and panic broke out. We rushed outside to find the hillside ablaze and burning out of control. We were running about like mad trying to douse the flames and send reports back to BBK. The local fire brigade turned up but due to the defended location could get nowhere near to the flames. In the end it transpired that the keen Multiple Commander was getting the place scrubbed up to Guards standards having taken over from the RA 'line-swine'. He had placed a load of rubbish in a burn pit which had then spread out. It had finally caught hold of the PAD/Claymore mines version which all went off in series, hence the explosions! PAD: Projectile Area Defence, a cheap British version of the Claymore! Still working and does the job. The main difference is that there is no writing on the Brit one; the yanks had to put 'THIS SIDE FACES ENEMY' on theirs!

The Multiple Commander was aghast, he had only taken over 3 hours previous and had now trashed the whole area.

1991: FERMANAGH

L/cpl Mark Overson, Duke of Edinburgh's Royal Regiment

I had only been in the Regiment a couple of years and, prior to Northern Ireland, I had been in Hong Kong and Catterick.

As a young man of 20, I had heard a lot of stories from the old 'sweats', whom, quite frankly, I was in awe of. This awe grew when I learned of several incidents they had been involved with in Dungannon and the regiment had also been in Enniskillen during the Poppy Day Massacre.

I had been trained in recce and COP [Close Observation Platoon] and when we reached Fermanagh, one of my roles was on overwatch of PVCPs in the area, doing 4 day ops each time. This was at Gortmullen and I was originally the RT man but I swapped roles and became the GPMG man! Anyway, on this one particular day, I was in a 4 man brick and we split into two to overwatch the PVCP below us, and both sets found the only cover available, two bits of very sparse bush.

I was with the 2IC and he was on sentry duty and I was on rest. This day – I can't remember if it was morning or afternoon – gunmen on the high ground to the east, over inside the Irish Republic, opened up on the PVCP with 2 or 3 machine guns; possibly GPMGs, or a Russian weapon or possibly an American M60. I can recognise the sound of 7.62 mm rounds so I knew that it had to be one of these. The sound of the attack woke me up and my 2IC shouted 'Come on, Ovie, let's bug the fuck out!' He then shouted – still not sure if it was an 'After you, old boy' kind of comment – 'I'll fire – you move!'

So, off I went, especially fast, as the gorse bush offered very little cover. In front of me were broken fields and I ran about 20 metres to the first hedgerow and flung myself into a drainage ditch. However, when I first set off from the gorse bush, the .50 cal of the lads in the PVCP opened up and started firing at the gunmen on the high ground. Ok, the .50 cal uses tracer on a one-round-in-five basis and as the gunmen were firing down the hill and our lads were firing up it, I could see the rounds crossing directly in front of me! I shouted to the 2Ic 'move' and soon we both had cover from both the IRA and our own men.

The entire incident took place in only 30 seconds or so, as the gunmen bugged out; I mean, who wants to be hit with .50 cal rounds?

I was both excited and scared, but it was a buzz and a break from the tedium of permanent PVCP overwatch!

(Mark was shot in the back by a gunman at Crossmaglen on a later tour)

MUSGRAVE PARK HOSPITAL, BELFAST: 1991

Lance Corporal Phillip Winstanley, Operating Theatre Technician

Royal Army Medical Corps

The events I am about to relate to you were described at the time, by the press, as 'Evil Without Limits' and also as 'Death on the Wards.'

I am writing this for Phil and Craig who both died, and on behalf of the rest of us who were lucky enough to survive. It was November 2, 1991 and it was about 15:40 as we were all watching England play Australia in the Rugby Union World Cup Final on the TV in the rest area, at the MPH in Belfast. At the time, England were losing 12–3.

Apparently the IRA had timed the bomb to go off at half-time in the game, just as the bar would be crowded with drinkers during the interval. Fortunately, only nine people were in the bar to watch the game and the bomb was late exploding as people had returned to their seats. The injuries and fatalities could have been far, far worse. The device had been planted in the fire escape tunnel behind the bar in the Junior Ranks club, known to us as the 'Keller Bar.' The device – 20lbs of Semtex – had been planted there the night before by a hospital porter who had gotten in through a door which had been deliberately unlocked. We never did find out who had left the door unlocked, but it was clearly done by someone (possibly a civvy) who had attended a function on the site.

So, there I was, a can of Coke in my hand, (couldn't drink as I was on call) enjoying the game which had just restarted, sitting on the left hand wall, TV to my left and the bar to my right. Minutes earlier, I had been sitting up on a partition, when Kev the barman ordered me to get down; unwittingly he saved my life. Suddenly, there was a huge bang, louder than anything I have ever heard in my life and, for an absolute split-second 'What the hell' flashed through my mind. I was thrown onto the floor and all the air was instantly sucked out of me; it felt as though someone huge was sitting on my chest and I was unable to breathe; then very hot air was forced into my lungs; I was gasping for breath but all I could breathe was hot air. I started retching and coughing.

The sound was a roar and then it all went black. Then, all I could see was sparks as the electrical wires which had been blasted, hung and crackled from the walls and ceilings. Then the silence hit me; it was deafening, if that makes any sense.

There I was, lying on the floor, covered in the debris and afraid to move in case any more of the wall fell on top of me, and there was an incredible ringing in my ears.

I'm not sure what the time frame was but it seemed like hours; perhaps people who have also been in blasts will understand what I mean. Eventually, I was able to get to my feet and began stumbling about, shouting out names and trying to make my way to where people had been before the explosion. I couldn't find anybody, even my mate Robbie, which was odd as he had been sitting right next to me! I tried to find the fire escapes, but these and every other exit were blocked by rubble. Later, I found out that the reason why no one was answering my calls was that they had all been knocked unconscious, but I really thought that they were all dead. What struck me was the vile smell; I can still smell it even now!

Aftermath of IRA bomb attack at Musgrave Park Hospital
(photo courtesy of Phil Winstanley)

Luckily, I found that one of the emergency lights was working, but even then, all I could see was blackness and the occasional sparks from torn and loose wires. Panic began to set in as I thought that I was the only one alive and I was absolutely terrified; I simply sat on the floor and sobbed my heart out. It was still difficult to breathe in all the smoke from the few small fires and my ears were still ringing; time just stood still. At that moment, Kev – the barman – shouted my name and I went to him. He told me that he been shouting my name for what seemed like ages; Kev had brought his daughter Sue, who was only 7, to help him behind the bar. He couldn't find her, so we both started looking frantically. The anguish on Kev's face is something I'll never forget. What we didn't realise was that the terrified kid had crawled into a cupboard under the bar to hide after the blast. It got to the point where we were struggling to breathe, both coughing and retching, the smoke was starting to sting our eyes. We started to look for a way out and found a small hole in the wall leading to the stairs, and crawled through helping each other get through the rubble. Then we heard voices and saw hands reaching through to help us.

I had no apparent physical injuries, and as I was part of the 'on call surgery team' I was asked to work and gladly did so. My mate Robbie was rescued and like me had no apparent physical injuries and was part of the 'on call surgery team.' So, we both worked, treating our stricken comrades; it was later that little Sue was found and pulled out.

After all the survivors had been pulled out and casevaced to the RVH (Royal Victoria Hospital), we were finally able to sit down in the coffee room, and it was then that a huge sledgehammer seemed to smash into me as the shock and adrenaline wore off. It hit me just what had happened. Both Robbie and I sobbed our hearts out and were inconsolable, such was the distress of the moment; all we knew at this moment was that one lad was dead and many others were injured.

We were the only ones in the blast not to be casevaced, and it was then that we were informed that two of the lads had been killed. WOII Phil Cross – our CSM – and Driver Craig Pantry, our RCT driver, had both been caught directly in the blast and killed instantly. Craig was killed by a piece of wood blasted straight at him. I am just so thankful that both lads didn't suffer for a single second; such was the power of the bomb.

Of the other seven, two were wounded badly and the others, including Robbie and myself, had injuries ranging from flash/superficial burns to cuts and bruises. We found out later that Robbie had also fractured his fibula. Two months later, my tour was ended prematurely and I was posted out of the Province.

CSM Philip Cross (33) was married with two children and was from the north-east of England. Craig Pantry was 20, single and was from the Gwent area of Wales.

A contemporary press report of the time, naturally outraged at this attack read:

'You Evil Cowards.' 'Even the heavens wept as a shocked world witnessed the depths plumbed in the IRA's latest example of man's inhumanity to man.

Rain has washed much of the blood and gore from the scene of yesterday's cowardly attack on the military wing at Belfast's Musgrave Park Hospital. A bomb blast left 2 soldiers dead, dozens hurt and 8 people seriously wounded including a 7 year old girl. But nothing can erase the stain caused by a nation's shame at a haven for the sick and dying being devastated by cold-hearted killers.'

Aftermath of IRA bomb attack at Musgrave Park Hospital.
(Photo courtesy of Phil Winstanley)

Phillip Winstanley

When I returned to Musgrave Park following sick leave, I was determined to make a memorial to Phil and Craig. So I was lucky enough to secure the last Webb Ellis Rugby Ball from Twickenham used in the final and I made a plinth for the ball from oak and a frame for the plaque. I was touched by the willingness of the lady at Twickenham, who took the reason I gave for the request at face value. and gave up the ball she had secured for herself, which she was going to auction for a local charity.

Chapter Twenty-Five

1992

A year of 419 bombings, 426 shootings and the deaths of 4 soldiers (the lowest figure in the 23 years since the troubles had been ongoing) 2 RUC officers, 59 civilians and 5 terrorists.

This year witnessed the continuing 'tit-for-tat' sectarian killings. In the January, the IRA killed 8 civilians with a bomb attack on a mini-bus near Cookstown; the UFF retaliated 3 weeks later, by shooting dead 5 Catholics in Sean Graham's bookmakers, Ormeau Road, Belfast.

It was also the year that the killings came to Derby. On April 14, Sergeant Michael Newman of the Royal Corps of Signals was shot and killed by Joseph 'Mad Dog' Magee of the INLA, in a car park near the Army Careers Office. He was lowering the flag at the end of the day's work, having only worked there for 2 weeks. Sergeant Newman had never served in Northern Ireland.

STRABANE, CO TYRONE: 2ND APRIL 1992

Darren Ware, Royal Green Jackets

In December 1991 I received instructions that I was to go on the Section Commanders' Battle Course for three months to earn my promotion to Corporal, therefore officially commanding a section of eight soldiers. This meant a gruelling course and three months away from my partner in Northern Ireland let alone the operational role that I was always eager to do. Nevertheless on the 27th March I successfully finished the course and returned to the battalion the next day. Unfortunately for me I had returned only three days before the company were to deploy to Castlederg as the Ops Company but the generosity of the CSM allowed me to have two days to myself to sort my kit out and spend a bit of time with my partner.

I had been itching to get back to operational stuff throughout the course and the time had soon come, however this was not to last for long as I was warned off by the company commander that I would be posted to the training depot the following January to train recruits. So, really I had only nine months or so left in Northern Ireland. I was always committed to my operational responsibilities and always reflected on the experience I got. The aim of the British Army in Northern Ireland was plain and simple, firstly to assist the RUC (now PSNI) in the defeat of terrorism and secondly to kill or capture the terrorists. Ever since my brother was killed in South Armagh only six months earlier the second objective was close to my heart. I wasn't really going out looking for the opportunity but thought that should it arise then I would be 'snapping its hand off.'

I led the patrol of eight soldiers on a routine foot patrol and exited the rear of Strabane RUC station just after 11pm on Friday April 2nd 1992. I infiltrated the northern part of the town using the remote rural area as my cover in an effort not to be compromised too soon. The route would take me along Church Street leading downhill into the town centre to Meetinghouse Street, which was in fact a very busy evening being a Friday. As I passed the large graveyard to my right with its church nestled in amongst the darkened grounds and high walls, the ambient street lights illuminated the Friday night busy town. A figure in the alleyway to my left fifteen metres in front drew my attention as he fumbled around near to parked vehicles amongst the darkened shadows. I halted the patrol and observed him for a few seconds through the SUSAT sight on top of my weapon, which afforded me an amount of magnification.

My suspicions were confirmed when I recognised the male as a known IRA terrorist. At the same time, but unaware to me the owner of a boarded-up shop on Main Street had reported suspicious activity to the police. I then instructed my 2i/c and his team to lay in wait in the graveyard whilst I waited nearby to appreciate my plan of action. I had contacted the ops room and instructed them to deploy the QRF to the main gates of the police station and instructed my 2i/c to observe and challenge the male should he move off. My 2i/c informed me that the suspect had moved off and I instructed him to follow and stop and search him. He was soon stopped and searched on Meetinghouse Street and found with nothing of any interest on him. I joined the patrol and confirmed that the male I had earlier observed through the sight of my weapon was this male. I could not believe my luck but was disappointed that nothing was found. Pursuing my suspicion I returned to the same alleyway to conduct a discreet search during which I found a CB radio secreted in the corner of a wall. Convinced that the same male would return and determined to pursue my suspicion I instructed my 2i/c to re deploy to the graveyard to observe the alleyway whilst I briefed the platoon sergeant and QRF at the police station gates, only a few yards away. During this quick brief my 2i/c informed me that the same male had returned and picked something up which was later identified as the same CB radio I had earlier located in the alleyway. My instructions were to detain him for police arrival which was done. When the police arrived their reaction was jubilant and described the situation as '... could not have happened to a nicer guy ... ' The suspect, having been arrested for conspiracy to cause an explosion and to murder members of the security forces was conveyed to Strand Road RUC Station where his detention was authorised.

Having analysed the suspicious activity earlier reported and the suspicious incident I had just dealt with I consulted my street map of Strabane. My attention was drawn to the area of Church Street and Meetinghouse Street and noticed, on the ground, that Church Street featured a boarded-up shop premises that afforded a clear view from the alleyway further up Church Street where the arrested male had been disturbed. I suggested that the area be put locally out of use by police and army patrols that night and that a search be conducted at first light. This was duly done and shortly before midday on Saturday 3rd April a bomb was located behind the boarded up shop at 61 Main Street consisting of 15lb of HME in a paint tin connected to a firing pack. The device was attached to a command wire laid ready to detonate. Also found at the scene was a compatible CB radio of exactly the same model found in the alleyway where the arrested male was detained. Both CB radios were tuned to the same channel and switched on. The ATO was tasked to clear the device and confirmed that the bomb was ready to detonate. For my actions and command and control that dark distant night I was to be awarded a Mention in Dispatches. My citation reads:

'By the Queen's Order, the name of LCpl (Acting Cpl) Darren Ware, The Royal Green Jackets, was published in the London Gazette on 12 October 1993 as Mentioned in a Dispatch for Distinguished Service in Northern Ireland. I am charged to record Her Majesty's Highest Appreciation.'

Following this incident I was jubilant and very pleased with my success and the dedication and professionalism of my section that night. I had made several quick-thinking decisions during the fast pace of the incident in an effort to succeed and mostly during this time I did not have time to brief the whole section but only my second in command. I had indeed achieved the aim and captured the terrorist and smiled to myself knowing that just revenge is so sweet. The terrorist was led away by the police in tears of sadness not knowing his fate.

Of course it was almost 18 months later, following the end of the battalion's tour, that my name was featured on the Queen's Northern Ireland Operational Awards List. By this time I had been training recruits as an instructor and on a field training exercise in Otterburn when the section commanders gathered for a platoon commander's O Group prior to a night time recce patrol.

'Cpl Ware, what have you done for meritorious service in Northern Ireland?' Confused, I said 'What do you mean boss?' 'Are you aware that you have just been awarded a Mention In Dispatches for distinguished service in Northern Ireland ?' That was just the icing on the cake I thought. I was so elated that I had been recognised for my command and control of that incident that not only led to the arrest of a terrorist but having aided in the location of the device had saved lives and prevented the attack.

I received many letters of congratulations on my award which surprised me very much. I had never known anyone else personally who had been in a similar position and was not aware of what happens. I got nine letters ranging from the Divisional Commander of the local policing division right up to Major Generals and Brigadiers. The best one of these was from the Brigade Commander of 8 Infantry Brigade Northern Ireland. I would never expect a personal letter from a Brigadier.

'A very well done on your award of a Mention in Dispatches in the operational honours and awards list. Although you were clearly a committed, loyal and professional patrol commander throughout your two year tour, it was your actions on the 3rd April 1992 for which you were particularly cited. In recognising a terrorist, who was not well known, and having the moral courage to pursue your suspicion with determination, you undoubtedly foiled an attempt to murder members of the security forces. You can take the credit for the subsequent conviction of that terrorist.'

That shiny bronze oak leaf attached to my Northern Ireland medal is proudly displayed on my wall in a boxed frame displaying the citation.

LONDONDERRY OR DERRY? NORTHERN IRELAND, 1992

Bombardier Andy Warren, Royal Artillery

27 Field Regiment Royal Artillery was given a secret warning order on Friday 11th October 1991 for a six month emergency tour of Northern Ireland (NI), commencing in January 1992. On instructions from HQ Arty 1 (BR) Corps, knowledge of the warning was initially restricted to those vital to the planning process.

The Regiment was informed of the tour at 0900 hours on Thursday 17 October 1991, four days before it was to have deployed to Munsterlager south ranges for a Regimental firing camp.

The Regiment's guns and armoured vehicles were put into Out of use Management and all equipments not required for the NI training were consigned to their stores within three days.

Training started on Monday 21st October 1991, with conversion of the Regiment to the SA80 rifle. There followed two and a half hectic months of training carried out under the expert tutelage of the Security Operations Training Advisory Team (SOTAT) at Sennelager and the valued guidance and advice from the Regiment's 'In Barracks Training Team', provided by 4th Field Regiment Royal Artillery. The Regiment went through SOTAT Sennelager Package during the period 20 November–4th December 1991 and the training culminated with a NI rural exercise 18–22 December 1991; this was conducted simultaneously with 45 Field Regiment Royal Artillery, who were training for their role as the Drumad roulement Battalion.

After a well earned (but short) Christmas break, the Regimental advance party deployed on 10th January 1992 by RAF Hercules to Ballykelly, Co Londonderry. From Ballykelly the party was flown by helicopter to Grosvenor barracks and St Angelo Camp, the 2 main base locations of the Fermanagh Roulement Battalion (FRB). During the succeeding week advance party conducted the preparations necessary to receive the main body and began to establish the Rapport with the FRB, 42 Commando Royal Marines, that was to prove so useful in the coming months.

The Regimental TAC HQ established a coordination cell at Grosvenor to provide the province-wide liaison between the Army Headquarters. RUC, civilian contractors and other Army and RAF units involved in the Operation.

On 16th and 17th January 1992 the Regimental main body arrived at Ballykelly by RAF Hercules. They were met by elements of the advance party who equipped them with all the stores required for their subsequent tasking. Regimental TAC HQ deployed directly to co-locate with TAC HQ of 42 Commando RM at Grosvenor Barracks, Enniskillen, whilst Regimental Echelon co-located with OPs company 42 CDO RM at St Angelo Camp.

D Troop from 6 Field Battery deployed directly as an independent troop to the HUMP permanent vehicle check point (PVCP), in Strabane, under operational command of the 2nd Battalion the Royal Green Jackets.

Following two days of briefings and preparation, the three gun batteries deployed by Chinook helicopters to the forward operating bases for phase 1 of this operation. N.b. – Although referred to as Gun batteries, we were working as Infantrymen and had no Artillery equipment in theatre.

An emergency in NI could amount to anything that requires further troops on the ground, in this case the refurbishment of permanent Vehicle Check Points (PVCPs) in Fermanagh. All British soldiers are Infantry first and trade second; the training we were put through for Northern Ireland was specific to the task at hand such as patrolling techniques, types of booby traps, immediate actions when making contact with an attacking group (I am a little loathe to call them the enemy for reasons I would rather not go into at this point).

Any ambushes as you call them would be carried out by specialist forces, for example, SAS; they were not something I was ever part of. Virtually all British Units regardless of their particular field would go through NI [hence the use of ACC and other HQ staff on the 'Star Trek' patrols with the Glosters], normally because it was the only fair way to do it and to get a good circulation of troops, so that no one unit would be stuck there forever and a day. The underlying benefit was of course that it was a good training environment for all troops.

Londonderry or Derry? Well call it what you will, I have no real feelings about the name, Derry?, Londonderry? it's all the same to me. It's been the topic of many a heated discussion but I don't really understand why? I mean I know the Protestants and the Catholics feel strongly about it but it's only a name; why not rename it and call it something completely different? This is the type of argument that although small and seemingly petty, will always get in the way of peace in the Province.

I am a Protestant but my wife is a Catholic and to show you that the differences in religion mean nothing to me, I have had my daughter Baptised a Catholic, at my wife's request. Religion, although the foundation of our existence, seems to me to have a hell of a lot to answer for throughout the ages !

I hope that in my lifetime or at least in my daughter's that we see peace in Ireland, it is rated as one of my top ten, most beautiful places in the world and it is full of genuinely pleasant and caring people.

TRAGEDY AT BESSBROOK MILL: 1992

Corporal Philip Gilbert, 1, Royal Scots

On my third tour in Northern Ireland (NI), we were situated in the infamous 'bandit country' of South Armagh, and, for us 'Royals' this was the start of a 'triple whammy' of tours in this area ... I was working in the buzzard cell of Bessbrook Mill, in one of the busiest heliports in Europe. This was a good, satisfying and yet, frustrating job moving men and equipment around 24/7. My job routine was 24 on, 24 off, a welcome change from patrolling the wet, damp NI countryside.

The tour had to this point gone pretty well for the Battalion; we had our fair share of contacts and minor incidents but nothing out of the norm. It was, however to change, very shortly, in fact, on the evening of the 24th November 1992. There were only 3 ways for helicopters to enter and exit Bessbrook Mill (recognised routes) and these were either over the back fence and onto one of the pads or into a lower pad called the 'Well' or to fly over the side fence and exit to the side of the Mill (the 'tube'); on the opposite side there was a street of local residents at the side of Bessbrook Town itself.

On the evening of the 24th, the weather was dry and cloudy, and the usual drone of both Lynx and Puma helicopters turning and lifting was as normal to us as was the daily postman on our married estate back in Inverness. I was settled in my room writing the mandatory 'bluey to the wife whilst watching television and enjoying some down time, when the sound of engines suddenly changed pitch. I looked out of the window down towards the helipads and witnessed an intermittent flashing green light (this was the illumination of the cockpit instruments). The engine groaning got louder until the lights from the residents windows silhouetted the Puma which was spiraling towards the back fence. A large explosion immediately followed when the aircraft clipped the back fence and hit the ground outside the camp. I immediately ran and informed the Medic Sergeant who was in the room next to mine and I then sprinted down towards the helipad.

The wreckage was fully alight and the smell of aviation fuel was all too evident; rounds were also igniting from the door gunner's GPMG. Throughout the night it became evident that the Puma had been approaching the helipad down the tube from the side of the Mill, whilst, at the same time a Gazelle was hovering to land in the 'well' Both aircraft collided and the Gazelle's blades folded but in the process they managed to chop the seat with the pilot attached out of the airframe. The Gazelle then flipped upside down and landed on a small footbridge by the well. Miraculously both Gazelle pilots survived and were helped away with minor injuries; very lucky, considering. Unfortunately the Puma crash was fatal and we can only assume the panic as the co-pilot tried to control the stricken aircraft with the loss of the pilot and the aircraft spiraling out of control.

This accident resulted in the temporary shut down of Bessbrook Mill helipad and the loss of 4 lives during this winter's night; another night in this country's conflict.

The lives lost that night were Major John Barr of the Prince of Wales' Royal Regiment and three RAF personnel: Squadron Leader Michael Haverson, Flight Sergeant Jan Pewtress and Flight Lieutenant Simon Roberts. These men are not recorded as deaths on active service by the MOD and I would like to rectify that here on this page.

Four days earlier, UDR soldier, Bryan Jones was killed and, yet again, the MOD failed to record his death as on active service.

BELFAST: 1992

Lance Corporal Phillip Winstanley, Royal Army Medical Corps

The summer after the Musgrave Park Hospital bombing, several of us were ordered back to Belfast in order to give evidence at the trial of the bomber. The man on trial was a hospital porter, and it was proved that he had carried a live device through a Children's' ward in order to plant it in the Junior ranks' Club. Both the IRA and surprise, surprise, Sinn Fein, managed to justify this.

The evidence I gave was of a factual nature; the function on the night before and the events of the actual day. The bomber's Q.C. tried, with the tone of his questions, to make us feel as though we were on trial; he was at the same time, both intimidating and condescending. Although the trial went on longer, we only gave evidence over 2 days; the bomber was found guilty and given two life sentences.

Captured IRA rocket launcher, responsible for many security force deaths

I.S. TRAINING AND SO FORTH: 1992

Mike H., RSM, NITAT (ex-Glosters, ex-UDR)

For every unit and every individual who went to Northern Ireland during the troubles, with the exception of the very earliest days and a few very 'specialised' units who had their very own training and methods of operations, there was Internal Security Training and this usually took place at one of two sites, NITAT (Lydd and Hythe) or NITAT (BAOR) Sennelager; there were a couple of places within the province for those individuals who slipped through the unit net, for one reason or another, with the main training unit, NIRT, at Ballykinler on the Antrim Coast.

NITAT (BAOR) changed its title in the early 1990's to SOTAT (Security Operations Training Unit) due to a growing hostility in Germany to this kind of training taking place on German soil and not part of NATO control or requirements, it also became much more diversified as the unit operational areas changed such as Iraq (1), Bosnia and Kosovo etc., came on line and required a level of specialist training for these deployments. Everything required was taught, or attempted during this phase of deployment, from control and arrest techniques of rioters and people required for detention, to search techniques of houses and vehicles. VCPs and CPC training, Vengeful and Jokers [the former was the classified system that the Army used to trace vehicle details and Jokers were the classified system used for the prevention of RCIED – remote controlled improvised explosive devices] cordons and medical training along with a host of different weapons and equipment, all had to be mastered as well as the various techniques for this situation or that eventuality.

'I don't think so!' Lance-Corporal Darren Croucher, A Company, 3rd Battalion
The Queen's Regiment standing over IRA graffiti at Coalisland.
(Photo courtesy of Darren Croucher)

Several clever and innovative practices were spawned such as 'Shot Boxes'
which were used to teach a soldier what it was like under fire and the recognition
of different types of weapons. Before this was used, a 'Crack and Thump'
demonstration was the only way and in this, a distant firer fired rounds over your
head and the distinction between the crack of the round passing over your head,
was followed by the thump of the report of the weapon some milliseconds later
and this would give the direction of the fire and its distance from you, which was
quite good for 'normal' warfare but in the tight confines of an urban setting such
as Belfast, with ranges of 50 metres and less, being a normal contact, it was of
little use. So, in one of the Martello Towers of the Cinque Ports, a Battle Range
was established which comprised a set of sangars around the interior wall,
looking out over a typical urban setting and around each aperture, was a sand box
of a predetermined depth and consistency where a weapon was fired into it from
a location close by and this gave a very realistic impression of being under fire,
what this felt like and how to identify the weapon or its type being used. The first
time of being subjected to this was very ass-grabbing, with the bright muzzle
flash, the crash of the weapon and the thump of the strike so very close to your
head, that realism was achieved and the adrenalin rush immense and adrenalin is
definitely brown, smelly and runs down your leg!

To be taught snatch squad techniques too was a definite sphincter muscle
contactor; in this, 4 nominated troops deploy to the riot in trainers, with batons
and little else. One guy carries the rifle, one the baton gun and the other two the
wooden batons reminiscent of Bobbies on the beat in the Victorian age, and at a

given signal from the commander the famous words 'man in the red T-shirt' would sound and the baton gunners, in the line, would fire their rubber bullets at him and with a great deal of good luck bring him down, the shield wall would then open and these intrepid four would dash out, into the rioting crowd, with the rifleman and baton gunner going slightly past the target to fend off the extremely pissed off and violent folk at that point, whilst the two others grabbed and frog marched the dazed individual back to the riot line. Not for the faint hearted.

The Urban Close Quarter Battle Range came into being, as we know it today, at Lydd and Hythe and it was designed to give soldiers a feel for an actual combat situation and to be able to practice and thus to feel and hear what it was like; this made it so much easier to deal with 'live' in Belfast or elsewhere. The range, a street patrol area, is very realistic with music, people, cars and the whole panoply of urban living going on whilst your 'brick' did its thing and was subjected to shootings and bombings etc and your reaction tested and recorded on film to be dissected later at the debriefing. The splats (a device used in the film industry to give the effect of the strike of a bullet) and the crack of the weapon being fired with your team firing back and racing into the pursuit or follow up mode or perhaps the dustbin you had stopped beside erupting in an explosion or the man in the public gents turning as you entered and having a gun in his hand instead of his willy, whilst you reacted with live rounds and therefore had to take note of who or what was in the line of fire, took realism to another level and the debrief after gave everyone a chance to see the incident, from every angle, warts and all!

Just before deployment, the final exercise took place at Rype Village or Tin Town depending on whether it was Kent or in Germany, and this consisted of living in company and platoon groups, as the unit would in the Province, and being subjected to a number of carefully planned 'Incidents' over that week or so and testing the ability of everyone in their role for the tour. Our first trip to Rype village near Lydd was from Blackpool in the mid 1970's and caused a stir for some of the older married guys because Rype Village was the old married quarters patch when Lydd was a unit station and the unit had been there in the early 1960s and this had, for some of the guys, been their homes and to misuse them so was a very strange feeling!

All of this kind of training had come at a heavy price in both monetary value and in lives lost or ruined, during these troubles but from the very early days of this conflict the British Army learnt and learnt well. It had started off in August 1969 very under-prepared, with its poor clothing and tactics, wrong weapons, equipment and attitude – along with this came a poor understanding of the Irish situation, not just one man one vote that it started with, but the fact that the IRA was still trying for a united Ireland and this was a superb platform to hijack and the use of PR and its importance and in this we gave the IRA all the ammunition, PR-wise, that it required. Our total reliance on the local Police and B Specials for our intelligence, gave us a very one side and distorted view of the facts and made us appear not only one-sided but out of touch with the Catholic population.

The poor quality of our staff officers, at the time, in how to deal with this kind of situation and our very poor tactics in how to deal with the people, made the situation worse and contributed to an increase in the length of the conflict. On the positive side, it was the professionalism of the British squaddie as he changed and adapted and learnt these lessons, often the hard way, that eventually held the ring stable enough and long enough, until everyone saw that the only way out was with dialogue and politics, not bomb and bullet. I have felt for a long time now that we who have served there, made the present situation in Northern Ireland possible and that no other Army could have done the same thing with so few, relatively speaking, casualties on all sides and whilst only history will recall our passing and our efforts, it gives me a warm glow of satisfaction in the darker moments of my despair at the present day woes and conflicts, and so I wish the next generation of squaddies good luck and I hope that they have as much success!

Squaddie, 'Scottish Regiment', Belfast

We had a couple of ACC [Army Catering Corps] guys with us who saw to our grub and stuff; basically, the food was piss-poor. We used to joke about the hardest course the Army offers. We decided it was the Chef's course, because no bugger had ever passed it! We also decided that the initials stood for 'Army Concrete Company'!

Chapter Twenty-Six

1993

A year of 351 bombs, 473 shootings, 8 soldiers, 6 RUC officers, 68 civilians and 2 terrorists killed.

On the British mainland, the IRA exploded bombs in a shopping centre in Warrington. They killed Jonathan Ball who was only 3 and 12 year old Timothy Parry.

In Northern Ireland, the 'bandit country' of South Armagh continued to live up to its deadly reputation and 6 of the 8 Army fatalities that year took place in that area. The other two were R.I.R. members killed off-duty and one, Lance Corporal Mervin Johnson, was shot outside his home with his child.

An IRA attack on a UDA office above a fish and chip shop in the Shankhill Road killed 10, including one of the bombers and 2 children.

XMG, 1993

Lieutenant Paul Muspratt, Duke of Edinburgh's Royal Regiment

XMG in 93 struck me as being just like what you'd imagine the 'wild west' to be like!

The RUC didn't go out unless they had 12 squaddies to look after them, and there was no movement by vehicle for either them or us; everything was either by foot or helicopter. The RUC tended therefore, to spend most of their 3 day rotation inside the station. I can't knock them for that though, as we spent only 6 months there, but for them there was no immediate end in sight. Inside their station they also had a wall covered in pictures showing all the RUC officers murdered in and around XMG; the dangers were always apparent.

After completing the NITAT training and flying in with the advance party, the first handover patrols we went on with the Royal Scots were surreal. It was easy to imagine that a DS would walk out from a bush and tell you to spread out more, or give you a hot debrief on what you'd just done wrong, or could do better. The Royal Scots took great delight in showing us around, explaining where the various incidents had happened (like the large hole in the brick work by the bank in XMG square where the round fired from the cemetery had passed through the LI soldier, and his bullet proof plate (?), before striking the wall) and introducing us to the various 'players'.

None of the locals ever acknowledged our presence, apart from the kids who swore at us, and no-one would speak to us. This seemed particularly noticeable in XMG, as when we took part in ops outside of our normal TAOR the locals would sometimes say things like 'Take care', which really put the shits up the blokes. Even the local priest wasn't above this – the graveyard that overlooked the square was a known firing point. When they tried to shoot down a Puma helicopter, which happened to be carrying the Brigade commander as it left the camp, they used a high sided truck mounted with a Russian 12.7mm Dushka HMG and GPMGs. It was parked in the chapel car park, between the church and the priest's house; he was in at the time but never heard or saw anything.

The tour started quietly enough. We knew at some point they were going to let us know what they could do, and we just carried on doing what we were doing until then. During a foggy morning, and just before my multiple was due to go out on a mortar baseplate patrol they managed to park a HGV in the Gaelic football club's car park, right next to the camp, and lobbed 3 'barrack busters' over the fence. We were sitting in the QRF room, attached to the concrete reinforced RUC station, when they hit. Everyone dived under the beds, but I sat on the floor watching the dust fall, wondering about the hatred of these people that drove them to do this – this was part of the UK after all, right? I ran round from the QRF room to the Ops room, as all the Comms were down, to see what they wanted us to do. The scene was utter devastation, with a large hole blown into a concrete reinforced wall of the RUC station. The army building was flimsy in comparison and any hit on that would have caused significant damage and probably casualties.

Later, they cleverly tried to blow up one of our helicopters as it landed in camp. Next door to the camp was a baker, with a red Hiace delivery van that normally parked next to the camp. So they got a ringer van, cut a hole in the roof and put a couple of small mortars in the van. Luckily the helicopter just took off as the rounds landed, but that was a close call. The only time they managed to down a heli in our tour was when one came in low over the football pitch and took a direct hit to the tail rotor from a football. It crash landed in the camp and stayed there over night until it could be repaired!

Ovie [L/cpl Mark Overson] was first to get shot, on one of the few patrols the CSM, 'Badger' went on. Ovie was about 2 feet taller than the CSM and so presented a much more attractive target to the sniper. The road around XMG seemed purpose-built for sniping; they were long and straight, with plenty of corner or dead ground to disappear into. The frequent telegraph poles and Republican flags provided excellent distance and windage markers.

PIRA tended to operate best at the weekend, as they had jobs too. Saturdays were never a good day to be out and about. That Saturday in July was a prime example. The rotation with one of the Golf towers had taken place either the night before or that morning, and the relieved multiple was patrolling back into camp. It was Sgt Zimmer's multiple, I think, which was making their way back into camp, and they were noticing some obvious and quite heavy dicking going on. Major Patrick Tomlinson, the OC of Support Company, tasked my multiple to do a short town patrol, I suppose to provide an extra distraction away from Sgt Zimmer's multiple and hinder any freedom of operations PIRA had, this was a usual tactic. We had a quick briefing before going out, I talked through Cpl 'Mac' McDermid and L/Cpl Jason Passey about what we were going to do and why and then we left.

My team headed across the square towards Carran road; Mac took his team parallel to the road and through a field along the back of the houses that opened up onto the road. Where the houses thinned out as you left town he crossed the road and went firm. Jason Passey took his team to the top of Carran Road and went firm in an alley there. My team proceeded to the road as well to where we were going to set up our snap VCP. The town was busy, it was Saturday, and the bars were full. Having turned down the road we walked on for another 50–100 metres away from the junction. Pte's Mead and Price, a Kiwi, were in front and L/Cpl Kevin Pullin and I were at the back. Kevin was, prior to the tour, the company's PTI and was therefore known and liked by all. He wasn't an ego inflated PTI, just a very fit, happy-go-lucky guy. He wasn't a regular as such either, he'd been in the TA and had volunteered for a stint in the regulars (pretty sure that's right, Ovie could probably confirm).

I remember him telling me he was looking forward to going for a run during our R&R that was coming up shortly; exercise was a bit limited for a squaddie in XMG. As we walked down the road I pointed for Kevin to go over to the right hand side of the road, I went to the left. We went firm and then I signalled to Kevin to start stopping the traffic, we usually took it in turns and as Kevin was a lance jack he was really in charge of the brick, whilst I concentrated on the multiple. The first car that came through, was a known player, this was probably the first time we'd had a good look at this bloke so Kevin called in the plates and had a chat, after that we went firm again, taking up squatting position on either side of the street behind whatever cover was available. Next thing there was a tremendous whizzing noise, not like a rifle shot at all. I looked across and could see Kevin was down, I stood up, looking down the road, but couldn't see anything, as the road dropped into dead ground, and ran over to Kevin. The first thing I noticed were his eyes; they had a vacant quality to them, and I shouted the other two over and we started to give him first aid.

He wouldn't respond to his name, and I remember shouting at him 'Cpl Pullin, Cpl Pullin' and Mead said to me 'His name's Kevin.' The entry wound appeared small but wasn't bleeding, I suppose I was getting pretty agitated now, and we couldn't find a pulse or put the drip in. Looking up the road I could see the bar had emptied and the drinkers had moved onto the street, we obviously provided better entertainment than the TV at that point. I called in the contact report and probably broke with SOPs by telling them his name rather than his number. They were to send the PIG out as an ambulance and I gave a casevac location in the field at the bottom of the road, it seemed closer at the time. After an age the PIG arrived, but someone had put the wrong fuel type in and they couldn't get it going. Of the three of us only Price thought he'd seen something, a car partly obscured, but that was it (it later turned out they were using a car with a hatch back and the seats removed on one side as a firing platform for their Barrett light 50). We'd been giving Kevin first aid for about 10 mins by now, it felt much longer, as soon as the PIG stopped we put Kevin on a stretcher and placed it in the vehicle. One of the medics from the camp was in there and he took over from us. It then drove down the road and we all ran down after it.

Jason Passey's team had sealed off the road behind us and was trying to move the drinkers on. Then other teams which were on patrol from the camp established a cordon. At the bottom of the road, Cpl Mac's team had run away from the firing point into the Lismore estate (?) at the sound of the shot as it was that loud and had been bounced around off the buildings nearby. They hadn't seen anything either and now sealed off the suspected firing point. We took Kevin out of the PIG, which was now trying to knock down a chain link fence so we could get access to the field where the helicopter was to land. As the helicopter flew in I threw smoke out and it landed. As they ran with Kevin to the helicopter, his arm fell and hung limply from the stretcher – I think that confirmed for me what I knew to be the truth from the moment I ran over to him. I believe Kevin died on the spot, maybe shortly after we got to him. The 50 calibre armour piercing round (?) entered about his navel, through his dog tags and below his flak jacket, the tip was later found in his water bottle. We maintained the cordon whilst the RUC went to work; I remember Patrick, the OC, coming up to me whilst still on the road and I cried whilst he spoke to me.

As more teams were being deployed we moved back into the camp – the other half of my platoon was there – Sgt Brierly and I walked around the helipad talking about what happened and what I should say to the platoon. We got them all together in the QRF room, but I think by then it'd been confirmed that Kevin had been killed – 'we have to go on' was about the best I could muster, some of the guys were in tears and I didn't want the level of professionalism that we had achieved to slip, nor did I want people to be afraid to go back out.

About an hour after that the OC got on the horn and asked us to deploy again as we were the QRF still. Some driver had been going through the cordon trying to knock down the soldiers as they tried to stop him. Patrick called a second time, just as the driver had pulled back onto the Carran Rd and was driving back up the road to where Kevin had just been shot, for the second time.

My team was first out and we ran directly to the junction, and just got there as he emerged from out of the cordon and stopped at the junction of the Castleblaney Rd. We knew that he was up to no good and were in no mind to muck about. I walked round the front of the car, probably the wrong thing to do, but I wanted to get a look at him and try to stop him from pulling off. The rules of contact were strict, rather than point my rifle at him, I couldn't fire unless he attempted to use lethal force against me, so I adjusted my grip to be ready to clobber him instead. Just as I got level with the driver and in front of the bonnet he took off, I swung down hard with the rifle, smashing but not breaking the windscreen. Luckily I managed to grab hold of the wiper arm and pulled myself onto the bonnet. He wasn't stopping and was already going into second gear as I rolled off the bonnet and hit the road – just prior to which, one of the guys in the brick opened fire. This was quite justified as he'd used the car as a weapon against us.

Unfortunately, he only fired one round and missed. We never found out who the driver was or why he'd done that, although our guess was that he was trying to win his PIRA spurs. They joked afterwards that I'd managed to call in the second contact for the day whilst surfing on the bonnet and it did the rounds as it was caught by the CCTV cameras on Borucki sangar. The incident did however settle our nerves and firmed our resolve.

The multiple went on R&R shortly after, during which the army psychologist visited the camp in our absence. We attended Kevin's funeral and were introduced to his parents. I had wanted to, but was unable to speak to his folks, as I wasn't sure what they'd been told about that day. I had then and continue to have, a feeling of guilt – I walked down that road and pointed to Kevin to go right, whilst I went left. I've heard that it's not uncommon for those who come out of these things when others around them don't, to feel guilty that they did. That others feel the same way, doesn't make it rational, nor go away. Every time I think about it I can feel the hairs on my neck stand up and the tears start to well up.

What made NI all the more frustrating and harrowing was that we were fighting shadows who took their opportunities when they best presented themselves. What could seem normal was suddenly shattered in a fraction of a second as mayhem came down around you, and then nothing again for weeks. In XMG we were put in harm's way and were almost the sport of PIRA. We knew who they were and where they all lived; we were never allowed to get them though ...

We won't forget you, ever, but I ask myself what we, or they, achieved?

XMG: 1993
Lance Corporal Mark 'Ovie' Overson, Duke of Edinburgh's Royal Regiment

We arrived in XMG in late March of that year for what was my second – and last – tour. I had been made up to Lance-Jack and I was in charge of a 4 man brick. We would do 2 weeks in the Golf towers and then this would be followed by 2 weeks of foot patrols.

I was in 5 Platoon and, as I said, I was a brick commander. A routine op for us in, say, a rural area would involve what we called 'roving VCPs' and this would involve 2 bricks of 4 men on our left and right on, generally, high ground and the other brick on the road. We would position one gut behind and one in front and these would be the 'cut off' men and their job would be to stop a suspect vehicle if it tried to flee and back us up when we were doing a check.

As we were under cover, an approaching car wouldn't spot us until the last minute as we jumped up and the driver had no time to stop and do a u-turn out of the place. One man – usually me – would radio in the plate details and a 'chat up' man would check the driver and generally keep him occupied whilst I did the checks over the RT.

Then one Saturday in April – it was almost inevitably on Saturdays when we were attacked, as I will explain later – we were doing a roving VCP on a quiet country road – Creggan Road – about 3 kilometres outside of XMG. It was the 3rd and my sister's birthday was the following day. My brick was on the road and we were all under cover; I remember that 'Sticks' the brick medic was on cut off and my chat up man was the CSM. That day he was just acting like an ordinary Private and I think that he just wanted to stretch his legs and get out of the base.

We saw a white 4x4 which might have been a Toyota Isuzu, but I can't be absolutely certain and, when it got close, we jumped up and indicated to the driver that we wanted him to stop. I then conducted a plate check over the radio whilst the CSM checked the driver and chatted to him and kept him distracted. The plate check came back as clear and I asked the CSM if he was happy and he nodded yes and I remember saying to the driver 'Ok, mate; on your way.'

The driver then said to me – jovially, I think: 'You might want to keep your heads down today, lads' and I laughed and waved him through. The vehicle drove up the hill towards a dip in the road and had only gone about 100 metres and I turned to get down under cover again.

I heard a terrifically loud crack and my first thought was that the CSM had had a ND [negligent discharge, accidental or careless firing] and I just called out 'Was that you?' 'Fuck off, Ovie – it weren't me – was it you?'

Looking back, I don't know why I said that as I knew that I had been shot! I felt an awful pain, as though someone had punched me in the back and then felt a burning sensation. I shouted 'Fuck me, I think I've been shot!' and the CSM just looked at me and replied 'Fuck me, you have!' Then, my knees buckled and I went down like a sack of shit!

Even though the CSM was, compared to me, only a little guy, bless him, he dragged me under cover at the side of the road. Both my arms had terrible pins and needles and, in the shock and confusion, I forgot my basic training and didn't immediately radio in "Contact". Despite going into shock, it should have been the first thing I did. Anyway, I got on the Storno and called in 'Contact – Wait – Out' and, as was SOP, the net went silent. Then the multiple commander on the hillside broke the silence. 'What's happening? Any casualties?'

Before I could reply, the CSM called out to 'Sticks' the brick medic: 'Get your arse down here; Ovie's been hit.' He started to patch me up and I began to flap, imagining the worst. I asked him how bad it was, and I remember him saying 'It's pissing with blood, but I think it's only a scratch.' His hands were shaking so much, I remember the CSM having to help him with the bandages. Suddenly, my training kicked in and I got back on the Storno to the multiple commander and informed him that we had one times casualty and that the potential firing point was about 300 metres to the north.

At this stage, the 2 bricks on both sides of the high ground began to run forward to seek out the gunman. Later, the Int boys felt that it was an infamous Provo group, the 'Cullyhanna crew' but that was never proved, sadly. I radioed through and gave a Cas-Rep and told him that we needed a casevac. When he asked who the casualty was, I gave him my own personal call-sign 'Oscar Victor 7123' and he was a little incredulous as he couldn't believe that I was reporting my own shooting! He did make me repeat my last statement!

Ten minutes later, a Puma helicopter landed in a field about 100 metres away and a female Captain jumped out and walked slowly towards where I was lying and just stood up in the road. Even though I was injured, I knew enough to grab her and pulled her down under cover. I remember apologising to her and calling her 'Ma'am' and that was it.

The round had severed a shoulder strap and then entered my day pack, then exited and ripped a huge chunk of flesh out of my back. I was so very lucky and it was only the accidental turning of my body as the gunman fired which saved my life.

There have been times when I have sat down and thought that I could have died. There would have been no wedding, no future.

Unfortunately we had two fatalities on the Crossmaglen tour – L/cpl. Kev Pullin (murdered with the Barrett.50) and Pte. Randall who were both shot and killed.

Fortunately for me I was very lucky and survived my incident and received the GOC's Commendation for relaying the incident to the OPs Room and helping with the subsequent follow up and my own Medevac.

[Having seen the damaged pack in Mark's parents' house in a Berkshire town, I can personally attest as to the entry and exit holes the round made; one small entry hole and a huge exit gash]

Mark listed the following events which involved his battalion on that tour:

1. Multi-weapon shoot against Borucki Sangar Crossmaglen SF base – 25th March 1993
2. Myself getting shot outside of Crossmaglen (Creggan road!) – 3rd April 1993
3. Triple Mk 15 Mortar attack against Crossmaglen SF Base – 7th April 1993
4. Single Mk 15 Mortar attack – 11th June 1993
5. Murder of Pte Randall at Newtonhamilton – 26th June 1993 (I was in Crossmaglen)
6. Murder of L/Cpl Kev Pullin – 17th July
7. Helicopter shoot, Crossmaglen to Cullyhanna – 24th September 1993.

E TYRONE 1993

Warrant Officer, Grenadier Guards

I deployed with a Multiple of 2nd Bn to assist the 1st Bn Coldstream Guards on a roulement tour of E Tyrone. We were manning sangars in Cookstown when a box of 'Quality Street' was dropped off by some 'well-wishers'. When they were taken back to the accommodation they were found to contain a full-on viable device. ATO was called and the device was neutralized; had it gone off it would have probably taken out 12–15 Guardsmen.

It was at this time that one of my lads had stripped his mags to clean them; he had lined up all his rounds on the wall to one side. Unfortunately he had placed them on a radiator and they eventually started boiling. Again a pissed-off ATO was called and dealt with the offending items!

We had a patrol out one night covering the 'Greenvale Hotel' a notorious night-spot in Cookstown; at about 0200hrs an extremely drunk and obnoxious group of scroats approached my team and started spoiling for a fight. It ended with one of the lads foolishly stating, 'My Dad is a Sinn Fein Councillor, and you dare not touch me'. Suffice to say we did and he ended up in a garden pond for his pains.

BELFAST AND BELLEEK: 1993

Corporal Paul 'Scouse' Hughes, Royal Welch Fusiliers

In 1993, I was a young Corporal in the 1st Bn the Royal Welch Fusiliers; during a six month tour of Fermanagh, one of the lads was hospitalised through injury, and was sent up to Musgrave Park Hospital (MPH) Belfast for a few days. Being the caring sort, my mate Jase Hill and I volunteered to drive up and see him. Amazingly, the OC allowed us to use his issued car for the trip, on the understanding it came back undamaged.

The journey up was pretty uneventful and we arrived at MPH. We got in to see our mate 'Bean', and after 20 minutes of calling him a lazy malingerer, he was glad to hear that we had to get back for that evening's patrol. It so happened that his wife at the time, from Belfast, was visiting and he had a pass to go out for the afternoon. Having joined them at a nearby MacDonald's, we were getting pressed for time. So his wife kindly suggested a quicker route back to the A1. Naively, we listened to her directions and set off on our return leg. All was going well until we realised that the paving stones, lampposts and murals were becoming a colour known as 'hint of Tricolour'. We soon realised that we were now on our very own little sightseeing tour of a Republican heartland! Then, Jase pointed out that I was in fact wearing a Northern Ireland football shirt, which really did not compliment the 'Celtic' shirts which covered the area. Nervous laughter began to give way to serious thoughts of needing to get out of the area rather rapidly, and all I could think about was those poor Corporals who drove into an IRA funeral in the late eighties.

With our pistols between our legs, for security, we decided to drive 'normally' so not to attract anymore attention than my football shirt was already doing. Finally we found our bearings, slightly embarrassed and very relieved we got back to Fermanagh. The OC was happy to see his car in one piece. We didn't have the heart, or the bottle to tell him it could have been so different; lesson learned.

During the same tour, we found ourselves in the border outpost of RUC Belleek. For those who are familiar with it, you will know that there is one road in and one road out, with the Irish Republic pretty much dominating three sides of the town. During one month in particular, much to the amusement of ourselves and the RUC, all patrolling kept getting cancelled. Obviously we were not important enough to know the reasons why, so we polished up on our scrabble skills! We never did find out the reason why. That was until I was discussing the tour with a guy from 22 [SAS] in Hereford, who was attached to us in Gorazde, Bosnia, two years later.

He was actually in Province at the time and recalled rather casually, 'Oh yeah, there was a fourteen man PIRA gun team on the border, waiting for you to leave the Police station!' Apparently they were even doing nighttime relief in place; sometimes, being kept in the dark about things isn't all that bad actually.

Paul's Regiment, the RWF, lost 7 men in their various tours of Northern Ireland; one man was lost on the 1993 tour. Corporal David 'Legs' Wright of the close observation platoon was killed in a road traffic accident just 9 days before Christmas. Most of their fatalities were in the period 1972–79, when 6 men were killed.

SOUTH ARMAGH 1993
Former Captain, Royal Gloucestershire, Berkshire & Wiltshire Regiment.

These are recollections which I was privileged to hear of from a previous tour in 1993 which reinforced the differences between tours in South Armagh pre- and post the peace process.

These recollections were from a platoon Sergeant whom I worked with later on my last tour in Ballykinler in 2001. In fact we were in Bessbrook Mill for a patrols stint in late 2001 and we started talking about South Armagh in general. This platoon sergeant had been a young private soldier in the early 1990s and had begun his military career in Crossmaglen.

He told me about how, as an 18 year old private soldier, he arrived with the company group into Crossmaglen SF base by chopper for the start of a 6 month tour in the early 1990s. As the chopper pulled away the mortar alarm sounded and as people dived for cover the PIRA hit Borucki sangar with a.50 cal sniper rifle. Luckily they all escaped injury. But the vast majority of patrols on that tour resulted in contacts.

He was also first on the scene following the shooting and subsequent murder of a Lance Corporal during that tour. As he watched the medic try to give first aid that summer's evening, local women and children came out of the bars in Crossmaglen town square to taunt the troops as they tried to evacuate the casualty. The young Lance Corporal was already dead. Nevertheless the sort of mental trauma that this leaves the soldiers on the ground with, frankly beggars belief. Even employing all of the drills taught during pre-tour training could not sometimes help you.

The dead team commander's multiple had gone out to protect the arrival of an inbound patrol – as was SOPs at the time, and yet still they were hit.

Within a month of being in Crossmaglen SF base this platoon sgt (at the time just an 18 year old 'Tom') said he had watched the more senior private soldiers (some with 8 years service or more) diving under their beds when mortar alarms sounded, reduced to tears and sobbing, praying that it wasn't them next. As someone at the start of his Army career, he said he found this particularly hard to deal with.

Another story that must be remembered was the PIRAs attempt to burn Borucki Sangar in Crossmaglen to the ground using a muckspreader to spray petrol over the sangar and then set it alight. The 4 soldiers inside ended up taking cold showers in the shower block to try and stay cool, as a rescue attempt was actioned. My understanding is that the Sangar Commander (a full screw) received either an MM or at least an MID for his leadership. I'm afraid I have no idea which unit this was but it was definitely a South Armagh battalion in the early/mid 90s.

For every squaddie on active service in the Province, whether he was a Private, a NCO, or an Officer, back home on the mainland was an anxious mother dreading the nightly news telling of the loss of another British soldier.

Lita Overson, Berkshire

My son did two tours of duty. The first was when he was 20 and he came home on leave and said that he was going but I just put it to the back of my mind.

I cried after he left and thought and worried every day for the next few weeks. When there was nothing on the news or he phoned or wrote, I calmed down and gradually felt convinced that he would come home safe.

However, with the second tour, things were different and for some reason when his [embarkation] leave was up and he went back to camp before flying out to Ireland, I was really worried and apprehensive. I was so worried, that I phoned both my sisters who are church members and asked them to pray for him. I couldn't pray for him myself, as I am not religious.

I found myself hunting for any news of Ireland; I looked in the media, on Teletext, Ceefax, anything. When my son survived the incident [Mark was shot near Crossmaglen] it was really strange. I stopped worrying; I was relaxed and was just waiting for him to come home.

When he was away, I had read of a poem used by a girl whose boyfriend had been killed in Ireland. Every time I read it, even today, it brings a lump to my throat. If anything had happened to my son, in Ireland or when he was in the Army, I would have put it on his headstone.

Do not stand at my grave and weep; I am not there, I do not sleep.
I am a thousand winds that blow; I am a diamond glinting in the snow.
I am the sunlight on reapened grain; I am the gentle autumn rain.
When you awaken in the morning hush, I am the uplifting rush of quiet birds in
encircled flight.
I am the soft stars that shine at night; do not stand at my grave and cry, I am not
there – I did not die.

BELFAST/PORTADOWN, 1993.

Private, Infantry Regiment

I did my one and only tour in 1993 and although the Bn went back I was in Germany and missed it. For many of us who did Northern Ireland, especially those chaps who were there in the 70s and 80s when it was shit, we have come to see ourselves as 'forgotten men' and I think that's why your book appeals so much. Sure, we all got our GSMs and we're all proud to wear them, but the Government gave out 300,000 of them. There were MMs and QGMs and a few MIDs and some other well-publicised gongs but we didn't get the recognition that other squaddies in other wars got.

I used to watch the news before I joined up and I noticed, even at a quite early stage that the death of a soldier would be fifth or sixth item on the news and gradually the news of a loss or even of NI altogether was either relegated to the middle of the newspapers or even not reported on at all. Sometimes, there would be a little paragraph about a bomb which had killed a soldier or a UDR man, but call Elton John 'gay' or something like that, and it was pages, one, two, three, four, five and even six! Talk to youngsters these days and say something like 'I served in Northern Ireland' and they'll look blank at you or ask 'What was that then?' and it seems as though the world, certainly our country at least, has consigned us to the dustbin of history without even an honourable mention.

Whenever they do a flick about the troubles, because it's usually a Yankee one, we're the bad guys and the IRA are the bleeding heroes. They even had Brad Pitt play a bomber and killer and they made him out to be a saint. In one flick I went to see, Tommy Lee Jones – a Yank – was playing a terrorist but he comes out a 'freedom fighter' and the public fell for it. We are the 'Nazis' and the IRA and the rest were resistance workers; such bollocks!

I have seen a comrade shot – in his throat – and although, thank God he lived, I had to hold my hand over the bubbling wound in his throat and he was crying and trying to say 'Mum' but the words wouldn't come out. Another time, we found a body that had been bound, hooded and gagged and his groin area was piss-stained as he must have panicked just before they shot him in the head. You know what? He had about a dozen burn marks on his body as they must have tortured him with lit fags. On one occasion, after a blast in a drinking club, we were trying to put bits of bodies together to make whole ones but it was impossible. Freedom fighters? I would like these Yankee film makers to have had time to come out on patrol with us.

I was a kid when the Falklands War was on, but I remember it ending on June 14, 1982 when we liberated Stanley. That meant nothing to the terrorists and they killed a squaddie on the same day just to celebrate!

[Believed to be Private Hugh Cummings of the UDR, shot as he left his place of work in Strabane.]

Keep telling our story mate, make us feel the pride that we should do and get us the recognition we deserve.

This was related to me over the phone by a soldier I know personally; several times during the interview, he had to ask for a break as he was overcome with emotion. Further comment from me is entirely superfluous.

NORTHERN IRELAND: 1993

Driver Philly Morris, 4 Sqdn, Royal Corps of Transport

I did the old 'tin city' in Sennelager, Germany and then out to Ulster where, as an RCT squadron you generally get split up and attached to the various Infantry Regiments around the Province. Some went to Londonderry, some down to the sticks in bandit country, a few to Lisburn as civvy drivers, and a few went to Limavady for the sneaky beaky stuff.

I, myself, got put in Moscow camp in the docks next to the airport where we were to look after the new Saxon patrol APCs and make the city know that we had plenty of them, and just drive them around the city, day and night, keeping people awake. We did our own top-cover [armed guard] which was always fun as the RCT lads maybe had one range-test just one day a year provided it did not clash with a BBQ.

Our rooms were pretty basic; metal walls and corrugated mesh roof and there were various regimental paintings from units such as the Paras, Marines, Guards, Green Jackets, REME, and the odd Navy slogan on every available wall inside and out across the whole base going back to the 70s which were great to read. It was then that it hit home that this had been going on for a long time. We shared the base with the Navy, but we were not allowed to cross over into their section, because there was a rumour it was the SBS [Special Boat Service; the Navy equivalent to the SAS] who did all the night time boat patrols around the province.

It became routine for something different to happen everyday, and I got my first fright not on the ground but lying on my bed on armoury duty. Suddenly, there was an almighty bang, and I jumped out of my bed and banged on my helmet and vest and jumped under my bed waiting for the sirens to start. I had never heard a bomb go off before and the walls had shaken; was it a mortar? I just didn't know but we did as we had been trained and took cover until further notice. After about ten minutes my mate Ashy came in with a hot dog, half- pissed and a porn mag rolled up under his arm. Casually, he sat on my bed and changed the TV channel, mumbling to himself. I was bemused and asked: 'what the fuck ya doing; aren't we being mortared?' He burst out laughing and informed me that it had been a car bomb about 2 miles away in a car park !

It was normal to be bricked and bottled, and you got used to it, but sometimes you just wanted to let a round off at their feet because you really could not be arsed ducking in and out of top cover every 10 feet, and these kids were good shots, plenty of practice from an early age.

In June, I think it was, we were on the Queen's Bridge doing car searches at a roadblock with the RUC when the Provos set off a massive bomb outside the Opera house by the Europa hotel. It was less than a mile away, but Jesus, there was glass coming past us and bits of window frame and all sorts of debris. Again the bang was a shock and we all jumped inside, the giggles were always the same – if giggles could be translated they would say 'fuck me.' We watched the News that night and I could not believe how much this fucker had wrecked the street; you had seen it in pictures but when you had been down there, the day before, it brought it all back to you.

July came around again and it was the annual marching season and it was a busy time for us – we didn't get too much sleep. We would go out in trucks with huge pull-out screens to block the views of the marchers from those in the Republican areas whom the Prods were trying to provoke. It was all-day, every day; a few hours on the Ardoyne, a few hours on the Crumlin Road, a few hours somewhere else. We would get there ahead of the marches, and then try and get to another part ahead of the tip of the march, and at these points there was massive RUC presence. We would have a small clear area between the 'Peeler' wagons and us and we would stand in there and were told to keep any press or the odd nutter from running through.

The Loyalist marches would stop where we were and just hurl abuse at the Republicans behind our screens; I could not believe how much anger there was. Of course you had heard about it and seen it in pictures but when you can hear every shout, see it in their eyes, and are having to rugby tackle them. All the time you were high on adrenaline; at times you just thought 'there's thousands of them and there's maybe 30 of us! If this goes off big time, I am dead'. I remember someone got past the screen and ran towards the RUC with something in his hand, and I ran over and swiftly kicked him in the stomach and got him to the ground. Whereupon, he started to scream: 'Press! Press! Don't shoot, please.' I got up and shouted at him: 'Fuck off, mate; you've just run through a road block with something in your hand!' It was in fact a small, black camera and I gave him a warning and told him to think next time before he did something like this. I checked his pass and then sent him on his way. He was from the 'Times' I think and I checked the next day to see if I had broken one of his ribs or something; nothing in it!

THE MURDER OF JOHN RANDALL

As told to me by Mark Overson, D.E.R.R.

On 26th June 1993, whilst on patrol to the south of the Village of Newtownhamilton in South Armagh he was murdered by a single shot; the lad was 19 years old.

Around 7pm, part of the patrol, under Corporal Travers, positioned themselves to the south-west of NTH, to provide cover to the other two sections as they patrolled across the valley (this runs from the base and to the south)

The forward of the two, as they were crossing fields near the Dundalk Road, took cover by a grass bank and immediately, a single shot was fired. The sound of the shot was partially muffled because of the sounds of drum and other music blaring out from the town. Apparently, the sound was heard quite clearly, away from the noise of the music.

The lads in the forward of the two sections were desperately trying to ascertain the firing point and a platoon commander, Lieutenant Telfer radioed to see if his team members were ok. All replied with one exception and it was realised that John Randell had not replied and the officer dashed from cover in order to search for him. Lieutenant Telfer searched for him amongst the reeds of a nearby stream, near which, the team had taken cover. Private Randall was found, lying wounded on the ground, clearly having taken the single round which had been fired; he had been mortally injured, as the round had hit him in the kidney area.

At this point, the lads in Corporal Traver's team had seen three civilians running towards a car, in which they climbed and drove off; the position was identified afterwards as the exact firing point. Despite incredible efforts by the team medic to save his life, he later died of his wounds in Newry.

His funeral service at Langley was well attended by all members of the Regimental Family, and in particular by his comrades from the 1st Battalion.

The killing of Private Randall – who was only 19 – was the sixth such border attack in a short period of time. The killer probably fired from behind the car which was observed by his comrades, which then immediately sped towards the border with the Irish Republic.

THE MURDER OF KEVIN PULLIN, CROSSMAGLEN

Related to me by a former D.E.R.R. soldier

L/Cpl Pullin was serving in 'C' Company based at Crossmaglen and was killed by a terrorist using a new large sniper rifle, the Barrett Light .50.

The local IRA ASU had launched several mortar attacks on SF bases in the area and they were clearly keen to continue this tactic and thus, the chance of further attacks was very high. The IRA seemed determined to inflict further damage on men and property and several anti-mortar searches were organised.

The idea was to discover potential launching sites in order to prevent further attacks. At least two companies were involved and in mid-July, we set up VCPs on the roads which led to the areas in which we were operating Nothing particularly helpful was found, but the local civilian populace appeared quite surprised at the timing and scale of our efforts. Despite this, we immediately began to attract the attention of known players and their helpers who were observing our troops. This process of observing and reporting was called 'dicking' or being 'dicked'. There was a feeling that we were vulnerable to attack and our instincts were sadly proven correct, although the skills we had learned over the years stood us in good stead and we never gave them the opportunity to attack us on that first day.

The next day, we patrolled again, but with greatly reduced numbers. We had intended to change over the personnel in an observation tower just south of Crossmaglen but this had been delayed due to the activities of the previous day. Whenever this changeover was effected, we were exposing ourselves to attacks from the town and so a patrol was actually put onto the streets in order to provide cover for the operation.

One of the platoon commanders, Lieutenant 'M' with three teams went into the town and we set up what we called a 'snap vcp' but no sooner had we done this, when a round was fired from the north. One of the lads, Lance Corporal Kevin Pullin, was hit as he positioned himself in a doorway and very seriously wounded. Two of the lads, Private Mead and Private Price, both fought desperately to save him, but, sadly, after he was casevaced by chopper, he died of his wound.

Lance Corporal Pullin was the last Duke of Edinburgh man to be killed in Northern Ireland, tragically so soon after John Randell. In total four men of the Regiment were killed in the Province, the other two being a Corporal Stephen Windsor and Private John Allen. Kevin Pullin was killed by a then new and terrifying weapon using a.50 round, the use of the weapon by the IRA would continue.

Driver Philly Morris, 4 Sqn, Royal Corps of Transport

The days were long and hot and I we all lost shit loads of weight that Marching season week; the good thing was you got to see your mates that you had not seen for months. These lads were out everyday, all day and had been hardened up by what they had experienced.

We were only ever out as top cover and recce and never really did any foot slogging and I was glad when it calmed down; it was exciting but I was goosed. Thirteen hours a day if not more; working with the RUC made our British police force look like girl guides and they were hard fuckers; they took no shit and would not show one bit of emotion toward either side of the fence. I remember an RUC woman stood and did not flinch while 10 or so Republicans shouted and screamed abuse at her from just 3 feet; big lads too and they could have ripped her to bits if they got more wound up. This girl was maybe 5 feet 6 and just stared them out, not even a blink, and I remember thinking that I wouldn't have wanted to get on the bad side of her.

A rioter had tried to throw a hand grenade at us, but it had gone off before he could launch it and it had taken his hand off, although, luckily, no-one else was hurt. He just lay there, next to us, in absolute agony and quickly, the place cleared and the RUC called for an ambulance. Of course, we all just looked at each other and said 'what do we do ?' We suggested helping him and putting a field dressing on his hand? This begged the question: ' what if he has one in his other hand or was armed?' Fortunately, the RUC put their hands up and gestured us to stay put and they went over and sat him up and got him seen to.

There was the time we had to block a road because a Republican had been killed planting a bomb. [The Shankhill Fish 'n Chip massacre which killed 10 people when the IRA tried to bomb the UDA offices] when it had gone off and killed him. The bomber's family lived in that road and a number of local well-known faces had turned up to comfort them. Just then,one of our lads came running down saying: 'fuck me; guess who is at the house?' We just looked blank and he said: 'Bryan Adams' [famous Canadian rock singer of the time] and ran off. We looked at each other and said 'Bryan Adams' and just giggled; again he came running back 'It's deffo Bryan Adams; I had him right in my [sniper scope] sights just to see what he looked like.' And again he ran off and we both by this time looked at each other and shrugged, thinking it was a hot day and he needed a cold drink. Finally he came running down and we were told by the RUC to let the next car out and as we did so, the guy said: 'look, here he is' and pointed at the car. We looked in and then turned to our excited mate and said 'That's Gerry Adams ya dickhead.' He said: 'oh, yeah; that's the one.'

When we left, two days later, the Provos declared a ceasefire! We all thought 'lucky bastards' as the lads who were replacing us would have an easy time.

Chapter Twenty-Seven

1994

1994 saw 222 bombing incidents and 348 shootings. It also saw the deaths of 3 soldiers, including 2 members of the Royal Irish regiment, which had come about as an amalgamation of the UDR and Royal Irish Rangers. 3 RUC officers were killed as were 48 civilians and 9 terrorists.

In this year, Private Reginald McCollum of the Royal Irish Rangers, who was only 19, was abducted and shot; the third member of his family to be killed by the IRA. One of his comrades, 46 year old Corporal Trelford Withers, was shot and killed at his shop in Crossgar, Co Down.

The only regular soldier to die was a member of the newly-formed Royal Logistics Corps, Lance Corporal David Wilson, killed by a bomb blast in Keady, Armagh on May 14.

The cycle of murders was decreasing, however, and, after the killing of RIR man Withers, officially only 3 more squaddies' families would be receiving that heart-stopping knock on their front door, often in the early hours of the morning by an Army welfare officer. The first of two major IRA ceasefires during this period came into effect.

LISNASKEA: 1994

Air Trooper Scott Buchanan, Army Air Corps

I had the opportunity for a relatively cushy number in the AAC, but at the age of 18 years and 2 days, I volunteered for a spell on the ground and, despite the scrapes which I will describe below, I do not have a second's regret, although I came close to some regrets after an incident at Carowshee.

We were based in a border post near Lisnaskea and although there were many boring days, there was always something which came along to snap us out of our boredom. On one particular day – changeover day – a Chinook was coming into land and from a nearby school field, dozens of the local yobs were hurling bricks and stones and trying to hit the rotor blades. No serious harm was done but the RAF boys were starting to wet their pants at the potential damage. The local kids delighted in taking every opportunity to cause us mischief.

This was harmless fun however, compared with an attempt by the IRA to blow us all up with a mortar attack launched from a white Transit van. One of their tactics was to either cut out the side or the side and the roof and launch them through this gap. They had all their coordinates and trajectories worked out and positioned the van-launcher by the fire station. As luck – good for us and bad for them – would have it, there was a fire alarm and as they were blocking the doors, they had to move their launcher back some distance. When they fired, the two mortars fell 10 feet short and fortunately failed to detonate. As I watched, I realised how close we had come to being blown into hundreds of pieces.

We had a VCP at one end of the Lisnaskea High Street, but unfortunately, the graveyard was on high ground and overlooked the checkpoint. An IRA sniper chose this exact point to fire at the RUC boys below. Both ourselves and the RUC considered this gunman a real pain in the arse, but we never were able to get the bastard, although we had our suspicions as to his identity.

Two more incidents come to mind during our time at Lisnaskea and one of them involved a Catholic enclave there called Carowshee Park. It was one big hotspot, a real breeding ground for the IRA and the Republicans and they hated us more there than anywhere else in Northern Ireland with the possible exception of XMG. In fact, right from the very top came the command: stay out of Carowshee Park; it is far too dangerous and volatile to patrol. So, this one night, a couple of bricks – 8 of us – decided that we would go down there and stir things up a bit as we were shortly due to leave the area.

Big mistake! Big mistake! The jungle drums must have been working overtime and within minutes, a mob of stone-throwing, stick-waving very angry Catholics came racing towards and the 8 of us shot out of the area like scalded cats.

My final memory of the time was the burger van down in the cattle market run by two Protestant girls; the scran was pretty tasty – just the kind of thing you wanted after a long night foot patrol. They served both sides of the community without too much hassle but when the Catholics, or more precisely, the Republicans got wind that they were serving soldiers, they were in for trouble.

Both girls were roughed up – I saw all their bruises – for serving us, but bless 'em, they never lost the courage to keep on serving us.

XMG: 1994
Company Sergeant Major 'D', Grenadier Guards

It was a cold and dark evening in March 1994. We had been in Crossmaglen for almost 6 months and during that time we had become used to regular IRA attacks on both the base and against our deployed patrols and observation posts. Earlier in the day, one of my Section Commanders mentioned to me that he felt the atmosphere in the town was wrong. I asked him exactly what he meant by this and he said he couldn't put his finger on exactly what was wrong, but he felt that we could be attacked very soon. It may seem strange to someone who has not served in XMG, but I took this remark seriously. XMG was like a pressure cooker at that time and you almost knew when something was going to happen, and when it did, it was almost like a relief, provided no one was hurt. There were combat indicators too; people being seen in certain places, certain patterns of life and things that we had noted from previous attacks, all these things added to the tension.

Even when you felt something was about to happen there was little that you could do. We were extra vigilant and took certain precautions, but life had to go on, after all, we had a job to do. At 1800hrs I took over as watch keeper in the operations room. I had checked the communications were working, I had familiarised myself with exactly who was where and what was going on or planned in our area of operations. Things had settled down and I was aware that a

Members of the ATO (bomb disposal) get a wheelbarrow ready to inspect a partially-exploded device under a bridge. (Photo courtesy of Darren Croucher)

Having a bit of fun with the RUC in a Londonderry police station.
(Photo courtesy of Darren Croucher)

Lynx helicopter was inbound to us with an under-slung load. The threat against helicopters during the day was extremely high at that time (The IRA had tried to bring down a Puma in XMG at the start of our tour) and to bring in one troop-carrying Puma we needed two armed Lynx in support. For this reason administrative and resupply flights were generally carried out in the dark, as this was deemed safer. Unfortunately this fact had not escaped the eyes of the South Armagh PIRA, as we would discover.

Helicopters landing and taking off were pretty routine in XMG, so when Lynx 5 was heard outside there was little reaction in the Ops Room, the boys on the helipad would 'sort it'. Suddenly the ops room was plunged into darkness, 'another bloody power cut' I thought. The emergency generator immediately kicked into life and the whirr of electronic equipment starting up could be heard. I had just started to complain about the 'bloody power' when there was a tremendous bang, the room shook and plaster and dust fell from the roof. We all realised immediately that this must have been a mortar attack and we were more concerned about getting the contact report off to Bessbrook than about taking cover. For a few seconds there was chaos as people flooded into the ops room and instructions were shouted. The operations officer quickly took over my duties and I rushed outside, as by this time we had remembered that we had a helo' on the pad.

As I took in the scene on the outside my worst fears were realised, immediately I was struck by a scene of devastation. Lynx 5 was sitting upright on its under-slung load, bright orange flames were coming from every door and window and its tail boom was completely missing. The outside of the base was covered in thick black oily smoke and there was a strong smell of aviation fuel. My first thought was about casualties, the cockpit of the helo was completely engulfed in flames and it looked really bad for anyone still on board. As I approached the scene, a seemingly lifeless body dressed in civilian clothes was dragged past me. One of the platoon commanders and a platoon sergeant were dragging the casualty clear, they were pulling him by the arms which were now above his head. His clothing had ridden up and I could see a huge open wound which started under his arm pit and stretched diagonally across his abdomen to his navel. I tried to lift the man's legs to ease the pressure on the wound but it was more important at this point to get him into some cover. The ammunition from the door gun had now started to 'cook off' and 7.62mm tracer rounds were starting to ricochet around the interior of the base. I had no idea who this casualty was and assumed that he had been a civilian contractor. It was a little while before I discovered that it was one of our RUC friends. 'Pete' had been returning from court and had not been wearing body armour. The Perspex window of the Lynx door had blown in and shrapnel had slashed him open, penetrating his chest. Pete was clearly in a bad way and was going to need rapid evacuation to hospital. I left him with our team medics who were already sealing his chest and inserting a drip into him.

I still had no idea who else was on the chopper at this point and the scene suggested that some, if not all, of the crew were probably dead. The boys had already reacted and large wheeled fire extinguishers had been turned onto the burning helo. Several frantic minutes followed as I dashed around the place trying to find the other casualties. The tracer rounds flying about the place were something of a concern and it was necessary to dash from cover to cover, fortunately we had built a substantial sandbag wall at the edge of the helipad and this provided some protection.

Amazingly the crew had all escaped relatively unscathed and to this day I cannot understand how. Having discovered that there were no other casualties, the company commander decided that the only option was to extract Pete from a field outside of the base. A couple of multiples were dispatched to secure the ground but the difficult part was to retrieve the Saxon Ambulance from the other side of the burning wreckage. It was necessary to reverse the ambulance to the casualty who was sheltered between some low buildings, rather than to expose the stretcher bearers to the ammunition still flying around the place. Cpl C——— — one of our RLC (Royal Logistics Corps) attachments [subsequently awarded the QGM for his outstanding courage in this incident] dashed across the helipad braving the exploding tracer rounds and retrieved the ambulance. Whilst this had all been taking place the RUC had telephoned a local doctor who had duly appeared complete with black bag. He was an elderly man who was panting heavily, he was invited to examine Pete but needed only a quick look to see that the young medics had done a superb job and he could do nothing more. We were all very surprised to see a civilian doctor at the scene, as the local doctor was infamous for her uncooperative attitude towards us 'Brits'. We later discovered that this chap had been a locum.

Pete was loaded onto the ambulance and was driven from the base to a greenfield extraction point. He was picked up by helicopter and flown direct to hospital. We were also surprised and delighted when the local part-time fire service arrived outside the main gate. The worst of the fire had by now died down but it was reassuring to have some fire brigade assistance.

The incident was of course ongoing until the firing point was located, cleared and any forensic evidence recovered. This stage of an incident was always dangerous because the threat of a secondary device or further ambush was ever present. Many lives had been lost to secondary attacks in XMG over the years. With Pete extracted to hospital we were now able to take a considered approach to the follow up operation. It was the afternoon of the following day before the incident was closed and we knew exactly what had happened.

The base plate of the improvised mortar was welded to the rear forks of a tractor and had been cleverly camouflaged with bales of straw. The tractor had been positioned in a sunken farm yard which was surrounded by a high wall. The main body of the tractor was actually under the shed and it was virtually impossible to see the location even from the air. The mortar was of the Mark 15 variety known to PIRA as 'The Barrack Buster'. The mortar had been initiated by use of a collapsing circuit and a domestic extension cable led to a mains plug socket in a building. The terrorists had simply turned off the power at an electrical power sub station and this had initiated the device. To ensure that they got the timing right, they must have had someone on a mobile phone overlooking the XMG base and the helicopter with an under-slung had been deliberately targeted as it would be much slower to manoeuvre. We now understood the reason for the power cut.

The wreckage of Lynx 5 had been shovelled into a skip by lunchtime and the base was open to helicopters once again. A fresh Lynx was flown in to replace the damaged one and the crew was extracted in this very chopper later during the day. Pete was quickly stabilised at the hospital and although he was critically ill for some time, he made a complete recovery from his injuries. At the time of writing he is still serving in the PSNI.

For us this was the culmination of a series of major attacks; this one, like some of the others, had been meticulously planned and executed. We often saw media reports referring to the IRA as highly professional. We never saw it this way, they always had the upper hand; they were in their own back yard and had been doing this for years. The local population were terrified of the Provos and the conduct of the so called 'Volunteers' was often worthy of Sicilian gangsters. We had a good idea who was responsible for this attack and unlike the media we knew that they were making a great deal of money under the cover of the 'troubles'. Unlike us they were not constrained by the rule of law. When the local SDLP councillor spoke out against this irresponsible attack, explaining how the local population could have been harmed, he was beaten senseless with Hurley sticks in his own home.

The real professionals were the 18 and 19 year old Guardsmen who endured the hardships and dangers and who lived under constant threat of attack 24 hours a day for 6 months. These young lads retained their discipline under extreme provocation and worked inside the rule of law at all times. They didn't like it, they thought that our hands were tied and that it was insulting to see the very same terrorists who had tried to kill us and to address them as 'sir', but they did it. Now that is professionalism and that is the reason why after 30 years of terror and mayhem N. Ireland remains a part of the UK where the majority of her population wants her.

LISNASKEA: 1994/5
Soldier, Light Infantry

There was a local player, a real scumbag by the name of Adamson, whom we had a lot of trouble with as he was not only suspected of attacks on the SF but would also give us a load of gob at every opportunity. We are pretty certain that he threw a coffee jar packed with explosives at an RUC patrol which detonated and severely damaged a young policeman's lower leg. We lifted him and I remember his abuse and insults as we took him in and I was tempted to give the scrote a good kicking but there were officers present!

His girlfriend worked in the local hairdressers and I remember the black looks she gave us as we walked by on foot patrol; this was nothing, however, to the looks she would shortly give us after a subsequent incident.

There was insufficient evidence to convict Adamson and he was released without charge and soon he was back at the camp gates taunting us. This particular day, he was on either a BMX or a mountain bike, just pissing around, swearing at us when his bike hit something and he was thrown backwards. His nut sack caught on the rear wheel literally ripping it open. There was blood everywhere and he was screaming like a pig; funnily enough, there was no rush from any of the amused military spectators and I certainly didn't jump in to help him.

Friday night and Saturday nights, although I shouldn't admit this, were the two nights of the week when we got our revenge on the players we couldn't lift even though we knew – and they knew that we knew – what they were doing. We would go into the town, raid the pubs and drag players outside for a bit of a bashing. Before you tell me that this wasn't 'British' let me tell you that these bastards were killing and maiming us and getting away with smirks on their faces. To make it worse, on VCPs and patrols, we had to call them sir ! We got a lot of pleasure from this player-bashing; it just evened things up a bit.

Whilst I was there, the local Proddies celebrated the 300th anniversary of the battle of the Boyne and 300 years of lauding it over the Catholics and they had flags everywhere and parades were planned. One night, a few of us drove into the town in a Land Rover and I shinnied up a lamp post and cut one of the flags down as a souvenir. Unfortunately for me, one of the locals who objected to my little treasure hunt spotted the number of the vehicle and reported us. I was hauled in front of the OC and fined £50 and I never got to keep the flag!

VARIOUS PLACES IN NORTHERN IRELAND: 1994
Lieutenant, Grenadier Guards

I did a couple of tours at a time when you might say, things were quieter than when some of my older, brother officers toured the Province. Although, statistically, things were safer than in the 70s and 80s, there was always that underlying menace, the threat, the implication of danger. The people, especially in the border land, hated us with a passion, but what they didn't seem to realise was that we were there to do a job and if they co-operated – or, at least let us in peace – then that job would be so much smoother for both sides.

The IRA was much more sophisticated, better armed, better trained and more skilful at what they had always been skillful at: killing us. The thing which rankled with all of us, not just brother officers, but the senior NCOs and the platoon chaps as well, was that we knew who all the players were; we could have lifted more than half of the South Armagh command overnight. We could certainly have taken them out or slotted them as was the parlance of the time; at worst, we could have arrested them but we were not allowed to. That was the most frustrating thing about it all; seeing the buggers in the towns and on the farms and sitting smirking at us from their cars when we pulled them at VCPs.

A lot of civilians who just read the press reports and who had these preconceived notions about the joviality and country simpleness of the Irish must have wondered what we were up against. They must have thought that we were – unfairly – fighting some carrot-haired bumpkin who used words like 'sor' and 'bejasus' and was only armed with World War I rifles and the kinds of bombs 'Blue Peter' could design. The reality was much, much different; a lot of them were no doubt committed to their perverted cause, but many were sociopaths and psychopaths who, had there not been a civil war, would have been gangsters anyway. They controlled the drugs and the prostitutes and ran the 'protection rackets' and we knew that they did and what is more important, they knew that we knew! Their violence and bloodlust was sickening and their followers were every bit as perverted; I have seen them spit at the bodies of dead soldiers and try to block ambulances from getting through. This is the image people back home didn't get to see because towards the end, our Government wanted the IRA to come to the conference table and they wanted to make Sinn Fein/IRA respectable.

They called us fascists and murderers, kiddie-killers and the like and claimed that they were freedom fighters and that they were resisting British tyranny. This was such absolute tosh! The SS and the South American juntas wouldn't have tolerated that nonsense; it would have been a quick line-up against the wall, a volley of shots and then move on, and leave a bloodied pile of corpses to serve as a warning. If we had have been fascists, we would have ended the whole sorry mess back in 1969–70 and the IRA instead of writing their bloody, sickening, callous page in history would be just another insignificant footnote in a brief period of civil unrest. We had to treat them with kid gloves and respect and we used force, deadly force when we had to; and we did that because we weren't the SS!

A lot of my platoon chaps stood up to the provocation and the spitting and the rioting and came out of the tunnel better human beings for it and they resisted the IRA and, whilst they didn't beat them outright, it was the IRA who eventually came to the conference table.

ROSSLEA: 1994

Air Trooper Scott Buchanan, Army Air Corps

One of the major incidents we had to contend with here was when the IRA – again using a hijacked white Transit van – fired two Mark 10 mortars at our positions from the car park of the Rosslea Arms. Their aim was off and they fell short, but what angered us the most, was the fact that the sentry whose main purpose was to warn us of an attack, actually fell asleep on duty. This is big shit and not easily forgiven. He was hauled before the officers and sent back to the mainland in disgrace. We did first, however, deal with him ourselves in a, let me say, 'appropriate manner'!

During our stay here and at Clonarty Bridge, the ceasefire kicked in and we took advantage of this to seek out some of the IRA hidey-holes, and usually a brick-strength crew plus RUC went looking for arms caches. The IRA were moving stuff on a regular basis and were extremely careful with their siting places. It actually surprised me just how ingenious their hiding places were, but most of the stuff we did find was old and dirty, and most of it belonged in museums.

Whilst the ceasefire was on, a Government Minister, Sir Patrick Mayhew, visited us for a couple of days and I managed to spend a little time chatting to him and getting to know him. He spoke like a squaddie and was friendly and chatty; a smashing guy and a real gentleman. After he left – without the IRA knowing – a lone sniper put one round into the sangar, just to send a message to him, in direct breach of the ceasefire. [It was not unknown for ceasefires to be ignored by local IRA units acting in a semi-independent manner]

We had a lot of trouble with two well-known players, the Gleeson brothers; it is true to say that they were both a pain the arse and we never seemed to have enough on them to lift them. We got a lot of pleasure in hassling them and disrupting their routine as often as we possibly could. One day, however, they turned the tables on us in general and me in particular and I ended up on the front page of the Republican News *An Phoblacht*.

On the day in question, they drove up to one of our VCPs which was manned by yours truly; out of our sight, a photographer had jumped out of the car and managed to secrete himself behind a hedge near where we were. We stopped the Gleeson's car and they immediately locked the doors and windows and pretended that they couldn't hear us. We were well prepared and put a warning sign in front of them, informing them that we would smash the windows. They continued to ignore us and so 'bang' in went several windows and we hauled the two brothers out by head, arms, legs or whatever part of their bodies we could reach and threw them onto the road. During this fracas, the photographer had appeared and took some lovely shots of us all. Air Trooper Scott Buchanan (myself) duly was the star of the next issue of *An Phoblacht*; right on the front page no less.

I was bollocked for this, but only for actually being seen !

We had a good relationship with the RAF boys who choppered us into positions to begin aggressive patrolling, but their pilots had wicked senses of humour. One of their guys used to love dropping us into bogs and marshy ground and then seeing us struggle from the knee-deep muddy water. On another occasion, they deliberately dropped us just over one mile, about a click-and-a-half, inside the border. We cursed the bastards as a patrol of the Garda Sichona then chased us like hell back to the Ulster border.

The final incident there was an IRA plan to kill a few of us in one fell swoop with a machine gun attack on the sangar. The VCP by the camp had a search pit which was pretty unique for Northern Ireland and we were able to get under a suspect car and give it a real good examination, much more effective than the mirrors on sticks.

Because of the layout of the camp and with high ground next to us, the IRA could see over the fence and see the trench we had built to try and get us safely to the sangar. We covered this with wriggly tin and, although not bullet proof at least hid us when we were changing positions. They had worked out our change over times and timed their attack to coincide with this and kill as many of us as possible.

This day, they hit the wriggly tin trench roof with 50–100 rounds – it looked like a colander afterwards – but because we were 10 minutes late, not one lad received a scratch!

Chapter Twenty-Eight

1995

This was the first year since 1970 in which no British soldiers were killed in Northern Ireland or anywhere in the world connected with the troubles. For the RUC, only one officer died through political violence; Constable Arthur Robert James Seymour, shot outside a police station in Co. Tyrone twenty-two years earlier, having been ill ever since. 6 civilians and 2 terrorists were also killed this year.

In a mad 9 day period, in December, a group claiming to be Direct Action Against Drugs shot dead 3 Catholic civilians, one of whom was a former IRA member. This same group shot and killed another Catholic civilian just two days into the New Year.

Additionally, there were only 2 bombing incidents and 50 shootings in what, by Northern Irish standards, was a very quiet year. The ceasefire appeared to be, generally, holding with only the occasional breach.

THE BORDER: 1995. DEATH OF AN IRA TOUT
Air Trooper Scott Buchannan, Army Air Corps

This was a particularly awful incident and one which sums up the IRA and I wonder how the Yanks who put money into buying arms for them might have viewed this.

One morning, very early, we were ordered out to a lonely country lane, just a few yards inside the Ulster border, as a body had been spotted, obviously dumped. It turned out to be the body of a female member of the IRA who had been 'turned' by our Int boys but they had discovered this and then tortured and killed her before tossing the body on the side of the road. They made a practice of booby-trapping bodies and it was not unusual to find a primed grenade or trembler device under the poor sod's body. They also had a habit of burying explosives in a ditch nearby and detonating them from their side of the border by remote control once the investigation team were on the spot.

This poor lady lay there for two days, before the ATO boys deemed it safe to remove her body. What a mess; the bastards had cut off both her breasts and dumped them next to her, she had been tortured with lit cigarette ends and worst of all, her body was burnt raw by a hot steam iron and the unmistakable shapes of the iron had been burned into her back in quite a few places. They did this as a warning to others not to inform on them. You couldn't call them animals as even animals don't behave in this way. I never did find out her name and her body was taken quietly away.

UDR: THE DRIVE HOME: 1995
UDR Soldier

One former UDR then latterly a Royal Irish Regiment soldier wrote that the main difference, for him, between the mainland or mainstream British soldier and his comrade in the UDR was the 'permanence' of the latter's predicament. Both the emergency (4–6 months) or resident battalion tour (18 months) ended eventually; that of the UDR didn't. These personnel, men and women, wore the same uniforms, used the same weapons and their bodies were equally vulnerable to a 9mm or 5.56mm bullet or a landmine or a mortar attack as were the regular soldiers. The one difference was that they didn't have the relative 'security' of the mainland or the Regimental depot.

The UDR men and women lived, ate and drank in the communities they had to patrol; they had to shop and relax amongst the very people they might have arrested or questioned or were actively seeking. For the UDR soldier –unlike the regulars – there was no escape into the community, knowing that their every move was being observed by the enemy within. IRA intelligence gathering on the domestic and working arrangements of these part-time soldiers was so good and so thorough that over 80% of UDR personnel killed were in one of these situations. This is a typical journey home in the life of a UDR man.

Most of us commute to and from work; some by rail, most by car, but I used to drive back and forth to work here – for a while I was part-time UDR – starting at 1930 and finishing at 0400. I had a twenty mile drive, through some 'areas of interest'.

"See you again lads". With this cheery, if tired farewell, I would go through the usual routine; beret, INIBA, webbing and combat jacket all would go into the boot. Cover with blanket. Take out baggy boiler suit and squeeze it over your uniform. Gloves on – smaller size, with the pad cut off the knuckles. Fit like pilot's gloves. Save your hands getting cut to ribbons if the windscreen comes in. Start up, seat belt on – not law yet, but might save your life if something happens.

OK, here we go; out the gate, give gate sentry the fingers, speed bumps, top of the road, no slowing, fast as she can take it, anyone could be waiting. Left? No, straight on, don't set a pattern; through the lights; red or not: stop for no man. Over the bridge, through the 'ville' keep going, no stopping, go, go, out into the country. Past the County Hall, floor it down the long straight; did a VCP here just a couple of hours ago. Through the 'hog hill' – a type of chicane in the middle of the village – and then change down and speed through the diamond. Real country now, no street lights, eyes get used slowly to the dark; now there are bumpy culverts, rutted, shadowy, too fast to dwell on them.

Down the long hill, try not to slow for the corner at the bottom and then fly down the long sloped straight; tight corner and then down to third; look around for following lights; picked anyone up? Big wall on the left, roadside monastery, tight left at the top; careful now. Past the cop shop, yellow sodium lights; did a LURK on a house near here last week. Change down and then left into the Glenone; wide market street, deserted; no cars, over the bridge and into 'their' patch. Now my antenna switches on and past the pub at the crossroads; the villages from here are in 'enemy' territory.' Good men have died in them. Through the village – VCP earlier too – down the hill, into the dark again with narrow roads, tension notches up a tad, past the corner, high hedges and then down to second for the last one, wait, wait for it, and then out into the open road, back up the gears, long straight, check the mirrors for lights. None; up to 75, 80, foot off gas for 'S' bends, crossroads; mirror again; bad road here, culverts again, close to their area again.

Stretch of concrete road, it dips into dead ground with blind corners, over the crest and 'Fuck!' Jam on brakes, fishtail to a stop, just short of a car on its roof; heart going nineteen to the dozen; there's room to pass. Sneak a look into the car; no-one in it, caused by some young lad with slower reactions than you. Phew! Up the hill and then floor it past the 'T' junction then left, no slowing, past bingo hall, over the crossroads and as fast as possible into the dark again. Now it's the fun part; road narrows and as it dips, turn off the headlights; that should confuse the bastards. If they are waiting, they'll still hear me but won't see me straight off; buy some time. Then I'm through and nearly home.

Houses in a clump to the left; a few street lights cast a weak light; sharp left and then pull up at the door. I switch off the engine and listen to the silence then get out and listen again and enjoy the cooling wind. I find the keys, open the door – quietly, noisy git – boots off, sweating in the boiler suit. Sit in the chair and she finds you still there, three hours later.

As harrowing as it was for this UDR man, it was very often the only way in which they could live to fight another day. 203 serving members of the UDR were killed during the Regiment's lifetime. 40 of these brave men and women were killed on duty; 163 were murdered in their homes, outside their homes, at work, driving to work or driving home from work or UDR service. This was precisely why this UDR man drove home the way he described.

Chapter Twenty-Nine

1996/1997

The twenty five month spell without a British soldier being killed came to an abrupt end on October 11 of this year, when W.O. James Bradwell of REME died of his wounds, four days after a bomb attack at Thiepval Barracks on the Lisburn Garrison.

In 1996 there were 25 bombing incidents and 125 shootings.

The INLA in an internal dispute made an attack on a fellow INLA member but instead killed 9 year old Barbara McAlorum at her home in Belfast.

1997: This year would see the last British Army's official fatality of the current troubles when Lance-Bombardier Stephen Restorick of the Royal Artillery was shot whilst manning a PVCP at Bessbrook Mill. 4 RUC men were killed as a result of political violence and 10 civilians and 5 terrorists were also killed. Interestingly enough, in addition to the loss of Stephen, a further 6 soldiers would lose their lives in the Province; only one, Private Richardson of the Light Infantry, has been explained to the author's satisfaction.

During 1997, 93 bombing incidents took place and there were 225 shootings. A UDA man was killed in a premature bomb explosion at Dunmurry near Belfast.

The IRA ceasefire came into effect very soon after Stephen Restorick's death; the ceasefire is still, apparently, holding.

BELFAST 1996
Warrant Officer, Grenadier Guards

I deployed as part of the Scots Guards on the most boring tour ever; I was desk bound. The only real things of note are when the IRA blew up the medical centre in Thiepval and I was the Ops Sgt at Whiterock in W Belfast. We had to mount OP BUCKINGHAM in order to stop all movement. I could never get the hang of the safe and therefore had a nightmare trying to open it whilst the Coy Commander was giving me grief. During this phase a suspect device was spotted on a location. I called the ATO in and we were observing it on the CCTV when a RUC Constable approached it. 'Well it isn't a pressure pad stated a bemused ATO. At which the RUC man kicked it, 'that's the tremble device option negated then' quoted the ATO whereupon the Constable opened the box. 'And its not a light sensitive device, my work here is done!' The ATO promptly left the office.

The tour was so boring I jacked up a rugby match at the New Forge Police sports club, we kept it quiet and got the RUC to smuggle us out of Whiterock to stop officers crowding the team. The match had only just started when I was called to the referee's area. One of the lads had broken his leg within 40 seconds of the whistle! We were not meant to be there so we got the bloke taken back to Whiterock covertly where we put him back into combats and laid him at the base

Bombardier Stephen Restorick, one of the last squaddies to be killed as a result of IRA
activity during the troubles

of some stairs by the cookhouse. When he was admitted to Hospital and his
combats were cut off the surgeon could not understand why he had mud and
white line markings all down his leg.

The Provisional IRA ceasefire had held for over 17 months when it abruptly came
to a halt on February 9 as an enormous bomb caused devastation at Canary Wharf
in London's docklands. Further, it killed two civilians and the sigh of relief the
British had permitted to escape from their lips was suddenly stifled. The Provisional IRA was back at war.

Back over in the Province, no British soldier, or UDR man had been killed in
action since August 8, 1994, when 48 year old part-time UDR soldier Trelford
Withers had been gunned down in his shop whilst off-duty. From the killing of
Withers through to the blast in the docklands area, over 17 months had elapsed,
but British troops still patrolled the streets of Belfast and Londonderry and the
rural areas of South Armagh and Fermanagh, in armoured vehicles and with loaded
SA80s.

The longest period of the troubles without the loss of military personnel came
to an abrupt halt with an apparent major lapse in Army security on the Lisburn
garrison. On October 7, two IRA bombs were smuggled into Thiepval barracks
and in one of the explosions, Sergeant Major James Bradwell of REME, who was
43, was critically injured. He died 4 days later in the RVH having fought bravely
for life; thus over 2 full years had elapsed without the death in action of a British
soldier in the Province. The ceasefire was over and British and UDR personnel

had, crucially to go back on guard as it was felt that they had relaxed and allowed their guard to slip. The final ceasefire was coming; but it wasn't there just yet.

Stephen Restorick died of his wounds on 12 February, 1997, following his shooting at a PVCP at Bessbrook Mill. He is accorded the tragic status of being the last squaddie to die on active service in Northern Ireland as a consequence of the troubles. However, four weeks later, Private A.J. Richardson of 3 Light Infantry, was killed in Belfast, having only just returned from leave spent in his home town of South Shields. He was killed in an 'incident' [author's inverted commas].

The following is an account of Pte Richardson's Death.

BELFAST: 1997
James Kirkby, Light Infantry

In brief, I believe to my knowledge that Pte Richardson died in Northern Ireland due to a planned attack, also called 'come on' by the IRA. Two of the armoured Land Rovers were on patrol when I was informed that an IRA member was waiting in an alleyway with a RPG ready to take out the rear APC (in which Pte Richardson was formally carrying out top cover). As the two vehicles drove on their route, a civilian car pulled out between the patrol cars and deliberately slowed down, causing the rear APC to also slow; this was a planned manoeuvre to aid the IRA to deliver his RPG on the intended target.

The driver of the Land Rover knew this was a 'come on' and decided to try to drive out of danger and tried to overtake the civilian vehicle; as it did so, the car then speeded up and would not let the APC back in. As a result, the armoured Land Rover then had no choice but to hit a central reservation on a roundabout causing it to flip over several times with Pte Richardson still on top cover alongside his comrade. He was crushed to death and his top cover partner flung out, hitting a lamp post square on.

The above info is to the best of my knowledge and I hope this will help you to decide if it was an accident. I feel this is what happened and see his death as a murder.

The death of Private Richardson occurred a full month after the murder of Lance-Bombardier Restorick and was clearly – viewed either objectively or subjectively – as a consequence of active service and was caused by the IRA. Why then do only the Light Infantry Reunited and NIVETS list this soldier on their roll of honour and no other agency or institution include him on their respective Rolls of Honour?

'Stevie', UDR, contributed the following 'answer':

That's a very good question ... other deaths due to RTA or 'accidental' shootings are mentioned in some sources but I feel that on some occasions it was considered 'not helpful' to ongoing negotiations with paramilitaries, especially around the time of Restorick's death. There is clearly a political aspect to this – e.g. examining *Lost Lives'* at one point there is a six-week gap with no military casualties – during a 'ceasefire' period. However reading the MOD's own list it is clear that soldiers were still dying in combat. Or not, depending on what the reports actually say.

Chapter Thirty

After Stephen Restorick: 1998 onwards

1 998 saw a killing at the rate of just over one person per week – 57 in total – despite the ceasefire; apparently, in some cases, as old scores were settled.

It must be remembered also, that over half of these fatalities took place in a single day. The so-called 'Real IRA' planted car bombs in Omagh. 29 civilians were killed by these bombs in the centre of a crowd in Market Street, Omagh. 2 pregnant women, 2 babies and 9 children among the dead. 2 of the dead were Spanish tourists.

The Northern Ireland Veterans' Association names 14 soldiers who lost their lives on active service during this year, a figure which is, apparently, disputed by the Ministry of Defence.

The year saw the final killing of an RUC officer in what was termed 'political violence' as on October 6, Officer Frank O'Reilly died of his wounds having been critically injured the day before in a bombing by Loyalist paramilitaries. Earlier in the year, former RUC Officer Cyril Stewart was shot in a supermarket by the INLA. Two years later, a Reserve Officer – William Thompson – was 'unlawfully' killed in Belfast whilst manning a checkpoint. To this date, no other RUC officer has lost his life through the euphemistically named phenomena, 'political violence'

The year also witnessed another IRA 'own goal' (or 'Premdet' in Army-speak) when 2 terrorists, including Brendan Burns, who was widely considered responsible for the bomb which killed 4 Royal Green Jackets and their RCT driver at Camlough in 1981, blew themselves up near Crossmaglen.

NEWTOWNHAMILTON – SOUTH ARMAGH 1998
Captain John Flexman
The Royal Gloucestershire Berkshire and Wiltshire Regiment

I would like to state that as someone who served in province in 1998 I simply cannot share the same experience as those who served in Ulster before the 1996 ceasefire. They served in an environment where on every patrol there was a high likelihood of contact, I did not.

I still gained useful experience during my tour and was a multiple commander on the ground when Newtownhamilton was car bombed by the INLA in June 1998. As a result of that incident, and a few other minor experiences, I feel I probably did as much as I could to earn my GSM. However on the one occasion each year when I wear that medal, I do recognise that in years gone by, people worked a lot harder and often went through much more trauma, for the same medal.

My first tour of the province started in late April 1998 just after the Good Friday agreement was signed. As a 21 year old Platoon Commander I flew in civilian clothes to Belfast International and found my way to the airport reception desk. Through a secure door and I met two members of the Battalion MT platoon who asked me to confirm that I had completed a pistol weapon handling test in the last 6 months. After this they then suggested that without a holster, the best place to stick my Browning High Power.was down my pants! Within a few minutes we were into a civilian vehicle and heading at speed to South Armagh. On arrival at Bessbrook Mill I met the Adjutant, the RSM and the CO briefly. I became acquainted with the small but pleasant Officers' Mess for just enough time to grab a coffee, and then I had to change and was on the move again. This time to the busiest heliport in Europe, just outside the Mill buildings, from where I was flown by Lynx on to B Company's base at Newtownhamilton.

Over the next four and a half months I was to learn my craft as a Platoon Commander. I was fully aware of the vast experience around me – there were many Glosters who had served in Ballykelly and many Duke of Edinburgh's Royal Regiment veterans who had served in South Armagh – both in much more violent times. I was keen to listen and learn from other people's experience. Luckily I had a Company Commander (an attached Highlander called Toby) who understood this and was very supportive of me. I think I broke the ice when I informed him I had been back-termed at Sandhurst. He then asked me who my Sandhurst Company Commander had been. It was then he realised it had been the same Air Corps Major who had lectured Toby at staff college and someone who he had thoroughly disliked. It makes me laugh looking back because I am sure that I instantly went up in his estimation that day. I sometimes wonder how many other back-termers would have admitted past failings; for some reason I thought it would be good to be honest.

My first 8 days were spent patrolling as a private soldier to enable me to get to know the ground, and the men of the company. There is no question that the blokes loved the opportunity to load me with the heaviest possible ECM kit. On stag too I fully appreciated the level of commitment and discipline required by Private soldiers in South Armagh. It only made me respect them more, except for the time they sent the Catholic Padre up to spend an hour with me in the base sangar. Father Basil (nickname 'The Madman') was thought to be clinically insane but as a left footer myself I was to see more of him then most. Sadly the blokes avoided him like the plague, so we ended up having to go through the personal files and root out all the Catholics so that he had a congregation for mass each Sunday. Mainly though Sunday mass consisted of the Company 2iC – Darren, myself and a very senior storeman, who at that stage was on his fifth tour of Ulster; and so understandably quite uninterested in religion.

That summer was the most fulfilling and educational of my 5 years as an officer in the Army. I felt like an amateur at the time, but I invested much energy in building relationships with my NCOs and senior Toms. They were key to enabling us to be successful as a multiple on the ground. In turn I vowed to repay the patience they showed me, by doing as much as I could to develop their careers and look after their welfare once we were back in the SF base. It was a two-way street in the end, but for the first few months it felt very much like one way traffic.

I fondly remember my multiple, and was very honoured to have been their boss. My primary team commander was a sure hand and an excellent navigator, my satellite team commander a proud ex-Gloster. He had once described to me the final parade of the Gloucestershire Regiment on Gloucester Dock and confessed that he, like many others, had shed a tear as the colours were marched off for the final time.

Our team of NCOs was well experienced, but the Private soldiers below them were very young, most of them only 18 or 19. Only 3 had been with the battalion to Bosnia. The mix of the younger soldiers was fascinating. Wide boy lads from Reading and Slough mixed with country boys from Wiltshire and proud young men from Bristol, Gloucester and the Forest of Dean. As you would expect much banter followed. Nevertheless when their skills were called upon under pressure, they delivered the goods. The only serious civilian casualty of the Newtownhamilton car bomb (a 10 year old boy) was dealt with at my team's cordon position.

Pte Dicks, our team medic, under the scrutiny of several journalists and at least one television camera, delivered life-saving first aid to a boy who suffered a chest laceration. Dicko was just 19 but he had come of age. I honestly think he was more nervous meeting the Brigade Commander the following day. He described the injury as a sucking chest wound, which made us all chuckle. What mattered though was the experience the platoon had been through. Previously a group of soldiers, we had now become a team. In addition we typified all that was good about an English county regiment. We had also developed an identity and a camaraderie which was neither Glosters nor Duke of Edinburgh's, but something special in its own right.

That week had seen our battalion deal with three separate serious incidents. The murder of Cpl Fenton outside Crossmaglen by a tanker driver. The first detonation of a mobile phone-operated IED outside Forkhill and a VBIED (the same size as the Omagh car bomb) in Newtownhamilton village square. My view is that it was only the professionalism of our private soldiers and NCOs, and the fact that our young officers were willing to listen (as well as lead), that saved us further fatalities. Without those attributes we could well have suffered more casualties.

Nevertheless I still look back on that 1998 tour with positive memories and I do count myself lucky that we were not there a few years earlier. I am sure we would have had a very different experience. Looking back now I try to dwell on the positives. In Newtownhamilton that day in June 1998, we helped the RUC to prevent what could have been a second Omagh. That remains today a massive point of pride for all of us who did our job that day.

SUMMARY

My own view is that a film should be made of the Infantry's experiences in South Armagh in the early 1990s. It would certainly raise awareness of the legacy of Ulster. The battle stress in those conditions in Crossmaglen must have been at least as bad, as what service personnel are experiencing in Iraq and Afghanistan right now.

In addition people out there need to understand what a very small number of locals in that part of Ireland are actually like. They would frankly be disgusted. It took the Omagh bomb to turn people against the 32 Counties Sovereignty Committee, 28 people and an unborn baby had to die before Irish people in Armagh and Monaghan realised how appalling a small number of people who lived next to them actually were. The loss at Omagh and the lack of justice for those families remains in my view one of the biggest miscarriages of justice in the history of our nation.

I had a friend from Sandhurst who led a platoon in collecting the body parts at Omagh in the immediate aftermath of the explosion. Again another NI veteran mentally scarred for life. The only comfort I had is that we learnt afterwards from Intelligence reports that the RIRA were forced to take the bomb (made in the south) around to the West as they could not get it through the roads in South Armagh. So at least as a Battalion we knew we had done all we could to stop Omagh. Sadly, of course, it wasn't enough.

LOOKING BACK

I particularly appreciated your [comments] about the cowardly murder of off-duty soldiers by the IRA on the British mainland. Something that has never, for me, received enough press attention. In my last job as a Company 2iC I had a company storeman who survived being shot 4 times by a pistol at close range on Darlington train station in the early 90s. He went on to have a full career in the Army, but as you and I know, he will carry that trauma with him for the rest of his life.

On June 22nd of that year, whilst manning a VCP at Crossmaglen, Corporal Gary Fenton, who was 29, was knocked down and killed by a lorry driven by a driver who refused to stop. Corporal Fenton who was 29, received a posthumous gallantry award.

Mark Overson writes:

Gary Fenton was a close friend of myself and many others and I attended his funeral (as an ex-squaddie) in Newbury on that same year and it was a fantastic turnout from all of his colleagues, friends and family.

THE KILLING OF GARY FENTON: SOUTH ARMAGH, 1998

Lt-Col Richard Hall, CO 1 RGBW

'The geography of South Armagh, with its porous border with the Republic, meant that it was a haven for smuggling. The distinction between smuggling for personal gain as opposed to raising funds for the IRA was ill defined. Due to the different tax regimes smuggling fuel was a reasonably common occurrence.

On 22 June 1998 Cpl Fenton's patrol stopped a fuel tanker at a vehicle check point close to the border. The driver's answers to the patrol's questions aroused their suspicions. The tanker was held whilst the RUC conducted checks on the veracity of his story. Before this could be completed the truck driver decided to make a dash for it. Cpl Fenton vainly tried to stop the truck from getting away and was run down and killed in the process. The patrol opened fire wounding the driver. They were however unable to stop the tanker from driving across the border.

SOUTH ARMAGH – MARCH TO SEPTEMBER 1998
Lt-Col Richard Hall, CO 1 RGBW

1 RGBW deployed to South Armagh in early March 1998 for a tour that was to prove to be challenging in a way that few could have predicted. Eight days into the tour an observation tower and the company base at Forkhill were the target of a synchronised mortar attack. Just 2 weeks later the Good Friday Peace agreement was signed, changing the political and security environment significantly.

The Peace Agreement produced a positive change in atmosphere throughout the province that percolated even down to South Armagh – 'Bandit Country' – an area of Northern Ireland where the rule of law was difficult to enforce and the sophistication, professionalism and ruthlessness of the Provisional IRA was notorious. There was widespread expectation, amongst the public, that the military presence would be reduced as the Army's 'demilitarisation' was perceived to have been part of the bargain for the Provisional IRA's agreement to the peace process. This was whipped up by Sinn Fein activists who, in particular, campaigned for the removal of our observation towers and a reduction in the use of helicopters, both of which were vital for our operations.

Our patrolling patterns and tactics were changed to reduce the military profile. This required thoughtful and understanding soldiers, who knowingly reduced their guard and increased their vulnerability at a time when the Provisional IRA had not disarmed and disgruntled Republicans, were forming a new organisation – the Real IRA. Failure to have adapted, however, would have discredited the sincerity of the Government's commitment to the peace process, and driven the sceptics back to violence.

It became increasingly difficult to remain on a reduced profile as the Real IRA gained in confidence. Their technology and expertise matched the Provisional IRA's and they launched a sustained campaign to discredit the peace process. Thus the Battalion had to carry out a delicate balancing act – reducing its military profile and activity without exposing soldiers to undue risk when combating the activities of the Real IRA.

The success of most tours is measured by the number of finds or terrorists arrested. This was a different sort of tour: the Battalion's success can be measured by failure of the Real IRA to gain popular support or Sinn Fein to make political capital out of the Battalion's operations. The Battalion kept the lid on a difficult and volatile situation, by accepting risks and demonstrating sensitivity to the local situation and in so doing prevented the peace process from being derailed.

IRA mortar tubes at Forkhill (photo courtesy of Mike Day, www.ijlb.com)

A TRIBUTE TO THE LIGHT INFANTRY
Geoff Smith

The 3 battalions of the Light Infantry have completed many tours in the province of Northern Ireland and in the process; they lost many good men to the cowardly tactics of the various organisations that call themselves 'Paramilitaries'. Just peruse the Roll of Honour for the three battalions to see the list of names of good, professional, highly trained, normal everyday men and boys that were sacrificed by the government of this country, in a futile and pointless exercise of trying to pacify various terrorist groups killing and bombing each other when in the end, it was quite obvious to everyone that people would have to sit down at a table and talk. In the end, people got around a table and talked. They are still talking and as long as they talk young soldiers will not die needlessly. Rest in Peace all those Light Infantrymen who fell in the name of 'Peacekeeping.' England, Scotland and Wales owe you a lot for your sacrifice. The people of Northern Ireland, who hopefully one day will find peace to live in, owe you 'EVERYTHING.' But as true professionals and just like soldiers the world over, who fight for their country's beliefs, you will be forgotten by the people you fought to protect or free from oppression; you will be nameless to them all. But that is the destiny of a soldier.

PENULTIMATE WORD

Northern Ireland ... Why I care.

The Private Views of an Ex-Serving British Soldier 1970 /73.

My name doesn't matter, enough just to say that I am one of the 300,000 British soldiers that served in Northern Ireland between 1969 and the present day. We are the faceless ones, ignored and ridiculed by all sides in the conflict, including our own masters, and yet, without our involvement, one of the worst civil wars that the world may have seen would have ravaged not only the Six Counties, but would, I believe, have spread far into the Republic.

It is so easy to forget the facts with relation to the British Army and the 'Troubles', depending of course on which side of the fence you sit. My aim is to broaden that fence into a triangle, so that the facts about the Army are also taken into account. It may hurt those whose doctrine has always been to believe the fables of the 1916 Easter uprising, or likewise those whose misguided love of King Billy rules their lives. Tough.

The British Army never asked, nor wanted, to become involved in the day-to-day security of Northern Ireland. Senior officers fought tooth and nail to keep the army out. Political intrigues by Brian Faulkner and others forced the issue onto a weak and foolish British Government.

The majority of British troops were pulled out of Germany to serve in Northern Ireland. These included many from the 'province', from both sides of the political divide, whose homes were there, and whose parents lived there. The make-up of the rank and file was a strange one, at the time; many soldiers came

Aftermath of 'Real' IRA attack on Omagh

from broken homes, many from the inner city slums of Salford, Birmingham, Liverpool and London. They were streetwise, having themselves been on the wrong side of the law before taking the Queen's Shilling.

We went as an army to protect the Catholic minority from being wiped from the face of the map. Without the British Army, that would have been the outcome. Troops were welcomed in both Catholic and Republican areas with open arms. Not something that Gerry Adams now likes to admit.

I thought it perhaps fitting, to leave the last voice to Mark Overson who toured Northern Ireland twice and was shot, nine days into his second tour on Creggan Road near Crossmaglen.

I phoned home and said: 'Mum, I've been shot.' She replied: 'Don't be so stupid. Don't tell lies and don't make jokes like that!'

Epilogue (or is it ?)

When I began writing this book, back on June 20, 2007, I didn't quite realise the depth and magnitude – which became a labour of love – of the task. I just thought that I would pay for an ad in *Soldier* magazine, sit back whilst the replies rolled in, a bit of cutting and pasting here, the odd phone call there and my masterpiece would be complete.

Not for the first time in my life did I receive a rather rude awakening. I drove or took the train to Berkshire, to South Wales, to Edinburgh and to Aberdeen to interview both serving and ex-squaddies. In the first 16 weeks alone I sent or received over 3,300 e-mails on Northern Ireland and I lost count long ago of the telephone calls I either made or received. However, when I made that first telephone call to *Soldier* and before I even typed the first word, I was under the impression that 741 British and UDR service personnel had been killed in or associated with, Northern Ireland.

I now believe that figure to be in excess of 1,000, thanks to the good offices of the Northern Ireland Veterans Association (NIVETS) and to several of their officers, to whom tribute has been made in the Acknowledgements section of this book.

For example, I had always been under the impression that Tommy Stoker, Light Infantry, had been killed by the IRA in Belfast on September 19, 1972, but was puzzled as to why his name did not appear on the various Rolls of Honour (ROH). As I dug further, it transpired that he had been accidentally killed in an Op on the Ardoyne by a fellow squaddie – one of three 'blue on blue' in a short period of time in the summer of that year.

After I had joined NIVETS I became privileged to read more about the lads who had died on active service connected with Northern Ireland, but who appear to have been ignored by the MOD. For example, it is generally accepted that, on February 6, 1971, Gunner Robert Curtis was the first British soldier to die in action. And yet, NIVETS list 30 names PRIOR to Curtis's murder, starting with a Trooper McCabe, who was killed whilst home on leave.

Conversely, on February 12, 1997, Lance-Bombardier Steven Restorick was shot and died of his wounds and is accepted as the last squaddie killed on active service, connected with the troubles. NIVETS list 70 (seventy, seven-zero) names who were killed or died afterwards. Light Infantry Reunited's site lists one of their men who was killed after Restorick. He was Private A.J. Richardson, who was killed in Belfast on March 12, 1997, i.e. 4 weeks after Steven Restorick. And what about the previously mentioned Gary Fenton killed at a VCP; why is he not accorded an honourable mention in the ROH?

The following came from a former member of the UDR who saw active service – a permanent state of affairs in the Regiment, and as he points out, afterwards and forever as well – who does not wish to be named.

What I got under the FOI Act from the MOD – you may have a copy of it from the NIVA site – was the 'Fatalities of service personnel in Northern Ireland from 1948'. A quite meaningless title, given that it starts in 1969 ...

It lists 1386 names – and the list itself requires some 'qualification'.

Firstly the heading letter that accompanied it stated that this is 'not a definitive list'. Examining the list and comparing it to *Lost Lives* and the Palace Barracks ROH, brings more disparities and also a large number of names in the MOD list that have no detail or mention in either of these sources.

These omissions can be 'explained' in a number of ways:

1) Bad record-keeping, lost records or deliberately destroyed records
2) Details withheld at the families' request
3) National security (50- or 100- year rule) due to the nature of the circumstances of the loss
4) Road accident, suicide, training accident or 'non-combat' loss.

The latter category is the biggest point contention – in that it is arbitrary, i.e. some RTA and accidental losses ('blue on blue') ARE mentioned in other sources, but there is no understandable pattern to govern inclusion/exclusion.

Also there is the difference between 'combat loss' – death due directly to a terrorist incident – and 'non-combat loss' which may be due to many other reasons like RTA, drowning, weapon 'accident' or similar – even at the hands of their own colleagues.

For example – Gunner Robert Curtis is 'traditionally' named as the 'first soldier killed violently', and his name is on page one of the MOD list – but at number 22. Tpr Anthony McCabe is first on the list, but as he was killed whilst on home leave he is not a 'combat loss'. In fact of the 39 names on this page I have details for only eight.

[The death of McCabe who was, not that it mattered, a Catholic, living in a Republican area, remains as shrouded in mystery as it was on the day he died. The 'official' version is that he was shot by the RUC during a night of rioting in the Divis Street area. McCabe was just 20 when he was struck by a round whilst on the roof the flats.]

I have trawled the regimental websites – not the official MOD ones, they are no help – for any mention of these 'lost dead' but with very little result. As time has passed memories dim, and perhaps in some cases it is not wise or prudent (even now) to remember openly how some people met their end.

So this is what any researcher is up against – I can provide the MOD list, which has name, rank, serial number and date of death – but that is all it gives.

I have recently sent a request to the MOD for any details, from any source, of three names from 1969 to see what it brings. If I am in any way successful I will simply continue to send in requests to fill in the gaps – it may take some time but I feel it a worthy task.

The same UDR man then explained the 'permanence' of active service or at least the permanence of pressure by being in, associated with, or just by virtue of being an ex-UDR member.

Our experience is different in some respects to that of the Regular soldier who came here by military transport, escorted by green vehicle to a fortified base, where they spent most of their 4 or 6 month tour. In uniform, on stag, kipping or patrolling – a bit of R+R in the middle and then downhill to the end of the tour. Pressurised and intense, yes – but at the end the experience is that of having been planted in 'enemy territory', working in such and surrounded by the 'enemy', innocent or terrorist. Something that can be set to one side once it has been done.

We lived in the community we worked in – we shopped, raised our kids, ate out, socialised, did everything that 'normal' life requires – but in the sight of our enemy. The same streets we lived on, we patrolled in uniform and did all the things the 'Regs' did, but then had to go home at the end of the day and live a life. Of the 197 UDR who were killed, the vast majority were killed in their own homes, in their own driveways, out shopping, at their civvy place of work, in front of their families, alone on country roads. And it didn't stop there – 57 ex-UDR members were killed in addition, some as long as ten years after leaving. Balance this against the experience of the Regular soldier and you begin to get the picture.

If you look at a lot of Army sites you will notice the same phrases – 'never got over it, even now 20 years on', 'nothing was the same afterwards', 'couldn't settle back into civvy street' – and they are all valid; but try to imagine living with that, not just for four months, but for ALL of your life. Even now – we will never switch off; the awareness will never leave us. It has been part of our lives for too long.

I am not in the business of blowing my own trumpet – not much there to blow really – but the true story of the UDR, in the format of personal stories, will never be told. There are too many people who are still happy to denigrate and demean our work and service, for various reasons; and sadly there are too many people willing to let them, also for various reasons. It's politics, and I don't have any interest it that, only in preserving the history of the UDR.

The current conflict – certainly so, at the time of writing – in Iraq is perceived by both public and press alike to be one in which honesty, in terms of casualty figures, appears uppermost. It is fairly apparent that, even when a death is non-battle re-lated, the MOD at least acknowledges that much and the unfortunate serviceman is at least accorded full military honours. There seems a distinct lack of parallel with the reporting of deaths in the Northern Ireland conflict, with, even if the NIVETS figures are wrong or even overestimated, at least 100 soldiers on their ROH which our government have failed to even acknowledge. One uses the term 'government' here in its most generic sense as no less than three Labour administrations and two Conservative ones sent troops to the province between 1969 and 2007 when Oper-ation Banner, finally, 38 years on, came to an end.

Why would the government be honest with the casualty figures in Iraq and Af-ghanistan and yet so meager with its veracity in relation to the conflict on our door-step? Both the author and several contributors have asked the MOD for an explanation but, certainly for the time being, at least, none appears to be forthcom-ing. Until they are prepared to explain their rationale or at least afford the honour of recognition to those, thus-far unnamed dead, the ROH at the end of this book will recognise as many as myself and the excellent offices of NIVETS can identify.

POSTSCRIPT 2003

Kingsman George Prosser, King's Regiment

On July 7, 2003, I returned to the Turf Lodge to the scene of the explosion that killed not just a fine NCO but more importantly, a fine young Kingsman. A couple of years earlier, I had driven up the outskirts of the estate, up the Monagh bypass and right along Springfield Road before finally turning left at the junction with the Falls Road. Although the Peace process was in place – albeit a fragile one at times – I felt uneasy about venturing into a place I now knew little about. I was going into a fiercely Republican enclave where strangers are viewed with suspicion and not welcomed. When I eventually felt that it was safe to go in there, I must say that I was taken aback at what I saw.

The ugly blocks of flats had all gone and the existing houses had gone through a considerable transformation in the twenty four years since I had walked those streets as a Peacekeeper. After parking the car, I decided to go for a walk around and the uncanny thing about the whole place was that it had the same feeling of calm as it did on the day of the explosion; the streets were deserted also. I stood in Ardmonagh Gardens on the spot where I stood on May 9, 1979 and it was almost too much to bear. Even now as I write, I fight to hold back the tears; the event is till very fresh in my mind and holds painful memories.

After pausing for a short while, I entered the building that now stands on the site of the old 'Disco block'. I politely asked the young lady at reception would it be ok if I took some photographs outside, but my request was at first viewed with suspicion. After telling her that a close friend had been killed there some years back and that I had returned to pay my respects, she was then very accommodating. I would like to thank her from the heart. While preparing to take the shots, I noticed a man in a window of a house directly behind where I was standing; he stared at me for a while because I was someone he did not recognise. At no time did I feel in danger, in fact, as I strolled around the estate, the local people were not hostile to me in any way. I was courteous at all times and asked for permission before attempting to take any more pictures. I had always felt the need to go back, the need to understand; at least now the answers to some of the questions have been found.

I think that it is an outrage that we have had to wait so long for the 'Ulster Ash Grove' at the National Memorial Arboretum to be commissioned. Now finally those who gave their lives to bring peace to the beleaguered people of Northern Ireland have been remembered. One must never forget that each tree represents not just a name but a person, a former colleague and most importantly a friend. To those brave men and women we shall be eternally grateful; Their Names Liveth For Evermore.

Afterword

In the period 1968 through to 2003, a total of 47,541* people were injured as a direct consequence of the troubles. Of these, 6,262 were soldiers of the British Army and UDR and 11,212 were members of the RUC. Utterly staggering figures, given both the geographical size of Northern Ireland and its 1.5 million population. These figures exclude the death toll, which most experts put at around 3,700.

This book looked at the period 1969–98 however, and the figures for this period were as follows: 40,273 injured, of whom 5,974 were British Army (including UDR and RIR) and 8,146 were RUC officers.

If the total figures were carried forward pro-rata to the remainder of the United Kingdom (minus Northern Ireland) with a population of c. 59.3 million, the amount of dead and injured would be around 2,027,800; a staggering figure in any conflict. Put another way, more than British losses, civilian and military in the entire Second World War.

With c. 3,700 people killed from all sides, if this were to be replicated on the same pro-rata basis, 146,273 people would have been killed on the British mainland. Again, put another way, more than were killed in the UK during the entire Blitz by the German Luftwaffe.

If I were to present this to some Hollywood moviemaker and suggest it as the basis for a movie about a country's collective insanity, my proposal would be rejected out of hand as being too far-fetched! 'Hey, man; what an imagination but, hey, nobody would believe ya.'

I talked with some Ulster people, a year or two back about our conduct and our role in Northern Ireland; some of it was positive as they remembered the terrible conditions of the late 1960s and how our arrival in July and August of 1969 not only gave them a measure of protection but at the same time, set the wheels in motion for social and political reforms– but mostly negative. There were many criticisms, however, about excesses and there was a description of the British Army being an 'occupying force.' But generally, they seemed to have accepted our presence as grudgingly expedient.

But when I criticised the IRA and the other terrorist groupings, they rounded on me and said that, whilst they accepted that some appalling things were committed in their names, that they were 'freedom fighters'.

Call me naïve, but my image of a freedom fighter would be the gallant resistance workers of the French Maquis, the Belgian underground, the Dutch soldiers of Orange who fought and died alongside the British and Poles at Arnhem and others who resisted the tyranny of Nazi Germany.

What kind of freedom fighter would lure the three Scottish soldiers to a drinking session and then execute them at the roadside on a 'pee break?' Or entice four off-duty Sergeants to a house with the promise of a party and then burst in and shoot them? What type of human being could sanction Ranger Best's murder in

Londonderry in May 1972 having previously assured his worried parents that he would be safe when he came home on leave from Germany?

What went through the mind of the spokesman for the Official IRA after they had killed an off-duty soldier, Thomas McCann of the RAOC, visiting his mother in the Republic when he announced 'We had no choice other than to execute him.'

What depths of depravity did it take to place bombs amongst unsuspecting drinkers in bars in Birmingham, in Woolwich and in Guilford or at the La Mon Restaurant? What type of person shoots dead an off-duty RAF man and his young child in a leafy lane in faraway Germany?

In God's name, how did the murder of 18 civilians by the IRA and UFF respectively, in an insane week in October 1993 advance EITHER of their causes?

I must confess to my own emotional failings when I explain that I am just incapable of getting inside the mind of the IRA gunman who shot UDR Corporal Herbert Kernaghan in front of dozens of children as he drove a delivery lorry into a school at Roslea, Fermanagh.

Will we ever, properly, know what went on in the heads of the mob who almost literally lynched the two Signals Corporals in the Milltown area of Belfast who had accidentally strayed into the path of a funeral procession, before they were murdered?

Finally, will the Godfathers of the IRA ever explain to the family of Pakistani immigrant Noor Baz Khan shot in Londonderry in 1973 because he served tea to soldiers? Will they offer an explanation to the parents of Pakistani tea boy Mohammed Abdul Khalid, shot 17 times by gunmen at Crossmaglen because he did catering work for the Army and his Dad was the camp barber? The body of the latter was riddled with bullets and dumped like a piece of rubbish at the side of an isolated country lane!

I need only read my own last few paragraphs to understand why this book was written from the perspective of the lost British voices of Northern Ireland.

We have to remember also, that, legally, politically and even practically, Ulster, Northern Ireland, or the 'Six Counties' is part of the United Kingdom. Had the killings and paramilitary excesses taken place in, and gripped Yorkshire, say or Lancashire or a part of the Midlands, would successive governments not have used troops to restore order, aid the police and fight terrorism?

It is easy to fall into the trap of resorting to the old adage one man's terrorist is another man's freedom fighter, but there were issues – still are – which needed resolution and the British Army, as always were there to be the 'pig in the middle', the 'meat' in a sectarian sandwich.

The reader must forgive my rhetoric, but it serves only to demonstrate that the writing of this book was so easy for me, given my absolute support for my fellow ex-squaddies.

I am not a hero, never have been and I never have done anything remotely heroic, but in the course of the research for this book, I spoke to, and met, lots of them!

Northern Ireland was a tragedy; there are those who would argue that it was a tragedy just waiting to happen. But it was a tragedy, nonetheless.

On the Bobby Sands wall mural on a house on the Lower Falls Road, part of an area the soldiers dubbed 'the murder mile' the artist has added the words: 'Everyone, Republican or otherwise has their own particular role to play.'

One wonders! Well over 3,000 of the dead, or 4 out of 5, would have preferred not to have played any role at all!

In conclusion, if this had taken place in Leeds or Liverpool, or Coventry or even London and British troops had been forced to wage war on terror in their own backyards, imagine the effect upon our lives. Difficult to imagine ?

But it did happen, just a few dozen miles, a few hours ferry ride or an hour by 'easyJet' away from the British mainland. And, it happened in our lifetimes.

* Figures courtesy of CAIN Web Service. See sources for internet address.

Alex 'Veteran's' Poetry (ex-RTR)

THE M62 COACH BOMB

'How could a woman kill innocent kids?' a nation of women cried down.
Reading a tale of the bold IRA, the killers of children with never a frown.
'Hangings too good for people like her' the nation cried out, its anguish complete.
For here was the woman that murdered them all, those people with semtex just under their feet.
For she had strolled up, that dark winters night, as cool as you please, and done her sick deed.
Condemning so many to horrible death, just doing her 'duty', fulfilling her creed.
By throwing that case in the boot of the bus, then watching the soldiers and children climb on,
she witnessed the victims of her semtex bomb.
She smiled at the young ones, walked swiftly away, night breeze in her hair,
the words drifted to her, 'Can we sit back there?'
So now the bus travelled through Manchester's Streets, the hour had gone midnight, the die had been cast.
The journey it travelled, with headlights ablazing, would now be its last.
And as the gears ground up the long Pennine slopes,
The passengers slumbered, their dreams and their hopes,
Would soon become nothing, for ticking below,
The clock in the suitcase was ready to show,
How the bold IRA murdered women and kids, to achieve its sick ends, to let the world see
How a united Ireland would be good for them all, and would teach you and me.
And the tales of this 'bravery' would echo for years,
Along with the shedding of millions of tears.
Twelve people lay dead on that cross Pennine road.
The coach had exploded, disgorging its load,
across all six lanes of the M62, and firemen wept as they counted the toll, of
women and children, whole families killed, by the ones with no soul.
And what of this women who planted the bomb, in bed with her lover as victims lay dead?
The wrong that she'd done never entered her head.
Her thirty year sentence cut short in its prime.
Her appeal upheld, by judges so stupid for cutting her time.
Now there's nothing to show on cold Hartshead moor, as the winter wind moans past the odd farmhouse door.
A small noise just whispers across fields so bare,

a young child asking, 'Can we sit back there?'

THE EMPTY PHOTO FRAME

I listen to the dull recording of his voice within my mind.
The words are plain, the voice is strong the accent one of my own kind.
The tape recorder in my brain repeats his words just as were said,
This final discourse written down in ink, inside my head.
And I can still remember where that last short talk took place.
Beside the road, near Crossmaglen, a spot now lost,
Without a trace
And as we chatted on that day, the devil's work came into play,
For soon my friend of countless chats would soon be lying dead.
The tarmac road of Cullaville the pillow for his resting head.
And through the mists of languid time I still call out his name,
His face has gone, and all I've left, is an empty photo frame.
What power is this that weaves its web, that takes away his face?
Is it because I blame myself for his sad fate, his shocking end,
That leaves my mind without a trace?
Or is it just that Father Time has marched the road where my thoughts live,
And somehow blanks his face from me, hoping to forgive?
Or is it just to see his face would tip me o'er the brink?
Would blow my mind, or ruin my soul, or tip me into drink?
These are the questions that I pose, to you, the reader of this prose,
Because I cannot find the answer for myself.
The answer lies, deep in my mind, upon some dusty brain-cell shelf.
It dangles here, before my eyes, mist shrouded, like a lurid game.
Nailed to the wall of my mind's eye, this empty photo frame.
One day, perhaps all will be told, the day I die, all grey and cold.
And I will leave this mortal coil, with dignity, and soul unsold.
And climb the escalator to that place, where judgments meet me,
Face to face.
And I will see those other lads, that I once knew, and shake their hands anew.
Then once again we'll crack a glass, to those who fought that stinking war,
And then I will be with my friends, who travelled on before.
The blinkers that have closed my eyes, will be removed, and I'll be sure,
Of all the things I see.
At last the shield that closed my mind will disappear, be gone from me.
So with the clarity of God, I will shout out his name,
And see hung there, in Odin's halls, his face, complete with photo frame.

Dedicated To Cpl Ian Henry Armstrong. Killed in action, 1500hrs, 29th August 1971, RIP.

Appendix II

Dougie Holden's poetry (ex 2 LI)

RETURN TO NORTHERN IRELAND 1969 – ?

Another tour, another bloody tour across the water,
Remembering sights of wanton slaughter.
Army and police in a mixed patrol,
The vehicle checkpoints and crowd control.

The spitting, the shouting, the abusive calls,
The sniper, the shot a comrade falls,
A barrage of bricks, the catapulted stones,
Torn bleeding flesh and splintered bones.

Beatings, kickings, kneecapping and killing,
Soldiers blown to pieces at Enniskillen.
The young, the old, the meek and mild,
No remorse shown for man or child.

More sectarian murders ready to greet,
Bullet scars on buildings down Leeson Street.
Unmoved bodies in a bullet-ridden car
Booby-trapped hedges across South Armagh.

Cursing and swearing from mouthy kids,
Petrol-bombs thrown at armoured pigs.
Searching eyes look out from Divis Flats,
Machine-guns poke below bullet-proof slats.

Time to leave again but I'm not alone.
Heading for Belfast, Derry or County Tyrone.
Seeing the sights of wanton slaughter,
To another bloody tour across the water.

Northern Ireland Roll of Honour

14th/20th King's Hussars and 15th/19th King's Royal Hussars

CPL IAN ARMSTRONG	29/8/71	Ambushed at Crossmaglen
2ND LT ROBERT WILLIAMS-WYNN	13/8/72	Shot by sniper in West Belfast
CPL MICHAEL COTTON	20/3/74	Killed in friendly fire Co Armagh
CPL MICHAEL HERBERT	20/3/74	Killed in same incident
SGT WILLIAM ROBERTSON	8/2/75	Shot by sniper Mullan, Co Fermanagh

17th/21st Lancers

CPL TERENCE WILLIAMS	5/5/73	Booby trap bomb Crossmaglen
TROOPER JOHN GIBBONS	5/5/73	Killed in same incident
TROOPER KENEALY	14/9/73	Killed in training accident Gosford Castle

16th/5th Lancers

CPL DAVID POWELL	28/10/71	Bomb attack Kinawley, Co Fermanagh
2/LT ANDREW SOMERVILLE	27/3/73	IRA landmine near Omagh

1st Regiment Royal Horse Artillery

GUNNER TIMOTHY UTTERIDGE	19/10/84	Shot on the Turf Lodge, Belfast

5 Regiment Army Air Corps

SGT I. C. REID	24/6/72	IRA landmine, Glenshane Pass, Co Antrim
L/CPL D. MOON	24/6/72	Killed in same incident
PTE C. STEVENSON	24/6/72	Killed in same incident
C/SGT A. PLACE	18/5/73	Booby trap bomb, Knock-na-Moe Hotel, Omagh
C. O. FH. B. R. COX	18/5/73	Killed in the same incident
SGT D. B. READ	18/5/73	Killed in the same incident
SGT S. YOUNG	18/5/73	Killed in the same incident
WO. D. C. ROWAT	12/4/74	Killed by IRA landmine, location unknown
MAJOR J. D. HICKS	18/12/75	Aircraft accident
WO. B. A. JACKSON	7/1/76	Aircraft accident
CAPTAIN M. J. KETT	10/4/78	Killed in helicopter accident
CAPTAIN. A. J. STIRLING	2/12/78	Killed in helicopter accident
CPL R. D. ADCOCK	2/12/78	Killed in helicopter accident
CPL. R. JACKSON	5/7/80	RTA
CPL B. McKENNA	6/4/82	Died of natural causes on duty
L/CPL. S. J. ROBERTS	28/11/83	RTA
L/CPL. T. ORANGE	20/10/87	RTA
S/SGT. J. N. P. CROFT	14/8/89	Violent or unnatural causes
CAPTAIN ANDREW NICOLL	22/12/3	Helicopter crash Londonderry
SERGEANT SIMON BENNETT.	22/12/3	Killed in same incident

5th Royal Inniskilling Dragoon Guards

SGT FREDERICK WILLIAM DRAKE	3/6/73	Died of wounds: bomb, Knock-na-Moe Hotel Omagh

Adjutant General's Corps

L/CPL PAUL MELLING	3/9/97	Natural causes

Argyll and Sutherland Highlanders

L/CPL DUNCAN MCPHEE	10/9/72	IRA landmine Dungannon
PTE DOUGLAS RICHMOND	10/9/72	Killed in same incident
2nd LT STEWART GARDINER	22/10/72	Shot by IRA sniper Drumuckaval, Armagh
PTE D. HARPER	12/11/72	Killed in train accident
CAPT WILLIAM WATSON	20/11/72	IRA booby trap Cullyhanna
C/SGT JAMES STRUTHERS	20/11/72	Killed in the same incident
PTE JOHN McGARRY	28/11/72	Friendly fire
PTE DOUGLAS MCKELVIE	20/8/79	RTA

CPL OWEN MCQUADE	11/11/80	Shot outside Altnagelvin hospital, Londonderry
CPL STEWART MARSHALL	20/8/98	RTA
PTE WILLIAM BROWN	20/8/98	RTA
PTE STEVEN CRAW	20/8/98	RTA

Army Catering Corps

PTE TERENCE M. ADAM	6/12/82	INLA bomb attack: Droppin' Well, Ballykelly
PTE PAUL JOSEPH DELANEY	6/12/82	Killed in same incident
PTE RICHARD R. BIDDLE	9/4/83	IRA booby trapped car, Omagh

Army Intelligence Corps

CORPORAL PAUL HARMAN	14/12/77	Killed on covert op by IRA Monagh Road, Belfast

Army Physical Training Corps

WO2 DAVID BELLAMY	19/11/79	IRA ambush, Springfield Road, Belfast

Black Watch

L/CPL EDWIN CHARNLEY	18/11/71	Shot by sniper in East Belfast
PTE MARK D. CARNIE	19/7/78	IRA bomb Dungannon

Blues & Royals

TROOPER ANTHONY DYKES	5/4/79	Shot by IRA snipers, Andersonstown RUC station
TROOPER ANTHONY THORNETT	5/4/79	Killed in same incident
LT DENIS DALY	20/7/82	Killed in Hyde Park bomb outrage
SQMC R BRIGHT	23/7/82	DoW from same incident
TROOPER SIMON TIPPER	23/7/82	Killed in same incident
L/CPL JEFFERY YOUNG	23/7/82	Killed in same incident

Cheshire Regiment

PTE D. A. SMITH	4/7/74	DoW after being shot, Ballymurphy Estate, Belfast
PTE NEIL WILLIAMS	6/12/82	IRA bomb Droppin' Well pub, Ballykelly
PTE ANTHONY WILLIAMSON	6/12/82	Killed in same incident
L/CPL DAVID WILSON-STITT	6/12/82	Killed in same incident
L/CPL STEVEN BAGSHAW	6/12/82	Killed in same incident
L/CPL CLINTON COLLINS	6/12/82	Killed in same incident
L/CPL PHILIP MCDONOUGH	6/12/82	Killed in same incident
PTE DAVID MURREY	6/12/82	Killed in same incident

Coldstream Guards

SGT ANTHONY METCALF	27/8/72	IRA sniper Creggan Heights, Londonderry
GUARDSMAN ROBERT PEARSON	20/2/73	Killed by IRA snipers, Lower Falls, Belfast
GUARDSMAN MICHAEL SHAW	20/2/73	Killed in same incident
GUARDSMAN MICHAEL DOYLE	21/2/73	Killed by sniper, Fort Whiterock, Belfast
GUARDSMAN ANTON BROWN	6/3/74	Killed by sniper, Ballymurphy Estate, Belfast
CAPTAIN ANTHONY POLLEN	24/4/74	Shot on a mission, Bogside, Londonderry
L/CPL SIMON WARE	17/8/91	IRA landmine explosion, Cullyhanna, Armagh

Devon & Dorset Regiment

PTE CHARLES STENTIFORD	21/1/72	IRA landmine, Keady, Co Armagh
PTE DAVID CHAMP	10/2/72	IRA landmine, Cullyhanna, Co Armagh
SGT IAN HARRIS	10/2/72	Killed in same incident
CPL STEVEN WINDSOR	6/11/74	Killed by sniper, Crossmaglen
CPL GERALD JEFFERY	7/4/83	DoW, IRA bomb, Falls Road, Belfast
L/CPL STEPHEN TAVERNER	5/11/83	Dow, IRA bomb, Crossmaglen

Duke of Edinburgh Royal Regiment

CPL JOSEPH LEAHY	8/3/73	DoW, booby trap, Forkhill, Co Armagh
S/SGT BARRINGTON FOSTER	23/3/73	Murdered off-duty by the IRA
CAPTAIN NIGEL SUTTON	14/8/73	Died in vehicle accident, Ballykinler
PTE MICHAEL SWANICK	28/10/74	IRA van bomb attack, Ballykinler
PTE BRIAN ALLEN	6/11/74	Killed by sniper, Crossmaglen

PTE JOHN RANDALL	26/6/93	Killed by sniper, Newtownhamilton, Co Armagh
L/CPL KEVIN PULLIN	17/7/93	Killed by sniper, Crossmaglen
MAJOR RICHARD ALLEN	2/6/94	Helicopter crash, Mull of Kintyre

Duke Of Wellington's Regiment

PTE GEORGE LEE	6/6/72	IRA sniper, Ballymurphy Estate, Belfast
CPL TERRENCE GRAHAM	16/7/72	Landmine attack, Crossmaglen
PTE JAMES LEE	16/7/72	Killed in same incident
2ND LT HOWARD FAWLEY	25/1/74	Landmine attack, Ballyronan Co Londonderry
CPL MICHAEL RYAN	17/3/74	IRA sniper at Brandywell, Londonderry
CPL ERROL PRYCE	26/1/80	IRA sniper, Ballymurphy Estate, Belfast

Gloucestershire Regiment

PTE ANTHONY ASPINWALL	16/12/71	DoW after gun battle in Lower Falls area, Belfast
PTE KEITH BRYAN	5/1/72	IRA sniper, Lower Falls area, Belfast
CPL IAN BRAMLEY	2/2/72	IRA sniper Hastings Street RUC station, Belfast
PTE GEOFFREY BREAKWELL	17/7/73	IRA booby trap, Divis St Flats, Belfast
PTE CHRISTOPHER PATRICK	17/7/73	Killed in same incident
PTE D. J. McCHILL	17/8/78	Died during the tour – not as a result of terrorist actions
L/CPL A P. BENNETT	4/6/80	Killed in vehicle accident, Limavady

Gordon Highlanders

WO2 ARTHUR MCMILLAN	18/6/72	Booby-trapped house in Lurgan, Co Down
SGT IAN MARK MUTCH	18/6/72	Killed in same incident
L/CPL COLIN LESLIE	18/6/72	Killed in same incident
L/CPL A. C. HARPER	8/8/72	RTA
PTE MICHAEL GEORGE MARR	29/3/73	Shot by sniper, Andersonstown, Belfast
L/CPL JACK MARSHALL	28/8/77	Shot in gun battle Ardoyne, Belfast

Green Howards

PTE MALCOLM HATTON	9/8/71	Shot by sniper, Brompton Park, Ardoyne
PTE JOHN ROBINSON	14/8/71	Shot by sniper in Ardoyne, Belfast
PTE GEORGE CROZIER	23/871	Shot by sniper Flax St Mill, Ardoyne
L/CPL PETER HERRINGTON	17/9/71	Shot by sniper, Brompton Park, Ardoyne
PTE PETER SHARP	1/10/71	Shot on Kerrara Street, Ardoyne
PTE RAYMOND HALL	5/3/73	DoW: Sniper attack, Belfast
PTE FREDERICK DICKS	5/6/74	IRA sniper, Dungannon
MAJOR PETER WILLIS	17/7/75	IRA bomb, Ford's Cross, Armagh
CPL IAN METCALF	15/6/88	IRA booby trapped lorry, Lisburn

Grenadier Guards

CAPTAIN ROBERT NAIRAC G. C.	14/5/77	Murdered by IRA on undercover mission
GUARDSMAN GRAHAM DUGGAN	21/12/78	Killed in attack on Army patrol, Crossmaglen
GUARDSMAN KEVIN JOHNSON	21/12/78	Killed in same incident
GUARDSMAN GLEN LING	21/12/78	Killed in same incident
CAPTAIN HERBERT WESTMACOTT	2/5/80	Killed on undercover mission in Belfast
GUARDSMAN DANIEL BLINCO	30/12/93	IRA sniper in South Armagh

Intelligence Corps

| CPL PAUL HARMAN | 14/12/77 | Killed after his vehicle was hijacked, Turf Lodge, Belfast |

Irish Guards

SGT PHILLIP PRICE	21/7/72	Killed by car bomb, 'Bloody Friday' Belfast
GUARDSMAN DAVID ROBERTSON	24/11/73	IRA landmine, Crossmaglen
GUARDSMAN SAMUEL MURPHY	14/11/77	Murdered in front of his mother whilst on leave, Andersonstown, Belfast
GUARDSMAN PAUL FRYER	13/11/79	IRA bomb, Crossmaglen

King's Own Royal Border Regiment

| C/SERGEANT WILLIAM BOARDLEY | 10/5/72 | Shot in Strabane by IRA gunman |
| CORPORAL JAMES BURNEY | 19/12/78 | IRA sniper, Newington, Belfast |

PTE O. C. PAVEY	11/3/80	Accidental shooting, Crossmaglen
PTE JOHN B. BATEMAN	15/3/80	IRA sniper, Crossmaglen
PTE SEAN G. WALKER	21/3/80	DoW, car bomb, Crossmaglen
L/CORPORAL ANTHONY DACRE	27/3/85	Bomb attack, Divis Street flats, Belfast
PTE HATFIELD	24/2/92	Vehicle accident, Londonderry
PTE M. K. THOMAS	17/5/95	Vehicle accident, Belfast
PTE D. R. MILRAY	21/2/95	Road accident
WOII M. C. WHITE		Training accident, Ballykinler

King's Own Scottish Borderers

S/SGT PETER SINTON	28/7/70	Violent or unnatural causes
L/CPL PETER DEACON SIME	7/4/72	IRA sniper, Ballymurphy Est. Belfast
L/CPL BARRY GOLD	24/4/72	DoW after gun battle at VCP in Belfast
C/SGT HENRY S. MIDDLEMASS	10/12/72	IRA booby trap, Turf Lodge, Belfast
S/SGT H. SHINGLESTON M. M.	25/11/76	Cause of death unknown
PTE P. B. SCOTT	10/10/79	Cause of death unknown
PTE JAMES HOUSTON	13/12/89	Killed at VCP in gun and grenade attack, Fermanagh
L/CPL MICHAEL JOHN PATERSON	13/12/89	Killed in same incident

King's Regiment

CPL ALAN BUCKLEY	13/5/72	Shot on Ballymurphy Estate, Belfast
PTE EUSTACE HANLEY	23/5/72	IRA sniper Ballymurphy Estate
PTE MARCEL DOGLAY	30/5/72	IRA bomb, Springfield Road, Belfast
PTE JAMES JONES	18/7/72	IRA sniper, New Barnsley, Belfast
PTE BRIAN THOMAS	24/7/72	IRA sniper, New Barnsley, Belfast
PTE RENNIE LAYFIELD	18/8/72	IRA sniper, Falls Road, Belfast
PTE ROY CHRISTOPHER	30/8/72	DoW after bomb attack, Cupar St, Belfast
PTE CHRISTOPHER SHANLEY	11/4/79	Ambushed and shot Ballymurphy Estate, Belfast
L/CPL STEPHEN RUMBLE	19/4/79	DoW from same incident
L/CPL ANDREW WEBSTER	19/5/79	Bomb attack, Turf Lodge, Belfast
PTE STEPHEN BEACHAM	24/10/90	Killed by IRA 'proxy bomb' Coshquin, nr Londonderry. 5 soldiers killed
L/CPL STEPHEN BURROWS	24/10/90	Killed in same incident
PTE VINCENT SCOTT	24/10/90	Killed in same incident
PTE DAVID SWEENE	24/10/90	Killed in same incident
PTE PAUL WORRALL	24/10/90	Killed in same incident

Life Guards

CPL of HORSE LEONARD DUBER	21/2/73	DoW after riot in Belfast

Light Infantry

1st Battalion

PTE. R. V. JONES	18/8/72	Shot by sniper in West Belfast
PTE. R. ROWE	28/8/72	Shot accidentally in Ardoyne, Belfast
PTE. T. A. STOKER	19/9/72	DoW after accidental shooting in Flex St Mill, Ardoyne
PTE. T. RUDMAN	30/9/72	Shot in Ardoyne, Belfast (brother killed in 1971 in Northern Ireland)
PTE. S. R. HALL	28/10/73	Shot in Crossmaglen
PTE. G. M. CURTIS	10/6/83	IRA bomb, Ballymurphy Estate, Belfast
PTE. N. I. BLYTHE	12/11/87	Killed in accident
PTE. J. J. WILLBY	6/2/88	Violent or unnatural causes
PTE. B. BISHOP	20/8/88	Killed in Ballygawley coach bombing; one of 8 soldiers killed
PTE. P. L. BULLOCK	20/8/88	Killed in same incident
PTE. J. BURFITT	20/8/88	Killed in same incident
PTE. R. GREENER	20/8/88	Killed in same incident
PTE. A. S. LEWIS	20/8/88	Killed in same incident
PTE. M. A. NORWORTHY	20/8/88	Killed in same incident
PTE. S. J. WILKINSON	20/8/88	Killed in same incident
PTE. J. WINTER	20/8/88	Killed in same incident
PTE. G. SMITH	3/12/88	Violent or unnatural causes

| PTE. A. J. RICHARDSON | 12/3/97 | Killed in attempted ambush by IRA after ceasefire. |

2nd Battalion

PTE. J. R. RUDMAN	14/10/71	Shot in Coalisland area
SGT. A. W. WHITELOCK	24/8/72	IRA sniper in Londonderry
CPL. T. P. TAYLOR	13/5/73	Killed in bomb attack, Donegall Road
PTE. J. GASKELL	14/5/73	DoW from same incident
PTE. R. B. ROBERTS	1/7/73	Shot by sniper in Ballymurphy Estate, Belfast
PTE. R. STAFFORD	20/7/79	Killed in car accident
PTE. P. TURNER	28/8/92	IRA sniper, Crossmaglen

3rd Battalion

PTE. P. K. EASTAUGH	23/3/71	Shot accidentally in the Ardoyne area of Belfast
CPL. I. R. MORRILL	28/8/72	IRA sniper, Belfast (Att from RGJ)
LCPL. A. KENNINGTON	28/2/73	IRA sniper, Ardoyne area of Belfast
LCPL. C. R. MILLER	18/9/73	Shot in West Belfast
PTE. R. D. TURNBULL	29/6/77	Ambushed and shot West Belfast
PTE. M. E. HARRISON	29/6/77	Killed in same incident
PTE. L. J. HARRISON	9/8/77	IRA sniper, New Barnsley, Belfast
CPL. D. P. SALTHOUSE	7/12/82	IRA bomb Droppin' Well pub, Ballykelly

North Irish Militia

| RANGER SAMUEL M. GIBSON. | 24/10/74 | Abducted and murdered off duty (TA) |

Parachute Regiment

PTE PETER DOCHERTY	21/5/70	Accidental death
PTE VICTOR CHAPMAN	24/6/70	Drowned
SGT. M. WILLETTS G. C.	25/5/71	Killed saving civilians in IRA bomb blast, Springfield Road, Belfast
PTE. R. A. BARTON	14/7/71	Shot protecting comrades, Andersonstown, Belfast
FATHER GERRY WESTON, M. B. E.	22/2/72	Killed in IRA bomb outrage, Aldershot
PTE. A. KELLY	18/3/72	Killed in accident, Holywood, Co Down
PTE. C. STEPHENSON	24/6/72	IRA landmine, Glenshane Pass, Londonderry
PTE. F. T. BELL	20/10/72	DoW after being shot on Ballymurphy Estate, Belfast
CPL. S. N. HARRISON	7/4/73	IRA landmine, Tullyogallaghan
L/CPL. T. D. BROWN	7/4/73	Killed in same incident
L/CPL. D. A. FORMAN	16/4/73	Accidentally shot, Flax Street Mill, Ardoyne
WO2. W. R. VINES	5/5/73	IRA landmine, Crossmaglen
A/SGT. J. WALLACE	24/5/73	IRA booby trap, Crossmaglen
PTE. R. BEDFORD	16/3/74	Shot in IRA ambush, Crossmaglen
PTE. P. JAMES	16/3/74	Killed in same incident
PTE. W. SNOWDON	28/6/76	IRA bomb, Crossmaglen
PTE. J. BORUCKI	8/8/76	IRA booby trap, Crossmaglen
L/CPL. D. A. JONES	17/3/78	Shot in gun battle, Glenshane Pass, Londonderry
PTE. J. FISHER	12/7/78	IRA booby trap, Crossmaglen
CPL. R. D. ADCOCK	2/12/78	Killed in helicopter accident
MAJ. P. J. FURSMAN	27/8/79	Killed in IRA double bomb blast, Warrenpoint. One of 16 Paras and 2 other soldiers killed
WO2. W. BEARD	27/8/79	Killed in same incident
SGT. I. A. ROGERS	27/8/79	Killed in same incident
CPL. N. J. ANDREWS	27/8/79	Killed in same incident
CPL. J. C. GILES	27/8/79	Killed in same incident
CPL. L. JONES	27/8/79	Killed in same incident
L/CPL. C. G. IRELAND	27/8/79	Killed in same incident
PTE. G. I. BARNES	27/8/79	Killed in same incident
PTE. D. F. BLAIR	27/8/79	Killed in same incident
PTE. R. DUNN	27/8/79	Killed in same incident
PTE. R. N. ENGLAND	27/8/79	Killed in same incident
PTE. R. D. U. JONES	27/8/79	Killed in same incident
PTE. T. R. VANCE	27/8/79	Killed in same incident
PTE. J. A. VAUGHAN-JONES	27/8/79	Killed in same incident

PTE. A. G. WOOD	27/8/79	Killed in same incident
PTE. M. WOODS	27/8/79	Killed in same incident
PTE. P. S. GRUNDY	16/12/79	IRA booby trap, Forkhill
LT. S. G. BATES	1/1/80	Shot accidentally, Forkhill
PTE. G. M. R. HARDY	1/1/80	Killed in same incident
A/SGT. B. M. BROWN	9/8/80	IRA booby trap, Forkhill
L/CPL. P. HAMPSON	24/12/81	Violent or unnatural causes
L/CPL. M. C. MAY	26/8/82	RTA
SGT. A. I. SLATER M. M.	2/12/84	Killed in anti-IRA operation, Fermanagh
SGT. M. B. MATTHEWS	29/7/88	DoW, IRA landmine, Cullyhanna
PTE. R. SPIKINS	25/3/89	RTA, Belfast
L/CPL. S. WILSON	18/11/89	IRA landmine, Mayobridge (3 soldiers killed)
PTE. D. MACAULAY	18/11/89	Killed in same incident
PTE. M. MARSHALL	18/11/89	Killed in same incident
PTE. A. HARRISON	19/6/91	Murdered by IRA in fiancé's home, East Belfast
L/CPL. R. COULSON	27/6/92	Drowned crossing a river
L/CPL. P. H. SULLIVAN	27/6/92	Drowned trying to rescue his friend
PTE. M. B. LEE	20/8/92	Violent or unnatural causes
PTE. P. F. J. GROSS	13/5/93	Accidental death at Holywood
PTE. C. D. KING.	4/12/94	Violent or unnatural causes
PTE. M. A. RAMSEY	21/8/97	Died in an accident

Prince of Wales' Own Regiment of Yorkshire

S/SGT ARTHUR PLACE	18/5/73	Booby trap bomb, Knock-na-Moe Hotel, Omagh
PTE DAVID WRAY	10/10/75	DoW after being shot Creggan area of Londonderry

Princess of Wales' Royal Regiment

MAJOR JOHN BARR	26/11/92	Helicopter crash, Bessbrook Mill

Queen's Lancashire Regiment

SGT JAMES SINGLETON	23/6/70	Natural causes
PTE MICHAEL MURTAGH	6/2/73	Killed in rocket attack Lower Falls area, Belfast
PTE EDWIN WESTON	14/2/73	IRA sniper Divis Street area, Belfast
PTE STEPHEN KEATING	3/3/73	IRA sniper, Manor Street, West Belfast
PTE GARY BARLOW	4/3/73	Gun battle, Lower Falls area, Belfast
PTE JOHN GREEN	8/3/73	Shot whilst guarding school in Lower Falls area, Belfast
PTE IAN O'CONNER	3/3/87	Grenade attack, Divis Street flats, Belfast
PTE JOSEPH LEACH	4/6/87	IRA sniper, Andersonstown, Belfast
L/CPL ANTONY HALTON	25/10/99	RTA

Queen's Own Highlanders

PTE WILLIAM MCINTYRE	11/10/72	DoW IRA landmine, Dungannon. Killed with 2 other soldiers from Argyll & Sutherlands
PTE JAMES HESKETH	10/12/73	Shot dead on Lower Falls, Belfast
PTE ALAN JOHN MCMILLAN	8/7/79	Remote-controlled bomb in Crossmaglen
L/CPL D. LANG	24/8/79	Killed in helicopter crash with another soldier
L/CPL D. A. WARES	24/8/79	Killed in same accident
LT/COL DAVID BLAIR	27/8/79	Killed in IRA double bomb blast, Warrenpoint (one of 18 soldiers killed in same incident)
L/CPL VICTOR MACLEOD	27/8/79	Killed in same incident
CPL R. D. TURNER.	27/2/90	Accidentally shot

Queen's Regiment

PTE DAVID PITCHFORD	27/6/70	RTA
PTE PAUL CARTER	15/9/71	DoW after being shot at Royal Victoria Hospital, Belfast
PTE ROBERT BENNER	29/11/71	Abducted and murdered by IRA off-duty at Crossmaglen
PTE RICHARD SINCLAIR	31/10/72	IRA sniper New Lodge, Belfast
PTE STANLEY EVANS	14/11/72	IRA sniper Unity Flats complex, West Belfast
PTE PETER WOOLMORE	19/3/79	Mortar bomb attack, Newtownhamilton, Co Armagh
PTE ALAN STOCK	15/10/83	Remote-controlled bomb, Creggan, Londonderry
PTE NEIL CLARKE	24/4/84	IRA sniper, Bishop Street, Londonderry

| CPL ALEXANDER BANNISTER | 8/8/88 | IRA sniper, New Barnsley, Belfast |
| SGT CHARLES CHAPMAN | 16/7/90 | IRA booby trap, Army recruiting office, Wembley, London |

Queen's Royal Irish Hussars

| TROOPER HUGH MCCABE | 15/8/69 | Killed by friendly fire, Divis Street, Belfast |

Royal Air Force

FLT SGT JOHN WILLOUGHBY	7/12/69	Natural causes
AIRMAN JOHN BAXTER	1/5/88	IRA booby trap, at Nieuw-Bergan, Holland
AIRMAN JOHN MILLER	1/5/88	Killed with his friend in the same incident
AIRMAN IAN SHINNER	1/5/88	Killed by IRA sniper in Roermond, Holland
CPL IAN LEARMOUTH		Cause of death unknown
CPL ISLANIA MAHESHKUMAR	26/10/89	Shot by IRA in Wildenrath, West Germany and killed alongside baby daughter, Nivruti (6 months old)
SQN LDR MICHAEL HAVERSON	26/10/92	Helicopter crash, Bessbrook Mill base, Armagh
FLT LT SIMON S. M. J. ROBERTS	26/10/92	Killed in same accident
FLT SGT JAN PEWTRESS	26/10/92	Killed in same accident

Royal Anglian Regiment

MAJOR PETER TAUNTON	26/10/70	Violent or unnatural causes
PTE BRIAN SHERIDAN	20/11/70	RTA
PTE ROGER WILKINSON	11/10/71	DoW after being shot on Letterkenny Rd, Londonderry
L/CPL IAN CURTIS	9/11/71	IRA sniper Foyle Road, Londonderry
2/LT NICHOLAS HULL	16/4/72	IRA sniper Divis Street flats, Belfast
PTE JOHN BALLARD	11/5/72	IRA sniper, Sultan St. Lower Falls, Belfast
CPL KENNETH MOGG	13/7/72	IRA sniper Dunville Park, Belfast
L/CPL MARTIN ROONEY	13/7/72	IRA sniper Clonnard St. , Lower Falls, Belfast
L/CPL JOHN BODDY	17/7/72	IRA sniper, Grosvenor Road area of Belfast
CPL JOHN BARRY	25/9/72	DoW after gun battle Lower Falls, Belfast
PTE IAN BURT	29/9/72	IRA sniper Albert Street, Lower Falls, Belfast
PTE ROBERT MASON	24/10/72	IRA sniper Naples St, Grosvenor Rd area, Belfast
PTE ANTHONY GOODFELLOW	27/4/73	Shot manning VCP Creggan Estate, Londonderry
PTE PAUL WRIGHT	8/10/79	Killed on covert operation, Falls Road area
PTE ANTHONY ANDERSON	24/5/82	Killed by vehicle in confusion after petrol bomb attack Butcher Street, Londonderry
PTE MARTIN PATTERN	22/10/85	Murdered off-duty Limavady Rd Waterside,Londonderry
MAJOR ANDREW FRENCH	22/5/86	Killed by remote-controlled bomb, Crossmaglen
PTE MITCHELL BERTRAM	9/7/86	Remote-controlled bomb Glassdrummond, Crossmaglen
PTE CARL DAVIS	9/7/86	Killed in the same incident
PTE NICHOLAS PEACOCK	31/1/89	Remote-controlled bomb Falls Road area, Belfast

Royal Army Medical Corps

| WOII PHILLIP CROSS | 2/11/91 | IRA bomb planted at Musgrave Park Hospital (killed with one other soldier) |

Royal Army Pay Corps

| PTE MICHAEL PRIME | 16/2/72 | Shot in ambush at Moira roundabout near Lisburn |

Royal Army Ordnance Corps

CAPTAIN D A STEWARDSON	9/9/71	Defusing IRA bomb Castlerobin, Antrim
WO2. C. J. L. DAVIES	24/11/71	Killed by IRA bomb in Lurgan
PTE T. F. McCANN	14/2/72	Abducted and murdered by the IRA, Newtownbutler
SSGT. C. R. CRACKNELL	15/3/72	IRA booby trap, Grosvenor Road, Belfast
SSGT. A. S. BUTCHER	15/3/72	Killed in same incident
MAJOR B. C. CALLADENE	29/3/72	IRA car bomb outside Belfast City Hall
CAPTAIN J. H. YOUNG	15/7/72	Defusing IRA bomb, Silverbridge near Forkhill
WO2. W. J. CLARK	3/8/72	Defusing IRA bomb at Strabane
SGT. R. E. HILLS	5/12/72	Attempting to make live shell safe Kitchen Hill
CAPTAIN B. S. GRITTEN	21/6/73	Killed inspecting explosives, Lecky Road, Londonderry
SSGT. R. F. BECKETT	30/8/73	Killed pulling bomb out of a post office Tullyhommon

CAPTAIN RONALD WILKINSON	23/9/73	Defusing IRA bomb, Edgbaston, Birmingham
2ND LT L. HAMILTON DOBBIE	3/10/73	IRA bomb, Bligh's Lane post, Londonderry
SSGT. A. N. BRAMMAH	18/2/74	Examining IRA roadside bomb, Crossmaglen
SSGT. V. I. ROSE	7/11/74	IRA landmine, Stewartstown, Tyrone
WO2. J. A. MADDOCKS	2/12/74	Examining milk churn bomb Gortmullen
WO2. E. GARSIDE	17/7/75	Killed with 3 other soldiers IRA bomb near Forkhill
CPL. C. W. BROWN	17/7/75	Killed in same incident
CPL DOUGLAS WHITFIELD	13/3/76	RTA
SGT. M. E. WALSH	9/1/77	Killed dismantling IRA bomb Newtownbutler
SIG. P. J. REECE	2/8/79	IRA landmine near Armagh
GNR. R. A. J. FURMINGER	2/8/79	Killed in same incident
WO2. M. O'NEIL	31/5/81	Examining IRA bomb near Newry
L/CORPORAL DEREK W. GREEN	15/6/88	One of 6 soldiers killed by IRA booby trap, Lisburn
WO2. J. R. HOWARD	8/8/88	IRA booby trap, Falls Road, Belfast

Royal Artillery

GUNNER ROBERT CURTIS	6/2/71	Shot by IRA gunmen, New Lodge area, Belfast
L/BOMB JOHN LAURIE	15/2/71	DoW after same incident
BOMBARDIER PAUL CHALLENOR	10/8/71	IRA sniper, Bligh's Lane post, Londonderry
GNR CLIFFORD LORING	31/8/71	DoW after being shot at VCP, Belfast
SGT MARTIN CARROLL	14/9/71	IRA sniper Creggan, Londonderry
GNR ANGUS STEVENS	27/10/71	IRA bomb attack, Rosemount RUC station, Belfast
L/BOMB DAVID TILBURY	27/10/71	Killed in same incident
GNR IAN DOCHERTY	31/10/71	DoW after being shot in Stockmans Lane, Belfast
GNR RICHARD HAM	29/12/71	Shot dead in the Brandywell area of Londonderry
BOMB ERIC BLACKBURN	10/4/71	Killed in bomb attack, Rosemount Avenue, Londonderry L/
BOMB BRIAN THOMASSON	10/4/71	Killed in same incident
GNR VICTOR HUSBAND	2/6/72	IRA landmine, Rosslea, Co Fermanagh
GNR BRIAN ROBERTSON	2/6/72	Killed in the same incident
SGT CHARLES COLEMAN	7/6/72	IRA sniper, Andersonstown, belfast
GUNNER WILLIAM RAISTRICK	11/6/72	IRA sniper Brooke Park, Londonderry
BOMBARDIER TERRENCE JONES	11/6/72	Shot in the back by IRA, Londonderry
GNR LEROY GORDON	7/8/72	IRA landmine, Lisnaskea, Co Fermanagh
L/BOMB DAVID WYNNE	7/8/72	Killed in same incident
MAJOR DAVID STORRY	14/8/72	Booby trap, casement Park base, Andersonstown
GNR ROBERT CUTTING	3/9/72	Accidentally shot, New Lodge area of Belfast
GNR PAUL JACKSON	28/11/72	Hit by bomb shrapnel Strand Road, Londonderry
GNR IDWAL EVANS	11/4/73	IRA sniper Bogside area of Londonderry
GNR KERRY VENN	28/4/73	IRA sniper Shantallow Estate, Londonderry
SGT THOMAS CRUMP	3/5/73	DoW after being shot in Londonderry
GNR JOSEPH BROOKES	25/11/73	Shot in IRA ambush in Bogside area of Londonderry
BOMBARDIER HEINZ PISAREK	25/11/73	Killed in same incident
SGT JOHN HAUGHEY	21/1/74	Remote-controlled bomb, Creggan Estate, Londonderry
GNR LEONARD GODDEN	4/2/74	Killed by IRA bomb on M62 in Yorkshire
BDR TERRENCE GRIFFIN	4/2. 74	Killed in same incident
GNR DAVID FARRINGTON	13/3/74	Shot by IRA gunmen at Chapel Lane Belfast city centre
LT/COL JOHN STEVENSON	8/4/74	Murdered by IRA gunmen at his home in Northumberland
GNR KIM MACCUNN	22/6/74	IRA sniper New Lodge, Belfast
SGT BERNARD FEARNS	30/7/74	IRA sniper New Lodge area of Belfast
GNR RICHARD DUNNE	8/11/74	IRA bomb in Woolwich, London pub bombings
GNR CYRIL MACDONALD	18/12/75	IRA bomb attack at Guildhall Square, Londonderry
GNR MARK ASHFORD	17/1/76	Shot at checkpoint, Great James Street, Londonderry
GNR JAMES REYNOLDS	13/3/76	RTA
GNR WILLIAM MILLER	3/7/76	IRA sniper at checkpoint Butcher Street, Londonderry
GNR ANTHONY ABBOT	24/10/76	Ambushed and killed by IRA, Ardoyne, Belfast
GNR MAURICE MURPHY	22/11/76	DoW from same incident
GNR EDWARD MULLER	11/1/77	IRA sniper at VCP in Old Park area of Belfast
GNR GEORGE MUNCASTER	23/1/77	IRA sniper Markets area, Belfast
GNR PAUL SHEPPARD	1/3/78	Shot in gun battle Clifton Park Avenue, Belfast
GNR RICHARD FURMINGER	2/8/79	Killed in IRA landmine attack with RAOC comrade, Cathedral Road, Armagh

GNR ALAN AYRTON	16/12/79	Killed with 3 others in landmine explosion, Dungannon
GNR WILLIAM BECK	16/12/79	Killed in same incident
GNR SIMON EVANS	16/12/79	Killed in same incident
GNR KEITH RICHARDS	16/12/79	Killed in same incident
L/BOMB KEVIN WALLER	20/9/82	Remote-controlled INLA bomb Divis St flats, Belfast
GNR LYNDON MORGAN	26/4/88	IRA booby trap Carrickmore
GNR MILES AMOS	8/3/89	IRA landmine, Buncrana Road, Londonderry
L/BOMB STEPHEN CUMMINS	8/3/89	Killed in same incident
MAJOR MICHAEL DILLION-LEE	2/6/90	Murdered outside his quarters in Dortmund, Germany
L/BOMB PAUL GARRETT	2/12/93	IRA sniper Keady, Co Armagh
L/BOMB STEPHEN RESTORICK	12/2/97	IRA sniper at VCP at Bessbrook Mill Army base
GNR JON COOPER	22/2/97	Violent or unnatural causes

Royal Corps of Signals

L/CPL MICHAEL SPURWAY	13/9/69	Friendly fire
SIGNALMAN PAUL GENGE	7/11/71	Shot by IRA whilst off-duty in Lurgan
CPL JOHN AIKMAN	6/11/73	Shot by IRA gunmen Newtownhamilton
SIGNALMAN MICHAEL E. WAUGH	4/2/74	Killed by IRA bomb, M62, Yorkshire
SIGNALMAN LESLIE DAVID WALSH	4/2/74	Killed in same incident
SIGNALMAN PAUL ANTHONY REID	4/2/74	Killed in same incident
SIGNALMAN DAVID ROBERTS	13/3/76	RTA
CPL A. K. FORD	7/1/76	Aircraft accident
SIGNALMAN PAUL J REECE	2/8/79	IRA landmine, Armagh
SIGNALMAN BRIAN RICHARD CROSS	4/7/81	Killed in road traffic accident, Lisburn
CPL MICHAEL WARD	1/4/82	Shot with REME soldier by IRA in Bogside, Londonderry
CPL DEREK T. WOOD	19/3/88	Beaten by mob, shot by IRA, Penny Lane, Belfast
CPL DAVID HOWES	19/3/88	Killed in same incident
L/CPL GRAHAM P. LAMBIE	15/6/88	Killed by IRA bomb, Lisburn (1 of 6 soldiers killed)
SGT MICHAEL JAMES WINKLER	15/6/88	Killed in same incident
SIGNALMAN MARK CLAVEY	15/6/88	Killed in same incident
CPL WILLIAM J. PATERSON	15/6/88	Killed in same incident
S/SGT KEVIN A. FROGGETT	16/9/89	Shot by IRA repairing radio mast Coalisland RUC station
SGT MICHAEL NEWMAN	14/4/92	Shot by INLA at Army Recruiting office, Derby, England
CPL IAN BIBBY	23/11/99	Violent or unnatural causes

Royal Corps Transport

MAJOR PHILIP COWLEY	13/1/70	Natural causes
DRIVER LAURENCE JUBB	26/4/72	Killed in vehicle crash after mob attack, Armagh
L/CPL MICHAEL BRUCE	31/5/72	IRA sniper Andersonstown, Belfast
S/SGT JOSEPH FLEMING	9/7/72	Shot dead by IRA in Grosvenor Road area of Belfast
DRIVER PETER HEPPENSTAL	14/7/72	IRA sniper Ardoyne area of Belfast
DRIVER STEPHEN COOPER	21/7/72	IRA car bomb on 'Bloody Friday' Belfast bus depot
DRIVER RONALD KITCHEN	10/11/72	IRA sniper at VCP in Old Park Road, Belfast
DRIVER MICHAEL GAY	17/3/73	IRA landmine, Dungannon
SGT THOMAS PENROSE	24/3/73	Murdered off-duty with 2 others, Antrim Road, Belfast
DRIVER NORMAN MCKENZIE	11/4/74	IRA landmine, Lisnaskea, Co Fermanagh
SGT WILLIAM EDGAR	15/4/77	Abducted and murdered by IRA whilst on leave in Londonderry
DRIVER PAUL BULMAN	19/5/81	Killed in IRA landmine attack along with 4 RGJs at Camlough, South Armagh
L/CPL NORMAN DUNCAN	22/2/89	Shot by IRA Waterside area of Londonderry
DVR C. PANTRY	2/11/91	Killed by IRA bomb at Musgrave Park hospital, Belfast

Royal Dragoon Guards

TROOPER GEOFFREY KNIPE	7/8/72	Armoured vehicle crashed after mob attack, Armagh

Royal Electrical & Mechanical Engineers

CFN CHRISTOPHER EDGAR	13/9/69	Violent or unnatural causes
SGT S. C. REID	24/6/72	IRA milk churn bombs at Glenshane Pass, Londonderry
L/CPL D. MOON	24/6/72	Killed in same incident
CFN BRIAN HOPE	14/8/72	IRA booby trap Casement Park, Andersonstown, Belfast

L/CPL COLIN HARKER	20/12/72	IRA sniper Lecky Road, Londonderry
SGT M. E. SELDON	30/6/74	
CFN COLIN MCINNES	18/12/75	IRA bomb attack on Army base in Londonderry
SGT MICHAEL BURBRIDGE	1/4/82	IRA sniper Rosemount barracks, Londonderry
SGT R. T. GREGORY	22/10/82	Died of natural causes on duty
WO1 (ASM) JAMES BRADWELL	11/10/96	DoW after car bomb attack by IRA on Army base Lisburn

Royal Engineers

SAPPER RONALD HURST	17/5/72	IRA sniper whilst working on base in Crossmaglen
S/SGT MALCOLM BANKS	28/6/72	Shot by IRA Short Strand area of Belfast
SAPPER EDWARD STUART	2/10/72	Shot whilst working undercover Dunmurry, Belfast
WO2 IAN DONALD	24/5/73	IRA bomb Cullaville, Co Armagh
MAJOR RICHARD JARMAN	20/7/73	IRA booby trap Middletown, Co Armagh
SAPPER JOHN WALTON	2/7/74	IRA booby trap Newtownhamilton
SGT DAVID EVANS	21/7/74	IRA booby trap Army base, Waterside, Londonderry
SAPPER HOWARD EDWARDS	11/12/76	IRA sniper, Bogside area of Londonderry
COLONEL MARK COE	16/2/80	Murdered by IRA gunmen at Army home in Bielefeld, Germany
SGT K. J. ROBSON	18/2/80	Aircraft accident
L/CPL MICHAEL ROBBINS	1/8/88	Killed by IRA bomb at Mill Hill Army camp, London
L/CPL C. M. MONTEITH	5/8/91	RTA
CPL M. D. IONNOU	15/4/95	RTA
S/SGT S. J. THOMPSON	30/6/95	Natural causes

Royal Gloucestershire, Berkshire and Wiltshire Regiment

CPL GARY LLEWELLYN FENTON	22/6/98	Run down and killed by lorry at VCP, Crossmaglen Posthumous Mention in Dispatches

Royal Green Jackets

L/CPL MICHAEL PEARCE	24/9/69	Violent or unnatural causes
RFN MICHAEL BOSWELL	25/10/69	RTA
RFN JOHN KEENEY	25/10/69	RTA
CPL ROBERT BANKIER	22/5/71	IRA sniper Markets area of Belfast
RFN DAVID WALKER	12/7/71	IRA sniper, Northumberland Street, Lower Falls, Belfast
RFN JOSEPH HILL	16/10/71	Shot by gunman during riots in Bogside, Londonderry
MAJOR ROBIN ALERS-HANKEY	30/1/72	DoW after being shot in Bogside area of Londonderry
RFN JOHN TAYLOR	20/3/72	IRA sniper, William Street, Londonderry
RFN JAMES MEREDITH	26/6/72	Shot in Abercorn Road, Londonderry
L/CPL DAVID CARD	4/8/72	Killed by IRA gunman in Andersonstown, Belfast
CPL IAN MORRILL	28/8/72	IRA sniper in Beechmount Avenue, Belfast
RFN DAVID GRIFFITHS	30/8/72	IRA sniper, Clonnard Street, Lower Falls, Belfast
RFN RAYMOND JOESBURY	8/12/72	DoW after being shot whilst in Whiterock area of Belfast
RFN MICHAEL GIBSON	14/12/74	Shot along with RUC constable at Forkhill on joint patrol
CPL WILLIAM SMITH	31/8/77	IRA sniper, Girdwood Park Army base, Belfast
LT/COL IAN CORDEN-LLOYD	17/2/78	Helicopter crash near Bessbrook
RFN NICHOLAS SMITH	4/3/78	IRA booby trap Crossmaglen
RFN CHRISTOPHER WATSON	19/7/80	Shot and killed off-duty in Rosemount, Londonderry
RFN MICHAEL BAGSHAW	19/5/81	Killed along with 4 others IRA landmine at Camlough
RFN ANDREW GAVIN	19/5/81	Killed in same incident
RFN JOHN KING	19/5/81	Killed in same incident
L/CPL GRENVILLE WINSTONE	19/5/81	Killed in same incident
L/CPL GAVIN DEAN	16/7/81	IRA sniper near Crossmaglen
RFN DANIEL HOLLAND	25/3/82	Killed with 2 others in gun attack on Springfield Road, Belfast
RFN NICHOLAS MALAKOS	25/3/82	Killed in same incident
RFN ANTHONY RAPLEY	25/3/82	Killed in same incident
WO2 GRAHAM BARKER	20/7/82	Killed in IRA bomb outrage, Regent's Park, London
BANDSMAN JOHN HERITAGE	20/7/82	Killed in same incident
BANDSMAN R LIVINGSTONE	20/7/82	Killed in same incident
CPL JOHN MCKNIGHT	20/7/82	Killed in same incident
BANDSMAN GEORGE MESURE	20/7/82	Killed in same incident

BANDSMAN KEITH POWELL	20/7/82	Killed in same incident
BANDSMAN LAURENCE SMITH	20/7/82	Killed in same incident
RFN DAVID MULLEY	18/3/86	IRA bomb, Castlewellin, Co Down
L/CPL THOMAS HEWITT	19/7/87	IRA sniper, Belleek, Co Fermanagh

Royal Hampshire Regiment

PTE JOHN KING	13/3/73	IRA booby trap, Crossmaglen
PTE ALAN WATKINS	3/8/73	INLA sniper, Dungiven, Co Londonderry
CPL JOHN LEAHY	3/8/73	DoW following IRA bomb, Mullaghbawn, Forkhill
DRUMMER FRANK FALLOWS	10/11/76	Died in accidental shooting, Magahera, Co Armagh
SGT MICHAEL P. UNSWORTH	2/6/77	Drowned after helicopter accident River Bann
PTE COLIN CLIFFORD	30/4/82	IRA landmine Belleek, Co Fermanagh

Royal Highland Fusiliers

FUSILIER JOHN B. MCCAIG	10/3/71	Abducted and murdered by the IRA at Ligoniel, Belfast
FUSILIER JOSEPH MCCAIG	10/3/71	Murdered in the same incident
FUSILIER DOUGALD P. MCCAUGHE	10/3/71	Murdered in the same incident
L/CPL DAVID HIND	2/1/77	Shot by IRA, Crossmaglen
CPL ROBERT M THOMPSON	20/7/80	IRA car bomb, Moy Bridge, Aughnacloy
FUSILIER S. G. WELLS.	25/6/1	Road traffic accident

Royal Hussars

S/SGT CHARLES SIMPSON	7/11/74	IRA booby trap, Stewartstown, Co Tyrone

Royal Irish Rangers

SGT THOMAS MCGAHON	19/1/71	RTA
RANGER WILLIAM J. BEST	21/5/72	Abducted and murdered when on home leave
RANGER CYRIL J. SMITH Q. G. M.	24/10/90	Killed saving colleagues during bomb attack at Newry
RANGER H. THOMPSON		RTA

Royal Irish Regiment

SGT ROBERT IRVINE	20/10/92	Shot by IRA in his sister's home, Rasharkin
L/CPL IAN WARNOCK	19/11/92	Shot by IRA as he met his wife in Portadown
PTE STEPHEN WALLER	30/12/92	Shot by IRA when on home leave, Belfast
L/CPL MERVYN JOHNSTON	15/2/93	Shot by IRA at his in-laws house West Belfast
PTE CHRIS WREN	31/5/93	Killed by IRA bomb under his car in Moneymore
PTE REGGIE MCCOLLUM	21/5/94	Abducted and murdered by the IRA whilst off-duty
CPL TRELFORD T. WITHERS	8/8/94	Shot in his shop, Downpatrick Street, Crossgar
PTE WILLIAM WOODS	3/9/97	Violent or unnatural causes
WOII ROBERT BELL	9/1/98	Natural causes
PTE MATTHEW FRANCE	1/5/98	Violent or unnatural causes
PTE RONALD MCCONVILLE	30/6/98	Natural causes
CPL JACKY IRELAND	13/7/98	RTA
PTE JOHN MURRAY	28/8/98	RTA
L/CPL STUART ANDREWS	16/9/98	Natural causes
CPL GERALD BLAIR	21/10/98	Natural causes

Royal Irish Regiment (V)

WO2 HUGH MCGINN	28/12/80	Killed by INLA in his own home in Armagh
SGT TREVOR A. ELLIOT	13/4/83	Killed by IRA at his shop in Keady
CPL TREVOR MAY	9/4/84	IRA bomb under his car in Newry outside his work

Royal Logistic Corps

L/CPL DAVID WILSON	14/5/94	Killed by bomb attack at VCP at Keady, Co Armagh
L/CPL RICHARD FORD	30/10/98	Natural causes

Royal Marines

BAND CPL DEAN PAVEY	22/9/89	Killed in IRA bomb outrage Marine Barracks, Deal
BAND CPL TREVOR DAVIS	22/9/89	Killed in same incident
BAND CPL DAVE McMILLAN	22/9/89	Killed in same incident
MUSICIAN RICHARD FICE	22/9/89	Killed in same incident

MUSICIAN BOB SIMMONDS	22/9/89	Killed in same incident
MUSICIAN MICK BALL	22/9/89	Killed in same incident
MUSICIAN RICHARD JONES	22/9/89	Killed in same incident
MUSICIAN TIM REEVES	22/9/89	Killed in same incident
MUSICIAN MARK PETCH	22/9/89	Killed in same incident
MUSICIAN ANDY CLEATHEROE	22/9/89	Killed in same incident
MUSICIAN CHRIS NOLAN	18/10/89	DoW from same incident

Royal Marine Commandos

40 Cdo

MARINE L. ALLEN	26/7/72	Shot by IRA Unity Flats, Belfast
MARINE ANTHONY DAVID	17/10/72	DoW after being shot by IRA on Falls Road
MARINE JOHN SHAW	26/7/73	DoW
MARINE ANDREW GIBBONS	28/5/83	Died Camlough Lake, Co Armagh

42 Cdo

MARINE IVOR SWAIN	23/3/73	RTA: North Belfast
MARINE GRAHAM COX	29/4/73	IRA sniper, New Lodge, Belfast
MARINE JOHN MACKLIN	28/3/74	DoW after being shot in the Antrim Rd, Belfast
CPL ROBERT MILLER	17/8/78	IRA bomb attack, Forkhill
MARINE GARY WHEDDON	12/11/78	DoW after bomb attack, Crossmaglen
MARINE ADAM GILBERT	15/6/89	Shot in friendly fire incident, New Lodge Road

45 Cdo

MARINE ROBERT CUTTING	28/8/72:	Killed in friendly fire incident, Turf Lodge
CPL DENNIS LEACH	13/8/74	IRA bomb, Crossmaglen
MARINE MICHAEL SOUTHERN	13/8/74	Killed in same incident
MARINE NEIL BEWLEY	21/8/77	IRA sniper Turf Lodge, Belfast
SGT WILLIAM CORBETT	23/8/81	Accidentally shot, Musgrave Park Hospital, Belfast

Royal Military Police

L/CPL WILLIAM G. JOLLIFFE	1/3/71	Killed in crash in Londonderry after petrol bombing
CPL THOMAS F. LEA	21/1/75	DoW 8 months after IRA bomb attack, Belfast
SGT DAVID ROSS	27/3/84	Killed in Londonderry after explosion

Royal Navy

| LT. A. R. SHIELDS. | 22/8/88 | IRA bomb in Belfast; was Naval recruiter |

Royal Pioneer Corps

PTE PHILIP DRAKE	26/8/74	IRA sniper, Craigavon, Co Armagh
PTE SOHAN VIRDEE	5/8/81	Murdered by the IRA whilst off duty
CPL DEREK HAYES	21/6/88	IRA booby trap, Crossmaglen

Royal Regiment Fusiliers

1st Battalion

FUSILIER. A. SIMMONS	15/11/74	Shot by IRA at Strabane
CPL. B. BARKER	25/1/81	Shot at VCP in Belfast
CPL. T. H. AGAR	18/5/84	Killed by IRA bomb under car at Enniskillen
L/CPL. R. V. HUGGINS	18/5/84	Killed in same incident
L/CPL. P. W. GALLIMORE	18/10/84	Died of heart attack after bomb attack, Enniskillen

2nd Battalion

MAJOR. J. J. E. SNOW	8/12/71	DoW after being shot by IRA in New Lodge area
FUSILIER. K. . CANHAM	14/7/72	IRA sniper in Lenadoon
FUSILIER. A. P. TINGEY	23/8/72	IRA sniper, West Belfast
CPL. D. NAPIER	9/3/73	RTA
FUSILIER. G. W. FOXALL	16/6/80	Violent or unnatural causes
FUSILIER. A. J. GRUNDY	1/5/92	IRA bomb at VCP at Killeen
L/CPL. M. J. BESWICK	9/2/93	DoW after IRA bomb in Armagh

3rd Battalion

CPL. J. L. DAVIS	15/9/72	Shot by IRA in Bogside, Londonderry
FUSILIER. C. J. MARCHANT	9/4/73	Shot in ambush at Lurgan
CPL. D. LLEWELLYN	28/9/75	RTA
CPL. E. GLEESON	9/10/75	IRA landmine, Lurgancullenboy
SGT. S. J. FRANCIS	21/11/75	IRA booby trap, Forkhill
FUSILIER. M. J. SAMPSON	22/11/75	Killed in major gun battle with IRA at Drumuckaval
FUSILIER. J. D. DUNCAN	22/11/75	Killed in same incident
FUSILIER. P. L. MCDONALD	22/11/75	Killed in same incident
CPL. D. TRAYNOR	30/3/76	IRA booby trap, Ballygallan
L/CPL. W. T. MAKIN	3/1/83	Violent or unnatural causes
CPL. T. O'NEIL (Dog Unit R. A. V. C.)	25/5/91	Killed by hand grenade, North Howard St, Belfast
L/CPL JAMES J. MCSHANE	4/2/74	Killed in IRA bomb outrage, M62, Yorkshire
FUSILIER JACK HYNES	4/2/74	Killed in same outrage
CPL CLIFFORD HOUGHTON	4/2/74	Killed in same outrage
FUSILIER STEPHEN WHALLEY	4/2/74	Killed in same outrage

Royal Regiment of Wales

L/CPL JOHN HILLMAN	18/6/72	IRA sniper Flax Street Mill, Ardoyne, Belfast
L/CPL ALAN GILES	12/6/72	Shot in gun battle with IRA, Ardoyne, Belfast
PTE BRIAN SODEN	19/6/72	IRA sniper in Ardoyne, Belfast
PTE DAVID MEEK	13/7/72	IRA sniper, Hooker Street, Ardoyne, Belfast
PTE JOHN WILLIAMS	14/7/72	Killed in gun battle with IRA, Hooker St. Ardoyne
WO1 (RSM) MIKE HEAKIN	12/8/88	Murdered at traffic lights by IRA, Ostende, Belgium
PTE WILLIAM DAVIS	1/6/90	Murdered in Litchfield railway station by IRA

Royal Scots

PTE RODERICK J D. W. C. BANNON	31/3/76	IRA landmine explosion, Co Armagh
PTE DAVID FERGUSON	31/3/76	Killed in same incident
PTE JOHN PEARSON	31/3/76	Killed in same incident
COL SGT N. REDPATH	2/2/81	Died of heart attack
PTE P. J. MCKENNA	15/3/81	Accidentally shot
PTE A. BRUCE	17/9/82	Road traffic accident
L/CPL LAWRENCE DICKSON	17/3/93	IRA sniper at Forkhill

Royal Scots Dragoon Guards

TROOPER IAN CAIE	24/8/72	IRA landmine attack at Crossmaglen

Royal Tank Regiment

L/CPL JOHN WARNOCK	4/9/71	IRA landmine attack, Derrybeg Park, Newry
TROOPER JAMES NOWOSAD	3/3/78	Shot by gunmen in 'Rag Day' killing, Belfast city centre; also killed was a civilian searcher.
CPL STEVEN SMITH	2/7/89	IRA bomb under his car, Hanover, Germany

Royal Welsh Fusiliers

CPL GERALD BRISTOW	16/4/72	IRA sniper Bishops Street, Londonderry
FUSILIER KERRY MCCARTHY	21/6/72	IRA sniper Victoria RUC station, Londonderry
CPL DAVID SMITH	21/6/73	IRA booby trap, Strabane
CPL ALAN COUGHLAN	28/10/74	Van bomb attack at Ballykinler Army camp
FUSILIER ANDREW CROCKER	24/11/76	Killed by IRA at Post Office robbery, Turf Lodge
LIEUTENANT STEVEN KIRBY	14/2/79	IRA sniper Abercorn Road, Londonderry
CORPORAL DAVID WRIGHT	16/12/93	RTA whilst on duty

Scots Guards

GUARDSMAN JOHN EDMUNDS	16/3/70	Drowned
GUARDSMAN BRIAN HALL	4/10/71	IRA sniper, Creggan Heights base, Londonderry
GUARDSMAN GEORGE HAMILTON	17/10/71	Ambushed and killed by IRA, Cupar Street, Lower Falls
GUARDSMAN NORMAN BOOTH	30/10/71	Killed in same incident
GUARDSMAN STEPHEN MCGUIRE	4/11/71	IRA sniper Henry Taggart base, West Belfast
GUARDSMAN PAUL NICHOLS	27/11/71	IRA sniper, St James Crescent, Falls Road, Belfast

GUARDSMAN JOHN VAN-BECK	18/9/72	DoW after being shot by IRA, Lecky Road, Londonderry
GUARDSMAN GEORGE LOCKHART	26/9/72	DoW after being shot by IRA, Bogside, Londonderry
L/SGT THOMAS MCKAY	28/10/72	IRA sniper, Bishop Street, Londonderry
GUARDSMAN ALAN DAUGHTERY	31/12/73	IRA sniper, Beechmount Avenue, Falls Road, Belfast
GUARDSMAN WILLIAM FORSYTH	5/10/74	Killed in IRA bomb outrage, Guildford (with 4 others)
GUARDSMAN JOHN HUNTER	5/10/74	Killed in same outrage
L/CPL ALAN SWIFT	11/8/78	Killed on covert ops, Letterkenny Rd, Londonderry
L/SGT GRAHAM STEWART	5/5/90	Killed on covert ops, Cullyhanna, Co Armagh
GUARDSMAN DAMIAN SHACKLETON	3/8/92	IRA sniper, New Lodge, Belfast

Staffordshire Regiment

S/SGT JOHN MORRELL	24/10/72	DoW after IRA booby trap, Drumargh, Armagh
2ND LT MICHAEL SIMPSON	23/10/74	DoW after being shot by IRA sniper, Londonderry
PTE CHRISTOPHER SHENTON	20/1/81	IRA sniper whilst in OP Bogside, Londonderry
L/CPL STEPHEN ANDERSON	29/5/84	IRA landmine, Crossmaglen

Ulster Defence Regiment

2nd Battalion

SERGEANT HARRY D. DICKSON	27/2/72	Murdered by the IRA at his home
PTE SIDNEY W. WATT	20/7/73	Ambushed by the IRA at a friend's house
PTE KENNETH HILL	28/8/73	Shot in Armagh City whilst attending an incident
CORPORAL JAMES A. FRAZER	30/8/75	Killed by IRA at a friend's farm
L/CORPORAL JOE REID	31/8/75	Murdered at home by IRA
L/CORPORAL D. JOHN BELL	6/11/75	Killed by IRA as he returned from work
C/SERGEANT JOE NESBITT	10/11/75	Shot by the IRA on his way to work
PTE JOSEPH A McCULLOUGH	25/2/76	Shot by IRA
CORPORAL ROBERT McCONNELLI	5/4/76	Murdered at his home in Tullyvallen, Newtownhamilton
L/CORPORAL JEAN LEGGETT	6/4/76	Ambushed and shot by IRA on patrol in Armagh
Lt JOE WILSON	26/10/76	Killed at work by the IRA
PTE MARGARET A. HEARST	8/10/77	Murdered at home by IRA near Middletown
CAPTAIN CHARLIE HENNING	6/10/78	Shot by IRA whilst at work
L/CPL THOMAS ARMSTRONG	13/4/79	Ambushed and killed by IRA on his way home
PTE JAMES PORTER	24/6/79	Murdered at home by IRA
PTE JAMES H. HEWITT	10/10/80	Killed by bomb under his car
L/CPL FREDDIE A. WILLIAMSON	7/10/82	Killed with a women prison officer in INLA-caused crash
SGT THOMAS G. COCHRANE	22/10/82	Abducted and murdered by IRA
CPL CHARLIE H. SPENCE	10/11/82	Shot by IRA as he left work in Armagh
CPL AUSTIN SMITH	19/12/82	Shot by IRA after parking his car near home
MAJOR CHARLIE ARMSTRONG	14/11/83	Killed by IRA bomb in Armagh City
PTE STEPHEN MCKINNEY	25/9/88	Murdered by IRA as he arrived home after quitting UDR
L/CPL DAVY HALLIGAN	17/11/89	Shot by IRA as he drove home
PTE PAUL D SUTCLIFFE	1/3/91	DoW after IRA mortar attack in Armagh
PTE ROGER J. LOVE	1/3/91	DoW from same incident
PTE PAUL R. BLAKELY	31/5/91	Killed in IRA bomb at the Glenane base with 2 others
PTE SIDNEY HAMILTON	31/5/91	Killed in same incident
L/CPL ROBERT W. CROZIER	31/5/91	Killed in same incident

3rd Battalion

L/CPL JOE JARDINE	8/3/72	Shot by IRA whilst working
CPL JIM D. ELLIOTT	19/4/72	Abducted and murdered by IRA; body then booby trapped by his killers
C/SGT JOHN RUDDY	10/10/72	Shot by IRA on his way to work
PTE JOHN MCCREADY	17/11/74	Shot by the IRA on duty
CPL CECIL GRILLS	12/1/78	Shot by IRA as he drove home from work
PTE JIM COCHRANE	6/1/80	Killed by IRA bomb at Castlewellen. One of 3 killed
PTE RICHARD SMITH	6/1/80	Killed in same incident
PTE RICKY WILSON	6/1/80	Killed in same incident
PTE COLIN H. QUINN	10/12/80	Shot by INLA as he left work
MAJOR W. E. IVAN TOOMBS	16/1/81	Shot by IRA in Warrenpoint where he worked
L/CPL RICHARD W. J. MCKEE	24/4/81	Shot by IRA at Kilcoo whilst on duty

CAPTAIN GORDON HANNA	29/11/85	Killed when IRA bomb exploded under his car at home
CPL D. BRIAN BROWN	28/5/86	Killed by IRA bomb when searching after a warning
PTE ROBERT W HILL	1/7/86	Killed when IRA bomb exploded under his car at home
CPL ALAN. T. JOHNSTON	15/2/88	Shot by the IRA as he arrived for work
PTE W. JOHN MORELAND	16/12/88	Shot in his coal lorry at Downpatrick
PTE MICHAEL D. ADAMS	9/4/90	Killed by IRA landmine with 3 others at Downpatrick
L/CPL J (BRAD) BRADLEY	9/4/90	Killed in same incident
PTE JOHN BIRCH	9/4/90	Killed in same incident
PTE STEVEN SMART	9/4/90	Killed in same incident

4th Battalion

PTE FRANK VEITCH	3/9/71	Shot by IRA at Kinawley RUC station
PTE JOHNNY FLETCHER	1/3/72	Abducted and murdered by IRA in front of his wife
L/CPL W. HARRY CREIGHTON	7/8/72	Murdered by IRA at his house near Monaghan
PTE JIMMY. E. EAMES	25/8/72	IRA booby trapped car at Enniskillen
L/CPL ALFIE JOHNSON	25/8/72	Killed in same incident
PTE TOMMY. R. BULLOCK	21/9/72	Murdered along with his wife at their home
PTE J. ROBIN BELL	22/10/72	Shot by IRA whilst with his father
PTE MATT LILLY	7/9/73	Shot by the IRA on his milk round
PTE ALAN R. FERGUSON	25/6/78	Killed in IRA landmine and gun attack
CPL HERBIE G. KERNAGHAN	15/10/79	Shot by the IRA as he delivered to his school; witnessed by dozens of children
CPL AUBREY ABERCROMBIE	5/2/80	Murdered by the IRA on his farm
PTE W. RITCHIE LATIMER	7/6/80	Shot by the IRA at his hardware store
PTE NORMAN H. DONALDSON	25/11/80	Shot by IRA as he collected charity money at RUC Station whilst off-duty
L/CPL RONNIE GRAHAM	5/6/81	Shot by IRA as he delivered coal; one of three brothers murdered by IRA
PTE CECIL GRAHAM	11/11/81	DoW after being shot by IRA at his wife's house
CPL ALBERT BEACOM	17/11/81	Murdered by IRA at his home
PTE JIMMY GRAHAM B. E. M.	1/2/85	Shot in front of school children by IRA
PTE JOHN F. EARLY	3/2/86	IRA landmine
CPL JIMMY OLDHAM	3/4/86	Shot by IRA gunmen as he arrived where he worked
CPL WILLIE BURLEIGH	6/4/88	Killed by IRA bomb under his car

5th Battalion

CAPTAIN MARCUS MCCAUSLAND	4/3/71	Abducted and murdered by the IRA
PTE THOMAS CALLAGHAN	16/2/72	Abducted and murdered in the Creggan, Londonderry
PTE SAMUEL PORTER	22/11/72	Shot and killed by the IRA as he walked home
PTE GEORGE E. HAMILTON	20/12/72	Shot by the IRA as he worked on repairs at a reservoir
CAPTAIN JAMES HOOD	4/1/73	Murdered by the IRA at home
SGT DAVID C. DEACON	3/3/73	Abducted and murdered by the IRA
CPL JOHN CONLEY	23/7/74	IRA car bomb in Bridge Street, Garvagh
PTE ROBERT STOTT	25/11/75	Shot by the IRA on the way home from work
PTE JOHN ARRELL	22/1/76	Shot on board his firm's mini bus
PTE JACK MCCUTCHEON	1/4/76	Shot at work by the IRA
S/SGT BOBBY H. LENNOX	2/4/76	He was a postman and the IRA deliberately lured him to an isolated farm and shot him
PTE ROBERT J. SCOTT	30/7/76	Killed by IRA booby trap at his family farm
CAPTAIN W. RONNIE BOND	7/11/76	Shot outside his home in Londonderry as he got home
L/CPL JIMMY SPEERS	9/11/76	Shot by the IRA at his garage in Desertmartin
L/CPL WINSTON C. MCCAUGHEY	11/11/76	Shot by the IRA as he stood outside his house in Kilrea
MAJOR J. PETER HILL	23/2/77	Shot by the IRA as he got home from work, Londonderry
PTE DAVID MCQUILLAN	15/3/77	Shot by the IRA as he waited for a lift to work, Bellaghy
L/CPL GERALD C. CLOETE	6/4/77	Shot by the IRA as he drove to work in Londonderry
LT WALTER KERR	2/11/77	DoW after IRA bomb under his car
CPL WILLIAM J. GORDON	8/2/78	Killed along with daughter (10) after IRA bomb exploded under their car
L/CPL SAMUEL D. MONTGOMERY	10/2/81	Shot by the IRA as he left work
PTE T. ALAN RITCHIE	25/5/81	Killed in IRA ambush at Gulladuff near Bellaghy
PTE ALLEN CLARKE	12/9/81	Shot by IRA as he walked through Maghera

L/CPL BERNIE V. MCKEOWN	17/12/83	Murdered by the IRA in front of his 13 year old son in their car
SGT BOBBY F. BOYD	18/11/85	Murdered by the IRA at his front door
SGT TOMMY A. JAMISON	8/3/90	Ambushed and killed by the IRA at work
PTE MICKEY BOXALL	6/11/91	Killed in IRA mortar attack at Bellaghy

6th Battalion

PTE WINSTON DONNELL	9/8/71	1st UDR man killed by the IRA; manning VCP at Clady, Tyrone
SGT KENNETH SMYTH	10/12/71	Shot whilst off-duty by the IRA
PTE TED MEGAHEY	9/6/72	DoW after IRA shooting
PTE WILLIAM J. BOGLE	5/12/72	Murdered in his car as he sat with his children
PTE ROBERT N. JAMESON	17/1/74	Shot by IRA as he got off a bus at Trillick
PTE EVA MARTIN	2/5/74	Killed by IRA in rocket and gun attack at Clogher
CPL W. DEREK KIDD	18/11/76	Shot and killed at work
CPL WILLIAM J. MCKEE	14/4/78	Shot and killed by gunmen as he drove a school bus
PTE JOHN GRAHAM	25/4/79	Shot by the IRA as he collected milk from farms
PTE JOHN A. HANNIGAN	19/6/79	Shot by IRA as he came out of a shop in Omagh
PTE JAMES A. ROBINSON	19/10/79	Shot and killed as he was on his milk round
PTE WILLIE J. CLARKE	3/8/80	Shot in the Republic visiting relatives
L/CPL JOHNNY MCKEEGAN	19/11/81	Lured to a house in Strabane and shot by IRA
LT J. LESLIE HAMILTON	27/4/82	Shot whilst delivering to a Londonderry supermarket
PTE H. A. (LEXI) CUMMINGS	15/6/82	Shot by IRA as he prepared to drive home from work
PTE RONNIE ALEXANDER	13/7/83	One of 4 men killed by IRA landmine at Drumquin
PTE OSSIE NEELY	13/7/82	Killed in same incident
PTE JOHN ROXBOROUGH	13/7/82	Killed in same incident
CPL THOMAS HARRON	13/7/82	Killed in same incident
CPL RONNIE D. FINDLAY	23/8/83	Shot by IRA as he left work
PTE GREG ELLIOTT	2/1/84	Shot as he got into his van at Castlederg
L/CPL THOMAS A. LOUGHLIN	2/3/84	Killed by IRA bomb planted underneath his works van
C/SGT IVAN E. HILLEN	12/5/84	Shot and killed at his farm in Augher by IRA
CPL HEATHER. C. J. KERRIGAN	14/7/84	One of 2 UDR men killed in IRA landmine, Castlederg
PTE NORMAN J. MCKINLEY	14/7/84	Killed in same incident
PTE W. VICTOR FOSTER	15/1/86	IRA bomb planted under his car at Castlederg
PTE THOMAS J. IRWIN	26/3/86	Shot and killed by IRA at his work in Omagh
PTE WILLIAM C. POLLOCK	8/4/86	Killed by IRA booby trap at home in Castlederg
CAPT IVAN R. K. ANDERSON	21/5/87	Shot by IRA as he drove home from his school
L/CPL MICHAEL DARCY	4/6/88	Murdered at home by IRA in Castlederg
PTE OLVEN L. KILPATRICK	9/1/90	Shot by IRA at his shoe shop in Castlederg

7th Battalion

PTE SEAN RUSSELL	27/3/81	Murdered at home by IRA, Belfast; daughter injured
PTE JOHN B. HOUSTON	29/11/75	Shot at work by the IRA
PTE PETER MCCELLAND	28/8/79	Killed at VCP
PTE JOHN D. SMITH	27/3/81	Shot by IRA as he walked to work in Belfast

8th Battalion

PTE W. DENNIS WILSON	7/12/71	Murdered at home in Curlough
L/CPL HENRY GILLESPIE	20/5/72	Shot by IRA patrolling near Dungannon
PTE FRED D. GREEVES	15/12/72	Shot by IRA as heft work in Armagh
CPL FRANK CADDOO	10/5/73	Shot by IRA at his farm in Rehagey
CAPTAIN CORMAC MCCABE	19/1/74	Abducted and murdered by IRA in Irish Republic
CPL ROY T. MOFFETT	3/3/74	IRA landmine on Cookstown to Omagh road
WO2 DAVID SINNAMON	11/4/74	IRA bomb in house in Dungannon
PTE EDMUND R. L. STEWART	29/4/76	Lured to relatives house and shot by IRA
L/CPL STANLEY D. ADAMS	28/10/76	Lured to remote farmhouse as mailman and shot by IRA
PTE JOHN REID	9/3/77	Ambushed and shot by IRA as he fed his cattle
CPL DAVY GRAHAM	25/3/77	DoW after being shot at work by IRA, Gortonis
CAPTAIN W. ERIC SHIELDS	29/4/77	Shot by IRA outside his home in Dungannon
2ND/LT ROBIN SMYRL	13/9/77	Shot by IRA as he drove to work at Plumbridge

PTE BOB J. BLOOMER	24/9/77	DoW after being shot at home by IRA in Eglish
SGT JOCK B EAGLESHAM (MID)	7/2/77	A postman, he was shot by IRA on his rounds
PTE G. SAMMY GIBSON	29/4/79	Shot by IRA as he cycled to work in Tyrone
CPL FRED H. IRWIN	30/10/79	Shot by IRA driving to work in Dungannon
PTE W. JACK DONNELLY	16/4/81	Shot by INLA at his local pub in Moy
L/CPL CECIL W. MCNEILL	25/2/83	Shot by IRA at his work in Tullyvannon
PTE ANDY F. STINSON	4/6/83	Killed by INLA booby trap on his digger at work
PTE CYRUS CAMPBELL	24/10/83	Shot by IRA at Carnteel as he drove to farm
PTE N. JIMMY JOHNSTON	8/5/84	Shot by IRA disguised as ambulance men at his hospital
PTE ROBERT BENNETT	7/9/84	Shot by IRA at his work in Pomeroy
PTE TREVOR W. HARKNESS	28/2/85	Killed by IRA bomb at Pomeroy on foot patrol
PTE MARTIN A. J. BLANEY	6/10/86	Shot by IRA as he drove home in Eglish
MAJOR GEORGE SHAW	26/1/87	Murdered by IRA at his home in Dungannon
PTE WILLIE T. GRAHAM	25/4/87	Shot by IRA at his farm in Pomeroy
CAPT TIM D ARMSTRONG	16/1/88	Murdered by unknown gunmen (Falklands veteran)
PTE JOHN STEWART	16/1/88	DoW after being shot by IRA at his home in Coalisland
PTE NED GIBSON	26/4/88	Shot by IRA as he worked on dustbins in Ardboe
PTE RAYMOND A. MCNICOL	3/8/88	Shot by IRA as he drove to work in Desertcreat
PTE JOHN HARDY	14/3/89	Shot by IRA as he drove his lorry to Granville
WO2 ALBERT D COOPER	2/11/90	IRA bomb planted in car left at his garage in Cookstown

9th Battalion

SGT MAYNARD CRAWFORD	13/1/72	Shot as he waited in a car at Newtownabbey
CPL ROY STANTON	9/6/72	Shot by IRA as he drove home
PTE HENRY J. RUSSELL	13/7/72	Abducted, tortured and shot by the IRA, Carrickfergus
CPL DAVID W. BINGHAM	16/1/73	Abducted and killed by the IRA
PTE THOMAS J FORSYTHE	16/10/73	Killed in a shooting accident
PTE STEVEN CARLETON	8/1/82	Shot by the IRA at petrol station in Belfast
PTE LINDENCOLIN HOUSTON	20/1/84	Murdered by the IRA at his home in Dunmurry

10th Battalion

PTE SEAN RUSSELL	8/12/71	Murdered by IRA at his home, New Barnsley, Belfast
PTE SAMUEL TRAINOR	20/3/72	IRA bomb, Belfast city centre
PTE ROBERT MCCOMB	23/7/72	Abducted and murdered by IRA in Belfast
PTE TERENCE MAGUIRE	14/10/72	Abducted and murdered in Belfast
PTE WILLIAM L. KENNY	16/3/73	Abducted and murdered on way to UDR barracks
CPL JOHN GEDDIS	10/5/77	Killed by UVF in explosion in Crumlin Road, Belfast
L/CPL GERALD W. D. TUCKER	8/6/77	Shot by IRA as he left work at Royal Victoria Hospital
CPL JAMES MCFALL	27/7/77	Murdered by IRA at his home in Belfast
CPL HUGH A. ROGERS	8/9/77	Shot by IRA as he left for work in Dunmurry
SGT ROBERT L. BATCHELOR	27/11/78	Shot by IRA as he left work in Belfast
PTE ALEXANDER GORE	6/6/79	Shot by IRA at UDR base, Malone Road, Belfast
PTE MARK A. STOCKMAN	29/9/81	Shot by INLA at work in Belfast
SGT RICKY CONNELLY	21/10/81	Murdered at his home by IRA, Belfast

11th Battalion

L/CPL VICTOR SMYTH	6/9/72	IRA bomb underneath his car, in Portadown
2ND/LT R. IRWIN LONG	8/11/72	Shot by IRA in Lurgan driving to collect his daughter
SGT ALFIE DOYLE	3/6/75	He and two friends shot dead by IRA as they returned from a meeting in Irish Republic
PTE GEORGE LUTTON	15/11/76	Shot by IRA on duty in Edward Street, Lurgan
PTE ROBERT J. MCNALLY	13/3/79	Killed by INLA bomb under his car, Portadown
PTE S. DAVID MONTGOMERY	8/3/84	Shot by IRA at his works, Moira on the Airport Road
PTE DAVID CHAMBERS	4/6/84	Shot by IRA as he arrived for work, Dollingstown
PTE WILLIE R. MEGRATH	23/7/87	Killed by IRA as he drove home to Lisburn
PTE COLIN J. MCCULLOUGH	23/9/90	Shot by IRA as he sat in his car with fiancé, Lurgan

4–6th Battalion

| L/CPL KENNY A. NEWELL | 27/11/91 | Abducted and murdered by IRA at Crossmaglen |

7-10th Battalion

SGT DENIS TAGGART	4/8/86	Shot dead outside his home by IRA in Belfast
PTE JOE MCILLWAINE	12/6/87	Shot by IRA at his work in Dunmurry
PTE G. JOHN TRACEY	26/6/87	Shot by IRA at his work in Belfast
PTE STEVEN W MEGRATH	17/9/87	Shot by IRA at his relatives' house
PTE JAMES CUMMINGS	24/2/88	Killed by IRA bomb in Belfast city centre
PTE FREDERICK STARRETT	24/2/88	Killed in same incident
L/CPL ROY W BUTLER	2/8/88	Shot dead by IRA in front of his family in West Belfast shopping centre
PTE BRIAN M LAWRENCE	17/6/91	Shot by IRA as he arrived for work, Belfast

UDR (Battalion unknown)

PTE THOMAS WILTON	22/10/70	Natural causes
PTE JOHN PROCTOR	24/10/70	RTA
L/CPL THOMAS MCDONNELL	8/6/97	Violent or unnatural causes
PTE FRANCIS ROBINSON	22/1/99	Natural causes

Ex Ulster Defence Regiment Soldiers killed in Northern Ireland

MR D. J. MCCORMICK	10/12/71	Shot by IRA on way to work
MR ISAAC SCOTT	10/7/73	Shot by IRA in Belleek, Co Armagh
MR IVAN VENNARD	3/10/73	Shot dead by IRA on his postal round, Lurgan
MR GEORGE SAUNDERSON	10/4/74	Shot by IRA at his school in Co Fermanagh
MR BRIAN SHAW	20/7/74	Abducted and killed, Grosvenor Road, Belfast
MR WILLIAM HUTCHINSON	24/8/74	Shot by IRA at work
MR GEORGE MCCALL	2/8/75	Shot by IRA in Moy, Co Tyrone
MR KENNETH WORTON	5/1/76	1 of 10 men murdered in Kingsmill Massacre
MR NICOLAS WHITE	13/3/76	Shot at youth club, Ardoyne, Belfast
MR SIDNEY MCAVOY	12/6/76	Shot at his shop in Dunmurry
MR JOHN FREEBURN	28/6/76	Shot in Lurgan
MR NORMAN CAMPBELL	15/12/76	Joined RUC and shot in Portadown
MR ROBERT HARRISON	5/2/77	RUCR: shot by IRA Gilford, Co Down
MR JOHN LEE	27/2/77	Shot by IRA in club in Ardoyne, Belfast
MR JAMES GREEN	5/5/77	Shot by IRA whilst working as taxi driver, Belfast
MR GILBERT JOHNSTON	19/8/78	Shot by IRA at his shop in Keady, Co Armagh
MR MICHAEL RILEY	7/6/78	Shot at his home by IRA in Shankhill Rd Belfast
MR ROBERT LOCHART	17/4/79	RUCR: killed by IRA bomb at Camlough
MR JACK MCCLENAGHAN	19/5/79*	Shot by the IRA whilst delivering bread in Fermanagh
MR DAVID STANLEY WRAY	20/5/79	Shot by IRA on his way to church in Claremont
MR DAVID ALAN DUNNE	2/6/79	RUCR: shot by INLA in Armagh
MR GEORGE HAWTHORNE	5/10/79	Shot by IRA in Newry
MR JAMES FOWLER	16/12/79	Shot by IRA as he drove his fish van in Omagh
MR CLIFFORD LUNDY	2/1/80	Shot at work by IRA near Bessbrook, Co Armagh
MR HENRY LIVINGSTONE	6/3/80	Shot by IRA at his farm at Tynan, Co Armagh
MR VICTOR MORROW	17/4/80	Shot by IRA at Newtownbutler, Co Fermanagh
MR JOHN EAGLESON	1/10/82	RUCR: shot by IRA on way to work
MR WILLIAM ELLIOT	28/6/80	Shot by IRA at cattle market in Ballybay, Co Monaghan
MR JOHN ROBINSON	23/4/81	Shot by IRA driving works van in Armagh
MR PTE JOHN PROCTOR	14/9/81	Shot by IRA at hospital after visiting his wife and newborn baby at Magherafelt
MR HECTOR HALL	5/10/81	Shot by IRA outside Altnagelvin hospital
MR CHARLES NEVILLE	10/11/81	Shot by IRA at work in Co Armagh
MR JAMES MCCLINTOCK	18/11/81	Shot by IRA on his way home from work, Londonderry
MR NORMAN HANNA	11/3/82	Shot by IRA at his works in Newry
MR THOMAS CUNNINGHAM	12/5/82	Shot by IRA whilst working in Strabane
MR WILFRED MCILVEEN	27/8/82	IRA bomb underneath his car in Armagh
MR CHARLES CROTHERS	5/10/82	Shot by IRA at Altnagelvin
MR ROBERT IRWIN	16/11/82	RUCR: shot by INLA at Markethill
MR SNOWDEN CORKEY	16/11/82	RUCR: killed in same incident
MR JAMES GIBSON	2/12/82	Shot by IRA driving school bus at Coalisland
MR JOHN TRUCKLE	20/9/83	IRA bomb underneath his car in Portadown

MR RONALD FUNSTON	13/3/84	Shot by IRA on his farm at Pettigoe, Co Fermanagh
MR HUGH GALLAGHER	3/6/84	Taxi driver; he was lured by IRA to Omagh and shot
MR MELVIN SIMPSON	8/10/84	Shot by IRA at work in Dungannon
MR DOUGLAS MCELHINNEY	25/2/85	Shot by INLA at friend's house in Londonderry
MR GEOFFREY CAMPBELL	25/2/85	RUCR. One of nine killed IRA mortar attack, Newry
MR HERBET MCCONVILLE	15/5/86	Shot dead by IRA whilst delivering in Newry
MR HARRY HENRY	21/4/87	Murdered by IRA at his home in Magherafelt
MR CHARLES WATSON	22/5/87	Murdered by the IRA at his home, Clough, Co Down
MR NATHANIEL CUSH	15/6/87	IRA bomb underneath his car in Belfast
MR WINSTON G FINLAY	30/8/87	Shot by IRA at his home in Ballyronan
MR JOHN GRIFFITHS	4/5/89	IRA bomb underneath his car
MR ROBERT J GLOVER	15/11/89	IRA bomb underneath his car near Dungannon
Mr DAVID STERRITT	24/7/90	RUCR: killed with 4 others by IRA landmine, Armagh
MR DAVID POLLOCK	20/10/90	Shot by an IRA sniper in Strabane
MR NORMAN KENDALL	10/11/90	Murdered with 3 others by IRA, Castor Bay, Lurgam
MR HUBERT GILMORE	1/12/90	Shot by IRA Kilrea, Co Londonderry
MR ERIC BOYD	5/8/91	Shot by IRA as he left work Cappagh, Co Tyrone
MR RONALD FINLAY	15/8/91	Shot at work by the IRA, Co Tyrone
MR DAVID MARTIN	25/4/93	IRA bomb underneath his car, Kildress, Co Tyrone
MR JOHN LYNESS	24/6/93	Shot by IRA at his home in Lurgan
MR JOHN ALEXANDER BURNS	30/10/93	Shot by UFF at Eglington
MR ALAN SMYTH	25/4/94	Shot by IRA in Garvagh
MR ERIC SMYTH	28/4/94	Shot by IRA at his home in Co Armagh
MR DAVID CALDWELL	1/8/02	Working on Army camp in Londonderry; killed by 'Real' IRA booby trap

Welsh Guards

GUARDSMAN SAMUEL MURPHY	14/11/74	Murdered whilst on home leave by the IRA, Belfast

Worcester & Sherwood Foresters

PTE MARTIN ROBINSON	16/4/72	Killed in gun battle at Brandywell base, Londonderry
PTE MARTIN JESSOP	20/9/82	Killed in rocket attack, Springfield Road RUC station
CPL LEON BUSH	27/9/82	IRA booby trap, West Circular Road, Belfast
CPL STEPHEN MCGONIGLE	4/5/89	IRA landmine, Crossmaglen

Women's Royal Army Corps

W/PTE ANN HAMILTON	5/10/74	Killed with 4 others in IRA bomb outrage, Guildford
W/PTE CAROLINE SLATER	5/10/74	Killed in same outrage
L/CPL ROBERTA THAIN	25/3/75	Accidentally shot dead in Londonderry

Regiment Unknown

HIGHLANDER S. HARRINGTON.	9/7/95	Accidentally shot (Palace Barracks memorial lists him under The Highland Regiment)
SGT MICHAEL PEACOCK	13/3/76	RTA

Civilian Searchers

NORMA SPENCE	3/3/78	Shot by IRA in Belfast City centre by IRA
BRIAN RUSSELL	28/9/78	Shot by IRA Waterloo Place, Londonderry

Security Services

MICHAEL G. DALTON
JOHN ROBERT DEVERELL
JOHN STUART HAYNES
ANNE CATHERINE MACDONALD
MICHAEL BRUCE MALTBY
STEVEN LEWIS RICKARD

The following Army women and children were also killed as a result of terrorism

MRS LINDA HOUGHTON	4/2/74	M62 Coach Bomb outrage

MASTER LEE HOUGHTON	4/2/74	Killed in same outrage
MASTER ROBERT H0UGHTON	4/2/74	Killed in same outrage
NIVRUTI MAHESKKUMAR	26/10/89	Murdered with her father, Wildenrath, Germany

Army Personnel killed in Aldershot bomb attack 22/2/72 IRA bomb outrage

THELMA BOSLEY
JOAN LUNN
MARGARET GRANT
JILL MANSFIELD
JOHN HASLAR
CHERIE MUNTON

The following soldier was killed or died during his time in Northern Ireland

The author invites anyone with further knowledge of him (e. g. Regiment or causes of death), to contact him on: ken_wharton@hotmail. co. uk. He is believed to have died *before* Robert Curtis.

SGT JOHN PLATT   3/2/71

I gratefully and wholeheartedly acknowledge the incredible services of Emma Beaumont, without whom the compiling of this comprehensive Roll of Honour could not have happened.

Bibliography

Unpublished material

Material for the Rolls of Honour supplied by the Northern Ireland Veterans Association and 'Britain's Small Wars'.

Printed sources

Arthur, M., *Northern Ireland: Soldiers Talking*, Sidgwick & Jackson, London, 1987

Barzilay, D., *The British Army in Ulster*, Century Books, Belfast, 1973–81, 4 vols

Barzilay, D. & M. Murray, *Four Months in Winter*, 2nd Battalion Royal Regiment of Fusiliers, Belfast, 1972

Curtis, N., *Faith and Duty: the True Story of a Soldier's War in Northern Ireland,* Andre Deutsch, London, 2003 (new edition)

Dewar, M., *The British Army in Northern Ireland*, Arms & Armour Press, London, 1985

Doherty, R., *The Thin Green Line: The History of the Royal Ulster Constabulary GC*, Barnsley, Pen & Sword, 2004

Gamble. R., *The History of E Company 5 UDR: The Last Coleraine Militia?* Regimental Association of the UDR, Coleraine Branch, Coleraine, 2007

Gilpin, D., *Weekends in Uniform*, Write Lines in Print, n.p., 2005

Hammill, D., *Pig in the Middle: The Army in Northern Ireland 1969–84*, Methuen, London, 1985

Lindsay, J., *Brits Speak Out: British Soldiers Impressions of the Northern Ireland Conflict*, Guildhall Press, Derry, 1998

McKittrick, D., *Lost Lives: The Stories of the Men, Women and Children who died through the Northern Ireland Troubles*, Mainstream, London, 2004 (second revised edition)

McKittrick, D. & D. McVea, *Making Sense of the Troubles*, Penguin, London, 2001 new ed.

Morton, Brig. P., *Emergency Tour: 3 PARA in South Armagh*, William Kimber, London, 1989

Nettleton, R.L., *Tales From the Less Darker Side*, privately published by the author, n.p., 2007 reprint

Potter, J., *A Testimony to Courage: The Regimental History of the Ulster Defence Regiment*, Barnsley, Leo Cooper, 2001

Restorick R., *Death of a Soldier: A Mother's Search for Peace*, Blackstaff Press, Belfast, 2000

Silkstone, J.A., *You Two: Fall In – In Three Ranks*, Lulu.com, 2007

Taylor, P., *Brits: The War Against the IRA*, Bloomsbury, London, 2001

Taylor, P., *The Provos: IRA and Sinn Fein*, Bloomsbury, London, 1997

Internet sources

Britain's Small Wars: www.britains-smallwars.com/ni/RM.html

CAIN Index of the Troubles: http://cain.ulst.ac.uk/sutton/alpha/S.html / http://
  cain.ulst.ac.uk/ni/security.htm#04
Glosters: http://www.rgbw-association.org.uk
Green Howards: www.ex-greenhowards.com
Guardian News Archive: http://www.guardian.co.uk/fromthearchive/story.
Light Infantry: www.lightinfantryreunited.co.uk
Lyrics of *Mountains of Mourne*: http://ingeb.org/songs/ohmaryth.html
Northern Ireland Veterans Association: http://nivets.org.uk//index.php
Palace Barracks, Belfast: http://www.palacebarracksmemorialgarden.org/
  Roll%20of%20Honour.htm
RUC Roll of Honour: http://www.policememorial.org.uk/Forces/RUC/
  RUC_Roll.htm
The music of Terry Friend (written about the Troubles): http://
  www.anothercountrysong.com
Wesley Johnston: http://www.wesleyjohnston.com/users/ireland/past/troubles/
  major_killings.html
Words to Rudyard Kipling's *Tommy*: www.web-books.com/classics/poetry/
  anthology/Kipling/Tommy
www.militaryimages.net

Photographs

Reproduced by kind permission of:

David Barzilay
Andrew Bennett
Andy Carr
Tim Castle
Tom Clarke
Barry Crane
Paul Crispin
Darren Croucher
Haydn Davies
Roy Davies
Mike Day
Ken Donovan
N Edwards
Jimmy Foster
Ronnie Gamble
Bob Gooch
Stephen Griffiths
Dave Hallam
Mike Heavens

Mike Hewlett
Barry Hughes
Marcus Lapsa
Andrew MacDonald
Jim Mackenzie
Eamon Melaugh
Pat Moir
Phil Morris
Richard Nettleton
Jim Parker
George Prosser
Regimental Museum of the Royal Welsh
David Roalfe
Ray Rose
Martin Starsmore
Mike Thomasson
Darren Ware
Phil Winstanley

Paul Crispin photography

Paul Crispin joined his local regiment, The King's Own Royal Border Regiment in 1979 after a years' specialized training in IJLB (Infantry Junior Leaders Battalion) and within 2 months was training for an emergency tour of Northern Ireland. His tour was brought to an abrupt end 2 months in when Paul and a fellow IJLB soldier were blow up in Crossmaglen. Paul suffered major burns and minor fractures to his arm; his colleague, Andy Walker, died of burns injuries sustained in the explosion 2 weeks later in hospital –a true baptism of fire to the troubles in N.I.

Paul served a total of almost 16 years with the British Army and saw further active service in Northern Ireland and the Gulf War. A lifelong photo enthusiast, his talents were recognized by 'the powers that be' and he was asked, amongst other things, to document an 'Op Banner' tour carried out by the 3rd Battalion the Royal Anglia Regt. in 1986–87. Paul's photos contained in this book are a small representation of about 600+ photos taken.

To see a more concise collection of the photographs taken visit: http://cain.ulst.ac.uk/crispin/index.html – The University of Ulster's conflict website

Paul Crispin's style of photography manages to 'get in and personal'. Not frightened to go the extra yard to achieve the photo he wants and always looking for that special angle or light to let the subject tell its own story has meant Paul's photography brings compassion, interest and power to his photos.

Paul now shares his time between Europe and Canada, photographing for such diverse subjects as industrial catalogues, landscape calendars or local news events. He feels though that his style of photography and his true talents lie in documenting adversity and conflict around the world and is therefore actively seeking commissions to be able to achieve this goal.

To contact Paul Crispin for photo journalistic commissions anywhere in the world where a powerful story is required, simply contact Paul by email at: paul@paulcrispinphtography.com

What the public say about Paul Crispin's photos:

"I rank Paul Crispin among the likes of Lee Miller, Phillip Jones Griffiths and Don McCullin, and if you take a look at his Northern Ireland photos, you will too" – Anni Rumble (UK)

"This is a fantastic set fo photos!!! Magnificent, Holy Cow and fabulous!! Great work here" – Glenn Perryman (USA)

"There are many, many great photographs on the Net as we all know. To my mind there are not nearly so many photos that are so memorable as Paul's on The Troubles. His Northern Ireland set is well observed, personal & technically excellent. Not only that, it symbolises hope in difficult times for the whole world that just sometimes – things get better" – Paul Busby (UK)

"I can say this is my favourite set of photographs till now. The photos are truly of a world journalist class … " – Kalsang Dhondup (Tibet)

"Your work is very touching. You have extreme talent that rarely is owned by many. It was hard to comment on just one" – Vikki Wiessner (USA)

"This set of photos is incredibly powerful. As someone who lived in North Belfast during the worst of 'The Troubles' I'm not ashamed to say some of these brought tears to my eyes" – Dave (N.Ireland)

"Wow, theses are the type of shots we could see on the front page of a major newspaper! Your whole series is quite impressive, truly photo-journalism" – Daniel Cheong (Singapore)

www.paulcrispinphotography.com

A request from the author

photo of Ken Wharton © Mike Day, www.ijlb.com

A sequel to this book is now underway and is another account of the 'troubles' from the perspective of the squaddie on the ground. The author welcomes contributions from all those who served, or loved ones of those who served, for the next volume.

The sequel will be published during 2009. A further collection of squaddies' views of the events in Northern Ireland 1969–97, it will focus on specific incidents and specific places – there will be a chapter which deals with the 'Murph, Turf Lodge, one which deals with the Ardoyne, one on the Lower Falls, one on the Bogside and the Creggan and so on. Part of the book will deal with the bandit country of South Armagh, including chapters on Crossmaglen (XMG), Belleek, Lisnaskea etc. I will invite former squaddies to describe their emotions felt during firefights, during IED detonations etc. Further, I will ask them to put into their own words their feelings in relation to the populace on both sides of the sectarian divide. In short: TO CONTINUE TO TELL THEIR STORY.

Ken Wharton

For further information, or to send your contributions see the author's website www.squaddiesvoices.com or contact Helion & Company Ltd, 26 Willow Road, Solihull, West Midlands, B91 1UE (telephone 0121 705 3393, email info@ helion.co.uk).

The publishers would particularly like to hear from Northern Ireland veterans who are interested in producing book-length accounts of their experiences in the Province. Our contact details are above.